TRANS-SIBERIAN HANDBOOK

B R Y N   T H O M A S

Fourth edition researched and updated by

**A T H O L   Y A T E S   &
T A T Y A N A   P O Z A R - B U R G A R**

TRAILBLAZER PUBLICATIONS

Bryn Thomas was born in Zimbabwe where he grew up on a farm. Since graduating from Durham University with a degree in anthropology, travel on five continents has included a Saharan journey in a home-built kit-car, a solo 2500km cycle ride through the Andes, five Himalayan treks and 40,000km of rail travel.

The first edition of this book, shortlisted for the Thomas Cook Travel and Guide Book Awards, was the result of several trips on the Trans-Siberian and six months in the Reading Room of the British Library. Subsequent publications have included guides to India and Britain which he co-authored for Lonely Planet. In 1992 he set up Trailblazer Publications, to produce the series of route guides for adventurous travellers that has now grown to twelve titles.

Athol Yates and **Tatyana Pozar-Burgar** updated this fourth edition of the *Trans-Siberian Handbook*. Athol has travelled extensively throughout Russia as a journalist and researcher. He has an engineering degree and graduate diploma in Soviet Studies and studied Russian at Melbourne University, Moscow's Patrice Lumumba University and Hungary's Egar Teachers' Institute. He is the author of *Siberian BAM Railway Guide* and *Russia by Rail* and now runs the internet travel agency, Russia-Rail, based in Melbourne.

Also based in Australia, Tatyana studied Russian at Melbourne and Moscow universities and has long been fascinated by Russia. As a photographer she found the country a perfect subject for her lens. Her work has been the subject of several exhibitions. Over the years she has amassed a large collection which is now the basis of a Russian photo library. She works for a Melbourne photographic company.

Trans-Siberian Handbook
First edition 1988; this fourth edition 1997

Publisher
Trailblazer Publications
The Old Manse, Tower Rd, Hindhead, Surrey, GU26 6SU, UK
Fax (+44) 01428-607571
E-mail: trailblazer@compuserve.com

British Library Cataloguing in Publication Data
A catalogue record for this book is available from the British Library

ISBN 1-873756-16-X

Editor: Patricia Major
Typesetting: Anna Jacomb-Hood
Cartography and index: Jane Thomas

Every effort has been made by the author and publisher to ensure that the
information contained herein is as accurate and up to date as possible. However,
they are unable to accept responsibility for any inconvenience, loss or injury sus-
tained by anyone as a result of the advice and information given in this guide.

Printed on chlorine-free paper from farmed forests by
Kelso Graphics (☎ 01573-223214) The Knowes, Kelso, Scottish Borders TD5 7BH

Acknowledgements

From Tatyana and Athol: Thanks to Gabriela and John Burgar for their years of support and understanding, Jacinta Nelligan for her enormous effort in editing the manuscript, Darko Burgar for his photography expertise, Elena Vvedenskaia for her translation checking, and Ilya & Inna Karachevtsev for digging up some amazing Russian stories. Also special thanks to Jan Wigsten (Eco Tour Productions), Susie Drost (The Mongolian Society), Becky Last (Monkey Business), Youry and Dennis Nemirovsky (Baikal Complex), Darcey Dahl, Frank Becker, Iko & Ann-Marie Burgar, Earlam Matthew, Herbert Groot Jebbink, Konstantine Tchervinski, J Ward Hills, Helen Fuge, Brent McCunn, Craig Patterson and everyone else who helped us.

From Bryn: I am greatly indebted to the numerous people who have helped me with the research and execution of this project in its four editions since the first publication in 1988. First, I should like to thank Jane Thomas for her extensive work in drawing the strip maps and town plans (without which this guide would be incomplete) and for the index. I'd also like to thank Patricia Thomas for her scrupulous editing of the text. Thanks to Athol Yates and Tatyana Pozar-Burgar for all their work in expanding and updating this edition of the book, to Dominic Streatfeild-James who updated the previous edition (and whose wry comments survive), to Douglas S-J for Beijing hotel prices, and to Anna Udagawa for updating the travel agents' section. I'm also grateful to Neil Magowan, Brian and Val Colyer, Neil Taylor, and André de Smet. Thanks also to Ron Ziel for the cover photograph. Previous editions have generated a considerable amount of feedback from readers. Thanks to:

Matz Lonnedal Risberg (Norway), Kenneth Lymer, Anthony Kay, Edward Wilson (UK), Werner Verschueren and Nieves Blasco (Belgium), Rodney Pinder (Hong Kong), Stuart Wilde, Dick Thompson, Jim Millar and Bob Huntley (UK), Lawrence R Cotter (USA), David Cowans (Australia), Guy de Bruyn (Netherlands), Abigail Browne, David and Janet Carr, Julian Wathen, Keith Walker, SCL Phillips (UK), Becky Last (Hong Kong), Christopher Knight (UK), Elizabeth Hehir (Netherlands), Annabel Boyes, Mary Fox, Susan Sexton (UK), Dolf van der Haven (Netherlands), David and Siriporn Brian (Hong Kong), Jacqui Williams (UK), Graham and Sue Small (New Zealand), Steven Caron, Boris Samarianov, Helen Nehonova, Ludmilla, Lingard and Maxim, Svetlana Rabdanova (Russia), Huang Rui Li (Beijing), Alex Malone and Rupert Dunbar-Rees (UK), Angels Castro and Genis Aymerich (Spain), Anne Lavelle and Pauline Wilson, Nick and Hilma (UK), Sandy Macmillan and John Podgora, Hal Sharpe (USA), Felix Patton (Australia), Andre Lvov (Russia), Ian Button (UK), Philip Robinson (UK, for the aside on Siberian post past), James Cherkoff (UK), Matthew Parsons (UK), Jovita da Silva (South Africa), Michael Crick (UK), Maarten Langemeijer (Netherlands), Cmndr RM Williams (Canada), Susan Pares, WD Webber, RC Rider, Colin Baker (UK), Heather and Steve Oxley (Japan), Bob and Hilda Helling (UK), Andrew and Val White, Christopher Turner, Keith Fothergill (Guernsey), Keith Watson (UK), Jeffrey de Forrestier (Canada), Joan Eriksson (Finland), Robert Bray, Joan Nicholls (UK).

Quotations used in Part 5 are from the *Guide to the Great Siberian Railway 1900*.

A note on prices and a request

Rapid inflation in Russia means that it would be pointless to give prices in roubles. US$ are used throughout but only roubles are accepted. The author and publisher have tried to ensure that this guide is as accurate and up-to-date as possible but things change quickly in Russia. If you notice any changes or omissions please write to Bryn Thomas at Trailblazer Publications (address on p2). A free copy of the next edition will be sent to persons making a significant contribution.

Front cover: A rare picture, taken in the early 1970s, of the Trans-Siberian being hauled by a steam engine. (Ron Ziel, USA)

CONTENTS

PART 4: CITY GUIDES AND PLANS

INTRODUCTION

There can be few people who have not, at some time in their lives, wondered what it must be like to travel on the Trans-Siberian Railway – to cross Russia and the wild forests and steppes of Siberia on the world's longest railway journey. The distances spanned by this famous line are immense: almost 6000 miles (a seven-day journey) between Moscow and the Pacific port of Vladivostok (for boat connections to Japan) and just under 5000 miles (five days) between Moscow and Beijing.

Ever since a rail service linking Europe with the Far East was established at the turn of the century, foreign travellers and adventurers have been drawn to this great journey. Most of the early travellers crossed Siberia in the comfort of the carriages of the Belgian Wagon Lits company, which were as luxurious as those of the Venice-Simplon Orient Express of today. Things changed somewhat after the Russian Revolution in 1917 and it became increasingly difficult for foreigners to obtain permits for Siberia. It was not until the 1960s that the situation improved and Westerners began to use the railway again for getting to Japan, taking the boat from Nakhodka (it now leaves from Vladivostok) for the last part of the journey. In the early 1980s, travel restrictions for foreigners visiting China were eased and since then many people have found the Trans-Siberian a cheap and interesting way to get to or from both the Middle Kingdom and Mongolia.

In this jet age, the great advantage of going by rail is that it allows passengers to absorb some of the atmosphere of the country through which they are travelling. On a journey on this train you are guaranteed to meet local people for this is no 'tourist special' but a working service; you may find yourself draining a bottle of vodka with a Russian soldier, discussing politics with a Chinese academic or drinking Russian champagne with a Mongolian trader.

Experimenting with democracy and the market economy, Russia is now undergoing phenomenal changes after years of stagnation. While the ending of the Cold War may have removed some of the mystique of travelling in the former USSR, the fact that Russia is now much more accessible means that there are new travel opportunities right across the country. With the opening of budget guest houses in Moscow, St Petersburg and also in Siberia, visiting the country is now cheaper than ever before.

Although travel in Siberia today presents few of the dangers and difficulties that it did earlier this century, a journey on the Trans-Siberian still demands a considerable amount of planning and preparation. The aim of this guide is to help you cut through the red tape when arranging the trip, to give background information on Russia and Siberia and to provide a kilometre-by-kilometre guide to the entire route of the greatest rail adventure – the Trans-Siberian.

PART 1: PLANNING YOUR TRIP

Routes and costs

*Best of all, he would tell me of the great train that ran across half the world ... He held me enthralled then, and today, a life-time later, the spell still holds. He told me the train's history, its beginnings ... how a Tzar had said, 'Let the Railway be built!' And it was ... For me, nothing was ever the same again. I had fallen in love with the Traveller's travels. Gradually, I became possessed by love of a horizon and a train which would take me there ...***Lesley Blanch** Journey into the Mind's Eye*

ROUTE OPTIONS

Travellers crossing Siberia have a choice of three routes: the Trans-Siberian, Trans-Manchurian and Trans-Mongolian. The Trans-Siberian is the most expensive route as it crosses the entire length of Siberia to the Pacific terminus at Vladivostok, from where, between late May and early October, passenger ships sail to Japan. The Trans-Manchurian travels through most of Siberia before turning south through Manchuria and ending in Beijing. The Trans-Mongolian also terminates in Beijing but travels via Mongolia which gives you the chance to stop off in Ulan Bator.

COSTS

Overall costs

How much you pay for a trip on the world's longest railway line depends on the level of comfort you demand, the number of stops you wish to make along the way and the amount of time you're prepared to put into getting hold of a budget ticket. Although the cheapest tickets for rail travel from Moscow to Beijing or vice versa currently cost £145/US$226, this price does not reflect what you'll end up paying for your trip. There are several major costs to add on: getting to your departure point and getting back at the end of your journey, accommodation in Moscow and Beijing, food etc. In the light of this, the package deals offered by travel agents can be better value than they might at first appear. Even more important, although you may be able to buy a ticket for as little as the above-mentioned price, a ticket is no use without a reservation on the train. Since certain trains may be fully booked for some time in advance, you may find the services of a travel agent invaluable. Packages on the Trans-Siberian between Moscow and Beijing, including transfers and a night's accommodation in Moscow, cost from £234/US$375.

From **London**, flights to Moscow cost around £150. Flights between London and Beijing are around £270 single. The cheapest fully inclusive Trans-Siberian holidays cost from around £1285 for a 12-day package including flights to and from London. If a four-week guided rail tour from Frankfurt to Vladivostok via Ulan Bator, with accommodation in private saloon cars pulled by old steam locomotives is more your idea of travelling then be prepared to part with £6995 (see GW Travel p25) .

From **New York**, flights to Moscow cost from US$450 one way. Flights between New York and Beijing cost from US$800 one way. The cheapest fully inclusive Trans-Siberian holidays cost from around US$2200 for a ten-day package including flights to and from New York.

From **Australia**, single flights to Beijing cost A$900 and to Moscow cost A$1600. The cheapest Trans-Manchurian holidays cost from around A$760 which includes the train ticket, three days in Irkutsk, Moscow and St Petersburg. A 17-day Vladivostok to St Petersburg budget package costs A$1300.

Travel in Russia – better value, fewer restrictions

Travel in Russia is becoming better value and a little less restricted than it was in the communist era. It is now far easier to get a visa (see p17); it is possible to travel independently (see p14); you do not have to deal with Intourist; you can get a hotel room without pre-booking, and train tickets are easier to get although this is partly because they're now more expensive.

During the Soviet period, all travel arrangements for foreigners were handled by the monolithic organisations of Intourist (for general travel), Sputnik (for youth travel) and CCTE (for government or business travel). This enforced division allowed them to charge monopoly prices and restrict travellers' options. Since the collapse of the Soviet Union, these organisations have been broken up and a number of new companies have sprung up. However, a loose confederation of formerly Intourist-owned companies and hotels still forms Russia's largest travel chain, and this has a monopoly on three and four star hotels in many cities.

Hotel costs

Since the collapse of Intourist, hotel prices have been reduced significantly. Moscow and St Petersburg are the only places with five star hotels (£220/US$350 to £310/US$500 a night) although there are a number of Trans-Siberian cities which have good four star hotels, for example Vladivostok and Khabarovsk.

Most travellers stay in the former Intourist hotels. A basic room with attached bathroom will cost £40-65/US$60-105 for a single or £45-70/US$70-115 for a double, booked from abroad. Note that in Russia most single rooms are only marginally cheaper than a double, so it pays to have a travelling companion. Breakfast is sometimes included in the price. If you book the hotel locally you may pay slightly less or a lot more, depending on the whim of the hotel manager.

There's better news for budget travellers as **guest-houses** have sprung up in Moscow, St Petersburg and Irkutsk. They charge about £9/US$15 for bed and breakfast. In other cities, it's possible to get a hotel room from as little as £13/US$20 but these hotels are often basic and have no English-speaking staff. **Homestay** is an option that is available in most Trans-Siberian cities. It costs about £22/US$35 a night including two meals. For more information on accommodation, see p63.

Train classes and prices

Foreigners are offered three levels of train berths. See p114 for more information about each. The prices shown in each category below range from the cheapest ticket bought from the railway ticket office in Moscow or Beijing to the most expensive ticket offered by a travel agent in the West. Note that because of the difficulty in getting reservations, the price that most travellers pay is nearer the higher figure in each category.

● **First/De luxe/Soft Class/SV, two berth:** On the **Moscow-Vladivostok route** prices are: £440-570/US$704-900 for the rail trip to Vladivostok. For the **Moscow-Beijing route**, prices are £275-375/US$440-600. De luxe Class is available only on the Trans-Mongolian train and comprises the most luxurious compartments of any train crossing Siberia, and the only ones containing showers.
● **First/Soft Class/SV, four berth:** Available only on the Trans-Mongolian Train Nos 3 & 4, prices for the **Moscow-Beijing route** are £230-310/US$366-500.
● **Second/Hard Class/Coupé, four berth:** Most people find the cheapest rail accommodation available to foreigners perfectly adequate. Prices for the **Moscow-Vladivostok route** are £225-350/US$359-550. For the **Moscow-Beijing route** prices range from £145-250/US$226-400.

Foreigners will usually find themselves sharing with other foreigners if they've booked through a large agency that deals mainly with non-Russians, and compartments are not single sex. When it comes to sharing compartments, I'm not sure which is worse – the elderly German who complains non-stop about the food or the female tractor driver from Krasnoyarsk who snores like a Massey-Ferguson.

BREAKING YOUR JOURNEY

Most people will want to break their journey and stop off along the way. This is a good idea not only because it gives you a chance to get off the train, stretch your legs and, most importantly, have a shower, but also because some of the places you pass through are well worth exploring; you won't learn much about life in Siberia by looking through a train window. All cities on the Trans-Siberian can be visited with the exception of the military cities of Krasnoyarsk-26 and Krasnoyarsk-45. Not all, however, are worth visiting (Omsk, for example). Plan your stops carefully: it's too late to decide to break your journey once you have started as you will have to buy a new ticket to continue your journey when you get off the train.

If your trip starts in **Moscow** (see p145) it's usually necessary to spend one night there but you'd need several days to see just the main sights. A side-trip to **St Petersburg** (p125) is highly recommended if only for a visit to the Hermitage. If your starting (or ending) point is Helsinki, you could go via St Petersburg. At the other end of the rails, it's worth spending several days in **Beijing** (p287).

Along the routes, Irkutsk and Ulan Bator are the most popular places to stop off at. **Irkutsk** (p220) is the eastern capital of Siberia and 64km from Lake Baikal, the world's deepest freshwater lake. It's possible to stay at **Listvyanka** (p234), right by the lake. **Ulan Bator** (Ulaanbaatar, p273), the capital of Mongolia, used to be so expensive to visit that few travellers could afford to stop but cheaper visits are now possible. South of Lake Baikal, **Ulan Ude** (p242) is interesting for the Buddhist monastery nearby. **Khabarovsk** (p254) is a pleasant place and **Ekaterinburg** (p191) is interesting. There's also **Novosibirsk** (p205), the capital of Western Siberia, Russia's religious capital at **Sergiev-Posad** (p174), the Kremlin at **Rostov-Yaroslavski** (p177) and **Vladivostok** (p263), eastern railway terminus and port for ships to Japan. Other places to visit in Siberia include **Bratsk** (p237), **Severobaikalsk** (p239), **Yakutsk** (p240), **Sakhalin Island** (p262), **Magadan** (with air connections to Alaska, see p262), **Perm** (p189), **Omsk** (p203), **Tyumen** (p201), **Krasnoyarsk** (p215) and **Chita** (p249).

❏ **Not the Trans-Siberian Express!**
Writers of travel articles may wax lyrical about trips on the fabled 'Trans-Siberian Express' but in fact no regular train service of that name exists. While the British generally refer to their trains by a time ('the 10.35 to Clapham'), the Russians and Chinese identify theirs by a number ('Train No 19', from Beijing to Moscow).

Just as in the West a few crack services have been singled out and given a name ('The Orient Express') some of the better services in Russia also have names, but 'Trans-Siberian Express' is not among them. 'Trans-Siberian', 'Trans-Mongolian' and 'Trans-Manchurian' are, however, convenient terms for the routes across Siberia and between Moscow and Beijing. The service which runs from Moscow to Vladivostok is train No 2, also known as the 'Rossiya'. Running from Vladivostok to Moscow, it's train No 1. The 'Baikal' is train No 9 from Irkutsk to Moscow, train No 10 when it runs in the other direction. The services which run between Moscow and Beijing are usually identified only by their numbers.

When to go

The mode of life which the long dark nights of winter induce, the contrivances of man in his struggle with the climate, the dormant aspect of nature with its thick coverage of dazzling snow and its ice-bound lakes now bearing horses and the heaviest burdens where ships floated and waves rolled, perhaps only a fortnight ago: – all these scenes and peculiar phases of life render a journey to Russia very interesting in winter.
Murray's Handbook for Travellers in Russia, Poland and Finland (1865)

For most people the mention of Siberia evokes a picture of snowy scenes from the film *Doctor Zhivago* and if they are not to be disappointed, then winter is probably the best time to go. It is, after all, the most Russian of seasons, a time of fur-coats, sleigh-rides and vodka. In sub-zero temperatures, with the bare birch trees and firs encased in ice, Siberia looks as one imagines it ought to – a bare desolate waste-land. The train, however, is kept well heated. Russian cities, too, look best and feel most 'Russian' under a layer of snow. St Petersburg with its brightly painted Classical architecture is far more attractive in the winter months, when the weather is crisp and skies clear. However, if you want to visit some of the Siberian cities, you'll probably find it more enjoyable to go in the late spring, summer or autumn, when there is more to do.

In Siberia, the heaviest snowfalls and coldest temperatures (as low as minus 40°C/F in some of the towns the train passes through), occur in late November and December. Between January and early April the weather is generally cold and clear. Spring comes late and then the warmest months are July and August, when it is warm enough for an invigorating dip in Lake Baikal. The birch and aspen provide a beautiful autumnal display in September and October.

In Moscow the average temperature is 17°C (63°F) in summer and minus 9°C (+16°F) during the winter; there are occasional heavy summer showers.

Tourist season
The tourist season reaches its peak between mid-July and early September. In the low season, between October and April, some companies offer discounts on tours; you'll also find it much easier to get a booking for the train at short notice at this time. During the summer it can be difficult to get a place on the popular Moscow – Beijing route without giving notice of several weeks.

Bookings and visas

ORGANISED TOURS OR INDIVIDUAL ITINERARIES?

Note that the regulations governing the issuing of Russian visas are particularly susceptible to change. Check the latest situation with your embassy or through the organisations listed on p18.

Group tours

The majority of visitors to Russia travel in organised groups for two main reasons. First, it's much easier as Russia is hard to get around without speaking Russian. Secondly the easiest way to get a visa to Russia is through a travel company offering group tours. This is also how the Russian authorities prefer you to travel. Groups are easier to control and tend to spend more money in the country than the itinerant back-packer. Going with a tour group takes all the hassle out of travelling. Most tours are accompanied by an English-speaking guide from the moment you arrive in Russia right up until you leave the country. Provided you are happy with the programme, it can also be the cheapest way to see the most in the shortest time. See pp22-39 for tour companies.

Semi independent travel

This is currently the most popular way for foreigners to travel on the Trans-Siberian: using a specialist agency who makes the accommodation and train bookings (with or without stops along the way) that are required in order to get a Russian tourist visa. You are able to choose the number and length of stops and departure dates; in effect you design your own package. Once you're in Russia, you're on your own; some agencies, however, also offer transfer services to or from the railway station in Moscow. A number of travel agents in the West will make these arrangements, or you can deal directly with one of the locally-based organisations (see p18 and p39) that offer packages on the Trans-Siberian.

Fully independent travel

Getting a fully independent visa, one that allows you to roam the country at will, stopping when and where you feel like it, is difficult because few embassies will issue any visa without confirmation of your accommodation. Some organisations (see p18) are able to add several days or sometimes several weeks onto an invitation based on accommodation booked with them for just one night. Bear in mind that few Russians outside the largest cities speak English, and that tourist infrastructure is very limited.

❏ Trans-Siberian on the Internet

The world's best Trans-Sib World Wide Web site – **http://www.xs4all.nl/~hgj** – is run by keen Trans-Cyber, Herbert Groot Jebbink. The site contains over 60 links to Trans-Siberian reports, photos, information sites, travel agencies, travel guides and videos. It also has a message page where you can leave comments, and the e-mail address is hgj@xs4all.nl. There is a mirror of the page at http://www.russia-rail.com/link.htm. A selection of Herbert's best sites:

Personal reports

- http://www.xs4all.nl/~hgj/logboek.html (in Dutch, Herbert Groot Jebbink – how about an English translation Herbert?)
- http://www.udel.edu/IntlProg/eli/92trip/trip1.html (Lowell Riethmuller)
- http://www.elec.qmw.ac.uk/~andy/london-hk/stage2.html (Andy Martin)
- http://www.u-net.com/~istar/d_tsr.htm (Steve Davies)
- http://solar.rtd.utk.edu/oldfriends/spbweb/lifestyl/125/headhome.html (Allison Lawler)
- http://www-karc.crl.go.jp/kss/xkozima/play/siberia/overview.html (in Japanese, Hideki Kozima)
- http://www.ego.net/tlogue/xsib/index.htm (Keith West)
- http://sunsite.icm.edu.pl/travel/SAJANY/eng/rosja.html (Przemyslaw Gamdzyk)
- http://www.commonb.com/issue3/travel/russia/ (Arnold Wechsler)
- http://www.ncgia.ucsb.edu/~ashton/biography/worldtxt.html (Ashton Shortridge)
- http://www.webcom.com/whills/Russia/Russia95a.html (J Ward Hills)
- http://www.icf.de/siberian_deal/rportpge.htm (Eva, Kathy & Tatjana)
- http://www.netcom.com/~whstlpnk/thlantry.html (TH Lantry's 1918 report)
- http://www.redcross.org/hec/1920-1939/transib.html (Red Cross 1919-1920)

Information sites

- http://www.qqq.com/russia/express.html (in Dutch, DT&T Nederlandse)
- http://www.russia-rail.com (Russsia-Rail)
- http://minyos.its.rmit.edu.au/~tbmlc/travel/places/siberia/index.html (Budget Travellers World)
- http://solar.rtd.utk.edu/oldfriends/travel/index.html (Friends and Partners)
- http://fllc.smu.edu/staffpages/keena/siberia.html (Keena Costlow's Virtual Tour of Siberia in Summer)
- http://pavel.physics.sunysb.edu/RR (Russian Railways Technical Information)
- http://www-cse.ucsd.edu/users/bowdidge/railroad/rail-home.html (Robert Bowdidge's Railroad Resources)
- http://www.lonelyplanet.com/dest/eur/rus.htm (Lonely Planet's Destination Russia)
- http://chorus.wazoo.com/eggs/egg19.html (Carl Faberge's Trans-Siberian Railway Egg)

Travel agencies

Many travel agents now have Web sites, which, provided they're kept up to date, can be a useful source of information about their services. See the travel agencies listed on pp22-39 for addresses.

ROUTE PLANNING

Planning your route across Siberia can be rather more complicated than
you might imagine, especially if you wish to make a number of stops.
These trains are not tourist specials but working services used by local
people and they're very popular. On most routes they run to capacity and
travel is usually difficult without a reservation.

Main services

For more information see p393 but note that all timetables are subject to
change, nowhere more so than in this part of the world. Local times are
given below.

No	Name	Departs	on	at	Arrives	on	at
1	Rossiya	Vladivostok	4-7 per week	1:05	Moscow	Day 7	6:45
2	Rossiya	Moscow	4-7 per week	14:00	Vladivostok	Day 7	9:45
3	via Mongolia	Beijing	Tue	7:40	Ulan Bator	Thr	13:20
3	via Mongolia	Ulan Bator	Thur	13:50	Moscow	Mon	19:00
4	via Mongolia	Moscow	Tue	19:50	Ulan Bator	Sun	9:00
4	via Mongolia	Ulan Bator	Sun	9:30	Beijing	Mon	15:33
5		Ulan Bator	Mon	13:50	Moscow	Fri	17:20
6		Moscow	Wed	21:25	Ulan Bator	Mon	8:00
9	Baikal	Irkutsk	4-7 per week	20:10	Moscow	Day 5	5:55
10	Baikal	Moscow	4-7 per week	12:05	Irkutsk	Day 5	6:30
19	via Manchuria	Beijing	Sat	22:40	Moscow	Fri	23:00
20	via Manchuria	Moscow	Fri	21:25	Beijing	Fri	6:32
23		Beijing	Sat	7:40	Ulan Bator	Sun	13:20
24		Ulan Bator	Thur	9:30	Beijing	Fri	15:33
89		Beijing	Tue/Fri	18:53	Ulan Bator	Thur/Sun	10:45
90		Ulan Bator	Tue/Fri	12:10	Beijing	Thur/Sun	6:20
263		Ulan Bator	Daily	21:00	Irkutsk	Day 3	8:45
264		Irkutsk	Daily	19:10	Ulan Bator	Day 3	6:40

Moscow to Vladivostok and Japan

If you're travelling to or from Japan you must begin by deciding the date
when you will sail into or out of Vladivostok. Details of the ferry service,
which runs only between May and October, are given on p272.

There are many trains that travel the railway between Moscow and
Vladivostok but there is only one good service that does the whole trip. It
is the famous and excellent No 1/2 Rossiya train. There are other good
trains which run between cities along the route such as No 9/10 Baikal
train (Moscow to Irkutsk) which increases your options if you are making stopovers along the way.

Moscow to Beijing: Trans-Manchurian or Trans-Mongolian?

You have two choices when travelling by train between Moscow and Beijing: No 3/4 Trans-Mongolian via Ulan Bator (Chinese Train) and the No 19/20 Trans-Manchurian via Harbin (Russian Train)

There are advantages and disadvantages with both. While only the Trans-Mongolian offers de luxe carriages (see p114), the coupé carriages on both routes are identical and this is what most travellers use. The Trans-Manchurian departs from Beijing at a more civilised time that the Trans-Mongolian and costs less. You need a Mongolian transit visa on the Trans-Mongolian but not on the Trans-Manchurian. The journey time on the Trans-Mongolian is about 12 hours less than on the Trans-Manchurian. The Trans-Mongolian gives you the chance to stop off in Ulan Bator. There is currently very little difference between the restaurant cars on the two routes.

Summer is the most difficult time to get bookings for these two routes so make arrangements several months in advance. There are weekly departures in each direction on the both trains, with an additional Trans-Manchurian service in the summer.

Stopping off in Mongolia

If you're taking the Trans-Mongolian route, breaking your journey in Ulan Bator is highly recommended. It's easiest to organise through a specialist agency since visa support is required, as for Russia.

Side trips

The possibilities for side trips are numerous. These include the Siberian **BAM Railway** (see p123), the **Silk Route** (see p124) and travelling to Pyongyang in **North Korea** via Ussurisk, near Vladivostok. It's also possible to continue by rail to **Vietnam** on the Beijing-Hanoi Express, a three-night journey.

VISAS

Visas are required by most nationalities visiting Russia, Mongolia and China. Getting a visa for Russia and Mongolia is not straightforward but China is not a problem. Visa regulations change regularly and even the border guards and police of the country often do not know the latest law. Check with travel agents or embassies.

You'll need to show your visa when staying at a hotel and often when buying a rail ticket.

Russian and Mongolian visa invitations

To get a visa to Russia or Mongolia, you need either an invitation or some written document that confirms your accommodation details (usually booked accommodation vouchers). Both of these must state your passport details, the duration of your stay and the cities you will visit. If you are going on a package tour, then your travel agents will organise everything and you will see none of the paperwork. Invitations are valid only if they are sent by a registered travel company in Russia or Mongolia. These companies will have a travel company number issued by the country's respective Ministry of Foreign Affairs. The invitations must contain the address of the travel company, and your name, passport data and itinerary. Normally, travel companies will issue an invitation only for the days that you have paid for. However there are a number of travel companies that are willing just to send you the Russian visa invitation and leave the rest to you. These include:

- **Russia-Rail Internet Travel Service** (http://www.russia-rail.com/, e-mail russia-rail@russia-rail.com).
- **Sindbad Travel** (☎ +7-812-327 8384, fax +7-812-329 8019, e-mail sindbad@ryh.spb.su), ul 3rd Sovetskaya 28, St Petersburg, Russia, You can also get invitations from their North America partner, **Russian Youth Hostels & Tourism** (☎ +1-310-379 4316, fax +1-310-379 8420, e-mail 71573.2010@compuserve.com).
- **Passport Travel** (☎ +61-3-9867 3888, fax +61-3-9867 1055, e-mail bmccunn@werple.mira.net.au) Suite 11, 401 St Kilda Rd, Melbourne, Victoria 3004, Australia.
- **Host Families Association (HOFA)** (☎/fax +7-812-275 1992, e-mail alexei@hofak.hop.stu.neva.ru) 5-25 Tavricheskaya, 193015 St Petersburg, Russia. This is a network of academic and professional families offering homestays throughout the country.
- **G & R International** (☎ +7-095-374 7366, fax +7-095-374 6132, e-mail grint@glas.apc.org), Block 6, Office 4, Institute of Youth, ul Yunosti 5/1, Moscow, Russia.
- **IRO Travel** (☎ +7-095-971 4059, 280 8562, fax +7-095-280 7686, e-mail tgh@glas.apc.org), 10th floor, ul Bolshaya Pereyaslavksaya 50, Moscow.
- **Andrew's Consulting** (☎ +7-095-126 9413, 232 3601), Moscow.

Visa invitation and in-country registration currently costs approximately:

 £20/US$30 for a one-month, single entry tourist visa invitation
 £32/US$50 for a one-month, double entry tourist visa invitation
 £32/US$50 for a three-month, single entry business visa invitation
 £47/US$75 for a three-month, double entry business visa
 £220/US$350 for a one-year, multiple entry business visa

Russian visa

The Russian visa is normally a three-page document rather than a stamp in your passport. This system is a cold war legacy from when Western countries discriminated against citizens who had visited the Soviet Union and this would be obvious if passport stamps were used. The visa contains all your passport information, entry and exit dates, the cities that you will visit, and the organisation that invited you. The Russian embassy requires a completed visa application form, three photos signed on the back, your passport (or photocopy of the first few pages of your passport), and a visa invitation or booked accommodation vouchers. Normally, visas will be issued within 10 working days.

Visa costs depend on where you apply, the type of visa you require, the urgency of the issuing of the visa and your nationality. Single entry tourist visas cost £10 (UK), US$40 (USA), A$60 (Australia), US$50 (Beijing); transit visas cost £10 (UK), A$50 (Aust), US$80 (Beijing).

Any foreigner visiting Russia for more than three months requires a doctor's certificate proving that they are not HIV/AIDS positive. This system was introduced as a political gimmick to appeal to anti-West forces in Russia.

● **Transit visa** The transit visa is normally given only to those who are in transit through Russia and are not staying overnight in any city. Most Russian embassies issue transit visas for only 72 hours; Russian embassies in China, however, will issue them for up to 10 days which will allow you to travel on the Trans-Siberian, stay in Moscow for two days and then leave. If you are intending to stay in Irkutsk for more than two nights, you will have to get a tourist visa. Extending a transit visa for up to seven days is possible but a lot of work. To get a transit visa you normally will need to show proof that you will be entering and leaving within 72 hours, such as rail tickets and onward visas.

● **Tourist visa** The tourist visa requires an invitation but allows you to stay for up to a year. You can get a double entry version.

● **Business visa** This allows you to stay for up to a year and requires an invitation from a registered Russian business. It is stamped in your passport. The inviting Russian company must get the Consular Division of the Russian Ministry of Foreign Affairs to send a telex to your Russian consulate authorising such a visa. It may be possible to obtain a business visa on the spot when you arrive at Moscow's or St Petersburg's international airports but this is a costly option (£125/US$200) and most airlines will refuse to carry you without a Russian visa.

● **Private visa** This visa is for those who are invited by Russian friends or relatives but it can take three months or more to get. The process involves your Russian friend getting an authorisation known as an *izveshchenia* (извещение) from the OViR office in their home town, and mailing the authorisation to you. You then need to take the authorisation to your Russian embassy which confirms it with OViR back in Russia. You can get a private visa for a stay of only up to three months though extensions are common in Russia.

❏ **Visa tips**
● When you are requesting an invitation to Russia, ask for it to cover several days on each side of your planned stay, as extending visas once you are in Russia can be time-consuming and expensive.
● It is best to have every city that you intend to visit listed on your visa as some hotels will not let you stay if you are not 'authorised' to be in their city.
● Take your visa invitation and three photos to Russia with you in case you have to extend your visa or replace it.

Russian visa extension Provided you have registered your visa within three working days of arrival, you can get normally get a visa extension. This usually involves the organisation which issued your visa invitation writing an official statement requesting an extension. Sometimes an international train ticket is all the proof you need. It is best to get your visa extended in Moscow (see p150) rather than in St Petersburg where it can be very difficult.

If Intourist issued your visa invitation, you can go to almost any Intourist hotel and ask for an extension. The rules are different in each hotel but in late 1996, one traveller reported being given a two-week extension from the Hotel Irkutsk-Intourist for US$60 plus the requirement that they stay a night in that hotel.

Russian visa registration All visitors staying in Russia for more than 72 hours must register with the local police or OViR within 72 hours of arrival. If you are staying at a hotel, this will be organised by the staff. The company that issued the invitation has to register your visa. If you are late in registering, you may be fined. If you do not register at all you may be fined at the border and the fine is totally subjective.

The back of your visa will be stamped when you register. In the Soviet era, it was important to have registration stamps covering every day to indicate your movements. Nowadays it is necessary to get only one stamp.

Mongolian visa

To get a Mongolian visa, you will need a valid passport, three photos, and usually an invitation. Visas generally cost the equivalent of £9-16/US$15-25 for a three to five-day wait or £32/US$50 on the spot.

Transit visas are for stays of 48 hours or less and cost about £9/US$15. You do not need an invitation from a Mongolian organisation but you will need to show your onward ticket and visa for the next destination – China or Russia. Some travellers have managed to get a transit visa at the border but since this was expensive and may not still be possible it's not worth the risk.

Tourist visas are issued for up to 90 days and there are single, double and triple entry versions. An official invitation from a Mongolian organisation or individual is required. If your trip is booked through a travel company, they will supply the invitation. If you are organising it yourself, you'll need to get an official letter (with lots of stamps on it). Travellers report that hawkers in front of the Mongolian embassy in Beijing will sell you such a letter. However, you might be buying a worthless invitation as the Beijing embassy may not accept any invitation unless it is from a Class A registered Mongolian travel agency (see p274). It appears that Mongolian embassies in Europe are less strict and virtually any letter or fax from Mongolia will suffice; you could try writing to any hotel in Ulan Bator, asking them to book you a room in return for a letter of invitation.

Mongolian visa extension Extending your visa once you are in Mongolia can be a trying experience. The Ministry of Foreign Affairs will invariably tell you that it is impossible but be persistent. Everything is possible although it might cost you a few dollars. To do this in Ulan Bator, see p274.

In 1996, a new law was passed that required travellers to get police permission before going to the countryside. This aggravating rule was apparently created to curb the operations of the growing numbers of foreign missionaries in the country. As a result, to legally go to the countryside you need to get the tourist agency which sends you your visa invitation to type up a fancy-looking document with stamps and signatures on it listing the places you plan to visit. You, and an agency representative, take this to the police who stamp the document to give it validity. If you fail to do this you might find yourself paying £40/US$60 or more in fines at each police checkpoint.

Mongolian visa registration It is essential that all travellers who hold tourist visas register with the police as soon as possible after arriving in Mongolia and definitely within 10 days of arrival. Visitors who fail to register will be stopped at departure, and fined. The delay could mean that you miss your train. For registration in Ulan Bator, see p274.

Chinese visa

The process of getting a visa is straightforward at most Chinese embassies; but if you're entering China via Russia or Mongolia, get a Chinese visa before you reach Moscow as the embassy there is not easy to deal with. Visas are generally given for up to a month but if your application form indicates that you will be in the country for less time than this you'll be given less. Extensions within China are easy to arrange in most cities.

MAKING A BOOKING IN BRITAIN

Note that Russia has no tourist office in Britain and no doubt in response to the numerous questions they receive some of the travel agents below produce very informative brochures. For the Chinese section of the journey visit the **China National Tourist Office** (☎ 0171-935 9427), 4 Glentworth St, London NW1 5PG, which is open 9.30am to 5pm, Monday to Friday.

● **Regent Holidays** (☎ 0117-921 1711; fax 0117-925 4866, e-mail: 106041.1470@compuserve.com; http//www.regent-holidays.co.uk), 15 John St, Bristol BS1 2HR. Recommended by several readers, they specialise in independent travel to the CIS, China and Mongolia but also offer group tours. Moscow-Beijing tickets for either the Trans-Mongolian or the Trans-Manchurian route cost from £300 including full board on the train to the Chinese or Mongolian border; Moscow to Vladivostok costs from £522 (excluding food on the train). Beijing-Moscow (either route) is from £477 including three nights' full board in Beijing but no meals on the train; all include the first night's hotel accommodation and transfers. They have stopover packages in Irkutsk and Ulan Bator. Bookings are accepted from outside the UK . They can arrange visas (allow at least six weeks for Russian visas), flights, tours and accommodation.

● **The Russia Experience** (☎ 0181-566 8846, fax 0181-566 8843, e-mail 100604.764@compuserve.com, http//travel.world.co.uk/russiaexp), Research House, Fraser Rd, Perivale, Middlesex UB6 7AQ. Recommended and now in co-operation with the Hong Kong Trans-Siberian agency, Monkey Business, the Russia Experience specialises in budget and medium-priced travel for individuals. Homestays can be arranged in St Petersburg and Moscow, as well as with Siberian villagers and Mongolian nomads. They offer a variety of packages including Moscow to Beijing from £290 including one night's accommodation in Moscow; Moscow to Beijing on the Trans-Manchurian route with one night in Moscow and two nights on Lake Baikal with a village stay and transfers from £470. They can also arrange Russian language courses in Moscow, and they provide a full complimentary visa-handling service.

● **Intourist Travel** (☎ 0171-538 8600/5965, fax 0171-538 5967, e-mail: info@intourus.demon.co.uk, http://www.intourus.demon.co.uk), Intourist House, 219 Marsh Wall, Isle of Dogs, London E14 9PD; Manchester (☎ 0161-834 0230) Suite 2F, Central Buildings, 211 Deansgate, Manchester M3 3NW; Glasgow (☎ 0141-204 5809, fax 0141-204 5807), 29 St Vincent Place, Glasgow G1 2DT. **Tours:** Intourist offers a 16-day Trans-Siberian tour from £1285 on the Trans-Manchurian route with two nights in Moscow and Irkutsk, seven nights on the train in all, and four nights in Beijing. The price includes flights from London, transfers, bed and breakfast in the cities, full board on the train and city tours. Visas can be arranged. **Independent travel:** Intourist's bookings on the Moscow-Beijing train include one night's accommodation in Moscow, meals on the train as far as the Russian border, and transfers in Moscow, from £282/311 in the low/high season. From Moscow to Vladivostok costs £366 year round. There's a range of stopover packages. Boat ticket for the Vladivostok-Niigata trip costs £200-230 depending on class. Single/double rooms in Intourist hotels are priced from £27/30 in Moscow, £33/36 in St Petersburg and £49/59 in Irkutsk.

● **Goodwill Holidays** (☎ 01438-716421, fax 01438-840228, e-mail: cwilding@msn.com) Manor Chambers, The Green, School Lane, Welwyn, Herts AL6 9EB, offer tickets from Moscow to Irkutsk from £175, to Beijing £305 and Khabarovsk £250. They can arrange homestay accommodation from £21 in Russia and £18 in Mongolia, half board. They also offer flights, a visa service (allow at least four weeks), transfers, and some package tours. A five-day hiking trip around Lake Baikal, with tented accommodation and all meals costs £187.

● **The Imaginative Traveller** (☎ 0181-742 8612, fax 0181-742 3045, e-mail: imagtrav@aol.com) 14 Barley Mow Passage, Chiswick, London W4 4PH, is the UK agent for Sundowners (see p34). This efficient company offers tickets for all the routes (Trans-Siberian, Trans-Mongolian and Trans-Manchurian) for individual travellers, as well as package tours. They can also arrange flights, visas, and accommodation en route.

● **China Travel Service and Information Centre** (☎ 0171-388 8838, fax 0171-388 8828), 124 Euston Rd, London NW1 2AL. The friendly and helpful staff here can help with tickets from Beijing to Moscow (in this direction only) as well as tours throughout China. Prices ex Beijing are from £260 to £400 for the Trans-Manchurian or the Trans-Mongolian route; from £175 to Ulan Bator, from £210 to Irkutsk. You'll be given a voucher which you exchange for a confirmed ticket in Beijing.

● **Progressive Tours** (☎ 0171-262 1676, fax 0171-724 6941, e-mail: 101533.513@compuserve.com) 12 Porchester Place, Marble Arch, London W2 2BS. Specialises in budget and youth travel to Russia and offers tickets on all routes. Moscow to Beijing from £285 in the off-season (Nov-Apr). Various packages are possible. Prices for direct trains (Moscow to Beijing) include one night full board in Moscow, berth on train, transfers, two sightseeing trips, English-speaking guide and meals on board the train until the Russian border. Moscow to Vladivostok costs from £250. They can arrange hotels in St Petersburg (from £26) and in Moscow from £25 for a twin room, flights to Moscow (from £190 single and £195 return), stopovers in various places including Ulan Bator and the ferry or flight from Vladivostok to Japan.

● **China Travel Service Ltd** (☎ 0171-836 9911, fax 0171-836 3121, e-mail: cts@ukcts.demon.co.uk, http://www.wtg-online.com/cts) 7 Upper St Martin's Lane, London WC2H 9DL. CTS will book individual itineraries across China as well as offering a 22-day tour from London to Hong Kong and back with three nights in Beijing and two in Xian, Guilin and Hong Kong. Prices start at £1545 for two or more people travelling together and from £1895 for an individual. The price includes flights from/to London, second class sleeper, and transfers. Individual tickets are sold only for the Trans-Mongolian and Trans-Manchurian trains; cheapest tickets from Moscow to Beijing are £290 (includes night in Moscow, full board until Russian border, transfers and two sightseeing tours) and from Beijing to Moscow £195 (rail ticket only). They can also arrange train travel in China and hotels in Moscow, Irkutsk and Ulan Bator.

● **Steppes East** (☎ 01285-810267, fax 01285-810693, e-mail: sales@steppeseast.co.uk, http://www.steppeseast.co.uk), Castle Eaton, Cricklade, Wilts SN6 6JU, have a range of of tailor-made individual Trans-Siberian itineraries from around £340.

● **STA Travel** has many branches in Britain,including: 117 Euston Rd, London (☎ 0171-465 0484); 38 Store St, London (☎ 0171-580 7733); 86 Old Brompton Rd London (☎ 0171-581 4132); 11 Goodge St, London (☎ 0171-436 7779); Bristol (☎ 0117-929 4399, fax 0117-929 4791) 25 Queens Road; Manchester (☎ 0161-839 7838) 75 Deansgate; Cambridge (☎ 01223-366966) 38 Sidney St; Brighton (☎ 01273-728282), 38/9 North Street; Oxford (☎ 01865-792800), 88 Vicar Lane; Glasgow (☎ 0141-338 6000, fax 0141-338 6022), 184 Byres Rd. A student travel centre which sells tickets for all routes for independent travellers, as well as flights.

● **Page & Moy** (☎ 0116-252 4433, fax 0116 -254 9949) 136-140 London Road, Leicester LE2 1EN. Recommended by several readers, their 12-day trip from Moscow to Beijing, stopping at Irkutsk along the way, is good value from £1295. Flights are included at either end of the trip.

● **Iris Mikof Ltd** (see p34) Although they do not yet have agents in the UK, this Australian-Russian joint venture company is worth contacting for their excellent accommodation.

● **Voyages Jules Verne** (☎ 0171-616 1000, fax 0171-723 8629, e-mail: sales@VJV.co.uk.), 21 Dorset Square, London NW1 6QG. The'Central Kingdom Express' will take you from Moscow to Beijing in the original Pullman carriages of the 'Nostalgic Orient Express'. The sixteen-day tour costs £2595 including flights from/to London.

Budget travellers booking from Britain should note that they can also arrange Trans-Siberian rail tickets through agencies based in Hong Kong (see p39) and Russia (p18 and p30).

Special interest tours
● **Great Rail Journeys** (☎ 01904-679969, fax 01904-679961) 71 The Mount, York YO2 2AX, have a three-week fully-guided rail trip from London to Beijing with a possible add-on to Vietnam. Accommodation is in three- and four-star hotels. This company also operates a range of interesting rail journeys to many other parts of the world.

● **GW Travel** (☎ 0161 928 9410, fax 0161 941 6101), 6 Old Market Place, Altrincham, Cheshire WA14 4NP, run distinctly upmarket tours chartering their own steam-hauled trains and luxurious carriages that come complete with chefs and attendants. The carriages are your main base while in Russia, you stay in hotels only in Moscow. A fully-escorted month-long tour from Moscow to Vladivostok with a side-trip to Mongolia costs £6995. A 14-day trip from Vladivostok to Moscow is £2800. For £115 per person per day (for six passengers) you can travel around Russia in your own private saloon car on a tailor-made tour.

● **Enthusiast Holidays** (☎ 0181-699 3654, fax 0181-291 6496, e-mail: vicallen@polxpres.itsnet.co.uk), 146 Forest Hill Road, London SE23 3QR. They arrange tours for railway enthusiasts and sell tickets for rail travel in Europe, including London to Moscow, but not for the actual Trans-Siberian route.

● **Dorridge Travel Service** (☎ 01564-776252, fax 01564-770117), 7 Station Approach, Dorridge, Solihull, B93 8JA.

● **Intourist** Special interest tours department: ☎ 0171-538 8600.

● **Industrial Railway Society** (☎ 01734 475 949, fax 01734 475 656), 16 Berrylands Rd, Caversham, Berks RG4 8NU

● **TEFS** (☎ 01509 262745, fax 01509 263636), 77 Frederick St, Loughborough, Leics LE11 3TL

● **Warwickshire Railway Society** (☎ 01564 826143), 145 Fulford Hall Rd, Tidbury Green, Solihull, West Midlands

● **LCGB**, Flat 5, 91 Albemarle Rd, Beckenham, Kent BR3 5JZ

● **Steam & Safaris** (☎ 01433 620805, fax 01433 620837), Eccles House, Eccles Lane, Hope, nr Sheffield S30 2RW

● **Leva** (☎ 01582 421203), 5 Hartley Rd, Luton, Beds LU2 0HX

Embassies in Britain
● **Russia** (☎ 0171-229 8027), 5 Kensington Palace Gardens, London W8 4QS. Open weekdays 10.00-12.30, not Wed. The queues here are extremely long so it may be worth paying for the visa services offered by most travel agents who deal in Russia (prices for this service vary considerably). Your passport is required, as well as a completed visa application form and three passport photos. A single entry visa costs £10, multiple entry £100 and a transit visa £10-15. In theory a visa can be issued in ten working days and by post in three weeks; travel agents now warn travellers that visas will take between four and six weeks to be issued.

● **China** (☎ 0891-880808 or, between 2 and 4pm, 0171-631 1430), 31 Portland Place, London W1 3AG. Open 09.00-12.00 (Mon to Fri). This is quite easy to do yourself. Two passport photos are required. A single entry visa valid for one month from the date of entry and three months from the date of issue costs £25 and takes three working days to issue. Check these dates before leaving the embassy.

● **Mongolia** (☎ 0171-937 0150), 7 Kensington Court, London W8 5DL. Open 10.00-12.30 (Mon to Fri). Transit visas cost £10, take three days to process (a one-day service costs £6 more) and rail confirmation is not required. If you're staying in Mongolia a tourist visa is required and for this you'll need a letter from Zhuulchin or another accredited travel agent. The tourist visa takes one week to process and costs £17 (a one-day service costs £6 more). Mongolia also has embassies in Moscow (p151), Irkutsk (p222) and Beijing (p288), along the route of the Trans-Siberian but it's best to get your visa before you go.

Getting to Moscow or Beijing from Britain

By air: Flights to Moscow start at around £150 one-way, £240 return; Aeroflot (☎ 0171-493 2410) usually offer the cheapest seats. Beijing is more expensive: at least £250 one way, £460 return. Air China are usually a good bet for cheap seats and can be booked from CTS (☎ 0171-388 8838). **By rail:** The completion of the Channel Tunnel means that British rails are at last linked with those of the Far Eastern Railway in Vladivostok. Tickets for the daily service to Moscow from London via Brussels can be booked through BR International (☎ 0171-834 2345) on either the Ostend (ferry) route or with Eurostar to Brussels. Prices on the ferry route are: £207 single, £406 return (£157/313 if you're under 26) second class, or £301/592 first class plus a sleeper fee (first class only) of £40-90 each way. There are reductions for OAP railcard holders. On the Eurostar route prices are £248 single, £410 return and first class £390/780 (no reductions for under 26 or OAP).

MAKING A BOOKING IN CONTINENTAL EUROPE

From Austria

● **Rail Tours** (☎/fax 43 1450 1488), Rosensteing 92/20, A-1170 Wien.

From Belgium

● **Intourist Benelux** (☎ 02-502 4440, fax 02-502 7913), Galerie Ravenstein 2, 1000 Brussels, arranges tickets for the Trans-Mongolian and Manchurian routes, flights, and accommodation en route and offers visa support. From BF16,590, or from BF24,100 with two nights in Moscow and two in Irkutsk.

● **Boundless Adventures** (☎ 02-426 40 30, fax 02-426 03 60), Ave Verdilaan 23/15/1080 Brussels - Ganshoren.

From Bulgaria
- **Sofintour** (☎/fax 2-880628) Burl Stambolijsky, 24, Sofia.

From Czech Republic
- **KHKD** (☎/fax 02-74 90 88), Jaroslav Krenek, na Podkovce 13, CS-147 00 Praha 4.

From Denmark
- **Kilroy Travels** (☎ 33 11 00 44, fax 33 32 32 69), Skindergade 28, DK-1159 Copenhagen K. They also have offices in Aarhus (☎ 86 20 11 44), Fredensgade 40, DK 8100, Aarhus C; Aalborg (☎ 99 35 11 00) Oesteraagade 23, DK 9000; Odense (☎ 66 17 77 80) Pantheonsgade 7, DK 5000; Lyngby (☎ 45 88 78 88) Lyngby Torv 6, DK 2800. These offices sell tickets for the Moscow-Beijing route (from DK2400) and can arrange hotels in Moscow, St Petersburg and Irkutsk, and visas.
- **Albatros** (☎ 33-32 24 88), Frederiksberggade15, DK-1459, Copenhagen K.

From Finland
- **Kilroy Travels** (☎ 90-680 7811), Kaivokatu 10 D, Helsinki; also in Oulu (☎ 981-372 720) Pakkahuoneenkatu 8; Tampere (☎ 931-223 0995) Tuomiokirkokatu 36; and Turku (☎ 921-273 7500) Eerikinkatu 2. These offices sell tickets for the Trans-Mongolian and the Trans-Manchurian routes and can arrange flights, accommodation in Moscow, St Petersburg and Irkutsk, and visas.
- **Sindbad Travel/Russian Youth Hostels** (Russia ☎ 812-329 8018, fax 812-329 8019, e-mail ryh@rhy.spb.su), PO Box 8, SF-53501, Lappeenranta. They are associated with Russian Youth Hostels and will make hostel reservations, provide visa support and sell air and train tickets. Letters are sent to RYH by Finnish post.
- **OY Finnsov Tours Ltd** (☎ 90-694 2267/2011, fax 90-694 5534, e-mail: webmaster@finnsov.fi, http//www.finnsov.fi/fs_trsib.html), Eerikinkatu 3, 00100 Helsinki.

From France
- **SARL Intourist** (☎ 01-47 23 80 10, fax 01-47 23 01 00) 25 rue Marbeuf, 75008 Paris.
- **Office de Tourisme de Chine** (☎ 01-42 96 95 48), 116 ave des Champs Elysées, 75008 Paris.
- **CTS**, 32 rue Vignon, 75009 Paris.

From Germany
- **Travel Service Asia Gmbh** (TSA-Reisen) (☎ 07371-8522; fax 07371-12593, e-mail 100140.3174@compuserve. com) Schulgasse 1, D-88499 Riedlingen. Rail prices: Moscow-Beijing on the Trans-Manchurian route from DM590 and on the Trans-Mongolian from DM630; Moscow to

Vladivostok direct from DM890. Worth contacting even if you don't live in Germany (an English brochure is available). The ferry from Vladivostok to Japan costs from DM810; Moscow to Beijing with two nights in Moscow, Irkutsk, Ulan Bator and Beijing including transfers and breakfast is from DM1665. They can also arrange tickets from Beijing to Moscow. Homestay is offered in many places from DM49. They will arrange visas if you send your passport or will provide visa support if you want to apply in your own country. They deal with **Baikal Complex** in Irkutsk (see p222) who provide hiking and trekking tours round Lake Baikal, with some new treks on Olkhon Island.

● **Lernidee Reisen** (☎ 030-786 50 56; fax 030-786 55 96) Dudenstrasse 78, 10965 Berlin. Siberian itineraries from this company range from a 2nd class ticket on the Moscow-Beijing train for DM625 (Beijing to Moscow DM775) to stopovers in Mongolia (four days/three nights DM819 including full board, English speaking guide. Other routes include Moscow to Vladivostok DM968. Homestay and hotel accommodation offered in several cities.

● **White Nights** (☎ 06211-400337, e-mail 06221400337-0001@t-online.de), Pfarrgasse 31, 69121 Heidelberg. Agent for budget travel operator based in St Petersburg.

● **STA Travel** has many branches in Germany some of which include: Hamburg (☎ 040-450 38400), Renzelstrasse 16, 20146 Hamburg; Bonn (☎ 0228-225579), Nassestrasse 11, 53113 Bonn; Berlin (☎ 030-311 0950), Goethestrasse 73, 10625 Berlin; Frankfurt/Main (☎ 069-703035), Bockenheimer Landstrasse 133, 60325 Frankfurt/Main; Mannheim (☎ 0621-10074) L14.11, 68161 Mannheim; Cologne (☎ 0221-442011), Zuelpicher Strasse 178, 50937 Cologne; Heidelberg (☎ 06221-23538), Haupstrasse 139, 69117 Heidelberg; Wuerzburg (☎ 0931-521716), Zwinger 6, 97070 Wuerzburg. A student travel centre which sells tickets for all routes for independent travellers, as well as flights.

● **SRS** (☎ 030-281 6741), Studenten Reiseservice GmbH, Marienstrasse 25, 1040 Berlin.

● **China Tourist Office** (☎ 069-520135), Ilkenhanstrasse 6, D-60433 Frankfurt/Main. Information office for Germany, Austria, Switzerland and Holland.

● **CTS** (☎ 069-250515), Dusseldorferstrasse 14, D-6000 Frankfurt.

● **Mongolia Zhuulchin Foreign Tourism Corporation** (☎ 030-474 2484, fax 030-471 8833) 2 Arnold Zweig St, 3R 13189 Berlin. This office will make bookings in Mongolia for non-Germans.

● **Mochel Reisen GMBH** (☎ 07821-43037, fax 07821-42998), Postfach 48, D-77922, Lahr/Schwarzwald.

● **Verein Frankische Reisefreunde** (☎ 0911-513 771), D-90409 Nurnberg, Aussere Bayreuther Str. 57.

● **Steam Loco Safari Tours** (☎/fax 02247-5376) D-5207 Ruppichteroth 4

From Hungary
● **Danubius Travels** (Ms Edit Rubos), (☎ 01-117 3652, fax 01-117 0210. Budapest 1051, Szervita 8.

From Italy
● **Hans Jurgen Rosenberger** (☎/fax 045 715 1751), I-37012 Bussolengo (VR), Via E Toti 3.

From the Netherlands
● **Eurocult** (☎ 030-243 96 34, fax 030-244 24 75, e-mail: euro.cult @inter.nl.net, http//www.xs4all.nl/~eurocult/13GRORUS.html) Balderikistraat 83 Utrecht. Check their Web site for the latest prices.
● **Global Travel** (☎ 020-696 75 85, fax 020-697 35 87) Anne Kooistrahof 15, 1106 WG Amsterdam; can make train reservations in 51 countries – worth contacting even if you don't live in the Netherlands.
● **Kontakt International** (☎ 020-623 47 71, fax 020-625 80 57, e-mail: kontakt@tip.nl, http//www.eurazie-overland.nl/TranssiExpress.html) Prins Hendrikkade 104, 1011 AJ Amsterdam. Claim to be the only company in Western Europe who can confirm train ticket reservations, for travel within Russia or starting from Russia, within 14 days. They can make reservations for all the routes and will send tickets to the client's home country.
● **White Nights** (☎ 050-3146749), Kleine Butjesstaat 38, 9712 Gronnigen. Agent for St Petersburg budget travel operator.
● **Tiara Tours** (☎ 076-565 28 79, fax 076-560 26 30, e-mail: tiara@ tref.nl, http//www.tref.nl/1167/comerci/tiara/tiara6.htm), Beukenlaan 2, 4834 CR Breda.
● **VNC Travel** (☎ 030-261 38 44, fax 030-262 77 34, e-mail: VNCTravel @inter.nl.net, http//www.qqq.com/vnc/index2.html) Mississippidreef 95, Postbus 79, 3500AB Utrecht.

From Norway
● **STA** (☎ 22 42 10 20. fax 22 33 21 02, e-mail kilroy@kilroy.no), Nedre Slottsgt 23, N 0157 Oslo. Also in Bergen (☎ 55 32 64 00) Parkveien 1, N 5007 Bergen; Stavanger (☎ 51 89 55 50), Breigata 11, N 4006 Stavanger; Trondheim (☎ 73 50 22 90), Jomfrugata 1, N 7011 Trondheim. These student travel centres sell package tours for the Trans Siberian and Trans-Mongolian routes – they deal with a Norwegian tour operator who provides the whole package including visas and accommodation.
● **Intourist** (☎ 22 42 28 99, fax 22 42 62 01), FR Nansens Plass 8, 0160 Oslo. They can arrange tickets for all routes (in either direction) as well as visas, accommodation and flights.
● **Kinareiser** (China Travel Ltd) (☎ 47 22-110 057, fax 47 22-360 544), Hegdehaugsveien 10, 0167 Oslo. This company represents Sweden's Eco Tour Production Mongolian adventure trips.

From Poland
● Intourist Warsaw (☎/fax 22-296370), ul Krucza 47, 00-509 Warsaw.

From Russia
Several organisations within Russia can arrange visa support (see p18). For other companies refer to the city guides: St Petersburg (p131), Moscow (p149), Novosibirsk (p207), Irkutsk (p222), Severobaikalsk (p239), Khabarovsk (p256), Vladivostok (p265).

From Slovakia
● **Intourist Bratislava** (☎ 7-333317, 7-330608), Venturska 2, Bratislava 81104, Slovakia

From Sweden
● **Frank Stenvall** (☎ 40-127 703, fax 40-127 700), Foreningsgatan 67, S-211 52 Malmo.
● **Fram Resor AB** (☎ 08-215934. fax 08-214060), Box 64, Kingsgaten 56, 11132 Stockholm.
● **STA** (☎ 08-234515), Box 7144. Kingsgatan 4, 10387 Stockholm.
● **Eco Tour Production** (☎ 46-0498 487 105, fax 46-498 487 115, e-mail janw.nomadic@gotlandica.se), Burge i Hablingbo, 620 11 Havdhem, Gotland. One of the best adventure travel agencies operating in Mongolia, they offer treks, horse riding and sports fishing. On a typical trek with six people, luggage and one *ger* (yurt) are loaded onto yak carts and the group is accompanied by a cook, herdsman-trailfinder and two horses or camels. Also contacable via Nomadic Journeys (fax 976 1 323 043, e-mail nomadic@ magicnet.mn). See p274 for details.

From Switzerland
● **White Nights** (☎/fax 031-333 8855) Haldenstr 5, 3014 Bern). Agent for St Petersburg budget travel operator.
● **Julian Pignat** (fax 022-340 1530) 2 Ch Mouille-Galland, 1214 Vernier. European representative for Bam Tour Co (see p239).
● **Stockli-Reisen AG** (☎ 01-242 8555, fax 01-242 8600), Stauffacher-strasse 26, 8004 Zürich.

MAKING A BOOKING IN NORTH AMERICA
From the USA
● **Russian Youth Hostels** (☎ 310-379-4316; fax 310-379-8420, e-mail 71573.2010@compuserve.com) 409 N Pacific Coast Highway #106, Suite 390, Redondo Beach, CA 90277. RYH organises visa support for independent travellers, and set up the St Petersburg youth hostel (p133).
● **Safaricentre** (☎ 310-546-4411; fax 546-3188; e-mail: info@safaricentre.com) 3201N Sepulveda Blvd, Manhattan Beach CA 90266. Agents for the popular Sundowners Adventure Travel trips (see p34).

● **Rahim Tours** (☎ 561-585-5305; fax 561-582-1353, toll free ☎ 800-556-5305), 12 South Dixie Highway, Lake Worth, Florida 33460. Offers Trans-Siberian tours and will also arrange individual itineraries. Moscow to Vladivostok from US$439, Moscow to Beijing from US$455, a four-night package tour covering Lake Baikal, Irkutsk and Listvyanka is from US$487. Homestays are offered in several cities, Moscow from US$30 and Irkutsk from US$36. They also arrange city tours and visas.

● **Intourist USA** (☎ 212-757-3884, fax 212-459-0031) 610 5th Ave, Suite 603, New York 10020, can organise Trans-Siberian tours and individual packages from Moscow to Beijing with stopovers in Siberia.

● **White Nights** (☎/fax 916-979-9381) 610 La Sierra Drive, Sacramento, CA 95864, is the US agent for the budget operator based in St Petersburg (Russia). Beijing to Moscow costs from US$210.

● **Petit Travel Consultants** (☎ 800-683-7403, fax 508-792-0065, e-mail: 70713.235@compuserve.com) 1405 Main St, Worcester, MA 01603, are specialists in budget travel on all routes across Siberia.

● **Mir Corporation** (☎ 206-624-7289, 800-424-7289, fax 206-624-7360, e-mail: mir@igc.apc.org, http://www.kiss.com/fr/mir/Trans-Siberian.html) 85 South Washington St, Suite 210, Seattle, WA 98104. This company has a wide range of individual and small group itineraries with accommodation in homestays or hotels.

● **China Voyages** (☎ 415-398-2244, 800-914-9133, fax 399-0827, e-mail: info@chinavoyages.com, http://www.chinavoyages.com/siber.html 582 Market St, San Francisco, CA 94104. They market a range of independent and group tours in Russia, Mongolia and China. A 21-day trip from Moscow to Beijing costs from US$1690.

● **World Rail Travel Specialists Inc**. (☎/fax 516 878 2260), PO Box 732, E Moriches, NY 11940-0732.

● **Rail Study Tours** (☎ 703 998 2362, fax 703 528 0356), PO Box 3468, Alexandria, VA 22302.

● **STA** (☎ 415-391-8407), 51 Grant Avenue, San Francisco CA 94108. STA has many branches in North America, some of which include: Boston (297 Newbury St, Boston, MA 02115, ☎ 617-266-6014), Santa Monica (120 Broadway, Apt 108, Santa Monica, CA 90401, ☎ 310-394-5126), New York (10 Downing St (6th Avenue and Bleecker), New York, NY 10014, ☎ 212-627-3111, fax 212-627-3387), Chicago (429 South Dearborn St, Chicago, Il 60605, ☎ 312-786-9050), Seattle (4341 University Way, NE, Seattle, WA 98105, ☎ 206-633-5000) and Miami (3115 Commodore Plaza, Miami Fl 33133, ☎ 305-461-3444). A student travel centre which sells tickets for all routes for independent travellers.

● **Russia Tours** (☎ 718-375-9500, fax 718-339-1376) 1324 East 15th, NY 11230.

● **General Tours** (☎ 800-221-2216), 53 Summer St, Keene NH 0343.

● **Russian Travel Bureau Inc** (☎ 800-847-1800, fax 212-490-1650, e-

mail: russtvl@interserve.com, http://www.asternet.com/get/russntrvl)
225 East 44 Street, New York, NY 10017. Features several Trans-Siberian
packages and can also organise individual itineraries.
● **Mongolian Tourism Corporation of America**, Inc (☎ 908-274 0088
fax 908-274 9181), Princeton Corporate Plaza, 1 Deer Park Drive, Suite
M, Monmouth Junction, New Jersey, 08852. This company represents
Mongolia's Zhuulchin Foreign Tourism Corporation.
● **Boojum Expeditions** (☎ 406-587 0125, fax 406-585 3474, e-mail boo-
jum@mcn.net, http://www.gorp.com/boojum/boojum.htm) 14543 Kelly
Canyon Road, Bozeman, MT 59715. Organises horse riding trips in the
Hovsgol region which is the northern-most province of Mongolia and lies
on the border with Siberia and Tuva.
● **Tread Lightly Ltd** (☎ 203-868 1710, 800 613 0060, fax 203-868
1718), One Titus Rd, Washington Depot, CT 06794. Represents Sweden's
Eco Tour Production Mongolian adventure trips.

Embassies There are **Russian Consulates** in Washington (☎ 202-939-
8907, 1825 Phelps Place NW, DC 20008); San Francisco (☎ 415-928-
6878, 2790 Green St, CA 94123), New York (☎ 212-348-0926, 9 E 91st
St, NY 10128) and Seattle (☎ 206-728-1910, 2323 Western Building, 201
6th Ave, Seattle, WA 98121.

There are **Chinese Consulates** in New York (☎ 212-330-7400, 520
12th Ave), Washington DC (☎ 202-328-5205), Houston (☎ 713-524-
0780), and San Francisco (☎ 415-533-4885).

The **Mongolian Embassy** (☎ 202-333-7117) is at 28-33 M Street
North West, Washington DC20001 and also in New York at 6 East 77th
St, New York, NY 10021 (☎ 212-861-9460).

Further information Neither Russia nor Mongolia maintains a tourist
office in North America but you can get information from Intourist USA
and the Mongolian Tourism Corporation of America (see above). You can
obtain information about China from: **China National Tourist Office** (☎
212-867-0271, fax 212-599-2892), Lincoln Building, 60 E 42nd St, Suite
3126, New York, NY 10165 and in Los Angeles, 333 West Broadway,
Suite 201, Glendale, Los Angeles, CA 91204, ☎ 818-545-7505).

Getting to Russia or China Numerous airlines fly from the US to
Russia. Aeroflot is among the cheapest with departures from many US
cities. From New York, flights to Moscow cost from US$450 one way.
Flights between New York and Beijing cost from US$800 one way. There
are now also weekly flights on Alaska Airlines and Aeroflot between
Magadan (on the north-east Pacific coast of Russia) and Seattle with a

---

(**Opposite**) **Top:** Each compartment is staffed by a *provodnitsa* (female attendant) or
a *provodnik* (male attendant). **Bottom:** The *Rossiya* is the name the Russians give to
the train which crosses Siberia from Moscow 9289km to Vladivostok. (Photos TPB).

stop in Anchorage. Magadan is linked by air to main cities in Siberia.

From Canada

● **Travel by Rail** (☎ 416-701-0756, fax 701-0751) 72 Prescott Ave, Toronto, Ontario M6N 3GS. Agents for Sundowners Adventure Travel (p34).

● **Adventure Centre/Westcan Treks** has several branches in Canada and operates a range of Trans-Siberian itineraries. A nine-day trip from Moscow to Beijing costs Can$855 with two nights in Moscow. They can arrange group tours as well as individual itineraries. There are offices in Toronto (☎ 416-922 7584, e-mail info@tor.trek.ca), 25 Bellair St, Toronto, Ontario M4Y 2P2; Vancouver (1965 West 4th Avenue, Vancouver BC V6J 1M8, ☎ 604-734 1066, e-mail: info@van.trek.ca), Edmonton (8412 109th St, Edmonton, Alberta T6G 1E2, ☎ 403-439 9118, e-mail: info@trek.ca) and Calgary (336 14th St NW, Calgary, Alberta T2N 1Z7, ☎ 403-283 6115, e-mail: westcant@cadvision.com).

● **Russian Tourist Office** (☎ 514-849 6394), 1801 McGill College Avenue, Suite 630, Montreal, Quebec H3A 2N4.

● **Intours Corporation** (☎ 416-766 4720, fax 766 8507), 2150 Bloor St West, Toronto, Ontario M6S 1M8, can organise trips on the Trans-Siberian for individuals or groups.

● **Exotik Tours** (☎ 514-284-3324, fax 514-843-5493), Suite 806, 1117 Ste-Catherine St West, Montreal, Quebec H3B 1H9. They sell packages for the Trans-Mongolian and Trans-Manchurian routes from Moscow to Beijing in 1st/2nd class from US$690/490 (Jan-Apr, Nov-Dec) or US$710/505 (May-Oct) including hotel and sightseeing tour and transfers in Moscow, full board until the Russian border. Other itineraries include stops and accommodation in places such as Novosibirsk and Irkutsk. Sightseeing tours in Mongolia are available, from US$285/1835 including transfers, accommodation, full board, guided visits and entrance fees as well as internal flights and land transportation. In addition they can arrange scheduled flights and visas for Russia, Mongolia and China.

Embassies in Canada There are **Russian Consulates** in Ottawa (☎ 613-236 7220, fax 238 6158), 52 Range Rd, Ottawa, Ontario K1N 8J5, and Montreal (☎ 514-843 5901, fax 842 2012), 2355 Ave du Musée, Montreal, Quebec H3G 2E1.

The **Chinese Consulate** is in Ottawa (☎ 613-789-3434), 515 St Patrick's St, Ottawa, Ontario K1N 5H3. There are consular representatives in Vancouver (☎ 604-734 0704), 3380 Granville St, Vancouver, BC V6H 3K3; and Toronto (☎ 416-324 6466), 240 St George St, Toronto, Ontario M5R 2P4. **Mongolia** does not have an embassy in Canada. You're advised to collect your visa in Beijing or Moscow.

(Opposite) Top: Soft sleeper coupé. **Bottom:** Russian Railways dining car. (Photos: Tatyana Pozar-Burgar)

MAKING A BOOKING IN AUSTRALASIA

From Australia

● **Passport Travel** (☎ 03-9867 3888, fax 03-9867 1055, e-mail bmc-cunn@werple.mira.net.au, http://www.travelcentre.com.au/) Suite 11, 401 St Kilda Rd, Melbourne, Victoria, 3004. Formerly Red Bear Tours, they can organise Trans-Siberian, visa invitations, group tours, BAM railway tours, Mongolian tours and individual travel arrangements.

● **Iris Hotels Pty Ltd** (☎ 02-9580 6466; fax 02-9580 7256, e-mail iris-tour@mpx.com.au), PO Box 60, Hurstville, NSW 2220. This Australian-Russian joint venture has offices in both countries but accepts bookings from abroad at the Australian office. The Russian partner is pioneering eye surgeon Professor SN Fyodorov, whose Mikof Group (MNTK) operates 13 hotels in Russia, each attached to an eye micro-surgery clinic. Aimed at mature travellers in self-formed groups (minimum 12 people) they offer stopovers in Vladivostok, Khabarovsk, Irkutsk, Novosibirsk, Ekaterinburg, Perm, Moscow and St Petersburg. Kiev and Warsaw options are also available. Staying in hotels beside clinics may sound unusual but you're guaranteed hot water, absolute cleanliness and if you happened to fall ill you couldn't be in better hands.

● **Russia-Rail Internet Travel Service** (http://www.russia-rail.com/, e-mail russia-rail@russia-rail.com). Russia-Rail can book rail tickets for anywhere in Russia, organise visas and provide timetable information. Russia-Rail is run by Athol Yates, author of two guidebooks to Russia.

● **Sundowners Adventure Travel** (☎ 03-9600 1934, fax 9642 5838, e-mail: sundownr@ozemail.com.au), Suite 15, 600 Lonsdale St, Melbourne, Vic 3000, has been recommended by several readers. They offer escorted and semi-independent Trans-Siberian, Trans-Mongolian and Trans-Manchurian trips. There's a 29-day fully escorted rail itinerary from Hong Kong via Xi'an to Beijing, Ulan Bator, Irkutsk, Moscow and St Petersburg, and an 18-day St Petersburg to Vladivostok trip (eight days on the train, ten in hotels). On their independent trips all bookings on the train and in hotels are made for you to a tailor-made itinerary but you travel independently. The itinerary can also include Vietnam using the Beijing-Hanoi rail-link.

● **Adventure World** North Sydney (☎ 02-9956 7766), 73 Walker St; Melbourne (☎ 03-9670 0125) 3rd Floor, 343 Little Collins St.

● **Gateway Travel** (☎ 02-9745 3333, fax 02-9745 3237, e-mail: gatrav@magna.com.au, http://www.magna.comau/~gatrav), 48 The Boulevard, Strathfield NSW 2135. They have a range of express routes and stopover packages between Moscow and Beijing from A$375-3275.

● **STA** (☎ 02-9212 1255), 1st Floor, 732 Harris St, Ultimo, Sydney NSW 2007. There are dozens of branches including Adelaide (☎ 08-9223 2426) 235 Rundle St; and Canberra (☎ 06-247 863) 13-15 Garema Place.

● **China Travel Service** (☎ 02 9211 2633) 757-759 George St, Sydney NSW 2000.

● **Baltic & Eastern Travel** (☎ 08-9 232 1228, fax 08-9244 5528) 1st floor, 2 Hindmarsh Square, Adelaide 5000.

● **Russian Travel Bureau** Sydney (☎ (02-9262 1144) Level 5, 75 King St; Melbourne (☎ 03-9600 0299) 3rd floor, 343 Little Collins St; Brisbane (☎ 07-6229 9716) 7th floor, 131 Elizabeth St; Perth (☎ 09-322 6812) 1st floor, 181 St Georges Terrace, offers semi-independent Trans-Mongolian and Trans-Manchurian trips.

● **Safeway Travel** (☎ 03-9534 4866, fax 03-9534 4206) 288 Carlisle St, Balaclava. Offers tours and hotel arrangements.

● **Access Travel** (☎ 02-9241 1128) 5th floor, 58 Pitt St, Sydney. Travel arrangements for China, Trans-Siberian from Beijing to Europe. Offer stop-overs in Ulan Bator, Irkutsk, Lake Baikal, St Petersburg and Moscow.

● **Classic Oriental Tours** (☎ 02-9261 3988) Level 4, 491 Kent St, Sydney, offers escorted and semi-independent Trans-Mongolian, Trans-Manchurian and Trans-Siberian trips.

Embassies in Australia The **Russian Embassy** (☎ 06-295 9033, 295 9474, fax 295 1847) is at 78 Canberra Ave, Griffith ACT 2603. There's also a **Russian Consulate** (☎ 02-9327 5065) at 7-9 Fullerton St, Woollahra NSW 2025.

There are **Chinese Consulates** at 539 Elizabeth St, Surry Hills, NSW 2010 (☎ 02-9698 7929), 75-77 Irving Rd, Toorak Vic 3142 (☎ 03-9822 0607), and 15-17 William St, Perth WA 6000 (☎ 08-9481 3278). The newly-opened **Mongolian Consulate** (☎ 02-9319 4797) is at 112/189 Philip St, Waterloo NSW 2017.

From New Zealand
● **Eurolynx** (☎ 09-379 9717), 3rd floor, 20 Fort St, Auckland, is the agent for Sundowners Adventure Travel (see Australia).

● **Suntravel** (☎ 09-525 3074, fax 525 3065) PO Box 12-424, 407 Great South Rd, Penrose, Auckland. Specialises in China, Russia and Mongolia with homestay and hotel accommodation.

● **Adventure World** (☎ 09-524 5118), 101 Great South Road, Remuera, PO Box 74008, Auckland.

● **STA** (☎ 09-309 9995), 10, High St, Auckland. STA also has branches at 223 High St, Christchurch (☎ 799 098) and 207 Cuba St, Wellington (☎ 850 561).

Embassies in New Zealand The **Russian Consulate** (☎ 04-476 6113) is at 57 Messines Rd. Karori, Wellington. The **Chinese Consulate** (☎ 04-472 1382) is at 2-6 Glenmore St, Wellington. **Mongolia** does not have an embassy in New Zealand.

MAKING A BOOKING IN SOUTH AFRICA

● **Student Travel** (☎ 11-447 5551, fax 11-447 5775), The Arcade, 62 Mutual Gardens, Corner of Oxford Rd and Tyrwhitt Avenue, Rosebank, Johannesburg 2196 and at 62 Strand St, Cape Town 8001 (☎ 21-418 6570, fax 21-418 4689).
● **Concorde Travel** (☎ 11-486 1850), 3rd fl, Killarney Mall, Riviera Rd, Killarney, Johannesburg 2193. Agents for Iris Hotels (see p34).
● **Travelvision** (☎ 11-482 5222), PO Box 4779, 9th fl, Metal Box Centre, Johannesburg 2000. Agents for Sundowners Adventure Travel (see p34).

MAKING A BOOKING IN ASIA

From Japan

The friendly and efficient **Euras Tours Inc** (formerly Japan Soviet Tourist Bureau, ☎ 03-5562 3381, fax 03-5562 3380), 7-3, Azabudai 1-chome, Minato-ku, Tokyo 106, will handle bookings for rail journeys to Europe. They offer a series of itineraries, combinations of flights and train journeys, and it's possible to fly from Japan (Niigata) to Khabarovsk or to arrange ferry tickets to Vladivostok. Note that the boat does not operate in the winter. They can also organise your journey via Shanghai, Beijing and Ulan Bator. Contact them for full details and prices.

Alternatively, you could take the boat from Kobe to Shanghai, make your own way to Beijing and organise your ticket there. The journey takes two days and although the boat is Chinese-run, the chef is Japanese, there are futons (mattresses) in the cabins and Japanese-style baths. Details of the weekly service and tickets from:

● **Japan-China International Ferry Co Ltd (JIFCO)** (☎ 03-5489 4800, fax 03-5489 4788), Daikanyama Pacific Bldg, 10-14 Sarugakucho, Shibuya-ku, Tokyo 150 and Room No 201, San-ai Bldg, 1-8-6, Shinmachi, Nishi-ku, Osaka 550. Services from Kobe or Osaka to Shanghai operate all year, from ¥18,400 one way. Tickets can also be bought from branch offices of Japan Travel Bureau and Kinki Nihon Tourist.
● **United Orient Shipping Agency** Co (☎ 03-3740 2061, fax 03-3740 2085), 7th Floor, Rikkokai-sogo Bldg, 32-3 Kita Shinagawa 2-chome, Shinagawa-ku, Tokyo 140. Sells boat tickets for the Niigata/Fushiki to Vladivostok trip. Current prices are ¥36,600-89,000, (US$340-830) including meals and the port tax at Vladivostok.
● **Tokyo Tourist Information Center** (☎ 03-3502 1461), 6-6, Yurakucho 1-chome, Chiyoda-ku, Tokyo. (Subway: Ginza/Yurakucho).
● **STA** Tokyo: 4th Floor, Nukariya Bldg, 1-16-20 Minami Ikebukuro, Toshima-Ku, Tokyo 171 (☎ 03-5391 2922, fax 03-5391 2923); 1st Floor, Star Plaza Aoyama Bldg, 1-10-3 Shibuya, Shibuya-ku, Tokyo 102, (☎ 03-5385 8380, fax 03-5485 8373); 2nd Floor, Toko Bldg, 1-5 Yotsuya,

Shinjuku-ku, Tokyo 160, (☎ 03-5269 0751, fax 03-5269 0759). Osaka: 6th Floor, Honmachi Meidai Bldg, 2-5-5, Azuchi-machi, Chuo-ku, (☎ 06-262 7066, fax 06-262 7065).

● **Intourist Japan Co Ltd** (☎ 03-3238 9118, fax 03-3238 9110), 5F Daihachi Tanaka Bldg, 5-1 Gobancho, Tokyo.

● **Mongol Zhuulchin Tours Co** (☎ 03-3486 7351, fax 03-3486 7440), Tokyo, Japan. This company is the Tokyo office of Mongolia's Zhuulchin Foreign Tourism Corporation.

● **Japan China Tourist Office** (☎ 03-3433 1461), 6F Hachidai Hamamatsu-cho Bldg, 1-27-13 Hamamatsu-cho, Minato-ku, Tokyo.

● **Russian Embassy** (☎ 03-3583 5982, fax 3503 0593), 1-1 Azabudai, 2-chome, Minato-ku, Tokyo 106; **Consulate** (☎ 06-848 3452, fax 848 3453), Toyonaka-Shi, Nizhimidorigaoka 1-2-2, Osaka-Fu.

● **Chinese Embassy** (☎ 03-3403 3381, fax 03-3405 3345), 3-4-33 Moto Azabu, Minatu-ku, Tokyo 106.

From China

● **CITS Beijing** (☎ 6515 8565), 28 Jianguomenwei Dajie can book rail tickets and they're open Mon-Sat, 08.30-17.00. The cheapest Trans-Siberian tickets you are likely to get anywhere are sold here, although a ticket is no good without a reservation and there can be a long wait in the summer. Tickets are currently around Y1600 to Y1800 for hard class to Moscow.

● **Monkey Business Infocenter** (☎/fax 6329 2244 ext 4406, e-mail: MonkeyChina@compuserve.com), Beijing Commercial Business Complex, No 1 Building Yu Lin Li, Office 406, 4th Floor, Youanmenwai, 100054 Beijing, are definitely worth a visit to pick up the latest travel information. Can arrange tickets, stopovers and accommodation in Moscow as well as excursions in Mongolia. See p39 for further information. Open daily 10.00-20.00, (Tuesday, Friday and Saturday till 18.00), Sunday from 14.00-20.00.

❏ **Tickets? Wo mei yo!**
Nineteen days to Christmas and the only response I could get from the booking clerk for trains to Europe was: 'Wo mei yo'. He said there were no places. The last train which would get us home for Christmas was leaving in eight days time. I tried offering a bribe: 'Wo mei yo'. The prospect of spending Christmas in cold, drab Beijing was not a merry one. I asked the clerk to check his reservations list again. We'd been in the office for over an hour by then and he was thoroughly bored with us. Throwing down the comic he'd been trying to read and, thrusting a form at me he said 'Okay'. Not really believing him I asked 'No 19 train okay?'. 'Okay, okay,' he replied. We'd got our reservations. For tickets in the summer, however, you'd need to allow much longer but given enough time, determination and patience, almost anything is possible in China.

Getting tickets In the summer trains fill up quickly so if you plan to spend some time travelling around China make Beijing your first stop and get your reservations. It may also be possible to reserve a place on the train in Shanghai (ask at the travel bureau in the Peace Hotel) and there's also a Russian embassy there (20 Huangpu Lu).

Once you've made your reservation and paid your deposit, do the rounds of the embassies and collect your visas. You'll need US$ in cash and a stock of passport photos.

Embassies in Beijing You'll need to visit the Russian embassy and, for the Trans-Mongolian route, the Mongolian embassy. Most European nationalities and Americans don't need visas for Poland; Canadians, Australians and New Zealanders still do. For most nationalities, visas can be obtained in any order. You used to have to get them in strict order starting with the last country you'll be visiting but this is no longer the case. If you need visas for the countries you'll be visiting after Moscow it may be better to get all your visas here rather than in Moscow.

● **Russia** (☎ 6532 1267), 4 Dongzhimen Beizhong Jie. Open 09.30-12.00 weekdays. It's possible to get a **transit visa** (valid for 10 days from departure date from Beijing) without having to show your ticket out of Russia but queues here can be very long. You'll need three photos and a photocopy of the personal pages of your passport; the service costs US$50 (three-day wait) or US$100 (one day). Some nationalities have to pay an additional consular fee (US$12 if you're from the Netherlands, US$100 if you're from Burkino Faso). If you're stopping in Irkutsk, or for more than two days in Moscow you'll need a **tourist visa**, which requires visa support; visa charges for most nationalities are US$50 for processing in five days, US$100 for an express visa.

● **Mongolia** (☎ 6532 1203), 2 Xiushui Beijie, Jianguomenwai. Open 08.30-11.30 weekdays except Wed. Queues are also long here. You'll need one passport photo and US$15 for a transit visa (three days to process); the express service costs US$30 (same day). You won't be allowed to stop off in Mongolia on a transit visa. You'll need visa support for a tourist visa (US$25-50). Monkey Business should be able to help.

For more information on **Beijing** and other embassies see p288.

From Hong Kong
Hong Kong can be a good place to arrange a ticket or stopover package on the Trans-Siberian, although things may change as the colony reverts to China. The agencies here offer a range of services and booking with them from abroad is usually no problem.

Trans-Siberian tours and individual itineraries Organising a Russian tour in Hong Kong can take several weeks. There's no Russian embassy, so your passport will have to be sent to Japan or Thailand.

● **Wallem Travel** (☎ 2876 8231, fax 2876 1220/1, e-mail: wtlhk@wallem.com), Hopewell Centre, 46th floor, 183 Queen's Rd East, Wanchai. They offer a variety of packages for independent travellers. Vladivostok to Moscow from HK$10,530; Beijing or Ulan Bator to Moscow from HK$5820. This includes train fare, en suite hotel accommodation with breakfast in departure and arrival cities (and a night in Irkutsk on the Trans-Siberian route), city tours, transfers and Russian visa fee. Tickets only from Beijing to Moscow, from HK$2540 on the Trans-Manchurian route and from HK$2710 on the Trans-Mongolian route.

Trans-Siberian tickets and stopover packages Several of the travel agencies in the Nathan Road area can arrange tickets at short notice (two weeks or under). Some will sell you a voucher to exchange at their branch in Beijing for a ticket with reservation. Others sell you an open ticket with a reservation voucher and you must get the ticket endorsed by CITS in Beijing. Getting the reservation is the difficult part so don't accept an open ticket without a reservation voucher. To visit Ulan Bator or Irkutsk you'll need tourist visas and for these you need visa support.

● **Monkey Business/Moonsky Star** (☎ 2723 1376; fax 2723 6653, e-mail: MonkeyHK@compuserve.com, http://www.monkeyshrine.com) E-Block, 4th floor, Flat 6, Chungking Mansion, 36-44 Nathan Rd, Kowloon (open 10am-6pm Monday to Saturday). The Monkeys are two Belgian brothers who've now put more than 12,000 budget travellers on the trains across Siberia. One's based in Hong Kong selling their packages and the other in Beijing at their **infocentre** (see p37) making sure everyone gets on the right train. The advantage of travelling with the Monkeys is that they provide the vital visa support you'll need for stopovers in Russia and Mongolia. They sell a range of individual packages from Beijing to Moscow (from US$340) and stopover packages including Ulan Bator (from US$695), Irkutsk and Listvyanka (from US$795) – the first night's accommodation in Moscow (three-star Hotel 'Aeroflop') is included in most packages. In the summer they run a popular six-day Mongolian stopover (from US$845) and a two-week Mongolia adventure tour by jeep, plane and train (from US$1290).

● **Time Travel Services** (☎ 2366 6222; fax 2739 5413, e-mail: timetrvl@hkstar.com), Block A, 16th floor, Chungking Mansions, 40 Nathan Rd, Kowloon. Also at the Hyatt Hotel (Shop No B22, Hyatt Hotel, 67 Nathan Road, Kowloon, ☎ 2722 6878). **Shoestring Travel** (☎ 2723 2306; fax 2721 2085, e-mail: shoetvl@hkstar.com), Flat A, 4th floor, Alpha House, 27-33 Nathan Rd, Kowloon. They sell tickets from Beijing to Moscow for the Trans-Mongolian and Trans-Manchurian routes as well as flights and visas.

● **Phoenix Services Agency** (☎ 2722 7378; fax 2369 8884), Room A, 7th floor, Milton Mansion, 96 Nathan Rd, Kowloon.

What to take

Woollen underwear is the best safeguard against sudden changes in temperature. High goloshes or 'rubber boots' are desirable, as the unpaved streets of the towns are almost impassable in spring and autumn; in winter felt overshoes or 'arctics' are also necessary. A mosquito-veil is desirable in E. Siberia and Manchuria during the summer. It is desirable to carry a revolver in Manchuria and in trips away from the railway. **Karl Baedeker** *Russia with Teheran, Port Arthur and Pekin, 1914,*

The best advice today is to travel as light as possible. Some people recommend that you put out everything you think you'll need and then pack only half of it. Remember that unless you're going on an upmarket tour, you'll be carrying your luggage yourself.

Clothes
For summer in Moscow and Siberia pack as for an English summer: thin clothes, a sweater and a raincoat. Clothes washing facilities in Russia are limited so it's best to take shirts and tops of a quick-drying cotton/polyester mixture and wash them yourself.

Winter in Russia and northern China is extremely cold, although trains and buildings are kept well-heated: inside the train you can be quite warm enough in a thin shirt as you watch Arctic scenes pass by your window. When you're outside, however, a thick winter overcoat is an absolute necessity, as well as gloves and a warm hat. It's easy to buy good quality overcoats/jackets in Beijing for about £20/US$30. If you're travelling in winter and plan to stop off in Siberian cities along the way you might consider taking thermal underwear. Shoes should be strong, light and comfortable; most travellers take sturdy running shoes. On the train, some people recommend slip-on kung-fu slippers available cheaply from sports shops in the West, Hong Kong or China. Russians wear track-suits or even pyjamas throughout the journey.

Dress casually; jeans are quite acceptable even for a visit to the Bolshoi Theatre. If you forget anything, clothes are expensive in Japan, cheap but shoddy in Russia, cheap and fashionable in Hong Kong, and very cheap but curiously dated in China.

Luggage
If you're going on one of the more expensive tours which include baggage handling, take a suitcase. Those on individual itineraries have the choice of rucksack (comfortable to carry for long distances but bulky) or shoulder-bag (not so good for longer walks but more compact than the rucksack). Unless you are going trekking in Russia or China, a zip-up

hold-all with a shoulder-strap or a frameless backpack are probably the best bet. It's also useful to take along a small day-pack for camera, books etc. Since bedding on the train and in hotels is supplied you don't need to take a sleeping-bag even when travelling in winter. However, sheets provided on the train are occasionally still damp from the laundry, so a sleeping sheet (a sheet used inside a sleeping bag) might be worth considering.

Medical supplies

Essential items are: aspirin or paracetamol; lip salve; sunscreen lotion; insect repellent (if you're travelling in summer); antiseptic cream and some plasters/bandaids; an anti-AIDS kit containing sterile syringes and swabs for emergency medical treatment. Note that Western brands of tampons and condoms are not easily available in Russia or China. Bring an extra pair of glasses or contacts lenses if you wear them.

You may want to take along something for an upset stomach ('Arrêt', for example) but use it only in an emergency, as changes in diet often cause slight diarrhoea which stops of its own accord. Avoid rich food, alcohol and strong coffee to give your stomach time to adjust. Paradoxically, a number of travellers have suggested that it's a good idea to take along laxatives. For vaccination requirements, see p47.

General items

A money-belt is essential to safeguard your documents and cash. Wear it underneath your clothing and don't take it off on the train, as compartments are occasionally broken into. A good pair of sun-glasses is necessary in summer as well as in winter when the sun on the snow is particularly bright. A compass is useful when looking at maps and out of the window of the train. Don't forget to take a good book (see p45). The following items are also useful: two-litre, solid plastic water bottle which

---

❏ **Luggage limits**

On my first Trans-Siberian trip from Beijing we had so much luggage that several taxi-drivers refused to take us to the station. Unfortunately all thirteen bags were necessary as we were moving back from Japan. On the train we'd managed to get some of them stowed away in the compartments above the door and under the seats when we were joined by a German girl travelling home after three years in China. Her equally voluminous baggage included two full-size theatrical lanterns which were very fragile. Then the man from Yaroslavl arrived with three trunks. We solved the storage situation by covering the floor between the bottom bunks with luggage and spreading the bedding over it, making a sort of triple bed on which we all lounged comfortably – eating, drinking, reading, playing cards and sleeping for the next six days. Dragging our bags around Moscow, Berlin and Paris was no fun, however. On subsequent journeys I didn't even take a rucksack, only a light 'sausage' bag with a shoulder strap and a small day-pack. Never travel with an ounce more than you absolutely need. Nowadays a 36kg luggage limit in compartments is strictly applied in Beijing and to a lesser extent in Moscow.

can take boiling water, a few clothes pegs, adhesive tape, ball-point pens, bike lock for securing your rucksack while you sleep, business cards, camera and adequate supplies of film (see p44), flashlight, folding umbrella, games (cards, chess -the Russians are very keen chess players -Scrabble etc), lavatory paper, calculator (for exchange rates), notebook or diary, penknife with corkscrew and can-opener (although there's a bottle opener fixed underneath the table in each compartment on the train), photocopies of passport, visa, air tickets, etc. (keep them in two separate places), sewing-kit, spare passport photographs for visas, string (to use as a washing-line), the addresses of friends and relatives (don't take your address book in case you lose it), thermos, insulated mug, spoon and knife, tissues (including the wet variety), universal bathplug (Russian basins usually don't have a plug), walkman (batteries are easily found locally), washing powder (liquid 'Travel Soap' is good).

Gifts

Not so long ago the sale of a pair of Levis in Moscow could cover your spending money for the entire trip but this is just not the case any more. Although you may have heard stories about how difficult it is to get hold of Western items in Russia it is now very hard for foreigners to trade anything on the black market.

Rather than things to trade, what you should bring in abundance is gifts. The Russians are great present givers and there's nothing more embarrassing than being entertained in a Russian home and then being presented with a truckload of souvenirs when you have nothing to offer in return. In the major cities, most Western goods can be purchased; however in Siberia it is a lot harder. Rather than give something that can be bought locally, bring things that are harder for Russians to get. These include postcards of your country, key rings and baseball caps. Bring a few foreign coins and badges as Russia is full of collectors. It is also worth bringing things to share (which can be bought locally): chocolate biscuits, sweets (but don't bother with Twixes, Mars Bars or Snickers bars, as they're all easily available). Cigarettes will always go down well.

It's also a good idea to bring things to show people: glossy magazines (as many glamorous pictures of celebrities as possible) and pictures of your family will all be interesting to someone who has never been abroad. The Chinese in particular adore looking at photographs of people.

❏ **What to give**

For gifts, don't take instant coffee – it's now ubiquitous. Real coffee would probably be more appreciated. No stamps for collectors as that hobby is out of favor amongst the young. Prettily wrapped gifts are specially appreciated as gift wraps are rarely seen. In Soviet times, newspaper was the only wrapping paper available. **Lawrence R Cotter** (USA)

❏ Platform food
I rather regretted having taken on so many supplies at Moscow before the journey, when I saw how much was on offer at the informal markets en route. Gastronomic offerings available from the hawkers at the various stations on the route included: fresh fruit and vegetables, bread, savoury pastries, pancakes, ice-cream, potatoes and various other hot dishes. Big city stations, however, often have no hawkers at all. **Anthony Kay** (UK)

Provisions

The range of food and drink available on the train is improving and you can now buy numerous things in the dining car that weren't previously available: alcohol, chocolate and sometimes even biscuits. There's also now a good selection of things to eat available from the hawkers on the platforms at the stations along the way. It's still wise to buy some provisions before you get on the train, though, especially if you are going the whole way without a break. A small bottle of Tabasco sauce or packet of chilli powder can come in handy if you like some heat in your food.

Some travellers bring rucksacks filled with food, though most people bring just some biscuits, tea-bags or instant coffee (with whitener and sugar if required); hot water is always available from the samovar in each carriage. Other popular items include drinking chocolate, beer and vodka (much cheaper on the platform than on the train), dried soups, tinned or fresh fruit, peanut butter, chocolate, crackers, cheese and pot noodles. If you forget to buy provisions at home there are Western-style supermarkets in both Moscow and Beijing where you can stock up with essentials.

Money

Moscow and St Petersburg are about the only cities where cashing travellers' cheques and getting credit card cash advances are not a problem. Most banks will do the exchange for between 2% and 4% commission. In the provinces, however you could be completely stuck.

Thus it is best to take as much US$ cash as you feel safe to carry and the rest in travellers' cheques, and hope that you make it to the capital. While other currencies may be acceptable (UK£, German DM and, in St Petersburg, Finnish Marks), everyone in Russia understands the word 'dollar'. The above is also true for Mongolia. In China travellers' cheques are widely accepted. Some places in China now also accept credit cards.

It's important that you bring notes of small denominations like US$1s and US$5s, and certainly not too many US$50 bills because it can be hard to get the correct change. Paying for a coffee in the Mongolian dining car with a US$20 bill will mean either donating the change to the waiter or accepting a suitcase full of togrogs. Make sure your US$ notes are in immaculate condition and not dated before 1990, as traders and even banks are likely to reject them if they are torn, badly creased or worn. Because of the circulation of outdated and worthless Russian banknotes, exchanging money on the street is not recommended. Always carry just a small amount of money in your pocket and the rest safely under your clothing.

Photographic equipment

Bring more film than you think you'll need, as you'll find there's a lot to photograph. Don't forget to bring some faster film for shots from the train (400 ASA). It's wise to carry all your film in a lead-lined pouch (available from camera shops) if you are going to let them go through Russian X-ray machines at airports.

Most major brands of film are available in Russia cities, but slide or high/low ASA film may be difficult to find outside Moscow and St Petersburg. In the large cities, you can have your film processed in one hour and the quality is acceptable but the price is high. Film development is naturally of a high standard in Japan but, unless you request otherwise, prints will be small. The large Friendship Stores and big hotels in Beijing may be all right. You certainly shouldn't risk having your photos developed in Mongolia.

Photography from the train

The problem on the train is to find a window that isn't opaque or one that opens. They're usually locked in winter so that no warmth escapes. Opening doors and hanging out will upset the carriage attendants if they

---

❏ **What not to photograph**

Taking pictures from the train used to be forbidden but now it's OK, although it would be wise not to get trigger-happy at aerodromes, military installations or other politically sensitive areas. In addition, many Russians still believe it is illegal to take any photos from a train and they may tell you in no uncertain terms to stop.

Remember that in Russia, as in most other countries, it's considered rude to take pictures of strangers, their children or possessions without asking permission. Often people are keen to have their picture taken but you must always ask. This is particularly the case during political demonstrations or rallies: the updater of the previous edition of this guide got stoned by a group of pensioners outside the White House in September 1993 for trying to get the next cover for *Time* magazine. Beware!

Refrain from photographing touchy subjects such as drunks, queues and beggars. Photography in churches is normally discouraged, and taking a photo of someone in front of an icon is considered disrespectful. A useful phrase is 'Mozhno vas snimat?' (Можно Вас Снимать) meaning simply, 'Can I take a photo of you?' When asking for permission, offer to send them a copy: and keep your word. If travelling in winter always carry your camera inside your pocket or elsewhere near your body as film gets brittle and batteries get sluggish in the intense cold.

catch you; if one carriage's doors are locked try the next, and remember that the kitchen car's doors are always open. Probably the best place for undisturbed photography is right at the end of the train: 'No one seemed to mind if we opened the door in the very last carriage. We got some great shots of the tracks extending for miles behind the train'. (Elizabeth Hehir, The Netherlands).

❏ **Window cleaning**
A squeegie, an instrument used by window-cleaners to remove water, can be easily obtained in a small size for car windows. This tool is an invaluable aid for cleaning the train's windows for photography, or for that matter just for passengers' viewing. **Robert Bray** (UK)

Background reading

A number of excellent books have been written about the Trans-Siberian, several of which are unfortunately out of print. If they're not in your library they should be available through the inter-library loans system. The following are well worth reading before you go:

● *Journey Into the Mind's Eye* by Lesley Blanch, is a fascinating book: a witty, semi-autobiographical story of the author's romantic obsession with Russia and the Trans-Siberian Railway.

● *To the Great Ocean* by Harmon Tupper (Secker and Warburg, 1965 and out of print) gives an entertaining account of Siberia and the building of the railway.

● *Guide to the Great Siberian Railway 1900* by A I Dmitriev-Mamanov, a reprint (David and Charles 1971 and also out of print) of the guide originally published by the Tsar's government to publicise their new railway. Highly detailed but interesting to look at.

● *Peking to Paris: A Journey across two Continents* by Luigi Barzini tells the story of the Peking to Paris Rally in 1907. The author accompanied the Italian Prince Borghese and his chauffeur in the winning car, a 40 horse-power Itala. Their route took them across Mongolia and Siberia and for some of the journey they actually drove along the railway tracks.

● *The Big Red Train Ride* by Eric Newby. A perceptive account of the journey, written in Newby's characteristically humorous style.

● *The Trans-Siberian Railway: A Traveller's Anthology*, edited by Deborah Manley, is well worth taking on the trip for a greater insight into the railway and the journey, as seen through the eyes of travellers from Annette Meakin to Bob Geldof.

● The *Princess of Siberia* is Christine Sutherland's biography of Princess Maria Volkonsky, who followed her husband to Siberia after he'd been exiled for his part in the Decembrists' Uprising. Her house in Irkutsk is now a museum.

● *Stalin's Nose* by Rory Maclean. Maclean explores the former Eastern Bloc in a battered Trabant with his elderly aunt Zita and a pig named

Winston. He recounts the histories of some of his more notorious relatives and it serves as a darkly humorous commentary on Communism and its demise. Highly recommended.

● *Among the Russians* by Colin Thubron (subtitled, 'Where Nights Are Longest') a humorous personal experience of travel in Soviet times.

● *A People's Tragedy – The Russian Revolution 1891-1924*, by Orlando Figes is a scholarly work that brings this turning point in Russia's history to life. Winner of the 1997 NCR Book Award.

● *Lenin's Tomb* by David Remnick is an historical account of the Gorbachev era to its end.

● *East of the Sun: The Conquest and Settlement of Siberia* by Benson Bobrick. Recently published (1993), this is a clear and readable narrative of the last four centuries of Siberian history.

However well written and accurate, these books are only the impressions of foreign travellers. You will get more of an idea of the Russian mind and soul from their own literature, even from the pre-Revolution classics. If you haven't already read them you might try some of the following:

● Dostoyevsky's *Crime and Punishment* (set in the Haymarket in St Petersburg).

● Tolstoy's *War and Peace*.

● Mikhail Bulgakov's weird but fascinating *The Master and Margarita*.

● *Dr Zhivago* by Boris Pasternak (whose grave you can visit in Moscow).

● *The Gulag Archipelago* by Alexander Solzhenitsyn.

● *Memories from the House of the Dead* is a semi-autobiographical account of Dostoyevsky's life as a convict in Omsk.

● *A Day in the Life of Ivan Denisovitch* by Alexander Solzhenitsyn details twenty-four hours in the life of a Siberian convict.

No guidebook can keep up with the changes in Russia so it's unfair to expect one to be totally up to date. The basic facts remain the same, though, and the following are recommended:

● *Russia, Ukraine & Belarus – a Lonely Planet travel survival kit* is very comprehensive. Other areas of interest to Trans-Siberian travellers that are covered by Lonely Planet include: North East Asia, China, Tibet, Japan, Hong Kong, Korea, Western Europe, Eastern Europe, the Baltic States, Poland, Hungary and Scandinavia. The new edition of their guide to **Mongolia** was released in mid 1997.

● *The Insider's Guide to Russia*, by Gleb Uspensky, is filled with anecdotes and insights that only a native can provide.

● *Holy Russia* by Fitzroy Maclean is probably the best historical summary (with walking tours) for the traveller.

● *The Russian Far East,* by Eric and Allegra Harris Auzulay, covers the cities of Vladivostok, Khabarovsk, Chita, Ulan-Ude, Yakutsk, Magadan, Petropavlovsk-Kamchatski and Yuzhno-Sakalinsk.

For further rail travels in Russia there are two comprehensive rail guides by Athol Yates. ***Russia by Rail including Belarus and Ukraine*** coves 50 cities and 300 towns along major rail lines. ***Siberian BAM Railway Guide: The Second Trans-Siberian Railway*** is the definitive guide to the 3400km long BAM (Baikal-Amur Mainline) railway in Eastern Siberia, with good coverage of the northern end of Lake Baikal.

For information on locomotives, ***Soviet Locomotive Types – The Union Legacy***, by AJ Heywood and IDC Button is invaluable. It's co-published by Luddenden Press (UK) and Frank Stenvalls (Sweden).

Health precautions and inoculations

No vaccinations are listed as official requirements for Western tourists visiting Russia, China, Mongolia or Japan. Some may be advisable, however, for certain areas (see below). If you plan to spend more than three months in Russia evidence of a recent negative AIDS test is required.

Up to date health information and on the spot vaccination services are available in London at **Trailfinders** (☎ 0171-938 3999) at 194 Kensington High Street, and at **British Airways Travel Clinic** (☎ 0171-439 9584), at 156 Regent St. **Nomad Travellers' Store & Medical Centre** (☎ 0181-889 7014) at 3-4 Turnpike Lane (Wellington Terrace), London N8 0PX offers travel medical advice, inoculations and supplies.

In the USA, the **Center for Disease Control and Prevention** (☎ 404-332 4559) in Atlanta is the best place to call for information. If you have a fax an automated service is provided on the above number to fax you back the latest health information for the countries you are visiting.

You should have **health insurance**, available from any travel agent, wherever you are travelling but especially if you are visiting Japan and Hong Kong where medical costs are astronomical.

INOCULATIONS

● **Diphtheria** There were outbreaks of diphtheria in Russia and the CIS in 1993. Check that you were given the initial vaccine as a child and a booster within the last ten years. The World Health Organisation recommends a combined booster dose of tetanus-diphtheria toxoid.

● **Tetanus** A booster is advisable if you haven't had one in the last 10 years: if you then cut yourself badly in Russia you won't need another.

● **Infectious hepatitis** Those travelling on a tight budget who will be eating in the cheaper restaurants in China run the risk of catching infectious hepatitis, a disease of the liver that drains you of energy and can last from three to eight weeks. It's spread by infected water or food, or by using utensils handled by an infected person. Gamma globulin injections give a certain amount of protection and are effective for six months. A more recent vaccine, 'Havrix', lasts twice that time but needs to be administered in two shots, two weeks apart.

● **Malaria** If you plan to go further south than Beijing you may need to take **anti-malarial tablets**. In parts of China, the parasite (carried by the *Anopheles* mosquito) that causes malaria is resistant to chloroquine, so you may need to take two kinds of tablet. Start taking the tablets one week before you go and continue for six weeks after you leave the malarial zone. If you're going to be in a malarial area you'd be foolish not to take the tablets: the disease is dangerous and on the increase.

● **Other** If you're planning to go off the beaten track in Mongolia and China it's advisable to have a vaccination against **meningococcal meningitis**. You may also wish to consider a pre-exposure **rabies** vaccination course, and a cholera shot if travelling to or through an epidemic area. (There was an outbreak of cholera near Ulan Bator in 1996). Ensure you've had recent typhoid and polio boosters.

> ❏ **Drinking water**
> Avoid tap-water in St Petersburg since it can cause a nasty form of diarrhoea (giardia), especially in summer. Although the water is all right in some other cities it's best to stick to mineral water or boiled water. In Irkutsk and Listvyanka you can drink the tap-water, which comes directly from Lake Baikal. Drink only boiled or bottled water in Mongolia and China; boiled water (in a thermos) is provided on trains and in hotels. Tap water is safe in Japan and Hong Kong.

MEDICAL SERVICES

Those travelling with tour groups will be with guides who can sort out medical problems; simple treatment from a doctor will usually be free. Serious problems can be expensive but you'll get the best treatment possible from doctors used to dealing with foreigners. If you're travelling independently and require medical assistance contact Intourist or an upmarket hotel for help. In Moscow or St Petersburg the best places to go in an emergency are the US Medical Centres. If you are in St Petersburg, Moscow, Ekaterinburg, Novosibirsk, Irkutsk or Khabarovsk, medical assistance is available at the MNTK clinics (see p34). Large hotels in China usually have a doctor in residence and in Beijing, Shanghai and Canton there are special hospitals for foreigners. Take supplies of any prescription medicine you may need. Medical facilities in Mongolia are limited; some medicine is unavailable.

(Opposite) Top: A constant supply of hot water is provided in each compartment by the samovar (*batchok*). **Bottom:** The best thing you can say about the meals served in canteens found in most Russian towns is that they're filling and cheap. (Photo: TPB)

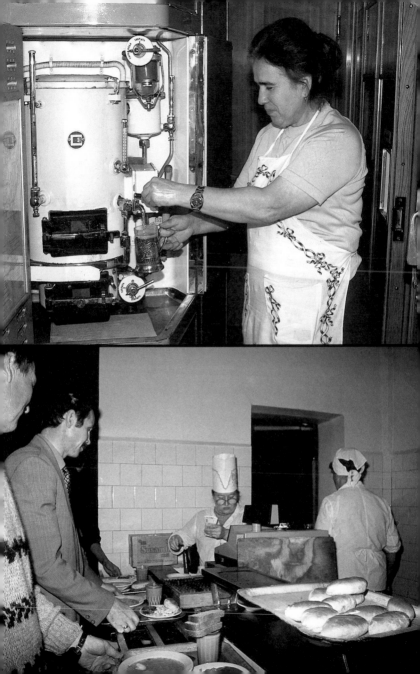

PART 2: RUSSIA

Facts about the country

GEOGRAPHICAL BACKGROUND

The Russian Federation includes over 75% of the former USSR. It is still the largest country in the world, incorporating 17,175,000 square km (over 6.5 million square miles) and stretching from well into the Arctic Circle right down to the northern Caucasus in the south, and from the Black Sea in the west to the Bering Straits in the east, only a few miles from Alaska. Russia is twice as big as the USA; the UK could fit into this vast country some 69 times.

Climate

Much of the country is situated in far northern latitudes. Moscow is on the same latitude as Edinburgh, St Petersburg is almost as far north as Anchorage in Alaska. Winters are extremely cold, and temperatures as low as -68°C (-90°F) have been recorded in Oymyakon in Siberia. It is not only the extremes of latitude which cause the severe winters: the physical make-up of the country is as much to blame. Most of the land is an open plain stretching up across Siberia to the Arctic. While there is higher ground in the south there are no mountains in the north to shield it from the cold Arctic air which blows down to fill this plain. To the west are the Urals, the low range which divides Europe and Asia. The Himalayan and Pamir ranges beyond the southern borders stop warm tropical air from reaching the Siberian and Russian plains. Thus blocked off, the plains warm rapidly in summer and become very cold in winter. Olekminsk, in north-east Siberia, holds the record for the place with the greatest temperature range in the world: from -60°C (-87°F) in winter to a record summer high of 45°C (113°F). Along the route of the Trans-Siberian, however, summers are rather more mild.

Transport and communications

Railways remain the principal transport system for both passengers and goods, and there are some 87,500km of track in the country. The heaviest traffic on the entire system and in the world is on certain stretches of the

---

(**Opposite**) Russian Orthodox priests outside St Basil's Cathedral, Moscow.

Trans-Siberian, with trains passing every few minutes. Although Russia's **road network** is comparatively well-developed (624,000km), few people own cars which means that, as well as the 47% of freight, 31% of all passengers also travel by rail.

The **rivers** of Russia have always been of vital importance as a communication network across the country. Some of these rivers are huge, and are navigable by ocean-going ships for considerable distances. Harsh winters preclude year-round navigation and air travel is gradually taking over. There has been a massive change in Russian **aviation** since the collapse of the Soviet Union. This has included the breakup of Aeroflot into 600 carriers. The safety level of these carriers is dubious and it is strongly recommended you travel only by train and if you have to fly, only go with the large carriers such as Aeroflot or Transaero.

Landscape zones: flora and fauna

The main landscape zones of interest to the Trans-Siberian traveller are as follows:

● **European Russia** West of the Urals the flora and fauna are similar to that found in the rest of northern Europe. Trees include oak, elm, hazel, ash, apple, aspen, spruce, lime and maple.

● **North Siberia and the Arctic regions** The *tundra* zone (short grass, mosses and lichens) covers the tree-less area in the far north. Soil is poor and much of it permanently frozen. In fact *permafrost* affects over 40 per cent of Russia and extends down into southern Siberia, where it causes building problems for architects and engineers. In this desolate northern zone the wildlife includes reindeer, arctic fox, wolf, lemming and vole. Bird life is more numerous: ptarmigan, snow-bunting, Iceland falcon and snow-owl as well as many kinds of migratory water and marsh fowl.

● **The Siberian plain** Much of this area is covered with *taiga* (pronounced 'tiger') meaning thick forest. To the north the trees are stunted and windblown; in the south they grow into dark impenetrable forests. More than 30 per cent of all the world's trees grow in this taiga zone. These include larch, pine and silver fir, intermingled with birch, aspen and maple. Willow and poplar line the rivers and streams. Much of the taiga forest along the route of the Trans-Siberian has been cleared and replaced with fields of wheat or sun-flowers. Parts of this region are affected by permafrost and in places rails and roads sink, and houses, trees and telegraph poles keel over drunkenly. Fauna in this region includes species once common in Europe: bear, badger, wolverine, polecat, ermine, sable, squirrel, weasel, otter, wolf, fox, lynx, beaver, several types of rodent, musk deer, roebuck, reindeer and elk.

● **East Siberia and Trans-Baikal** Much of the flora and fauna of this region is unique (see p323) including, in Lake Baikal, such rarities as the world's only fresh-water seals. Amongst the ubiquitous larch and pine there grows a type of birch with dark bark, *Betula daurica*. Towards the south and into China and Mongolia, the forests give way to open grassy areas known as *steppes*. The black earth (*chernozem*) of the northern steppes is quite fertile and some areas are under cultivation.

● **The Far Eastern territories: the Amur region** Along the Amur River the flora and fauna are similar to that found in northern China and it is here that the rare Amur tiger (see p356) is found. European flora makes a reappearance in the Far Eastern region including such trees as cork, walnut and acacia.

HISTORICAL OUTLINE

The first Russians
Artefacts recently uncovered in Siberia suggest that human history may stretch back very much further than had previously been believed, perhaps between one and two million years. Around the thirteenth millennium BC there were Stone Age nomads living beside Lake Baikal.

By the second millennium BC when fairly advanced civilisations had emerged here (see p83), European Russia was inhabited by Ural-Altaic and Indo-European peoples. In the sixth century BC the Scythians (whose magnificent goldwork may be seen in the Hermitage) settled in southern Russia, near the Black Sea.

Through the early centuries of the first millennium AD trade routes developed between Scandinavia, Russia and Byzantium, following the Dnieper River. Centres of trade grew up along the route (Novgorod, Kiev, Smolensk, Chernigov) and by the sixth century AD the towns were populated by Slavic tribes known as the Rus (hence 'Russian'). The year 830 saw the first of the Varangian (Viking) invasions and in 862 Novgorod fell to the Varangian chief, Rurik, Russia's first sovereign.

Vladimir and Christian Russia
The great Tsar Vladimir (978-1015) ruled Russia from Kiev and was responsible for the conversion of the country to Christianity. At the time the Slavs worshipped a range of pagan gods and it is said that in his search for a new religion Vladimir invited bids from the Muslims, the Jews and the Christians. Since Islam and the consumption of vodka were not compatible and Judaism did not make for a unified nation, he chose Christianity as the state religion and had himself baptised at Constantinople in 988 AD. At his order the mass conversion of the Russian people began, with whole towns being baptised simultaneously.

The eleventh century was marked by continual feuding between his heirs. It was at this time that the northern principalities of Vladimir and Suzdal were founded.

The Mongol invasion and the rise of Muscovy

Between 1220 and 1230, the Golden Horde brought a sudden halt to economic progress in Russia, burning towns and putting the local population to the sword. By 1249 Kiev was under their control and the Russians moved north, establishing a new political centre at Muscovy (Moscow). All Russian principalities were obliged to pay tribute to the Mongol khans but Muscovy was the first to challenge their authority. Over the next three centuries Moscow gained control of the other Russian principalities and shook off the Mongol yoke.

Ivan the Terrible (1530-84)

When Ivan the Terrible came to the throne he declared himself Tsar of All the Russias and by his successful military campaigns extended the borders of the young country. He was as wild and blood-thirsty as his name suggests and in a fit of anger in 1582 he struck his favourite son with a metal staff, fatally injuring him (a scene used by Ilya Repin as the subject of one of his greatest paintings). Ivan was succeeded by his mentally-retarded son, Fyodor, but the real power was with the regent, Boris Godunov. Godunov later became the Tsar and ruled from 1598 to 1605. The early part of the seventeenth century was marked by dynastic feuding which ended with the election of Michael Romanov (1613-45), the first of a long line that lasted until the Revolution in 1917.

Peter the Great and the Westernisation of Russia

Peter (1672-1725) well deserved his soubriquet 'the Great' for it was due to his policy of Westernisation that Russia emerged from centuries of isolation and backwardness into the eighteenth century. He founded St Petersburg in 1703 as a 'window open on the West' and made it his capital in 1712. During his reign there were wars with Sweden and Turkey. Territorial gains included the Baltic provinces and the southern and western shores of the Caspian.

The extravagant building programme in St Petersburg continued under Catherine the Great (1762-96). While her generals were taking the Black Sea steppes, the Ukraine and parts of Poland for Russia, Catherine conducted extensive campaigns of a more romantic nature with a series of favourites in her elegant capital.

Alexander I and the Napoleonic Wars

In Russia during the nineteenth century, the political pendulum swung back and forth between conservatism and enlightenment. The mad Tsar Paul I came to the throne in 1796 but was murdered five years later. He was succeeded by his son Alexander I (1801-25) who was said to have had a hand in the sudden demise of his father. In the course of Alexander's reign, he abolished the secret police, lifted the laws of censorship and would have freed the serfs had the aristocracy not objected so strongly to the idea. In 1812 Napoleon invaded Russia and Moscow was burnt to the ground (by the inhabitants, not by the French) before he was pushed back over the border.

Growing unrest among the peasants

Nicholas I's reign began with the first Russian Revolution, the Decembrists' uprising (see p94), and ended, after he had reversed most of Alexander's enlightened policies, with the Crimean War against the English and the French in 1853-6. Nicholas was succeeded by Alexander II (1855-81) who was known as the Tsar Liberator, for it was he who freed the serfs. His reward was his assassination by a student in St Petersburg in 1881. He was succeeded by the strong Tsar Alexander III, during whose reign work began on the Trans-Siberian Railway.

Nicholas II: last of the Tsars

The dice were heavily loaded against this unfortunate Tsar. Nicholas inherited a vast empire and a restless population that was beginning to discover its own power. In 1905 his army and navy suffered a most humiliating defeat at the hands of the Japanese. Just when his country needed him most, as strikes and riots swept through the cities in the first few years of this century, Nicholas's attention was drawn into his own family crisis. It was discovered that the heir to the throne, Alexis, was suffering from haemophilia. The Siberian monk, Rasputin, ingratiated himself into the court circle through his ability to exert a calming influence over the Tsarevich. His influence over other members of the royal family, including the Tsar, was not so beneficial.

October 1917: the Russian Revolution

After the riots in 1905, Nicholas agreed to allow the formation of a national parliament (Duma) but its elected members had no real power. Reforms came too slowly for the people and morale fell further when, during the First World War, Russia suffered heavy losses. By March 1917 the Tsar had lost all control and was forced to abdicate in favour of a provisional government led by Alexander Kerensky. The Revolution that abruptly changed the course of Russian history took place in October 1917, when the reins of government were seized by Lenin and his Bolshevik Party. Nicholas and his family were taken to Siberia where they were murdered (see p197). Civil war raged across the country and it was not until 1920 that the Bolsheviks brought the lands of Russia under their control, forming the Union of Soviet Socialist Republics.

The Stalin era

After the death of Lenin in 1924, control of the country passed to Stalin and it was under his leadership that the USSR was transformed from a backward agricultural country into an industrial world power. The cost to the people was tremendous and most of those who were unwilling to swim with the current were jailed for their 'political' crimes. During the Great Terror in the 1930s, millions were sentenced to work camps, which provided much of the labour for ambitious building projects.

During the Second World War the USSR played a vital part in the defeat of the Nazis and extended its influence to the East European countries that took on Communist governments after the war.

Khrushchev, Brezhnev, Andropov and Chernenko

After Stalin's death in 1953, Khrushchev became Party Secretary and attempted to ease the strict regulations which governed Soviet society. In 1962 his installation of missiles in Cuba almost led to war with the USA. Khrushchev was forced to resign in 1964, blamed for the failure of the country's economy and for his clumsy foreign policy. He was replaced by Brezhnev who continued the USSR's policy of adopting friendly 'buffer' states along the Iron Curtain by ordering the invasion of Afghanistan in 1979 'at the invitation of the leaders of the country'. When Brezhnev died in 1982, he was replaced by the former head of the KGB, Yuri Andropov. He died in 1984 and was succeeded by the elderly Chernenko, who managed a mere thirteen months in office before becoming the chief participant in yet another state funeral.

Gorbachev and the end of the Cold War

Mikhail Gorbachev, the youngest Soviet premier since Stalin, was elected in 1985 and quickly initiated a process of change categorised under the terms *glasnost* (openness) and *perestroika* (restructuring). The West credits him with bringing about the end of the Cold War (he received the Nobel Prize in 1990) but it would be misguided to think that he was the sole architect of the changes that took place in the USSR: it was widely acknowledged before he came to power that things had gone seriously wrong.

Gorbachev launched a series of bold reforms: Soviet troops were pulled out of Afghanistan, Eastern Europe and Mongolia, political dissidents were freed, laws on religion relaxed and press censorship lifted. These changes displeased many of the Soviet 'old guard,' and on 19 August 1991, a group of senior military and political figures staged a coup. Gorbachev was isolated at his Crimean villa and Vice President Yanaev took over, declaring a state of emergency. Other politicians, including the President of the Russian Republic, Boris Yeltsin, denounced the coup and rallied popular support. There were general strikes and, after a very limited skirmish in Moscow (three casualties), the coup committee was put to flight.

The collapse of the USSR

Because most levels of the Communist Party had been compromised in the failed coup attempt, it was soon seen as corrupt and ineffectual.

Gorbachev resigned his position as Chairman in late August and the Party was abolished five days later. The Communist Party's collapse heralded the demise of the republic it had created, and Gorbachev commenced a desperate struggle to stop this happening. His reforms, however, had already sparked nationalist uprisings in the Baltic republics, Armenia and Azerbaijan.

Despite his suggestions for loose 'federations' of Russian states, by the end of 1991 the USSR had split into 15 independent republics. Having lost almost all his support, Gorbachev resigned and was relieved by Yeltsin.

Yeltsin vs the Congress of Deputies

Yeltsin's plans for economic reforms were thwarted at every turn by the Congress of People's Deputies (parliament). Members of Congress, elected before the collapse of communism, were well aware that by voting for reforms they were, in effect, removing themselves from office. In the Western press this struggle was described as the fight between the reformists (Yeltsin and his followers) and the hard-liners (Vice President Alexander Rutskoi, Congress's Speaker Ruslan Khasbulatov, and the rest of Congress). Yeltsin's hard-won referendum in April 1993 gave him a majority of 58% but this didn't give him a mandate to overrule parliament.

On 22 September 1993, Yeltsin suddenly dissolved parliament and declared presidential rule. (Some have suggested that this swift action was to avert another coup attempt). The Congress denounced his action, stripped him of all powers and swore in Rutskoi as President. The Constitutional Court ruled that, having acted illegally, Yeltsin could now be impeached. Khasbulatov accused him of effecting a 'state coup' and appealed for a national strike. The deciding factor in the confrontation between parliament and president was the question of whom the military would support. Rutskoi, an Afghan war veteran with a keen military following, ordered troops to march on Moscow. They never did, but some 5000 supporters surrounded the White House. Inside, the Congress voted to impeach Yeltsin, who retaliated by severing their telephone lines. The White House vigil turned into a siege; electricity lines were cut and the building surrounded by troops faithful to Yeltsin.

On 3 October a crowd of 10,000 communist supporters converged on the White House where Rutskoi exhorted the people to seize the Kremlin and other strategic locations around the city. All through the night there were confrontations as rioters attacked the mayor's office, the Tass news service building and the main TV station. At dawn on 4 October Yeltsin's troops stormed the White House. Fighting went on for most of the day but by the evening the building, charred and battered, was taken. By the end of the week, when order had been restored, 171 people had been killed.

Zhirinovsky and Chechnya

The state elections, held in December 1993, supported Yeltsin's draft constitution, which outlined Russia's new democratic architecture. Although the immediate threat was seen to have been the constitution's rejection (Yeltsin warned that this might lead to civil war), the election revealed a new problem in the form of the Liberal Democrat Party. Its leader, Vladimir Zhirinovsky, espouses some extremely sinister policies. Particularly worrying are his comments about reuniting the former USSR, his racist jibes and his aim to re-establish a Russian empire reaching 'from Murmansk to Madras'. In a move to demonstrate Yeltsin's strong leadership, to warn other republics considering separation and to regain control over oil industry in the region, Yeltsin ordered Russian troops into the breakaway Russian republic of Chechnya in November 1994. This military solution to a political problem was doomed to failure. By the time a truce was signed in mid-1996, over 80,000 Russian and Chechnan soldiers and civilians had died.

1996 Presidential elections

Zhirinovsky's star had fallen by the start of the 1996 election and for some time it appeared that the winner would be the communist leader, Genardi Zyuganov. At the start of the campaign, Yeltsin was written off as a contender with under 20% of the primary vote. At the end of the first round of voting, however, Yeltsin had proved his enormous campaign ability winning first place with a fistful of electoral bribes, strict control of the media, and the backing of the nation's richest businesses. Interestingly, Gorbachev polled less than 3% of the vote. The popular General Alexander Lebed posed a last minute threat having polled over 15% of the primary vote. Courted by Yeltsin and Zyuganov he finally supported Yeltsin in return for appointment as chairman of the powerful National Security Council. This tipped the election scales in Yeltsin's favour.

Immediately after Yeltsin's victory, he disappeared from public view and it soon became obvious that the campaign had taken a serious toll on the hard drinking president. For nearly four months until his heart bypass operation in November 1996, Russia was leaderless and power-plays were the only decisions being made in the Kremlin. In early 1997, Yeltsin regained control of the Kremlin but his reduced ability may not be enough to guide Russia through the difficult years ahead.

ECONOMY

Russia has vast natural resources and in this sense it is an extremely rich country. It has the world's largest reserves of natural gas as well as deposits of oil, coal, iron ore, manganese, asbestos, lead, gold, silver and copper that will continue to be extracted long after most other countries have exhausted their supplies. The forested regions in Russia cover an area almost four times the size of the Amazon basin. Yet, owing to gross economic mismanagement under communism, the country is experiencing severe financial hardship and has been receiving Western aid since 1990. A series of reforms first under Gorbachev and now Yeltsin means that change is on the way via market liberalisation and privation.

The reforms are yet to have significant beneficial effect and by 1997 the economy was still shrinking at about 5% a year. A major problem limiting the government's ability to turn around the economy let alone tackle social problems is the severe payments crisis. Companies do not pay suppliers or workers for months and huge tax arrears build up. In 1996, only 16% of Russian enterprises paid their taxes in full and on time and only 14 regions out of Russia's 75 paid their tax bills in full. A major tax evasion crackdown by the heavily armed Federal Tax Police secured a massive US$6 billion in the first nine months of 1996. Even though the government coffers are slightly fuller, nearly one in four workers had not been paid for at least three months by the end of that year. The total unpaid wages bill was US$8 billion and growing at 6% per month.

Privatisation

Mass privatisation started in the early 1990s and in an attempt to create public approval of the process, in October 1992, every citizen received vouchers worth 10,000 roubles (about US$60 at time of issue). The vouchers could be sold for cash or exchanged for shares in the growing number of private companies. Although the idea of buying and selling stocks is catching on, there's some confusion over how exactly the market works. Western economic advisers are often asked such questions as 'If I own part of the company, why can't I take the computer home?'

Despite the fact that over 150,000 organisations were privatised, it is now obvious that privatisation did nothing to benefit the average Russian. The country's valuable raw materials and viable industries were mostly sold at closed auctions to officially-preferred banks and tycoons, while economically unviable factories and collective farms were purchased by their workers. Consequently a relatively small number of well-connected business people pocketed Russia's wealth while millions of workers were lumbered with worthless investments.

Hyperinflation

When the markets for most commodities, previously artificially regulated, were freed on 2 January 1992, prices immediately soared by 300-400%. Inflation was already being fuelled by a law passed in 1990, allowing possession of hard currency, which led to a rush for dollars. Another factor adding to inflation was that in some instances the debts of former Communist Bloc countries to Russia were payable in roubles. These countries reserved their right to print Russian banknotes and simply set their presses running, releasing their own debts but fuelling the Russian problem. In an effort to limit the amount of Russian currency on the streets, a law passed in August 1993 withdrew all old rouble notes, replacing them with new ones. By late 1993, inflation was still running at around 25% per month. Following a year of tight monetary policy, the monthly inflation rate was a mere 2% a month by the end of 1996.

THE PEOPLE

Russia is the sixth most populous nation in the world with just under 150 million people (about half the population of the former USSR). Of these, a high proportion (82%) are actually Russian. The rest belong to any one of nearly 100 ethnic minorities, most commonly Tartar (4%) and Ukrainian (3%). In the former USSR it was always unwise to refer to people as 'Russian' because of the vast number of other republics they might have come from. With the establishment of independence for many of these states you must be even more careful: Kazakhs or Ukrainians, for example, will not appreciate being called Russians.

Russia is divided up into *oblasts* (the basic administrative unit), *krays* (smaller territories) and *autonomous republics* (containing ethnic minority groups such as the Buryats in Siberia). Siberia forms part of the Russian Federation and exists only as a geographical, not a political, unit.

Government

Russia moved briskly down the political path from autocracy to 'socialist state', with a period of a few months in 1917 when it was a republic. From November 1917 until August 1991 the country was in the hands of the Communist Party, and until September 1993 it was run by the Congress of People's Deputies. This 1068-seat forum was elected from throughout the USSR. At its head sat the Supreme Soviet, the legislative body, elected from Congress. Since only Party members could stand for election in Congress, only Party members could ever run the country.

The confirmation of the new Russian Constitution in December 1993 means that the country is now governed by a European-style two-tier parliament very similar to that of France. The head of state remains the Russian president, currently Boris Yeltsin.

Despite the theory, Russia is far from democratic. The power of the country is vested in a few hundred chief executives of huge corporations who picked up enormous wealth through the corrupt privatisation of the state enterprises under communism. These people now monopolise the media, gas and oil, military production and banking sectors, in effect controlling the entire Russian state. Seven of these tycoons bankrolled the 1996 Yeltsin re-election and were rewarded with powerful government positions. With these oligarchic, criminal and monopolistic power merchants securely lodged in the Kremlin, true democracy is a long way off.

Education and social welfare

Education and health care are provided free for the entire population but standards for both are now falling. School is compulsory between the ages of seven and seventeen with the result that Russia has a literacy rate of almost 100%. Although funding for research is currently at an all-time low, until a few years ago the country used to plough 5% of its national income directly into scientific research in its 900 universities and institutes. Russia's present inability to maintain its scientists has led to serious fears of a brain drain; certain states in the Middle East are very keen for Russian scientists to help them with their nuclear programmes. The national health care programme is likewise suffering through lack of funds. Russia has produced some of the world's leading surgeons yet recent outbreaks of diseases extinct in the developed world have demonstrated that health services here were never comprehensive. The most publicised epidemic in the last year has been diphtheria: hundreds of Russians who should have been inoculated at birth have died.

On re-election in July 1996, Yeltsin promised that the government would give higher priority to social reform and raising the living standards of ordinary Russians, to take into account the downside of the market reforms. These reforms have seen real incomes fall by about 40% between 1991 and 1996, unemployment reach 6.6 million, and in 1996 nearly 26% of Russian households existed below the poverty level, considered to be US$70 a month. The average monthly wage in 1996 was US$150 (£93) and the average pension was US$60.

The new government programme aims to stabilise living standards, gradually reduce poverty and stop mass unemployment, and in its second phase (1998-2000) to create the conditions for real growth in incomes and the end to poverty. Even the most optimistic Russian believes that this programme has virtually no chance of success.

❏ Homelessness

Homelessness is a major problem in Moscow and other cities. Police estimate that there are 20,000 homeless people in Moscow out of a total population of eight million and just 25 beds for homeless people. As a comparison, there are about 100,000 homeless in New York City and 25,000 government-provided shelter beds. By the end of 1997, Moscow expects to have 800 beds.

Most Russians have little sympathy for the beggars huddling in subway stations who came to the big city in search of a job, and the old women swindled out of their homes when real estate was privatised. The government solution is to round up the homeless and return them to the villages where they grew up or were last registered as permanent residents. This is despite the post-Communist Russian Constitution guaranteeing the right to freedom of movement. Aleksandr V Zolin, one of the Moscow mayor's legal advisers, justified the action: 'We don't want our city to look like the streets of New York or the shantytowns of Latin America'. Technically all Russian are entitled to accommodation but with more than 20 million on city lists for housing, entitlements mean little.

Religion

Russia was a pagan nation until 988 when Tsar Vladimir ordered the mass conversion of the country to Christianity. The state religion adopted was that of the Greek Orthodox Eastern Church (Russian Orthodox) rather than Roman Catholicism. After the Revolution, religion was suppressed until the late 1930s when Stalin, recognising the importance of the Church's patriotism in time of war, restored Orthodoxy to respectability. This policy was reversed shortly after the war and many of the country's churches, synagogues and mosques were closed down. Labour camps were filled with religious dissidents, particularly under Khrushchev.

Gorbachev's attitude towards religion was more relaxed and the Freedom of Conscience law, passed in 1990, took religion off the black-list. Numerous churches are now being restored to cater for the country's 35-40 million Orthodox believers. In 1991 Yeltsin even legalised Christmas. Russian Christmas Day, celebrated on 7 January, is now an official public holiday again.

Numbers of Christian sects are growing. Sects as diverse as the so-called 'Old Believers' (who split from the Orthodox church in the 17th century), Scientology and Jehovah's Witnesses are attempting to find converts here. This has worried some Russians, and on 14 June 1993 the Supreme Soviet passed an amendment to the 1990 Freedom of Conscience law, banning foreign organisations from recruiting by 'independent' religious activities, without permission. On 10 July 1996 the Russian Duma approved the first reading of new legislation regulating religious organisations. The legislation resulted from the perceived lawlessness of new and foreign religions and pseudo-religions, the negative impact of new religions on children and families, and conflicts between religious freedom and a secular state. If passed all religions will have to be re-registered by 1999 and any deemed unsuitable or a threat to the state and its people will be banned.

Russian Jews, historically subject to the most cruel discrimination, have been less trusting of the greater religious freedoms. In 1990 more than 200,000 moved to Israel, pouring in at a rate of up to 3000 per day; fewer are emigrating now and there are still large Jewish communities in Moscow and St Petersburg.

In Buryatia, the centre of Russian Buddhism, many of the monasteries have reopened. Since all are a long way off the tourist track, they have not been kept in good repair as museums, unlike churches in European Russia.

With the independence of the Central Asian Republics there are now few Moslems in the country.

Practical information for the visitor

DOCUMENTS, TICKETS AND VOUCHERS

(Also see Part 1: Planning Your Trip.) The essential documents are your passport, Russian visa (supplied as a separate document) and a visa for the first country that you'll be entering after Russia. If you are travelling with Intourist, don't forget your rail and hotel vouchers, and if you've arranged a Beijing-Moscow ticket from abroad, don't forget your voucher to exchange for a ticket at CITS in Beijing. It's worth bringing some additional identification (eg driver's licence) as your passport will be confiscated by the hotel when you check in. It is now possible to rent self-drive cars in Moscow and St Petersburg for which you'll need an international driving licence (available from your country's automobile club).

> ❑ One 19th century English traveller left his passport and tickets behind in London and yet still managed to travel across Siberia carrying no other document than a pass to the Reading Room at the British Library. Entry requirements for foreigners are somewhat stricter nowadays.

International student cards were never much use in the USSR but now that prices are tiered, it's worth bringing one. Part of the IS card is written in Russian, too, which might impress someone. Note that if you're arriving from Africa or South America you may be required to show a yellow fever vaccination certificate. Travellers arriving from countries where there have been recent outbreaks of cholera may be asked to show proof of vaccination.

CROSSING THE BORDER

Customs declaration form

At the Russian border you will be given a Customs Declaration Form on which you must declare the total amount of money you are carrying (cash and travellers' cheques) and the number of pieces of luggage you have. You must keep this form until you leave, when it may be checked; note that on departure you must fill out another identical form. The purpose of these forms is to deter people from giving away or selling their foreign currency or valuables. Now that the use of foreign currency has been outlawed in Russia it's likely that these forms may be more thoroughly checked than in the last few years, when US$ could be spent in shops in Russia. When you exchange money ensure that you get given either an exchange certificate or have your Customs Declaration Form officially endorsed. Keep any certificates together with your Customs Declaration Form for presentation when you leave Russia.

China also requires visitors to fill in a customs form. Don't give away or sell anything you have listed on the form or you may be expected to account for it later. If anything is stolen, get a letter from the local Public Security Bureau (police station) to that effect. Make a photocopy to give to customs, as the original must go to your travel insurance company if you want to claim compensation.

Customs allowances: entering or leaving the country

Russia's customs laws are being reformed so you should check current regulations before arrival. You should not, however, have any problems bringing in a litre of spirits and two litres of wine.

When leaving the country note that you need a special permit to export 'cultural treasures', a term used to include almost anything that looks old or valuable. Paintings, gold and silver items made before 1968, military medals, and coins attract the attention of customs officials and may be confiscated or charged at 600% or more duty if you do not have a permit from the Ministry of Culture.

Border crossing procedure

The border crossing procedure between Russia-China, China-Mongolia and Mongolia-Russia takes anything from two to six hours. The first step is for customs officers of the country you are leaving to check your passports and visas, and collect your customs forms. Remove all loose papers from your passport and make sure you get it back. The compartments will then be searched by border guards looking for stowaways before the train crosses the border and the entire procedure is run through again.

As rails in Russia and Mongolia are set to a wider gauge than those in China and most of Europe, the bogies have to be changed at the borders. The carriages are lifted individually, the bogies being rolled out and replaced. If you do not want to stay on the train as the bogies are being changed, you can wait at the border station. If you do get off, the carriage attendants won't normally let you get back on before the official board-

❏ **Border etiquette**

While it's never a good idea to act smart in front of border guards this is perhaps nowhere more true than in Russia. A disturbing study reported by the Russian ITAR-TASS news service (17 November 1995) states that about 60% of Russia's border guards are so unstable they shouldn't be allowed to carry guns. The study, which was released two days after a guard in eastern Siberia killed five of his colleagues on a shooting rampage, was based on tests conducted by doctors, psychologists and lawyers following a series of similar shootouts by border guards over the previous two years.

ing time which is when the train returns to the station to pick up the passengers. Don't leave valuables behind. Bear in mind that during the entire border crossing procedure, the train's lavatories remain locked. This is not purely for security reasons since changing the bogies requires workers operating beneath the train.

HOTELS

Russian hotels are usually of gargantuan proportions and about as architecturally interesting as the average multi-storey car park in the West. This having been said, some of the old hotels in Moscow and St Petersburg have recently been restored to a very high standard in joint ventures with foreign companies. Many of the 'Soviet modern' hotels can accommodate over 2000 people. Moscow's Hotel Rossiya, once the world's largest hotel, with 3200 rooms and beds for 6000 guests, fell to second place in 1990 with the opening of the 4032-room Excalibur Hotel in Las Vegas.

Main types of accommodation
Top hotels These are normally owned by large Western chains such as Radisson and Novotel. While they look glitzy like international hotels everywhere, the service still has a touch of Soviet reticence about it. Their restaurants are normally excellent, they have banking facilities, room service and shops, and their staff are motivated. These hotels are mostly found in Moscow, St Petersburg, Khabarovsk and Vladivostok. Because of lack of competition these places can charge high prices – £200-300/US$350-500 per night.

The hotels of the MNTK hotel chain across Russia also receive an excellent hotel rating although their facilities are not as good as similar class hotels in Moscow. MNTK is owned by the wealthy Russian, Professor Svyatoslav Fedorov, who pioneered conveyor belt eye microsurgery. One floor in each of his eight, multi-storey, Finnish-built eye clinics has been converted into a hotel. The quality of the food and the motivation of the staff are unusually high. Rooms cost around US$110 and, on the Trans-Siberian route there are MNTK hotels in Moscow, Ekaterinburg, Novosibirsk, Irkutsk and Khabarovsk. The main Western agent is Iris Hotels in Australia (see p34).

Standard hotels These are mostly the solid old Intourist hotels. They have all the tourist facilities of restaurants, banks and shops. Their rooms were once good but lack of maintenance and interest, have resulted in their becoming a bit run down. In capital cities, standard hotel rooms cost from £65-130/US$100-200 and in others US$50-70. A basic room with attached bathroom will cost US$60-105 for a single or US$70-115 for a double, booked from abroad. Rooms booked locally usually cost more.

Basic hotels Once impossible for foreigners to stay in, as they were considered to reflect badly on the country, these places are invariably clean if basically equipped. Basic hotels normally have a restaurant but no shops, foreign exchange or room service. The rooms are simple with a TV and fridge; about 50% will have a bathroom. The best rooms are called *lyuks* (meaning 'luxury') and most hotels have at least one such room. *Lyuks* is a relative term and it just means that it is the best of all the rooms in that one hotel. Basic hotel rooms range from £6-18/US$10-30.

Very basic hotels/hostels These come in many forms; some are quite good and others lousy. They're often attached to an industrial enterprise or a market to accommodate visiting workers or farmers. Sometimes foreigners are refused a room at these hotels because staff feel that this isn't quite the sort of place a foreigner should stay in. If you have been refused, be persistent or return later when the reception staff have been changed. These hotels will often not even have a restaurant or café. Very few rooms will have an attached bathroom and rooms will have up to four beds. At most stations there's a Rest Room (Komnata Otdykha Комната отдыха) where you can stay overnight with a ticket for a train the next morning. Rooms at very basic hotels cost from £1.90-6/US$3-10.

Other types of accommodation

Youth hostels The only cities in Russia with youth hostels are Moscow, St Petersburg, Irkutsk and Novgorod. These are mainly run by foreigners and dormitory beds cost about £9/US$15 a night including breakfast. Information on these can be obtained from Russian Youth Hostel Association in St Petersburg (see p133).

Holiday homes (Dom Otdykha Дом отдыха) In the Soviet era these were holiday destinations for city dwellers. They were like country hotels and offered meals and some organised activities. Today the ones that still operate are mostly run down and often do not have even a restaurant. A few are excellent and remain the holiday choice of the country's élite.

Sanatoriums (Sanitorti Санитори) are similar to holiday homes with the addition of a sauna, therapeutic services and mud or spring pools. You do not have to be sick to stay at one and many locals visit them once a year as they believe that this will keep them healthy for another year.

Homestays can be organised in most cities on the Trans-Siberian route; they cost about £22/$35 a night including meals. To minimise the possibility of misunderstandings, ask beforehand how much it will cost before agreeing to stay and set an upper limit on how much you can afford to pay, establish set times each day for your meals, and be prepared to pay for additional services such as organising theatre tickets, sightseeing and taxis. Also be prepared to supplement the household's food shopping when you visit the markets: buy fruit or goods that they normally do not have.

Checking in at hotels

Checking in is not always the swift procedure it should be. After the receptionist has kept you waiting for a while, she will relieve you of your passport and hand you a small pass-card without which you will be unable to get into your room; in some of the upmarket hotels, however, you may actually be given your key by the receptionist. Keys are usually kept by the *dezhurnaya* (floor attendant), very often an elderly female busybody who passes the time drinking tea in a little den, keeping an eagle eye on all that goes on her floor. You may be able to get hot water or a kettle from her for drinks.

Bedrooms

Unless you are staying in the most expensive accommodation, you will be surprised by the shoddiness of your new home, considering the fact that you probably had to fork out a small fortune for it. In some of the older hotels the rooms are vast and comfortable but they're rather smaller in the more modern places. They are generally furnished in the worst possible taste. One room I stayed in had one wall papered with pink roses and the others in a bold orange geometric design; purple nylon curtains completed the schizophrenic decor. Beds are often too short, usually of orthopaedic hardness and bedding consists of blankets in a duvet-cover. There's usually an internal phone and wake-up calls may be arranged at the reception desk; but don't rely on them in the cheaper places.

Bathrooms

Except in the best hotels, bathrooms are equipped with broken fittings and dripping taps, lavatories with dislocated seats and there are no plugs in either bath or basin. Don't forget to take a universal bathplug, soap and loo paper.

During summer, you will find that your hotel may not have hot water. This is because hot water is centrally supplied and each year the water has to be turned off so that the pipes can be cleaned. This means that for a four week period (eight weeks in some Siberian cities) every building in a city will be without hot water. The only exceptions are the expensive hotels which have their own independent hot water systems. If your hotel does not have hot water, you will not get a discount off the bill.

TOURS

Although Intourist lost its monopoly over foreign travellers in 1990, a loose confederation of hotels and travel agencies under the banner of Intourist still dominates the travel market. Intourist offers tours, theatre ticket booking, travel ticket booking, guides and local transport. The problem with their services is that they are expensive. While you will always be able to get what you want cheaper elsewhere, it will usually require a lot more effort, so most people pay up and go along with Intourist. An alternative is the MNTK hotel chain (see p34) which offers a good range of services in six cities in this book. In Moscow, the cheapest places to get tours and other services from English speakers is from IRO Travel, G&R International, Heritage Hostel and Hotel Aeroflot. In St Petersburg, try Sindbad Travel and Peter TIPs. An escorted half day tour usually costs about £15/US$25.

While guided tours allow you to cover a lot of ground quickly, you can easily get around by yourself, particularly in Moscow and St Petersburg. You'll learn more on the buses and metro than you will inside a tour bus.

LOCAL TRANSPORT

When you are arranging your trip you may be encouraged to purchase 'transfers' so that you will be met at the airport or station and taken to your hotel. The prices charged for this service can be high (£19-45/US$30-70) but it can sometimes be worthwhile. If you are planning to take a taxi from the airport when you arrive it's probably better to arrange a transfer in advance, if only to keep yourself out of the hands of the taxi mafia. Moscow taxi drivers will charge you a minimum of US$60 from the international airport to the city. Whether you buy transfers for the rest of your trip or not will depend on how enterprising you want to be and what time you'll be reaching each city. It would be foolish to wander around looking for a hotel or guesthouse after dark. Transfers from the hotel to the railway station have less to recommend them. Don't believe that whoever is organising the transfer is responsible if you miss your train; check departure times.

Taxis

Virtually every car in Russia is a taxi: stand in the street with your arm outstretched and within two minutes someone will be pulling over and asking where you want to go. It's illegal, of course, but if drivers are going your way it makes perfect sense for them to take along paying passengers. While this may be very convenient, it could also be dangerous, as you have no idea of the driver's intentions. For this reason, women travelling alone would be unwise to hitch rides and no-one should get into a car that already has more than one occupant. Don't put your luggage into the boot or your driver could simply pull away when you get out to retrieve it. Russians seem to delight in worrying about crime and if you ask them they'll tell you numerous stories about unwary passengers being driven into the countryside and robbed.

Official taxis are safer but more difficult to find. You'll recognise them by the chequerboard pattern on the door and the green 'for hire' light. Although they have meters, owing to the meteoric decline of the rouble these require constant recalibration which is rarely done. You should agree on a price before you get in but, of course, once the driver realises you're a foreigner he'll bump up the price accordingly. You're more likely to be charged local rates if you don't pick up taxis outside big hotels or major tourist spots.

Metro

The metro is a very cheap way to get around with a flat fare of about £0.25/US$0.40 and trains every few minutes. In Moscow it's worth using the metro just to see the stations, which are more like subterranean stately homes, with ornate ceilings, gilded statues and enormous chandeliers. There are no tickets: just put a token into the turnstile to get in. Be careful not to fall over getting on the escalators: they move twice as fast as those in the West. Russian metro systems are built deeper underground than their Western counterparts, perhaps to act as shelters in the event of aerial bombing. Because they're so far down, escalators need to be extremely long as well as swift. The world's longest escalator is, in fact, in St Petersburg (Ploshchad Lenina), and has 729 steps, rising 59 metres.

In the street, metro stations are indicated by a large blue or red 'M'. Lines are named after their terminal stations, as on the Paris metro. One peculiarity you'll notice is that where two lines intersect the station is given two names, one for each line. As trains move off from the station, the next station is announced. The counter above the end of each tunnel indicates how long it's been since the last train. In Siberia, there are metros in Novosibirsk and Ekaterinburg.

Buses

In all cities there's a bus service (fixed fare and often very crowded) and usually also trolley-buses and trams. Some buses have conductors, some ticket machines and in others tickets are purchased from the driver in strips or booklets. If there's no conductor you must punch the ticket yourself, using one of the punches by the windows. If the bus is crowded and you can't reach, pass your ticket to someone near the machine and they'll do it for you. Occasionally, inspectors impose on the spot fines for those without punched tickets. Beware of the St Petersburg public transport scam (see p130).

Domestic flights

Domestic flights usually involve long delays and far too much sitting around in airports. Safety standards are not high: if you must fly use one of the larger carriers such as Aeroflot or Transaero. Getting airline tickets in Russia is now considerably easier than getting tickets for some trains. This is because most Russians can't afford to fly. Upmarket hotels have air ticket booking offices; tickets for foreigners are about 15% more expensive than for Russians.

Boat

Most of the cities you will visit are built on rivers and short trips on the water are usually possible. In St Petersburg the best way to reach Petrodvorets is by hydrofoil. You can also get to Lake Baikal by boat up the Angara from Irkutsk. Possibly the most exciting river trip you can make is from Yakutsk to the Lena Pillars (see p241).

Car rental

In St Petersburg and Moscow it is possible to rent self-drive cars. Charges are high and you will need an international driving licence.

ELECTRICITY

In almost all Russian cities electricity is 220v, 50 cycles AC. Sockets require a continental-type plug or adaptor. In some places the voltage is 127v so you should enquire at the reception desk before using your own appliances. Sockets for electric razors are provided on trains.

TIME

Russia spans ten time zones and on the Trans-Siberian you will be adjusting your watch an hour almost every day. Russian railways run on Moscow time and timetables do not list local time. It can be disconcerting to cross the border from China at breakfast-time to be informed by station clocks that it is really only 2:00am. Moscow time (MT) is three hours ahead of Greenwich Mean Time. Siberian time zones are listed throughout the route guide and the main cities are in the following zones: Novosibirsk (MT+4), Irkutsk (MT+5), Khabarovsk (MT+7), Vladivostok (MT+7). Also remember that 'summer time' runs from the last Saturday in March to the last Saturday in September.

MONEY

(See also p43). The rouble is the basic unit of Russian currency. This is theoretically divided into 100 kopecks but since the exchange rate in early 1997 was 5800 roubles to US$1 you're unlikely to see any kopecks or many of the smaller denomination rouble bills. New notes in circulation are 100, 200, 500, 1000, 5000, 10,000, 50,000, and 100,000 roubles. Coins are 1, 5, 10, 20, 50 and 100 roubles. Note that roubles issued before 1993 are no longer valid; be sure that no one tries to palm any off on you. All notes are clearly stamped with the date.

Following the reforms of January 1994, the rouble is now the only legitimate currency, and it is illegal for anyone to ask you to pay in US$ with the exception of a few sectors of the economy such as airlines tickets and payment for visas. If anyone else tries to make you pay in dollars tell them that you know this is illegal and insist on paying in roubles.

People still want dollars for security, although as the rouble becomes more steady, they should gain confidence in their own currency. Note that in this guide prices are given in dollars, since rapid inflation would render any rouble price out of date almost immediately.

Other currencies which are easy to convert to roubles are German DMs and UK pounds. In St Petersburg you can also easily exchange the Swedish kroner and Finnish marks, while in the Russian Far East you can exchange Japanese yen.

> ❏ **Which dollar bills to bring**
> Bring low denominations (US$1, 5, 10 and 20) for cash outlays and high denominations (US$50 and 100) for changing dollars into roubles. The bills should be new enough to have the vertical watermark stripe, which can be seen by holding the bills up to the light. The newly designed US$100 bills, issued since 1996, provide increased protection against counterfeiting. Soiled, or torn bills are not accepted, nor are any which have writing or ink stamps on them.
> Carefully check any dollar bills you are given in Russia.

Exchanging dollars for roubles

There are hundreds of official currency exchange offices (*Obmen Valyuty*) in hotels, banks, stores and kiosks in most cities. Keep currency exchange receipts as you may have to show them to customs on departure if you are carrying a large amount of money out of the country. The exchange rate as of early 1997 was 5800 roubles to US$1. In banks, the difference in the buying and selling rate is about 3-5% but it can be as high as 10% when the rouble is unstable. The rates offered in stores and restaurants are usually not very good. The rates vary according to supply and demand and whether banks are open. Out of hours you will get a worse deal than during bank hours.

The black market

With little difference between the bank rate and the black market rate the risks involved in changing money this way far outweigh the benefits. There's also no advantage to be gained from 'speculation': bringing in articles from the West to sell in Russia. Most Western goods can now be bought locally.

Tipping

Soviet policy outlawed tipping. It was seen as nothing less than bribery: the thin end of the corruption wedge. Glasnost soon changed all this, though, and you'll find that certain people (taxi-drivers, waiters etc) have come to accept the practice. It's really up to you but Russians generally don't. As hotels and restaurants occasionally add a 5-15% service charge to your bill as well as a 20% value added tax, don't feel obliged to tip them. Pay porters about US$1 a bag. If you want to thank your guide or your carriage attendant on the train, the best way of doing so is not with money but with a small gift, preferably something that is obviously Western (ie exotic). Scented soap, perfume, cosmetics, tights, cigarettes, or any Western food product will all go down well.

POST AND TELECOMMUNICATIONS

Post, fax and telegram

Outbound airmail to the UK and USA takes about three weeks and is reliable. Inbound mail is less reliable and can take more than three weeks. Be warned that letters are likely to be opened in transit by thieves looking for money, so don't send anything valuable or important. To send a parcel from Russia, you have to go to a post office where it will be wrapped and sealed with a wax stamp.

Addresses on international mail into and out of Russia may be written in English and in standard Western format. The usual order of writing an address within Russia is the following and all should be in Russian:

> Six digit postal code of the city or town
> City or town
> Street name
> Name of addressee
> followed below by the return address.

The main city post offices often have **fax** machines and a typical international fax costs about £3/US$5 a minute.

The cheapest way to send an urgent message is by **telegram**. These can be sent from most post offices. Costs are US$0.10-0.30 per word depending on destination.

Phone

To make a **local call** from a street phone (*Taksofon*), you need a token which is available from metro stations and post offices and costs about US$0.20. Officially your call lasts for three minutes before it is cut off. To call **between cities** you will need to go to a post office. You can either place a call with the cashier or buy a special token for an Intercity Telephone (*Mezhdugorodnyy Telefon*). You can book **international calls** at the post office or through your hotel reception. The best hotels in most large Russian cities also have credit card or debit card phones in their foyers. The cards are often unique to each hotel and only available there. These sorts of calls are very expensive.

BROCHURES, MAPS AND NEWSPAPERS

The service bureaux in hotels will supply you with glossy brochures detailing local sights. Most Intourist hotels also have a small bookshop where you can occasionally buy Western papers, local guide-books and maps. Newspaper kiosks and bookshops in most towns also stock maps.

In Moscow, the two papers to look out for are the *Moscow Times* and the *Moscow Tribune*. In St Petersburg, the best paper is the *Saint Petersburg Times*. These papers are all dailies, are free and can be found in the hotels, hostels and supermarkets which foreigners frequent.

HOLIDAYS

National holidays
If a holiday falls on Thursday, then Friday and Saturday may also be holidays. If a holiday falls on Saturday or Sunday, then Monday will be a holiday.
- 1 Jan: New Year's Day
- 7 Jan: Russian Orthodox Christmas Day
- 13 Jan: New Years Day according to the old Julian calendar
- 15 Feb: Defenders of the Motherland Day
- 8 Mar: International Women's Day
- 22 Apr: Lenin Memorial Day
- Late April-May Russian Orthodox Easter
- 1 May: Day of Spring and Labour (formerly May Day or the International Working People's Solidarity Day). The next working day is also a holiday.
- 9 May: Victory Day, to commemorate the end of World War II (the 1941-45 Great Patriotic War)
- 12 June: Independence Day for Russia
- 22 Aug: Holiday in honour of the defeat of the 1993 coup
- 7 and 8 Nov: Formerly the Anniversary of the Communist October Revolution and now called Grief Day or The Day Of Reconciliation
- 12 Dec: Constitution Day

School and university holidays
Schools start 1 September and finish 31 May with a week's vacation in November, two weeks in January at the New Year and one week in March.

Universities usually start on 1 September and finish on 25 June with the winter break from 25 January to 8 February.

FESTIVALS

Annual arts festivals in Moscow include Moscow Stars (5-15 May) and Russian Winter (25 Dec to 05 Jan).

The most interesting festival is St Petersburg's White Nights, held around the summer solstice, when the sun does not set. The days are separated by only a few hours of silvery light: a combined dusk and dawn. Theatres and concert halls save their best performances for this time and a festival is also held at Petrodvorets.

❏ RUSSIAN CUSTOMS AND ETIQUETTE

Customs

❏ A bottle of wine, cake, box of candy or bouquet of flowers are traditional gifts if you're invited to dinner in someone's home. A small gift for any children is always appropriate. If you bring flowers, make sure the number of flowers is uneven; even numbers of flowers are for funerals.

❏ Do not shake hands or kiss across the threshold of the door step; this is traditionally bad luck.

❏ Take off your gloves when shaking hands.

❏ Be prepared to remove your shoes upon entering a home. You will be given a pair of slippers (*tapki*) to help keep the apartment clean.

❏ Do not cross your legs with the ankle on the knee. It's impolite to show people the soles of your shoes. When in the metro or sitting on a bus, don't let your feet even come close to the seat or another passenger.

❏ Smoking is common and accepted in Russia

❏ Be prepared to accept all alcohol and food offered when visiting friends, and this can be quite a lot. Refusing a drink or a toast is a serious breach of etiquette. An open bottle must often be finished.

❏ Be prepared to give toasts at dinners, etc. Be careful, the vodka can catch up with you.

❏ Dress for the theatre. Check your coat and any large bags at the garderobe.

❏ Be careful in complimenting something in a home. Your host may offer it to you.

❏ Russian men still expect women to act in a traditional manner. You're not supposed to be assertive in public, carry heavy bags if walking with a man, open doors, uncork bottles or pay for yourself in social situations. A woman alone in a restaurant or hotel risks being taken for a prostitute.

❏ Dress casually for dinner in someone's home. In cold weather, wear a hat or old ladies will lecture you on your foolishness.

❏ In a Russian Orthodox church, women should cover their heads with a scarf or hat and wear a skirt. Men should remove their hats.

❏ Putting your thumb between your first two fingers is a very rude gesture.

Superstitions

Russians are still remarkably superstitious; many of the following were once also common in Europe:

❏ Never light a cigarette from a candle. It will bring you bad luck.

❏ Do not whistle inside or you will whistle away your money.

❏ Never pour wine back handed, it means you will also pour away your money.

❏ A black cat crossing your path is bad luck.

❏ If you're a woman and find yourself sitting on the corner of a table you'll be single for the next seven years.

❏ If you spill salt at the table you will be plagued by bad luck unless you throw three pinches over your left shoulder immediately.

❏ If someone gives good wishes, or you talk about your good fortune, you must spit three times over your left shoulder and knock on wood to keep your good fortune.

FOOD AND DRINK

No one ever came to Russia for the food alone but that doesn't mean you won't have some really good meals. There's rather more to Russian cuisine than borscht and chicken Kiev but if you're eating most of your meals on the train, you won't have much of a chance to discover this. You will probably leave with the idea that Russian cooking is of the school dinner variety, with large hunks of meat, piles of potatoes and one vegetable (the interminable cabbage), followed by ice-cream.

Food is no problem if you have money. Even in remote Siberia, you can still get a Mars bar although it may be expensive. Although there are food shortages in some parts of the country, Westerners are well catered for. A substantial breakfast will provide you with enough energy to tackle even the heaviest sight-seeing schedule. The first meal of the day consists of fruit juice (good if it's apple), cheese, eggs, bread, jam and *kefir* (thin, sour yoghurt). Lunch and dinner will be of similarly large size, consisting of at least three courses. Meat dishes can be good but there is still a shortage of fresh fruit and vegetables except at the best hotels.

Zakuski

Russian hors d'oeuvres (*zakuski*), consist of some or all of the following: cold meat, sausages, salmon, pickled herring, paté, tomato salads, sturgeon and caviare. Large quantities of vodka are drunk with zakuski.

Soups

Soups are usually watery but good, meals in themselves with a stack of brown bread. Best known is *borscht*: beetroot soup which often includes

---

❏ **Caviare**

The roe of the sturgeon is becoming more expensive as the fish itself becomes gets rarer. Four species are acknowledged to produce the best caviare: beluga, sterlet, osetra and sevruga, all from the Caspian and Black Seas. To produce its characteristic flavour (preferably not too 'fishy') a complicated process is involved. First the female fish is stunned with a mallet. Her belly is slit open and the roe sacs removed. The eggs are washed and put through strainers to grade them into batches of a similar size. The master-taster then samples the roe and decides how much salt to add for preservation.

Processed caviare varies in colour (black, red or golden) and also in the size of the roe. It is eaten either with brown bread or served with sour cream in *blinis* (thin pancakes). You can get it in most tourist hotels and on the black market. Red caviare is occasionally available on the train.

A 1996 report from the WWF warns that the sturgeon is on the brink of extinction because of aggressive fishing by Russia. The report says up to 90 percent of caviare is now obtained illegally and the Russian authorities are doing nothing because of corruption.

other vegetables, (potatoes, cabbage and onion), chopped ham and a swirl of sour cream (*smetana*). Cabbage soup or *shchi* is the traditional soup of the proletariat and was a favourite of Nicholas II, who is said to have enjoyed only plain peasant cooking (to the great disappointment of his French chef). *Akroshka* is a chilled soup made from meat, vegetables and *kvas* (thin beer). *Rassolnik* is a soup of pickled vegetables.

Fish

Fish common in Russia include herring, halibut, salmon and sturgeon. These last two may be served with a creamy sauce of vegetables. In Irkutsk you should try *omul*, the famous Lake Baikal fish, which has a delicious, delicate flavour.

Meat

The most famous Russian main course is chicken Kiev (fried breast of chicken filled with garlic and butter). Almost as famous is *boeuf stroganov*, a beef stew made with sour cream and mushrooms, and named after the wealthy merchant family who financed the first Siberian explorations in the 1580s.

> ❏ **You don't eat meat?!**
> Vegetarians find it difficult to eat a balanced diet in this country of dedicated carnivores; bring some supplies and vitamin pills.
> 'The Russians don't seem to comprehend what a vegetarian is. They would just take the meat off a plate or out of a meat-based soup and call it 'vegetarian'. We found a packet of Complan very useful'. **Hilda Helling** (UK).

Other regional specialities that you are likely to encounter on a trip across Siberia include *shashlik* (mutton kebabs) and *pilov* (rice with spiced meat) from Central Asia, chicken *tabaka* (with garlic sauce) from Georgia, and (to be avoided at all costs) *salo* which is pig's fat preserved with salt, from the Ukraine. From Siberia comes *pelmeni*, small dumplings filled with meat and served in a soup or as a main course. If you're expecting a rump steak when you order *bifstek* you'll be disappointed: it's just a compressed lump of minced meat.

Puddings

Very often the choice is limited to ice-cream (*morozhenoye* – always good, safe, and available everywhere) and fruit compôte (a disappointing fruit salad of a few pieces of tinned fruit floating in a large dish of syrup). You may, however, be offered *blinis* with sour cream and fruit jam; *vareniki* (sweet dumplings filled with fruit) or rice pudding. Unless you are staying in one of the more expensive hotels there will be very little fresh fruit although it is now easily available from street vendors.

Bread

Russian bread, served with every meal, is wholesome and filling. Tourist literature claims that over one hundred different types are baked in

Moscow. Communist 'bread technology' was said to be so much in demand in the West that Soviet experts were allegedly recruited to build a brown bread factory in Finland.

Drinks
Non alcoholic Most popular is tea, traditionally served black with a spoonful of jam or sugar. Milk is not always available so you may want to take along some whitener. The Russians have been brewing coffee since Peter the Great introduced it in the 17th century but standards have dropped since then; take a jar of instant with you. Bottled mineral water is available everywhere but it often tastes rather too strongly of all those natural minerals that are supposed to be so good for you.

There are several varieties of bottled fruit juice (*sok*), of which apple seems to be the most consistently good. The Pepsi and Coca Cola companies fought bitterly over distribution in the USSR and during the 1980s Pepsi was awarded sole rights. Now both are easily obtainable, as are other Western soft drinks.

Alcoholic Vodka predominates, of course, and Russians will be disgusted if you do anything other than drink it straight. It should be served ice cold and drained in one from single shot glasses. Note that a shot of vodka ought to be followed immediately by zakuski (see above): only drunkards drink without food.

The spirit originated in Poland (although some say that it was brought back from Holland by Peter the Great) and means 'little water', something of an understatement. If you tire of the original product, there's a wide range of flavoured vodkas to sample: lemon, cherry, blackberry or pepper.

Wines tend to be rather sweet for the Western palate but Russian champagne is surprisingly good and very cheap. Beer is widely available. You should also try *kvas* (a fermented mixture of stale brown bread, malt sugar and water). A popular drink sold on the streets during the summer, its alcohol content is so low it's hardly noticeable at all.

BUYING YOUR OWN FOOD

The once sparse self-serve Soviet supermarkets *(universam)* have rapidly modernised their facilities and improved the quality and selection of goods. Canned and packaged goods, juices, pots, tableware, soap, paper products, dry goods, as well as meat, bread, fruits and vegetables can be found here. A *gastronome* is a delicatessen; a *dieta* sells food for those on special diets, such as diabetics.

Markets (*rynok*) range from small groups of old people selling garden produce around the metro exits to large, covered markets with dozens of stalls selling everything from honey to dried mushrooms and meat to imported pineapples. *Produkty* stores are the most common food shops in Russia and sell a limited range of fresh vegetables, fruit, bread, meat, eggs and manufactured products. There are now even some Western-style supermarkets in the largest cities.

❏ Food and drink prices

Many food stores have been privatised and now set their own prices. Only a few products such as bread, milk, and eggs are still subsidised and regulated. Some examples of current prices:

Hot dog	US$0.47
Georgian cheese bread	US$0.28
McDonald's Quarter-pounder	US$3.50
Large loaf of tasty white bread	US$0.47
Russian 'Edam' style cheese (1kg)	US$4.10
Large jar of Nutella spread	US$2.80
Cheapest bottle of Russian beer (330ml)	US$0.56
Good Russian beer 330ml	US$1.00
Imported small can of Heineken	US$1.13
Cheapest vodka (500ml)	US$1.30
Moskovskaya vodka (500ml)	US$2.30
Gzhel Crystal vodka (500ml)	US$30.00
Georgian red wine (1l)	US$4.30
Sekt Russian champagne	US$4.70

When you buy vodka check the seal on the bottle to make sure it hasn't been diluted. It's wise to go for the bigger brands as there are reports of the smaller distilleries cutting costs to produce low grade alcohol which has resulted in blindness amongst some drinkers.

RESTAURANTS

It used to be very difficult to get a good meal in Russia. Because all restaurants were state-run, waiters were not keen to serve you, chefs couldn't be bothered to cook for you and you considered yourself lucky if you managed to bribe your way to a table. With the advent of co-operatives, joint ventures and private restaurants, the situation has improved greatly but for Western service everyone pays Western prices.

Until the opening of these new restaurants, hotel restaurants were often the best places to eat and in some Siberian cities they still are. Budget travellers may find these restaurants too expensive, but some have cheaper dining rooms attached to them where similar food is served without the upmarket decor and service. The cheapest places to eat are the self-service cafés found in most shopping streets. There are also branches of McDonald's and Pizza Hut in Moscow and St Petersburg.

When Russians go to a restaurant, they go in large groups and like to make a meal last the evening. Waiters do their best to ensure no dish arrives too quickly and give you more than enough time to try to interpret the menu. Many of the dishes that have prices pencilled against them will in fact be unavailable. While you wait for your food a dance-band entertains with folk-songs and Western hits from the sixties at so high a volume that you can't ignore it. Nevertheless, a visit to a local restaurant can be an entertaining and drunken affair, especially if you get invited to join a Russian party. Note that tsarist traditions die hard: if a man wishes to invite a woman from another table to dance he will ask permission of the men at her table before she joins him on the dance-floor.

In some upmarket restaurants, additional costs may include charges for entertainment and glasses and can add up to about 10% of your bill.

WHAT TO DO IN THE EVENING

If you're expecting a wild nightlife during your stay in Russia, you may be disappointed unless you are in Moscow or St Petersburg. In these cities there are lots of night clubs, discos and bars. In the other cities, your major night life options are the hotels' bars and discos, casinos and cultural activities such as opera, theatre, ballet or circus. Tickets for these last four can be arranged through the hotel service bureaus or bought from the kiosks in the street or at the box-office. Touts sell tickets outside theatre entrances just before the show; check the date on the ticket before you buy. Note that there are plans to introduce separately priced tickets for foreigners. Performances usually start early: between 18:00 and 19:00. Don't be late as the ushers may not let you in until half time. When you arrive, check in your coat and, if necessary, rent opera glasses.

Ballet

Many of the world's greatest dancers were Russians from the Bolshoi and Kirov companies. Some defected to the West including Rudolf Nureyev (Kirov), Russia's most famous ballet star, who was 'shaken out' of his mother's womb on the Trans-Siberian as it was rattling along towards Lake Baikal.

Don't miss the chance of a night at the magnificent Bolshoi Theatre; the season runs from September to May. Note that many touring groups dance at the Bolshoi so it may not be the famous company you see.

Opera and theatre

In the past, opera was encouraged more than theatre as it was seen as politically neutral. Glasnost, however, encouraged playwrights to produce drama that reflected Russian life as it is, rather than as the government would like people to see it. This has led to a number of successful new theatre groups opening in Moscow and St Petersburg. Details of plays and operas are available from hotel service bureaux. There are also several puppet theatres which are highly recommended if you have time.

Cinema and television

In the 1980s the Soviet film industry also benefited from the greater freedoms that came with glasnost. In early 1987, one of the most successful
and controversial films was *Is It Easy To Be Young?*, which was deeply
critical of the Soviet war in Afghanistan. In the 1990s the pessimism of
the people towards life is reflected in films made in the country. *Little
Vera* (1990) is the story of a provincial girl who sinks into small-time
prostitution and finally drowns herself. Gorbachev walked out of it saying he disapproved of the sex scenes. In *Executioner* (1991) a female
journalist takes on the mafia in St Petersburg and loses.

Nowadays Western and American movies are everywhere, with the
result that Stallone and Schwartzeneggar are as famous in Russia as they
are everywhere else. There are cinemas in every town and shows start
early in the evening. Films are shown as a whole programme with a couple of short educational films before the main feature. There is a thriving
black market in bootlegged American movies; don't be surprised to find
Total Recall showing in your restaurant car.

Russian television has evolved fast in the last few years; news and
current affairs programmes are now of quite high quality. For the majority of the population there is one programme worth watching at the
moment: *The Rich also Cry*, a distinctly mediocre *Dynasty* wanna-be
from Mexico. The star, Veronica Castro, has reached cult status
unequalled even by the Beatles: a certain Mrs Maslova in Tatarstan made
the headlines in 1992 when she stabbed her husband to death after he
made a disparaging remark about the actress.

Rock concerts and sports matches

Rock concerts and various sports fixtures are invariably held in stadiums.
These are usually well worth attending and very safe as the arenas are
swarming with police and soldiers to keep the order.

SHOPPING

Shopping was an incredibly complicated and frustrating affair in the
USSR. Shops were crowded and if they weren't this was a sign that there
was nothing worth buying in them. One Russian story tells of the wife of
a Soviet official who, visiting London, concluded from the lack of queues
that no one could afford any of the fancy goods for sale. The common
view on market reform is that while twenty years ago there wasn't much
in the stores, at least everyone could afford what there was. Now the
shelves are overflowing with goods but no one has the money to buy
them. This is the chief reason for the nostalgia for the old days. The situation, one hopes, will improve as wages increase. Despite the fact that the
majority of Russian shoppers tend to flock to the stores with the lowest

prices, you are unlikely to see food queues. Having said this, Russians still carry around their *avoska* (a 'just in case' bag) and are quick to notice a queue forming, joining it even before they know what it is for in the hope that they may snap up a bargain.

For foreigners shopping is no problem at all: you only have to wander into the main street to see the wide variety of goods on sale and if you walk into a privately-owned shop or the electronics section of a department store you'll find quality merchandise on a par with anything available in the West. Whereas previously this was all sold for hard currency, now it's for roubles; the change still doesn't mean that ordinary people can afford it, though.

Making a purchase
The procedure for actually purchasing something is rather more complicated than in the West and exactly the same as the outmoded purchasing process in the department stores of New Delhi. First you must decide what you want to buy and find out the price (the assistant may write this down on a ticket for you). Then go to the cash desk (where an abacus may be used to calculate the purchase price of the goods you want) and pay, getting a receipt. This must then be taken back to the first counter and exchanged for your purchases.

Department stores
Department stores (*Univermag*) sell a variety of manufactured goods such as clothing, linens, toys, homewares and shoes. Often they have separate boutiques selling selections of imported goods.

No visit to Moscow would be complete without a visit to GUM, the largest department store in Russia. It comprises an enormous collection of arcades, now partly taken over by upmarket chains and boutiques from the West and is housed in an impressive glass-roofed building, rather like a giant greenhouse. There is another department store chain: TsUM, which has branches in Moscow and most of the larger cities.

Kiosks
Outdoor kiosks are shops in small booths on the sidewalks, squares, markets and around the metros and stations. They often remain open late and a few are open 24 hours. Most sell alcohol, drinks and cigarettes, while others also specialise in newspapers, ticket sales, lotto, milk, souvenirs, fruit and vegetable, bootleg cassettes and clothing. It is best not to buy vodka from kiosks as dishonest operators will pass off watered down industrial alcohol or home-brew as genuine factory vodka.

Opening hours
Large department stores are open from 09:00 to 20:00 Monday to Saturday. Smaller stores have a wide range of opening times, anywhere

from 08:00 to 11:00, closing between 20:00 and 23:00, with an hour's lunch-break either from 13:00 to 14:00 or 14:00 to 15:00. Most shops are closed on Sundays. Many modern shops and large department stores now work without a lunch-break.

WHAT TO BUY

Handicrafts

These include the attractively decorated black lacquer *palekh* boxes (icon-painters started making them when religious art lost popularity after the Revolution); enamelled bowls and ornaments; embroidered blouses and tablecloths from the Ukraine; large black printed scarves; guitars and *balalaikas*; lace tablecloths and handkerchiefs; jewellery and gemstones from Siberia and the Urals and painted wooden ornaments, including the ubiquitous *matrioshka* dolls which fit one inside the other. Modern variations on the matrioshka doll include leaders of the former USSR, the Beatles and even American all-star basketball teams. Old communist memorabilia have long been removed from the shops but are still sold to tourists and make interesting souvenirs.

Beware of buying paintings, especially if they are expensive, as a 600% duty may be imposed on them when you leave the country. If you are going to buy one, make it a small one so that it will fit into your bag easily. If the painting looks old and as if it might be really valuable, it may well be confiscated by customs officials unless you have a permit (see p62).

Books

You'll find few English-language books in the shops but upmarket hotels usually have a small selection of novels in their gift shops. Russian-language art books are worth buying for their reproductions and they can be very cheap. There are branches of Dom Knigi (House of Books) in Moscow, St Petersburg and most other large cities.

Records and CDs

Whilst the records themselves are not of as high quality as in the West, they are incredibly cheap. There is a fairly wide range of classical records and folk music as well as Beatles' oldies and local pop groups blossoming in the aftermath of glasnost. The Beatles have always had a large following in Russia but it was only in March 1986 that their records went on sale outside the black market. Compact discs are available, although they are all imported from Europe and the USA. There's no Russian artwork that might make a CD worth buying here rather than at home.

Clothes

Most Russian clothes are imported from China and are cheap but shoddy. There are now also dozens of trendy foreign fashion shops. Russian or

Soviet military clothing is a popular buy for foreigners but this should be concealed as you leave the country or it may be confiscated.

CRIME

Protection racketeering is big business in Russia. There are believed to be over 8000 gangs operating in the country, many of whom, using 'heavies'

❑ **Safety tips for Trans-Siberian travellers**
There are many stories of crimes on railways. The majority are exaggerations, distortions or complete fabrications. The most outrageous story in recent years was the so-called 'Sleeping Gas Incident' on a Moscow-St Petersburg train. This story involved an entire carriage supposedly being put to sleep by gas and everyone being robbed. After a week of international media coverage, the Russian journalist who wrote the story admitted that it was fictitious but she still maintained that she did lose her purse when she was asleep!

Crime does exist on railways but a few simple precautions will substantially reduce your chances of anything untoward happening to you.

❑ Lock the cabin from the inside when you are asleep, by using both the normal door handle lock and the flick down lock, putting your bags under the sleeping bench which means that they can't be reached without lifting your bed, dressing down on trains, not displaying cameras, talking softly and always carrying valuables on your body. The railways are currently installing a new type of lock on coupé doors in trains which they claim is not openable from the outside.

❑ Some people padlock their bags to the compartment wall but this is excessive. It is a good idea always to leave someone in the cabin to look after the luggage. If everyone has to leave, ask the *provodnik* (conductor) to lock your cabin. Although valuables can be left in a small safe that is located in the chief provodnik's cabin, this is not recommended.

❑ Carry only a small amount of roubles and US$ in your wallet. Don't show large amounts of money, especially hard currency. Large amounts of money and important documents should always be carried in a money belt under your clothing. Even sleep with it on.

❑ Carry only non-essential goods in bags over your shoulder.

❑ Have a pocket torch/flashlight handy as many entrance halls and stairways have no lights. This is really important in winter when it gets dark very early.

❑ Never get into a taxi carrying anyone other than the driver. Look at the driver and condition of the car. If in doubt, wave the taxi on. Taxis ordered by phone or through organised services at hotels are often a better bet.

❑ Change money only at kiosks and banks.

❑ Watch out for street urchins and gipsy children as they are the most visible and aggressive thieves. Unless you ignore them they'll swarm around you like bees, begging and even grabbing your legs or arms to distract you. Before you realise it, they'll have opened your bag or pulled out your wallet. Their 'controller' is often a dishevelled woman beggar with a small infant in her arms. If you're approached, don't look at them but walk away quickly. It you look like becoming a victim, go into a shop or towards a group of Russians who will usually send them packing.

recruited from the army, extort money from businesses. Protection payments running into millions of roubles are demanded of the proprietors. Restaurant owners must pay up or face their properties being set on fire. Taxi-drivers have been threatened with having their cars damaged or families attacked. There have even been cases of contract killing – 45 people in 1995 and there are occasional shoot-outs between rival gangs in the streets of Moscow and St Petersburg. Moscow is the believed to be the most dangerous city in which to operate a business, followed by St Petersburg and then Krasnoyarsk. It seems that it's not the local councils but the mafia who now run Russia's cities.

Most of the really serious crime does not involve tourists, and, despite the above, Russia is still a safe place for tourists to visit. A little more care should be taken these days, however. Crimes against tourists were almost unimaginable ten years ago but now a new branch of the police force has had to be set up especially to protect foreigners. The situation is not as bad as in New York or even some other European capitals but you shouldn't wander around late at night, especially in Moscow or St Petersburg.

Don't dress too ostentatiously or wear expensive jewellery or watches. Travellers have reported that petty pilfering from hotel rooms has increased quite considerably over the last few years. Don't take valuables with you. A money-belt for your passport, travellers' cheques and foreign currency is essential.

PART 3: SIBERIA AND THE RAILWAY

Historical outline

EARLY HISTORY

Prehistory: the first Siberians

Recent discoveries at Dering Yuryakh (100km south of Yakutsk) have indicated that man may have lived in Siberia for far longer than had previously been thought. Unconfirmed evidence from this site suggests human habitation stretching back as far as 1-2 million years ago, which would place the site on a par with Professor Leakey's discoveries in East Africa. There is evidence of rather more recent human life in the Lake Baikal area. In the 13th millennium BC, Stone Age nomads were roaming round the shores of the lake, hunting mammoths and carving their tusks into the tubby fertility goddesses that can been seen in the museums of Irkutsk today. Several of these sites in the Baikal area have been discovered and the railway passes through one at the village of Malta, 45 miles west of Irkutsk, where a camp dating back to this early period has been excavated.

By the Neolithic Age (twelfth to fifth millennia BC) there is far more archaeological evidence and it shows that the nomadic tribes had reached the Arctic Circle and moved into North America through Alaska. These northern tribes trained dogs to pull their sledges but were left behind technologically, remaining in the Stone Age until Russian colonists arrived in the mid-seventeenth century.

In the south, however, several Bronze Age cultures emerged around the central parts of the Yenisei River. Afanassevskaya, south of Krasnoyarsk, has given its name to the culture of the people who lived in this area in the second millennium BC. They made pottery and decorated it with a herring-bone pattern. The first evidence of permanent buildings has been found near Achinsk, where the Andronovo people built huge log cabins in the first millennium BC. Excavations of sites of the Karassuk culture, also dated to the first millennium BC, have yielded Chinese artifacts, indicating trade between these two peoples.

Early civilisations

The Iron Age sites show evidence of more complex and organised societies. The clear air of the Altai Mountains has preserved the contents of numerous graves of the Tagar Culture which existed here in the second

century BC. Their leaders were embalmed and buried like Egyptian
pharaohs with all that they might need in the after-life. In their burial
mounds archaeologists have found perfectly preserved woollen blankets,
decorated leather saddles and the complete skeletons of horses, probably
buried alive when their master died.

The Huns moved into the region south of Lake Baikal in the third century BC where the Buryats, their descendants, now live. Their move west
continued slowly over the next five centuries when their infamous leader
Attila, the 'Scourge of God', having pillaged his way across Europe,
reached Paris where he was defeated in 452 AD.

The ancestors of the Kirghiz people were the Tashtyks from west
Siberia, who built large houses of clay (one found near Abakan even has
an underfloor central heating system), moulded the features of their dead
in clay death masks and decorated their bodies with elaborate tattoos.
Tiny Kirghizstan in the extreme south of the CIS is all that remains of a
once mighty empire that stretched from Samarkand to Manchuria in the
twelfth century AD. In the following century, the Kirghiz were taken over
by the rapidly advancing Mongols. Genghis Khan's Mongol empire grew
to become the largest empire ever, including the Tartars of South Russia,
and the peoples of North Asia, Mongolia and China.

The first Russian expeditions to Siberia
In mediaeval times, Siberia was known to Russians only as a distant land
of valuable fur-bearing animals. There were occasional expeditions from
Novgorod in the fifteenth century. These became more frequent in the
sixteenth century, once the lands of South Russia had been released from
the grip of the Mongols by Tsar Ivan the Terrible who seized Kazan and
Astrakhan, opening the way to Siberia. Yediger, the leader of a small
Siberian kingdom just over the Urals, realised his vulnerability and sent
Ivan a large tribute of furs, declaring himself a vassal of the Tsar.

Yediger's son, Kuchum, was of a more independent mind and, having
murdered his father, he put an end to the annual tribute of furs, proclaim-
ing himself Tsar of Siberia. Since Ivan's armies were occupied on his
western frontiers, he allowed the powerful Stroganov family to raise a
private army to annex the rebel lands. In 1574 he granted them a twenty-
year lease on the land over the Urals as far east as the Tobol River, the
centre of Kuchum's kingdom.

Yermak: the founder of Siberia
The Stroganovs' army was a wild bunch of mercenaries led by ex-pirate
Yermak, the man now recognised as the founder of Siberia. They crossed
the Urals and challenged Kuchum, gaining control of his lands after a
struggle that was surprisingly long, since the Russians were armed with
muskets, the enemy with swords and bows and arrows. On 5th November
1581, Yermak raised the Russian flag in Isker (near modern Tobolsk) and

sent the Tsar a tribute of over 2500 furs. In return Ivan pardoned him for his past crimes, sent him a fur-lined cape that had once graced the royal shoulders and a magnificent suit of armour. Over the next few years Yermak was constantly harassed by Kuchum. On 16th August 1584, the enemy ambushed them when they were asleep on an island in the Irtysh. The story goes that Yermak drowned in the river, dragged under by the weight of the armour given him by the Tsar. His name lives on as the top brand of Russian rucksack.

The quest for furs
Over the next fifty years Cossack forces moved rapidly across Siberia, establishing *ostrogs* (military outposts) as they went and gathering tributes of fur for the Tsar. Tyumen was founded in 1586, Tomsk in 1604, Krasnoyarsk in 1628, Yakutsk in 1633 and by 1639 the Cossacks had crossed the width of the country reaching the east coast. Like the Spanish Conquistadors in South America they dealt roughly with the native tribes they met, who were no match for their muskets and cannons. The prize they lusted after was not gold (as it was for the Spaniards in Peru and for later Russian adventurers in Siberia) but furs. In the days before fur farms certain pelts were worth far more than they are today and from the proceeds of a season's trapping in Siberia a man could buy and stock a large farm with cattle and sheep; the chances that such a man would be successful in finding his way into or out of the dark, swampy forests of the taiga were not very high but quite a few did.

Khabarov and the Amur
In 1650, a Russian fur merchant named Khabarov set out from Yakutsk to explore the Amur region in what is now the Far Eastern Territories. He found the local tribes extremely hostile as the Russians' reputation for rape and pillage had spread before him. The land was fertile and rich in fur-bearing animals and Khabarov and his men committed such atrocities that the news reached the ears of the Tsar, who ordered him back to the capital to explain himself. Bearing gifts of fur, he convinced the Tsar that he had won valuable new lands which would enrich his empire. The local tribes, however, appealed to the Manchus, their southern neighbours, who sent an army to help them fight off the Russians. The Tsar's men were gradually beaten back but periodic fighting went on until 1689, when the Russians were forced out of Manchuria and the Amur by the Treaty of Nerchinsk.

Eighteenth-century explorers
Peter the Great became Tsar in 1696 and initiated a new era of exploration in the Far East. By the following year the explorer, Atlassov, had claimed Kamchatka for Russia. In 1719 the first scientific expedition set out for Siberia. Peter commissioned the Danish seaman, Vitus Bering, to try to

find a northern sea-passage to Kamchatka and the Sea of Okhotsk (unaware that the route had been discovered by Deshnev eighty years before). However, the Tsar did not live to see Bering set out in 1725.

Between 1733 and 1743 another scientific expedition, comprising naval officers, topographers, geodesic surveyors, naturalists and astronomers, made detailed charts of Russians lands in the Far East. Fur traders reached the Aleutian Islands and the first colony in Alaska (on Kodiak Island) was founded in 1784 by Gregory Shelekhov. (His grave is in the cemetery of the Church of the Holy Saviour in Irkutsk.) The Russian colony of Alaska was sold to the United States in 1868 for the bargain price of two cents an acre.

THE NINETEENTH CENTURY

There were two developments in Siberia in the nineteenth century which had a tremendous effect upon its history. First, the practice of sentencing criminals to a life of exile or hard labour in Siberia was increased to provide labour for the mines and to establish communities around the military outposts. The exile system, which caused a great deal of human misery, (see below) greatly increased the population in this vast and empty region. Secondly, and of far greater importance was the building of the Trans-Siberian Railway in the 1890s (described in a later section).

Colonisation

By the end of the eighteenth century, the population of Siberia was estimated to be about one and a half million people, most of whom belonged to nomadic native tribes. The policy of populating the region through the exile system swelled the numbers of settlers but criminals did not make the best colonists. As a result, voluntary emigration from overcrowded European Russia was encouraged by the government. Peasant settlers could escape the bonds of serfdom by crossing the Urals but Siberia's reputation as a place of exile was not much of an incentive to move.

As the railway penetrated Siberia, the transport of colonists was facilitated. Tsar Alexander's emigration representatives were sent to many thickly-populated regions in European Russia in the 1880s. They offered prospective colonists incentives including a reduced rail fare (6 roubles for the 1200 mile journey) and a free allotment of twenty-seven acres of land. Prices in Siberia were high for most things and colonists could expect get up to 100 per cent more than in European Russia for produce grown on this land. Many peasants left Europe for Siberia after the great famine of 1890-91.

Further exploration and expansion

Throughout the century scientists and explorers continued to make expeditions to Siberia, recording their discoveries in the region. In 1829, an expedition led by the German scientist, Baron von Humboldt, who had become famous for his scientific explorations in South America, investigated the geological structure of the Altai plateau (southern Siberia).

In 1840, the estuary of the Amur was discovered and colonisation encouraged, after Count Muraviev-Amursky, Governor General of Eastern Siberia, had annexed the entire Amur territory for Russia. This was in flagrant violation of the Russo-Chinese Treaty of Nerchinsk, which had been signed in 1689. However, the Chinese were in no position to argue, being threatened by the French and English as well as by internal troubles in Peking. By the Treaty of Peking (1860) they ceded the territory north of the Amur to Russia, and also the land east of the Ussuri, including the valuable Pacific port of Vladivostok.

THE EXILE SYSTEM

The word 'Siberia' meant only one thing in Victorian England and nineteenth century Russia: an inhospitable land of exiled murderers and other evil criminals who paid for their sins by working in the infamous salt mines. To a great extent this was a true picture of Siberia except that the prisoners were mining gold, silver and coal rather than salt. Some of the first exiles sent over the Urals did indeed work in salt mines which may be why people associated Siberia with salt.

By the year 1900, over one million people had been exiled and made the long march over the Urals to the squalid and overcrowded prisons of Siberia.

George Kennan

In 1891 a book entitled *Siberia and the Exile System*, written by George Kennan, was published in America. It exposed the truly horrific conditions under which prisoners were kept in Siberia and aroused public opinion in both America and Britain. Kennan was a journalist working for the *New York Century Magazine*. He knew Siberia well, having previously spent two years there. He was then unaware, however, of quite how badly the convicts were treated and in a series of lectures before the American Geographical Society he defended the Tsarist government and the exile system.

When his editor commissioned him to investigate the system more thoroughly, the bureaucrats in St Petersburg were happy to give him the letters of introduction which allowed him to venture into the very worst of the prisons and to meet the governors and convicts. The government hoped, no doubt, that Kennan would champion their cause. Such had been the case with the Rev Dr Henry Landsell who had travelled in Siberia in 1879. In his account of the journey, *Through Siberia*, he wrote that 'on the whole, if a Russian exile behaves himself decently well, he may in Siberia be more comfortable than in many, and as comfortable as in most of the prisons of the world.' After the year he spent visiting Siberian prisons, Kennan could not agree with Landsell and the inhumanity of the exile system, the convict mines and the terrible conditions in the overcrowded prisons were all revealed in his book.

The first exiles

The earliest mention of exile in Russian documents of law is in 1648. In the seventeenth century, exile was used as a way of getting rid of criminals who had already been punished. In Kennan's words: 'The Russian criminal code of that age was almost incredibly cruel and barbarous. Men were impaled on sharp stakes, hanged and beheaded by the hundred for crimes that would not now be regarded as criminal in any civilised country in the world, while lesser offenders were flogged with the knut (a whip of leather and metal thongs, which could break a man's back with a single blow) and bastinado (cane), branded with hot irons, mutilated by amputation of one or more of their limbs, deprived of their tongues, and suspended in the air by hooks passed under two of their ribs until they died a lingering and miserable death.' Those who survived these ordeals were too mutilated to be of any use so they were then driven out of their villages to the lands beyond the Urals.

Exile as a punishment: the convict mines

With the discovery of valuable minerals in Siberia and the shortage of labourers available to mine them, the government began to use criminals to work them. Exile was thus developed into a form of punishment and extended to cover a range of crimes including desertion, assault with intent to kill and vagrancy (when the vagrant was of no use to the army or the community). It was also the punishment for offences that now seem nothing short of ridiculous. According to Kennan, exile became the punishment for fortune-telling, prize-fighting, snuff-taking (the snuff-taker was not only banished to Siberia but also had the septum between his nostrils torn out) and driving with reins. (The old Russian driver had been accustomed to ride his horse or run beside it – using reins was regarded as too Western, too European.)

Abolition of the death penalty

In the eighteenth century demand for labour for the mines continued to grow and the list of crimes punishable by exile was further extended to include drunkenness and wife-beating, the cutting down of trees by serfs, begging with a pretence to being in distress, and setting fire to property accidentally.

In 1753, the death penalty was abolished (for all crimes except an attempt on the life of the Tsar) and replaced by exile with hard labour. No attention was given to the treatment of exiles en route, they were simply herded like animals over the Urals, many dying on the way. The system

The Siberian Boundary Post (circa 1880) In this melancholy scene, friends and relatives bid exiled prisoners farewell by the brick pillar that marked the western border of Siberia, on the Great Post Road.

was chaotically corrupt and disorganised, with hardened murderers being set free in Siberia while people convicted of relatively insignificant offences perished down the mines.

Reorganisation in the nineteenth century

In the nineteenth century the system became more organised but no less corrupt. In 1817 a series of *étapes* (exile stations) was built along the way to provide overnight shelter for the marching parties. They were nothing more than crude log cabins with wooden sleeping platforms. Forwarding prisons were established at Tyumen and Tomsk, from where prisoners were sent to their final place of exile. From Tyumen, convicts travelled by barge in specially designed cages to Tomsk. From here some would be directed on to Krasnoyarsk or else to Irkutsk, a 1040-mile, three-month march away. The prisoners would be sent from these large centres to smaller prisons, penal colonies and to the mines. The most infamous mines were on the island of Sakhalin, off the east coast, where convicts dug for coal; the mines at Kara, which Kennan states were producing an annual average of 3600 pounds of pure gold in the late nineteenth century; and the silver mines of Nerchinsk.

Records were started in 1823 and between this date and 1887, when Kennan consulted the books in Tomsk, 772,979 prisoners had passed through on their way to Siberia. They comprised *katorzhniki* (hard labour convicts) who were distinguishable by their half-shaved heads; *poselentsi* (penal colonists); *silni* (persons simply banished and allowed to return to Russia after serving their sentence), and *dobrovolni* (women and children voluntarily accompanying their husbands or fathers). Until the 1850s convicts and penal colonists would be branded on the cheek with a letter to indicate the nature of their crime. More than half of those who crossed the Urals had had no proper trial but were exiled by 'administrative process'. As Kennan states: 'Every village commune has the right to banish any of its members who, through bad conduct or general worthlessness, have proved themselves obnoxious to their fellow citizens.'

Life in the cells

The first prison Kennan was shown round on his trip in 1887 was the Tyumen forwarding prison. He records the experience thus: 'As we entered the cell, the convicts, with a sudden jingling of chains, sprang to their feet, removed their caps and stood in a dense throng around the *nari* (wooden sleeping platforms).... "The prison" said the warden, "is terribly overcrowded. This cell for example is only 35 feet long by 25 wide, and has air space for 35, or at most 40 men. How many men slept here last night?" he inquired, turning to the prisoners. "A hundred and sixty, your high nobility", shouted half a dozen hoarse voices.....I looked around the cell. There was practically no ventilation and the air was so poisoned and foul that I could hardly force myself to breathe it in.'

The hospital cells

None of these dreadful experiences could prepare Kennan for the hospital cells, filled with prisoners suffering from typhus, scurvy, pneumonia, smallpox, diphtheria, dysentery and syphilis. He wrote afterwards: 'Never before in my life had I seen faces so white, haggard, and ghastly as those that lay on the gray pillows in the hospital cells....As I breathed that heavy, stifling atmosphere, poisoned with the breaths of syphilitic and fever-stricken patients, loaded and saturated with the odor of excrement, disease germs, exhalations from unclean human bodies, and foulness inconceivable, it seemed to me that over the hospital doors should be written "All hope abandon, ye who enter here".' From the records he discovered that almost thirty per cent of the patients in the prison hospital died each year. This he compared with 3.8 per cent for French prisons of the time, two per cent for American and 1.4 per cent for English prisons.

Corruption

As well as the grossly inhuman conditions he saw in the prisons, Kennan found that the whole exile system was riddled with corruption. Bribes were regularly accepted by warders and other officials. One provincial administrator boasted that his governor, the Governor of Tobolsk, was so careless that he could get him to sign any document he was given. As a wager he wrote out 'The Lord's Prayer' on an official form and placed it before the Governor who blindly signed it. The government in St Petersburg was too far away to know what was going on in the lands beyond the Urals.

Political exiles (circa 1880), many of whom came from aristocratic families, were free to adopt whatever lifestyle they could afford within the confines of Siberia.

Many high-ranking officials in Siberia were so tightly bound by bureaucratic ties that change was impossible, even if they desired it. An officer in the Tomsk prison confided in Kennan: 'I would gladly resign tomorrow if I could see the (exile) system abolished. It is disastrous to Siberia, it is ruinous to the criminal, and it causes an immense amount of misery; but what can be done? If we say anything to our superiors in St Petersburg, they strike us in the face; and they strike hard – it hurts!'

Political exiles

Life for the so-called 'politicals' and 'nihilists', banished to prevent them infecting European Russians with their criticisms of the autocratic political system that was choking the country to death, was luxury compared to that of the prisoners (see p91). Many came from rich aristocratic families and, after the move to Siberia, life for them continued in much the same way as it had west of the Urals. The most famous political exiles were the 'Decembrists': the men who took part in the unsuccessful coup in 1825. Many were accompanied into exile by their wives. Some of the houses in which they lived are now preserved as *Dom* ('house') museums in Irkutsk (see p230).

Kennan secretly visited many of the politicals in Siberia and was convinced that they did not deserve being exiled. He wrote later: 'If such men are in exile in a lonely Siberian village on the frontier of Mongolia, instead of being at home in the service of the state – so much the worse for the state.' A few politicals were sentenced to exile with the native Yakut tribe within the Arctic Circle. Escape was impossible and life with a Stone Age tribe must have seemed unbearable for cultured aristocrats who had until recently been part of the St Petersburg court circle.

Temporary abolition of the exile system

The exile system was abolished in 1900. However corrupt the system and inhuman the conditions in these early Siberian prisons, worse was to come only thirty years later. Under Stalin's regime, vast concentration camps (in European Russia as well as in Siberia) were set up to provide a huge slave-labour force to build roads, railways and factories in the 1930s and '40s.

The camps were strictly off-limits to twentieth century George Kennans but former inmates have reported that the prisoners were grossly overworked and undernourished. The mortality rate in some of these camps is said to have been as high as thirty per cent. Reports of the number of people sentenced to these slave labour camps range from between three million and twenty million. Some reports place the death toll up to the late 1950s as high as eighteen million.

Early travellers

VICTORIAN ADVENTURERS

This was the great age of the gentleman (and gentlewoman) adventurer. These upper-class travellers spent the greater part of their lives exploring the lesser-known regions of the world, writing long and usually highly-readable accounts of their adventures and encounters with the 'natives'. Siberia attracted almost as many of this brave breed as did Africa and India. Once they had travelled across the great Siberian plain using the normal forms of transport of the time (carriage and sledge) they resorted to such new-fangled inventions as the bicycle (R.L.Jefferson in 1896), the train (from 1900) and then the car (the Italian Prince Borghese in an Itala in 1907). Some even crossed the country entirely on foot.

THE GREAT SIBERIAN POST ROAD

Before the railway was built, there was but one way for convicts, colonists and adventurers to cross this region: a rough track known as the Post Road or *Trakt*. Posting stations (see photograph opposite p112) were set up at approximately 25 mile intervals along the route, where travellers could rent horses and drivers. Murray, in his *Handbook for Russia, Poland and Finland* (1865 edition) told his travellers: 'Three kinds of conveyances are available: the *telega*, or cart without springs, which has to be changed at every station, and for which a charge of about 8d is made at every stage; the *kibitka* or cart (in winter a sledge) with a hood; and the *tarantass*, a kind of carriage on wooden springs which admits of the traveller lying down full length and which can be made very comfortable at night. The two latter vehicles have to be purchased at Perm, if the *telega*, or postal conveyance be not accepted. A *tarantass* may be bought from £12 to £15.'

George Kennan called the Imperial Russian Post System 'the most perfectly organised horse express service in the world'.

The discomforts of Siberian travel

Since a visit to Siberia could rarely be completed in a single season, most travellers experienced the different modes of transport used in summer and winter. They found the sledge more comfortable than the tarantass and indeed no nineteenth century travelogue would be complete without a detailed description of this unique vehicle. The tarantass had a large boat-shaped body and travellers stored their belongings on the floor, covering them with straw and mattresses on top of which they lay. Although this may sound comfortable, when experienced at speed over atrocious roads and for great distances, by contemporary accounts it was not. S.S.Hill wrote in 1854: 'The worst of the inconveniences arose from the deep ruts which were everywhere...and from the necessity of galloping down the declivities to force the carriage upon the bridges. And often our carriage fell with such force against the bridges that it was unsafe to retain our accustomed reclining position...'

Kate Marsden, a nurse travelling in 1894, recalled the agony of days spent in a tarantass in the following way: 'Your limbs ache, your muscles ache, your head aches, and, worst of all, your inside aches terribly. "Tarantass rheumatism" internal and external, chronic, or rather perpetual, is the complaint.'

The yamshchiki

The driver (*yamshchik*) of the tarantass or sledge, was invariably drunk. He had to be bribed with vodka to make good time between the post stations and Murray's 1865 guide-book thoughtfully includes in its 'Useful Russian Phrases' section, the words 'Dam na vodki' ('I will give you drink money').

Accidents were commonplace and R.L. Jefferson (on a trip without his bicycle in 1895) wrote that his yamshchik became so inebriated that he fell off the sledge and died. The same fate befell one of Kate Marsden's sledge-drivers who had gone to sleep with the reins tied around his wrists. She wrote: 'And there was the poor fellow being tossed to and fro amongst the legs of the horses, which, now terrified, tore down the hill like mad creatures.... In a few minutes there was a fearful crash. We had come into collision with another tarantass and the six horses and the two tarantasses were mixed up in a chaotic mass'.

The horses

Sledges and tarantasses were pulled by a *troika*, a group of three horses. These were small furry specimens, 'not much larger than the average English donkey', noted R.L.Jefferson. They were hired between post stations and usually belonged to the yamshchik.

S.S.Hill was shocked at the way in which these animals were treated. He remarked: 'The Arab is the friend of his horse. The Russian or Siberian peasant is his severe master who exacts every grain of his strength by blows accompanied with curses....lodges him badly or not at all, cares little how he feeds him, and never cleans him or clips a hair of his body from the hour of his birth to that of his death.' Horses were worked literally until they died. R.L.Jefferson recalls that two of his animals dropped dead in harness and had to be cut free.

(Above) Until the building of the Trans-Siberian, the Great Post Road formed the life-line for hundreds of tiny communities such as this. (Below) There were few bridges on the Road – crossing frozen rivers and lakes was treacherous in early winter and spring.

Dangers

Travel in Siberia was not only uncomfortable, it was also dangerous. Wolves and bears roamed the forests and when food was scarce would attack a horse or man (although you were safe in a tarantass). In the Amur region lived the world's largest tiger, the Amur tiger. Just as wild as these animals, and probably more dangerous, were the *brodyagi*, escaped convicts in search of money and a passport to readmit them to Europe.

> ❏ **Siberian hotels circa 1894**
> Hotel rooms were universally squalid. Kate Marsden gives the following advice to anyone entering a hotel bedroom in Siberia: 'Have your pocket handkerchief ready...and place it close to your nostrils the moment the door is opened. The hinges creak and your first greeting is a gust of hot, foetid air.'

Dirt and disease

As well as the discomfort of the 'conveyance' and the dangers along the Trakt, travellers were warned about the dirt and disease they could encounter. R.L.Jefferson wrote: 'No wonder that Siberia is looked upon by the traveller with abhorrence. Apart from its inhabitants, no one can say that Siberia is not a land of beauty, plenty and promise; but it is the nature of its inhabitants which make it the terrible place it is. The independence, the filth and general want of comfort which characterize every effort of the community, serve to make a visit to any Siberian centre a thing to be remembered for many years and an experience not desirable to repeat.'

Insects

Especially in the summer months, travellers were plagued by flies and mosquitoes. Kate Marsden wrote: 'After a few days the body swells from their bites into a form that can neither be imagined nor described. They attack your eyes and your face, so that you would hardly be recognised by your dearest friend.'

At night, travellers who had stopped in the dirty hotels or posting stations were kept awake by lice, bed-bugs and a variety of other insects with which the bedding was infested. R.L.Jefferson met a man who never travelled without four saucers and a can of kerosene. In the hotel room at night he would put a saucer filled with kerosene under each bed-leg, to stop the bugs reaching him in bed. However, Jefferson noted that: 'With a sagacity which one would hardly credit so small an insect, it would make a detour by getting up the wall on to the ceiling, and then, having accurately poised, drop down upon the victim – no doubt to his extreme discomfort.'

Bovril and Jaeger underwear: essential provisions

R.L.Jefferson, who made several trips to Russia (three of which were on his Imperial Rover bicycle) never travelled without a large supply of

Bovril and a change of Jaeger 'Cellular' underwear – 'capital stuff for lightness and durability' he wrote after one long ride. Kate Marsden shared his enthusiasm for Dr Jaeger's undergarments: 'without which it would have been quite impossible to go through all the changes of climate; and to remain for weeks together without changing my clothes', she wrote. On the subject of provisions for the trip, Murray recommended taking along basic foodstuffs. Miss Marsden packed into her tarantass 'a few boxes of sardines, biscuits, some bread, tea and one or two other trifles which included forty pounds of plum pudding'.

S.S.HILL'S *TRAVELS IN SIBERIA*

This account of Hill's Siberian adventures was the result of a journey made in the early 1850s to Irkutsk and then Yakutsk (now in the Far Eastern Territories). Armed with a pistol loaded with goose-shot (for the law forbade a foreigner to shoot at a Russian, even in self defence), he travelled by tarantass and existed on *shchi* (soup) and tea for most of the time. He makes some interesting observations upon the culinary habits of the Siberians he met along the way.

He records that on one occasion, when settling down to a bowl of shchi after a long winter's journey 'we found the taste of our accustomed dish, however, today peculiar'. He was made aware of the main ingredient of their soup later, 'by the yamshchik pointing out to us the marks of the axe upon the frozen carcass of a horse lying within a quarter of a verst of the site of our feast'. In some places even tea and shchi were unavailable and they could find only cedar nuts ('a favourite food article with the peasants of Eastern Siberia'). He ate better in Irkutsk, where, at a dinner party, he was treated to *comba* fish, six feet in length and served whole. 'I confess I never before saw so enormous an animal served or cooked whole save once, an ox roasted at a 'mop' in Worcestershire', he wrote later. He was shocked by the behaviour of the ladies at the table, who, when bored, displayed 'a very droll habit of rolling the damp crumb of rye bread... into pills'. He remarks with surprise that in Siberian society ' a glass of milk terminates the dinner'.

KATE MARSDEN VISITS SIBERIAN LEPERS

Miss Marsden was a nurse with a definite mission in Siberia. In the 1880s she learnt, through travellers' accounts, of the numerous leper colonies to the north of Yakutsk. There were rumours of a special herb found there, that could alleviate the symptoms of the disease. After an audience with Queen Victoria, during which she was given useful letters of introduction, she travelled to Moscow. She arrived, in mid-winter, wearing her thin cotton nurse's uniform and a white bonnet, which she immediately exchanged for thick Russian clothes.

Crossing Siberia

When she had met the Empress Marya, who gave her a thousand roubles for her relief fund, she started on her long sledge ride. It was not a dignified send-off – 'three muscular policemen attempted to lift me into the sledge; but their combined strength was futile under the load'. She got aboard eventually and was soon experiencing the extreme discomfort of Siberian travel. She said it made her feel more like 'a battered old log of mahogany than a gently nurtured Englishwoman'.

Distributing tea, sugar and copies of the Gospels to convicts in the marching parties she encountered along the Post Road, she reached Irkutsk in the summer. She boarded a leaky barge on the Lena River, north of Lake Baikal and drifted down to Yakutsk, sitting on the sacks of potatoes with which the boat was filled. Of this part of the journey she wrote: 'Fortunately we had only about 3,000 miles of this but 3,000 miles were enough'. Her goal was still a 2,000 mile ride away when she reached Yakutsk. Although she had never been on a horse before, this brave woman arranged an escort of fifteen men and rode with them through insect-infested swamps and across a fiery plain, below which the earth was in a constant state of combustion, until she reached the settlement of Viluisk.

The Lepers of Viluisk

On her arrival, the local priest informed her that 'On the whole of the earth you will not find men in so miserable a condition as the Smedni Viluisk lepers'. She found them dressed in rags, living in hovels and barely existing on a diet of rotten fish. This was in an area where, in winter, some of the lowest temperatures in the world have been recorded. Unfortunately she did not find the herb that was rumoured to exist there but left all the more convinced that finances must be raised for a hospital.

Although she managed to raise 25,000 roubles towards the enterprise, her task was not made any easier by several individuals who took exception to her breezy style of writing, accusing her of having undertaken the journey for her own fame and fortune. Some even suggested that the journey was a fiction invented so that Miss Marsden could collect charitable sums for her own use. In the end she was forced to sue one of her attackers who wrote a letter to *The Times* describing her journey as 'only a little pleasure trip'. Nevertheless she achieved her aim: a hospital opened in Viluisk in 1897. It still stands and her name is still remembered in this remote corner of Russia.

JEFFERSON'S BICYCLE TRIPS

R.L.Jefferson was an enthusiastic cyclist and traveller who made several journeys to Siberia in the 1890s. A year after bicycling from London to Constantinople and back, he set out again from Kennington Oval for

Moscow on his Imperial Rover bicycle. Twelve hours out of Moscow, a speeding tarantass knocked him down, squashing the back wheel of his 'machine'. Repairs took a few days but he still managed to set a cycling speed record of just under fifty days for the 4281 mile journey from London to Moscow and back.

His next ride was to the decaying capital of the Khanate of Khiva, now in Uzbekistan. The 6,000 mile journey took him across the Kirghiz Steppes in south-west Siberia, along the coast of the Aral Sea and over the Karakum Desert. When the bicycle's wheels sank up to their axles in the sand he had the Rover lashed to the back of a camel for the rest of the journey. While in Central Asia he lived on a diet of boiled mutton and *koumis* (fermented mares' milk). He travelled in a camel-hair suit (Jaeger, of course) and top boots, with a white cork helmet to complete the outfit.

Across Siberia

Jefferson made two more trips to Siberia. In *Across Siberia by Bicycle* (1896), he wrote that he left Moscow and 'sleeping the night in some woodman's hut, subsisting on occasional lumps of black bread, bitten to desperation by fearful insects, and tormented out of my life during the day by swarms of mosquitoes, I arrived in Perm jaded and disgusted'. He then cycled over the Urals and through the mud of the Great Post Road to Ekaterinburg. Here he was entertained by the Ekaterinburg Cyclists' Club whom he described as 'friends of the wheel – jolly good fellows all'.

Declaring that 'from a cyclist's point of view, Russian roads cannot be recommended', he abandoned his Rover in 1897 for the adventure described in *Roughing it in Siberia*. With three chums, he travelled by sledge from Krasnoyarsk up the frozen Yenisei ('jerking about like peas in a frying pan') to the gold mines in Minusinsk district, spending several weeks prospecting in the Syansk Mountains.

Building the railway

The first railway to be built in Russia was Tsar Nicholas I's private line (opened in 1836) which ran from his summer palace at Tsarkoye Selo (Pushkin) to Pavlovsk and later to St Petersburg, a distance of 14 miles. The Tsar was said to have been most impressed with this new form of transport and over the next 30 years several lines were laid in European Russia, linking the main cities and towns. Siberia, however, was really too far away to deserve serious consideration since most people only went there if they were forced to as exiles. And as far as the Tsar was concerned, traditional methods of transport kept him supplied with all the gold and furs he needed.

PLANS FOR A TRANS-SIBERIAN RAILWAY

Horse-powered Trans-Siberian Express?

The earliest plans for long distance railways in Siberia came from a number of foreigners. Most books which include a history of the Trans-Siberian give a passing mention to an English engineer, if only because of his wildly eccentric ideas and his unfortunate name. Thus a Mr Dull has gone down in history as the man who seriously suggested the building of a line from Perm across Siberia to the Pacific, with carriages being pulled by wild horses (of which there were a great many in the region at the time). He is said to have formally proposed his plan to the Ministry of Ways of Communication, who turned it down.

The Englishman's name was, in fact, not Dull but Duff and it's not only his name that has been distorted through time. His descendants (John Howell and William Lawrie) have requested that the story be set straight. Thomas Duff was an enterprising adventurer who went out to China to seek his fortune in the 1850s. He returned to England via Siberia, spending some time in St Petersburg with wealthy aristocratic friends. Here he was introduced to the Minister of Ways of Communication and it was probably during their conversation that he remarked on the vast numbers of wild horses he had encountered on his journey. Could they not be put to some use? Perhaps they might be trained to pull the trains that people were saying would soon run across Siberia. It is unlikely that this remark was intended to be serious but it has gone down in history as a formal proposal for a horse-powered Trans-Siberian Express.

More serious proposals

At around this time the American Perry McDonough Collins was exploring the Amur river, having persuaded the US government to appoint him as their commercial agent in the region. He had been given an enthusiastic welcome by Count Amurski Muravyev, the Governor-General of Siberia, before setting off to descend the Amur in a small boat. Collins envisaged a trade link between America and Siberia with vessels sailing up the Amur and Shilka rivers to Chita, where a railway link would shuttle goods to and from Irkutsk. He sent his plans for the building and financing of such a line to the government but these too were rejected. Collins' next venture, a telegraph link between America and Russia, also failed but not before he had made himself a considerable fortune.

It took a further twenty years for the government to become interested enough in the idea of a railway in Siberia to send surveyors to investigate the feasibility of such a project. Plans were considered for the building of lines to link the great Siberian rivers, so that future travellers could cross Siberia in relative comfort by a combination of rail and ship. European lines were extended from Perm over the Urals, reaching Ekaterinburg in 1878.

Tsar Alexander III : the railway's founder

In 1881 Alexander III became Tsar and in 1886 gave the Trans-Siberian project his official sanction with the words: 'I have read many reports of the Governors-General of Siberia and must own with grief and shame that until now the government has done scarcely anything towards satisfying the needs of this rich, but neglected country! It is time, high time!'

He was thus able to add 'Most August Founder of The Great Siberian Railway' to his many other titles. He rightly saw the railway as both the key to developing the land beyond the Urals and also as the means to transport his troops to the Amur region which was being threatened by the Chinese. When the commission looking into the building of the new line declared that the country did not have the money to pay for it, the Tsar solved the problem simply by forming a new committee, dismissing the first.

THE DECISION TO BUILD

The new commission took note of the petitions from Count Ignatyev and Baron Korf, the Governors-General of Irkutsk and the Amur territories, respectively. They proposed rail links between Tomsk and Irkutsk, Lake Baikal and Sretensk (where passengers could board ships for the journey down the Shilka and Amur Rivers to the coast) and for the Ussuri line to Vladivostok. Baron Korf considered that it was imperative for the Ussuri line to be built as soon as possible if the valuable port of Vladivostok was not to be cut off by the advancing Chinese. The Tsar took note and declared: 'I hope the Ministry will practically prove the possibility of the quick and cheap construction of the line'.

Surveys were commissioned and detailed plans prepared. In 1891 it was announced that the Trans-Siberian Railway would indeed be built and work would start immediately. It was, however, to be constructed as cheaply as possible using thinner rails, shorter sleepers and timber (rather than stone) for the smaller bridges.

The route

The railway committee decided that the great project should be divided into several sections with work commencing simultaneously on a number of them. The West Siberian Railway would run from Chelyabinsk (the railway over the Urals reached this town in 1892) to the Ob River where the settlement of Novo Nikolayevsk (now Novosibirsk) was being built. The Mid-Siberian Railway would link the Ob to Irkutsk, the capital of Eastern Siberia. Passengers would cross Lake Baikal on ferries to Mysovaya, the start of the Transbaikal Railway to Sretensk. From here they would continue to use the Shilka and Amur River for the journey to Khabarovsk, until the Amur Railway could be built between these towns.

The Ussuri Railway would link Khabarovsk with Vladivostok. There were also plans for a shortcut from the Transbaikal area to Vladivostok, across Manchuria. This would be known as the East Chinese Railway.

Nicholas lays the foundation stone

After the decision to start work, the Tsar wrote the following letter to his son, the Tsarevich, who had just reached Vladivostok at the end of a tour around the world: 'Having given the order to build a continuous line of railway across Siberia, which is to unite the rich Siberian provinces with the railway system of the interior, I entrust you to declare My will, upon your entering the Russian dominions after your inspection of the foreign countries of the East. At the same time I desire you to lay the first stone at Vladivostok for the construction of the Ussuri line forming part of the Siberian Railway...'

On 31 May 1891, Nicholas carried out his father's wishes, filling a wheelbarrow with earth and emptying it onto what was to become part of the embankment for the Ussuri Railway. He then laid the foundation stone for the station.

RAILWAY CONSTRUCTION: PHASE 1 (1891-1901)

● **The Ussuri, West Siberian & Mid-Siberian Railways (1891-98)**
Work started on the Ussuri line (Vladivostok to Khabarovsk) some time after the inauguration ceremony and proceeded slowly. In July 1892, the construction of the West Siberian (Chelyabinsk to the west bank of the Ob River) was begun. In July 1893 work started on the Mid-Siberian (east bank of the Ob to Irkutsk). The West Siberian reached Omsk in 1894 and was completed when the rails reached the Ob in October 1895. The Ussuri Railway was completed in 1897 and in the following year the final rails of the Mid-Siberian were laid and Irkutsk was linked to Moscow and St Petersburg.

● **The Transbaikal Railway (1895-1900)** The rail link between the Lake Baikal port of Mysovaya and Sretensk on the Shilka River was begun in 1895. In spite of a flood which swept part of the track away in 1897, the line was completed by the beginning of 1900.

Passengers could now travel to Irkutsk by train, take the ferry across Lake Baikal and the train again from Mysovaya to Srtensk, where steamers would take them to Khabarovsk.

● **The East Chinese Railway (1897-1901)** Surveys showed that the proposed Amur Railway between Sretensk and Khabarovsk would be expensive to build because of the mountainous region it would have to pass through and the large supplies of explosives required to deal with the permafrost. In 1894 the Russian government granted China a generous loan to help pay off China's debts to Japan. In exchange for this financial help,

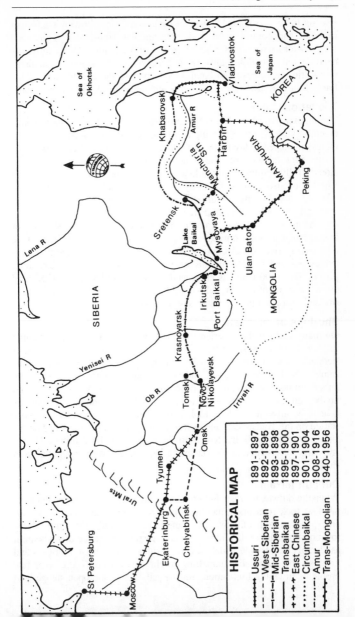

HISTORICAL MAP

+++++ Ussuri	1891-1897
– – – West Siberian	1892-1895
–ı–ı– Mid-Siberian	1893-1898
———— Transbaikal	1895-1900
+‡+‡+ East Chinese	1897-1901
·········· Circumbaikal	1901-1904
–··–··– Amur	1908-1916
▼▼▼▼ Trans-Mongolian	1940-1956

a secret treaty was signed between Russia and China allowing the former to build and control a rail link between the Transbaikal region and Vladivostok, across the Chinese territory of Manchuria. Every difficulty encountered in building railways in Siberia (severe winters, mountains, rivers, floods, disease and bandits) was part of the construction of the East Chinese Railway, begun in 1897 and opened to light traffic in 1901.

The labour force

The greater part of the Trans-Siberian Railway was built without heavy machinery by men with nothing more than wooden shovels. They never-theless managed to lay up to two and a half miles of rail on a good day. Most of the labour force had to be imported as the local peasants were already fully employed on the land. They came not only from European Russia but also from as far away as Italy and Turkey. Chinese coolies were employed on the Ussuri Railway but overseers found them unreli-able and terrified of the Amur tigers with which the area was infested.

The government soon turned to the prisons to relieve the shortage of labour and gangs of convicts were put to work on the lines. They were paid twenty-five kopecks (a quarter of a rouble) a day and had their sen-tences reduced – eight months on the railways counted for a year in prison. The 1500 convicts employed on the Mid-Siberian worked hard but those brought in from Sakhalin Island to work on the Ussuri line ran riot and terrorised the inhabitants of Vladivostok.

Shortage of materials

On many parts of the Siberian Plain engineers discovered that although there were vast forests of trees, none of them was suitable for using as sleepers (ties). Timber had to be imported over great distances. Rails came from European Russia and some even from Britain. They were either shipped via the Kara Sea (a southern part of the Arctic Ocean) and up the Yenisei River to Krasnoyarsk, or else right around the continent by boat to Vladivostok (which took two months). From here, when work started on the Transbaikal line in 1895, materials had to be shipped up the Ussuri, Amur and Shilka Rivers to Sretensk (over 1000 miles). Horses and carts were scarce in Siberia and these, too, had to be brought in from Europe.

Difficult terrain

When the railway between St Petersburg and Moscow was being planned, the Tsar took ruler and pencil and drew a straight line between the two cities, declaring that this was the route to be followed, with almost every town by-passed. For the Trans-Siberian, Alexander ordered that it be built as cheaply as possible which is why in some places the route twists and turns so that expensive tunnelling might be avoided. There were few problems in laying foundations for the rails across the open steppe land of the Siberian plain but cutting through the almost impenetrable forests of the taiga proved extremely difficult. Much of this area was not only thickly forested but swampy in summer and frozen in winter until July. Consequently the building season lasted no more than four months in most places.

In eastern Siberia parts of the ground were locked in permafrost and, even in mid-summer, had to be dynamited or warmed with fires before rails could be laid. The most difficult terrain was the short line around the southern end of Lake Baikal, the Circumbaikal Loop, which required over 200 trestles and bridges and 33 tunnels.

Conditions

For the workers who laboured in Siberia, conditions were hardly the most enjoyable. All were far from home, living in isolated log cabins that were not much cleaner or more comfortable than the squalid prison in Tyumen, graphically described by George Kennan in *Siberia and the Exile System*. Winters were very long and extremely cold. The brief summer brought relief from the cold but the added discomfort of plagues of black flies and mosquitoes in the swamps of the taiga. There were numerous outbreaks of disease. Workers on the East Chinese Railway were struck first by an outbreak of bubonic plague in 1899 and cholera in 1902. In many places the horses were wiped out by Siberian anthrax.

There were other dangers in addition to disease. In Manchuria and the Amur and Ussuri regions, the forests were filled with Amur tigers for whom the occasional railway labourer no doubt made a pleasant snack. In Manchuria construction camps were frequently raided by *hunghutzes* (bandits) who roamed around the country in gangs of up to seven hundred men. As a result, the Russian government was obliged to allocate considerable sums of money and men to the policing of the region.

There were several set-backs that no one could have foreseen. In July 1897 severe flooding swept away or damaged over two hundred miles of track near Lake Baikal on the Transbaikal line, also destroying settlements and livestock. Damage was estimated at six million roubles. In other areas landslides were caused by torrential rainfall.

RAILWAY CONSTRUCTION: PHASE 2 (1898-1916)

Reconstruction

As the first trains began to travel over the newly-laid tracks, the short-sightedness of the policy of building the railway as cheaply as possible soon became clear. Many of the materials used in its construction were either sub-standard or unsuitable to the conditions they were expected to withstand. The rails were under half the weight of those used in America and fashioned of iron of an inferior quality. They soon bent and buckled and needed replacing. The ballast under the sleepers was far thinner than that put down on the major railways of Europe. As a result, the ride in the carriages was bumpy and uncomfortable and speed had to be kept down to 13 mph for passenger trains, 8 mph for freight. Foreign engineers proclaimed the whole system unsafe and were proved correct by the frequent derailments which took place.

In 1895 Prince Khilkov became Minister of Ways of Communication. On a tour of inspection along the West and Mid-Siberian lines he quickly realised that a massive rebuilding programme would have to be put into operation. Extra trains were also needed to transport the hundreds of thousands of emigrants who were now flooding over the Urals. In 1899 100 million roubles were allocated for repairs, work which would have been unnecessary had sufficient funds been made available from the start.

● **The Circumbaikal Loop Line (1901-1904)** In 1901 work began on the 260km Circumbaikal Loop line around Lake Baikal's southern shores. The initial project had been shelved in 1893, since the terrain was considered too difficult. Passengers used the ferry service across the lake but it was soon found that the ships couldn't cope with the increased traffic. The situation became critical at the start of the Russo-Japanese war in 1904, when troops and machinery being sent to the East by rail were delayed at the lake. Construction of the new line continued as fast as possible and by the end of the year the final section of the Trans-Siberian was opened. Passengers were at last able to travel from Calais to Vladivostok entirely by train.

● **The Amur Railway (1907-1916)** The original plans for a railway from Sretensk to Khabarovsk along the Shilka and Amur Rivers were abandoned because the route would entail expensive engineering work. After the Russo-Japanese war in 1904-5, the government realised that there was a danger of Japan taking control of Manchuria and the East Chinese Railway. This was the only rail-link to Russia's naval base at Vladivostok. It was therefore decided that the Amur Railway must indeed be built. Work began at Kuenga in 1908. There were the usual problems of insects, disease and permafrost but with the rest of the railway operational, it was easier to transport men and materials to the Amur area. When the bridge over the Amur at Khabarovsk was finished in 1916, the Trans-Siberian Railway was at last complete. Over 1000 million roubles had been spent on building all the sections (including the East Chinese line) since 1891.

THE FIRST RAIL TRAVELLERS

Rail service begins

As each of the sectors of the Trans-Siberian was completed, a rail service was begun. To say that there were teething troubles would be a gross understatement; there was a shortage of engines and carriages, most of the system operated without a timetable and there were frequent delays and derailments along the shoddily constructed line. Nevertheless, in order to attract foreign travellers, luxury trains and 'Expresses' were introduced. Those run by the government were known as Russian State Expresses while another service was operated by the Belgian 'Compagnie Internationale des Wagons-Lits'. In 1900 the Ministry of Ways of Communication published their detailed *Guide to The Great Siberian Railway* in English.

The Paris Exhibition

The Russian government was keen to show off to the world the country's great engineering feat and at the Paris 'Exposition Universelle' of 1900, a comprehensive Trans-Siberian exhibit was staged. Amongst photographs and maps of Siberia, with Kirghiz, Buryat and Goldi robes and artifacts, there were several carriages to be operated by the Wagons-Lits Company on the Great Siberian Railway. They were furnished in the most sumptuous style, with just four spacious compartments in the sleeping carriages, each with a connecting lavatory. The other carriages contained a smoking-room done up in Chinese style, a library and music-room complete with piano.

In the two restaurant cars, decorated with mahogany panelling and heavy curtains, visitors to the exhibition could dine on the luxurious fare that was promised on the journey itself. To give diners the feeling of crossing Siberia, a length of canvas on which was painted a Siberian panorama of wide steppes, thick taiga and little villages of log cabins, could be seen through the windows. In order to complete the illusion that the train was actually chugging across the Great Siberian Plain, the painted panorama was made to move past the windows by mechanical means.

Visitors were intrigued and impressed and more than a few soon set off on the epic trip. The reality, they were to discover, was a little different from what they experienced at the exhibition.

Early rail travellers

When R.L.Jefferson set out to investigate the Minusinsk gold-mining region in 1897, he was able to take the train (travelling for once without his Imperial Rover bicycle but no doubt taking along a good supply of Bovril and 'Cellular' underwear) as far as Krasnoyarsk.

The first English woman to travel the entire length of this route was Annette Meakin, who took her aged mother for company on the journey made in 1900. They travelled via Paris to see the Siberian display at the Paris Exhibition. Having crossed Siberia, they went by ship to Japan and then to North America, crossing that continent by train too. Having circumnavigated the globe by rail, Miss Meakin recorded her experiences in the book she called *A Ribbon of Iron*. Two years later, in 1902, Michael

Myres Shoemaker took *The Great Siberian Railway from St Petersburg to Pekin* (the name of his account of the journey). He wrote enthusiastically: 'This Railway will take its place amongst the most important works of the world .... Russia is awakening at last and moving forward.'

It is interesting to compare the descriptions these travellers give of the trains they took, with the carriages displayed at the Paris Exhibition as well as with the service operated today by Russian Railways.

The carriages

Advertising brochures informed prospective Trans-Siberian travellers, in gushing prose, that the carriages in which they were to be conveyed would be of a standard equal to those used by European royalty. In addition to the luxurious sleeping compartments and dining cars shown at the Paris Exhibition, there would be a bathroom with marble bath-tub, a gymnasium equipped with a stationary bicycle and other exercising machines, a fire-proof safe, a hair-dressing salon and a darkroom equipped with all the chemicals a photographer would need. The carriages would be lit by electric lighting, individually heated in winter and cooled by under-floor ice-boxes in summer.

❏'The Siberian express is a kind of "Liberty Hall", where you can shut your door and sleep all day if you prefer it, or eat and drink, smoke and play cards if you like that better. An electric bell summons a serving-man to make your bed or sweep your floor, as the case may be, while a bell on the other side summons a waiter from the buffet....Time passes very pleasantly on such a train.' **Annette Meakin** *A Ribbon of Iron*

Although more than a few of those luxurious appointments, which they had seen in the carriages of the Siberian exhibit in Paris, were missing on their train, Annette Meakin and her mother found their accommodation entirely satisfactory. The ride was not so comfortable for the Meakins from Mysovaya on the Transbaikal Railway. Only fourth class carriages were provided and they were forced to take their travelling rugs and picnic hamper to the luggage van, where they spent the next four days.

Travelling in 1902, Michael Myres Shoemaker was very impressed with the bathing arrangements on the train and wrote: 'I have just discovered that there is a fine bathroom in the restaurant car, large and tiled, with all sorts of sprays, plunges and douches. This bath has its separate attendant and all the bath towels you may demand.' He was less enthusiastic about his travelling companions, a French Consul and family whose fox terrier 'promptly domesticated itself in my compartment'.

The restaurant car

At the Paris Exhibition visitors were led to believe that a good part of the enjoyment of travelling on the Trans-Siberian would be the cordon bleu cuisine served in the restaurant car. It was claimed that the kitchens were even equipped with water tanks filled with live fish. The waiters would be multi-lingual and a truly international service was promised.

Travellers found the above description to be something of an exaggeration. Annette Meakin reported the existence of a Bechstein piano and a library of Russian novels in the restaurant car. Shoemaker wrote: 'The restaurant car is just like all those on the trains of Europe. There is a piano, generally used to hold dirty dishes. There are three very stupid waiters who speak nothing save Russian. The food is very poor.'

Travellers were warned by their guide-books that there were occasional food shortages and advised to take along a picnic hamper. The Meakins found theirs invaluable on their four-day jaunt in the luggage van. In fact, for the first few years after the service began, there had been no restaurant cars. R.L.Jefferson wrote that at meal-times, the train would stop at a convenient station and all passengers (and the engine-driver) would get off for a meal at the station. Travelling in 1901, John Foster Fraser reports, in *The Real Siberia*, that locals did good business on the platforms selling 'dumplings with hashed meat and seasoning inside....huge loaves of new made bread, bottles of beer, pails of milk, apples, grapes, and fifty other things'. This is still true today.

The church car

Behind the baggage car was a peculiar carriage known as the church car. It was a Russian Orthodox Church on wheels, complete with icons and candelabra inside, church bells and a cross on the roof, and a peripatetic priest who dispensed blessings along the way. This carriage was detached at stations and settlements where churches had not yet been built and services were conducted for railway workers and their families.

Transport of emigrants

While foreign visitors discussed whether or not their accommodation was all that the Siberian exhibit in Paris had led them to believe, emigrants travelled in the unenviable conditions described by R.L.Jefferson: 'The emigrants' train is simply one of the cattle trucks, each car being marked on the side "Forty men or eight horses". There are no seats or lights provided, and into each of these pens forty men, women and children have to herd over a dreary journey of fourteen or fifteen days...They have to provide their own food but at every station a large samovar is kept boiling in order to provide them with hot water for their tea.'

By the end of the century they were crossing the Urals to Siberia at the rate of about a quarter of a million peasants each year.

Stations

Little wooden station buildings mushroomed along the railway. Russian stations were traditionally given a class number from one to five. Of the stations listed in the official *Guide to the Great Siberian Railway*, none was of the first class and the majority were no more than fifth class. Beside most stations there towered a water-tank to supply the steam engines. Many of these towers, their eaves decorated with ornate fret-work, can still be seen today. Most of the larger stations also had their own churches and resident priests. If the train did not have a church car, stops would be made for lengthy services at these railside churches, especially on the eve of an important saint's day.

R.L.Jefferson found that in the early years of the railways, the arrival and departure of every train at a Siberian station was quite an event, being 'attended with an amount of excitement that it is hard to associate with the usually stolid Russian. Particularly is this so in Eastern Russia where railways are new and interesting.' A man 'performs a terrific tintinabulation on a large suspended bell. All the conductors blow whistles.' Jefferson goes on to explain that none of the passengers was allowed out of the train until the engine driver had got down and shaken hands with the station-master and his staff.

Delays
Because the original line was so badly laid, the ride in the carriages was rough and uncomfortable and speed had to be kept down. There were frequent derailments and long delays. Annette Meakin complained: 'We stopped at a great many stations; indeed on some parts of the route we seemed to get into a chronic state of stopping'. 'All day long at a dog trot,' wrote Shoemaker, 'Certainly no more than ten miles an hour.' Over some sections the train went so slowly passengers could get out and pick flowers as they walked along beside it. Still, the delays did give one time to catch up on current affairs, as Miss Meakin observes when her train was delayed for four hours ('a mere nothing in Siberia') at Taiga. She writes: 'As we sat waiting in the station the good news was brought that Mafeking had been relieved.'

Bridges
Although the rails were badly laid and of poor quality, the bridges that were made of stone were built to such a high standard that many are still in use today. They were largely the work of Italian masons, who laboured throughout the winter months, the bridge-building season, since no work could be done on the snow-covered line. Many labourers caught hypothermia while they worked in temperatures as low as -40°C, dropping to their death on the ice below.

If a bridge was not finished in the winter when the railway lines reached it, engineers had had the brilliant idea of laying rails across the ice. The sleepers were literally frozen onto the surface of the river by large amounts of water being poured over them. When R.L.Jefferson's train reached the track laid across the Chulim River, passengers were made to get out and walk, in case the train proved too great a weight for the ice to bear. He wrote: 'As it passed us we felt the ice quiver, and heard innumerable cracks, like the reports of pistols in the distance, but the train got across the centre safely.'

Breakdowns

These were all too frequent. A wait of twenty-four hours for a new engine was not regarded as a long delay. Annette Meakin recorded the following incident: 'Outside Kainsk the train stopped. "The engine has smashed up," said a jolly Russian sailor in broken English. "She is sixty years old and was made in Glasgow. She is no use any more"....The poor old engine was now towed to her last berth....I had whipped out my "Kodak" and taken her photograph, thinking of Turner's "Fighting Temeraire".'

Cost of the journey

The *Guide to the Great Siberian Railway* informed its readers that, for the journey from London to Shanghai: 'The conveyance by the Siberian Railway will be over twice as quick and two and a half times cheaper than that now existing' (the sea passage via the Suez Canal). The cost of a first class ticket for the sixteen-day journey was to be 319 roubles. From Moscow to Vladivostok the price was 114 roubles.

THE RAILWAY IN THE TWENTIETH CENTURY

After the Revolution

'When the trains stop, that will be the end,' announced Lenin and the trains continued to run, the Trans-Siberian included, throughout those troubled times.

When the new Bolshevik government pulled out of the First World War in early 1918, a Czech force of 50,000 well-armed men found themselves marooned in Russia, German forces preventing them getting back to western Europe. Receiving permission to leave Russia via Vladivostok, they set off on the Trans-Siberian. Their passage was not a smooth one for the Bolsheviks suspected that the Czechs would join the White Russian resistance movement while the Czechs suspected that the Bolsheviks were not going to allow them to leave. Violence erupted, several Czechs were arrested and the rest of the legion decided they would shoot their way out of Russia. They took over the Trans-Siberian line from the Urals to Lake Baikal and travelled the railway in armour-plated carriages.

The Civil War in Siberia (1918-20)

At this time Siberia was divided amongst a number of forces, all fighting against the Bolsheviks but not as a combined unit. Many of the leaders were nothing more than gangsters. East Siberia and Manchuria were controlled by the evil Ataman Semenov, half-Russian, half-Buryat and supported by the Japanese. He charged around Transbaikalia murdering whole villages and, to alleviate the boredom of these mass executions, a different method of death was adopted each day. Then there was Baron General von Ungern Sternberg, one of the White Russian commanders whose cruelty rivalled that of Semenov. The Americans, French, English and Japanese all brought troops into Siberia to evacuate the Czech legions and to help Admiral Kolchak, the Supreme Ruler of the White Government which was based at Omsk. Kolchak, however, failed to win the support of the people in the Siberian towns, his troops were ill-disciplined and in November 1919 he lost Omsk to the Bolsheviks. He was executed in Irkutsk in early 1920 and the Allies abandoned the White Russian cause. The Japanese gave up Vladivostok in 1922 and all Siberia was then in Communist hands.

Reconstruction

After the Civil War, the Soviet Union set about rebuilding its battered economy. High on the priority list was the repair of the Trans-Siberian line, so that raw materials like iron ore could be transported to European Russia. The First Five Year Plan (1928) set ambitious goals for the expansion of industry and agriculture. It also included new railway projects, the double-tracking of the Trans-Siberian and the building of the Turk-Sib, the line between Turkestan and Novosibirsk. Work began on two giant industrial complexes known as the Ural-Kuznetsk Combine. Iron ore from the Urals was taken by rail to the Kuznetsk in Siberia, where it was exchanged for coal to take back to the Ural blast furnaces. For all these giant projects an enormous, controllable labour force was needed and this was to a large extent provided by prisoners from the corrective labour camps.

The Second World War

Siberia played an important backstage role in the Great Patriotic War as Russians call the Second World War. Many factories were moved from European Russia to Siberia and the populations of cities such as Novosibirsk rose dramatically. The Trans-Siberian's part was a vital one and loads of coal and food were continuously despatched over the Urals to Europe throughout the war years.

(Opposite) Post Houses (Posting Stations, see p93) were set up at 25-mile intervals along the Great Siberian Post Road in the 19th century providing travellers with fresh horses, squalid accommodation and inedible meals. This is a fortified example (*ostrog*) to be seen at the open air museum near Irkutsk.

The Trans-Siberian today

THE TRAIN

Engines

If you imagined you would be hauled across Siberia by a puffing steam locomotive you will be sadly disappointed. Soviet Railways (SZD), now Russian Railways (RZD), began converting the system to electricity in 1927 (now 3kV dc or, more commonly, 25kV ac 50Hz) and the Trans-Siberian line is now almost entirely electrified. Passenger engines are usually Czech Skoda ChS2's (line voltage 3kV dc; max output 4620kW; max speed 160kph; weight 126 tonnes) and ChS4T's (25kV 50 Hz; 5200kW; 180kph; 126 tonnes) or Russian-built VL10's, VL60's and VL65's type. On the Moscow-St Petersburg route the latest Czech-built engines are used: the CS200 (3kV dc; 8400kW; 200kph; 157 tonnes) and the CS7 developed from it. The most common freight engines are the large VL80S and the newer VL85.

Where electrification has yet to be completed (Vyazemskaya-Ussuriisk on the Far Eastern Railway in East Siberia), diesel rather than steam engines are used. They are usually Russian-built 2TE10L/M/V types (with overhanging windscreens) or sometimes a 2M62U or 3M62U twin or triple-unit. If you're continuing on the Trans-Mongolian or Trans-Manchurian routes to Beijing, it is quite likely that a steam loco will be hitched to your carriages at the China border, at least for shunting duties. Although steam engines have officially been phased out in Russia, there were still 5900 on the books in 1992, many lining the tracks in remote sidings along the way. Their numbers are shrinking fast now as they are sold off to Western Europe and China for scrap and parts. See below for identification information and class numbers.

Carriages and carriage attendants

Most of the carriages now used are of East German origin, solidly-built, warm in winter and each staffed by an attendant (*provodnitsa* (female), *provodnik* (male) in Russian, *fuwuyuen* in Chinese), whose 'den' is situated at one end of the carriage. Their duties include collecting your tick-

---

(**Opposite**) **Top:** Waiting for the train. **Bottom:** A 2TE10M diesel locomotive, used on the few remaining non-electric sections of the journey. These locos were built in Lugansk between 1981 and 1990; maximum speed is 100kph. (Photos: Tatyana Pozar-Burgar).

ets, letting down the carriage steps at stations, coming round with the vacuum-cleaner and providing you with tea (good but without milk) or coffee (utterly disgusting). You pay for what you've drunk on your trip (usually less than £2.50/US$4 in total) just before you reach your destination. The attendant also maintains the **samovar** which is opposite the attendant's compartment at one end of the carriage, and provides a continuous supply of boiling water for drinks. There are doors at both ends of the carriages and if you're a smoker the only place where you're allowed to indulge your habit is in this area between the carriages (unheated in winter). Travellers on some trains, Nos 3/4 in particular, have reported that if there are a lot of smokers on board this rule is waived.

> ❏ The Chinese staff on the No 3/4 Beijing Moscow train must be the laziest sleeping car attendants in the world. They do absolutely nothing but cook for themselves and chat to their colleagues.
>
> Russian cars are clean and fairly new (my Moscow-Irkutsk car was built in 1992, my Moscow-Vladivostok car in 1994). The Chinese cars are dirty – mine was not vacuum cleaned until after Mongolia.
>
> Many travellers say the cars are very warm – I far from agree and often found them chilly. However, as a Scandinavian I, like the Americans, also found it cold in Poland, while the Continental Europeans found the temperature on board just fine and the Britons complained about it being too warm! **Matz Lonnedal Risberg** (Norway)

The best carriages are air-conditioned in summer but in order to operate properly all windows is the carriage must be kept shut, since the system works on the pressure difference between the inside and outside of the carriage and takes about an hour to get going. The initial instinct (and certainly that of the Russian passengers) is to open all the windows, and the carriage attendant wages a constant battle with everyone to keep them closed. Music (either radio or cassettes) is piped to the compartments from the attendant's den; the knob above the window controls the volume.

Compartments

On the Trans-Siberian and Trans-Manchurian, there are two main classes of compartments – SV and coupé. On the Trans-Mongolian Train No 3 & 4, there is three main classes of compartments – de luxe, SV and coupé). The reason for the difference is that Train No 3 & 4 is a Chinese made train and has a slightly different layout to the Russian ones.

● **De luxe First Class (Trans-Mongolian Train Nos 3 and 4 only)** The closest you can get to luxury accommodation while crossing Siberia on standard services, these two-berth compartments have attached showerrooms (hand-held showers but the only showers on any of the trains), wider bunks, wood panelling, a wind-down window, armchair, tablelamp with frilly shade and plush green carpet.

● **SV/Soft/First Class** On Russian trains, SV is a two-berth compartment which may or may not have a washbasin. On the Trans-Mongolian Train No 3 and 4, SV is a four-berth compartment of an identical layout to the coupé compartment except 16cm wider. As you pay significantly more for this compartment compared to a coupé, it is not good value.

● **Coupé/Hard/Tourist/Second Class** These four-berth cabins are the most popular with travellers as they are reasonably comfortable and cheap.

● **Platskartny/Third Class** is not really recommended; it's a cheap but rough way of travelling. Platskartny carriages are open plan, similar to Hard Class in China, with doorless compartments containing four bunks in tiers of two with another bunk opposite them, beside the corridor. While these carriages are adequate for an overnight trip, do not even contemplate them for the Trans-Siberian.

Bedding is provided and sheets are supposed to be changed every three days. In the newer carriages, it is possible to move the lower bed up to 10cm away from the wall which gives you a wider sleeping area.

Luggage

Each passenger can take up to 35kg of luggage with them for free on the Trans-Siberian. In Beijing, this limit is rigidly enforced as your baggage is weighed before you are allowed onto the platform.

You can take additional luggage totalling up to 75kg into your compartment providing you pay excess baggage. If you are departing from Moscow, go to the station early on the day of departure and pay the excess luggage fee (about US$11 per 10kg). You will be asked to show the receipt before boarding the train. If you are departing from Beijing, bring the excess baggage to the Luggage Shipment Office the day before departure. This office is located on the right hand side of the main station and is open 8:00-10:30 and 11:20-18:15. Bring your passport, ticket and customs entry declaration.

Luggage in the carriage can be stored in the box under the seat (57x134x24cm), in the free space next to the box under the seat (57x28x24cm) and in the space above the door (33x190x67cm).

Bathroom

Sadly the marble bath-tub (ingeniously designed so that the water would not spill as the train rounded a corner) and the copious supplies of hot water and towels that Michael Myres Shoemaker enthused over on his trip in 1902 are no more. The lack of proper bathing facilities is usually the biggest grumble from people who have done the trip. Apart from the De luxe First Class compartments of the Trans-Mongolian, there are no showers on the train – a ridiculous oversight. With most of the rail system now electrified there is a cheap power source for heated shower units but no doubt it will be years before they are installed.

Today, in every carriage there's a 'bathroom' at each end and it now appears to be standard practice for the carriage attendants to keep one locked for their personal use. Complaining about this is unlikely to achieve anything but a strategic friendly gift might gain you access. This small cubicle contains a basin and a lavatory, with or without a seat. To flush the lavatory, fully depress the foot pedal, hold it down and lean back out of the way, as the contents have a nasty habit of going the wrong way if the train is moving fast.

> ❏ If you'd like a shower when travelling in Second Class (Hard Sleeper), it may be worth bringing along a length of garden hose or a similar tube (say one metre long) and an attachment for the tap (such as the rubber type used in the UK). This seems to be what the provodnitzas use, and it will enable you to hose down the toilets. **Edward Wilson** (UK)

The taps on the basin are operated by pushing up the little lever located under the tap outlet. You should get hot water by turning the left hand wheel above the sink (the right hand wheel controls the cold water). However the flow of hot water depends on the whim of the attendant who may not want to switch the system on. Don't forget to bring along a universal plug (or a squash ball) for the basin, soap and lavatory paper. One of these items is usually available but never all three together. There's a socket for an electric razor but you may need to ask the attendant to turn the power on. Don't try to charge video camera batteries from these sockets: one traveller reported blowing the fuses attempting this.

There are two ways to have a shower in these bathrooms. Either fill the basin and use a mug to scoop out the water and pour it over yourself, or fit a flexible shower hose over the tap nozzle. Some attendants carry these hoses and you may be able to rent one from them. Don't worry about splashing water around as there is a drain in the floor.

Restaurant cars

One of the myths that has sprung up amongst prospective travellers is that you'll get better food if you take the Chinese (Trans-Mongolian) train. As is the custom with international rail travel, restaurant cars belonging to the country through which the train is travelling are attached to the train at the border. Regardless of which train you're on, when you're travelling through China you'll be eating in a restaurant car supplied by Chinese Railways; at the border with Mongolia this will be replaced by a Mongolian restaurant car; while the same train is on Russian territory meals will be provided by a restaurant car from Russian Railways.

Note that on the Trans-Mongolian train there is usually no restaurant car service between the Russian border and Ulan Bator.

❑ **Getting better service**

The food you're served in the Russian restaurant car seems to depend entirely on your relationship with the staff. I thought greasy lumps of compressed beef with fried eggs and rice were *de rigeur* until a recent trip with a flamboyantly friendly Australian/Ukrainian lady, who made a point of introducing herself and her friends to the staff of each car. Not only did she discover that the waiters and cooks were all invariably distant relatives or old family friends but the food was spectacular. Excellent *pelmeni*, tasty Stroganov: the cooks all rustled up their 'specials' for the crazy Australian and her entourage. Over at the adjacent tables, meanwhile, glum Russians tucked into greasy chunks of beef with eggs on top.

Dominic Streatfeild-James (UK)

● **Russian restaurant car** You may be feasting on caviare as you rattle across the Siberian steppes but only if you've brought along your own supplies. The food was never much to write home about and financial hardship in Russia has not made things any better, but it's true to say that the quality of the food seems to vary very much between one Russian restaurant car and the next. Rather than cooking, staff seem more interested in buying and selling produce at stations along the way.

On entering the restaurant car (having averted your eyes from the grubby kitchen to preserve your appetite) you may be presented with the menu, almost invariably in Russian and often running to ten pages or more. The only dishes available will be indicated by a pencilled-in price or added in an almost indecipherable scrawl. The choice includes egg or tomato salad (the white sauce is not mayonnaise but sour cream, actually rather good), *shchi* (thick cabbage soup with meat), *solyanka* (meat soup, thick and nourishing), meat-balls and mash or macaroni, smoked *teshka* fish (like hunks of smoked salmon), *skumbria* fish (usually fried and quite good), beef Stroganov, boiled chicken or duck, tea and coffee, and occasionally cakes. Piles of bread and various fizzy drinks (*napitok*) and fruit juice (*sok*) are also on sale. A full meal will cost about £3.75/US$6. There are usually two people serving, each with their own half of the restaurant car (one won't serve you if you're in the other section). Small gifts or tips given early on in the trip will help encourage attentive service.

The trend towards free trade means that the restaurant car staff can now sell all sorts of goodies on the side. Banned for several years, alcohol is now sold on the train. You should be able to get chilled Russian champagne (£4.50/US$7), vodka, chocolate bars and cartons of fruit juice. Some restaurant cars even show videos, charging passengers an entry fee to watch bootleg copies of American movies.

Note that you can pay only in roubles; US$ are not accepted.

● **Mongolian restaurant car** The main differences between the Mongolian and the Russian restaurant cars are that in the Mongolian car you're likely to get a menu in English and everything comes with mutton.

If you are travelling on trains Nos 3/4, 89/90 or 23/24, you will have to pay in US$ as there is no opportunity to change any hard currency into Mongolian togrogs. Take lots of small denomination US bills as the waiters will pretend never to have any change.

Delicacies include main course with roast potatoes, main course with rice, main course with noodles and main course with cabbage; all priced from US$3-5. Tea is US$0.50 and coffee US$1; a Pepsi costs US$1. Some Mongolian cars have extensive stocks of duty free goods and even souvenirs. Mongolian beer is highly recommended.

Train Nos 5/6 and 263/264 rarely have a restaurant carriage inside Mongolia.

Chinese restaurant car Travellers tend to agree that the food in the Chinese car is the best, and there's a bit more choice. For US$3 you'll get a breakfast of eggs, bread, jam and tea. Lunch and supper consist of tomato salad (US$2), cold chicken or sauté chicken with hot sauce and peanuts (US$3), fish (US$2.50), sweet and sour pork (US$3), sauté beef or egg plant with dried shrimp. Drinks include beer (US$0.50), cola (US$1) and mineral water (US$1).

LIFE ON THE TRAIN

Most people imagine they'll get bored on so long a journey but you may be surprised at how quickly the time flies. Don't overdo the number of books you bring: *War and Peace,* weighing in at 1,444 pages is a frequent choice, although I know of only one person who actually managed to finish it on the trip. There are so many other things to do apart from reading. You can have monosyllabic conversations with inquisitive Russians, meet

---

❏ **Local travellers**
Unlike the Orient Express, most trains that cross Siberia are working trains, not tourist specials. Russian passengers are extremely friendly and genuinely interested in foreign travellers. Sharing her compartment with three Russians, a winter traveller writes: 'Inside the carriage there's interest on both sides. Five hours ago my Walkman was borrowed (with only one tape inside it). It has just been returned with a helpless gesture -the battery (surprise, surprise) has run out. Great concern all round about my travelling unaccompanied and questions as to the whereabouts of my parents. Much shaking of heads and 'tutting'. There's plenty for me to find out. The thin man (with cold eyes that have gradually thawed over the last two days) has five children and is going to Moscow to get stomach medicine for one of them (or for himself?). The large motherly babushka in the corner who has been so kind to me is an artist, going to visit her son (or is the son an artist?). The fourth member of the compartment played chess with me last night, totally baffled by my tactics (there weren't any) so that we ended with a stalemate. He hasn't offered again. So much can be achieved with not a word of language in common.' **Heather Oxley** (UK)

the other Westerners on the train, play cards or chess, visit the restaurant car or hop off at the stations for a little exercise. 'Time passes very pleasantly on such a train', as Annette Meakin wrote in 1900.

The Trans-Siberian time warp

During his trip on the Great Siberian Railway in 1902, Michael Myres Shoemaker wrote: 'There is an odd state of affairs as regards time over here. Though Irkutsk is 2,400 miles from St Petersburg, the trains all run on the time of the latter city, therefore arriving in Irkutsk at 5pm when the sun would make it 9pm. The confusion en route is amusing; one never knows when to go to bed or when to eat. Today I should make it now about 8.30 -these clocks say 10.30 and some of these people are eating their luncheon.'

You will be pleased to know that this is something that hasn't changed, although the system now operates on Moscow time (no different from St Petersburg time). Crossing the border from China after breakfast, the first Russian station clock you see tells you that it's actually 01:00 hours. All timetables quote Moscow time. The restaurant car, however, runs on local time. Passing through anything up to seven timezones, things can get rather confusing. The answer is to ignore Moscow time and reset your watch as you cross into new time zones (details given in the Route Guide). A watch that can show the time in two zones might be useful, otherwise just add or subtract the appropriate number of hours every time you consult the timetable in the carriage corridor.

Stops

Getting enough exercise on so long a journey can be a problem and most people make full use of the brief stops: 'We even managed to persuade our carriage attendant (never seen out of her pink woollen hat) to take part in our efforts to keep fit on the platforms. Several Russian passengers were happy to participate in our foreign antics while others, dressed in the ubiquitous blue track-suits, watched from the windows of the train. However, if your attendant indicates that you shouldn't get off at a stop, take her advice. At some stops another train pulls in between the platform and yours, making it almost impossible for you to get back on board.' Jane Bull (UK). Always carry your passport and valuables with you in case you miss your train.

Traders' trains

The growth of free trade in Russia led to some Trans-Siberian routes becoming monopolised by Chinese, Mongolian and Russian shuttle traders in the mid-1990s. Excess baggage charges, and a reduction in the duty-free allowance from US$2000 to US$1000 has now stemmed the flow but you may still find yourself sharing a compartment on the Trans-Mongolian route with a trader and anything from pile of imitation Adidas trainers to several thousand yellow plastic ducks.

RAIL TICKETS

Booking rail tickets in Russia is considerably easier today than at any time in the past since increased prices mean that supply is greater than demand. Despite the price rise, overnight rail tickets are still considerably cheaper than in the West.

Stations in Moscow will issue tickets up to 45 days in advance; large stations in the rest of the country issue them up to 30 days in advance.

Prices

The cheapest ticket is the four-berth coupé ticket. The two-berth SV ticket is about 1.5 to 2 times the cost of a coupé ticket. Tickets on special, more comfortable services, called *firmenny* trains, cost about 1.2 to 1.5 that of non-firmenny tickets. Foreigners have to buy Intourist tickets which are between 15% to 30% more than tickets for Russians. The only places where foreigners can legally buy Russian tickets are from those stations which do not sell foreigner tickets, such as small stations. If you try to use one of these tickets, the provodnik may demand that you make up the difference in ticket prices. You will get an official receipt which you must keep in case a ticket inspector gets on your train. While you may be able to get locals' tickets only from small stations, if you have obtained one dishonestly from a station that sells foreigner tickets, you may have to pay a fine as well as making up the difference. You can try to bribe the provodnik and may get away with paying less.

Names on tickets

To get a ticket, you normally have to show your passport. The name on the passport is written down on the ticket. Ticket sellers will often only sell you as many tickets as you have passports. This system was introduced to stop speculators from buying tickets and reselling them for a profit when the train is all sold out. The only way for a ticket to be legally renamed once it is bought is for the ticket selling staff to overstamp the original name with an official stamp and write your name on it.

Getting off in the middle of a journey

It is possible to break your journey once on any ticket, however it is not really worth the effort. You have to get the station master to validate your ticket within 30 minutes of arriving. Secondly you have to re-book a berth for the onward journey which will often only be done by the chief ticket officer. If you don't speak Russian, don't even attempt this.

Visas and tickets

In the Soviet era, a rail ticket would be sold only to foreigners if the destination was written on their visa. Nowadays, this situation occurs rarely and mostly with rail staff in rural areas who do not know that the law has changed. Show only your passport and not your visa when you buy a rail ticket.

❏ BUYING A TICKET

In most large cities on the Trans-Siberian, tickets for trains departing on the day of purchase can be bought only at the station from which the train is departing. Tickets for trains departing on the following day up to 30 days are normally bought from the Advance Purchase Ticket Booking Offices or the station from which the train is departing. Also see the ticket purchasing sheet on p398.

Which train?

Check the timetable which is displayed in the booking hall. It states the train's number, time of departure and the days on which it travels.

❏ The train number indicates which way it is heading. If the number is even it means that it is going to the east or north and if odd, the train is heading west or south.

❏ The time quoted on timetables is invariably Moscow Time. Across a network covering eight time zones (the country is 11 zones), this is the only way the system would work. The clock in the booking hall is normally set to Moscow Time. Some station clocks (eg Khabarovsk) have two hour hands, black for Local Time and red for Moscow Time.

❏ Most trains depart every day, however some run on odd numbered days (1st, 3rd, 5th etc) and some on even days.

Which ticket window?

At railway stations and Advance Purchase Ticket Booking Offices there are several sorts of ticket windows, known as *kassa*. It is important to queue at the correct one otherwise you can waste hours. If the station has an Intourist window, go there immediately. Sometimes it will not be marked as Intourist and instead say in Russian Иностранцы (*inostrantsy* meaning *foreigner*). If there is no obvious window for foreigners, go to the information window. Ask if there are any tickets for the train you want to go on, which window they are sold from and how much they cost. You may have to pay US$0.50 for this information. Before queuing, check the opening hours of the window. It may be better to queue up at a closed kassa which will open in an hour than wait in a long line where the kassa might close before you get to the head of the queue.

Leave your bags with your partner so that you can push your way through the queue without worrying about your belongings. If there are three of you, two should queue with one shielding the other from the people trying to push in ahead. The person guarding the luggage should stack it in a corner near the information window, the safest place in the hall.

Which ticket?

When you get to the window, tell them the train number; date of departure; class of cabin: Л (Л = two-berth *SV*), М (М = four-berth *SV*), К (К = *coupé*), П (П = *platskartny*), О (О = *obshchi*); and your destination. There are several types of tickets for long-distance trains but the most common is the long, paper, computer printed ticket. It contains not only information about the train but also your name so don't buy someone else's ticket from them. The traveller-type is printed on the ticket: Полный (polny = adult), Детский (detski = child), Студенческий (studencheski = student), Бесплатный для жд (besplatny dlya zhd = free for railways). On the train, the conductor tears off a portion of the ticket which prevents it from being used again. If the ticket is for a train that originates elsewhere, the berth number is given only once you board the train.

STEAM LOCOMOTIVES IN SIBERIA

In 1956, the USSR stopped producing steam engines, and the official policy was to phase out these locomotives by 1970. As with most official plans in the country, this one overran a little and a second official end of steam was announced for the end of 1987, when the number of locos stood at over 6000. Some of these have been sold as scrap to Germany and Korea but many are still stored as a 'strategic reserve' in remote sidings and used very occasionally for shunting work -there are some to be seen along the Trans-Siberian line (see Route Guide for locations). In Northern China, there are large numbers still at work.

In 1836, the first locomotive was delivered in St Petersburg, a Hackworth 2-2-2, to pull the Tsar's private carriages over the fourteen miles of six-foot gauge track to his palace at Tsarskoye Selo. The Russians have always been (and still are) conservative by nature when it comes to buying or building engines. Usually large numbers of a few standard locomotives have been ordered so there's not much of a range to be seen today. They seem to be uniformly large, standing up to 17 feet high, and larger than British locos (partly because the Russian gauge is 3.5 inches wider than that used in Britain). They are numbered separately by classes, not in a single series and not by railway regions. If variations of the class have been built, they are given an additional letter to follow the main class letter. Thus, for example, the first type of 0-10-0 freight locomotive was Class E and those of this class built in Germany were Class Eg. Classes you may see in Siberia should include some of the following (Roman alphabet class letters given in brackets; * = very rare):

- **Class O (O)** The first freight trains on the Trans-Siberian route were pulled by these long-boilered 0-8-0 locos (55 tons) which date back to 1889. The 'O' in the class name stands for *Osnovnoi Tip* meaning 'basic type'. Although production ceased in 1923, as late as 1958 there were 1500 of these locomotives still at work.
- **Class C (S)*** 2-6-2 (75 tons) A highly successful passenger engine. 'S' stands for *Sormovo*, where these locos were built from 1911. **Class Cy (Su)** ('u' for usileny, meaning 'strengthened') was developed from the former class and in production from 1926-51.
- **Class E (Ye)** 2-10-0 (imported from the USA in 1914). There were 1,500 Ye 2-10-0s imported.
- **Class Эу/Эм/Эр (Eu/Em/Er)*** (subclasses of the old type (E) 0-10-0, 80 tons, built in Russia from 1926-52. The old type E was also produced in Germany and Sweden, as Esh and Eg subclasses.
- **Class Ea (YeA)*** 2-10-0 (90 tons) Over 2,000 were built in the USA between 1944 and 1947 and shipped across the Pacific.
- **Class Л (L)** 2-10-0 (103 tons) About 4130 were built between 1945-56.
- **Class П36 (P36)** 4-8-4 (133 tons) 251 were built between 1950 and

1956 – the last express passenger type built for Soviet railways. 'Skyliner'-style, fitted with large smoke-deflectors, and painted green with a cream stripe. Preserved examples at Sharya, Taiga, Sibirtsevo, Skovorodino, Belogorsk, Mogzon, and Chernyshevsk

The classes **Class O, C/Cy, E (O, S/Su, YE)** have all disappeared from the steam dumps but you will see the occasional one on a plinth.

For more information refer to the comprehensive *Soviet Locomotive Types – The Union Legacy* by AJ Heywood and IDC Button (1995, Frank Stenvalls/Luddenden Press).

BAM: A SECOND TRANS-SIBERIAN

In the 1930s another Herculean undertaking was begun on the railways in Russia. The project was named the Baikal-Amur-Magistral (BAM): a second Trans-Siberian railway, 3140km long, running parallel but to the north of the existing line. It was to run through the rich mining districts of northern Siberia, providing an east-west communications back-up to the main line. Work began in Taishet and the track reached Ust Kut on the Lena River before the project was officially abandoned at the end of the war. Much of the 700km of track that had been laid was torn up to replace war-damaged lines in the west. Construction continued in secret, using slave labour until the gulags were closed in 1954.

In 1976 it was announced that work on the BAM was recommencing. Incentives were offered to labourers to collect the 100,000 strong work-force needed for so large a project. For eight years they laboured hero-ically, dynamiting their way through the permafrost which covers almost half the route, across a region where temperatures fall as low as -60°C in winter. In October 1984 it was announced that the way was open from Taishet to Komsomolsk-na-Amur. Although track-laying had been com-pleted, only the eastern half was operational (from Komsomolsk to BAM station, where traffic joined the old Trans-Siberian route).

By 1991 the whole system was still not fully operational, the main obstacle being the Severomuisk Tunnel, bypassed by an unsatisfactory detour with a 1 in 25 gradient. It took from 1981 to 1991 to drill eight of the ten miles of this tunnel in the most difficult of conditions. Many were already questioning the point of a railway that was beginning to look like a white elephant. Work has more or less stopped now; the main sections of the line are complete but traffic is infrequent. The BAM was built to compete with shipping routes for the transfer of freight but the cost has been tremendous: there has been considerable ecological damage and there is no money left for the extraction of the minerals that was the other reason for the building of the railway. It is possible to travel along the BAM route starting near the north of Lake Baikal and ending up at Khabarovsk. *Siberian BAM Railway Guide*, by Athol Yates (Trailblazer Publications), covers this line in detail.

YAKUTIA RAILWAY

Work has started on this branch line from the BAM (starting in Tynda) pushing north eventually to Yakutsk, to transport the huge reserves of coal and other minerals to be found in Yakutia. The project was scheduled for completion at the same time as the BAM but is now at a standstill for lack of funds, although passenger services operate as far as Aldan.

SAKHALIN RAILWAY

The island of Sakhalin (north of Japan) is currently linked to the Russian mainland by rail ferries operating between Vanino and Kholmsk. Steam specials are occasionally run on the island's 3ft 6in-gauge rail system.

SECOND ASIA-EUROPE LAND BRIDGE

In September 1990 the rail link between Urumqi in northwest China and the border with Kazakhstan was completed, opening a new rail route between east Asia and Europe via the Central Asian Republics. China built this new link to create the shortest rail route (2000kms shorter than the Trans-Siberian) between countries on the western Pacific coast and the eastern Atlantic coast, enabling freight to be transported faster and more cheaply than by ship.

Rail travellers on the Silk Route

Opened also to passenger traffic in 1992, the Silk Route offers a new opportunity for those wishing to travel from Moscow to Beijing (or vice versa): a journey along the old Silk Route, through the old Central Asian capitals of Khiva, Bukhara and Samarkand, and the Chinese cities of Dunhuang, Luoyang and Xi'an. For the adventurous, the trip represents a unique travel opportunity. Full details are given in *Silk Route by Rail* by Dominic Streatfeild-James (1997, Trailblazer Publications).

THIRD ASIA-EUROPE LAND BRIDGE

The 295km railway linking Turkmenistan and Iran was officially opened on 13 May 1996. The US$216 million railway links landlocked Central Asia with the Persian Gulf and, via Turkey, the Mediterranean. In addition the railway connects Central Asia to the Istanbul-Beijing railway. This has the potential to become a new silk route connecting Southern Europe and the Far East, cutting the travel time by up to 10 days. Work on the Meshhed (Iran)-Sarakhs-Tedzhen (Turkmenistan) railway started in 1992 and is a milestone as it breaks Russia's transport stronghold on the Central Asian countries. It is estimated that 500,000 passengers will travel the route in 1997 and this will rise to about 1 million passengers annually by the year 2000.

PART 4: CITY GUIDES AND PLANS

St Petersburg
Санкт-Петербург

Less than 300 years old, St Petersburg is a young city compared to Moscow and yet there is probably as much, if not more, to see here. Many visitors prefer this northern city, perhaps because it is of more manageable proportions than the sprawling capital. It is certainly more beautiful, having been laid out in 18th-century Classical style by Peter the Great on a grand scale. A trip to St Petersburg is well worth it if only for a visit to the Hermitage Museum, one of the world's most spectacular collections of European art, partly housed in the fabulously ornate Winter Palace.

You can visit Manchester's twin city by taking a side-trip from Moscow on the overnight train and staying a night or two but you really need at least four days to do justice to the sights. Alternatively, you can route your Trans-Siberian journey through St Petersburg by starting (or ending) your trip in Helsinki (200km from St Petersburg) or by travelling directly between St Petersburg and Warsaw (bypassing Moscow. The city is especially attractive in winter, when the snow shows up the brightly painted facades of the buildings. In summer, the most important cultural festival in Russia, 'White Nights', is held here in the last week of June.

HISTORY

Window on Europe
Peter the Great decided to build his new capital here to give Russia a 'window on Europe'. He felt that his country was becoming introverted and backward with its capital isolated from the West. The building of this European capital, St Petersburg, was the first step in Peter's crusade for Russia's modernisation. The site selected for the new capital was particularly inhospitable: the marshy estuary of the River Neva. Work began on the Peter and Paul Fortress in May 1703 and in 1712 the capital was moved here from Moscow. St Petersburg grew quickly and stylishly, for Peter employed the finest Italian architects for the palaces and many other important buildings.

Cultural and revolutionary centre
St Petersburg soon developed into the cultural centre of Russia and in the nineteenth century was one of the great cultural centres of Europe. It has been the home of such composers as Tchaikovsky, Glinka, Mussorgsky,

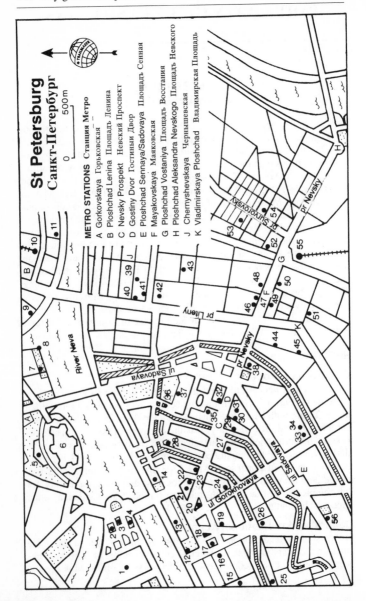

St Petersburg
Санкт-Петербург

0   500m

METRO STATIONS Станциия Метро
A Gorkovskaya Горьковская
B Ploshchad Lenina Площадь Ленина
C Nevsky Prospekt Невский Проспект
D Gostiny Dvor Гостиныи Двор
E Ploshchad Sennaya/Sadovaya Площадь Сенная
F Mayakovskaya Маяковская
G Ploshchad Vostaniya Площадь Восстания
H Ploshchad Aleksandra Nevskogo Площадь Невского
J Chernyshevskaya Чернышевская
K Vladimirskaya Ploshchad Владимирская Площадь

12 Decembrists' Square Площадь Декабристов
13 Admiralty Адмиралтейство
14 Winter Palace/Hermitage Зимний Дворец/Эрмитаж
15 Central Post Office Главпочтамт
16 St P'burg Trvl Co Ст. Петербургская Компания Путешествий
17 St Isaac's Cathedral Иссакиевкий Собор
20 Air Terminal (buses to airports) Агентство Воздушных
21 Former General Staff Building Здание Главного Штаба
22 Telephone Office Централний Переговорный Пункт
25 Yusupovsky Palace Юсуповский Дворец
26 Mariinski Palace Мариинский Дворец
27 Kazan Cathedral Казанский Собор
28 Pushkin House Дом Пушкина
29 Rail Ticket Office Центральные Железнодорожные Кассы
30 Theatre Booking Office Театральная Касса
31 Gostiny Dvor Универмаг Гостиный Двор
32 Industry and Construction Bank Банк
34 American Medical Ctr Американский Медицинский Центр
36 Church of Resurrection Церковь Воскресения Христова
37 Russian State Museum Русский Государственый Музей
38 Anichkov Palace Аничков Дворец
39 US Consulate Консульство США
41 Central OVIR ОВиР
42 Cathedral of the Transfiguration of Our Saviour Собор
44 Maly Theatre Малый Театр
46 Peter TIPS Travel Information Бюро Информации
51 Dostoevsky House-Museum Музей Ф.М. Достоевского
53 Polish Consulate Консольство Польши
55 Moscow Station Московский Вокзал
56 Railway Museum Железнодорожный Музей

HOTELS AND RESTAURANTS
9 Hotel St Petersburg Гостиница Санкт-Петербург
11 Holiday Hostel Гостиница Holiday
18 Tandoor Indian Restaurant Индийский Ресторан Тандур
19 Astoria Hotel Гостиница Астория
23 Café Literaturnoe Кафе Литературное
24 Pizza Hut Пицца Хат
33 Restaurant Na Fontanke Ресторан на Фонтанке
35 Grand Hotel Europe Гостиница Grand Hotel
40 Rose Pub Бар Роза
43 Hotel Rus Гостиница Русь
45 Mollie's Irish Bar Молис Ирландский Бар
47 Aphrodite Restaurant Ресторан Афродита
48 Restaurant Nevsky Ресторан Невский
49 Nevsky Palace Hotel Гостиница Невский Дворец
50 John Bull Pub Бар John Bull
52 Oktyabrskaya Hotel Гостиница Октябрьская
54 HI St Petersburg Hostel and Sindbad Travel

OTHER
1 University Государственый Университет
2 Literature Museum/Geological Museum Музей Русской
  Литературы/Карпинский Геологический Музей
3 Naval Museum Военно-Морской Музей
4 Anthropology Museum Музей Антропологии
5 Artillery Museum Артиллерийский Музей
6 Peter and Paul Fortress Петропавловская Крепость
7 Peter the Great's Log Cabin Домик Петра
8 Aurora Cruiser Аврора
10 Finland Station Финляндский Вокзал

Rimsky-Korsakov and Shostakovich, and writers such as Gorky, Pushkin, Turgenev and Dostoyevsky. It was a centre of new ideas and among them, inevitably, were revolutionary ideals. On 14 December 1825, these were translated into action for the first time in Russia's history, when a group of revolutionaries from the nobility (the 'Decembrists') refused to swear allegiance to Nicholas I and led their troops into Senate Square. Quickly disarmed, they were exiled to Siberia.

The Revolutions of 1905 and 1917

The second 'revolution' took place in 1905 when, on 22 January (Bloody Sunday), the Tsar's troops fired on a crowd that had marched to the Winter Palace to ask his help in improving working conditions. Ninety-two people were killed and several hundred wounded but more tragic for the country was the fact that the people's faith in their Tsar was finally shattered. Strikes and civil disorder followed and on 25 October 1917, a cannon shot from the cruiser *Aurora* provided the signal for the start of the Revolution proper.

Leningrad: 'Hero City'

In 1914 Tsar Nicholas II changed the city's name to the more Russian-sounding Petrograd; following Lenin's death ten years later, it was renamed Leningrad. In 1945 it was awarded the title 'Hero City' for its stand against the Germans during the Second World War. From September 1941 to January 1943 the city was besieged and bombarded with an average of 250 shells per day. Ultimately, however, most of the 641,803 inhabitants who died during the blockade died of starvation.

St Petersburg today

St Petersburg has been almost entirely rebuilt since the war but fortunately the planners opted for restoration of many of the historic buildings rather than replacement. The building programme continued until the 1980s but is now almost stationary owing to a lack of funds. Work on an ambitious flood barrier around the edge of the Gulf of Finland has recently been halted in its final stages, the best part of US$1 million having been spent.

In June 1991, after a heated public debate, 55% of Leningrad's citizens voted to change the city's name back to St Petersburg. The modern city is in a chaotic state of flux: a severe shortage of housing means that many inhabitants still live in communal flats, and there is a terrible pol-

(**Opposite**) **St Petersburg – Top:** The Hermitage Museum is the world's largest gallery with nearly three million works of art in its collection. To walk through each of the 300 galleries you'd cover a total distance of almost 25km! **Bottom left:** St Peter and St Paul Cathedral. (Photo: TPB). **Bottom right:** The Church of the Resurrection, built in the style of St Basil's in Moscow (Photo: Tatyana Pozar-Burgar).

lution problem owing to the industrial plants on the city's outskirts.

Throughout its short history, St Petersburg has always been at the forefront of change in the country. Since 1990 the city's council has been attempting to turn it into a free economic zone; and as you wander through the streets you'll come across numerous Western-standard shops. The windows of the ornate shops of Nevsky Prospekt, once filled with stacks of tinned fruit juice and bottled beetroot that nobody wanted, now glitter with Western delicacies few can afford.

ARRIVING IN ST PETERSBURG

By air

There are two airports: **Pulkovo II** (20km south of the city) for international and some domestic flights (bus No 13 from Moskovskaya metro station) and **Pulkovo I** for domestic flights (bus No 39 from Moskovskaya metro station or the express bus from the Air Terminal at the Agency of Air Communications (formerly Aeroflot Office) on Nevsky Prospekt). You should get to the airport two full hours ahead of scheduled take-off, since baggage and passport control queues are long. On domestic flights, still bring along your own food and beverages for long trips.

What with getting to and from the airports and the usual delays, it's better to take the train from Moscow to St Peterburg rather than fly.

By train

There are five railway stations in St Petersburg. The three most important are: **Finland** (metro station: Ploshchad Lenina) for trains to and from Helsinki; **Moscow** (metro: Ploshchad Vosstaniya) for Moscow trains; and **Warsaw** (metro: Frunzenskaya) for trains to Warsaw, Berlin and other Western cities.

LOCAL TRANSPORT

In this city of canals and rivers, the 'Venice of the North', you might expect the local transportation system to be dominated by gondolas or punts but it's just like any other city in Russia.

There's a good metro system; although not as impressive as Moscow's metro, it's the quickest way around the city. Some of the stations have automatic safety doors; be aware that it may make finding the station you need confusing. Stay alert and count the stops. The metro stations rival Moscow's in their Baroque decor and trains run from 05:35 to 00:30. As well as the metro there are buses, trams and trolley-buses.

(**Opposite**) St Basil's Cathedral, Moscow.

ST PETERSBURG METRO PLAN (ROMAN SCRIPT)

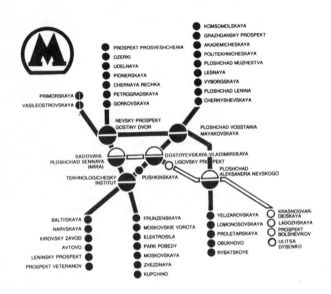

KOMSOMOLSKAYA
GRAZHDANSKY PROSPEKT
AKADEMICHESKAYA
POLITEKHNICHESKAYA
PLOSHCHAD MUZHESTVA
LESNAYA
VYBORGSKAYA
PLOSHCHAD LENINA
CHERNYSHEVSKAYA

PROSPEKT PROSVESHCHENIA
OZERKI
UDELNAYA
PIONERSKAYA
CHERNAYA RECHKA
PETROGRADSKAYA
GORKOVSKAYA

PRIMORSKAYA
VASILEOSTROVSKAYA

NEVSKY PROSPEKT
GOSTINY DVOR

PLOSHCHAD VOSSTANIA
MAYAKOVSKAYA

SADOVAYA
PLOSHCHAD SENNAYA
(MIRA)

DOSTOYEVSKAYA-VLADIMIRSKAYA
LIGOVSKY PROSPEKT

PLOSHCHAD
ALEKSANDRA NEVSKOGO

TEKHNOLOGICHESKY
INSTITUT   PUSHKINSKAYA

BALTIISKAYA   FRUNZENSKAYA   YELIZAROVSKAYA   KRASNOGVAR-DEISKAYA
NARVSKAYA   MOSKOVSKIE VOROTA   LOMONOSOVSKAYA   LADOZHSKAYA
KIROVSKY ZAVOD   ELEKTROSILA   PROLETARSKAYA   PROSPEKT BOLSHEVIKOV
AVTOVO   PARK POBEDY   OBUKHOVO   ULITSA DYBENKO
LENINSKY PROSPEKT   MOSKOVSKAYA   RYBATSKOYE
PROSPEKT VETERANOV   ZVEZDNAYA
                    KUPCHINO

The same flat fare (US$0.15) is payable on the metro, trolley-buses, buses and trams. A taxi ride to the airport should cost around US$20 but if you pick one up at the airport on arrival you are likely to pay two or three times this amount. There are also buses to and from the airport (see p129).

It's possible to rent a car at **Innis** (☎ 210 5858) at the Hotel Astoria, or **Interavto** (☎ 277 4032) at 9/11 Ispolkomskaya.

❏ **Public transport scam**
Foreigners are often caught out by a scam on trams, buses and trolley buses. The unwary victim enters the vehicle and either because of ignorance or because of the crowd fails to self-punch a pre-purchased ticket. The watching conductor quickly makes a bee-line for the passenger and starts demanding that they pay a fine for not having a ticket. Soon, several other conductors swarm around all yelling 'fine' while pretending not to understand English. Your options are to pay the hugely inflated fine, get off and start yelling for a militsia man who may or may not help you, or get off and run away. Incidentally, the fine should be about US$5 and most Russians refuse to pay it unless the conductor is accompanied by a militsia.

ST PETERSBURG METRO PLAN (CYRILLIC SCRIPT)

ORIENTATION AND SERVICES

St Petersburg stands at the mouth of the Neva, where the river meets the Baltic Sea's Gulf of Finland. The centre of the city is the 4km Nevsky Prospekt with the Hermitage Museum and the city's top hotels at its north-western end.

Intourist has been replaced by a number of independent travel organisations, some of which have service desks in hotels. The **St Petersburg Travel Company** (formerly Intourist) (☎ 315 5129) operates from the building opposite St Isaac's Cathedral.

Peter TIPS (☎ 279 0037) is at Nevsky Prospekt 86, inside House of Actors ('Dom Actyor'). The friendly staff will assist you any way they can. **Sindbad Travel** (☎ 327 8384, fax 329 8019, e-mail sindbad@ ryh.spb.su) at ul 3rd Sovetskaya 28, offers train and plane tickets, visa support, city tours, theatre tickets and information for hostelling in Russia, the Baltic States and worldwide. They sell and service all student and youth air tickets on all international carriers. **American Express** has a travel agency in the Hotel Grand Europe.

There are a number of useful guides to St Petersburg including *The Traveller's Yellow Pages Saint Petersburg* (US$8) which is revised twice a year, *Where in St Petersburg* (US$13.50), and the entertaining and informative, locally-produced guide *The Fresh Guide to St Petersburg*.

For current information on events around St Petersburg you can pick up one of the local English language newspapers. These are free and available in most hotels, hostels and western supermarkets on and around Nevsky Prospect. The only daily paper is the *Saint Petersburg Times*, while other regular papers include *Neva News* and *Pulse St Petersburg*.

Visas and extensions

If St Petersburg is your first stop in Russia, remember that you must register your visa within three working days (see p20). To get a visa extension, you need to visit the Visa and Registration Department (OViR) with your passport, visa, proof of hotel reservations, official letter of extension and a translator if you don't speak Russian. The **Central OViR office** (☎ 278 3486) is at ul Saltkova-Shchedrina 4 (metro Chernishevskaya) and is open 09:30-17:30 (Mon and Wed) and 14:00-16:00 on Friday. As the visa extension situation changes from month to month, contact your sponsor, hotel or hostel, rather than trekking down to OViR for the latest rules

Transit visas are generally not extended for longer than five days. This might mean that you will have to leave Russia and get a new visa in one of the Baltic States or Finland. Sindbad Travel and Peter TIPS are the best if you have any visa problems.

Diplomatic Representation

- **China** (☎ 114 6230), nab Griboyedova Kanala 134
- **Czech Republic** (☎ 271 0459, fax 271 4615), ul Tverskaya 5
- **Estonia** (☎ 233 5548, fax 233 5309), ul Bolshaya Monetnaya 14
- **Finland** (☎ 273 7321, 272 4256 (visas), fax 272 1421),
  ul Chaykovskovo 71
- **Germany** (☎ 273 5598, 279 3207, fax 279 3242), ul Furshtadtskaya 39
- **Hungary** (☎ 312 6753, 312 6458, fax 312 6432), ul Marata 15
- **Latvia** (☎ 315 1774, 230 3974, fax 554 3619), ul Galernaya 69
- **Lithuania** (☎ 314 5857), ul Gorokhovaya 4
- **Poland** (☎ 274 4318, 274 4170, fax 274 4318), ul 5th Sovetskaya 12
- **Sweden** (☎ 218 3526, 213 4191 (visas), fax 213 7198),
  ul 10th Liniya 11
- **UK** (☎ 119 6036, 325 6166, 325 6036, fax 325 6037),
  pl Protetarski Diktatury 5
- **USA** (☎ 274 8689, 274 8568, fax 110 6479), ul Furshtadtskaya 15

Tours

Independent sightseeing is easy, although the service bureau in your hotel should be able to arrange the following half day tours: the **Hermitage** (about US$25); **Peter and Paul Fortress** (US$20); **city tour** (US$25). There are also architecture tours, metro station tours and excursions to **Petrodvorets** (US$25), or to **Pushkin** and **Pavlovsk** (US$35). **HI St Petersburg Hostel** and **Peter TIPS** also offer great deals.

Between May and September, sightseeing **boats** leave from the Hermitage and Decembrists' Piers. Unfortunately most commentaries are in Russian so check first before paying.

WHERE TO STAY

Budget accommodation

A number of international companies organises **homestays** in St Petersburg including G&R (p18) and Passport Travel (p18). Locally they can be organised through *Peter TIPS* and the *Host Families Association, Bed and Breakfast in Russia* (☎ 275 1992, 535 7824), ul Tavricheskaya 5, kv 25. Sometimes at the Moskovsky Station you can find people offering a room for overnight stays but you should be cautious when pursuing these options.

Summer Hostel (☎ 252 7563, 252 4011, fax 252 4019), ul Baltiyskaya 26, offers beds for US$8 a night in the renovated 3rd floor wing of the Industrial Teacher's College. The closest metro stations are Narvskaya and Ploshchad Vosstaniya.

The *HI St Petersburg Hostel* (☎ 329 8018, fax 329 8019, e-mail ryh@ryh.spb.su), at ul 3rd Sovetskaya 28, was the first hostel to open in St Petersburg. You can make reservations from North America by contacting Russian Youth Hostels & Tourism ☎ +1 (310) 379 4316, fax 379 8420, e-mail 71573.2010@compuserve.com). A bed in a three-bed dormitory costs US$17 summer (US$12 winter) including breakfast. The building is clean and well-organised and it's an excellent place to meet other travellers and pick up the latest travel information. English language movies are shown nightly. Ticket bookings are handled here at reasonable rates via Sindbad Travel, as are visa invitations and extensions (they can only help extend your visa if you have booked it through them – see p20). As the hostel is well known, in summer it is often full. If making a booking via Moscow's Travellers Guest House, hold on to your receipt. Communication between the two hostels is unreliable. To get to the hostel from Moscow train station, turn right onto Staraya Nevsky, then left at the first traffic lights onto pro Suvorovky (a Philips Electronics Store is on the left), then right at the second traffic light into ul 3rd Sovetskaya.

If you are arriving from Finland, *Holiday Hostel* (☎ 542 7364 fax 325 8559, e-mail postmaster@hostelling.spb.su) at ul Mikhaylova 1 is very

The St Petersburg area code is ☎ 812. From outside Russia dial +7-812.

convenient. It is a five-minute walk from the Findlandsky station and metro Ploshchad Lenina. Bed and breakfast costs US$15 in a double room and US$12 in a 3/5-bed room (winter time), US$22 and US$18 respectively in summer. It's beautifully located on the waterfront and despite being next door to Kresty Prison this is a peaceful area. The entrance is now via the Zdorovyak fast-food restaurant, owned by the Holiday Hostel.

Midrange hotels

There are numerous two- and three-star hotels in the city. The *Hotel St Petersburg* (☎ 542 9411, fax 248 8002), at Nab Pirogovskaya 5/2, is only a five minute walk from Finlandsky railway station (metro Ploshchad Lenina) and now a UK/Russian joint venture. Its rooms, which start at US$75, have majestic view of the Neva River.

Cheaper options include the *Hotel Oktyabrskaya* (☎ 277 6330) at Ligovsky Prospekt 10 (metro Ploshchad Vosstaniya) Old but comfortable, rooms start from US$25 for a single, and US$60 for a double room. *Hotel Rus* (☎ 279 5003, fax 279 3600), at ul Artilleriyskaya 28 is a large modern hotel with prices from US$40/50 for a single/double room. Similarly-priced is the *Hotel Rossiya* (294 6322), at ul Chernysevskovo 11, a Soviet-era hotel. It is about 3km south of the city centre near the metro station, Park Pobedy.

Upmarket hotels

The two most centrally located hotels have been completely refurbished and now offer luxury facilities at seriously luxurious prices. The *Grand Hotel Europe* (☎ 329 6000, fax 329 6001), at 1/7 Nevsky Prospekt, is reputed to be the best hotel in the country; doubles here start at US$295. It has four restaurants and bars.

The *Astoria Hotel* (☎ 210 5757), ul Bolshaya Morskaya 39, built in 1913 and furnished in beautiful Art Nouveau style, is now a Finnish/Russian joint venture. It's opposite St Isaac's Cathedral and prices are from US$180 for a double. Good tours can be arranged from here.

The *Nevsky Palace Hotel* (☎ 275 2001, fax 310 7323), a new five-star place, is at the other end of Nevsky Prospekt (number 57). A standard single costs US$290 and a double US$355. The Finnish-built *Pulkhovskaya Hotel* (☎ 264 5122, 264 5022, fax 264 6396) is at Ploshchad Pobedy 1, (metro: Moskovskaya) with comfortable and clean rooms starting from US$120. Its restaurants offer Russian and Finnish cuisine. *MNTK* (☎ 178 9536) is at ul Yaroslava Gasheka 21; rooms start from US$115.

Slightly further away and of a lower standard is the *Pribaltiskaya Hotel* (☎ 356 0001, fax 356 4496, rooms from US$80), at ul Korablestroiteley 14 (metro Primorskaya) which faces the Gulf of Finland. It contains several restaurants and Casino Spielbank.

WHERE TO EAT

The city's top restaurants charge anything from US$20 to US$50 plus for a meal. Recommended places include the *Aphrodite* (☎ 275 7620) Nevsky Prospekt 86 for seafood; the *Tbilisi* (☎ 232 9391) ul Sitninskaya 10 for Georgian food including excellent shashlik; the *Imperial* (☎ 234 1742) pro Kamenovstrovsky 53 for good Russian food, and the *Europe Restaurant* (☎ 113 8066) at the Grand Hotel Europe. The Bacchanalian Sunday brunch (12:00 to 15:00) at the Grand Hotel Europe, with live jazz is popular. *Kalinka* (☎ 213 3751, 218 2866) is one of St Petersburg's best with very good traditional Russian cuisine and folk music. It's on Sezdovskaya liniya 9. *Na Fontanke* (☎ 310 2547, 310 0689), at nab Fontanki Reki 77, is a Russian/European restaurant with gypsies dancing and an orchestra playing all night long.

The *Café Literaturnoe*, where Pushkin had his last meal before his fatal duel, is at Nevsky Prospekt 18. It offers classical music and traditional Russian fare and has an entry charge. It's best to make a reservation here (☎ 312 8543).

The *Pizza House* at ul Podolskaya 23 offers 13 types of Finnish (thin crust) pizza, salad and beer; and a delivery service (☎ 316 2666, open 12:30-23:00). *Pizza Hut* is on the corner of nab Moyki Reki and ul Gorokhovaya (open 11:00-21:00).

Other places worth trying are the *Balkany Café*, Nevsky Prospekt 27 which is a little café serving ptta bread, felafel and moussaka at reasonable prices, *Russkie Bliny Café* ☎ 279 0559), ul Furmanova 13, which is renowned for serving Russian *bliny* pancakes in a relaxed environment where patrons share wooden tables, and *Springtime Bistro* (☎ 279 1855), ul Chernyakhovskovo 33, which has a good selection of cheap middle Eastern specialities.

Tandoor (☎ 312 3886) at pro Voznesensky 2, which serves great vegetarian Indian cuisine. The Hare Krishna *Troitsky Most Café*, at ul Malaya Posadskaya 2, is another vegetarian restaurant.

St Petersburg also boast a cyberspace café, the *Tetris Internet Café* (☎ 164 8759) at ul Chernyakhovskovo 33., open daily 12:00-24:00.

Bars

There are dozens of bars in St Petersburg and most offer a relaxed and convivial evening of good spirits, music, and pub food. The better ones are *Mollie's Irish Bar*, ul Rubinshteyna 36 (open 11:00-03:00), the *Night Sky Bar* on the Hotelship Peterhof (open 10:00-02:00), *Relax Bar*, pro Morisa

❏ **Drinking water**
Avoid St Petersburg's tap water, even to brush your teeth with as it can cause giardia, a particularly nasty infection which leads to diarrhoea, stomach cramps and nausea. Buy bottled water and peel all fruit.

Toreza 34 (open 24 hours), **Senat-Bar**, ul Galernaya 1 (11:00 -05:00), **Shamrock Irish Bar**, ul Dekabristov 27 (12:00-01:00) and **Rose Pub**, pro Liteynyy 14 (11:00-05:00).

Worth a special mention is **Daddys' Bar** at Daddy's Steak Room which serves the best Tex-Mex in St Petersburg. It's at pro Moskovsky 73 (open 12:00-24:00).

❏ **Bridge Raising**
If you plan to be out late on the opposite side of the river to your hotel, remember that the metro trains across the river stop running at 00:30, and the bridges open up for ships at 02:00 for up to two hours. The length of times varies depending on traffic but if you have to wait the river front is the perfect place to watch the sun rise.

WHAT TO SEE

The Hermitage Museum

Bigger than the British Museum or the Louvre, this museum surpasses both in the lavishness of its setting and the comprehensiveness of its collection of paintings. It comprises two huge buildings, the **Winter Palace** and the **Hermitage**. The Winter Palace, designed by the Italian architect, Rastrelli, was completed in 1762. The dozens of rooms and halls contained within its Baroque exterior were decorated in the reign of Catherine the Great who favoured the Classical style. Catherine ordered the building of the Hermitage, next door to her palace, as a place of retreat where she could contemplate the art collection she had begun.

The Hermitage is so large it would be impossible to see more than a small part of it in one visit. It comprises the following departments:

1. The History of Russian Culture

2. Ancient History (Don't miss the exquisite goldwork in the Scythian collection. You might be allowed in only if you are with a tour group. It's worth checking this in advance.)

3. Central Asian Department

4. The Middle East, China and Japan

5. Ancient Greece and Rome

6. European Art This is the section that draws the tourists. There are works by Leonardo da Vinci, Raphael and Michelangelo (Halls 207-30); El Greco, Velazquez, Murillo and Goya (Halls 239-40); Van Dyck, Rembrandt and Rubens (Halls 245-54). French artists are well represented in Halls 272-297 and the Impressionists can be seen in Halls 317-345.

The works of Reynolds, Gainsborough and other English artists are displayed in Halls 289-303.

The setting for these masterpieces could not be more magnificent: grand marble halls with gilded columns, mosaic floors and vast crystal chandeliers. As the place is so big, it may be worthwhile getting a guided tour one day and coming back the next day to wander at your leisure.

While the museum is open 10:30-17:30, closed Monday, the front doors close at 17:00. Entrance is US$9, or US$2.50 with a student card. (It's US$0.40 for Russians). You have to pay extra to use cameras (US$3.00) and video cameras (US$7.00). No tripods or flashes allowed. Ticket queues can be long.

❑ **Rules for social conduct**
When Catherine the Great held a dinner party the lucky few who were honoured with an invitation were bound by a list of social rules displayed by the doors to the dining room. Guests were ordered to 'put off their title and rank as well as their hats and swords'. Pretensions were to be left outside; guests were to 'enjoy themselves but break nothing and spoil nothing'; be sparing with their words; eat and drink with moderation and avoid yawning. Those who violated the above rules were obliged to undergo the following punishment: the drinking of one glass of fresh water (ladies not excepted) and the recital of a page of poetry.

The museum has a Web site at http://www.hermitage.ru/.

Decembrists' Square

This square was the scene of the uprising by the group of officers on 14 December 1825 (see p128). They came to be known as the Decembrists and were sent to Siberia for their treachery,

The **Bronze Horseman**, a monument to Peter the Great, stands in the square. The statue was commissioned by Catherine II and the work carried out by the French sculptor, Falconet, in 1782.

St Isaac's Cathedral

South of Decembrists' Square is St Isaac's Cathedral (built between 1819 and 1859) with its vast gilded dome and ornate interior. In pre-Revolutionary days, the Cathedral would be packed with up to 14,000 people for major celebrations like Easter and St Isaac's birthday.

Recently reconsecrated, services are held here only at major Christian festivals but it's possible to view the spectacular interior daily except Wednesday from 11:00 to 18:00. There's an US$8 admission charge to the church plus US$8 for cameras and US$21 for videos.

You can climb part of the way up the dome for a great view over the city. It costs US$3 to walk up around the outside of the dome plus US$3 for using cameras and US$11 for videos.

A walk down Nevsky Prospekt

Nevsky Prospekt has been the main shopping street and most fashionable place to be seen in St Petersburg since the foundation of the city. A walk along this once grand street, past palaces and churches, over canals and beside faded buildings is a walk through the history of the city itself. Nevsky Prospekt starts near the Admiralty Building and, as you walk south-east from here, you can identify the buildings by the numbers beside the doors. The following may be of interest:

No 7 Gogol wrote *The Government Inspector* here in the 1830s.

No 9 This building was modelled on the Doges' Palace in Venice, for the Swedish banker, Wawelberg. Now it's the **Agency of Air Communication** and Air Terminal for buses to the airports.

No 14 Note the blue and white sign here which dates from the Siege of Leningrad in WWII and advises pedestrians to walk on the other side of the street during shelling.

No 17 This impressive building, designed by Rastrelli and built in 1754, was once the palace of the wealthy Stroganov family. Although they are more famous for the beef stew named after them, it was the Stroganovs who initiated the conquest and colonisation of Siberia by sending their private army to the Urals in the 1570s.

No 18 The **Café Literaturnoe** was Pushkin's favourite café and is still popular among Russian intellectuals. It charges an entry fee which includes high class entertainment such as violin concerts.

No 20 The former **Dutch Church**, built in 1837, now an Agfa shop.

No 24 Once the showrooms of the court jewellers Fabergé (creators of the golden Easter eggs now on display in the Kremlin).

No 27 Balkany Café, a little place serving pita bread, felafel and moussaka at reasonable prices. Open from 11:00-23:00.

No 28 The former showrooms of the Singer Sewing Machine Company with their trademark (a glass globe) still on the roof. Now it's home to **Dom Knigi Bookstore**, the largest bookshop in the city.

Kazan Cathedral was designed by Voronikhin and completed in 1811. Prince Peter Kropotkin, writing in 1911, called it 'an ugly imitation on a smaller scale of St Peter's in Rome'.

The large, domed cathedral is approached by a semi-circular colonnade. There is a statue at each end of the colonnade. The one on the left is Mikhail Kutuzov who prayed here before leading an army to fight Napoleon. After the victory over the French in 1812, the cathedral became a monument to Russia's military glory. In an act of supreme tastelessness, the Soviets turned it into a Museum of Atheism, later renamed the Museum of Religions. Part of the cathedral still houses exhibits on the history of religion, the rest has been returned to the Orthodox Church.

Looking north along the Griboyedova Canal, you'll see the onion-domed **Church of the Resurrection** (also known as the Church of the Resurrection Built on Spilt Blood) which is reminiscent of St Basil's in Moscow. It was built on the spot where Alexander II was assassinated in 1881.

No 31 This building housed the City Duma (Municipal Council) in Tsarist times. The tower was used as a fire-lookout. The little portico around the corner is a **Theatre Booking Office**. Foreigners may buy tickets here. Opposite the Duma, is ul Brodskovo which runs north into Arts Square (Ploshchad Iskustvo) which is where the **Russian State Museum** is located. The museum was the former Mikhailovsky Palace and now houses over 300,000 paintings, drawings and sculptures. It is open 10:00-18:00, closed Tuesday, admission US$2. The **Maly Theatre** and the **St Petersburg State Philharmonia** are situated near the museum. The **Grand Hotel Europe** is a short distance down ul Brodskovo 32.

No 32 In the **Church of St Catherine,** Stanislaw Poniatowski, the last king of Poland and one of the lovers of Catherine the Great, is buried. Local artists sell their sketches and watercolours outside.

No 38 The **Industry and Construction Bank** is one of the best places to cash Travellers Cheques in St Petersburg.

No 40 Dr. Oetker Nevsky 40 Restaurant is a German style beer house and restaurant, with good atmosphere, good draft beer and reasonable food. Open 12:00-24:00 daily.

No 41 St Petersburg Mosaic Dance Theatre (☎ 274 1287) has Russian folklore dances.

Gostiny Dvor, the city's largest department store, fills the whole of the next block (south side). It's a good place to buy souvenirs. It is being renovated but even when it is finished, it will not be as inviting as **Passazh Department Store** on the opposite side of the street. Passazh was the city's first privately owned department store and has a range of goods similar to any large Western department store. There is a large supermarket in the basement.

From the street, you can see a **statue of Catherine the Great**, surrounded by her lovers (or 'associates' as some guides coyly put it) and other famous people of the time. In the park behind the statues is the Pushkin Theatre.

No 56 Eliseevsky Gastronome was a delicatessen that rivalled the Food Hall at Harrods in Tsarist days when it was presided over by Mr Eliseyev. After the Revolution it became Gastronom Number One and the ornate showcases of its sumptuous interior were heaped with jars of boiled vegetables. It is a wonderful example of classic St Petersburg interior design. Exotic Western fare is now on offer here.

The building on the south side of the street beside the Fontanka Canal is known as the **Anichkov Palace**, after the nearby **Anichkov Bridge** with its famous equestrian statues.

No 82 Art Gallery of the Master's Guild (Gildiya Masterov) offers a good range of graphics, tapestries, ceramics, batik, jewellery and glassware by well-known artists. Open 11:00-16:00 weekdays.

No 86 The Finnish-French **Aphrodite Restaurant** has excellent seafood and French decor. It is open 12:00 to 24:00.

Continuing east along the Nevsky Prospekt, it's one km from here to Ploshchad Vosstaniya where Moskovsky railway station (for trains to Moscow) is situated. From Ploshchad Vosstaniya it's a further 700m to the end of the avenue at Ploshchad Aleksandra Nevskovo. The interesting **Alexander Nevsky Monastery**, with seven churches in the grounds, is situated here across the square from the **Hotel Moskva**.

Peter and Paul Fortress
In 1703 work began on this fortress, situated on an island in the very heart of the city. It was used as a maximum security prison until 1921, when it was turned into a museum. If you're here at midday don't be surprised by the sound of a cannon. It's the daily noonday cannon that St Petersburgers check their watches by. At the centre of the fortress is the **Peter and Paul Cathedral**, with its soaring, needle-like spire (122m). It now serves as a mausoleum for Peter the Great and his successors and is crammed with their ornate tombs. There are plans to bury here the remains of Nicholas II, Russia's last monarch, who was killed in 1917 in Ekaterinburg. The cathedral is open daily except Wednesday, and the fortress is open 10:00-18:00, closed Wednesday and last Tuesday of the month.

Leaving the fortress, crossing the bridge and walking east along the river you will come to a small brick building amongst the trees in a square. This outer shell protects **Peter the Great's Log Cabin**, the earliest surviving building in the city, built in 1703, and now preserved as an interesting little museum (open 10:00-18:00, closed Tuesday).

Other sights
Since the city boasts over sixty museums, it is impossible to give details of more than a few in a guide of this type. As well as those places of interest listed above there are art museums (**Monastery of the Holy Trinity**

and **Alexander Nevsky**); museums of social history (the **Cruiser Aurora** from which the signal for the Revolution was fired); literary museums (homes of **Dostoyevsky** and **Pushkin**) and scientific museums (the history of rail transport in the CIS at the **Railway Museum**; the **Museum of the Arctic and Antarctic** and the **Natural History Museum**, where a fully preserved baby mammoth dug out of the Siberian permafrost, is on display).

Excursions

Thirty kilometres west of the city lies **Petrodvorets** (Peterhof), built as Peter the Great's Versailles by the sea. It is most famous for its spectacular fountains, with the gilded figures which appear in all the tourist literature. Open daily (though the main palace is closed on Monday) from 11:00 to 20:00. In the summer you can get there by hydrofoil from Hermitage Pier (several boats each hour, US$5 each way).

At **Pushkin** (25km outside St Petersburg) is the grand palace (closed Tuesday) that was the home of the Imperial family. Set in a beautiful park, it was formerly known as Tsarskoye Selo (the Tsar's village). Four km south of here is **Pavlovsk**, built by Catherine the Great for her son Paul. Pavlovsk is closed Fridays. Trains for Pushkin and Pavlovsk leave from Vitebsky railway station (metro: Pushkinskaya). **Lomonosov (Oranienbaum) Palace** with its beautiful park attracts far fewer tourists than the above three and is a peaceful place to visit. It is closed Tuesday and in winter. Trains leave from Baltiisky railway station (metro: Baltiiskaya). Ilya Repin's house **Penaty** (closed Tuesday) is at Repino and can be reached by the suburban train from Finlandskii station.

NIGHTLIFE

St Petersburg is probably the most interesting city in Russia for nightlife: everything from sitting around in the bars mentioned above to a night out at the ballet. For current information on events around St Petersburg, pick up one of the local English language newspapers listed on p132 or look for the posters around the city. Ask at the service bureau for a programme of **ballet** (Kirov US$50, Maly US$20), **opera, concerts** and the **circus**. You can also buy tickets as the Russians do from the Theatre Booking Office off Nevsky Prospekt (see p139) or from the hostels who put a surcharge on them. Or you can try the touts outside the theatre just before the show.

There are more than 30 casinos in St Petersburg. The best are the **Eldorado** at the Hotel Kareliya, ul Tukhachevskovo 7/2 (open 20:00-05:00), and **Nevskaya Melody**, nab Sverdlovskaya 62.

The best large disco nightclub complexes are **Fekel**, ul Soviyskaya 44, which has live Russian bands, and **Stiers Club**, pl Stachek 4, which offers dancing and a game room (open 22:00-05:00).

MOVING ON

By air

Most European airlines have offices in St Petersburg. There are daily international flights from Berlin, Helsinki, Prague and Warsaw and regular weekly flights to most other European capitals. All international flights land at Pulkovo-2 while domestic flights land at Pulkovo-1. For information on getting to the airports, see p129.

Air tickets for within Russia can be obtained from Aeroflot offices or the **Central Agency of Air Communications** (☎ 314 6963) at pro Nevsky 7/9 or at pro Kamennoostrovsky 27. Both offices are open weekdays from 8:00-19:00 and weekends 8:00-18:00. **Transaero** (☎ 327 84 50) is at pro Liteynyy 48.

By rail

Check **departure times** with the hotel service bureau and arrive half an hour before the train is due to leave. If you don't know the stations, give yourself extra time to find the right platform as the sheer size of the stations can be daunting. Long distance and suburban trains may depart from the same station. Russian trains rarely depart late and have been known to roll out of the station a few minutes ahead of schedule.

Printed intercity **train schedules** are available at all stations and if you can speak Russian, you can call for railway information on ☎ 168 0111 (general), ☎ 162 3344 (domestic) and ☎ 274 2092 (international).

Tickets Tickets for **same day departure** can be purchased only at the station of departure at the 'same-day window' (*sutochnaya*) or Intourist window. Last minute tickets can sometimes be obtained from speculators, but at a high price. It is also risky because of the name-on-ticket/passport rule (see p121).

Advance tickets for departures from the following day up to 45 days in advance can be purchased at the Central Railroad Ticket Office (*Tsentralnye Zheleznodorozhnye Kassy*) at nab Kanala Griboyedova 24. The closest metro is Nevsky Prospekt. The office is open 08:00-20:00 on Monday to Saturday and 08:00-16:00 on Sundays. They sell tickets for all long distance and international train routes but not suburban rail tickets. Foreigners normally purchase tickets at windows 13, 14, or 15 or in the Intourist hall to the left of the entrance. You can try to buy the tickets at the station from which your train departs but unless they have an Intourist window (both Finland and Moscow stations have Intourist windows), you will probably be told to go to nab Kanala Griboyedova. Occasionally the Intourist Office will not sell you a ticket without your passport. Intourist charges a US$4 premium above the price of the Russian ticket and as conductors also often compare the name on your passport against that on the ticket, it is not worth buying a local's ticket.

At the Moscow Station, foreigners were being told in early 1997 that they could buy tickets only at the Business Centre in the building. This centre charges a massive US$25 commission.

If you do not want to go to the hassle of buying tickets yourself, you can get them from most hotel service desks (who add a sizeable commission) or from Sindbad Travel (who add a smaller one).

International trains If you plan to return to Europe by train from here, you will have to pass through one or more of Latvia, Lithuania, Estonia and Belarus. See p387 for the visa requirements of each country. You will be able to get all your visas in St Petersburg with the exception of the Belorussian one. Unfortunately, information on the need for a

---

❏ **Moscow to St Petersburg by train**

There are about 20 trains a day between Moscow and St Petersburg. A berth in a two-berth cabin (SV) costs US$90 and in a four-berth cabin (coupé) it's US$60.

The 650km line is Russia's busiest and most prestigious railway. Consequently, high standards are maintained, both in terms of carriage conditions and service. When the line was opened in 1851, the average travel time was 25 hours. Today most of the overnight trains take eight hours, with the once a week, high speed ER-200 train taking just five hours. This compares to over 10 hours if you travel by car on the shosse Peterburgskoe (St Petersburg Highway).

The most scenic time of the year on this route is between April and October and in particular during autumn when the leaves turn. Most travellers prefer an overnight journey as it saves accommodation costs and maximises daytime sight-seeing.

Service is excellent. You will be given a lunch box on daytime trains or breakfast box on overnight trains. The dining cars are usually open all night and on the best trains, security guards patrol the corridors all night. The best overnight trains are Nos 1/2, 3/4 and 5/6 and the ones to avoid are Nos 9/10 and 35/36.

Origin	No or name	Travel time	Dep	Arr	Destination
Moscow	2 Red Arrow	8hrs 30min	23:55	8:25	St Petersburg
Moscow	4	8hrs 30min	23:59	8:29	St Petersburg
Moscow	6 Inturist	7hrs 25min	23:10	7:35	St Petersburg
St Petersburg	1 Red Arrow	8hrs 30min	23:55	8:25	Moscow
St Petersburg	3	8hrs 29min	23:59	8:30	Moscow
St Petersburg	5 Inturist	7hrs 10min	23:33	7:43	Moscow
Moscow	8 Neva	7hrs 25min	22:15	6:40	St Petersburg
Moscow	14 Avrora	8hrs 30min	20:35	5:05	St Petersburg
St Petersburg	7 Neva	8hrs 25min	22:45	7:10	Moscow
St Petersburg	19	9hrs 23min	21:55	6:18	Moscow
Moscow	158 ER-200*	4hrs 59min	12:21	17:20	St Petersburg
St Petersburg	157 ER-200¶	4hrs 59min	12:15	17:14	Moscow
Moscow	134	8hrs 55min	9:38	18:33	St Petersburg
St Petersburg	135	10hrs 39min	10:55	21:34	Moscow

* Fridays only ¶ Thursdays only

Belorussian visa is contradictory. In Moscow they claim no transit visa is required providing you have a valid Russian visa (if you only have a single entry Russian visa, this will be taken from you at the Russia/Belarus border), while in St Petersburg, they say that you need one. Get a Belorussian visa before you leave your home country or in Moscow to save any problems at the border.

Train No 25 to Berlin via Warsaw goes through the Baltic states avoiding Belarus, train No 57 goes to Warsaw via Belarus, and train No 183 goes to Prague via Belarus and Ukraine.

Some international trains and journey times from St Petersburg are as follows: Berlin (32 hours, train No 25), Budapest (44 hours), Warsaw (22 hours, train No 57), Prague (48 hours, train No 183), Helsinki (8 hours), Riga (12 hours), Tallinn (9 hours), Vilnuis (13 hours).

By bus

If you've had enough of trains and planes, **Finnord Bus Agency** (☎ 314 8951, fax 314 7058) at ul Italianskaya 37, operates an overnight coach service to Helsinki for US$46 (less with student card). It departs at 3:30pm and arrives at 10pm. Another option is the **St Petersburg Express Bus Service** which offers a daily bus from Hotel Astoria for US$44. Sovavto also offers daily departures to Helsinki from the Grand Hotel Europe at 8:45, arriving at 15:45. A ticket costs US$46.

Sovavto also has regular departures for the routes: St Petersburg-Helsinki-Turku-St Petersburg, and St Petersburg-Vyborg-Lappeenranta-Yvyaskyulya-St Petersburg. Tickets can be purchased from several hotels, including the Pulkovskaya, Astoria, Grand Hotel Europe, and Saint Petersburg, and also from Sovavto offices (☎ 264 5125) at pl Pobedy 1 and pro Kamennoostrovski 39.

By ship

Baltic Shipping Company (☎ 355 1616, 355 6140) runs ferries between St Petersburg and Helsinki, Stockholm and Riga. The timetable changes depending on the season and in 1996, a one way, overnight bed in a four berth room cost US$70. Tickets can be purchased from the company, Peter TIPS and Sindbad Travel and its agents in Helsinki (3589-665 755), Stockholm (☎ 460-200 029) and USA (Euro Cruises, ☎ 800 688 3876, 212-691 2099).

❏ **Finland border charge**

If you are leaving Russia via Finland, you must pay a US$10 border charge regardless of your means of transport.

Moscow
Москва

All railway lines in Russia lead to the capital, so you'll be spending some time here, even if it's just a quick visit to Red Square as you change stations. Moscow is a fascinating city to explore, made more so by recent tumultuous political events, so any time here is well spent: bank on three days as a minimum to see the main sights. Finding a place to stay, whatever your budget, is not a problem and extending a transit visa is currently a straightforward process.

HISTORY

The archaeological record shows that Moscow has been inhabited since Neolithic times. However, the first written mention of the city was not until 1147, when Prince Yuri Dolguruky was said to have founded the city by building a fort on a site beside the Moskva River, in the principality of Vladimir. The settlement which grew up around the wooden fort soon developed into a major trading centre.

The Mongols

Disaster struck the Russian principalities in the early thirteenth century in the form of the Mongol invasion. Moscow was razed to the ground in 1238 and for the next two and a half centuries was obliged to pay an annual tribute to the Mongol Khan. During this time the principality of Muscovy (of which Moscow was capital) emerged as the most important state in Russia. In 1326, Moscow became the seat of the Russian Orthodox Church. Prince Dimitri Donskoi strengthened the city's defences and built a stone wall around the Kremlin. In 1380 he defeated a Mongol-Tatar army at Kulikovo but it was not until 1476 that tributes to the Khan ceased.

The years of growth

The reign of Ivan III (Ivan the Great: 1462-1505) was a period of intensive construction in the city. Italian architects were commissioned to redesign the Kremlin, and many of the cathedrals and churches date from this period. Prosperity continued into the sixteenth century under Ivan IV (Ivan the Terrible) and it was at this time that St Basil's Cathedral in Red Square was built.

The early seventeenth century was a time of civil disorder, and a peasant uprising culminated in the invasion of Moscow by Polish and

Lithuanian forces. When they were driven out in 1612 the city was yet again burnt to the ground. Rebuilt in stone, Moscow became the most important trading city in Russia by the end of the century. It remained a major economic and cultural centre even when Peter the Great transferred the capital of Russia to St Petersburg in 1712.

The final sacking of the city occurred in 1812 when Napoleon invaded Russia. As much of the damage was probably caused by retreating Muscovites as by the French armies but three quarters of the buildings were destroyed. Recovery was swift and trade increased after the abolition of serfdom in 1861.

Revolution

Towards the end of the century Moscow became a revolutionary centre and its factories were hit by a series of strikes and riots. Michael Myres Shoemaker, who was here in 1903, wrote in *The Great Siberian Railway from St Petersburg to Peking*: 'Up to the present day the dissatisfaction has arisen from the middle classes especially the students, but now for the first time in Russia's history it is spreading downward to the peasants... but it will be a century at least before that vast inert mass awakens to life.' In 1905 there was an armed uprising and twelve years later 'that vast inert mass' had stormed the Kremlin and established Soviet power in the city. The civil war saw terrible food shortages and great loss of life.

The capital once more

In March 1918 Lenin transferred the government back to Moscow. In the years between the two world wars the city embarked on an ambitious programme of industrial development and the population doubled to four million by 1939. During the Second World War many of the factories in the European part of the USSR were re-located to the other side of the Urals, which turned out to be sensible move. By October 1941, the German army had surrounded the city and the two-month Siege of Moscow had begun. Moscow was rebuilt following the war and grew in size, grandeur and power. However by the late 1980s, the city's clean appearance and services had started to collapse under Gorbachev's reforms and the breakdown of communist power. The few years following the 1991 disintegration of the Soviet Union was a time when little worked in the city and road, buildings and public utilities were continually on the verge of complete collapse.

Moscow today

The only thing that can be said with certainty about Moscow is that the changes that have transformed it over the last five years are not about to stop now. On the one hand the restructuring here seems to be part of a beneficial transition to a market economy: new hotels spring up, joint-venture restaurants open and private shops flourish. On the other hand it's impossible to ignore the widespread poverty: old women in the streets stand for hours trying to hawk their one hairbrush or plastic bag, ragged war veterans sleep in the subways and everywhere, it seems, there are beggars. The fact that the new generation of foreign shops, bars and restaurants offer all the latest in Western luxuries highlights the contrasts. Most Muscovites can only afford to window shop in such places.

Crime, ranging from petty pilfering to gang warfare on the streets is on the increase and many businesses are forced to pay protection money to local 'mafia' gangs. Certain areas in the city are being compared to Chicago in the 1930s. There is also a chronic shortage of housing which has worsened with the arrival of thousands of ethnic Russians from the other CIS republics.

Moscow is currently in a complete state of flux. Just what will be the final result of this metamorphosis remains to be seen.

ARRIVING IN MOSCOW

By air

International flights land at **Sheremetyevo International Airport**, 35km from the city centre. Buses from just across the parking lot here will ferry you to or from the metro stations Rechnoi Vokzal (bus No 551) or Planernaya (bus No 517), departing every half hour (6am to 11pm). There are also special orange airport buses. Taxis charge US$40-60 to the city centre; for your own safety take an official cab rather than just any car whose driver offers you a lift.

Domestic flights use one of Moscow's four local airports.

By train

There are nine railway stations, the four you are most likely to use being: **Belorusski** (metro: Belorusskaya), for trains to and from Western Europe (note that the station is sometimes called Smolenski); **Leningradski** (metro: Komsomolskaya) for Helsinki and St Petersburg; and, next door to it, **Yaroslavlski** (metro: Komsomolskaya) for Trans-Siberian trains (except No 26 to Novosibirsk via Kazan, which leave from Kazanski) and **Kazanski**, opposite Leningradski, for trains to Central Asia. **Kievski** (metro: Kievskaya) is for trains to Budapest; note that departures require a Ukrainian visa. See p170 for information on **leaving Moscow.**

LOCAL TRANSPORT

Metro

The palatial metro sytem (see map pp162-3), a tourist attraction in itself, is the best way to travel around Moscow.

The network is extensive and straightforward. The metro uses single use tokens or multiple use magnetic cards which can be purchased inside the metro station building, near the entry barriers. You can travel any distance and change trains as often as you want without exiting. Trains arrive every minute in peak hours and you have to wait a maximum of five minutes even at midnight. All stations open from 06:00 to 01:00. During peak hours, from 07:00 to 10:00 and 15:00 to 19:00, trains are very crowded.

When you leave a station, a recorded message announces the name of the next station, warns you not to lean against the doors, and following the terrorist campaign during the Chechnya war, reminds you not to forget your luggage. The current price of the metro US$0.35, an amount that is said to cover only a quarter of the real cost of a trip.

❑ **The Moscow metro and the secret metro**

Construction of the metro began in the early 1930s and it was planned that the first line would be opened on May Day 1935. In late April 1935, Stalin was invited to inspect the system but his train tour came to an unexpected halt for 30 minutes following a signal failure. Expecting imprisonment or worse, the engineers nearly collapsed with relief when Stalin simply suggested that it might be better to fix all the problems and delay the opening until 15 May. The honour of driving the first metro train, which consisted of local copies of the 1932 New York carriages, went to the strangely named Ivan Ivanovich Ivanov.

As well as transporting passengers, the metro served as a bomb shelter in 1941 and 1942. Male Moscovites slept on wooden platforms assembled every evening in the tunnels while women and children slept on camp stretchers on the platforms. Following the start of the Cold War, the metro was modified to contain fall out shelters and evidence of both the World War and Cold War preparations can still be seen today. These include large recessed blast doors at the entrances of the metros on ground level, collapsible platform edges which become steps, and large storerooms on the platforms for medical supplies.

A second, 'secret' metro was finished in 1967 which would enable government leaders to flee Moscow in the face of a nuclear attack. The 30km line runs from the former Central Communist Headquarters building on Staraya Square (near metro station Kitai-Gorod) to the government's underground bunker complex in the Ramenki region (near metro station Universitet) to the government's airport, Vnukovo-2. Closed to the public, the line is said to be still operational.

Over the next few years, new N5 metro carriages from Moscow's Mytishchi railway factory are being phased in. They are significantly quieter, smoother and safer, due to automatic fire quenchers and extensive use of fireproof material.

It is interesting to note that while women drive many of Moscow's buses and trams, until recently only men were train drivers. The reason for this is the belief that men better handle the stress of suicidal passengers who jump into the path of the oncoming metro trains.

You can discover the history of the metro in the **Moscow Metro Museum**. This five hall museum contains maps, working models and documents about the history of Moscow's public transport and metro from the beginning of the 19th century. The museum is part of the Sportivnaya metro station and it is advisable to book a visit. Address: Khamovnicheski val 35, metro Sportivnaya, ☎ 222 7309. Open 11:00-18:00 Monday, 9:00-16:00 Tuesday to Friday, closed Saturday and Sunday.

Bus and **tram** services are comprehensive but overcrowded. Virtually any Russian car will be a **taxi** but don't get in if there are already passengers (see p66). Self-drive **hire cars** (from hotel service bureaux) might be worth considering for some of the sights outside the city but are not recommended for city sightseeing.

There's a pleasant **river trip** which leaves from the Kiev River Terminal (near Kievskaya metro station) and passes Lenin Hills and Gorky Park on its way towards the Kremlin. The 1.5-hour trip ends at the Novospassky Bridge terminal which is about 2km past the Kremlin.

ORIENTATION AND SERVICES

At the very centre of the city are the Kremlin, Red Square and St Basil's Cathedral. The most conveniently placed (and generally expensive) hotels are in this area. The metro system is efficient, however, so it's not vital to have a hotel right on Red Square.

The main branch of **Intourist** (☎ 292 2365) is located at ul Mokhovaya 13, around the corner from the Intourist Hotel and beside the National Hotel. Open daily from 09:00-20:00, it books tours, rail tickets (☎ 292 2294) and air tickets (☎ 292 2293). Another centrally located travel company is **R-Tours** (tel & fax 298 1600, e-mail rtours@glasnet.ru) which has offices in the Hotel Rossiya (office 10-160) and Hotel Mezdynarodnaya. Most large hotels also have a service bureau which offers a range of standard tours.

A highly recommended travel company is **G & R International** (☎ 374 7366, fax 374 6132, e-mail grint@glas.apc.org), Block 6, Office 4, Institute of Youth, ul Yunosti 5/1.

You can rent a car from **Avis** (240 9932) in the centre of Moscow at nab Berezhkovskaya 12 or at the Sheremetevo 2 airport (☎ 578 5646).

Telecommunications

You can book **international calls** from a private phone on ☎ 8194 or from your hotel on ☎ 333 4101. The operators speak English.

Medical

The **European Medical Centre** at per 2nd Tverskoi-Yamskoi 10 offers medical (☎ 250 5523), dental (☎ 250 1302) and emergency (☎ 251 6099) services; as does the **American Medical Centre** (☎ 956 3366) on proezd Shmitovsky 3. For emergency evacuation, contact **Assist 24 Medical Evacuation** (☎ 229 6536, 564 8316, fax 229 2138).

There is a **dental clinic** (☎ 488 8279) at the Pullman Iris Hotel, shosse Korovinskoye 10.

Pharmacies include **Farmakon** (☎ 292 0301) at ul 4th Tverskaya-Yamskaya 2/11; **Eczacibasi** (☎ 928 9189) at per Telegrafny 5/4 or at ul Maroseyka 2/15; and the **American Medical Centre** (above).

Money

Hard currency used to be the number one requirement for travellers in Moscow but as the currency reforms take effect there's less demand for it. **Travellers' cheques** are becoming more widely accepted but are time-consuming to cash. The best place to cash them is the Olympic Penta (pro Olympski 18/1, metro Prospekt Mira) which charges 3% commission. The worst is Radisson Slavyanka Hotel which charges 5%. The average commission currently charged by the various Russian banks are Credo Bank 3.75%, Credit-Moskva 2.5% and Menater 2%.

For **credit card cash advances**, the best is the Inkombank chain which charges 1% for Visa and Menater Bank which charges 2% for Visa, 0% for JVC and 3% for Mastercard. Commissions charged by other banks are Most Bank 1.5% and Credit-Moskva 2.93%.

American Express, on ul Sadovo Kudrinskaya 21A (metro Maykovskaya) will change only their own cheques. Open weekdays 9:00-17:00, Saturday 9:00-13:00.

Russian visa extensions

UViR (as OViR, the state visa office, is known in Moscow) is at ul Pokrovka 42 (formerly ul Chernishevskogo) which is near metro Kurskaya and Krasnye Vorota. It is open Monday, Tuesday, Thursday and Friday from 10:00-13:00 and 15:00-18:00 (17:00 close on Friday). It is also open on Saturday from 10:00-13:00 but only for emergencies. The visa extension situation changes from month to month but five-day extensions (US$30 in roubles) are currently easy to obtain if you have a day to spend getting the right documents. Longer extensions or a second extension are not so straightforward and may be refused.

To get an extension, take your passport, train ticket out of the country and visa to Room No 1 on the ground floor. You need to fill in a form and hand it in. You will then be given a chit to take to the nearby Sberegatelny Bank (Savings Bank) about 30m west of UViR on the other side of the street. The bank (ul Pokrovka 31) is open weekdays 8:30-14:00 and 15:00-19:30. At the bank, you must show your chit, fill in another form and pay the fee in roubles. You will get a receipt back and take this back to UViR and your visa will be stamped with an extension.

Because of the complications that sometimes occur, it is advisable to take a Russian speaker or a letter from the organisation which gave you your visa invitation saying that they will provide for you.

As the extension starts from the date of your application, go to UViR only a few days before your visa expires. To extend your Intourist issued visa, see p20. If you have difficulty, contact one of the specialist visa agencies listed in the classified section of the *Moscow Times* and *Moscow Tribune* newspapers.

Local publications

The two best English language newspapers are the daily *Moscow Times* and *Moscow Tribune*. These can be picked up for free from most hotels and Western supermarkets. The Moscow Times has a travel section on the weekend and a what's on guide on Friday. There is also a weekly *Living Here* newspaper which is a small cynical tabloid focusing on what's happening in Moscow. The poorly translated *Moscow News* is published weekly (US$1) as is the glossy *Moscow Magazine* (US$5).

The best place to find a job is in the *Career Forum* which comes out monthly and is free.

Diplomatic representation

- **Australia** (☎ 956 6070) per Kropotkinski 13
- **Austria** (☎ 201 7317) per Starokonyushenni 1
- **Belarus** (embassy ☎ 924 7031, visa 924 7095, general fax 928 6403) ul Maroseka 17/6
- **Belgium** (☎ 291 6027) ul Malaya Molchanovka 7
- **Canada** (☎ 291 6027) per Starokonyushenni 23
- **China** (☎ 143 1540, 143 1543 (visa)) ul Druzhby 6, (metro Universitet). Open weekdays 09:00-11.30. Service here is extremely slow. It is best to arive at least by 07:00 in order to get a place (some will be here by 05:00). If there are more than 20 people in front of you in the queue you are unlikely to get in that day. Most travellers think it's worth paying the extra US$20 on-the-spot express fee so that they don't have to return and go through the queuing process again.
- **Czech Republic** (☎ 251 0540) ul Yuliusa Fuchika 12/14, (metro Mayakovskaya)
- **Denmark** (☎ 201 7860) per Prechistenski 9
- **Estonia** (☎ 290 4655, 290 5013) per Kalashny 8, (metro Tverskaya)
- **Finland** (☎ 246 4027) per Kropotkinski 15/17
- **France** (☎ 236 0003) ul Bolshaya Yakimanka 45
- **Germany** (☎ 956 1080) ul Mosfilmovskaya 56; consulate (☎ 936 2401), pro Leninsky 94A,
- **Hungary** (☎ 146 8611) ul Mosfilmovskaya 62, (metro Kievskaya)
- **Ireland** (☎ 288 4101, 230 2763) per Grokholski 5
- **Israel** (☎ 238 2732, 230 6700) ul Bolshaya Ordynka 56
- **Italy** (☎ 241 1533) per Denezhny 5
- **Japan** (☎ 291 8500) per Kalashny 12
- **Kazakhstan** (☎ 208 9852, 927 1836) bul Chistoprudny 3A
- **Latvia** (☎ 925 2707) ul Chaplygina 3, (metro Chistye Prudy)
- **Lithuania** (☎ 291 2643) per Borisoglebski 19, (metro Arbatskaya)
- **Mongolia** (☎ 290 6792) per Borisoglebski 11; consulate (☎ 244 7867), per Spasopeskovski 7, (metro Smolenskaya). Open weekdays 10:00-12:00, 15:00-17:00.

- **Netherlands** (☎ 291 2999) per Kalashny 6
- **New Zealand** (☎ 956 3579) ul Povarskaya 44
- **Norway** (☎ 290 3872) ul Povarskaya 7
- **Poland** (☎ 255 0017, 254 3621 (visa) ul Klimashkina 4, (metro Barrikadnaya)
- **Slovakia** (☎ 251 0540, 251 1070) ul Yuliusa Fuchika 12/14
- **South Africa** (☎ 230 6869) per Bolshoi Strochenovski 22/25
- **UK** (☎ 956 7400) nab Sofiyskaya 14
- **Ukraine** (☎ 229 3422, 229 1079, 229 3442, fax 229 3542) ul Stanislavsky 18, (metro Tverskaya)
- **USA** (☎ 252 2451) bul Novinski 19/23

Tours

Tours of the main sights can be arranged in any of the upmarket hotels or at the Intourist office, at ul Mokhovaya 13. The Intourist Hotel offers the following: **Armoury and Kremlin** (four hours, US$25, not Thurs), **city sightseeing** (three hours, US$25, daily), **Kremlin grounds tour** (two hours, US$10, not Thurs), **Pushkin Fine Arts Museum** (three hours, US$15, not Mon), **Tretyakov Art Gallery** (four hours, US$20 not Mon), a **metro tour** and tours to many museums. Cheaper tours are offered by guides who hang around at the Tomb of the Unknown Soldier; if they are registered they will have ID cards to prove it.

It's worth enquiring about the mysterious **KGB Tour** that is occa-sionally offered by Intourist. If this is running you'll be treated to demon-strations of miniature cameras, microdots, bugging techniques and more at the **Federal Counterintelligence Service (KGB) Museum**.

WHERE TO STAY – (Map p159)

Budget accommodation

The *TGH Travellers Guest House Moscow* (☎ 971 4059, fax 280 7686, e-mail tgh@glas.apc.org) on the 10th floor at ul Bolshaya Pereyaslavskaya 50, is a magnet for the city's budget travellers; it's an excellent place to pick up the latest travel tips and visa information. A bed in a four-bed room costs US$15, single rooms are US$35 and double rooms are US$40-50. There's a restaurant and bar, kitchen and laundry facilities and a travel agency. They will book tickets for you even if you're not staying here but they'll be unable to do anything about extend-ing your visa unless you've booked it through them (see p20). They can also make free bookings for you for accommodation in St Petersburg and Irkutsk and they sell Trans-Siberian tickets and stopover packages. If booking accommodation at TGHM for St Petersburg International Hostel, make sure you retain your receipt in case there is no record of your book-ing when you arrive in St Petersburg. Trolleybus No 14 from Leningradski Station takes you right past TGHM. If you're coming by metro it's a 15-minute walk from the closest metro station, Prospekt Mira. Walk north for ten minutes. (Note that there are two exits from the metro but both open onto the large road, Prospekt Mira). Take the third turning on the right (pereulok Banniy) which leads to a T-junction. Turn left and the building is immediately on your right.

If the TGHM is full, try the ***Hotel Molodezhnaya*** (☎ 210 4565, fax 210 4311), a big blue monster of a place built for the 1980 Olympics, at shosse Dmitrovskoe 27. Ask at reception and you'll be quoted prices of US$25-40 for a double but go straight up to the 20th floor and you should be offered a bed in a triple room for under US$15. It's a ten-minute walk from Timiryazevskaya metro station and visible from the station itself.

Cheaper and more basic is the ***Hotel Ipkir*** (☎ 210 7148) where a single bed is US$7; there's a communal kitchen between every two rooms. It's 400m south of Dmitreyevskaya metro station at ul Butirskaya 79, opposite a cluster of trees.

The well known G & R International (☎ 374 7430, fax 374 7366, e-mail grint@glas.apc.org) has rooms in the ***Institute of Youth Hostel*** from US$17 a night. The Institute of Youth (*Institut Molodyozh*), ul Yunosti 5/1, is set in parklands and their office is in Block 6, Office 4. The closest metro station is Vykhino which is about 40 minutes out from the centre of Moscow. Then catch bus Nos 196 or 197 to the stop Institut Molodyozh.

Prakash Guest House (☎/fax 334 2595) runs a hostel with beds from US$10 a night at ul Profsoyuznaya 83. The closest metro station is Belyaevo.

New on the scene is the ***Heritage Hostel*** (☎ 975 3501 fax 975 3619, e-mail evgen@az-tour.msk.ru, http:www.arimsoft.ru/astour.html) at ul Kosmonavtov 2. The hostel is located about 10km from the city centre near the metro station VDNKh. Across the road from the metro station is Hotel Cosmos and to the right of the hotel is ul Kosmonavtov. The hostel is easy to find as it is a five-storey brick building with big blue letters on the roof. A bed in a three-bed room costs US$15 including breakfast and a double room with facilities and breakfast costs US$27. The hostel also offers a range of reasonably priced tours.

Other low priced choices include ***Hotel Kievskaya*** (☎ 240 1234), ul Kievskaya 2, US$50 for a double room (metro Kievskaya); ***Hotel Sputnik*** (☎ 938 7106,), pro Leninski 38, US$50 for a double (metro Leninski Prospekt); ***Hotel Tsentralnaya*** (☎ 229 8589), ul Tverskaya 10, US$50 for a double (metro Tverskaya); and ***Hotel Ural*** (☎ 917 4258), ul Pokrovka 40, US$60 for a double (metro Krasnye Vorota).

The popular concept of **bed and breakfast** (homestays) now exists in Moscow. Private rooms or fully furnished apartments are available and additional meals if required. Guided tours, tickets for theatres, and translators can also be arranged. Costs start from US$40 per day. A large number of homestays are advertised in the *Moscow Times*, and these include Rezon (☎ 369 6231), Vita Agency (☎ 265 4948) and Ya Servis (☎ 231 0053, per Pyatnitsky 8).

Mid-range accommodation

Hotel Aeroflot (☎ 155 5624, 151 0442), on pro Leningradsky 37, offers excellent value at US$48 per person. The hotel is between metros Dynamo and Aeroport. This recently renovated hotel has 120 rooms, each with a separate bathroom. The fourth floor is used by Monkey Business and Russia Experience whose major clients are budget Trans-Siberians. The hotel boasts a 24-hour restaurant, bar, sauna and laundry.

Hotel Moskva (☎ 292 1000, fax 925 0155), on Okhotni Ryad 2, is well located and costs US$45 twin share per person. The closest metro station is Okhotny Ryad. The *Hotel Rossiya* (☎ 298 5400, fax 298 5541), at ul Varvarka 6 (formerly ul Razina), is the world's second biggest hotel and also the closest hotel to Red Square, and starts from US$45 twin share per person. The closest metro station is Katai-Gorod. Both of these hotels are renowned mafia hangouts, however, and there have been numerous reports of petty pilfering from rooms.

Hotel Izmaulovo Block D (☎ 166 4127, fax 166 7486), at Izmaulovski Sosshe 71 is a giant hotel divided into six blocks, with Intourist having an office in Block D. Rooms cost US$44 twin share per person. The closest metro station is Izmaulovski Park.

At US$45 per person in a double room, the *MNTK budget guesthouse* (☎ 483 0460, fax 485 5954), at bulvar Beskudnikovski 59A, is good value. Being right next door to the Hotel Pullman Iris, even a taxi driver should be able to find it.

Other choices with double rooms for around US$110 are *Hotel Belgrad* (☎ 248 1643, fax 230 2129), ul Smolenskaya 8 (metro Smolenskaya); *Hotel Budapest* (☎ 924 8820, fax 921 1266), lini Petrovskie 2/18 (metro Kuznetski Most); *Hotel Kosmos* (☎ 217 0785, fax 215 8880), pro Mira 150 (metro VDNKh); and *Hotel Ukraina* (☎ 243 3030, fax 243 3092), pro Kutuzovski 2/1 (metro Kievskaya).

Upmarket hotels

The luxurious *Hotel Metropol* (☎ 927 6000, fax 927 6010), close to Red Square at Teatralni proezd 1, is as much a historic monument as a hotel for it was here that Rasputin is said to have dined, and Lenin to have made several speeches. Its beautiful Art Nouveau interior featured in the film *Dr Zhivago*. Rooms cost from US$200 twin share per person to US$1500 for a suite.

Other five-star international hotels include the *Hotel Savoy* (☎ 929 8590, fax 230 2186) at ul Rozhdestvenka 3, also close to Red Square, charging from US$175 twin share per person (metro Lubyanka); the *Hotel Pullman Iris* (☎ 203 0131) at 10 Korovinskoye shosse, with swimming-pool and single rooms from US$200; and the similarly-priced *Marco Polo* (☎ 202 28 48) at 9 Spiridonevsky.

The *Hotel Radisson Slavyanskaya* (☎ 941 8020, fax 941 8000, 240 6915) at nab Berezhkovsaya 2, charges US$126 twin share per person. The closest metro station is Kievskaya.

The *Hotel Aerostar* (☎ 224 80 00), at 37 Leningradsky Prospekt (seven km from the centre of town towards the airport), has rooms from US$215.

The *Hotel Intourist* (☎ 956 8426, fax 956 8450), at ul Tverskaya 3/5, is a popular choice since it's very close to Red Square. Prices start from US$75 twin share per person reaching up to US$225 for a two room, three bed apartment. Breakfast costs US$5. The closest metro station is Okhoti Ryad.

You can see the Kremlin and Red Square from the windows of the *Hotel National* (☎ 258 7000, fax 258 7100) next door at Okhotny Ryad 14/1. Prices starts at US$210 twin share per person. The closest metro station is Okhoty Ryad.

WHERE TO EAT

The restaurant scene in Moscow is changing very fast with new places opening daily. The food you are likely to get, however, will either be the standard Russian fare ('cutlet', very cheap) or something served up by joint-venture restaurants which is Western food at Western prices. Nowadays all shops and markets are well stocked; by buying your own food and drink, you will cut costs considerably.

Some Moscow restaurants slap a **cover charge** on your bill as well as a service charge. These extras can mount up to US$10. As they won't be printed on the menu, ask before you order if there will be any extra charges on top of the food cost.

Budget restaurants
These generally fall into two categories: cheap Russian restaurants and cheap fast food outlets. Restaurants in the former category can be very cheap if you're with a Russian speaker but if not you may well be ripped off. Some serve champagne and caviare, so bills can mount up if you're not careful. In this group, try the *Praga*, a Soviet-style vault on the edge of Arbat St, the *Arbat* further up (there's a big Aeroflot globe above the entrance) or the *Café Margarita* (by Patriarch's Pond, metro: Mayakovskaya) – excellent value, with blinis and caviare for US$4, but

---

The Moscow area code is ☎ 095. From outside Russia dial +7-095.

it can get very crowded. For a meal with a view, try the revolving *Seventh Heaven Restaurant* on the top of the Ostankino television tower (metro: VDNK) where prices, surprisingly, are quite reasonable. To get into the Ostankino tower you need to show your passport.

If you simply want cheap fast food, try *Rostik's* fried chicken bar in GUM: Col Sanders has little to worry about but it's not bad and is considerably more interesting than a visit to one of the ever-multiplying branches of *McDonald's*. If you do go there you will find a Big Mac for US$2. Other McDonald's branches are at ul Arbat 50 near metro Smolenskaya, per Gazetny 6 near metro Okhotny Ryad, pro Mira near metro Prospekt Mira, and Sokolniki near metro Sokolniki, and pl Pushkina 29 near metro Pushkinskaya. The pl Pushkina McDonald's claims to be the world's busiest and serves an average of 50,000 customers per day.

There are several new cafés and bars on **ul Arbat** which might be worth a look. Those staying at the TGHM will doubtless make use of the *Kombis* sandwich bar on Prospekt Mira 46-48, which produces excellent filled rolls (US$2-4), or the *Flamingo* chicken restaurant next door (more expensive) at Prospekt Mira 152 or ul Tverskaya 2. A little further up the street is an *Italian bar* which even serves

Vegetarian restaurants

The *Indian Tandoor* (☎ 299 5925) at ul Tverskaya 30/2 (metro Maykovskaya) is recommended. US$12 buys a banquet and US$20 a big night with drinks.

The *Starlite Diner* (☎ 290 9638) at ul Bolshaya Sadovaya 16 (metro Maykovskaya) oozes Americans and serves a great vegiburger for US$8. The *Georgian Guriya* (☎ 246 0378) at pro Komsomolski 7/3 (metro Park Kultury) has great soups, thick Georgian bread and tasty eggplant.

Taganka Blues (☎ 915 1004) at ul Verkhnyaya Radishchevskaya 15 serves Russian food and US$20 gets you great zakuski, pelmeni and drinks in a lively exciting atmosphere. Great service and entertainment including jazz. The *Skazka Café* (☎ 271 0998) at per Tovarishchesky 1 offers good traditional Russian food served amidst cosy Hans Christian Andersen decor. You'll eat well for US$10.

Upmarket restaurants

The best restaurants are still to be found in the expensive hotels (see above). Other places to try include *La Cantina*, the Tex Mex bar by the Hotel Intourist. Service is provided by American language students, giving an almost authentic Texan atmosphere. The food's not bad but quite expensive at US$12-16 for a main course and beer at US$3. There's another Tex Mex bar, *Armadillo*, behind GUM. *Patio Pizza,* opposite the Pushkin Museum, is highly recommended. The *Spanish Bar and Restaurant* is on the ground floor of the Hotel Moskva. A main course should cost about US$8 here. Just around the corner, the *Paradise Restaurant* is more expensive (US$6 for a gin and tonic or US$15 for a hamburger).

Other foreign restaurants include the *Shamrock Pub* in the Irish Arbat department store on ul Novy Arbat 19, where you can get draught Guinness for US$4 and various bar snacks. *Rosie O Grady's*, at ul Znamenka 9 (metro: Biblioteka Lenina) is another Irish place. A large meal here will cost you US$8, with Guinness also at US$4. It really does look authentic and is a good place to meet homesick travellers. Credit cards are accepted for orders over US$50 and it's open at weekends until 1am.

Pizza Hut on ul Tverskaya serves some fairly average pizzas. Unless you buy a slice on the street, however, this is the expensive branch, so bank on paying US$6-12 for a small pizza. Russian beer is US$3. A cheaper outlet is at Kutusovsky Prospekt 17 (metro: Kievskaya).

Supermarkets

Well stocked supermarkets include **Super Siwa** (ul Slavyanksi 6), **Garden Ring** (ul Bolshaya Sadovaya 1, pro Leninsky 113 and ul Serafimovicha 2, metro: Mayakovskaya), **Novo-Arbatski Gastrom** (ul Novy Arbat 13) and **Irish Arbat department** store (ul Novy Arbat 19). As food sampling is currently a big fad in Moscow, the really poverty stricken can always get a free feed in one of these supermarkets.

❏ **Mummification for the masses**

The Centre for Biological Researches, responsible for the preservation of Lenin's body, recently announced the offer of full mummification services to anyone for a mere US$300,000.

Previous clients are a testimony to their considerable skill. An independent team of embalmers recently inspected Lenin's corpse and declared it to be in perfect condition. After his death on 21 January 1924, an autopsy was carried out and a full report published in *Pravda*. The public were treated to a list of weights and measurements of most of the internal organs of their dead leader (his brain weighed 1340g – far larger than average). Then the embalmers began their work. One wonders if the decision the Central Executive Committee took in 1924 to preserve Lenin's body, had anything to do with Howard Carter's discovery of the Pharaoh Tuthankamun fourteen months earlier.

In 1997 Lenin was put back on display after a three-month cosmetic make-over. The debate over what to do with him continues with liberal politicians suggesting that Russia should bury its past and Communists arguing that to move Lenin now would be a denial of the country's history. Meanwhile the former leader continues to be an excellent advertisement for the services of the Centre for Biologiocal Researches. Dr Zbarsky, who headed the original team of embalmers, boasted that Lenin's body would remain unchanged indefinitely. This claim is reiterated by Dr Yuri Denisov-Nikolsky, who hopes to attract rich American corpses.

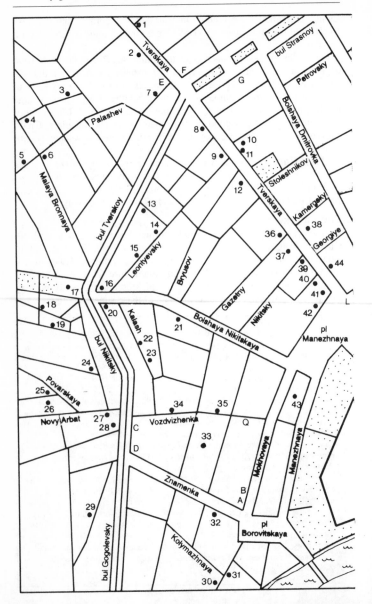

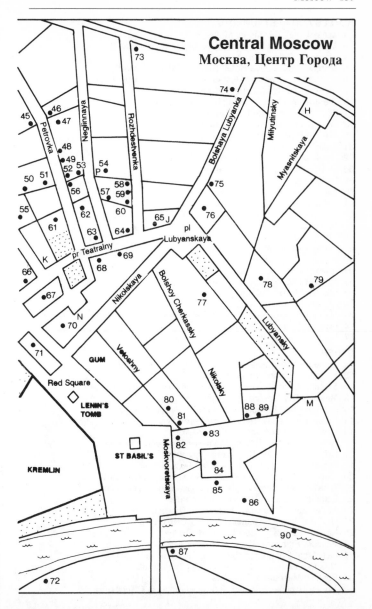

Central Moscow
Москва, Центр Города

HOTELS AND RESTAURANTS
1 Minsk Hotel Гостиница Минск
3 Moskovskie Zori Restaurant Ресторан Московские Зори
4 Margarita Café Кафе Маргарита
5 Marco Polo-Preshya Hotel Гостинца Марко Поло-Пресня
6 Scandinavia Swedish Restaurant Ресторан Скандинавия
7 McDonald's Restaurant Макдоналдс
10 Tsentralnaya Hotel Гостиница Центральная
11 Pizza Hut Restaurant Пицца Хат
13 Junk Boat Chinese Restaurant Ресторан Junk Boat
28 Prague Restaurant Ресторан Прага
31 Patio Pizza Патио Пицца
32 Rosie O'Grady's Pub Бар Рози Огрэдис
36 McDonald's Restaurant Макдоналдс
39 La Kantina Restaurant Ресторан La Kantina
40 Intourist Hotel Гостиница Интурист
41 National Hotel Гостиница Националь
44 Kombi's Restaurant Ресторан Kombi
47 Budapest Hotel Гостиница Будапешт
48 News Pub Бар
53 Rocky Restaurant Ресторан Rocky
60 Pizzeria Пиццерия
64 Savoy Hotel Гостиница Савой
67 Moskva Hotel Гостиница Москва
68 Metropol Hotel Гостиница Метрополь
80 Armadillo Bar Бар Armadillo
81 Manhattan Express American Restaurant Ресторан Manhattan Express
84 Rossiya Hotel Гостиница Россия
87 Baltschug-Kempinski Hotel Гостиница Балчуг-Кемпинский

OTHER
2 Museum of Russian Revolutions Музей Революции
8 Nightflight Disco Дискотека
9 Moscow Drama Theatre Московсий Драмитический Театр
12 Moscow City Goverment Building Мэрия
14 Azerbaidzhan Embassy Посольство Азербайджана
15 Ukraine Embassy Посольство Украины
16 ITAR-TASS news agency ИТАР-ТАСС
17 Grand Ascension Church Большая Вознесеная Цекровь
18 Georgia Embassy Посольство Грузии
19 Tadjikistan Embassy Посольство Таджикстана
20 Mayakovsky House-Museum Дом-Музей Маяковского
21 Tchaikovsky Conservatory Консерватория имени Чайковского
22 Estonia Embassy Посольство Эстонии
23 Netherlands Embassy Посольство Нидерландов
24 USA & Canada Institute Институт США и Канады
25 Norway Embassy Посольство Норвегии
26 Belgium Embassy Посольство Бельгии
27 Irish Arbat Department Store Ирландский Дом
29 Turkmen Embassy Посольство Туркменистана
30 Pushkin Museum of Fine Arts
   Музей Изобразительных Искусств имени А С Пушкина

33 Russian State Library Российская Государственная Библиотека
34 Friendship House Дом Дружбы
35 Military Department Store Воинторг
37 Central Post Office Центральный Телеграф
38 Finnair & Malev Airline Offices Finnair Malev Авиа Касса
42 Intourist Travel Agency Интурист
43 Central Exhibition Hall Центральный Выставочный Зал
45 Intourtrans Travel Agency Интуртранс
46 Aeroflot Airlines Office Касса Аэрофлотаа
49 Petrovsky Passazh Department Store Универмаг Петровский Пассаж
50 SAS Airline Office SAS Авиакасса
51 JAL Airline Office JAL Авиакасса
52 Atlas Map Shop Магазин Атлас
54 Moldova Embassy Посольство Молдавии
55 Operetta Theatre Театр Оперетты
56 Air China Airline Office Air China Авиакасса
57 Hungry Duck Disco Дискотека Hungry Duck
58 Iberia Restaurant Ресторан Иберия
59 City Excursion Bureau Московское Городское Экскурсонное Бюро
61 Bolshoi Theatre Большой Театр
62 TsUM Department Store ЦУМ
63 Maly Theatre Малый Театр
65 Detskiy Mir Children's Department Store Универмаг Детский Мир
66 State Duma Parliament House Государственная Дума
69 Arkadia Jazz Club Джаз Клуб Аркадия
70 Former Lenin Museum Бывший Центральный Музей Ленина
71 State Historical Museum Государственный Исторический Музей
72 UK Embassy Британское Посольство
73 Nativity of Our Lady Cathedral Рождественский Собор
74 Church of Vladimir Mother of God Церковь Владимирской Богоматери
75 KGB Museum Музей КГБ
76 Former KGB Headquarters Лубянка
77 Moscow City History Museum Музей Истории Города Москвы
78 St Nicholas Church Никольская церковь
79 Belarus Embassy Посольство Белоруссии
82 St Barbara's Church Церковь Святово Варвары
83 Monastery of the Sign Belltower Колокольня Знаменского Монастыря
85 Central Concert Hall Центральный Концертный Зал
86 Church of St Anne's Conception Церковь Святой Зачатия Анны
88 St George's Church Церковь Святово Святово Георгия
89 17th Century Art Museum Художественний музей 17 века
90 Boat Landing Пристань

METRO STATIONS Станция Метро

A Borovitskaya Боровитска
B Biblioteka im Lenina
   Библиотека имени Ленинаz
C Arbatskaya 1 Арбатская
D Arbatskaya 2 Арбатская
E Tverskaya Тверская
F Pushkinskaya Пушкинская
G Chekhovskaya Чеховская
H Turgenevskaya Тургеневская

J Lubyanka Лубянка
K Teatralnaya Театральная
L Okhotny Ryad Охотный Ряд
M Kitai-Gorod Китай-Город
N Ploshchad Revolyutsi
   Площадь Революции
P Kuznetsky Most
   Кузнецкий Мост
Q Aleksandrovski Sad
   Александровский Сад

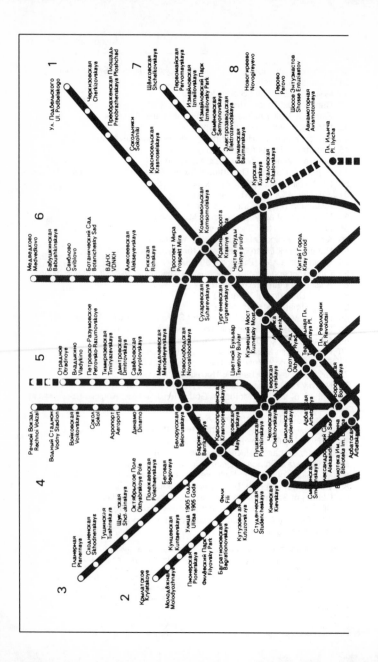

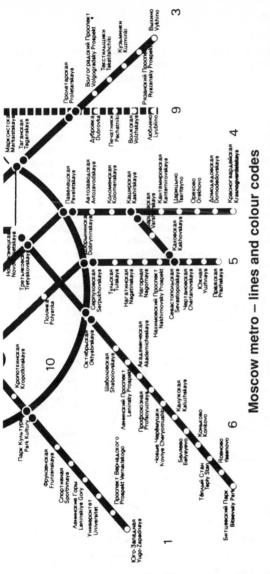

Moscow metro – lines and colour codes

1 (Red) Sokolnicheskaya Сокольническая
2 (Light blue) Filevskaya Филевская
3 (Purple) Tagansko-Krasnopresenskaya Таганско-Краснопресненская
4 (Light green) Zamoskvoretskaya Замоскворецкая
5 (Grey) Serpukhovsko-Timryazevskaya Серпуховско-Тимирязевская

6 (Orange) Kaluzhsko-Rizhskaya Калужско-Рижская
7 (Dark blue) Arbatsko-Pokrovskaya Арбатско-Покровская
8 (Yellow) Kalininskaya Калининская
9 (Dark green) Line under construction Строящиеся Линии
10 (Brown) Circular Кольцевая

WHAT TO SEE

Red Square

This wide cobbled square, *Krasnaya Ploshchad* in Russian, extends across the area beside the north-eastern wall of the Kremlin. The main sights around the square are St Basil's Cathedral, Lenin's Mausoleum, the GUM Department Store and the Kremlin.

St Basil's Cathedral

Also known as the Church of the Saviour and nicknamed the Pineapple Church by Victorian travellers, this whimsical architectural creation is as much a symbol of Moscow as Tower Bridge is of London. Commissioned by Ivan the Terrible, it was completed in 1561 and so pleased with the result was the Tsar that he had the architect's eyes put out so that he would never be able to produce anything to equal or surpass it. Apparently the architect went on to produce other buildings, so perhaps this is a tall story, but it's a good one fitting the Tsar's character perfectly. St Basil's is a quite incredible building, with its nine brightly-painted, dissimilar domes and the stone-work decorated with intricate patterns more usually found on the wooden buildings of the time. For many years a museum, it has been returned to the Church.

Moscow - The Kremlin

1 War Memorial
2 Kutafya Tower
3 Trinity Tower
4 Palace of Congress
5 Church of the Twelve Apostles
6 Church of the Deposition of the Virgin's Robe
7 Cathedral of the Assumption
8 Tsar Cannon
9 Bell Tower of Ivan III
10 Tsar Bell
11 Cathedral of the Archangel
12 Cathedral of the Annunciation
13 Faceted Palace
14 Saviour Cathedral
15 Terem Palace
16 Grand Kremlin Palace
17 Armoury
18 Poteshny Palace
19 Arsenal
20 Senate
21 Supreme Soviet
22 Spassky Tower
23 Ticket Kiosks
24 Patriarch's Palace

Lenin's Mausoleum
Built onto the side of the Kremlin in 1930, the red granite mausoleum and its mummified occupant are something of an embarrassment to the current regime. Tourists still queue up to file past the once-revered corpse, laid out in its dark suit and polka-dot tie. Lenin currently receives visitors from 10:00-13:00, but not on Monday or Friday.

The mausoleum was the centre of a cult that flourished for almost 70 years. The cubist design is the work of A.V.Shchusev who envisaged the cube, like the pyramid, as a symbol of eternity and it was his plan that every Soviet home would have its own little cube to the memory of the dead leader. Until the early 1990s, no Soviet town was without a Lenin statue, and no public office lacked a Lenin portrait.

There are plans to move Lenin's body to the family plot in St Petersburg after the more important reburial of the Tsar and his family has been completed. Behind the mausoleum are the graves of other communist heroes, including Brezhnev and Stalin, and these will be moved to Novodevichy Cemetery. The fate of the building itself is uncertain. Campaigners want it demolished and replaced with the statue of Kuzma Minin and Prince Pozharsky (famed for saving Moscow during the 'Times of Troubles' in the early 17th century) that originally stood on the spot but is now in front of St Basil's.

GUM
The remarkable glass-roofed GUM building (pronounced 'goom') was constructed in 1894 as a shopping mall where individual traders could set up their stalls. It was nationalised after the Revolution and turned into a huge state store, a monument to Soviet shortages, but following the recent market reforms the Western chains have moved in. You can now buy anything from a Benetton sweater to the latest compact disc, but most Muscovites can afford only to browse. There are a couple of bars and restaurants here as well as fast-food stands.

The Tomb of the Unknown Soldier
It is traditional for bridal couples to visit this monument in the Aleksandrovski Gardens on their wedding day, to be photographed beside the eternal flame. Beneath the marble lies the body of one of the soldiers who helped to stop the German advance on Moscow in 1941.

The Kremlin
The heart of Moscow and the seat of the Russian government, the Kremlin is, in fact, a large walled castle. Although the site has been continuously occupied for at least the last 800 years, the walls and many of the cathedrals date from the fifteenth century. There are 20 towers, the most famous being the **Saviour Tower** above Red Square. Russian officials drive through its gate to work. The Kremlin's main entrance and

ticket office is in **Kutafya Tower**, on the opposite side to Red Square. Note that you may not take large bags or rucksacks in, and that you won't get past the guards if you are wearing shorts.

You buy a ticket to the Kremlin grounds (US$0.20) and then additional tickets for each major museum or group of churches. All the tickets can be bought at the Kutafya Tower or the ticket office in the Aleksandrovski Park. Check large bags into the left luggage office under the Kutafya Tower. As tours for some of the museums start at particular times, your tickets may have a time printed on them. To prevent disappointment, you can always buy your tickets a few days ahead. You can also buy tickets for the individual museums and churches at their respective doors. The Kremlin grounds are open 10:00-17:00, closed Thursday.

Cathedral Square

In the centre of the Kremlin is a square around which stand four cathedrals and the **Bell Tower** of Ivan the Great (81m/263ft high), which Napoleon attempted to blow up in 1812. Beneath the tower stands the **Tsar Bell**, at 200 tons the heaviest in the world. The piece of the bell that stands beside it broke off during the fire of 1737. Nearby is the largest calibre **cannon** in the world.

The **Cathedral of the Assumption**, the work of an Italian, was completed in 1479 and was the traditional place of coronation for Russia's tsars. During the last coronation, on 26 May 1896, something happened that was taken by those who saw it as a bad omen: as Nicholas II walked up the steps to the altar, the chain of the Order of St Anthony fell from his shoulders to the floor. Inside are three thrones; the wooden one to the right as you enter belonged to Ivan the Terrible.

The **Cathedral of the Archangel Mikhael** (1505-09) looks classically Russian from the outside but the hand of its Italian architect Alevisio Novi can be seen in the light interior. Forty-six tsars (including Ivan the Great and Ivan the Terrible) are buried here. The smaller **Cathedral of the Annunciation** (1484-89), the private chapel of the tsars, was the work of Russian architects and contains icons by the great master, Andrei Rublyev. The **Church of the Deposition of the Robe** (1484-5) was designed as a private chapel for the clergy. The Patriarch worshipped in the **Church of the 12 Apostles** next door to his residence.

Other buildings The **Great Kremlin Palace**, now a government building, is not usually open to visitors. One wall of the Italian-designed **Faceted Chamber** (so-called because of its facade of pointed stone blocks) faces Cathedral Square. The **Golden Tsarina Palace** or Terem Palace has a striking red and white tiled roof. The seat of Russian government is the modern **Palace of Congress**. The **Armoury** should not be missed (entry is US$14, or US$7 for students) as it contains a dazzling display of various tsars' jewellery and regalia, weapons and armour. Of special interest to Trans-Siberian passengers is the ornate **Great Siberian Easter Egg** (probably the finest of the 56 famous Imperial Easter Eggs made by Carl Fabergé), which contains a clockwork model of the train, complete with golden engine (with a ruby for the headlight), five gold coaches and a church-car (Hall III).

Tretyakov Art Gallery
The best collection of icons and sculpture in Russia is housed here. There are icons painted by Andrei Rublyev; *Christ's First Appearance to the People* which took Alexander Ivanov 20 years to complete; and two halls devoted to the great Russian masters, Ilya Repin and Vasily Surikov. The gallery is at 10 Lavrushinsky Perelok, (Metro: Tretyakovskaya). The museum (☎ 230 7788) is at pro Lavrushinski 12 and is open daily (except Mon) 10:00 to 19:00.

Pushkin Museum of Fine Arts
Most interesting for its large collection of Impressionist paintings including many famous canvases (Manet's *Déjeuner sur l'Herbe* for example, and Monet's *Boulevard des Capucines*). There are also galleries of Egyptian antiquities and Old Masters. Well worth a visit, the gallery is at 12 ul Volkhonka, (metro: Kropotkinskaya). The museum (☎ 203 9578) is at ul Volkhonka 12 and is open daily (except Mon) 10:00 to 19:00.

Old Arbat Street (Stari Arbat)
This pedestrianised shopping street is very popular with tourists. As in Covent Garden, there are buskers, street artists and swarms of souvenir sellers hawking everything from matrioshkas to military jackets. Bargain hard and watch out for pickpockets. At the western end, you'll find one of the eight McDonald's in Russia.

Novodevichy Convent
This beautiful sixteenth century walled convent is well worth visiting. Dating back to the sixteenth century it has been used at various times as a fortress (it held out against the Poles during a siege in 1610) and a prison (it was here that Peter the Great banished his sister Sophia, among others). Although Napoleon tried to blow it up in 1812 it remained undamaged: one brave nun rushed in and extinguished the fuses to the powder kegs at the last minute. The **cathedral** is famous for its frescoes and highly ornate, multi-tiered iconostasis (the backdrop to the altar), all recently restored. It also contains a small museum. Novodevichy is open 08:00-18:00 daily but closed Tuesday and the first Monday of the month. (Nearest metro: Sportivnaya).

Behind the convent is the **cemetery**. As well as graves of many influential people (including Khrushchev, Chekhov and Prokofiev), there are some outlandish gravestones: one soldier lies under a model tank. Stalin, Gagarin and Brezhnev will probably be moved here from Red Square.

Other museums, galleries and churches in Moscow

There is simply not room in a guide-book of this type to give details of
more than a few of Moscow's 150 museums and exhibitions. However a
few of the best are the **Andrei Rublyov Ancient Russian Culture and
Art Museum** (☎ 278 1467), pl Andronyevskaya 10, open 10:00-18:00,
closed Wed; **Museum of Astronauts** (☎ 286 3714), ul 1st Ostankinskaya
41/9; **Borodino Battle Field Panorama** (☎ 148 1965), pro Kutuzovski
38, open 10:30-20:00, open Sat to Thur; **Federal Counterintelligence
Service (KGB) Museum** (☎ 224 1982), ul Lubyanka 12/1s; and **Former
Political Prisoners Museum** (☎ 925 0144), ul Chaplyghina 15. There are
other museums devoted to Gorky, Tolstoy, Dostoyevsky, Pushkin,
Chekhov, Gogol, Glinka, Lermontov.

DAY TRIPS FROM MOSCOW

A visit to the cathedrals and churches of **Sergiev Posad** (formerly
Zagorsk, see p171), 75km from Moscow, is the most interesting day trip.
Until 1988, it was the seat of the Russian Orthodox Church and today, it
is still the site of one of the most important seminaries in the country.

A half day trip to Russia's **Star City** (Zvezdny Gorodok), 30km from
Moscow, is a must if you are interested in outer space. This is the centre
responsible for controlling all manned spacecraft and space station activities. Of particular interest is the Star City Museum, the Space Station
Simulators Hall and the Neutral Buoyancy Simulator. See p298.

NIGHTLIFE

Tickets for the **Bolshoi Theatre** (☎ 292 0050), ul Theatralni, are easy to
come by if you don't mind paying US$50 for them: try the service bureau
in your hotel or the Intourist office. There's a ticket office at the theatre

---

❏ **Abramtsevo Estate** (Абрамцево)
About 80km from Moscow is **Abramtsevo Estate,**one of the most important
centres of Russian culture in the second half of the 19th century. Today it's a
museum and well worth a day trip. The estate was originally known as
Obromkovo Pustosh when the current wooden house was built in the 1770s.
Bought in 1843 by the Slavophile writer Sergei Aksakov it became the regular
haunt of eminent Russian writers and actors including Gogol and Turgenev. In
1870, the estate was purchased by the railway tycoon and art connoisseur, Savva
Mamontov. It was then turned into a colony for artists who shared a belief in the
greatness of Russian native art and architecture but were concerned that it faced
extinction by rapid industrialisation – ironic considering the estate's patron.

From Moscow, take a suburban train from Yaroslavski station bound for
either Sergiev Posad (Сергиев Посад) or Aleksandrov (Александров), both to
the north of Abramtsevo. Get off at Abramtsevo. This trip takes 70 minutes. It's
a 15 minute walk from the station.

but all tickets are usually bought up by black marketeers. If you want a cheap ticket, stand around outside the opera house before the performance and they'll find you. You'll be quoted prices of US$10-40 depending on how gullible they think you are. Barter and remember that the later you leave it before the performance the more anxious they'll be to get rid of their tickets. Check the date and time of the performance on the ticket before you hand over any cash.

The **Moscow State Circus** performs two shows daily at the arena beside Tsvetnoye Blvd metro station. Tickets are readily available and cost US$2. The human performers are generally excellent but Western visitors tend to be dismayed by the animal acts.

There are dozens of **night clubs** in Moscow. Get your Russian friends to ring them before you go so that you can get an idea of their clientele. Don't be put off by the Kalashnikov toting bouncers. Try **0-11 Club** (☎ 245 3272), ul Sadovaya-Kudrinskaya 19, building 2, just behind American Express, entry US$10; **Arkadiya Jazz Club** (☎ 926 9008), pro Teatralny 3, which specialises in free jamming and its US$5 entry charge includes free drink; **Hungry Duck Club** (☎ 923 6158), ul Pushechnaya 9) US$4 entry which promises 'reckless dancing on the bar'.

Techno, Underground and **Dance clubs** include **Galaktika**, cinema Progress, pro Lomonosovsky 17 (metro Universitet); **Treasure Island** (☎ 318 6795), Hotel Sevastopol, metro Sevastopolskaya; **X-Dance** (☎ 425 8000), Hanoi cinema, bul Litovsky 7; **Utopia** (☎ 229 0003), Rossia cinema, pl Pushkinskaya 2; and **MegaDance-2 Club**, Tbilisi cinema, ul Novocheremushkinskaya 53.

WHAT TO BUY

Most foreigners end up buying their matrioshkas, ceramic boxes and furry hats from street sellers, although you'll need to check quality first and then bargain hard. The best place to go is Ismailovsky Park at a weekend: you'll find everything from stolen icons to Stalin pictures. It's easy to get to as you go to metro Ismailovsky Park and then just need to follow the crowds to the market, which is about a five-minute walk away.

MOVING ON

By air

Moscow is not the best city in which to buy international air tickets as you rarely get a discount. Aeroflot is generally the cheapest airline. The main airlines are **Aeroflot International**, (☎ 156 8019), ul Petrovka 20; **Aeroflot Domestic**, ul Petrovka 15; **Air China** (☎ 292 6896), ul Kuznetsky Most 1/8; **Air France** (☎ 234 3377), ul Korovy Val 7; **Alitalia** (☎ 923 9840), ul Pushechnaya 7; **ANA**-All Nippon Airways (☎ 253 1546) nab Krasnopresnenskaya 12, office 1405; **British Airways** (☎ 253

2492), Krasnopresnenskaya 12, office 1905; **Delta Airlines** (253 2658), Krasnopresnenskaya 12, office 1102a; **Finnair** (☎ 292 8788), per Kamergerski 6; **JAL** (☎ 921 6448), ul Kuznetski Most 3; **KLM** (☎ 258 3600, 956 1666), Krasnopresnenskaya 12, office 1307; **LOT** (☎ 2380 003), ul Korovy Val 7, office 5; **Lufthansa** (☎ 975 2501), pro Olympiyski 18/1; **MIAT**-Mongolian Airlines (☎ 241 3757), per Spasopeskovsky 7/1; **SAS** (☎ 925 4747), ul Kuznetski Most 3; **Swissair** (☎ 253 8988), Krasnopresnenskaya 12, office 2005; **Transaero** Russian Airlines (☎ 292 7513, 292 7526), Hotel Moskva, ul Okhotny Ryad 2.

From Moscow's various local airports, there are frequent flights to St Petersburg (US$95), and many cities in Siberia including Ekaterinburg (US$175), Irkutsk (US$300), Khabarovsk (US$475), Novosibirsk (US$315), Ulan Ude (US$350) and Vladivostok (US$378): all daily.

By rail

Trains from Siberia arrive either at Yaroslavski or Kazanski stations (both at pl Komsomolskaya). For Moscow and St Petersburg trains, see p143.

Getting railway tickets and information There are a number of places around Moscow to get tickets for foreigners. These include the railway stations, Transport Agency, Central Railway Booking Agency and resellers. If you want to get the cheaper tickets for locals but run the risk of a fine, try any of the normal windows at the first three places. Railway information (in Russian) can be obtained on ☎ 266 9000-9.

Railway stations sell tickets only for trains that depart from their station. In most there is an Intourist window selling foreigner tickets.

● **Tsentralnoe Zheleznodorozhnoe Agentstvo** (Central Railway Booking Agency), beside the Yaroslavski station (☎ 266 0004, metro Komsomolskaya) is the easiest place to buy your own Trans-Siberian ticket. The only sign indicating which windows to queue up in front of is in Russian and it has the word Иностранцы painted on it. It may be also worth trying window 2 for tickets to destinations within the ex-USSR and windows 5 to 8 for other destinations. Until recently, tickets could also be bought at the Transport Agency (*Transagenstvo*), also beside Yaroslavski station. However nowadays only foreigners with a residential visa can purchase tickets from here.

The Central Railway Booking Agency has three other offices around the city. The offices are open from 8:00 to 13:00 and 14:00 to 19:00:

● **Tsentralnoe Zheleznodorozhnoe Agentstvo** ul Maly Kharitonevsky 6/11 (formerly ul Griboedova) (☎ 262 9605, 262 7935, 262 0604, fax 921 7934). The closest metros are Chistye Prudy and Krasnaya Vorota. For tickets to ex-USSR destinations, go to windows 1 to 3 in Hall 1 of Building (Korpus) 1. Tickets will be sold for departures on the following day up to 10 days. For tickets to other countries, go to windows 7 and 8 on the ground floor of Building 2. Tickets will be sold for departures on the following day up to 30 days ahead.

● **Tsentralnoe Zheleznodorozhnoe Agentstvo** pro Leningradskaya 1, (☎ 262 3342). The closest metro is Belorusskaya. To get to it from the Belorussia Station, cross the railway bridge and you will see it on the corner of pro Leningradskaya and ul Nizhnyaya. It is entered from the lane on the west side of pro Leningradskaya. Tickets are sold for departures on the following day up to 30 days from windows 9 and 10.

● **Tsentralnoe Zheleznodorozhnoe Agentstvo** ul Mozhayski val 4/6, (☎ 240 0505). The closest metro is Kievskaya which is about 1km away.

There are a number of resellers around Moscow who mark up foreigner tickets a further 5-20%. If you do not speak Russian, then they're worth using. There are few English speakers at Intertrans, however it is still worth a try as it is conveniently located in the centre of the city.

● **G & R International** (☎ 374 7366, fax 374 6132, e-mail grint@glas.apc.org), Block 6, Office 4, Institute of Youth, ul Yunosti 5/1. Closest metro is Vykhino; from in front of the station, take buses No 197 or 697 for 5 or 7 stops to the Institute of Youth, *Institut Molodyozhi*.

● **Intourist** (☎ 292 2294) is at ul Mokhovaya 13, around the corner from the Intourist Hotel and by the National Hotel. Open 9:00-20:00.

● **IRO Travel** (☎ 971 4059, 280 8562, fax 280 7686, e-mail tgh@glas.apc.org), 10th floor, ul Bolshaya Pereyaslavksaya 50, at the Travellers Guest House. Open 10:00-18:00.

● **Intertrans** (☎ 927 1181), 2nd floor, ul Petrovka 15, which is near the Bolshoi Theatre. The closest metro is Kuznetski Most. Open 9:00-20:00 weekdays, 9:00-19:00 weekends.

❏ **Luggage Lockers** (Автоматические Камеры Хранения)

It's worth explaining how to use the combination-lock luggage lockers, called *avtomaticheskie kamery khranenia*, at stations because they're not as straightforward as they look. To store luggage, get a token from the supervisor,and choose a locker within view of the supervisor. On the inside of the door is a set of four combination locks. Select a combination of three numbers and one Cyrillic character. Write the combination and the locker number down immediately. Put in the token and close the door and twirl around the knobs on the outside of the locker. To get your luggage out, set the combination on the knobs and wait two seconds until you hear the electric lock click back. Some lockers require you to put in a second token before the electric lock clicks back. If there is a problem call the supervisor. (Bribes are not necessary). They can open any locker but first you must describe what your luggage looks like. The supervisor can open up to three lockers at once for you. If you want more opened because you have forgotten which locker you put your luggage in, the supervisor has to call a militia officer. After finding your things, you pay a small fine, fill in a form and show the supervisor your passport. Don't forget to write down the code – never rely on your memory as the opening process can take an hour and you may miss your train. You can only leave luggage in the lockers until 23:59 of the next day before it is cleared. The coin operated lockers operate 24 hours a day but are closed several times a day for breaks of up to 30 minutes.

Sergiev Posad
Сергиев Посад

Sergiev-Posad is the most popular tourist attraction in the Golden Ring (see p299) and a must for even those who are 'all churched out'. The city contains Russia's religious capital: the Exalted Trinity Monastery of St Sergius (Troitse-Sergiyeva Lavra). Entering the white walled, 600 year old monastery is like taking a step back into medieval Russia with long bearded monks in traditional black robes and tall *klobuki* hats, and continuous chanting emanating from lamp lit, incense filled churches.

HISTORY

The monastery was founded in 1340 by Sergius of Radonezh (1321-1391) who became the patron saint of Russia. The power of Sergius's monastery grew quickly because he was closely allied to Moscow's princes and actively worked for the unification of Russian lands by building a ring of 23 similar monastery-fortresses around Moscow. The friendship between Moscow's ruler Grand Prince Mitry Donskoi and Sergius was so strong that the when Dmitry asked for the church's blessing in 1380 before he left to battle the Tatar-Mongols at Kulikovo, Sergius himself delivered the service. While the resultant victory had already indicated to Sergius's followers that he had God's ear, 17 years after his death it became obvious that Sergius also had divine protection. The 'proof' of this appeared in 1408 when the Tatar-Mongols levelled the monastery and the only thing that survived unscathed was Sergius's corpse.

Between 1540 and 1550, the monastery was ringed with a massive stone wall and 12 defensive towers. Never again was the complex to fall, not even after an 18 month siege by 20,000 Poles against 1500 defenders in 1608. Both Ivan the Terrible and Peter the Great hid here after fleeing plotting princes in Moscow.

Besides its military function, the monastery was a great centre of learning. It became famous for its *sergievski* style, hand copied books adorned with gold and vermillion letters. Several of these books are on display in the monastery's museum. It is also believed that Russia's first printer, Ivan Fedorov, studied here.

During the 18th century the monastery's spiritual power grew considerably. In 1744, it was elevated to a *lavra* monastery which meant that it was a 'most exalted monastery'. At the time, there were only four lavra monasteries in Russia with the other three being the Kievo-Pechorskaya in Kiev, the Aleksandro-Nevskaya in St Petersburg and Pochayevsko-Uspenskaya in Volyn. In 1749 a Theological College was opened at Sergiev-Posad and in 1814 an Ecclesiastical Academy was created.

Two years after the communists came to power, the monastery was closed down and it was reopened only in 1946 after Stalin fulfilled his side of a pact with the Orthodox Church for their support during the Second World War. The monastery was home to the Patriarch of Russia until 1988 when this was moved to Danilovsky Monastery in Moscow.

WHERE TO STAY

Hotel Druzhba, also known as Hotel Zagorsk, is on pl Sovetskaya. Rooms cost US$34 per person in a double room.

WHERE TO EAT

There are three standard restaurants in town; **Restaurant Russky Dvorik** opposite the Monastery, the **Restaurant Zolotoe Koltso** (also known as Restaurant Golden Ring) which is where most tour groups eat, and the restaurant at the **Hotel Druzhba**.

WHAT TO SEE

Exalted Trinity Monastery of St Sergius

The monastery is spread over six hectares and ringed by a white-washed, 1km long wall which is up to 15m thick. Of the 13 defensive towers, the Duck Tower is interesting as it has a metal duck on its spire, put there for the young Peter the Great to use for archery practice.

Many of the churches are open for services. You can enter those holding services but you may be turned away if you are wearing shorts or have bare shoulders. Photography is generally frowned upon and you should never take photos with a flash, as this damages the icons, nor have your photo taken in front of an icon which is considered disrespectful.

The monastery grounds are open 10:00-18:00 daily and entry is free. You have to pay to get into the monastery's three museums, which are all open 10:00-15:00, closed Mondays. Tickets for the museums are sold in the kiosk at the north end of the Art Museum.

About 200m from the monastery on the road to Moscow are two churches. Both the **Church of St Pareskeva Pyatnitsa** and the **Church of the Presentation of the Mother of God** were built in 1547 which was the year Ivan the Terrible was crowned Tsar. On the opposite side of the road is the attractive **Pyatnitsa Well Chapel**. One of the most popular photographs of Sergiev Posad is taken from just across the river with Pyatnitsa Well Chapel in the foreground and the Church of the Presentation of the Mother of God and the monastery in the background.

HOTELS AND RESTAURANTS

  1 Hotel Druzhba Гостиница Дружба
26 Restaurant Russky Dvorik Ресторан Русский Дворик
27 Restaurant Zolotoe Koltso Ресторан Золотое Колцо
32 Café Minutka Кафе Минутка

OTHER

  2 Stables Конный Двор
  3 Duck Tower Уточья Башня
  4 Pilgrim Gate Tower Каличья Воротная Башня
  5 Bathhouse Баня
  6 Tsar's Palace Царские Дворец
  7 History Museum in Hospital & Church of Saints Zosima & Savvaty
     Исторический Музей (Больничные палаты) и Церковь
     Зосимы и Савватия
  8 Smolensk Church Смоленская Церковь
  9 Bell-tower Колокольня
10 Asumption/Dormition Cathedral Успенский Собор
11 Holy Gates & John the Baptist Gate Church
     Святые Ворота и Надвратная Церковь Иоанна Предтечи
12 Museum Ticket Kiosk Касса
13 Art Museum in former Treasurer's Wing
     Художественный Музей (Казначейский Корпус)
14 Chapel above the Well Надкладезная Часовня
15 Old Art Museum in the Vestry
     Музей Древнерусского Прикладного Искусства (Ризница)
16 Trinity Cathedral Троицкий Собор
17 Descent of the Holy Spirit Church Духовская Церковь
18 St Micah's Church Михеевская Церковь
19 Refectory & St Sergius's Church
     Трапезная Палата и Церковь Святого Сергия
20 Metropolitan's Chambers Митрополичьи Палаты
21 Former Hospital of the Trinity Monastery of St Sergei
     Больница-Богадельня Троице-Сергиевой Лавры
22 Water Gate/Tower Водяные Ворота/Башня
23 St Paraskeva Pyatnitsa Church Пятницкая Церковь
24 Presentation of the Mother of God Church Введенская Церковь
25 Krasnogorskaya Chapel Красногорская Часовня
28 Chapel over St Paraskeva Pyatnitsa's Well
     Часовня Пятницкого Колодца
29 Kazan Church Казанская Церковь
30 Elijah the Prophet's Church Ильинская Церковь
31 Toy Museum Музей Игрушки
33 Ascension Church Вознесенская Церковь
34 Dormition Church Успенская Церковь
35 Bus Station Автовокзал
36 Railway Station Железнодорожний Вокзал

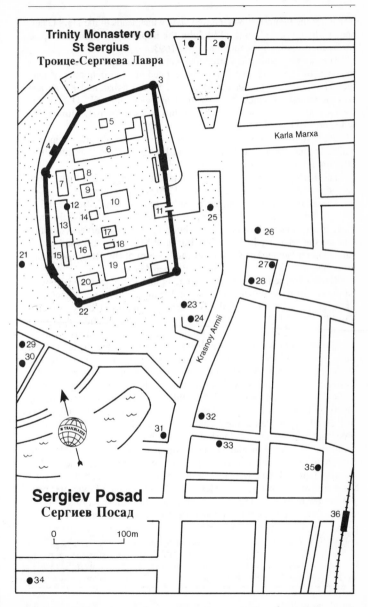

Trinity Monastery of St Sergius
Троице-Сергиева Лавра

Karla Marxa

Krasnoy Armii

Sergiev Posad
Сергиев Посад

0   100m

You enter the monastery via the Red Gate which leads to the Holy Gates, above which is the **Church of St John the Baptist**. The church was paid for by the wealthy Stroganov family in 1693.

The sky blue and gold starred, five cupola **Assumption Cathedral** is the heart of the monastery. It was consecrated in 1585 in honour of Ivan the Terrible's victory over the Mongols near Astrakhan and Kazan and was the church in which many of the Tsars were baptised. Outside the western door of the cathedral is the **tomb of Tsar Boris Godunov**, his wife and two of their children.

The **Chapel over the Well** was built over a sacred spring which is claimed to have appeared during the Polish siege of 1608. Pilgrims fill up drinking bottles with holy water here.

The **Bell-tower** is the monastery's tallest building, 93m high. Work started on this five tiered bell-tower in 1740 and took 30 years.

The **Refectory and Church of St Sergius** was built from 1686 to 1693 and served as a dining hall for pilgrims. You can't miss this red, blue, green and yellow chequered building with its carved columns. Outside the refectory is the squat **Church of St Sergius** crowned with a single golden dome. The **Church of the Descent of the Holy Spirit** contains the grave of the first Bishop of Russian Alaska.

Trinity Cathedral is the most sacred place in the monastery as it is on the site of the original wooden church built by St Sergius. It contains St Sergius's corpse in a dull silver sarcophagus donated by Ivan the Terrible. Built in 1422 in honour of St Sergius's canonisation, the cathedral contains 42 icons by Andrei Rublev, Russia's most famous painter.

Church of Our Lady of Smolensk was built to house the icon of the same name in 1745. Decorated in baroque style, it resembles a rotunda .

You have to buy separate tickets for each of the museums, and the Art Museum has specific entry times on the tickets. The museums are open 10:00-17:00, closed Mondays. The **Old Art Museum** is located in the Vestry and contains one of Russia's richest collections of religious art as well as gifts presented to the monastery. As the gifts are displayed in the order they were given, it is interesting to see how tastes changed over the centuries. The **Art Museum** contains Russian handicrafts from the 14th century to the present. The **History Museum** is in the former hospital.

The **Tsar's Palace** was built at the end of the 17th century to be the residence of the visiting Tsar Alexei and his entourage of over 500 people. It now houses a Theological College and Ecclesiastical Academy.

It is possible to climb **Pilgrim Gate Tower** and walk along the wall.

❏ Sergiev-Posad has always been associated with carved wooden toys as St Sergius used to give them to children. Locally produced *matryaskhas* are distinctive as they are painted with gouache and covered with varnish. Before you buy one, visit the **toy museum** so that you see the variety available.

Rostov-Yaroslavski
Ростов-Ярославский

Also known as **Rostov-Veliki**, this is one of the most attractive Golden Ring cities to visit. Packed with interesting places it's a small city in a beautiful location beside scenic Lake Nero.

Found in 862, Rostov-Yaroslavski played a major role in the formation of Russia and at one time was as big as the mighty capitals of Kiev and Novgorod. Yuri Dolgoruky, who founded Moscow in 1147, gave Rostov the honourable and rare title of *veliki* meaning great. Rostov-Veliki soon became an independent principality.

Rebuilt after the Tatar-Mongol sacking, Rostov-Veliki continued to have political importance for two more centuries until the local prince sold the remainder of his hereditary domain to Moscow's Grand Prince Ivan III in 1474. The city remained an important ecclesiastical centre as it was the religious capital of northern Russia and home to the senior religious leader called the Metropolitan. In the 17th century, however, the Metropolitan was moved to the larger city of Yaroslavl. No longer called Rostov the Great, the city became known as Rostov-Yaroslavski, rapidly became a backwater and has remained one ever since.

Much of Russia's lousy coffee originates here as there is a factory for roasting chicory roots which are substituted for, or added to, coffee beans.

ORIENTATION AND SERVICES

To get from the railway station to the kremlin and the main bus station, take bus No 6. To get from the main bus station to St Jacob Monastery, take bus Nos 1 or 2; for St Avraamy Monastery, take bus No 1.

Intourist (☎ 312 44) is located in the kremlin.

WHERE TO STAY

One of the most appealing places to stay in all of Russia is in the *Rostov Kremlin*. The former servants' quarters have been turned into a basic hotel run by the International Tourist Centre (☎ 318 54). The rooms cost US$22 per person in a double. There is a café in the same building.

Other places to stay are the standard *Hotel Intourist* (☎ 659 066), ul Engelsa 115; the basic *Hotel Rostov* (☎ 391 818), ul Svedlova 64; and *Hotel Moskovskaya* (☎ 388 700), ul Engelsa 62, which is similar.

As well as at the café in the International Tourist Centre, you can get a reasonable two course meal at *Restaurant Teremok* for US$12.

WHAT TO SEE

The Rostov Kremlin

The white walled Rostov Kremlin is one of the most photogenic in the country. It is spread over two hectares, has six churches and is ringed by 11 towers. The kremlin was founded in 1162 by Prince Andrei Bogolyubsky, son of Yuri Dolgoruky but all traces of the original buildings disappeared in the 17th century when the kremlin was rebuilt.

Despite its mighty 12m high and 2m thick walls and towers, this reconstructed kremlin is actually an imitation fortress. All the elements of real fortifications are missing. The ambitious 17th century Metropolitan, Ion Sisoyevich, wanted a residence to reflect his importance. After the 17th century when the Metropolitan was moved to nearby Yaroslavl, the kremlin became derelict. Today most of the buildings have been restored to their 16th and 17th century condition.

The kremlin grounds are always open as the gate on the eastern wall is never locked. The museums are normally open 10:00-17:00, closed Wednesday.

The **Assumption Cathedral** in the northern part of the kremlin, is a 16th century, 60m high, five-domed building with white stone friezes decorating the outside. The cathedral contains the tomb of the canonised Bishop Leontius who was martyred by Rostov's pagans in 1071 during his Christianity drive. The Metropolitan Ion is also buried here. The **bell-tower** contains superb examples of 17th century Russian bells, the largest weighing 32 tons. There are 13 bells in all and they can be heard up to 20km away. They're rung at 13:00 on Saturday and Sunday.

The central part of the kremlin contains five churches. The religious part of each church occupies only the 2nd floor as the ground floor was left for animal husbandry, storage and accommodation.

The kremlin's **main entrance** is on its western side through the **St John the Divine Gateway Church** built in 1683, which has a richly decorated facade. The ticket office is in this building.

The entrance to the kremlin's northern part from the central part is through the **Resurrection of Christ Gate Church** built in 1670. This church has a stone iconostasis instead of the traditional wooden one.

The **Transfiguration of the Saviour above the Cellars Church** is one of the gems of the kremlin as it was the private church of the Metropolitan. It is quite austere from the outside but its interior is lavish. This church is the tallest in the kremlin and has a single dome. The **White Chamber** next door was designed as a sumptuous dining hall; it now houses a museum on local Rostov crafts.

The **Church of the Virgin Hodegetria** was erected 20 years after the death of Metropolitan Ion and has a Moscow baroque interior. It now contains an exhibition on church vestments.

Rostov-Yaroslavski
Ростов-Ярославский

Nero Lake

0   300m

1 Railway Station   Железнодорожний Вокзал
2 Church of St Nicholas (Nikola) in the Field   Церковь Святого Никола
3 Church of St Isidore the Blessed   Церковь Вознесения
4 Church of the Virgin Birth   Церковь Рождества Богородицы
5 Saviour on the Market Place Church   Церковь Спаса на Торгу
6 Rostov Kremlin and Hotel   Ростовский Кремль и Гостиница
7 Bus Station   Автовокзал
8 Restaurant Teremok   Ресторан Теремок
9 Metropolitan's Horse Stables   Конный двор и Музей
10 Hotel Rostov   Гостиница Ростов
11 Church of the Tolg Virgin   Церковь Толгской Богоматери
12 Hotel Intourist   Гостиница Интурист
13 Hotel Moskovskaya   Гостиница Московская
14 St Jacob Monastery   Яковлевский Монастыр

The **Prince's Chambers** is the oldest building here, dating from the the 16th century. It's claustrophobic with small dark passages, narrow doors and slit windows filled with slivers of mica. This is a good place to get an impression of the life of 16th century Russian nobility.

The **Metropolitan's House** is now a museum and has a large collection of stone carvings, wooden sculptures, and 14th and 15th century doors from local churches. The **Red Chamber**, built as a residence for visiting tsars and their large retinue is now the hostel of the International Youth Tourism Centre.

Other places of interest

In front of the eastern entrance of the kremlin is the **Saviour on the Market Place Church**. It was built in the late 1600s and is now a library. The name comes from the rows of shops and stalls around the church that have stood there for centuries. Beside the church is the Arcade built in the 1830s and on the opposite side of the street is the Traders' Row.

The neoclassical **St Nicholas in the Field Church** on ul Gogola was built in 1813 and has a golden iconostasis with *finift* enamel decorations and icons from the 15th to 19th centuries. It was one of two main churches in Rostov that conducted services during the communist era (the other was the **Church of the Tolg Virgin**). The single-domed **Church of St Isidore the Blessed**, ul Karla Marxa, dates from the 16th century and was originally called Ascension Church.

In front of the kremlin's main gate on the western side, ul Kamenny Most, are the **Metropolitan's Horse Stables**. It was planned to demolish this nondescript two-storey building recently. After the plaster was knocked off the walls, however, it was discovered that the building was part of a 300 year old complex which included stables, rooms for tack, sledges and carriages, and quarters for grooms, coachmen and watchmen.

You can hire rowing boats at the **river station** near the kremlin.

❏ **Finift**

Rostov-Yaroslavski's most famous handicraft is *finift* multi-coloured enamel work. This craft originated in Byzantium: the name derives from the Greek *fingitis* meaning colourful and shiny. Finift was used to decorate icons, sacred utensils and bible covers, as well as in portraits of people. The enamel's greatest advantages are that it cannot be damaged by water and does not fade with time.

The process of making the enamel is extremely complex and involves oxidising various metals to produce different colours. Iron produces yellow, orange-red and brown, copper produces green and blue, tin produces a non-transparent white, and gold with tin produces a cold ruby red.

Finift has been produced here since the 12th century. The Rostov Finift Factory has been operating since the 18th century. While there are no regular tours of the Rostov Finift Factory, you can organise one through Intourist or by talking to the factory's director (☎ 352 29).

Yaroslavl
Ярославль

Yaroslav's old central section and the tree-lined streets and squares make this one of the most attractive cities in Russia. In many ways, Yaroslavl's buildings surpass those of Moscow as they have not suffered as much from the ravages of war and rapid industrialisation.

Yaroslavl is the Volga River's oldest city, founded in 1010 by Grand Prince Yaroslav the Wise. With the expansion of river trade from the 16th century, Yaroslavl became the second most populous city after Moscow. Until the opening of the Moscow-Volga River Canal in 1937, which gave Moscow direct access to the Volga, Yaroslavl was Moscow's main port.

ORIENTATION AND SERVICES

There are two railway stations. **Yaroslavl-Glavny** (*Yaroslavl-Main*) is on the north side of the Kotorosl River and **Yaroslavl-Moskovski** is on the south side. All trains to Yaroslavl go through Yaroslavl-Glavny while only those trains travelling along the east and west line (such as from Ivanovo and St Petersburg) go through Yaroslavl-Moskovski.

To get from the station to pl Volkova (for Hotel Yaroslavl), catch trolley-bus No 1. From the station to Hotel Kotorosl, take tram No 3. The airport is to the north and its closest railway station is Molot (Мотол) on the line to St Petersburg. Bus No 140 from pl Sovetskaya runs to the airport.

Yaroslavlskoye Travel Agency/Intourist (☎ 224 594, 221 613, fax 229 306), is in Hotel Yubileynaya, office 230A, nab Kotoroslennaya 11A.

WHERE TO STAY

The best option is the *Hotel Yubileynaya* (☎ 224 159), nab Kotoroslennaya 11A, at US$42 for a double room. *Hotel Kotorosl* (☎ 212 415), ul Bolshaya Oktyabrskaya 87, is a standard place charging US$54 for a double; and the basic *Hotel Volga* (☎ 229 131), ul Kirova 10, formerly known as the Bristol Hotel, charges US$26 for a double.

Beside one another are the *Hotel Vest*, ul Respublikanskaya 79, US$24 (double); and the *Hotel Yuta* (☎ 218 793), ul Respublikanskaya 79, US$48 (double). *Hotel Yaroslavl* (☎ 221 275), ul Ushinskovo 40, and with an entrance also at ul 2 Svobody, is noisy. A double room is US$84.

There are restaurants in all the hotels. Other good places to eat are the *Restaurant Staroe Mesto*, and the *Restaurant Volga* which only opens in the evening in the River Station.

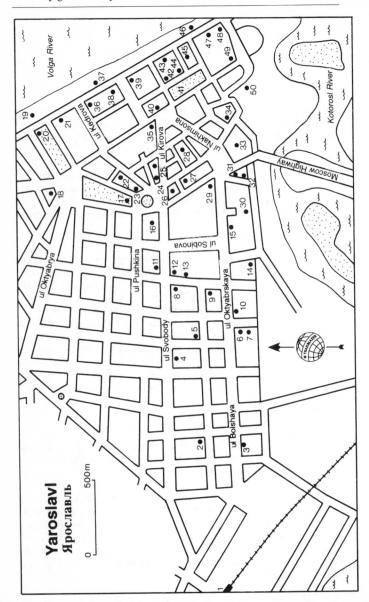

HOTELS AND RESTAURANTS
3 Hotel Kotorosl Гостиница Которосль
12 Hotel Vest Гостиница Вест
13 Hotel Yuta Гостиница Юта
16 Hotel Yaroslavl Гостиница Ярославль
21 Café Lira Кафе Лира
25 Hotel Volga Гостиница Волга
30 Hotel Yubileynaya Гостиница Юбилейная

OTHER
1 Yaroslavl Main Station Урославль-Главный Вокзал
2 Church of Vladimir Mother of God
   Церковь Владимирской Богоматери
4 Circus Цирк
5 Bell-tower of St Nicholas Колокольня Николы
6 Church of St Nicholas on the Waters
   Церковь Святого Николы
7 Church of Tikhvin Virgin Церковь Тихвинской Богоматери
8 Youth and Puppet Theatres Театры Юного Зрителя и Кукол
9 Seminary Духовная Семинрия
10 House of Ivanov Дом Иванова
11 House of Nikin Дом Никина
14 Church of Metropolitan Peter Церковь Петра
15 Church of St Demetrius of Thessalonica
   Церковь Дмитрия Солунского
17 Volkov's Theatre Драматический Театр имени Волкова
18 University Университет
19 River Station Речной Вокзал
20 Nekrasov Monument Памятник Некрасову
22 Planetarium Планетарий
23 Philharmonic Hall Филармония
24 Book Store Дом Книги
26 Vlasyevskaya Tower Власьевская Башня
27 Arcade Гостиный Двор
28 Market Рынок
29 Post Office Почтамп
31 Epiphany Church Церковь Богоявления
32 Descent of the Holy Spirit Consistorium
   Духовная Консистория
33 Transfiguration of our Saviour Monastery
   Спасо-Преображенский Монастырь
34 Church of St Michael the Archangel
   Церковь Михайла-Архангелск
35 Government Offices Присутственные Места
36 Church of the Nativity Церковь Рождества Христова
37 Provincial Governor's Rotunda-Pavilion Павильон
38 Church of St Nicholas-Naden
   Церковь Цвятого Николы Надеина
39 Art Museum Художественный Музей
40 Church of Elijah the Prophet Церковь Ильи Пророка
41 Chelyuskintsev Park Парк Челюскинцев
42 House of Matreev Дом Матреева
43 Physicians Society House Дом Врачов
44 House of the Vakhrameevs Дом Вахрамеевых
45 Medical Institute Мелицинский Институт
46 Volga Tower Волжская Башня
47 Church of Patriarch Tikhon Церковь Патрarha Тихона
48 Metropolitan's Chamber Митрополичьи Палаты
49 Church of St Nicholas in Log Town
   Церковь Святого Николы
50 Church of Saviour in the Town Церковь Спаса

WHAT TO SEE

Transfiguration of Our Saviour Monastery

This attractive white monastery was founded in the 12th century but the oldest building to be seen today dates from 1516 when the wooden walls were replaced with stone and brick. Considered impregnable, part of the tsar's treasury was stored here, protected by a garrison.

The **Transfiguration of Our Saviour Cathedral** occupies central place in the monastery. This three-domed cathedral was built in 1516 after the original building was destroyed in a fire in 1501 and is currently being renovated. Sixteenth century frescoes include depictions of John the Baptist on the eastern wall, Christ Pantokrator on the cupola in the central dome, and the Last Judgement on the western wall.

The **Refectory** was built in the 16th century. On the second floor a single mighty pillar supports the vaults, creating a large open dining area. It's now a history museum. The **Nativity Church**, which is also known as the Refectory Church, is now a natural history museum.

Climb the **bell tower** for a panoramic view of the city. Directly above you is the main bell which was cast in 1738. The bell-tower's clock was installed in 1624 after being brought from the Saviour (Spassky) Tower in the Moscow Kremlin.

The **Monks' Cell Block** consists of four buildings and was built at the end of the 17th century. It now contains a large museum of Old Russia which includes icons, handicrafts, weapons, armour and books.

Entry into the grounds (open daily) is free but you will have to pay for each of the museums (open 10:00 to 17:00 daily except Monday).

Around the monastery

This area is rich in churches and other historic buildings. Directly opposite the monastery on the Moscow Highway is the **Epiphany Church**. The five-domed church was completed in 1693 and has nine large windows which make the interior extraordinarily light. It is an excellent example of the Yaroslavl school of architecture with its glazed tiles and festive decorations. It is now a museum, open from 1 May to 30 September, 10:00-17:00, closed Tuesday.

The **House of Ivanov**, ul Chaikovskovo 4, is a typical two storey residence of a well-to-do town dweller built at the end of the 17th century. The ground floor was used for storage and the upper floor contains the sleeping and living rooms.

The five-domed **Church of St Nicholas on the Waters**, ul Chaikovskovo 1, was built from 1665 to 1672 and has marvellous glazed bands around the altar windows.

The **Church of the Tikhvin Virgin** is a small church designed for winter worship as it can be heated. It has extensive glazed tile work on its exterior.

The Volga River Embankment

A stroll down the landscaped high right bank of the Volga River from the river station to the Metropolitan's Chambers is an enjoyable way of exploring this area. At the end of ul Pervomaiskaya is the **river station**; one section is for long distance hydrofoils, and slightly downstream, there's another for local passenger ferries.

The tent-roofed **Nativity Church**, ul Kedrova 1, built over nine years starting in 1635 is famous as the first church to use glazed tiles for external decoration. This practice was soon adopted everywhere and led to the development of the Yaroslavl Architecture style. The names of those involved in the building of the church have been inscribed on the tiles and if you look closely, you can still see them.

St Nicholas-Nadeyina Church, per Narodny 2a, was funded by the wealthy merchant, Nadey Sveshnikov, hence its name. The Annunciation Chapel here was built for Nadey's private use so that he could pray in the company of only his closest friends. It has an interesting iconostasis framed in ornamental lead. The church is now a museum, open from 1 May to 30 September, 10:00-17:00, closed Sunday and Monday.

The small **Art Museum** is housed in the former governor's residence and it contains artwork from the 18th century and onwards. It is located at nab Volzhskaya 23 and is open 10:00-17:00, closed Friday.

The **Volga Tower**, also known as the Arsenal Tower, sits on the river bank at nab Volzhskaya 7. It is one of two towers which remain from the former Yaroslavl Kremlin. This citadel consisted of earth ramparts with wooden fortress walls and stone towers. This tower was finished in 1668 and is now a naval club.

The **Metropolitan's Chamber**, nab Volzhskaya 1, was built in the 1680s for the Metropolitan of the nearby city of Rostov-Yaroslavski. The two storey building is now one of the country's richest museums of old Russian Art. While Yaroslavl's most revered icon, *The Sign of the Virgin,* painted in about 1218, now sits in Moscow's Tretyakov Gallery, the museum contains a number of other notable icons. Particularly interesting are the 13th and 14th centuries Mongolian icons. The Museum of Old Russian Art is open 10:00-17:00, closed Friday.

❏ **Yaroslavl style**

The Yaroslavl school of architecture dates from the second half of the 16th century and is epitomised by tall, pointed tent roofs, free standing bell-towers, large airy churches with side chapels, external glazed tiles, and large interior frescoes and mosaics. Yaroslavl has many buildings in this style as its evolution coincided with a massive reconstruction drive after the great fire in 1658. The city had developed a rich merchant class which commissioned churches to its own taste. As this style also appealed to hereditary nobles and peasants, it became widespread throughout Russia, much to the chagrin of the conservative clergy.

Yaroslavl centre

The centre of the city is Soviet Square (pl Sovetskaya). On the east side of the square is the Church of St Elijah the Prophet and on the north side is a government office building of the 1780.

The imposing **Church of St Elijah the Prophet** is well worth seeing for its superb 17th century frescoes, still in excellent condition, The church was commissioned by one of the richest and most influential Russian merchant dynasties, the Shripins. It's now a museum and is open from 1 May to 30 September, from 10:00 to 18:00, closed Wednesday.

The **Vlasyevskaya Tower**, ul Pervomaiskaya 21, is the second of the two towers that remain from Yaroslavl's original kremlin. The tower is also known as the Sign (Znamenskaya) Tower.

The **Volkov Drama Theatre**, pl Volkova, was built in 1911 and is named after Fedor Volkov (1729-1763) who is considered the founder of Russian national theatre. He inherited his step-father's factories in Yaroslavl which enabled him to organise his own private theatre company before moving onto bigger and better things. Amongst his claims to fame was that he organised the first staging of *Hamlet* in Russia.

Although the Rostov Finift Enamel factory is based in the nearby city of Rostov-Yaroslavski, the **factory shop** is here at ul Kirova 13, next to the Hotel Volga. It has a great range of *finift* enamel gifts.

Korovnitskaya Sloboda Historic District

Korovnitskaya Sloboda, which means 'cattle breeding settlement on the outskirts of town', sits on the right bank of the Kotorosl River as it flows into the Volga River. The district's focal point is the **Church of St John Chrysostom**, nab Portovaya 2, which was built from 1649 to 1654. It has four domes and two tent-shaped side chapels which makes it appealingly symmetrical. As it was built at the height of the decorative arts in Yaroslavl, its ornamentation is very elaborate. The **Church of Vladimir Mother of God** is very similar in style but significantly smaller.

The most obvious building in this historic area is the pointed 37m high bell-tower which carries the nickname of the Candle of Yaroslavl.

Church of St John the Baptist

In the Tolchkovski district, once famous for its leather work, this impressive 15-domed church (1671-87) is considered the architectural pinnacle of Yaroslavl. From a distance it looks as if it is trimmed in lace and carved of wood but this deception is created by carved and patterned bricks. It consists of two side chapels, unusual in that they are practically as tall as the church and each is crowned with five domes. Inside is a mass of frescoes – reputedly more than in any other church in Russia. It is now a museum, open 10:00-18:00, closed Tuesday.

You can see this church as you cross over the Kotorosl River on the train.

Kirov/Vyatka
Киров/Вятка

Kirov was founded in 1181 on the banks of the Vyatka River, and was originally named Klynov. It developed into a fur-trading centre entirely dependent on the river for transport and communication with the rest of the country. In the eighteenth century it fell under the rule of Moscow and was renamed Vyatka, soon gaining a reputation as a place of exile. In 1934 its name was changed once more and it became Kirov, in honour of the communist leader assassinated earlier in the same year. Kirov was, at one time, so close to Stalin that most people assumed that he would eventually succeed him as General Secretary of the Party. However, in the 1930s he broke away and it is more than likely that Stalin had a hand in his murder. His death served as the excuse for Stalin's Great Purge in the mid-1930s during which several million people died in labour camps.

Modern Kirov, now also known as Vyatka again, is a large industrial and administrative centre with a population of 490,000. It's not of great interest but there's enough to keep you occupied for a day and the river front is attractive.

ORIENTATION AND SERVICES

Kirov is spread out and has no real main street which means that you need to do a lot of walking to get around. To get from Kirov-1 railway station to the Hotel Administratsi Oblast and Drama Theatre, take bus 23 from in front of Detski Mir department store. To get from Kirov-1 railway station to the Hotel Vyatka, take trolley bus Nos 2, 3 or 6 also from Detski Mir.

Intourist (☎ 90 949), ul Volodarskovo 127, offers tours of the city (3 hours), the Trifon Monastery (1 hour), and the **Bakulev Museum of Heart Surgery** in the nearby town of Slobodskoi (2 hours), as well as a four day **rafting trip** down the Velikaya River. **Aeroflot** (☎ 44 472, 25 287), is at ul Gorkovo 56.

You can only buy tickets for trains departing that day at the station and for advance bookings, you need to go to the **Advance Railway Ticket Booking Office**.

WHERE TO STAY

The only two hotels frequented by foreigners are the ***Hotel Vyatka*** (☎ 648 396), pr Oktyabrski 145, which charges US$34/80 for a single/double room; *Hotel Administratsi Oblast* (☎ 691 018), ul Gertsena 49, US$25 single; and *Motel Kolos* (☎ 679 324), ul Bolshoe Bolshevikov, which has beds in the dormitory for US$8 and single rooms for US$34.

The best restaurant is the *Rossiya*, ul Lenina 80 which is near the M E Saltykov-Shchedrin House-museum. There is a restaurant in the Hotel Vyatka and three canteens near the puppet theatre. The restaurant at Kirov-1 station is not bad.

WHAT TO SEE

Russia's answer to Joseph Conrad was AC Grin (1880-1932) who was born 35km away at Slobodskoi. Grin's adventure novels set in mysterious places are still popular today and his works are on display in the **AC Grin Museum**, ul Volodarskovo 44, open 10:00-18:00, closed Monday.

Other museums include the **Museum of Aviation and Space**, ul Engelsa, open 10:00-18:00, closed Monday; the **Museum of Vyatka Local Handicrafts**, ul Drelevskovo 4B, which has a large collection of Dymkovo clay toys, and the large **United Historical Archive and Literary Museum**, ul Lenina 82.

The **Exhibition Hall of the Kirov Region**, ul Gertsina, open 10:00-16:00, closed Monday, exhibits works of local artists and each month has a different exhibition. The staff are very helpful and some speak English.

The **Assumption Cathedral** at the Trifon Monastery dates from the late 17th century.

❏ **Kirov to Vyelikoryetskaya Pilgrimage**

Every year on 3 June, 1000-odd worshippers take part in the Russian Orthodox Church's longest procession; a 170km trek starting from Kirov and ending in Vyelikoryetskaya village. Leading the procession is the Icon of St Nikolai, the miracle curer.

According to religious lore, a peasant in 1383 found this icon up a tree surrounded by candles on the outskirts of Vyelikoryetskaya. The villagers agreed to house the icon in Kirov providing that it was brought back to the village in the yearly procession. This condition has been met every year since then, even during the communist era when the icon was hidden, the tree in Vyelikoryetskaya chopped down and the devout had to pretend that they were out strolling.

Today the procession is gaining popularity as more people seek the miracles that they believe result from participating. Everyone is welcome but you must bring your own blanket, food and drink for three days of walking.

Perm
Пермь

The city of Perm, gateway to Siberia, lies in the foothills of the Ural Mountains. It's an industrial city of over one million people and the focus of the region. The surrounding area is good for hiking and skiing. Some operators now offer white water rafting trips.

Perm dates back to 1723 when construction of the Egoshikhinski copper foundry began. It was started by VN Tatichev who was one of the close associates of Peter the Great. The location on two major trading rivers ensured that Perm grew as not only an industrial but also a trading city. Salt caravans arrived along the Kama River while wheat, honey and metal products from the Urals travelled along the Chusovi River. The arrival of the railway in 1878, the discovery of oil in the region, and the transfer of factories from European Russia during WWII all boosted the local economy further.

The city's most familiar product is the Kama bicycle which while rarely seen on the streets of Russian cities, is still widely used in the country. Nearly all of Russia's domestic phones are made here but Perm's most specialised products are the first stage motors for the Proton Heavy Lift rockets.

Despite its industries, Perm has a long history of culture and scholarship. This can mostly be attributed to the revolutionaries, intellectuals and political prisoners who were exiled here in the 19th century. Perm had the first university in the Urals and its most famous student was Alexander Popov (1859-1905) who, according to Russian historians, invented the wireless. He first demonstrated his invention in 1895, the same year that Marconi also proved his concept. Popov was born in nearby Krasnoturinsk.

From 1940 to 1957 Perm was called Molotov after the disgraced Soviet Foreign Minister who signed the 1939 Ribbentrop-Molotov Pact, dividing up Poland with the Nazis.

ORIENTATION AND SERVICES

The town extends for 80km along the Kama River with the centre being around Perm 1 station on the left (eastern) bank. At the southern end of Perm, also on the left bank, is Perm 2 which is the station at which the Trans-Siberian stops. There are suburban trains that run the 5km between Perm 2 and Perm 1. The city has two airport: the new Bolshoe Savino

Airport which handles most traffic and is 20km to the west, and the old
Bakharevka Airport which is 10km to the south in the suburb of Balatovo.

A recommended travel company is **Galakon** (☎ 338 087, fax 341
568), ul Kuibysheva 14. They can offer a half-day trip to the Khokhlovka
open air museum, a day boat trip along the Kama and Chisovaya Rivers,
and a day trip to the Kungur ice caves. Perm also has a small **Intourist**
(☎ 333 843) at ul Popova 9.

Aeroflot (☎ 334 668) is at ul Krisanova 19 and you can also buy tickets from the Ural and Prikamiye Hotels.

Rail tickets can be purchased from Perm 1 and 2 stations as well as
the Advance Ticket Booking Office on ul Krisanova.

WHERE TO STAY

The best place to stay in Perm is the standard *Ural Hotel* (☎ 344 417), ul
Lenina 58. It's a fairly new place charging US$33/66 for a single/double
room. *Hotel Prikamiye* (☎ 348 662), ul Komsomolskaya 27, is not bad
and has singles for US$30. Not recommended is the grubby *Hotel Turist*
(☎ 342 494), ul Ordzhonikidze 43, and you should certainly avoid the
Hotel Tsentralaya and *Hotel Sportivnaya*. All the hotels have restaurants
or buffets; the one in Hotel Prikamiye is the best.

A wonderful place to stay is the German built *Ushatchka Resort*
which is about 50km out of Perm. Recently opened it has four-star facilities. Contact Galakon (☎ 338 087) for more information.

WHAT TO SEE

The most interesting part of town is the old quarter around Perm 1 station.
Old churches here include the baroque **Cathedral of Peter and Paul**
(1757-1765 with a 19th century belfry) and the Empire style **Cathedral
of the Saviour of the Transfiguration Monastery** (1798-1832). There
are also numerous examples of eclectic and art nouveau styles of which
the old building of Perm 2 station is one. The river station is near Perm 1.

Perm Art Gallery, pr Komsomolski 2, is one of the largest in Russia.
Its collection of wooden sculptures is interesting and includes a figure of
Jesus with Mongolian features. It's open 11:00-18:00, closed Monday.
The city also boasts a **terrarium** in Gorky Park, a **planetarium**, and a
Museum of Local Studies.

About 45km out of town near the village of **Khokhlovka** is an open-
air ethnographic museum which has a collection of 16-20th century
buildings. This museum is open all year around. About 100km from Perm
are the fabulous **Kungur Ice Caves**, some of the biggest in the Urals
region with a total length of 5.6km including 58 grottos, 60 lakes, and
hundreds of stalactites and stalagmites. About 1.3km of the caves are
open to the public and fitted with electric lights. Take warm clothes.

Ekaterinburg
Екатеринбург

Ekaterinburg's role in shaping Russian history has been both immense and paradoxical: ushering in the Socialist era in 1918 with the murder of the Romanov family, providing the setting for the 1960's 'U2 Affair' (effectively a caricature of the Cold War itself), and giving the country Boris Yeltsin, who played a key role in dismantling the Soviet myth. The city seems to act as Russia's litmus paper: as a harbinger of whatever is to come.

Its historical significance alone justifies a visit and while there is not much to see here in real terms, the wealth of pre-Stalinist architecture makes a change from other Siberian cities, harking back to the days before the Revolution, when Ekaterinburg was already the centre of a rich mining region. From 1924 to 1992 the city was known as Sverdlovsk.

HISTORY

The earliest settlers in the area were the 'Old Believers', religious dissidents fleeing the reforms of the Russian Orthodox Church in 1672. They created the *Shartash* township here and were the first to discover that the area was rich in iron ore. This discovery was the key to later development: Peter the Great, in the process of fighting the Great Northern War against Sweden, gave instructions for new sources of iron to be found, and the first ironworks were established here just as the war ended in 1721. A fortress was built a year later and the town was officially founded in 1723. The city was named Ekaterinburg in honour of Peter's new wife, Catherine. The railway reached the town in 1888 bringing foreign travellers on their way to Siberia.

The murder of the Romanovs

The Romanov family was moved from Tobolsk to Ekaterinburg in May 1918 and imprisoned in a house belonging to a rich merchant, Ipatev. Here they spent the last two months of their lives being tormented by the guards, who openly referred to Nicholas as the 'Blood Drinker' and scrawled lewd pictures on the walls depicting the Tsarina with Rasputin.

Several attempts were made to save the royal family, and eventually the Bolshevik government, deciding that the Tsar was too great a threat to its security, ordered his elimination. Shortly before midnight on 16 July, Nicholas, Alexandra, their four daughters and their haemophiliac son,

Alexis, were taken down to the cellar where they were shot and bayonetted to death. The bodies were then taken to the Four Brothers Mine, 40km outside the city, where the guards spent three days destroying the evidence. The corpses were dismembered, doused with petrol and burned.

A week later the White Army took Ekaterinburg and their suspicions were immediately aroused by the sight of the blood-spattered walls of the cellar. In the garden they found the Tsarevich's spaniel, Joy, neglected and half starved. However, it was not until the following January that investigators were led to the mineshaft, where they found fragments of bone and pieces of jewellery that had once belonged to members of the Imperial Family. They also found the body of Jimmy, Anastasia's dog, that the murderers had carelessly flung down the mineshaft without bothering to destroy. All the evidence was identified by the Tsarevich's tutor, Pierre Gilliard. At first the Bolsheviks would not admit to more than the 'execution' of Nicholas, accusing a group of counter-revolutionaries of the murders of his family. Five of them were tried, 'found guilty' and executed. However, in 1919 after the death of Party official Yacob Sverdlov, it was acknowledged that it was, in fact, he who had arranged the massacre. In his honour the town was renamed Sverdlovsk.

The U2 Affair
The next time the town became the focus of world attention was in May 1960 when the American U2 pilot, Gary Powers, was shot down in this area (see p310). US Intelligence was no doubt unhappy to hear that he had survived the crash, parachuting into the arms of the Soviets and confirming that he had been spying. The ensuing confrontation led to the collapse of the Summit conference in Paris.

The city today
Ekaterinburg is now one of Russia's most important industrial cities, with a population of nearly 1.5 million. The city's most famous son is, of course, Boris Yeltsin: coup-buster, economic reformer, referendum winner, dissolver of parliament and Russian President.

Industries include heavy engineering, chemical production with 200 complexes and a transport hub with seven radiating railway lines. It is educationally rich with more than 200 schools, 50 technical schools and 14 higher education institutions. It also has over 600 libraries, including the Belinski Library which has more than 15 million books and was founded in 1899. The city used to focus on armaments research and production but munitions factories, including the vast 'Pentagon' building in

---

(Opposite) Top: The continental divide: Europe/Asia Border Obelisk beside the railway line at Km1777 (see p308). Bottom: The site of the Romanov murders in Ekaterinburg. (Photos: Tatyana Pozar-Burgar)

the eastern part of the town, are now being closed down. If Ekaterinburg is an indicator of the state of affairs in Russia, things don't look too good: I asked if anything important had happened here recently and was told only that there had been 'a number of mafia funerals'.

LOCAL TRANSPORT

Ekaterinburg has a good bus and trolley-bus system, and also a rather limited metro. To get to the centre from the station, take bus Nos 1, 13, 21, 23, 31 or trolleybus Nos 1, 3, 5, 9, 12. From the station to Hotel Tsentralnaya, take trolleybus Nos 1, 5, 9 down ul Karla Libknekhta. For Hotel Iset, Hotel Yubileynaya and Hotel Bolshoi Ural, take tram Nos 27 and 29 which go down ul Lunacharskovo then pro Lenina. For MNTK, take bus No 41 westward from the junction of pro Lenina and ul Karla Libknetka. This bus passes the hotel about 500m from its terminus.

To get to the airport, catch a bus from the Air Station (*aerovokzal*) beside the Aeroflot office at ul Bolshakova 99A.

ORIENTATION AND SERVICES

The main street, pro Lenina, runs from east to west through the city and is bisected by the River Iset. The point where the road and the river cross is more or less the city centre and most of the hotels, restaurants and sights are within walking distance of it.

Travel Agents include Intourist, (☎ 518 434, fax 518 230), ul Lenina 40; Sputnik (☎ 513 743, fax 513 483), ul Pushkina 5; Miklukho-Maklay (☎ 237 596, fax 518 087), ul Shaumyana 100; Globe Tour (☎ 589 819, fax 516 455), ul Dzerzhinski 2. **Aeroflot** (☎ 299 298), is at ul Bolshakova 99A. For **rail tickets**, you have to go to the second floor of the **Central Railway Ticket Booking Office** located in a new building on the west side of the main railway station. There is a special window for foreigners. The building also has showers. You can also get tickets at the **Advance Purchase Rail Ticket Booking Office**, ul Sverdlova 22. Railway information can be obtained in Russian on ☎ 519 924.

The **Central Post Office**, ul Lenina 51, has an excellent business centre which offers international faxes, e-mail and www facilities.

There's a **Mongolian Consulate** (☎ 445 453) at ul Furmanova 45, and a **US Consulate** (☎ 564 619, fax 564 515), at ul Gogolya 15A.

(Opposite) Top: There are still some traditional wooden buildings to be seen in Siberian cities, such as this in Irkutsk (see p220). **Bottom:** The library at Ivolginsky Monastery (Datsan), 25km outside Ulan Ude (see p247) contains priceless Buddhist texts and a colourful model of the Buddhist paradise.

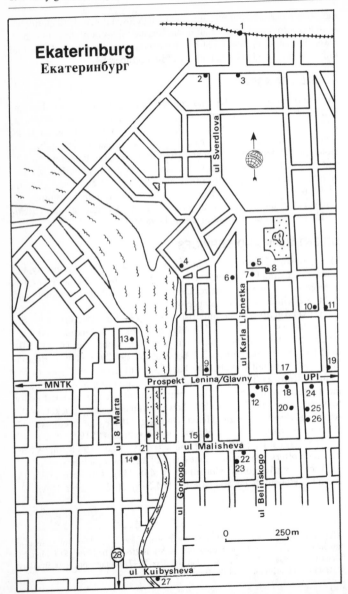

Ekaterinburg
Екатеринбург

HOTELS AND RESTAURANTS

2 Restaurant Staraya Krepost Ресторан Старая Крепость
3 Hotel Sverdlovsk Гостиница Свердловск
4 Restaurant Kosmos Ресторан Космос
10 Ural Chicken Restaurant Ресторан Уральские Цыплята
12 Restaurant Okean Ресторан Океан
13 Dom Mir-i-Druzhby (House of Peace & Friendship) Дом Мира и Дружбы
16 Hotel Yubilena Гостиница Юбилейная
20 Hotel Bolshoi Ural Гостиница Большой Урал
22 Hotel Tsentralnaya Гостиница Центральная
24 Food Store Гастроном Центральный
25 Bar Vesna Бар Весна
26 Restaurant Tsentralny Ресторан Центральный
27 Restaurant Harbin Ресторан Харбин

OTHER

1 Ekaterinburg Railway Station Вокзал
5 Former Estate of Rastorguev-Kharitonov (1794-1836)
  Быв. Усадьба Расторгуева-Харитонова
6 Romanov Memorial (Ipatev House) Белый Крест (Быв. Дом Ипатьева)
7 Monument to the Ural's Komsomol Young Communists
  Памятник Комсомолу Урала
8 Ascension Cathedral Церковь Вознесения
9 Central Post Office Почтамт
11 Military Museum in the House of Officers (U2)
  Музей «Боевая Слава Урала»
14 Museum of Local History Краеведческий Музей
15 Svak Bank Свак-Банк
17 Sverdlov Statue Памятник Свердлову
18 Opera & Ballet Theatre Театр Оперы и Балета
21 Museum of Decorative Arts Музей Изобразительных Искусств
23 Popov's Radio Museum Музей радио имени Попова
28 To Bus Station Автовокзал

WHERE TO STAY

Hotels worth trying include the *Hotel Tsentralnaya* (☎ 551 109) on ul Malisheva 74, with singles for US$50 and doubles for US$140; and the *Hotel Yubilena* (☎ 578 028) on pro Lenina 40, with singles for US$40, de luxe twin rooms for US$114, and an Intourist office on the 4th floor. The *Hotel Bolshoi Ural* (☎ 556 896) ul Krasnoarmeiskaya 1, is right next door to a 'secret' weapons technology plant and a little cheaper.

Directly opposite the railway station is the rather dirty *Hotel Sverdlovsk* (☎ 536 261), ul Chelyuskintsev 106, which is a conventional, Intourist-style place. The rooms range from US$28 to US$100 per person. Breakfast is US$4 extra.

.

MNTK (☎ 289 145, fax 286 292), ul Bardina 4, is a 20-30 minute bus ride from the city centre. To get here, take bus No 18, which starts opposite UPI (see p193) and stops right outside the building (it's on the right). The spotless rooms start from US$115. MNTK also has a railway ticket issuing agency in its building.

The best place to stay can be difficult to arrange, although with luck you might just be able to walk in off the street and get a room: *Dom Mir-i-Druzhby* (House of Peace and Friendship) is at 1/2 Nab Rabochei Molodeshi, on the western bank of the river, 200m north of pro Lenina. They have luxurious apartments or rooms at knock-down prices (eg a flat with three double bedrooms, two bathrooms, kitchen, hall and dining-room for US$60). When the 18-room hotel here is full they can also arrange homestays. Call or fax in advance (☎ 51 77 52, fax 51 86 47). If you do manage to get in here, you have the added bonus of knowing that you're staying in the former residence of one B Yeltsin.

The *Hotel Iset* (☎ 556 943), pro Lenina 69/1, has overpriced single/double suites for US$122/226 and a few cheaper rooms. This dilapidated construction was built to resemble a hammer and sickle from above. The sickle, which one imagines would be the tricky bit, turned out well but the hammer never really quite happened.

A top quality hotel is the excellent *Hotel Oktyabrskaya* (☎ 445 146), ul Sofi Kovalevskoi 17, with very comfortable rooms for US$298/340.

If you arrive by plane, you can stay at the *Uktus Airport Hotel* (☎ 219 365).

Homestays can be organised by the Moscow based G&R International for US$25 including breakfast. For contact information, see p171.

WHERE TO EAT

The best, most interesting and most expensive restaurant in town is the Chinese *Harbin* (☎ 617 571). There's hardly a chopstick in sight but the food is surprisingly good. Around US$25 will get you a set four-course meal for one which will probably be more than enough for two. It may well be topped off with the restaurant's pièce de resistance – a large deep-fried fish flambéd at the table. I asked my wide-eyed Russian companion what the fish was: 'It's...on fire!' was the reply. Harbin is at ul Kuibysheva 38 which is very near the circus and the concrete communications tower to the south of pro Lenina (both visible from the river). To get here take tram Nos 4, 14, 26 or 34 from the city centre to the stop on ul Belinskogo, or trolleybus Nos 1, 5 or 9 from the railway station.

Next best bet is the *Kosmos*, a trendy ex-Party restaurant with a casino (and a large neon sign). Food is standard Russian/European fare. Smaller and cheaper is the *Ural Chicken Restaurant*, opposite Dom Officerov. It tends to be pretty busy (always a good sign) and a set meal here will cost you about US$3. The pelmeni at **Hotel Iset** are good, although the place is a bit dingy and service can be casual. Near the railway station, beside the Sverdlovsk Hotel restaurant, the **Staraya Krepost** just across ul Sverdlova, is better.

The restaurant **Teatralnoe** (ul Mamin-Sibiryak opposite the Opera and Ballet Theatre) is recommended although it serves rather small portions so you need to fill up on bread. Mushrooms in sour cream cost US$5, meat soup is US$4 and shashlik costs US$10. Also in the building is the **Kafe Pizza** where you'll get a pizza, ice-cream and shakes for US$9. Next door is the **Vesna Bar** which offers pelmeni for US$2, sandwiches at US$0.50 and beers for US$4.

WHAT TO SEE

The Romanov Memorial

The site of the murder of the Imperial family is simply a patch of bare earth marked by a **white metal cross** and a **plaque** inscribed with the names of the Romanov family. Yeltsin had the original building (Ipatev House) demolished in 1976.

A small wooden **chapel** dedicated to St Elizabeth (Elizabeth Fyodorov) was built on the site in the late 1980s. Elizabeth was Alexander II's sister-in-law and following the Romanov murders, was thrown down a mineshaft and left to die. Local villagers claimed to have heard her miserable wailings for two days as she prayed for the souls of her attackers who, when they realised that she was still alive, piped poisonous gas into the well and then filled the hole with earth. The chapel

---

❏ **The discovery of the Romanov remains**

The story behind the discovery of the Romanov remains is almost as bizarre as that of their 'disappearance'. In July 1991 it was announced that parts of nine bodies had been found and that these were almost certainly those of the Imperial Family. Perhaps the most intriguing aspect of the discovery was the fact that three of the skulls, including that of the Tsar himself, had been placed in a wooden box. In fact the bodies had been discovered some 20 years before by a local detective novel writer named Geli Ryabov. He deduced, by the skulls' immaculate dental work, that these were indeed the bodies of the Royal Family, but reburied them for fear of persecution by the secret police.

In December 1992, testing at the Forensic Science Service laboratory in Aldermaston matched DNA samples from the bodies with DNA taken from a blood sample from Prince Philip, Duke of Edinburgh, (Tsarina Alexandra's sister was Philip's maternal grandmother).

The state burial of the royal remains has been delayed following a disagreement between surviving members of the Romanov family, who want the bones to be returned to Ekaterinburg as a memorial to the millions killed by the Communists, and the government, who favour burial in St Petersburg.

is occasionally set alight by anti-monarchists. In late 1996, the charred remains of this church could been seen and another larger, permanent church is being built near the white cross.

The grand building opposite the Romanov site now houses the headquarters of the Children's Movement. It was commissioned by one of Ekaterinburg's wealthy merchants, Rastoguiev, and legend holds that he was so rich that he used to mint his own gold coins in the basement. Apparently he was a cruel man: having bailed an architect out of jail, he offered to buy the man's freedom if he designed him a beautiful enough house. The architect laboured hard to complete his side of the bargain but, when Rastoguiev did not keep his promise, hanged himself.

Next door to this building is **Ascension Cathedral**, impressive from the outside but containing nothing of particular note. It was closed following the Revolution, its treasures removed and its murals painted over.

Military Museum

The remains of Gary Powers' U2 aircraft are exhibited in the Military Museum at the House of Officers (Dom Officerov) near the city centre but staff here are sometimes unwilling to let foreigners in or occasionally seem to be ignorant of the fact that the plane is even here at all. The exhibit itself is impressive but what was state-of-the-art espionage equipment in 1960 is today only the remains of an old aeroplane. Pride of place goes to the U2 camera which so impressed Nikita Khrushshev: 'It must be said that the camera is not a bad one,' he said, 'the photographs are very accurate. But I must say that our cameras take better pictures and are more accurate'.

The House of Officers is easily recognisable by the massive armoury outside, and around the back is a collection of Soviet military hardware including a couple of fighter planes, a helicopter, a long line of tanks and the cosmonauts' re-entry capsule from the rocket Soyuz. The Military Museum (☎ 552 106) is open 11:00-18:00 on Saturday and bookings are necessary for the rest of the week.

Museum of Decorative Arts

There's a fine collection of nineteenth century iron sculpture here, a gallery of Russian paintings, including works by Ivanov and Tarakanova, a portrait of PA Stroganov (of Beef Stroganov fame), and a famous painting of Christ by Polenov. Pride of place goes to the iron pavilion, which won first prize in the Paris Exposition in 1900. It's very impressive but you can't but wonder what it's for. Open daily 09:00-17:00.

Museum of local history

The museum of local history (☎ 511 819) is at ul Malysheva 46, relocated from the old museum in Alexander Nevsky Cathedral. There are interesting displays on 19th century Ekaterinburg, the revolution and the murder of the Romanovs and the discovery of their remains. It's well worth a visit and is open daily from 11:00 to 17:00.

Other things to see in Ekaterinburg

The **Ural Geology Museum** (☎ 223 109) at ul Kuibysheva 30 is good; try to track down the curator, who speaks perfect English and seems to enjoy showing visitors around. It is open 11:00-18:00, closed Tuesday.

Other museums include the **Literary Quarter Museum**, ul Tolmacheva 41; the **Museum of Political Development in the Urals**, ul Karla Libknekhta 32, open 11:00-18:00, closed Friday; and **Popov's Radio Museum**, ul Rozy Lyuksemburg 9.

There are a number of interesting buildings in the city including the classical style **Mining Office** (1737-1739), and the former estate of **Rastorguev-Kharitonov** (1794-1824) ul Karla Libknehkta 44. At the eastern end of pro Lenina is **UPI**, the Urals Polytechnical Institute, an impressive building which often features on postcards. In fact it was recently re-termed a university but the old name has stuck. The building beside it with the cannons outside is the city's military college.

The **Opera and Ballet Theatre** (☎ 558 057) at pro Lenina 46a is the third most important in Russia after Moscow and St Petersburg. The programme changes every night.

There is also a depressing **zoo** which looks more like a prison at ul Mamin-Sibiryak 189.

Excursions from Ekaterinburg

● **Europe/Asia marker** About 40km to the west along the main road to Moscow (*Novi Moscovski Trakt*) the German scientists, Gumboldt and Roze, selected the border between Europe and Asia in 1829 while doing barometric surveying along the Trakt. The original marker was destroyed in the 1920s and replaced with a concrete obelisk faced with granite. Intourist runs trips to this obelisk. There's a another marker beside the railway line, 36km to the west at Vershina (Вершина).

● **Museum of wooden architecture** It's a long way away (60km to the north) and not as good as the one outside Irkutsk but bus No31 from the railway station will get you here. The most interesting building is the old church. Closed since the Revolution, craftsmen began its restoration recently and were surprised to find many of the carved floor tiles missing. As work proceeded, the lost tiles began to show up, brought in by pensioners who had long ago removed pieces of their church as momentos. Incredibly, all the tiles have now been returned.

● **Other sights** Visitors are occasionally taken to either the **Alapayevsky jade mines** 300km to the east, or to **Tchaikovsky's house** 300km to the north-east. A visit to either of these sites could take in the mineshaft where Elizabeth Fyodorov was murdered but there's nothing to see at this rather grim site.

Tyumen
Тюмень

1 History Museum Complex (Saints Peter & Paul
Church & Cathedral of Trinity Monastery
Музей Истории Города (Петропавловская
Церковь и Троицкий Собор Троицкого
Мужского ММонастыря)
2 Elevation of the Cross Church
Крестовоздвиженская Церковь
3 Remains of Kremlin Walls Остатки Земляных
Валов быв. Кремля
4 1941-1945 Monument & Eternal Flame
Монумент Победы и Вечный Огонь
5 Local Studies Museum Краеведческий Музей
6 University Университет
7 Household Goods & Architecture Museum
8 Church of Mikhaila Maleina
Церковь Михаила Малеина
9 Puppet Theatre Театр Кукол
10 Cathedral of Holy Cross Знаменский Собор
11 Church of the Saviour Спасская Церковь
12 Philharmonic Hall Филармония
13 Art Gallery Картинная Галерея
14 Hotel Quality Tyumen Гостиница Tyumen
15 Hotel Prometei Гостиница Прометей
16 Central Square Центральная Площадь
17 Police Station Милиция
18 Central Post Office Почтамт
19 Tsentralni Stadium Стадион Центральный»«
20 City Park Парк
21 Circus Цирк
22 Drama Theatre Театр Драмы
23 Department Store Умивермаг
24 Market Рынок
25 Fire Technology Museum Музей
26 Old Cemetery Старое Кладбище
27 Book Shop Дом Книги
28 Hotel Vostok Гостиница Восток
29 Hotel Tura Гостиница Тура
30 Aeroflot Касса Аэрофлота
31 Hotel Turist Гостиница Турист
32 Pizza Tyumen Пицца Тюмень
33 Parliament House Дом Советов
34 Café Chebureki Кафе Чебуреки
35 Credo Bank Кредо Банк
36 Sputnik Travel Agency Спутник
37 House-Museum of Masharov Дом-музей
Машарова
38 Library Библиотека
39 Restaurant Slabutich & Café Olyushka
Ресторан Слабутич и Кафе Олюшка
40 Bar Nedra Бар Недра

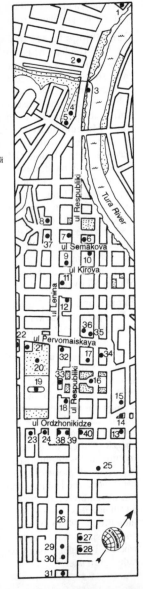

Tyumen
Тюмень

The only city in Asia to have hosted a European cup, Tyumen is the booming oil capital of Western Siberia and its wealth is illustrated by the expensive goods in the shops.

Founded in 1586, Tyumen's location on a major trading river, the Tura, made it an important transit point for goods between Siberia and China. It was also a major transit point for settlers and convicts destined for Siberia and the Russian Far East. By 1900, over one million convicts had tramped through Tyumen. During WWII, much of European Russia's factories, treasures and population were relocated to Siberia. The greatest treasure to be transferred from Moscow to Tyumen during this time was Lenin's corpse. For years he rested secretly in a building of the Agricultural Institute, tended by a team of specialists.

Prior to the drilling of the first well in the region in 1960, Tyumen was just a dusty backwater of 150,000 inhabitants. Since then its population has tripled. The importance of oil to the city can be seen in the two giant crude oil pipelines running through it. Tyumen is a pleasant enough place and certainly feels more affluent than many other Siberian cities.

ORIENTATION AND SERVICES

From the train station, all trolley buses and buses take you along ul Pervomaiskaya then either down ul Lenina or ul Respubliki.

Travel agencies include **Intourist** (☎ 250 027), ul Gertsena 74, and **Sputnik** (☎ 240 713), ul Respubliki 19. **Aeroflot** (☎ 223 252, 262 946) is at ul Respubliki 156, and you can get information about flights from the airport (☎ 232 124).

Credit card **cash advances** can be obtained from the exchange office in Hotel Prometei and the Credo Bank office at ul Pervomaiskaya 8 for 4% commission.

WHERE TO STAY

The cheapest accommodation is also the worst. The *Komnata Otdikha* (☎ 292 073), at the station, charges US$5 a single room, US$10 a double room, and US$12 a triple. Bathrooms are in the corridor. The entrance to the Komnata Otdikha is on the street in the front of the station.

Basic hotels are the *Hotel Turist* (☎ 273 573), ul Respubliki 156; and *Hotel Vostok* (☎ 225 205), ul Respubliki 159, with singles from US$44 with attached bathroom. To get to Hotel Vostok from the Central Square on ul Respubliki, take trolleybus 14.

There are two standard hotels in the city: *Hotel Prometei* (☎ 251 423), ul Sovetskaya 20, and *Hotel Quality*, ul Ordzhonikidze. Both have single rooms for around US$40, or US$70 for a de luxe single.

The top hotel in town is the newly-opened Western-quality *Hotel Tura* (☎ 229 969), ul Melnikaite 103A. A single room with attached bathroom costs US$120.

WHERE TO EAT

The best place for snacks is the *Pizza Tyumen* (☎ 261 868), ul Lenina 61 (opposite the City Park) which has a good range of fast food such as pizza (US$0.60), pelmini (US$1), salad (US$1). In summer, the patio upstairs is open and becomes the *Café Letnee*.

Other places for a quick snack are the *Café Olyushka* behind the Restaurant Slabutich, *Café Chebureki* at ul Voldarsko 43, and *Bar Nedra* across the road from Restaurant Slabutich.

Restaurant Slabutich (ul Respubliki 62) is Tyumen's best Russian restaurant with friendly service and large portions. It has a vast range of meals including assorted salads (US$2), *varenki* (potato filled dumplings) (US$3), stuffed tomatoes (US$2) and soups (US$2). The place is popular with wealthy locals who all seem to want a turn on the piano singing old folk songs.

WHAT TO SEE

The most interesting buildings are at the **History Museum Complex** (☎ 262 412) at ul Kommunisticheskaya 10, open 9:30-17:00. The complex includes the Museums of Siberian Religious History and the History of the City and Trinity Cathedral built in 1616, the Church of Saints Peter and Paul, and the walls of the monastery. This monastery is unusual in Siberia as it was one of only a few built from stone. All museums in Tyumen are closed Monday and Tuesday.

Particularly interesting is the wooden **Household Goods and Architecture Museum** which was formerly the Blyukher Museum (ul Respubliki). The wooden house was built in 1804 and its owners included the 1830s Tyumen mayor, Ikonikov. The **House-Museum of Masharov** (☎ 261 310, 262 976) ul Lenina 24, provides an insight into the life and times of a wealthy 19th century factory owner. Specialist museums include the **Fire Technology Museum** on ul Gorkovo, and the **Geology, Oil and Gas Museum** (☎ 227 426) on ul Respubliki 42. The **City Park** is the local Hari Krishna hangout.

Bookstores sell old Tsarist coins. As it is illegal to take them out of the country, don't declare them at customs when you leave.

Omsk
Омск

Omsk is the second largest city in Siberia, founded in 1719 when a small fortress was set up on the west bank of the Om. This was the military headquarters of the Cossack regiments in Siberia. The fortress had been considerably enlarged and included a large *ostrog* (prison). It was here that Dostoyevsky did four years hard labour for political crimes in 1849. His unenviable experiences were recorded in *Buried Alive in Siberia*. He was twice flogged, once for complaining about a lump of dirt in his soup; the second time he saved the life of a drowning prisoner, ignoring a guard who ordered that the man be left to drown. Dostoyevsky received so severe a flogging for this charitable act that he almost died and had to spend six weeks in the hospital.

During the Civil War, Omsk was the capital of the White Russian government of Admiral Kolchak, until November 1919 when the Red Army entered and took the city. The population grew fast after the war and now more than a million people live here. Textiles, food, agricultural machinery and timber-products are the main industries. There is also an important petro-chemical industry here, supplied by a pipeline from the Ural-Volga oil region.

Omsk has a sister city relationship with Milwaukee, Wisconsin.

ORIENTATION AND SERVICES

Most of the hotels and museums are located in the city centre which is about 2.5km from the station at the junction of the Om and Irtysh rivers. **Intourist** (☎ 311 490) is at pr Karla Marxa 4, and **Turist** (☎ 250 624), ul Gagarina 2. The main office of **Aeroflot** (☎ 223 252, 262 946) is at ul Respubliki 156, with branches at the river terminal (☎ 312 266), and railway station.

Train tickets can be purchased only at window 15 at the **Ticket Booking Office** on ul Pushkina, not at the station.

WHERE TO STAY

The best of the hotels located in downtown Omsk is the ***Hotel Mayak*** (☎ 315 431), ul Lermontova 2. There are single rooms for US$67, doubles for US$75, and executive suites consisting of two large rooms from US$150. It has very clean rooms and rather kitch Russian decor. They offer student discounts. Other good choices are the ***Hotel Tourist*** (☎ 316

414), ul Tito 2: double room US$50 with bathroom, de luxe single US$84; and the *Hotel Sibir* (formerly Hotel Evropa) (☎ 312 571), ul Lenina 22: single US$40, double de luxe room US$90.

Only the standard *Hotel Omsk* (☎ 310 721), Irtyshskaya nab 30, and very basic *Hotel Avtomobilist*, pro Karla Marxa 43, are within walking distance (but only just) of the railway station.

WHERE TO EAT

Numerous cafés are springing up all along ul Lenina and most are fairly ordinary. *Salon Sharm* at ul Masilenikovo deserves a special mention as it is a combined beauty salon and expresso bar. It serves real coffee for US$1.50 which probably isn't worth it unless you're desperate for a real caffeine fix. Very cheap meals are available at the *Canteen Blini*.

WHAT TO SEE

Omsk prides itself on having numerous parks and there isn't really a lot to see here unless you're into museums of the 'Former Home of Unknown Artist and Obscure Soviet Poet' variety. The **Dostoyevsky Museum** (☎ 242 965), ul Dostoevskovo, is fairly interesting, however. The **Military Museum**, ul Taube 7, has displays on WW1, WW2, the Afganistan and Chechnya conflicts. Most museums are closed on Monday. Near the junction of the Om and Irtysh Rivers are the ramparts and the **Tobolsk Gate** of the old Omsk Fortress.

Tobolsk

Probably the most interesting thing to do in the area is to take a trip 235km north to the historic town of **Tobolsk**. This was the capital of Siberia until 1824 and some of the old buildings survive. Tobolsk Kremlin sits high above the river; the Bishop's Chambers, Gostiny Dvor and Bell-tower are also worth seeing and there are daily hydrofoil trips along the Irtysh River.

You can reach Tobolsk by train from Tyumen. If you catch the No 274 at 05:03 you'll arrive at 10:00. There's a train leaving Tobolsk at 16:10 which reaches Tyumen at 20:55. If you've more time, the boat from Tyumen can be a pleasant way to reach Tobolsk.

River trips

There are two river stations in Omsk. Long distance vessels, such as those for Tobolsk, leave from the **Long-Distance River Station**. The timetable and ticket office are in the large station building.

Tourist trips along the Irtysh River depart from the **Excursion River Station**. Tickets and timetables are available from the kiosk under the Lenin bridge. A one-hour trip costs about US$3. The river is navigable from late May to September.

Novosibirsk
Новосибирск

With a population of over 1.6 million people, this is the largest city in Siberia and its industrial centre but, of the cities along the Trans-Siberian that foreigners usually visit, Novosibirsk has the least to offer the tourist. It's a relatively young city and has few buildings of historic interest.

You can visit the enormous opera house, the museums and the nearby town of Akademgorodok, the Scientists' City where three thousand scientists live in a purpose-built town, a Soviet academic experiment. Winters here are particularly harsh, with temperatures falling as low as minus 50°C. Novosibirsk is the starting point of the 'Turksib' railway line; enterprising travellers could catch a train from here to Almaty in Kazakhstan and then continue west into China.

HISTORY

Novosibirsk didn't exist before the Trans-Siberian was built and its spectacular growth this century is largely due to the railway. In 1891 it was decided that a railway bridge over the Ob should be built here and in 1893, a small settlement on the river bank sprung up to house the bridge builders. The town was named Novo-Nikolayevsk in honour of the accession of the new Tsar.

By 1900 over 15,000 people lived here and the numbers grew as railway and water-borne trade developed. As far as tourists were concerned, there was only one reason for getting off the Trans-Siberian in Novo-Nikolayevsk, as Baedeker's 1914 *Guide to Russia* points out: 'It is a favourite starting point for sportsmen in pursuit of the wapiti, mountain sheep, ibex and other big game on the north slopes of the Altai'. The town suffered badly during the Civil War when 30,000 people lost their lives. During the first four months of 1920 a further 60,000 died of typhus. In 1925 Novo-Nikolayevsk was re-christened Novosibirsk ('New Siberia').

Between 1926 and 1939 the population increased greatly as the city's iron-making furnaces were built and fed with coal from the nearby Kuznetsk Basin and iron ore from the Urals. In the early 1930s, the 900-mile Turksib Railway was completed linking Novosibirsk with Turkestan in former Soviet Central Asia, via Semipalatinsk and Almaty. Grain from the lands around Novosibirsk could then easily be exchanged for cotton, which grew best in Central Asia. The building of this railway, the jewel in the new government's first Five Year Plan, was filmed and is still

HOTELS AND RESTAURANTS

 2 Hotel Novosibirsk Гостиница Новосибирск
 6 Restaurant Sobek Ресторан Собек
11 Hotel Sibir, Intourist & American Business Centre Гостиница Сибирь
14 Canteen Столовая
17 Kafe Yunost Кафе Юность
20 Hotel Tsentre Rossi and German Consulate Гостиница Центр России и
   Консольство Германии Sibirski Torgovy Bank Сибирский Торговый
   Банк Tsentralny Kompleks Центральный Комплекс
21 Hotel Tsentralnaya/Restaurant Druzhba Гостиница Центральная
   Ресторан Дружба
23 Zolotoye Kolos Булочная «Золотой Колос»
26 Canteen Столовая
29 Hotel Sapfir Гостиница Сапфир
31 Hotel Tsentre Rossi Гостиница Центр России
34 Hotel Ob/River Station Гостиница Обь/Речной Вокзал

OTHER

 1 Central Railway Station Железнодорожний Вокзал
 3 Railway ticket office for foreigners travelling within CIS
   Железнодорожная Касса для Иностранцев
 4 Cathedral of the Ascension/Circus Вознесенский Собор/Цирк
 5 Aeroflot Касса Аэрофлота
 7 Market Рынок
 8 Banya Баня
 9 Museum of Local Studies Краеведческий Музей
10 TsUM Department Store ЦУМ
12 House-Museum of Kirov Дом-Музей Кирова
13 Puppet Theatre Театр Кукол
15 Tsentralny Dom Knigi Bookstore Центральный Дом Книги
16 Medical Institute Медицинский Институт
18 Opera & Ballet Theatre Театр Оперы и Балета
19 Regional Centre of Russian Folklore and Ethnography
   Областной Центр Фольклора и Этнографии
22 Sibirski Bank Сибирский Банк
24 Central Post Office Почтамт
25 Long-distance Telephone Office Междугородний Переговорный Пункт
27 Railway ticket office for foreigners travelling outside CIS
   Железнодорожная Касса для Иностранцев
28 Steam Engine Паровоз
30 Chapel of St Nicholas Часовня Святителя Николая
32 Bus Station Автовокзал
33 Oktyabrski Commercial Port Октябрьский Порт

METRO STATIONS Станция Метро

A Ploshchad Garina-Mikailovskovo Площадь Гарина-Михайловского
B Ploshchad Lenina Пл Ленина
C Ploshchad Gagarinskaya Пл Гагаринская
D Krasny Prospekt Красный Проспект
E Ploshchad Oktyabrskaya Октябьская
F Rechnoi Vokzal Речной Вокзал

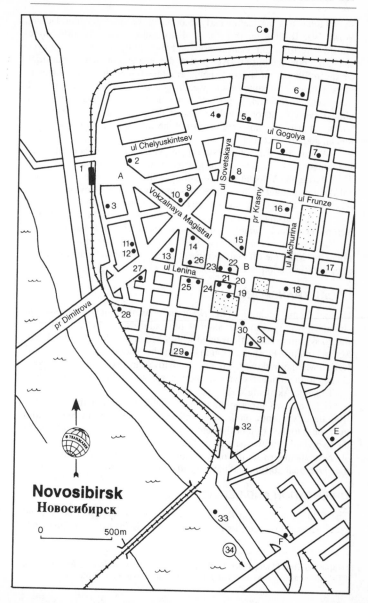

ul Chelyuskintsev

ul Sovetskaya

ul Gogolya

ul Frunze

pr Krasny

ul Michurina

Vokzalnaya Magistral

ul Lenina

pr Dimitrova

Novosibirsk
Новосибирск

0   500m

shown today as a fascinating early example of documentary film. During World War II large numbers of civilians and complete factories were moved here from European Russia, and the city has been growing ever since. It's now the busiest river port in the area and the major industrial centre in Siberia, most people being employed in engineering or metallurgy factories. In spite of the wealth generated by the area's natural resources, Novosibirsk is no better run than other Russian cities. On almost every occasion that I've visited the place there's been no hot water, not just in the hotel but in most of the city. Apparently it's been like this on and off since 1917!

1990 saw pro-democracy rallies here, with a number of students staging hunger strikes in the square in front of the opera house. In October 1993 during the Yeltsin/Congress struggle, there were once again political demonstrations in the square, this time pro-Soviet. Novosibirskians who've had enough of politics have been concerning themselves with the problem of raising money for a statue in honour of Mexican starlet Veronica Castro, leading lady in the soap opera, *The Rich Also Cry*.

Novosibirsk's centenary, in 1993, was marked with major celebrations, including the official opening of the Chapel of St Nicholas, closed after the Revolution (see p212).

LOCAL TRANSPORT

On foot, Lenin Square is about twenty minutes from the railway station, straight down Vokzalnaya (Station) Magistral. Novosibirsk has a good **metro** system (some stations lined with Siberian marble). To get to Lenin Square (metro: Ploshchad Lenina) from the station (metro: Ploshchad Garina-Mikhailovskovo), go one stop to Sibirskaya/Krasny Prospekt, change to the Studentskaya line and it's one stop to Ploshchad Lenina.

To get to Akademgorodok, see p214.

There are two airports; the international **Tolmachovo airport**, 23km from the city's centre on the western bank, and the domestic **Sverny airport**, 6km to the north of the centre. Buses No 122 and 111 run between the two via the railway station and bus station.

Near the metro station of Rechnoi Vokzal (meaning *river station*) is the **river boat station** and the **long distance bus station**.

ORIENTATION AND SERVICES

The fifth largest city in Russia, Novosibirsk was designed on a grand scale. Krasny Prospekt, its main street, extends for over ten kilometres.

(Opposite) Top: Plinthed loco by the line at Km3333, Novosibirsk . **Bottom:** Hare Krishna devotees on the streets of Tyumen. (Photo: Tatyana Pozar-Burgar)

The mighty River Ob bisects the city, leaving the main hotels, sights and the railway station on the east bank. Although there were plans to rid the city of its Communist era street names, the signs are still in place.

Intourist (☎ 237 870) is in Hotel Sibir at ul Lenina 21. Recommended local agents include the adventure travel company, **Sibalp** (☎ 495 922, fax 469 059, e-mail: sibalp@niee.nsk.su), ul Nemirovicha-Danchenko 155/1, kv 47; **Magic Tours** (☎ 204 252), pro Krasny 62 (specialists in the Altai); and **Tourist Guide Union** (☎ 297 561, fax 239 529), ul Lenina 30/2 (specialists in sports).

Airlines here include: **Aeroflot** (☎ 291 999), ul Pyatovo Goda 83; **Sibir Aviation** (☎ 669 078, fax 227 572); **Lufthansa** (at airport) (☎ 696 377, fax 227 151), **Transaero** (☎ 231 917, fax 230 321) ul Krasny.

There are three places where foreigners can get rail tickets. For trips **within the CIS**, same day and advance tickets can be purchased from ul Shamshurina 10. The ticket office is open 9:00-13:00 and 14:00-17:00, Monday to Friday. For Mongolia or China, same day and advance tickets can be purchased from pro Dimitrova 2 (☎ 982 333). The office is inside the Bank Vostok building, and is open 9:00-12:00 and 13:00-18:00, Monday to Friday. For information: general (☎ 207 711), international tickets (☎ 293 530). For **same day tickets**, you can try the station at windows 11 to 14 or the Advance Purchase Rail Ticket Office (☎ 207 721), ul Sovetskaya 72. The Advance Ticket Office normally sells to Russians only, for tickets not on the day of departure but they're fairly relaxed about this rule so you may be lucky.

The **SAIC American Business Centre** is at Suite 731, Hotel Sibir, ul Lenina 21, ☎ 235 569, fax 235 762, e-mail: abc@saic.nsk.su.

Money can be exchanged at most banks and at the Central Post Office on ul Lenina. Sibirski Bank, ul Lenina, offers Visa card cash advances.

Novosibirsk University offers reasonably priced Russian **language courses**. Contact Gwendolin Fricker, KASSI Language, Novosibirsk University, ☎ 352 653, fax 397 124, e-mail admin@kassi.nsu.nsk.su, http://www.cnit.nsk.su/univer/english/kassi.htm.

Tours

The travel desks at most hotels offer a morning tour of the city as well as tours to the sights and museums described below. Tours to Akadem-gorodok usually include a visit to the geological museum and a boat-trip on the Ob Dam in summer. They will also arrange tickets for the circus (closed in summer) and for opera and ballet at the Opera House. You can organise your own boat trip from the landing stage near Rechnoi Vokzal metro station to Korablik Island, which is popular with Novosibirskians for swimming and sunbathing from May to September.

(Opposite) Traditional shuttered house, Listvyanka (see p234)

WHERE TO STAY

A good value hotel is *Hotel Ob* (☎ 667 401), ul Obnaya 49. Unfortunately the hotel is about 3km south of the city's centre, on the banks of the Ob River, next to the River Station. However it is easy to get to as it is near the Rechnoi Vokzal metro station. Singles start from US$20 and double rooms from US$35. A very cheap and basic hotel is *Hotel Sapfir*, ul Oktyabrskaya 49. with single rooms from US$15.

The *Hotel Novosibirsk* (☎ 201 120) is well located right opposite the railway station at Vokzalnaya Magistral 1. Single rooms start from US$50, double rooms from US$52 and these are without bathroom. Double rooms with bathrooms are from US$80.

While *Hotel Tsentralnaya* (☎ 227 660) is right in the city centre on ul Lenina 3, it is dingy and not good value. Prices start from US$55 single, US$84 double room. A double room with bathroom is US$102.

A good but overpriced place is *Hotel Tsentre Rossi* (☎ 234 562), pr Krasny 23. Singles start from US$130, a double from US$260, while a de luxe room costs a whopping US$250 per person.

The excellent *MNTK* is some way from the centre of town to the west of the river, at ul Kolkhidskaya 10 (☎ 410 155, fax 403 73); rooms start from US$115. To get here, take bus Nos 2 or 37 from pl Stanislavskaya.

By far the most upmarket place is the *Hotel Sibir* (☎ 231 215), ul Lenina 21, a Polish/Russian joint venture and Intourist's standard pad. Rooms are US$100 single, US$130 double. The rooms are clean and well maintained. There's a classy souvenir shop in the foyer.

Near Tolmachovo airport is the *Novosibirsk Airport Hotel* (☎ 281 430), ul Lenina 23. Singles start from US$24, a double US$36, cold water only and each room has only a basin, bathrooms are not attached. Only the de luxe rooms, costing US$68 per person, have hot water.

WHERE TO EAT

You can get a reasonable meal at the *Tsentralny Kompleks*, a department store on ul Lenina. Restaurant Tsentralny is on the ground floor, there's another restaurant is on the first floor and the Desert Bar is in the basement. Everything on the menus is under US$5 but the restaurant on the first floor charges US$2.50 entry.

For snacks, try *Café Yunost* (formerly Café Jazz), behind the Opera and Ballet Theatre. Snacks cost under US$3 and there are meals from US$5. In the afteroons they have a great selection of cakes and after 7pm there is live jazz. There is a surprisingly good snack bar in *TsUM* where the pastries are excellent and the coffee thoroughly drinkable.

The Novosibirsk area code is ☎ 3832. From outside Russia dial +7-3832.

Zolotoye Kolos is a recommended bakery opposite the Hotel Tsentralnaya and a good place to stock up for the Trans-Siberian trip as it sells a range of bottled and tinned foods. There is decent *canteen* at ul Lenina 9. Next door is a bar which serves beer, pizzas and shashliks for US$2 each.

A night at the *Sobek* (☎ 205 867), ul Dostoevsky 19, a Russian/Korean joint venture restaurant, can be exciting. It's an intimate little place that's packed with racketeers and mafia men. The food's not bad, about US$6 per person, live ammunition extra.

A reasonable choice is the *Hotel Sibir*. In the restaurant downstairs, service is good, as is the food (the chicken Kiev is recommended); but it tends to fill up with leather-jacketed, shell-suited 'businessmen' in the evenings. Directly above it, the second floor restaurant is better and has live Dixieland jazz every night. Expect to pay US$20 without drinks; if you want wine it's best to buy it in the kiosk outside the restaurant. The best restaurant in the city is the *Restaurant Druzhba*, next door to Hotel Tsentralnaya. It's a little cheaper than the Hotel Sibir.

WHAT TO SEE

Lenin Square and the Opera House

This is the centre of the city and the square is dominated by the vast **Opera House**, one of the largest in the world, with its silver dome. It was completed in 1945, when most of the builders had been sent off to join the war effort. Its completion is seen as all the more heroic in that it was to some extent due to the city's women and children, who helped the few remaining builders. You get tickets from the kiosk on the left side of the theatre or book seats on ☎ 223 866.

In the middle of the square is a **statue of Lenin**, his coat blowing behind him in the cold Siberian wind, a rather more artistic representation of the man than the many others produced. He is flanked by three soldiers on his right and by two 'Peace' figures on his left, who look as if they are directing the traffic that flows around the great square. In the winter there are troika rides here, and people build ice-sculptures. The low building above the metro station is the oldest stone structure in the city.

Museum of Local Studies

The Museum of Local Studies (☎ 218 630) is at ul Vokzalnaya Magistral 11. The bulk of this collection is housed in the ground floor (entrance at the side) of the block right behind TSUM. It's an interesting museum, although you will need a guide to explain the significance of some of the historical exhibits. There's a display showing life before the Revolution including a Singer sewing machine, a rusty British Norton motorbike (built in 1909) and an early piece of rail (stamped 'Birmingham 1899'). There's also a special section recording the troubled times during the civil war, when the city was occupied by the White Russians and then the

Bolsheviks, before being devastated by an outbreak of typhus in 1920. The extensive display of Siberian flora and fauna includes some of the 50 species of mammals, 30 species of fish and 30 species of birds that are found only in Novosibirsk oblast. There's also a collection of Siberian trees and grasses, a geological display and the skeleton of a mammoth. The labels on the natural history exhibits are in Latin as well as Russian: for a translation see p401.

Other things to see

Alexander Nevsky Cathedral, at the south end of Krasny Prospekt near the river, is now fully restored and is well worth a look. Closer to the centre of town, however, is the **Chapel of St Nicholas**, opened during the 1993 centenary celebrations and built on the spot that marks the exact centre of the country. The original church here was destroyed after the Revolution.

The **Dom Museum Kirov** is devoted to Kirov, a rising Communist Party leader who was assassinated in 1934 on Stalin's orders. It is housed, next to the Sibir Hotel, in an attractive log cabin, one of the few that have survived. In the neighbouring apartment block there is a small exhibition of local handicrafts, mainly wood-carvings. There is a good **Art Gallery**, pr Krasnyi 5 (near the regional administration building, on Sverdlovsk Square. It is open 11:00-19:00, closed Tuesday.

The **Regional Centre of Russian Folklore and Ethnography** (☎ 218 630) at pro Krasny 23, has three main sections; archaeology, ethnography and contemporary history. It is open 10:00-18:00, closed Monday and Tuesday.

ENTERTAINMENT

Novosibirsk boasts numerous theatres and cultural groups beside the Opera House. These include the **Chaldony Song and Dance Company** (☎ 418 889), ul Zabaluyeva 47; the **Circus** (☎ 237 584), ul Sovetskaya 11; the **Puppet Theatre** (☎ 221 202), ul Revolyutsi 6; the **Siberian Dixieland Jazz Band** (☎ 235 642), ul Kirova 3; the **Siberian Russian Folk Chorus** (☎ 202 269), ul Krasnoyarskaya 117; and the **Symphony and Chamber Orchestras Halls** (☎ 224 880), ul Spartaka 11.

WHAT TO BUY

There are the usual souvenir shops in the hotels. The main street for shopping is Vokzalnaya Magistral. The market is one block east of Krasny Prospekt. The Tsentralny Dom Knigi Bookstore, on pl Lenina, has a good selection of maps. TsUM Department Store next door to the Museum of Local Studies is surprisingly well stocked. There is also a large department store complex next to Hotel Novosibirsk.

EXCURSIONS

River Cruises

The Ob River which flows through Novosibirsk is the busiest river in Siberia. The most popular trip is the 65-minute round trip from the river station to Korablik Island. Most passengers get off here as it is a popular swimming spot. The ferry travels this route three times a day from May to September. To get to the river station, take the metro to the Rechnoi Vokzal station and you can see it from the exit.

Akademgorodok Academic City (Академгородок)

Established in the 1950s to house the scientists of the Siberian branch of the USSR's Academy of Sciences, Akademgorodok comprises 26 special research institutes and a staff of over 10,000. In this pleasant sylvan setting, students spend five years studying physics, chemistry, mathematics, history or economics (a recently restructured course, no doubt).

Akademgorodok is ranked third in the university tables after Moscow and St Petersburg but as government funding drops times are getting harder. It was once worth visiting just to see how the élite of the Soviet system lived. As with its Olympic athletes, the Soviet Union believed in training its academics from a very early age, spiriting them away from home to attend special boarding schools for the gifted. Nowadays the place is looking rather run down and there's little happening over the summer but the setting is pleasant, a relaxing opportunity to get away from polluted Novosibirsk.

The **Geological Museum** in the Institute of Geology and Geophysics is open to tours only. You could follow one in or just say, 'Moozay' to the doorman, and you may be let into the museum which is straight ahead, up the stairs. The overpowering mineral wealth of Siberia is displayed here, including the purple mineral chaorite, found only in this part of the world.

There is only one hotel in Akademgorodok which foreigners can stay in. *Hotel Zolotaya Dolina* (formerly Hotel Soran) (☎ 3832-356 609), ul Ilicha 10, charges US$35 for a double room. It has a good **restaurant**. For cheap food try the café on the first floor of the **Torgovi Centre** nearby. In the same street is a **bookshop** which has a small selection of maps, posters and books in English.

After looking round Akademgorodok you can walk through the birch forest and over the railway-track to the beaches of the **Ob Dam**. It was created by the building of the Novo-Sibirskaya power station, Siberia's first large hydro-electric project. This is a good place to swim as the water is surprisingly warm. It is 18°C for 2-3 months a year and reaches 22°C for about one month, usually July. In winter, **cross-country skiers** converge on Akademgorodok as it is the site of some good tracks maintained by the Alik Tulskii ski centre.

To get to Akademgorodok, from Novosibirsk take a train from the suburban station located south of the Central Railway Station to Obskoe More (Обское Море). The terminus for the train to Obskoe More is Bredek (Бредек) and a timetable can be found at the entrance to the suburban station on the street. Expect a slow 50-minute trip; one-way tickets cost under US$1.00. Trains run hourly from 06:02 to 23:17. To get to Akademgorodok from Obskoe More station, walk 100m away from the Ob Dam, cross over shosse Berdskoe, which runs parallel to the railway line, and continue on any of the dirt paths through the park. In about 10 minutes you reach the bus station and if you keep going, you get to the Torgovi Centre and Hotel Zolotaya Dolina.

There are several buses from Novosibirsk. Catch bus Nos 8 or 22 from in front of Rechnoi Vokzal metro station, Nos 2 or 22 from the Central Railway Station, or Nos 2 or 8 from in front of Studentskaya metro station. A taxi from Novosibirsk costs about US$20 one way.

AKADEMGORODOK

1 Bus Station
2 Bus to Novosibirsk
3 Supermarket & bookshop
4 Bakery
5 Cafe
6 Geological Museum
7 Market
8 Zolotaya Dolina Hotel
9 Obskoye More Station

Krasnoyarsk
Красноярск

Krasnoyarsk is a major industrial centre, producing one quarter of Russia's aluminium (749,100 tons per year), almost a quarter of its refrigerators and millions of truck and car tyres a year. Don't be entirely put of by this, however, as the old part of the city is quite attractive. With hills on the outskirts, Krasnoyarsk is certainly more pleasantly located than some other large Siberian cities, Novosibirsk, for example.

Russian settlement dates back to 1628 when a fort was built. Long since disappeared, it was situated on a hill overlooking the river and was first known as Krasny Yar meaning 'beautiful steep bank'. By 1900, the population was 27,000 and the town boasted 20 churches and two cathedrals, a synagogue, 26 schools, a railway technical college and a botanical garden reputed to be the finest in Siberia.

RL Jefferson visited Krasnoyarsk in 1897 and was impressed: 'Its situation cannot fail to elicit admiration – the tall mountains rear up around it.' Most of the townsfolk he met here were ex-convicts. So used were they to their own kind, that they were particularly suspicious of anyone who lacked a criminal record. He was told of a certain merchant in the city who found it difficult to do business, never having been behind bars. To remedy the situation he travelled all the way to St Petersburg and deliberately committed a crime that was punishable by exile to Siberia. After a short sentence in Irkutsk he returned to his business in Krasnoyarsk and 'got on famously' thereafter.

During the Second World War, many factories were evacuated from European Russia and rebuilt here. The city grew as a trading centre and during the Soviet's early five-year plans, underwent massive industrialisation to become Siberia's third largest city.

LOCAL TRANSPORT

For the airport catch bus No 135 from the bus station (US$0.50) or take a taxi (US$23). To get from the station to Hotel Krasnoyarsk, take trolley bus No 2 and get off at the bus station. To get to Hotel Turist from the bus station, take any tram along ul Veinbauma.

ORIENTATION AND SERVICES

Krasnoyarsk is divided into two parts, separated by the Yenisei River. The **north bank** is a mass of terraces and is bounded on the north by a steep

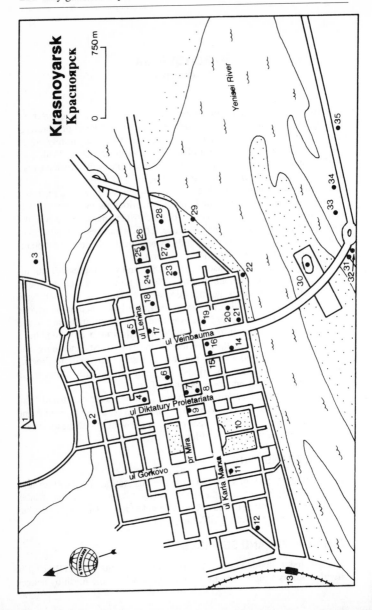

Krasnoyarsk
Красноярск

750 m

0

Yenisei River

ul Lenina
ul Veinbauma
ul Diktatury Proletariata
pr Mira
ul Gorkovo
ul Karla Marxa

HOTELS AND RESTAURANTS

7 Café Shakhmatnoe Кафе Шахматное
15 Hotel Krasnoyarsk Гостиница Красноярск
20 Hotel Enisei Гостиница Енисей
27 Hotel Oktyabrskaya Гостиница Октябрьская
31 Hotel Turist Гостиница Турист

OTHER

1 Chapel of St Parasceva Pyatnitsa
   Часовня Святой Великомученницы Парескевы Пятницы
2 Market Рынок
3 Trinity Church Троицкая Церковь
4 House-Museum of Surikov
   Дом-Музей В И Сурикова
5 Literature Museum
   Литературный Музей
6 Book Shop Книжный Мир
8 TsUM Department Store ЦУМ
9 Sinto Bank Синто Банк
10 Central Park
   Центральный Парк Культуры и Отдыха
11 Catholic Church Католическая Церковь
12 Palace of Culture of the Combine Harvester Builders (!)
   Дворец Культуры Комбайностроителей
13 Railway Station
   Железнодорожный Вокзал
14 Opera & Ballet Theatre
   Театр Оперы и Балета
16 Bus Station Автовокзал

OTHER (cont)

17 Central Post Office
   Почтамт
18 Intercession Church
   Покровская Церковь
19 City Administration Building
   Здание Городской Администрации
21 Museum of Local Studies
   Краеведческий Музей
22 River Station
   Речной Вокзал
23 Surikov Art Museum
   Художественный Музей В И Сурикова
24 Avtobaz Bank Автобазбанк
25 Annunciation Cathedral
   Благовещенский Собор
26 Art Gallery Художественная Галерея
28 Main Concert Hall
   Большой Концертный Зал
29 SS Nikolai Steamship
   Пароход «Св. Николай»
30 Stadium Lenin Komsomol
   Центральный Стадион имени Ленинского Комсомола
32 Aeroflot Office Агентство Аэрофлота
33 Concert & Dance Theatre
   Концертно-Танцевальный Зал
34 Monument to the Tsarist Convict Route
   Памятник Кандальный Путь
35 Circus Цирк

hill known as Karaulnaya Mountain and on the west by the forested Gremiachinskaya Ridge. The railway station, museums and hotels are located on this side. Just south of the station is the academic area (another Akademgorodok). The south bank is relatively flat and is mostly factories and multi-storey apartment blocks.

Krasnoyarsk's main **airport** (Emelyanovo) is 40km north of the station. Krasnoyarsk boasts offices for **Aeroflot** (☎ 222 156) ul Matrosova 4 and **Krasnoyarsk Airlines** (☎ 236 366, fax 234 896). Krasnoyarsk Airlines offers infrequent air service between New York and Krasnoyarsk over the summer. The flight is not direct as you have to change airports in Moscow.

Intourist (☎ 273 715) is in Hotel Krasnoyarsk and offers a range of tours. Visa and MasterCard cash advances are available from Avtovazbank at pro Mira 39 and Sinto Bank at pro Mira 87.

The Yenisei River is a major communications link and passenger ferries sail nearly 2000km along it from Krasnoyarsk. Tickets are available from the River Station. Contact the **Yenisei Steamship Line** (☎ 236 651, fax 236 883), ul Bograda 15, for information.

WHERE TO STAY

The best value hotel is the large, standard *Hotel Krasnoyarsk* (☎ 273 769), ul Uritskovo 94, charging US$30/60 for a single/double. Intourist groups usually stay at the standard 103-room *Hotel Oktyabrskaya* (☎ 271 916), ul Mira 15, with rooms from US$40/80 with attached bath. This hotel has a casino.

Avoid the basic *Hotel Turist* (☎ 361 470), ul Matrossova 2 (US$50 for a double) and the *Hotel Enisei* (☎ 278 262), ul Dubrovinskovo 80, US$30 for a single.

While all the hotels have restaurants, the best is *Hotel Krasnoyarsk* as it has a range: three cafés, a restaurant and a bar. You can get a reasonable meal for US$15 in the restaurant. Another good choice is *Café Shakhmatnoe* (pro Mira 85).

WHAT TO SEE

The terraced hill around the old part of town is an interesting place for a walk. The most interesting buildings here are the **Annunciation Cathedral** on ul Lenina and the old **Catholic Church**, which has an organ. The recently restored **Chapel of St Parasceva Pyatnitsa** is worth visiting and it takes about 40 minutes to reach from Hotel Krasnoyarsk. There are a number of general museums including the **Surikov Art**

The Krasnoyarsk area code is ☎ 3912. From outside Russia dial +7-3912.

Museum (☎ 272 558), ul Parizhskoi Kommuny 20, open 10:00-18:00, the **Museum of Local Studies**, ul Dubrovinskovo 84. The House-Museum of V I Lenin, who stayed here for all of two months in 1897 is now the **Literature Museum**, and the **SS Nikolai Steamship**, the ship on which Lenin sailed to exile in Shushenkoe, is now a commercial base.

EXCURSIONS

Stolby Nature Sanctuary (Заповедные Столбы)

An excursion to this 17,000 hectare recreational area is probably the most pleasant thing to do in Krasnoyarsk. It's a few kilometres upstream of the Yenisei River and there are over 100 large rock pillars, some up to 100m high, that look like people and have been given fanciful names like The Grandfather and The Woman. To get to Stolby take the suburban train to Ovsyanka (Овсянка), 5km from the city or to Turbaza (Турбаза). Or you could take bus No 7 from pl Predmostnaya (Площадь Пред-мостная) and get off at the Turbaza (Турбаза) stop but it is still a good 5km uphill walk to the first of the pillars. If you stay on the bus until the village of Bazaikha (Базайха), a few stops further on, you can take a chair lift (if it is working) to the top and walk to the pillars from there.

Divnogorsk (Дивногорск)

About 30km away on the railway past Stolby Nature Sanctuary is the town of Divnogorsk and the Yenisei Hydro-Electric Dam. The 100m high hydro-electric dam is technically interesting as it has a large moving basin to transport ships over the dam. The basin is about 5m by 15m and after the ship above the dam enters it, the basin's doors close, and the entire basin and enclosed ship move up to the top of the dam on a cog-railway. The basin is then rotated and lowered the 100m on the other side of the dam to river level. You can see this unusual system operating until 25 October which is when the river freezes over. Hydrofoils travel between Krasnoyarsk's River Station and Divnogorsk from 1 May to 31 August and depart every two hours. The trip takes about 45 minutes. There are also buses from the long distance bus station behind Hotel Krasnoyarsk, or you can catch a suburban train (three times a day). You can stay at the *Hotel Biryusa*, ul Naberezhnaya, US$40 for a double.

❏ Travelling intellectuals at the turn of the 20th century were advised to visit the library of Krasnoyarsk merchant, Yudin. This bibliophile assembled a collection of 100,000 volumes, including almost every publication ever issued in Siberia. At the end of the 19th century, while sentenced to exile in Krasnoyarsk, Lenin spent several months working in this library. In 1906 Yudin sold his valuable collection to the Library of Congress, for just US$40,000 even though it was valued at US$114,000. He did this 'with the sole idea of establishing closer relations between the two nations,' he wrote to the Congressional Librarian.

Irkutsk
Иркутск

If you can afford only one stop on the Trans-Siberian, you should make it Irkutsk. In this city, which was once known as the 'Paris of Siberia', you'll find the people rather more friendly and relaxed than the people in European Russia. Along many of the streets you can still see the cosy-looking log cabins (eaves and windows decorated with intricate fretwork) which are typical of the Siberian style of domestic architecture. Sixty-four kilometres from Irkutsk is Lake Baikal, set amongst some of the world's most beautiful countryside. Trekking, camping, boat excursions and riding are just a few of the pursuits that are now available in this out-door paradise.

HISTORY

Military outpost

Irkutsk was founded as a military outpost in 1652 by Ivan Pakhobov, a tax-collector who had come to encourage the local Buryat tribesmen to pay their fur tribute. By 1686 a church had been built and a small town established on the banks of the Angara. Tea caravans from China passed through Irkutsk, fur-traders sold their pelts here and the town quickly developed into a centre for trade in Siberia. By the beginning of the nineteenth century, Irkutsk was recognised as the administrative capital of Siberia. The Governor, who lived in the elegant white building that still stands by the river (opposite the obelisk), presided over an area twenty times the size of France. Being the capital of Siberia, it was the destination of many exiled nobles from Western Russia. The most celebrated exiles were the Decembrists, who had attempted a coup in St Petersburg in 1825. The houses in which some of them lived are now museums.

Boom town

With the discovery of gold in the area in the early 1800s, 'Gold Fever' hit Irkutsk. Fortunes were made in a day and lost overnight in the gambling dens. By the end of the century, in spite of a great fire in 1879 which destroyed 75 per cent of the houses, the city had become the financial and cultural centre of Siberia. Its cosmopolitan population included fur traders, tea merchants, gold prospectors, exiles and ex-convicts. Irkutsk had become 'a city of striking contrasts, with the magnificent mansions of the rich at one end of the pole and the dilapidated shanties of the poor at the other' as an Intourist brochure pointedly remarks. Those prospectors who were lucky became exceedingly rich, some amassing personal fortunes that would be equivalent to £70 or £80 million today. Often no more than illiterate adventurers or ex-convicts, they spent their money on lavish houses, French tutors for their children and clothes from the Paris fashion houses for their wives.

By far the most exciting occasion in the Irkutskian social calendar for 1891 was the visit of the Tsarevich (later Nicholas II) who stayed only a day but still had time to visit the museum, gold-smelting laboratory and the monastery, to consecrate and open the new pontoon bridge over the Angara (replaced only in 1936), to review the troops and to attend a ball.

The first rail travellers arrive

On 16 August 1898 Irkutsk was linked by rail to Europe with the arrival of the first Trans-Siberian Express. The train brought more European tourists than had dared venture into Siberia in the days when travelling meant weeks of discomfort bumping along the Trakt (the Post Road) in a wooden tarantass (carriage). Their guide books warned them of the dangers that awaited them in Irkutsk. Bradshaw's *Through Routes to the Capitals of the World* (1903) had this to say about the town: 'The streets are not paved or lighted; the sidewalks are merely boards on crosspieces over the open sewers. In summer it is almost impassable owing to the mud, or unbearable owing to the dust. The police are few, escaped criminals and ticket-of-leave criminals many. In Irkutsk and all towns east of it, the stranger should not walk after dark; if a carriage cannot be got as is often the case, the only way is to walk noisily along the planked walk; be careful in making crossings, and do not stop, or the immense mongrel mastiffs turned loose into the streets as guards will attack. To walk in the middle of the road is to court attack from the garrotters with which Siberian towns abound.'

The dangers that Bradshaw warned his travellers against were no exaggeration for at the time the average number of reported murders per year in Irkutsk was over 400, out of a population of barely 50,000.

Irkutsk today

Today's Irkutskians are rather better behaved, although mafia-related crime is on the increase. A city of over half a million, Irkutsk is still one of the largest suppliers of furs to the world markets, although engineering is now the main industry.

For too long Irkutskians have had to allow Moscow to make all their political, economic and environmental decisions for them. Control is slowly being decentralised and there has been a number of victories recently. The wood pulp mill built on the edge of Lake Baikal is still an eyesore but filtration systems now ensure that waste water is purified before being returned to the lake. The city now needs to have direct access to the hard currency earned by its exports, so that the money can be spent improving the lot of the people of Irkutsk rather than disappearing into the bottomless coffers of Moscow. It seems likely, however, that the city will benefit from tourism with the increasing numbers of visitors stopping off on their way to Lake Baikal.

LOCAL TRANSPORT

Since most of the sights, restaurants and shops are within walking distance of the hotels, this is the most pleasant and interesting way to get around. There's no metro but the usual bus service operates. Bus No 20 runs between the station and the airport down ul Lenina. Trams 1 and 2 go from the station over the bridge and into the centre of town. Tram No 4 goes out to the airport (25 mins) and back from outside the former Hotel Sibir.

ORIENTATION AND SERVICES

Irkutsk railway station is on the west bank of the river; the city centre and the tourist hotels are on the east. The city centre is along two intersected main streets: ul Lenina and ul Karla Marxa. Ul Lenina runs north-south from the administrative and public transport cente of pl Kirova, while the main shopping and museum street of ul Karla Marxa runs east-west. Any bus heading north from the railway station should take you over the bridge; from here all the main hotels are within walking distance.

A great budget agency is **Baikal Complex** (☎ 359 205, fax 432 060, 432 322 (marked attn Baikalcomplex), e-mail: youry@baikal.irkutsk.su,

---

❏ **Getting to Mongolia**

Irkutsk has a Mongolian Consulate, travel agents specialising in Mongolian travel and daily trains to Mongolia.

The **Mongolian Consulate** (☎ 242 370, fax 342 445), ul Lapina 11, is open 09:00-18:00 weekdays. It is possible to get a transit visa here in only 45 minutes (bring two passport photographs, US$30 and your ticket out of Mongolia). To get a tourist visa, you will need an invitation (see Irkutsk travel agents that offer Monglian services), US$30 and two photos. Allow five working days for your application to be processed. Getting a Mongolian visa can be difficult if you do not speak Russian or Mongolian so using a local travel agent is advisable.

Travel agents that can organise train tickets, accommodation and tours to Mongolia include Baikal Complex, Intourist and Sputnik. Baikal Complex offers the cheapest deals.

To buy **train tickets** from Irkutsk to Mongolia, go to the International Ticket Office on the first floor of the Irkutsk railway station. To get to the ticket office, you have to go through the waiting hall. You normally will have to pay to enter the waiting hall, but if you say that you want to buy an international ticket, you will probably get in for free. Train No 264 leaves daily for Ulan Bator at 19:33 local time. Ask for wagon 15 which is the best quality carriage. A coupé ticket costs US$57.

http://www.icc.ru/baikalcomplex), PO Box 3598, Irkutsk-29. The **Intourist office** (☎ 290 264, fax 277 872) is at the Hotel Irkutsk-Intourist, bul Gagarina 44; the people here are helpful and speak good English.

Other agencies are **AquaEco** (☎ 334 290), ul Karla Libknekhta 12; **Baikal House** (☎ 335 378, fax 335 378), ul Karla Marxa 3113; **Sputnik** (☎ 341 727), ul Dzerzhinskovo 48, which organises both local and Mongolian trips; and **Maria Travel** (☎ 341 486), ul Kievskaya 2, kv 211, e-mail maria@pop.irk.ru, http://riaph.irkutsk.su/maria.

Aeroflot (☎ 276 917), is at ul Gorkovo 29; and next door is the new airline, **Air Baikal**. This company operates a Boeing 757 on the Moscow-Irkutsk route. **Transero** has an office at bul Gagarina 38. Tickets for any airline can also be purchased from the Flight Ticket Office (☎ 293 415) in Hotel Angara.

A great source of information on the city is the **Irkutsk Electronic Yellow Pages** which can be found at http://www.icc.ru/fed/yellow.html. Locally, you can get good **maps** from the Hotel Irkutsk-Intourist, and Sibtorg Bookshop at ul Karla Marxa 24. **Faxes** can be sent from the Central Telegraph Office and the Central Post Office.

Visa credit card **cash advances** can be obtained from Inkom Bank on ul Gorkovo and they charge 6% commission. To exchange **travellers cheques**, go to Inkom Bank on ul Lenina; they charge 4% commission.

Irkutsk State Teachers' Training Institute of Foreign Languages (☎ 333 246, fax 333 244), Room 201/203, ul Lenina 8, has **Russian language courses** lasting anything from a week to four years. The cost is US$350 per month tuition and US$60 a month for accommodation.

Tours

Intourist and Baikal Complex offer a two-hour **city tour** (US$20 not including the churches) and a **Baikal tour** (US$50 for a car but if there's a bus tour going you may be able to join it for US$15). The tour to Baikal leaves at 08:00 and gets back at around 18:00. Intourist occasionally runs its own boat trip to Listvyanka and this might be worth enquiring about if you don't want to arrange things yourself.

Baikal Complex, run by the friendly Yuri Nemirorsky, has a range of day trips and **adventure tours** such as hiking, skiing and trekking from US$44 per day per person for two to four people in a group. They also offer a two-day trip along the **Circumbaikal Railway Line**. See p331 for information on this trip. Maria Travel offers **scuba diving** (US$50 per hour), **horse riding** (US$10 per hour), and a four-day trip to **Olkhon Island** (200km north in Lake Baikal) costing about US$60 a day per person. You stay in the wooden hotel (no hot water) in Khuzhir village, and visit several Buryiat sacred sites and a Stalin era gulag camp.

The Irkutsk area code is ☎ 3952. From outside Russia dial +7-3952.

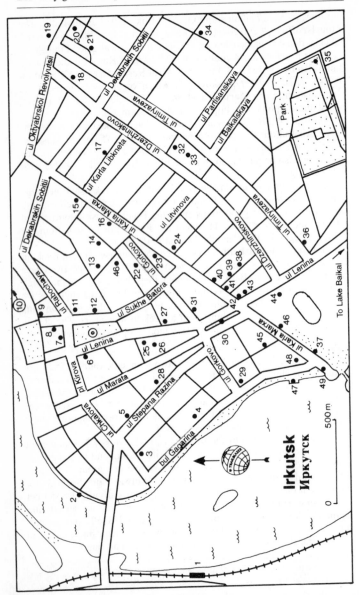

Irkutsk
Иркутск

OTHER (cont)

8 Church of Our Saviour
  Краеведческий Музей-Спасская Церковь
9 Epiphany Cathedral Богоявленский Собор
10 Znamensky Convent Знаменский Монастырь
11 Polish Catholic Cathedral Органный Зал-Польский Костёл
17 Synagogue Синагога
18 Trubetskoi House Музей-усадьба Трубецкого
19 Bus Station Автовокзал
20 Church of the Transfiguration Преображенская Церковь
21 Maria Volkonsky's House Музей-усадьба Волконского
22 Aeroflot & Air Baikal Касса Аэрофлота и Air Baikal
23 Exhibition Hall/Art Museum
  Выставочный Зал Художественного Музея
27 Art Museum Художественный Музей
28 Central Post Office Почтамт
29 Transaero Авиакомпания Трансаэро
30 Inkom Bank (For travellers cheques) ИнкомБанк
31 Inkom Bank (For visa card cash advances) ИнкомБанк
32 Market Рынок
34 Mosque Мечеть
35 Aistenok Puppet Theatre Театр Кукол Аистенока
36 Church of the Elevation of the Cross
  Крестовоздвиженская Церковь
37 Museum of Local History Краеведческий Музей
38 Mongolian Consulate Кунсульство Монголии
46 Central Telegraph Office Центральный Телеграф
47 Gagarin Pier Причал Гагарина
48 White House/Irkutsk University Белый Дом/Университет
49 Trans-Sib Monument Обелиск Транссибирской

HOTELS AND RESTAURANTS

4 Hotel Irkutsk-Intourist Гостиница Иркутск-Интурист
5 Café Uyut Кафе Уют
12 Hotel Angara Гостиница Ангара
13 Circus & Restaurant Aura Цирк и Ресторан Аура
14 Hotel Arena Гостиница Арена
15 Café Yunost Кафе Юность
16 Niva Bakery Пекарня Нива
24 Restaurant Baikal Ресторан Байкал
25 Site of Hotel Sibir Быв. Гостиница Сибирь
26 Hotel Rus Гостиница Русь
33 Restaurant Tsentralny Ресторан Центральный
39 Café Sever Кафе Север
40 Restaurant Arktika Ресторан Арктика
41 Café Piotr Pervy Кафе Пётр Первый
42 Café Moroznoe Кафе Мороженое
43 Restaurant Bylina/Café Karlson
  Ресторан Былина/Кафе Карлсон
44 Fikhtelberg Casino Restaurant
  Ресторан Казино Фихтельберг
45 Restaurant Drakon Ресторан Дракон

OTHER

1 Railway Station Железнодорожний Вокзал
2 River Station Речной Вокзал
3 Planetarium in the Trinity Church
  Планетарий в Троитской Церкви
6 Pl. Kirova (Kirov Square) bus stop
  Остановка «Пл. Кирова»
7 Government Headquarters Дом Правительства

WHERE TO STAY

The *Hotel Irkutsk-Intourist* (☎ 290 166, fax 277 872), bul Gagarina 44, is the best in town. Singles range from US$60 to US$90 and double rooms from US$75 to US$95. All rooms have bathrooms attached and the price includes breakfast. The hotel offers a wide range of services including car rentals, medical services and hair dressing.

The *Hotel Angara* (☎ 241 631), ul Sukhe-Batora 7, was the main hotel used for foreigners until the Irkutsk-Intourist was built in the late 1980s. Today it is a tired, dilapidated-looking place. Singles are US$40, doubles US$50, all with attached bathrooms. The *Hotel Sibir*, ul Lenina 8, was destroyed by fire in the summer of 1995 but it may be rebuilt.

On the western side of the river is *MNTK* (☎ 462 569, fax 461 762), at ul Lermontova 337. Rooms start from US$115. Take trolleybuses Nos 1, 2 or 7 from pl Kirova or trolley bus No 6 from the airport.

Hotel Rus (☎ 343 715), ul Sverdlova 19, is a reasonable deal, charging from US$40 to US$75 for a single room including all facilities, and from US$130 for a double room. It has a great restaurant.

For budget travellers by far the best choice is the *American House* (☎ 432 689), ul Ostrovski 19, a very relaxed place run by a friendly Russian couple, Marko and Tatyana, who speak a little English. It has three single rooms, two double rooms and overflow areas. Bed and breakfast costs US$15. From the railway station, you have to either take a taxi or walk as no public transport goes past it. On foot (15 minutes) leave the station and cross the road. An opening between the row of kiosks takes you to some stairs. At the top of the stairs, a dirt road leads between apartment blocks to a large dirt road. This goes up a very steep hill and near the top on the left is a newly built brick church. Opposite, on the right, is ul Ostrovski. Ask locals for 'Americansky Dom' if you can't find it. Coming from the centre of Irkutsk, bus No 11 from in front of Hotel Angara takes you across the river, and along ul Mayakovskovo, before turning left into ul Chaikovskovo. Get off at the first stop along this street which is on the corner of the dirt road which leads to the railway station. Walk down the street for about 20m and you will see the church on the right; turn left down ul Ostrovski.

Budget hotels in the city area include *Hotel Akademicheskaya* (☎ 463 872), ul Lermontova 271, US$30 double room; *Hotel Vizit* (☎ 432 908), ul Pushkina 36; *Hotel Elochka* (☎ 336 384), pos Patrony; *Hotel Kolos* (231 943), ul 1st Nevskovo 105; *Hotel Retro* (☎ 333 981, 333 251), ul Karla Marxa 1; *Hotel Taiga* (☎ 465 971, 466 452, 465 986), ul Borodina 25; and *Hotel Taezhnaya* (☎ 436 096), ul Gogolya 92/3.

Homestay

Baikal Complex offers homestay in Irkutsk, Listvayanka and Bolshie Koty for about US$15 including breakfast.

WHERE TO EAT

The *Restaurant Aura* (☎ 336 139), on the first floor of the circus build-ing, is the best place to eat in Irkutsk. It's a clean, well-organised private restaurant whose only drawback is the fact that there are striptease shows here at weekends. (An entry fee will indicate that there's a show in progress). The food is good, authentic Siberian fare: their pelmeni are recommended. A good meal without drinks is US$15.

For the widest range of food, try the numerous restaurants and bars in the *Hotel Irkutsk-Intourist*. Choices consist of the expensive Chinese Peking Restaurant that's usually full in the evenings, the Russian Irkutsk Restaurant and the Russian Siberian Trakt Restaurant. All serve reason-able food but service can be very slow unless you're with a group. Try the delicious *omul*, from Lake Baikal, if it's on the menu here. You can also get snacks or just drinks in the hotel's numerous bars. Try the Berlin Beer Bar or Express Bar if you just want a drink as they don't sell food.

The *Fikhtelberg Casino Restaurant* (☎ 336 101), on ul Lenina 46, isn't bad at all and serves an excellent steak with sour cream and wild gar-lic sauce for US$10. If you are a vegetarian stay away from this place as its meals are mostly meat. Unfortunately there's a house band, and it gets rather hot and stuffy here on summer evenings.

An excellent restaurant serving traditional Siberian meals is *Restaurant Rus* in Hotel Rus (☎ 277 315), ul Sverdlova 19. A three course meal costs US$15.

The best oriental food is at the *Chinese Restaurant Drakon* at ul 5th Armii 67 but it's difficult to get in for dinner without a reservation.

There are numerous cafés, with the best being the *Café Piotr Pervy*, ul Karla Marxa, which serves reasonable meals with live entertainment and the occasional karaoki session; *Café Yunost*, ul Karla Marxa, which serves a quick pizza; and *Café Karlson*, ul Lenina, which is decorated in a fairy tale style. There's a *Pizzeria* (☎ 340 373) at ul Karla Marxa 45.

The best bread in town comes from the *Niva Bakery*, ul Karla Marxa.

WHAT TO SEE

Cathedrals and War Memorial

In Irkutsk in 1900 there were two cathedrals. The splendid Cathedral of Our Lady of Kazan, bigger than Kazan Cathedral in St Petersburg, was damaged during the Civil War. It was demolished and now the ugly bulk of the **Central Government Heaquarters** stands in its place, opposite the **WWII Memorial**. The second cathedral, the **Cathedral of the Epiphany** (1724), is across the road. In the great fire of 1879 it was badly damaged and the heat was so intense that it melted one of the 12-ton bells. It used to contain an icon museum, but is now a practising church. The icons have been relocated to the Art Museum.

Church of Our Saviour

This boat-shaped church contains the **Museum of Local Studies**. There are some interesting frescoes on the exterior which depict, from left to right, Buryats being baptised, Christ being baptised and the local bishop, Innocenti, being canonised. The museum inside contains a small display of stuffed local animals. Upstairs there's an interesting religious history display including the robes, rattle of human bones and feathered head-dress of a *shaman* (see below); masks and robes used in Tibetan Buddhist mystery plays; prayer wheels and Buddhist texts from the monasteries south of Irkutsk. Up a very narrow staircase is a small exhibition of bells. Open 10:00-18:00, not Tuesday. Entry is US$2.50 and there's a camera charge of US$2.

Polish Catholic Church

Opposite the Church of Our Saviour is a church with a tall steeple, the Catholic Church. It is the only (mock) Gothic church in Siberia and was built in 1883 by exiled Poles. Services are held on Sundays for the descendants of Poles exiled to Siberia. During summer there are usually organ concerts held on Sundays and Wednesdays, starting around 19:30.

Museum of Local History

This museum, situated beside the river just south of the Hotel Irkutsk-Intourist, has some interesting exhibits. Upstairs is a 'local achievements' gallery including a model of part of the BAM railway. Above the stairs is a panorama showing the Great Irkutsk Fire of 1879. The ethnographic galleries are downstairs and exhibits include flints and bones from the archaeological site of Malta, just outside Irkutsk where evidence of human habitation has been found dating back 24,000 years; the inside of a settler's house from earlier this century with carved wooden side-board and HMV gramophone and 78rpm records; a set of robes worn by a *shaman*, together with his antlers and drum; photographs showing what life was like for past inhabitants and the convicts; and also a most peculiar article of clothing: a suit made completely of fish skins, the standard summer costume of the Goldi tribe who lived in the Far Eastern Territories. The museum (☎ 333 449), ul Karla Marxa, is open 10:00-16:00, not Monday. Entry is US$2.50.

Other Churches

At the turn of the century, Irkutsk boasted fifty-eight places of worship. This fell to only three or four after the Revolution but with glasnost has risen to ten today.

Znamensky Convent (Apparition of the Virgin Nunnery) lies to the north-east of the city, over the bridge. The frescoes inside are very impressive but recent restoration has left the interior looking rather modern, a bit like the bizarre centre of some 60s sect. Don't wear shorts or you won't be allowed in. Services are held here regularly). Note that the adjacent 'hotel' is for the clergy only. Beside the church are the graves of Yekaterine Trubetskoi (see p230) and also Gregory Shelekhov, who founded the colony of Alaska in 1784 (sold to the USA in 1868). His grave is marked by an obelisk decorated with cartographic instruments. To get here, take trolleybus No 3 from the south end of pl Kirova.

It's also interesting to visit the **synagogue**, ul Karla Libknekhta 23, a large blue building, the lower storey of which has been converted into a factory. Enter through the door on left with the three stars above it. You may need to knock loudly to get the caretaker's attention and he'll then shuffle down in shirtsleeves and braces to open up. He'll check that you have some kind of head covering (there are a few caps you can borrow) and may give you a photocopy of the Ten Commandments. There is also a **mosque** at ul Karla Libknekhta 86.

Art museum

This is the most impressive art gallery east of the Urals and includes works by eighteenth and nineteenth century Russian, German, Flemish, French, Italian and English painters. The collection was begun by Vladimir Sukachev in the 1870s and 'donated' to the city after the Revolution. There are, however, the inevitable modern Soviet master-pieces: A A Plastov's *Supper of Tractor Operators* and A V Moravov's *Calculating of Working Days*, for example. The gallery devoted to nine-teenth century local scenes is particularly interesting and in the gallery of

---

❑ **Shamanism**

This is a primitive form of religion centred around the shaman, a kind of medium and healer. Although the concept of the shaman is fairly common throughout the world, the word itself originally derives from the Tungus tribes of Siberia.

Wearing spectacular robes, the shaman would beat his drum and go into a trance in order to communicate with the spirits. From them he would discover the cause of an illness, the reason for the failure of the crops, or he would be warned of some approaching disaster. Commonly, spirits were thought to select their shamans before they were born and brand them with distinguishing features: an extra finger or toe or a large birthmark. During their adolescence they would be 'tortured' by the spirits with an illness of some kind until they agreed to act as shaman. Often such people were epileptic, mentally disordered or physically weak. Through their spiritual power they gained authority and often large amounts of money for performing rituals.

'Shamanism played an extremely negative role in the history of the Siberian peoples... In status, activity and interests, the shamans were hand in glove with the ruling cliques of the indigenous populations', wrote the Marxist anthropologists M.G.Levin and L.P.Potapov, in *The Peoples of Siberia*. Other anthropologists have been less severe, noting that shamanism gave those with mental and physical disorders a place in society at a time when most other societies shunned the handicapped.

Western Art (XV-XIX centuries) you will find a small canvas with the label 'Landsir 1802-73' which is *The Family of Dogs* by Sir Edwin Landseer, who designed the lions in Trafalgar Square. The Art Museum (☎ 244 336, 242 528), ul Lenina 5, is open 10:00-18:00, closed Tuesday; entry is US$2.00. There is also an exhibition hall, a branch of the museum, nearby on ul Karla Marxa.

Trubetskoi house

The wooden house once occupied by Sergei and Yekaterine Trubetskoi (who is buried in the graveyard of the Church of the Holy Saviour) and other nobles involved in an unsuccessful coup in 1825 is preserved as a museum, kept as it was when the exiles lived here. In the cellar there is an interesting display of old photographs showing life in the Nerchinsk silver mines and a prison cell in Chita. There is also a picture of Maria Volkonsky (see below) and her child. At ul Dzerzhinskovo 64 (☎ 275 773), it's open 10:00-18:00, closed Tuesday. Entry is US$2. ('With thermopane windows it would be a great place'. Louis Wozniak (USA): Visitors' book in this museum.)

Maria Volkonsky's house

The large and attractive blue and white house of this famous Decembrist who followed her husband into Siberian exile is open to the public. If you've read Caroline Sutherland's *The Princess of Siberia* then you must visit Maria Volkonsky's house. It is a grand old building but it's a pity it's so sparsely furnished as it doesn't have the lived-in feel of the other house museums. Displays include Maria's clothes, letters, furniture, and church robes of 18th and 19th centuries. In the yard there are several wooden buildings and a well. At per Volkhonskovo 10 (☎ 277 818), it is open 10:00-18:00, closed Monday.

Angara steamship

The *Angara*, commissioned in 1899, was partially assembled in England and then sent to Irkutsk in pieces by train. Until the completion of the Circumbaikal line she ferried rail passengers across the lake, together with her bigger sister, the *Baikal*. Following the line's completion in 1904, the *Angara* performed a series of menial tasks before being abandoned, partially submerged, in 1958. The boat was restored and became the Museum of Nautical Navigation. In 1995, the ship was again converted and this time became the office of a local newspaper. Unfortunately you can't wander around the vessel today. Bus No 16 south from pl Kirova (towards the hydrofoil terminal) passes by.

Other sights

In the summer, touring companies perform in the imposing **Drama Theatre**, built at the turn of the century, in ul Karla Marxa. There are also

boat trips (1-2hrs) along the river to the dam and power station. They leave daily from the Gagarin Pier near the **Trans-Siberian Builder's Monument**. This statue has Yermak and Count Muravyev-Amursky on its sides and the double-headed Imperial eagle on the railings surrounding it. The building beside the obelisk may look like a mini Sydney Opera House but its main use is for dog shows.

In the **Fur Distribution Centre**, on the southern outskirts of the city, visitors are shown some of the 18 varieties of mink and also the pelts of the Barguzinsk sable, which sell for over £500/US$750 each. It's open to tours only, and only between October and May.

Also worth a visit is the **House of Artists** (Dom Khudozhnikov) at ul Karla Marxa 38, which has the occasional exhibition.

ENTERTAINMENT

For an alternative theatre experience, try the **Vampilov Youth Theatre** which is in the basement of Café Morozhenoe. There's also a **circus**, the **Aistenok Puppet Theatre** (☎ 270 666), at ul 1st Sovetskaya 1; and the **Philharmonic Hall** (☎ 345 873), at ul Dzershinskovo 2. .

WHAT TO BUY

The heart of the city is the **market**, which extends for several hundred metres behind the main shopping street, ul Karla Marxa. It's not hard to find: long before you see it you'll hear the many bootleg cassette dealers demonstrating their 'latest' releases. Tapes sell for about US$2. Other stalls sell everything from Sindy dolls and Snickers bars to sports shoes and switchblades. The **Detsky Mir Children Store** is the best proper shop in the market area. You can buy Kodak film here, or have your photographs processed in an hour.

The best local bookshops are **Military Books**, ul Uritskovo 15; **Rodnik Books**, ul Litvinova 1; and **Sibtorg**, ul Karla Marxa 24. Next to Sibtorg is an **art shop** which sells semi-precious gems, such as chariot, which are found only in the Baikal area.

Rip-off of the Year Award goes to the Irkutsk-Intourist shop for selling Baikal water ('saturated with pure ozone-containing oxygen', 'Bring a piece of Baikal to your home') at US$5 per litre.

RIVER CRUISES AND LISTVYANKA

Rivers are navigable from mid May to September. There are three river stations in Irkutsk, each for a different destination.

● **Scenic cruises** These depart from Gagarin Pier which is at the intersection of bul Gagarina and ul Gorkovo. Boats travel upstream to the Angara Hydro-Electric Power Station dam and departures for the eighty

minute return trip leave every hour. Tickets can be bought at the pier.
● **Long distance Angara River trips** Boats that travel down the Angara
River depart from the River Station at the base of the bridge over the
Angara. When you cross this bridge from the railway station, you can see
it on the left. To get to it from pl Kirova, walk down ul Chkalova which
runs to the bridge. Avoid this area after dark as it's notoriously dangerous.
Hydrofoils from here run to Bratsk via Angarsk.
● **Lake Baikal** Boats for Lake Baikal and Listvyanka depart from the
Hydrofoil Pier (☎ 238 072), above the Angara Dam which is 5km
upstream (to the south) of Irkutsk. Bus No 16 runs there from pl Kirova;
the trip takes 45 minutes. For detailed information on how to get to
Listvyanka, see 233.

Hydrofoil timetable

Route	Via	Departure days of week	Depart	Arrive	Cost
Irkutsk-Bratsk*	Angarsk	3 times a week	08:30	21:00	$30
Irkutsk-Nizhneangarsk**	Port Baikal, Severobaikalsk	about 4 times a week	7:50	19:50	$42
Irkutsk-Ust Barguzin**	Listvyanka, Bukhta Peschannaya, MRS, Khyzhir	Mon (returns Tue)	9:00	19:00	$29
Irkutsk-MRS**	Listvyanka, Bukhta Peschannaya	Thur, Sat	8:00	15:00	$20
Irkutsk-Bukhta Peschannaya**	Listvyanka, Goloustnoye	Wed, Fri, Sun	9:00	12:30	$13
Irkutsk-Bolshie Koty**	Listvyanka	3 times a day	10:00 11:00 14:30	11:40 12:40 16:10	$6

* departs from the River Station   ** departs from the Hydrofoil Pier

Lake Baikal
Озеро Байкал

The world's deepest lake
Sixty-four kilometres (forty miles) south of Irkutsk, Lake Baikal is 1637
metres (5371 feet) deep and is estimated to contain more than 20,000
cubic km of water, roughly 20% of the world's freshwater supplies. If all
the rest of the world's drinking water ran out tomorrow, Lake Baikal
could supply the entire population of the planet for the next 40 years.

Known as the 'Blue Eye of Siberia' it is also the world's oldest lake,
formed almost 50 million years ago. It is among the largest lakes on the
planet, being about 400 miles long and between 20 and 40 miles wide.
The water is incredibly clear and, except around Baikalsk and the Selenga

delta, completely safe to drink owing to the filtering action of numerous types of sponge which live in its depths, along with hundreds of other species found nowhere else.

Holy Sea

Russian colonists called Baikal the 'Holy Sea' since there were so many local myths and legends surrounding it. The Buryats believed that the evil spirit Begdozi lived on Olkhon Island in the middle of the lake, though the Evenki shamans held that this was the home of the sea god, Dianda. It is hardly surprising that these primitive tribes were impressed by the strange power of the lake for at times sudden violent storms spring up, lashing the coast with waves up to seven feet high. It freezes to a depth of about ten feet for four months of the year, from late December. The Angara is the only river that flows out of the lake and since the dam and hydro-electric power station were built on the Angara in 1959, the water-level of the lake has been slowly rising.

Environmental threats

The remoteness of the lake kept it safe from the threat of environmental damage until the building of the Trans-Siberian at the end of the last century. Damage to the environment is increasing, with the building of new towns on the northern shores for the construction of the BAM line, and also owing to industrial waste from Ulan Ude (the Selenga River flows past this city into the lake via one of the world's last large wetlands, the Selenga delta). The most famous campaigner for the protection of the lake is author Valentin Rasputin. Demonstrations in Irkutsk in 1987 resulted in filtration equipment being installed in the wood pulp mill at Baikalsk, on the edge of the lake but current reports suggest that it is inefficient and that pollution is continuing. A coastal protection zone was established around the edge of the entire lake in 1987 but campaigners bemoan the fact that the government's anti-pollution laws have no teeth. They believe that the lake should be placed under the independent protection of UNESCO. For more information, contact **Greenpeace's Baikal Campaign** Coordinator, Roman Pukalov in Moscow at fax (095) 251 9088 or by e-mail gpmoscow@glas.apc.org.

GETTING TO LAKE BAIKAL

The two ways of getting from Irkutsk to Lake Baikal are by boat (see opposite) or by bus. Buses depart from Irkutsk's long distance bus station on ul Oktyabrskoi Revolutsii. The trip takes about 90 minutes. During summer, buses depart from Irkutsk at 9:00, 14:30, 16:30 and 19:00 and from Listvyanka at 7:00, 11:50, 16:45 and 18:00. The bus will stop on request virtually anywhere with major stops at the Open Air Museum, Baikal Ecological Museum, Listvyanka village and Listvyanka pier.

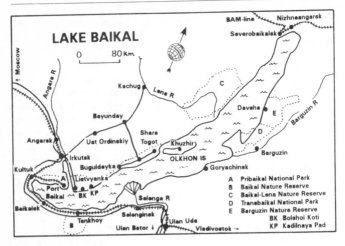

Open Air Museum

On the road between Irkutsk and Listvyanka is the Museum of Wooden Architecture (☎ 145 249, an interesting collection of reconstructed, traditional wooden houses. It is located at the km47 marker from Irkutsk, which is the km23 marker from Listvyanka – ask the bus driver for the 'moozay'. There is a large farmhouse, a bathroom with a vast wooden tub and, a short way along a path, a water-mill and a post-house, complete with the Imperial crest on its roof-top. When the only way to cross Siberia was by road and river, fresh horses and simple accommodation were available from post-houses. The museum is open only in the summer but you can wander round outside in spring and autumn.

LISTVYANKA

Listvyanka is an attractive village of wooden houses lying at the end of the Irkutsk-Lake Baikal road. There's a shop, two small cafés and the jetty. The Baikal Ecological Museum and the Hotel Baikal-Intourist above it are about one km before the village on the road from Irkutsk.

Where to stay

Near the Baikal Ecological Museum is the pleasant *Hotel Baikal-Intourist* (☎ 3952-290 391) where most tours stop for lunch. Rooms are from US$64 per person in a double. Various services are offered here including bike hire (US$6 per day), skiing, sleigh rides, boat trips and riding. There is an expensive sauna, too. Behind the hotel is a hill that gives a good view over the water to the Khamar Daban Mountains. The half-hour hike up is well worth it. At the top there's a little shelter and a tree decorated with paper ribbons that people have tied to it for good luck, a very old Siberian superstition.

You can also stay at the **Sand Bay Holiday Home** (Turbasa Bukhta Peschanaya) about 80km north of Listvyanka on the shores of Lake Baikal by booking it at Turbasa Bukhta Peschanaya's office (☎ 243 515) in Irkutsk ul Karla Marxa 22, kv 17.

Baikal Complex (see Irkutsk) offers **homestays** in Listvyanka for US$28 a night.

Where to eat

The restaurant in **Hotel Baikal-Intourist** is excellent; try their omul soup. The only other places to eat are two **cafés** (which usually only have hot-dogs) in Listvyanka village. During summer, you can always pick up freshly smoked or barbequed omul from local traders on the jetty.

Baikal Ecological Museum

The Baikal Ecological Museum (formerly the Limnological Museum, ☎ 460 324), has a number of fascinating displays of the unique marine life and animals in the Baikal area. Entry is US$1.

Over 80 per cent of the species in Lake Baikal cannot be found any-where else in the world. These include 1085 types of algae, 250 mosses, 450 lichens, 1500 vascular plants, 255 small crustaceans, 83 gastropods, 86 worms and 52 fish. The exceptionally high oxygen levels in the lake create the ideal environment for many creatures which have long since become extinct elsewhere. These include the freshwater seals, found only here and until recently threatened with extinction by the Buryats who turned them into overcoats. They are now a protected species, listed in the *Red Book of Endangered Species*, and currently number about 60,000. A

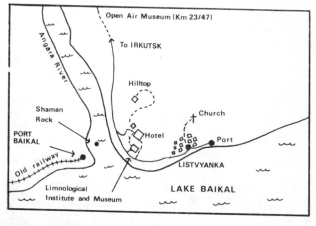

unique Baikal fish is the tiny *golomyanka* which, composed almost entirely of transparent fat, lives at depths up to 1.5km. Surprisingly, it gives birth to its young alive and fully formed. The museum also contains a model of the *Angara*, some examples of the tasty *omul*, and a collection of the sponges which keep the water so clean. The colonists' wives discovered that they were also very useful for polishing the samovar.

Listvyanka Church

A pleasant ten-minute walk through the village takes you to a tiny church in which an old woman sells cheap-looking icons. Although the village is worth seeing, one feels that this church has been part of the Intourist 'milk-run' for a long time. 'No smoking on the territory of the Church', warns a sign in English. Concessions to tourists have their advantages: five-star lavatories are thoughtfully located behind the building.

Shaman Rock

In the stretch of water between the Baikal Ecological Museum and Port Baikal it's just possible to make out the top of a rock sticking out of the water. The legend relating to its origin is as follows: Old Man Baikal had 336 sons (the number of rivers which flow into the lake) and one daughter, the beautiful but headstrong Angara. She enraged him by refusing to marry the weak and feeble Irkut, preferring the mighty Yenisei (Russia's longest river). The old man chained her up but one stormy night she slipped her bonds and fled north to her lover. As she ran her furious father hurled a huge boulder after her. She got away but the rock remains to this day, a small point showing above the water. The level of the lake has since risen and very little of Shaman Rock is now visible.

PORT BAIKAL

Across the water from Listvyanka is the attractive village of Port Baikal. Before 1904, the western end of the Trans-Siberian terminated here and passenger had to cross the lake by steamer to Mysovaya which is where the eastern end of the Trans-Siberian finished. The largest steamer was a 290-foot ice-breaker, *Baikal*, which transported the carriages from the

---

❏ **Life-enhancing waters**

Guides never fail to recount the superstition concerning the power of Baikal water. Dip your hands in, they say, and you will live a year longer than you otherwise would. Dip your feet in too and this will be extended to five years. Brave the icy waters for a swim and, if the shock doesn't kill you instantly, you'll be around for twenty-five extra years.

A world record was set in here in 1991, as a team of relay swimmers managed to cross the width of the lake in 17 hours. Even these intrepid athletes had trouble, though: because of the extreme cold, the longest period any one of them could spend in the water at one time was 30 minutes.

train on her deck. She was built by the English firm of Sir W G Armstrong, Whitworth and Co. in Newcastle, UK, delivered by train in kit-form and she sank in 1919 during the Civil War. Her sister ship, the smaller *Angara*, supplied by the same firm, survived (see p230).

Four ferries a day run between Port Baikal and Listvyanka from May to December. The first leaves Port Baikal at 06:30 and Listvyanka at 07:00, and the last leaves Port Baikal at 20:00 and Listvyanka at 20:30. A hydrofoil also runs from Port Baikal and Listvyanka all the way along Lake Baikal to Severobaikalsk (see p232).

Baikal Complex organises trips to Port Baikal along the old Circumbaikal Railway.

❑ **Riding the Circumbaikal Railway**

A trip on the Circumbaikal Railway (see p332) should not be undertaken lightly. There are two daily trains each way but they're unreliable and very slow. As there is no accommodation in Port Baikal, and it is difficult to get between Port Baikal and Listvyanka you should be well prepared – you may be up all night. Confirm the times of all services before you set out. Theoretically it is possible to catch a train at the weekend from Irkutsk to Slyudyanka, then take the after-noon Circumbaikal train to Port Baikal. You should reach the station in time for the last ferry from Port Baikal to Listvyanka which departs at 20:00. Don't expect everything to run to schedule. The easiest way to travel this route is to take one of the tours organised by Irkutsk travel agents (see p222). Baikal Complex charges around US$20 for theirs.

BOLSHIE KOTY

Bolshie Koty is a small village north of Lystvyanka. Its main attraction is Irkutsk University's Limnological Institute where the students do their practical work. Gold used to be extracted from the Bolshie Koty River and the rusting dredges can still be seen 1km beyond the village. If you miss the boat back, you will have to walk the 18km to Lystvyanka along a dirt track. Be aware that the track is sometimes covered by the tide. Baikal Complex organises trips here, offering *homestays* (US$15).

Other Siberian excursions

BRATSK (Братск)

Three hundred miles north of Irkutsk lies one of the largest dams in the world. The enormous hydro-electric power station at Bratsk, the second largest in Russia after the one at Krasnoyarsk, is the chief attraction of this town. Originally founded in 1631, it was never more than a tiny village until construction of the dam started in 1955. It reputedly produces an enormous 4.5 million kW which is a great deal but not as much as the Raul Leoni power station in Venezuela which currently holds the world's title, producing 10.3 million kW.

Despite being one of the top ten most polluted cities in Russia, Bratsk is still awe-inspiring considering the massive achievement of constructing a modern city, a giant dam and massive industrial enterprises in just two decades. Bratsk is on the BAM line but unless you're stopping off on this line, or unless you're especially interested in power stations, there seems little reason to come here. Bratsk is covered in depth in the *Siberian BAM Railway Guide*.

Orientation and hotels

Bratsk is not one town but a ring of connected settlements around the man-made Bratsk Sea, which is a large reservoir created by the Bratsk dam. From the south in a counter-clockwise direction, the towns are Novobratsk Port (Порт Новобратск), Bratsk More (Братское море), Bratsk Tsentralny (Центральный район) which is the administartation centre, Padun (Падун), Energetik (Энергетик) on the dam's west bank and Gidrostroitel (Гидростройтель) on the east bank.

The station of Padunskie Porogi services the suburbs of Padun and Energetik. This station is the closest to Hotel Turist. Padun contains the most attractive part of Bratsk as it has a pleasant promenade, with an old log watchtower and the city's only church. Bratsk airport is to the north of Padunskie Porogi and can be reached by a 40 minute bus trip which starts from in front of the station.

The best accommodation is the standard *Hotel Taiga* (☎ 39531-443 979), ul Mira 35, US$50 in a twin share room. Intourist is on the second floor. Other choices are the standard *Hotel Turist* (☎ 39531-370 995), Energetik, ul Naymushina 28, and the basic *Hotel Bratsk* (☎ 39531-446 44), ul Deputatskaya 32, US$24-46 for a single room.

What to see

The top site is the impressive **Bratsk Hydro-Electric Station** and the dam. Bus Nos 4, 102, 103, 104, and 107 run along the dam, and you can also visit the powerhouse. On the outskirts of Angara Village there's an open-air **ethnographic museum** containing an Evenki camp, a watchtower and a fort. There's a history museum at ul Komsomolskaya 38.

Getting to Bratsk

From Irkutsk, you could take the hydrofoil (US$30 one way), which leaves Irkutsk at 08.30, arriving in Bratsk at 20.50. On the return journey it leaves at 07.50 arriving at 20.40 in Irkutsk. Hydrofoils travel three times a week from May to September. There are daily trains between Bratsk and Irkustsk and the trip takes 18 hours.

SEVEROBAIKALSK (Северобайкальск)

Severobaikalsk is the capital of the northern end of Lake Baikal on the BAM railway. The town provides excellent access to the North Baikal attractions, which include trekking and mountaineering in the Baikal Mountains, indigenous villages, a Stalin era gulag, downhill skiing, sailing around the north end of the lake and seal watching.

Orientation and hotels

Everything in Severobaikalsk is within walking distance, with the exception of the port from which the hydrofoil departs. To get to the port, take Bus No 1 from the central bus station in front of the railway station. Bus No 3 goes past the BAM railway museum and near Hotel Sever.

BAMTour is a recommended company organising tours on the BAM and in the north Lake Baikal region. It's run by Rashit Yakhin who worked on the railway in the early 1970s. BAMTour Co, 671717, Severobaikalsk, ul Oktyabrskaya 16-2 ☎/fax 30139-21 560.

The best place to stay is at the excellent *BAM Railway Cottages*, a 10 minute walk from the station, and with a view of the coast. Booking is done via BAMTour and costs US$25 a night per person. The best hotel is the standard *Hotel Nord* at the port where the hydrofoil arrives. The hotel is expensive at US$80 for a single room.

What to see

Railway places of interest are the **BAM Museum**, ul Mira 2, open 10:00-18:00 closed Monday, and the **BAM Art Museum**, ul Druzhba.

Akikan Gulag (Акикана ГУЛаг) was a mica mining camp that operated in the late 1930s. The remnants of those terrible years consist of several collapsed wooden and stone buildings, towers and barbed wire fences. The camp is a two-hour walk from Kholodnoe (60 minutes by bus or train from Severobaikalsk); BAMTour can provide guides.

For more information see *Siberian BAM Railway Guide*.

Getting to Severobaikalsk

The easiest way to get between Severobaikalsk and Irkutsk is by hydrofoil (see p232). You can also get there by train from Taishet on the Trans-Siberian. Unfortunately there is no direct Severobaikalsk-Irkutsk train: change at Taishet or Bratsk.

NIZHNEANGARSK (Нижнеангарск)

Nizhneangarsk is 40km east of Severobaikalsk, wedged on a narrow strip between Lake Baikal and steep mountains. The 20km-long town has a large port for a small fishing fleet. The harbour was built for the contruction of the BAM but the railway arrived before it was needed.Despite being the regional power, Nizhneangarsk is smaller than neighbouring Severobaikalsk. The town is pleasant to stroll around with its mainly wooden buildings. Despite most of it being built since the mid 1970s, Nizhneangarsk is not dominated by multi-storey concrete flats and pre-fabricated buildings. Even the two-storey City Council building is wood-en. An architectural oddity is the wooden boat rental and water rescue sta-tion on the lake's edge. The **fish processing factory** can be visited and gives an interesting insight into Russian methods and working conditions. The plant makes delicious smoked or salted *omul*.

YAKUTSK

This is the capital of the vast Yakut Autonomous Region (see p346). Lying only 600km south of the Arctic Circle, it is one of the world's cold-est cities (average temperature in January is minus 32°C) although sum-mers are pleasantly mild (plus 19°C in July). It is also one of Siberia's oldest settlements, founded in 1632 on the banks of the mighty Lena River as a base for exploration and a trading centre for gold and furs. There is little left of historic interest in this polluted city, but it is worth visiting for the excursions on the Lena and to see the effects of per-mafrost. All the buildings here have to be built on massive stilts or they would sink into the ground as the heat from them melts the permafrost.

Only about 30% of the people are ethnic Yakuts, the majority of the rest being Russians and Ukrainians. Like other minority groups in Russia the Yakuts are now making themselves heard in Moscow. They have been exploited since the region was first colonised 350 years ago and even now a large amount of the foreign exchange earned from their fabulously rich region stays in Moscow.

In 1996, the Russian media voted Yakutsk the most expensive city in the country for food and goods. The telephone area code is ☎ 4112.

Getting to Yakutsk

Until the rail link is finished (which will be many years from now as there is still 800km to cover) the only way in is by plane from Irkutsk, Moscow or several other cities. A single economy flight from Yakutsk to Moscow costs from US$350 to US$450; a return is exactly double. There are sometimes direct flights between Yakutsk and its twin city, Fairbanks in Alaska. Local airline agencies (Sakha Air and Russian Air) are located at ul Ordzhonikidze 45 (☎ 42 0204, 42 5139). A new airport was built by the Canadians in 1995 after the last one was burned down.

Where to stay

An inexpensive hotel is the basic *Hotel Yakutsk* (☎ 250 700), ul Oktyabrskaya 20/1. A single room costs US$35. *Hotel Sterkh* (242 701, satellite fax 7-509 854 5001) pro Lenin 8 is a better choice with singles from US$75. The hotel was known as Hotel Lena until it was rebuilt in 1992. The *Canadian Hotel Ontario* (☎ 422 066, fax 259 438), Viliusky trakt 6, was built in 1992 and has 12 rooms, a restaurant and bar. It is in a quiet location in a park zone about 20 minutes out of the city centre. It's somewhat overpriced at US$94 a single. The best hotel is the *Hotel Tygyn Darkhan* (formerly the President Hotel), (☎ 435 109, fax 435 004), ul Ammosov 9. Recently renovated by a Swiss company, it's in the heart of the city. It has 46 rooms, and single rooms cost from US$100 to US$200. The restaurant here is excellent but very pricey.

What to see

The most interesting place to visit in Yakutsk is the **Permafrost Institute**. You are taken 12 metres underground to see part of the old river bed, where the temperature never varies from -5°C. Permafrost is said to affect 25% of the planet and 50% of Russia. Outside the Institute is a model of the baby mammoth (now in St Petersburg Natural History Museum) that was found preserved in permafrost.

The **Yakutian State History and Culture Museum**, housed in what was formerly the Bishop's Palace, is one of the oldest museums in Siberia. It is said to include over 140,000 items illustrating Yakut flora, fauna and anthropology. Outside is an *ostrog* (wooden fort). The **Museum of Yakut Music and Folklore**, at ul Kirova 8, has an interesting display about Yakut shamanism. There's also the **Yakut Literature Museum**, with a large yurt outside it and the **Geological Museum**, crammed full of all the geological wealth of Yakutia. A Museum of the Mammoth is planned. Tours can be arranged to reindeer breeding farms.

Excursions on the Lena River

The geological formations known as the **Lena Pillars** have fascinated travellers here since the 17th century. About 140km upriver from Yakutsk, the rock of the cliffs alongside the river has been eroded away into delicate shapes of a reddish brown colour. Hydrofoil excursions leave around 08:00, often with breakfast (followed by vodka and cognac) on board. You reach the landing spot about four hours later and it takes about an hour's strenuous climb to reach the top for a magnificent view of the river and the cliffs. A picnic is usually organised. Be very careful disembarking: one of our party (who'd overdone the vodka at breakfast) toppled off the flimsy gang-plank into the chilly waters.

On the way to the Lena Pillars you pass the archaeological site of **Dering Yuryakh**, where, in 1982, evidence of man dating back 1-2 million years was discovered, putting the site on a par with excavations in Africa. There's not much to see but there are plans for a museum.

The luxury cruise ships *M/S Demyan Bedny* and *M/S Mikhail Svetlov* do 7-10 day trips along the Lena River starting from Yakutsk, passing the Lena Pillars and continuing to the river port of Lensk. It's also possible to make a trip down the Lena from Yakutsk to Tiksi on the Arctic Ocean. Information on Lena River Ship Company (LenaRechFlot) trips can be obtained from their Web site: http://www.travelcentre.com.au/vakut.htm.

Ulan Ude
Улан Уде

Ulan Ude is well worth a stop if only to visit the **Ivolginsky Datsan** (35km outside the city), the centre of Buddhism in Russia. Rail enthusiasts may also be interested in a visit to the **locomotive repair workshops**. The people of Ulan Ude are very friendly and hospitable and the place has a relaxed atmosphere to it, with quite a few traditional Siberian wooden buildings still standing. Ulan Ude is a 45 minute flight, or a 7.5 hour train journey, from Irkutsk. Air links with Ulan Bator have been established and a new service to Beijing is planned.

HISTORY

Military outpost
In 1668 a military outpost was set up here in the valley between the Khamar Daban and Tsaga Daban mountain ranges. Strategically located beside the Selenga and Ude rivers, it was named Verkhneudinsk. A cathedral was built in 1745 and the town became a key trading centre on the route of the tea caravans from China. The railway reached the town in 1900 and in 1949 the branch line to Mongolia was opened.

Ulan Ude today
Capital of the Buryat Republic, Ulan Ude is now a pleasant city of nearly 400,000 people (only 21% of whom are Buryats, the rest mainly Russians). Local industries include the large railway repair workshop and locomotive plant, food processing, helicopter assembly and glass making.

Buildings here require firm foundations since the city is in an earthquake zone. The most recent 'quake, measuring 9.5 on the Richter scale, was in 1959 but because its epicentre was directly beneath Lake Baikal nobody in Ulan Ude was killed. The military bases in the area kept Ulan Ude off-limits to foreigners until the thaw in East-West relations. In 1990, Princess Anne led the tourists in with the first royal visit to Russia since the Tsar's execution. A local official declared that her visit was probably the most exciting thing to have happened since Genghis Khan swept through on his way to Moscow in 1239.

LOCAL TRANSPORT

Most places, except the Datsan and the Open-air museum, are within walking distance. Buses No 7 or 10 from in front of the station run along pl Sovetov and past Hotel Baikal. Bus No 7 terminates at the central bus station and bus No 10 continues to the airport. Bus No 35 travels between the airport and pl Sovetov. **Taxis** congregate in the usual places: outside the hotels and by the railway and bus stations, but are not in great supply.

ORIENTATION AND SERVICES

To reach the centre of town from the railway station, cross the line via the pedestrian bridge. It takes about 15 minutes to walk to pl Lenina. The main hotels and the Intourist office are all in this area.

The **Intourist** office is in the Hotel Geser (☎ 292 67); and **Sputnik** Travel (☎ 208 34), is at pr Pobedy 9. **Aeroflot** (☎ 222 48) is at ul Yerbanova 14. There's a **Mongolian Consulate** based in Hotel Baikal.

Tours
Intourist offers tours to all of the major sights. The resurgence of Buddhism in the area has resulted in the reopening, reconstruction, or construction of a large number of Buddhist temples and monasteries. Intourist is quite willing to take you to any of them, the closest being **Ivolginsky Datsan**. A day trip to **Tamcha Datsan** which is 150 km away costs US$80 for a car or US$20 if you go as part of a group on a bus tour. A visit to **Atsagat Temple**, 50km away, costs US$50 for a car or US$12 on a group tour. Other tours go to **Lake Baikal**, some of the old cities along the tea route to China (**Kyakhta, Novoselenginsk** etc), or to remote villages with interesting ethnic roots (**Bolshoi Kunali**).

WHERE TO STAY

The *Hotel Buryatia* (☎ 218 35) at pr Pobedy is the city's newest hotel and rooms cost US$23/46 for a single/double room. The old Communist Party hotel, the *Hotel Geser* (☎ 258 35) at ul Ranzhurova 12, charges US$25/50. There are numerous cheaper hotels but none is particularly good. The best seems to be the *Hotel Barguzin* (☎ 219 58) at ul Sovetskaya 28 which charges US$20/40. It has friendly staff and a stuffed bear in the foyer. The *Hotel Baikal* (☎ 280 44) at ul Erbanova 12 is very basic and charges US$14/28. Less pleasant hotels include the *Hotel Odon* (☎ 434 80) at ul Gagarina 43 which charges just US$10 for a double, and the *Zolotoye Kolos* at ul Sverdlova 34.

WHERE TO EAT

The best restaurants in Ulan Ude are those in the hotels. *Hotel Geser* serves reasonable food and the service is good; there's also a buffet down the hall. *Hotel Buryatia* has some tasty dishes but service can be slow.

The Ulan Ude area code is ☎ 30122. From outside Russia dial +7-30122.

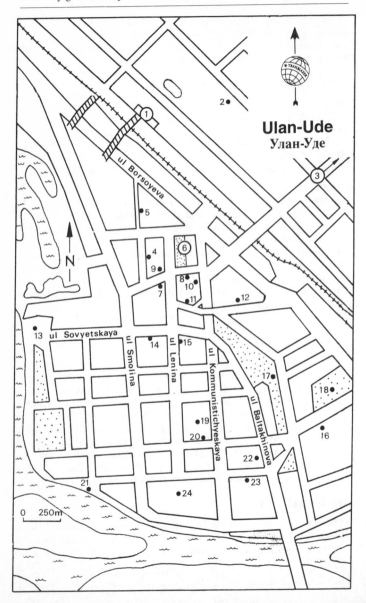

Ulan-Ude
Улан-Уде

HOTELS AND RESTAURANTS

2 Hotel Odin Гостиница Один
5 Hotel Geser Гостиница Гейзер
8 Hotel Baikal Гостиница Байкал
10 Café Buterbrodnya Кафе Бутербродня
11 Hotel Buryatia & Mongolian Consulate
    Гостиница Бурятия и Кулсульство Монголии
14 Hotel Barguzin Гостиница Баргузин
23 Hotel Zolotoi Kolos Гостиница Золотой Колос

OTHER

1 Railway Station Железнодорожний Вокзал
3 To Open Air Museum
4 Buryat Teaching Institute Бурятский Педагогический Институт
6 Giant Head of Lenin (Main Square) Бюст Ленина
7 Opera and Ballet Theatre Театр Оперы и Балета
9 Philharmonic Hall Филармония
12 History Museum Музей Истории
13 Bus Station Автовокзал
15 Nature Museum Музей Природы
16 Buryat Drama Theatre Бурятский Театр Драмы
17 T-34 Tank Monument Памятник-монумент «Танк Т-34»
18 Trinity Church Церковь Троицы
19 Arcade Гостиный Двор
20 Buryat Art Museum Бурятский Художественный Музей
21 River Station Речной Вокзал
22 Market Рынок
24 Virgin Hodegetria Cathedral Одигитриевский Собор

The *Hotel Barguzin* restaurant is on the second floor and is also good. Next door to the Hotel Barguzin is the *Restaurant Turistsky* which is fine, though sometimes a bit noisy. *Restaurant Baikal* at ul Erbanova 8, serves bland but reasonable meals.

Myf (Myth) is a recommended place at ul Mayakovskovo 17, that serves Russian and Buryat dishes. It's quite far from the main hotels, near the football stadium on the way to the open air museum. Buses 3, 8, 29 and 30 stop nearby – ask for the stop 'Kinema Oktyabra'. A meal here will cost you about US$8 without drinks. Other places to eat include *Café Okhotnik* at ul Mayakovskovo 3, and *Café Bagulnik* ul Trubacheeva 20.

WHAT TO SEE

Giant Lenin Head

The pl Sovetov (Square of the Soviet Councils) is dominated by the sinister bulk of **Lenin's head**, the biggest in the world; standing in front of him you feel like Dorothy meeting the Wizard of Oz.

History Museum

The History Museum, at ul Profsoyuznaya 29, covers the Russian history of the region and includes icons dating back to the 17th century; and day-to-day objects from the houses of the rich traders of Kyakhta.

Buryat Art Museum

The fantastic collection of items relating to Lamaism (Tibetan Buddhism) and the spiritual culture of the Buryats should now have been moved from the Virgin Hodegetria Cathedral to the Buryat Art Museum at ul Kuibysheva 29. Assembled from monasteries closed after the Revolution, the collection includes Buddha figures; the robes of a Buryat shaman; musical instruments (conches and horns and a beautiful guitar with a carved horse's head); a large collection of masks used in Buddhist mystery plays; and a valuable collection of Tibetan *thangkas* (paintings) including healing thangkas used by monks practising Tibetan medicine. There is also a unique *Atlas of Tibetan Medicine*. It is worth getting an Intourist tour around the museum. It's open 10:00-19:00, closed Monday.

Natural History Museum

Some of the interesting displays here include a Lake Baikal panorama with flora and fauna (ask an attendant to turn on the 'authentic Siberian' soundtrack for you) and a model of the mini-submarine Pisces XI which reached a depth of 1410m in the lake in 1977; there are two large galleries of local wildlife include eagles, wolves, bears and reindeer. Since one of the world's few remaining wetlands is the Selenga Delta on the edge of Lake Baikal, there is also a comprehensive display of local birds. Labels are in Cyrillic and Latin (see p403). It's open 10:00-18:00, closed Monday and Tuesday. Entry is US$0.20.

Open-Air Ethnographic Museum

One of the best of the numerous open-air museums in the country, this collection of reconstructed buildings is about 6km north of Ulan Ude. Exhibits include a Bronze Age stone circle; Evenki camp with birchwood wig-wam, a shaman's hut with wooden carvings outside it: birds on poles, animals and fish. There is a dreadful zoo with camels standing in the mud, bears in tiny cages and disconsolate reindeer (the more people complaining to the guides about this the better). The Buryat area contains *ghers* (yurts) of felt and wood and also a log cabin in which there are silk robes and day-to-day items. There are also houses of Kazakhs, Cossacks and 17th century Orthodox Christians, built around large brick ovens with sleeping platforms above them. Except in mid-summer it gets very cold walking round here; bring warm clothing.

It's open 10:00-18:00 in summer and 10:00-17:00 in winter. Bus No 35 from pl Sovetov goes directly to the museum: the more frequent bus No 8 drops you at a T-junction from which it's a 20-minute walk.

Locomotive Works

Ulan Ude's railway factory is definitely worth a visit even if you are not interested in trains. The conditions under which people work are surprising, as is the age of most of the equipment.

The factory was founded in 1932 to repair locomotives and passenger carriages and from 1938 to 1956 it built large SO series freight steam locomotives. After a massive refit in 1959, the factory concentrated on rebuilding electric locomotives and passenger carriages. Today it repairs VL60 and VL80 locomotives and passenger carriages. Intourist organises visits to the factory for about US$10 per person.

There's a preserved SO17 on the right hand side of the road to the Open-Air Ethnographic Museum.

Other sights

It's worth spending some time wandering around the town as there are still quite a few interesting buildings to be seen here. The small, attractive **Troitskaya Church**, built in 1798, has recently reopened and is undergoing renovation. Only a small section of the interior is currently open but it looks good; new bells were added in 1993. As at many Russian churches, begging babooshkas crowd around the entrance.

The **Virgin Hodegetria Cathedral**, which was built from 1745 to 1785, is now being renovated. The **Opera and Ballet Theatre** has excellent socialist paintings and murals inside. The theatre was built by some of the 18,000 Japanese prisoners of war who were interned in the Buryat Republic between 1945 and 1948. Over the bridge at the south end of town is the **Russian Orthodox Church** where services are held regularly. The **Geological Museum**, ul Lenina 57, is open 10:00-16:00 on Tuesday and Friday only.

WHAT TO BUY

There is a **Buryat Crafts Store** in the Arcade. Other good places to pick up souvenirs are **Art Store**, ul Lenina 33, **Podarki Gift Shop**, ul Lenina 40, and **Yantar Amber Jewellery Store**, ul Lenina 40. Interesting Siberian alcohol is brewed at ul Novokuznetskaya 1. Under the brand name 'Crystal', it comes in a range of colours and it's worth buying a bottle just for the label which states 'The smell of Siberian taiga which you'd never visited gives you a happy recollection of last summer'. Sounds rather like a crossword clue.

IVOLGINSKY DATSAN (MONASTERY)

The centre of Russian Buddhism stands on a wide plain 35km outside the city and it's a fascinating place to visit. Before the Revolution there were hundreds of similar monasteries in the area with the largest and most important at Selenginsk. Almost all were closed and the monks sent to the gulags in the 1930s but when Stalin sanctioned greater religious tolerance in the 1940s, astrologers selected this site for a new monastery and it was built in 1946. There are now 30 lamas, some of them very elderly but novices still join each year and most spend up to five years studying in Ulan Bator. Tibetan Buddhism is practised here and the Dalai Lama has visited the Datsan five times.

Getting there

Bus No 104 from Ulan Ude's Central Bus Station passes the Datsan and goes as far as Kalenovo village. There are three departures a day and the trip takes 45 minutes. Another not very convenient option is to catch bus No 130 which runs past Ivolga village. From here walk straight ahead out of the village, then turn right after about 3km, and from here you can see the Datsan.

Visiting the Datsan

As you walk around the Datsan don't forget that you should walk clockwise around objects of Buddhist veneration (prayer wheels, temples and stupas); hats must be taken off inside the buildings. Visitors are shown round by a smiling monk. Be sure to make a donation, bearing in mind the tremendous cost of the rebuilding projects that are now being carried out at the old monasteries throughout the region.

The **largest temple**, a three-storey building constructed in 1971, burnt down four months after completion, with the loss of numerous valuable *thangkas* (paintings). It was rebuilt in just seven months. Inside, its joyous technicolour decoration seems rather out of place in grey Russia: golden dragons slide down the sixteen wooden columns supporting the upper galleries (where there is a library of Tantric texts), and hundreds of incarnations of the Buddha line one wall. Easy to recognise is Manla, with the dark blue face, the Buddha of Tibetan medicine. The largest thangka hanging above the incarnations is of the founder of this 'Yellow Hat' (Gelukpa) sect. Juniper wood is burnt and food and money offered to the incarnations.

Beside this is a smaller pagoda, and the **green temple** behind it is the oldest building in the complex, constructed in 1946. The octagonal white building houses a model of **Paradise** (*Devashin*) and a library of several hundred Tibetan and Mongolian texts, each wrapped in silk. In the big **white stupa** nearby are the ashes of the most famous former head lama of the Datsan, Sherapov, who died in 1961. There is even a **Bo tree** growing very successfully in its own greenhouse from seeds brought in 1956 from Delhi. Visiting Buddhists stay in the 'hotel' and students now come from all over the CIS to spend time studying Buddhism here.

Snacks are available at the kiosk outside, which is where the buses go from. You could also try hitching a ride back in a tour-bus.

Chita
Чита

Chita is the junction of the Trans-Siberian and the Trans-Manchurian railway lines. The city was closed to foreigners until the late 1980s as it was the military centre for the sometimes tense Siberian/Chinese border. There's just about enough to keep you occupied for a day here: a Decembrists museum, a museum full of military hardware and an interesting Army Officers' Club where non-members are welcome.

HISTORY

Founded in 1653, Chita became a *sloboda* (tax-exempt settlement) in 1690, populated by Cossacks and trappers. It was famous in the 1800s when it became the place of exile for many revolutionary Decembrists. George Kennan was here in 1887 and wrote: 'Among the exiles of Chita were some of the brightest, most cultivated, most sympathetic men and women we had met in Eastern Siberia.'

By 1900 more than 11,000 people lived here. There were nine churches, a cathedral, a nunnery, a synagogue, thirteen schools and even a telephone system. Soviet power was established in the city on 16 February 1918 but by 26 August, the city was captured by the White Army. However, by 22 October it was firmly back in the hands of the Soviets.

Chita is now the major industrial and cultural centre of Eastern Siberia, and still of military importance. The numerous army buildings around the city look much like ordinary office buildings but have their foyers hidden from the streets with armed guards just inside the door.

ORIENTATION AND SERVICES

The railway station is only a short walk away from the centre of the town and most hotels. The central bus station is in front of the railway station. The airport is 13km east of the city (bus Nos 4 or 14 from pl Lenina).

Intourist (☎ 31 246) is at ul Lenina 56, and **Sputnik** (☎ 32-985) is at ul Kalinina 68. **Chitakurort Services** (☎ 323 79) , ul Angarskaya 15, represent the numerous health spas in the region. **Aeroflot** (☎ 343 81) is at ul Leningradskaya 36. **Railway information** (☎ 321 19) can be obtained from the station and tickets can also be booked at the railway booking office at ul Lenina 55.

If you are interested in traditional medicine, the **Centre of Eastern Medicine** (☎ 665 20) is at ul Lenina 109.

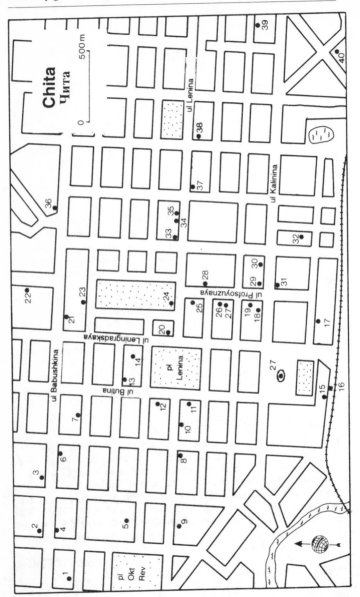

HOTELS AND RESTAURANTS

2 Restaurant Moran Ресторан Моран
4 Hotel Kommohalnaya
   Гостиница Коммунальная
9 Café Bar Кафе или Бар
17 Café Bar Кафе или Бар
18 Hotel Dauriya Гостиница Даурия
19 Hotel Obkomovskaya
   Обкомовная Гостиница
20 Hotel Zabaikale Гостиница Забайкалье
25 Café Sibir Кафе Сибирь
26 Hotel Ingoda Гостиница Ингода
32 Café Кафе
36 Hotel Turist Гостиница Турист
37 Restaurant Argol Ресторан Аргол
38 Café Tsyplyata Tabaka Кафе Цыплята Табака

OTHER

1 Market Рынок
3 Old Church Старая Церковь
5 Old Market Старый Рынок
6 Teaching Institute & Lenin Museum
   Педагогический Институт и Музей Ленина
7 Stamp Shop Филателия
8 Book Shop Дом Книги
10 Centre of Eastern Medicine Центр Восточной Медицины
11 Central Post Office Почтамт
12 City Administration Дом Советов
13 Aeroflot Office Касса Аэрофлота

OTHER (cont)

14 Delfin Swimming Pool Бассейн «Дельфин»
15 Bus Station Автовокзал
16 Railway Station
   Железнодорожний Вокзал
21 Museum of Local Studies
   Краеведческий Музей
22 Medical Institute Медицинский Институт
23 Art Museum Художественный Музей
24 Military Museum & Officers' Club
   Музей Истории Войск и Дом Официров
27 Stadium Trud
   Стадион «Труд»
28 Drama Theatre
   Драматический Театр
29 Sputnik Спутник
30 Book Shop Дом Книги
31 Museum of Minerals
   Минералогический Музей
33 Shumov Palace & Site of future Museum of Local Studies
   Дворец Шумова и Будущий Краеведческий Музей
34 Art Shop
   Художественный Магазин
35 Intourist Интурист
39 Tatar Mosque
   Татарская Мечеть
40 Decembrists Museum in Archangel Michael Church
   Музей Декабристов Михайло-Архангельской Церкови

WHERE TO STAY

The best of the cheapies is the *Hotel Dauriya* (☎ 623 65), ul Profsoyuznaya 17, which charges US$13 per person in a double room. There's also the extremely basic *Hotel Zabaikale* (☎ 645 20), ul Leningradskaya 36, charges US$14 per person in a double room. Even more basic is the *Hotel Taiga* (☎ 390 48), ul Lenina 75, more of a hostel than a hotel, with beds for US$5 in a small dormitory.

In the middle price range, with single/double rooms for around US$30/50, there's the *Hotel Obkomovskaya* (☎ 65 270), ul Profsoyuznaya 18; the *Hotel Turist* (☎ 652 70), ul Babushkina 42; and the *Hotel Kommohalnaya* (☎ 375 77), ul Baboshkina 149. Out of town on the way to the airport is the *Krasni Drakon Motel* (☎ 11 973), ul Magistralnaya. To get to it take bus No 14 and tell the driver 'motel' so he lets you out at the stop just before the motel.

WHERE TO EAT

The most expensive restaurant in town is the *Restaurant Krasni Drakon* at the motel of the same name. Bookings (☎ 142 88) are recommended as it is a long trip there. The best of the inner city restaurants is *Café Tsyplyata Tabaka* at ul Ostrovskovo 20, which does excellent roast chicken. *Restaurant Moran* at ul Bogomyakova 23, claims to be a Korean restaurant but everything seems to be Russian.

WHAT TO SEE

The **Army Officers' Club**, ul Lenina 80 is well worth a visit. On the second floor, opposite the bar, is the entertainment room with eight full-size billiard tables, and this is surrounded by chess tables with another balcony above, also full of tables. Despite the fact that few people speak, the noise level is unbelievable as each chess player punches his time clock every 30 seconds. The bar is quite good and is open 12:00-23:00 every day except Monday. The **Military Museum** is next door, open 10:00-18:00 Wednesday, Thursday and Friday, and 10:00-17:00 on weekends.

The **Decembrists Museum** (☎ 348 03), is housed in the former Archangel Michael Church, ul Dekabristov 3b. It's open 10:00-18:00, closed Monday.

The **Museum of Local Studies** is closed for capital repairs and may move from its current address at ul Babushkina 113 to ul Lenina 84. Call first to find out on ☎ 355 30.

Birobidzhan
Биробиджан

A little bit of Israel in the Far East, Birobidzhan is the capital of the Jewish Autonomous Region, a remote site selected in 1934 as the 'homeland' for Soviet Jews. An effective propaganda campaign and starvation in the east, encouraged 41,000 Soviet Jews to move here but by 1938, 28,000 of them had fled the region's harsh conditions. There were Jewish schools and synagogues in Birobidzhan up until the 1940s, when a resurgence of religious repression led to their closure. Despite the low number of Jews, considerable effort was put into giving the city a Jewish feel. This includes providing street signs in Hebrew and Russian, making Hebrew the official language of the region, and printing Russia's only Hebrew paper, the *Birbobidzhaner Sterm*. Today less than 5% of the population have Jewish ancestry but students are again offered classes in Hebrew and Yiddish. Birobidzhan's most famous export is the rice combine harvester made at the Dalselmash factory on the western outskirts of the town.

Birobidzhan is not a 'must see' but could make an interesting short stop on the Trans-Siberian journey, or a day trip from Khabarovsk, 180km east.

ORIENTATION AND SERVICES

Everything is within walking distance of the station. The town's only travel agent is **Intour-Birobidzhan** (☎ 42145-61573), ul Sholom-Aleikhema 55. The only hotel is the standard *Hotel Vostok* (☎ 42145-65330), ul Sholom-Aleikhema 1. They charge US$35 for a single and US$50 a double. There's a restaurant here and several in the town.

WHAT TO SEE

The **Museum of Local Studies**, ul Lenina 24, is open 09:00-17:50, closed Mondays. The **Art Museum** is on ul Pionerskaya. Cultural performances are often scheduled at the **Philharmonic Hall** (☎ 656 79), pro 60th SSSR. The **synagogue** is on the eastern outskirts of town, ul Mayakovskovo 11; take bus Nos 5, 16 or 22 eastward from Hotel Vostok.

There's a **beach** on the Bira River which is packed at summer weekends. To get there, keep walking down ul Gorky until you reach the river and you'll see it on the left beside Park Kultury. It is only 800m past the Art Museum.

Khabarovsk
Хабаровск

Khabarovsk is a relaxed provincial city of 600,000 people, pleasantly situated beside the Amur River. It's well worth stopping here for a day or two. In summer, holiday crowds flock to the sandy river banks, giving the place the atmosphere of a friendly English seaside resort; (but for some reason sunbathing in Russia is often done standing up). It's bitterly cold here in winter and when the river freezes, people drive their cars onto it and fish through holes chopped in the two-foot thick ice. Apart from the river, the other sights include an interesting Museum of Local History, a Military Museum and the arboretum, which was founded over one hundred years ago to supply the numerous parks and gardens in the city.

HISTORY

In 1858 a military settlement was founded here by Count Muravev-Amurski, the governor general of East Siberia who did much to advance Russia's interests in the Far East. It was named Khabarovka, in honour of the Cossack explorer who conquered the Amur region in the 17th century, and whose statue now stands in the square in front of the railway station. By 1883 the town was known as Khabarovsk and the following year, when the Far Eastern Territories were made a region separate from Eastern Siberia, it became the administrative capital and home of the governor general of the area.

Until the railway arrived, the town was just a trading and military post picturesquely situated on three hills on the banks of the Amur River, where it is joined by its tributary, the Ussuri. It was a junction for passengers who arrived by steamer from west Siberia, along the Shilka and Amur rivers. Here they would transfer to another ship for the voyage down the Amur and Ussuri to Vladivostok.

From 1875 onwards several plans were submitted for the building of the Ussuri Railway, which now runs along the great river between Khabarovsk and Vladivostok. Work began in 1893 and on 3 September 1897 a train completed the first journey between these two towns. A railway technical school was opened in the following year on the street that is now named ul Karla Marxa.

Early visitors

As more of the sections of the Trans-Siberian Railway were built, greater numbers of foreign travellers arrived in Khabarovsk. The *1900 Guide to the Great Siberian Railway* did not encourage them to stay long, reporting that: 'The conditions of life in Khabarovsk are not attractive, on account of the absence of comfortable dwellings, and the expensiveness of some products and of most necessary articles ... Imported colonial goods are sold at a high price and only fish is very cheap.' Tourists at the time were also advised against trying Mr Khlebnikov's locally produced wine, made from the wild vines that grow in the area because: 'it is of inferior quality and without any flavour'. Recommended sights included the wooden triumphal arch (now demolished) erected in commemoration of the visit of the Tsarevich Nicholas in 1891 and the bronze statue of Count Muravev-Amurski on the promontory above the river. After the Revolution, the Count was traded in for an image from the Lenin Statue Factory.

The city today

The railway brought more trade than tourists, and though it suffered during the Civil War, the town quickly grew into the modern city it is today. Few of the old wooden cabins remain but there are some attractive stone buildings from Imperial times. It is the capital of Khabarovsk Territory and one of the regions with the richest mineral deposits in the CIS, although the land is little more than a gigantic swampy forest. Khabarovsk is now a major industrial centre involved in engineering, petroleum refining and timber-working. In the last few years the Japanese and South Koreans have moved in, opening factories and businesses.

LOCAL TRANSPORT

There's no metro but there are regular bus, trolley-bus and tram services. From the station, bus No 1 travels down ul Karla Marxa and ul Muraveva-Amurskovo and then back to the station along ul Lenina. Bus No 2 from the station runs down ul Serysheva (which is parallel to bul Amurski) and back up to the station via ul Karla Marxa and ul Muraveva-Amurskovo. To get to MNTK, take tram No 5 from the station; the trip takes 45 minutes. Trolleybus No 1 runs between the airport and pl Komsomolskaya.

Boats along the Amur River operate from May to October. Both local ferries and long distance hydrofoils depart from the river station at ul Shevchenko 1. While Intourist can organise tickets for a trip it's easy enough to do this yourself.

ORIENTATION AND SERVICES

Khabarovsk is a large city; the railway station and the Hotel Intourist are about 3-4kms apart, a half-hour walk. The Intourist office is at this hotel and many of the tourist sights are within walking distance of it. The main street is ul Karla Marxa which becomes ul Muraveva-Amurskovo as it goes around the city's central , pl Lenina. There are numerous travel agencies here including **Intourist** (☎ 337 634), in the Hotel Intourist; **Dalni Vostok Company** (☎ 388 079, fax 338 679); and **Michael Travel Agency** (☎ 334 992).

Diplomatic representation
● **Japanese Consulate** (☎ 331 918, satellite ☎ 50985-21 002, fax 331 912), ul Pushkina 38/A, open Mon-Fri, 9:00-12:30, 14:00-17:30 for visas.
● **Chinese Consulate** (☎ 348 537, fax 348 537), Lenin Stadium, Southern Korpus, open 9:30-12:00 Mon, Wed and Fri for visas.
● **United States** (☎ 337 923, 336 923), ul Turgeneva 69.

Railways
There is an **Intourist booking office** at the railway station (☎ 342 192). The advance purchase rail **ticket office** is at ul Leningradskaya 56 (☎ 383 164). You can also get tickets through the private company **Eurasia Trans Inc** (☎ 226 067, fax 332 726), ul Turgeneva 64.

Airlines
Aeroflot (☎ 335 346), is at bul Amursky 18. This office is for international departures; the domestic departures office is opposite. Other airlines include **Alaska Airlines** (☎ 378 804); **Asiana Airlines** of South Korea (at airport ☎ 348 024); **Chosonminhang Airlines** of North Korea (at airport ☎ 373 204); Japan Airlines **JAL** (at airport ☎ 370 686); and **Chinese Northern Airlines** (☎ 373 440).

Tours
The service bureau (☎ 399 919) in the Hotel Intourist offers the following tours: **city tour** (2.5hrs by car: US$35); **museum tours** (US$10); the **arboretum** (1hr: US$10); **city sightseeing from above** (2 hrs: US$300 for the flight); **Nanai village folk show** (4hrs: US$45). They will also arrange **boat trips**, with a folk group performing on deck, and they sell tickets for the **Drama Theatre**, the **Musical Comedy Theatre** and the **circus**. Note that these are all closed on Mondays and that tickets must be booked before 13:00 on the day you wish to go to a performance.

WHERE TO STAY

The most centrally located hotel and the best value is the basic *Hotel Tsentralnaya* (☎ 336 731), ul Pushkina 52. Double rooms with attached bath cost US$30. The basic *Hotel Mayak* (☎ 330 935), ul Kooperativnaya 11 and near the railway station, is not bad, They charge US$15/30 for a single/double. *Hotel Amur* (☎ 335 043, fax 221 223), ul Lenina 29, has rooms for US$25/40 but they're hardly spotless. *Hotel Turist* (☎ 370 417), ul Karla Marxa 67, is much better but more expensive: US$45/58 with bathrooms attached. Cheaper places include the refurbished *Hotel Dalny Vostok* (☎ 335 093), ul Muravieva-Amurskovo 18; and the *Hotel Vassily Payarkov* (☎ 398 201) which is on a boat tied at the City Pier.

Hotel Lyudmila (☎ 388 665) ul Muravieva-Amurskovo 33, is a good mid-range choice. You'll get a large double room here for US$100. *Mar Kuel Apartment Hotel*, at per Derzhinski 3, (note that this is not ul Derzhinski, but a small road between ul Derzhinski and ul Zaparina toward the Amur River from ul Lenina), has studio apartments with kitchen for US$80.

MNTK (☎ 399 401, fax 352 121) is situated a fair way away from the centre of town, at ul Tikhookeanskaya 211. The rooms, however, are clean and comfortable; they cost from US$115.

The main tourist hotel is the *Hotel Intourist* (☎ 336 507) at per Arseneva 7 which is expensive (double rooms only, at US$120) but is, however, surprisingly well organised and pleasant. There's a number of good shops on the ground floor, an excellent restaurant on the eleventh, and the service bureau on the second offers a wide range of excursions. In its brochure, the hotel is described as 'a twelve storey modern style building with a clear-cut architectural silhouette'.

There is an ever increasing number of excellent hotels and these are popular with business travellers. You're unlikely to be able to get in unless you book well in advance. *Hotel Sapporo* (☎ 332 702, fax 332 830) at ul Komsomolskaya 79 is the best of them and caters to Japanese business people, charging US$200 for a double room. *Hotel Parus* (☎ 33 72 70, fax (7-509) 31 436 123 via Sprint) is at ul Shchevchenko 5, and has single rooms for US$120. *Hotel Amethyst* (☎ 334 699, fax (509) 01-600131), ul Tolstovo 5a, has singles/doubles for US$80/120; *Hotel Maly* (☎ 225 802, fax 225 567), ul Kalinina 83a, charges US$100 for a double.

WHERE TO EAT

The two best restaurants in town are both foreign. The *Harbin* (☎ 331 356) at ul Volochaveskaya 118, has two halls which have different prices. Food can be excellent but the service is variable.

The Japanese restaurant, *Unikhab* (☎ 399 315) on the top storey of the Hotel Intourist, is more reliable but expensive. For some reason the floor here slopes to the right on the southern side of the building, promoting a somewhat unsteady feeling even before the vodka appears but the food more than makes up for this.

The *Sapporo Restaurant* (☎ 330 8082) on ul Muraveva-Amurskovo 3 is the next best place to eat but it's expensive. It has three floors of food with Russian cuisine on the first two and Japanese on the third.

The Khabarovsk area code is ☎ 4210. From outside Russia dial +7-4210.

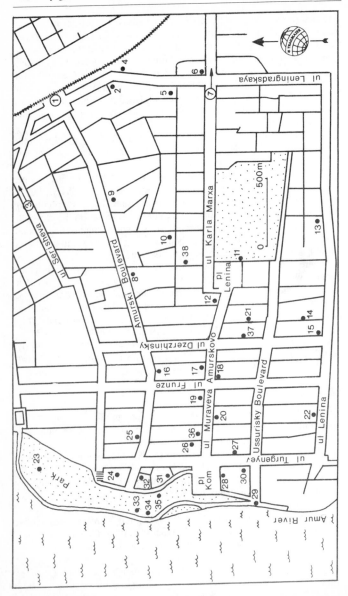

Khabarovsk
Хабаровск

HOTELS AND RESTAURANTS

5 Hotel Zarya Гостиница Заря
6 Hotel Turist Гостиница Турист
9 Hotel Mayak Гостиница Маяк
10 Hotel Amethyst Гостиница Аметист
11 Hotel Tsentralnaya Гостиница Центральная
12 Hotel Lyudmila Гостиница Людмила
13 Restaurant Okean Ресторан Океан
14 Hotel Sever Гостиница Север
15 Hotel Amur Гостиница Амур
17 Café Dauria & Cinema Кафе Даурия и Кино
20 Hotel Dalny Vostok Гостиница Далний Восток
21 Restaurant Harbin Ресторан Харбин
26 Hotel Sapporo Гостиница Саппоро
28 Restaurant Khamali Ресторан Камалий
32 Hotel Intourist Гостиница Интурист
34 Café Tower Кафе Башня
36 Restaurant Rus Ресторан Русь
37 Pizzeria Пицца

OTHER

1 Railway Station
   Железнодорожный Вокзал
2 Church Церковь
3 Bus Station Автовокзал

OTHER (cont)

4 Advance Purchase Rail Ticket Office
   Предварительная Железнодорожная Касса
7 To War Cemetery
8 Market Рынок
16 Aeroflot International Office
   Касса Аэрофлота
18 Central Post Office Почтамт
19 Tainy Remesla Art Store
   Художественный Магазин Тайны Ремесла
22 Geological Museum
   Геологический Музей
23 Open Air Pool
   Открытный Бассейн
24 Church of St Innocent
   Иннокентьевская Церковь
25 Aeroflot Domestic Office
   Касса Аэрофлота
27 Eurasia Trans Inc
   Предприятие Eurasia
29 River Station Речной Вокзал
30 United States Foreign Office
   Американский Торговый Центр
31 Military Museum Музей Истории Краснознаменного
   Дальневосточного Военного Округа
33 Casino Amur Казино Амур
35 Museum of Local Studies
   Краеведческий Музей
38 Japanese Consulate
   Кулсульство Японии

On Komsomolskaya Square, is the inexpensive Georgian **Khamali** (☎ 333 845) where the speciality is *khinkali* which are giant meat-filled dumplings. Most dishes are under US$5.

If you're staying at MNTK, the closest restaurant is the **Chinese Samovar** (Kitayski Samovar). There are some dubious dealings going on behind the scenes but the food's not bad. Despite being only 50m from the main road, it's difficult to find. Take tram No 5 to Avtodorozhny Technikum.

By far the best snack bar in Khabarovsk is the **Café Tower**: good coffee, excellent ice cream and meringues. Take a chair out onto the balcony for a superb view over the river. Another great find is the **Pizzeria** at ul Dzerzhinskovo 36. Khabarovsk's bright young things hang out at **Café Dauria**, ul Muraveva-Amurskovo 25.

WHAT TO SEE

Museum of Local History

The museum, based on the extensive collection of Baron Korff, a former governor general of the Amur region, was opened in 1894. In 1897 it was moved into the three-storey building in which it is now housed. With donations made by hunters and explorers over the last 90 years, the collection has grown into an impressive display of local history, flora and fauna. Labels are in Cyrillic and Latin (see p401).

Among the animals in the galleries on the ground floor are two Amur tigers. Also known as the Siberian or Manchurian tiger (*Felis/Panthera tigris altaica*), this is the largest member of the cat family and can weigh up to 350kg, about twice the average weight of an African lion. In the same gallery are various fur-bearing animals including the large sea-otter or Kamchatka beaver (*Enhydra lutris*) from which come the highest-priced pelts in the world. Before protection of the animal began in the early 1900s single pelts were selling for over £1300/US$2000.

The upper galleries are devoted to local history and ethnography. The area was inhabited by several tribes at the time of the Revolution. The Goldi and Orochi lived near the mouth of the Ussuri; the Olchi and the Giliak beside the Amur. All tribes had their *shamans* and some of their robes and equipment are on display as well as a suit made entirely from fish-skins. The skin of a common fish, the *keta*, was not used only for clothing but also for tents, sails and boots. There's also a display of early settlers' furniture, samovars and other utensils, including some bread baked by the original colonists. The museum is at ul Shevchenko 11; open 10:00-18:00, closed Monday.

Military Museum

Fifty metres up the street from the Museum of Local History, this museum provides a record of military activity here since the city was founded.

There are numerous pictures of Russian soldiers, as well as photographs of British, French, Italians and Americans in Vladivostok in 1918. The museum's walls are decorated with medals and old weapons, including a weather-beaten Winchester rifle and a few Smith and Wesson pistols. There's a small display on Mongolia including a picture of Lenin and Sukhe Bator sharing a joke. Upstairs is a large quantity of WWII memorabilia. Behind the building there's a row of armoured vehicles and tanks, a Mig fighter plane and a train carriage used by the commander of the Russian Far East military forces in the 1930s. Entry is US$0.50; it's open 10:00-18:00, closed Monday and Tuesday.

Other sights and things to do

The **Geological Museum**, on the corner of ul Lenina and ul Pushkina, contains a well laid-out display of local minerals. You've heard how rich Siberia is in natural resources, now come and see what they actually look like. Paradoxically, pride of place goes to some rocks from the moon, small fragments under a microscope. Open 10:00-18:00 (not Monday), entry is US$0.50.

Founded long before the railway arrived in Khabarovsk, the **arboretum** is an interesting place to visit. Originally set up to provide trees and shrubs for the new town's parks, it now claims to have a specimen of every plant species found in the Far Eastern Territories. The arboretum is located at ul Volochaevskaya, and open 9:00-18:00 weekdays. Take bus No 1 to the corner of ul Volochaevskaya and ul Lenina, then bus No 25 to the Ussurisky stop.

The **Amur River** is a focus of interest in both winter and summer. In the winter when it freezes locals drill holes through the ice and set up little tents to sit in while they fish. In the summer the beaches along the banks become crowded with swimmers. The water is certainly not crystal clear but it's refreshing on a hot summer's day. You should watch out for the strong current though. There are also boat trips on the river.

There are regular services at the **church** on ul Leningradskaya, the interior of which is beautifully decorated.

The excellent **sauna** (☎ 331 729), ul Moskovskaya 7, is very popular with foreigners. The sauna also includes a pool, billiards room and a restaurant. Bookings are not necessary; a visit costs US$10.

ENTERTAINMENT

Khabarovsk doesn't offer much in terms of nightlife but gamblers may be interested to know that there are two casinos. The **Casino Amur** (☎ 334 782) at 15 ul Shevchenko (just opposite the Tower Café), is almost certainly the main rendezvous of all the petty criminals, hangers-on and hookers in the city, so watch your wallet if you go. The casino's literature offers comfort to worried punters, promising 'True service and guarantee of safety' which is not exactly reassuring. It's open every night from 20:00 to 06:00. **Casino Tourist** (☎ 370 473) is the city's other gambling den and it is located in the Hotel Tourist, ul Karla Marxa 67.

WHAT TO BUY

Interesting local products include ginseng and a special blend of vodka and herbs known as *Aralievaya Vodka*. The attractive, tree-lined ul Muraveva-Amurskovo is the place to go shopping, although the shops close from 14:00 to 15:00 for lunch. The best souvenir shops are the **Tainy Remesla** art store, Muraveva-Amurskovo 17; **Art Salon**, ul Muraveva-Amurskovo 17; and **Art Shop**, ul Karla Marxa 15. **Hotel Intourist** also has a good selection.

The best open air clothing market is the **Vyborgskaya Market**, ul Vyborgskaya. Other markets outside the city centre include one at ul Seryshev 60 and one in a former sewing factory on ul 60th Let Oktobr.

Excursions from Khabarovsk

Khabarovsk is an ideal base from which to start trips into the Siberian outback. The service bureau at Hotel Intourist here offers special interest tours to various distant and not so distant regions and can be contacted in advance on ☎ 4212-39 99 19; fax 1-509-689 42 22 51. Some of the excursions and tours currently being offered are listed below but as the region opens up to tourism many other places will become available.

Sakhalin is an island just off the East Siberian coast. The main attraction here is the great variety of wildlife which foreigners may explore, photograph, study, ride horses amongst, or kill. The most popular tours are the hunting and fishing trips, US$700 for 5-10 days salmon fishing. Vanino, from where you catch a ferry to Sakhalin Island, is on the **BAM Railway**.

Excursions to **Birobidzhan** (see p253), the capital of the Jewish Autonomous region, take a full day.

Other destinations in Eastern Siberia and the Far Eastern Territories that can be visited from Khabarovsk include **Yakutsk** (see p240), **Kamchatka** (for fishing and hunting), **Perelk** in the Arctic Circle (to see the Northern Lights) and **Magadan** (a former gulag centre). Weekly flights now link Magadan with Anchorage.

Vladivostok
Владивосток

Vladivostok, eastern terminus of the Trans-Siberian line and home of the Pacific Fleet, was off-limits until 1990. Soviet citizens needed special permits to visit and foreigners, with a few notable exceptions (Gerald Ford, 1975), required nothing short of divine intervention.

Ferries for Japan now leave from Vladivostok (from the dock next to the railway station). Whether you're coming from the east or heading that way it's well worth stopping off to explore one of the former USSR's major Cold War secrets.

HISTORY

The Vladivostok region has been inhabited for many thousands of years, certainly back at least to the second millennium BC; inhabitants were largely nomadic, however, so few relics remain. Eastern chronicles reveal that this area was considered part of the Chinese empire at a very early stage but also that it was so remote and conditions so harsh that they left it well alone.

The Russians arrive

In the mid-19th century the Russians were concentrating on expanding their territory eastwards at China's expense. At the head of the exploratory missions was Count Muravyev-Amurski (see p87) who, in 1859, chose the site for a harbour here from his steamer, the *Amerika*. A year later a party of forty soldiers landed to secure the region. The port was named Vladivostok, or 'Rule the East'.

In 1861 the first shipments of soldiers arrived to protect Russia's new eastern frontier and settlers were not far behind. It soon became apparent just how important a find this city was: one of the few deep water ports on the east coast, Vladivostok's coastline remains unfrozen for longer than other parts of Siberia, being inaccessible for only 72 days per year on average compared with Nakhodka's 98. The city's strategic location resulted in the movement of the Russian eastern naval base here in 1872 from Nikolaevsk-na-Amur (where the water remains frozen for an impressive 190 days per year).

Conflict in the east

In 1904 the Russo-Japanese war broke out. Vladivostok was heavily bombarded during the fighting and trade virtually ceased but while large parts of the port were destroyed, the war was ultimately to prove beneficial: peace settlements with Japan left Vladivostok as Russia's prime east coast port although Japan gained Port Arthur and parts of Sakhalin Island.

During the First World War the city served as the chief entry point for supplies and ammunition from the USA. At the same time, foreign troops (British, Japanese, American, Canadian and Italian) flooded in to support the White Russians' struggle against the Bolsheviks. The most notorious foreign 'visitors' were the Czech legions which had fought their way east all the way from the Ukraine in a desperate bid for freedom (see p111). Many of their graves, and those of other foreigners, can still be found in the cemetery here.

Ultimately, as it became clear that the Bolsheviks were gaining the upper hand, the foreign forces departed. Most troops had left by 1920 although some Japanese stayed on until October 1922. Finally, on 25 October, the city was 'liberated' and Soviet power established, prompting Lenin's famous comment about Vladivostok, 'It's a long way away. But it's ours'.

The Soviet period

The Soviet period was good for the city. Money poured in, along with orders to develop the port and build more ships. In the last days of the Great Patriotic War Vladivostok assumed a key role as the centre of operations from which the fight against the Japanese in Manchuria was co-ordinated. Twenty-five ships from here were sunk in four years and some 30,000 sailors perished.

The city was then sealed off completely from the outside world as the Cold War set in, and the Pacific Fleet expanded fast. The West heard little more of this protected port until 1986 when Gorbachev made his 'Vladivostok Initiative' speech, in which he highlighted a grand new plan for Soviet economics and military commitments in the Far East. Echoing Peter the Great, he announced that Vladivostok was to become 'A wide open window on the East'.

Vladivostok today

The city is keen to establish itself as a major player on the Pacific Rim. There are even periodic murmurs of an independence movement whereby the entire Primorsky region would become an independent economic zone; attempts to encourage this have included the offer of free passports to Hong Kong Chinese. While there is, doubtless, enormous potential in the area, mafia gangs from all over Russia have been drawn here by the availability of hard currency; and there's a thriving criminal underworld dealing in every commodity imaginable.

Vladivostok was 'honoured' in 1995 by being featured on Russia's new 1000 rouble note. Locals were unimpressed, saying that this virtually worthless denomination reflected Moscow's attitude to the provinces.

LOCAL TRANSPORT

The **airport** is 30km outside Vladivostok near Artem-Primorski railway station. A taxi to Vladivostok railway station costs about US$50. Bus No 101 runs from the airport to the central bus station (not actually very central as it's 9km to the north of Vladivostok railway station and just in front of Vtoraya Rechka railway station). There are regular suburban trains between the two stations. The cheapest way to get from the airport to Vladivostok is also the most time consuming. Take bus No 7 to Artem-Primorski railway station and get on a local train heading west. Get off at the fourth stop (Amurski Zaliv) and change trains for Vladivostok.

The **railway station** is a delightful, two-storey building from the last century. To leave the station walk up to the top floor which is at street level. To get to the Hotel Pensionat and Vlad Motor Inn, take the suburban train six stops to the station Sanatornaya (Санаторная). Behind the station is a modern **ferry terminal**.

There are numerous daily ferries from the **local ferry station** opposite the Submarine Museum. Destinations include the popular swimming spots of Russia Island, Popov Island, Reiniky Island, Cape Peshanaya, and Slavyanka Beach (two hydrofoils a day).

ORIENTATION AND SERVICES

Vladivostok is built along the Muravyev Peninsula, which stretches south-west into the Sea of Japan. Scattered around it is a series of islands, of which Russia Island remains the most important. It's still very much off-limits and protected by ferocious guard dogs so don't try any sightseeing there.

The focal point of the city is Zolotoi Rog (Golden Horn) Bay, so called because of its resemblance to the Golden Horn of Istanbul, and it's here that most of the ferries, warships and fishing boats dock. The railway station is conveniently located on the waterfront, ideal if you're transferring directly to the ferry terminal. Opposite this is pl Lenina and between the square and the station is ul Aleutskaya (previously known as 25 Oktabrya). The central hotels are within walking distance of the station, to the east.

Vladivostok: Your Essential Guide (Azulay US$6.50), is useful if you're here for any length of time. It's on sale at Vlad Motor Inn, the American Business Centre, and Nostalgia Art Salon. The English language fortnightly *Vladivostok News* is a great source of local information. You can get copies from its office, pro Krasnovo Znameni 10, or on the internet at http://www.tribnet.com and http://www.vladnews.ru.

The best adventure travel agency is **Primoski Klub Travel Service** (☎ 318 037), 4th floor, ul Russkaya 17, Vtoraya Rechka. There's also **Intourist** (☎ 256 210, fax 258 839), pr Okeanski 90; and **ACFES Tour**

Centre (☎ 319 492) in the Hotel Acfes Seiyo, pr 100th Vladivostoka 103.

Airlines include: **Aeroflot** (☎ general 260 880, ☎ international 222 581), ul Posetskaya 17; **Alaska Airlines** (☎ 227 645), located at the airport; **Transaero Airlines** (☎ 267 124); **Korean Air** (☎ 261 407), ul Aleutskaya, room 308; and **Orient Avia** (☎ 264 440), ul Posetskaya 17..

Both long-distance and local train tickets are available from the **Central Railway Station** (☎ 210 440). The **Central Bus Station** is in front of Vtoraya Rechka suburban railway station.

Diplomatic representation

● **US Consulate** (☎ 268 458, fax 268 445), ul Pushkinskaya 32; American citizen services 14:30-16:00 weekdays.

● **Australian Consulate** (☎ 228 628, fax 228 778), ul Uborevicha 17, floor 4; open 9:00-17:00 weekdays.

● **Japanese Consulate** (☎ 267 502, satellite ☎ 509-851 1001), ul Verkhneportovaya 46; open 10:00-12:00 weekdays except Wed.

● **South Korean Consulate** (☎ 227 822), ul Aleutskaya 45, 5th floor; open 9:00-18:00 weekdays.

● **Indian Consulate** (☎ 228 110, fax 228 666, satellite ☎ 509-851 1015), ul Aleutskaya 14; open 9:30-12:00 for visas.

Tours

All of the sights are within easy walking distance so there's not really any need for a tour. If you want to see something further away, however, contact one of the travel agencies above. **Boat trips** around the harbour are highly recommended: the chance to take pictures of Russian nuclear submarines doesn't arise that often. One-hour ferry cruises around Vladivostok's harbours and straits leave from Sportivnaya Gavan Pier approximately every hour between 11:00 and 16:00 in summer. A tour guide will give a history of sights (in Russian) including Russia Island, Skryplev Strait, Tokarevski Hill and the lighthouse at the end of Egersheld. The boat has a bar and the trip costs US$2.

❏ **Eco-tours from Vladivostok**

Local environmental organisations offer a variety of nature tours. The **Tiger Company** (☎ 277-91192) has tours in the area of Lazo nature reserve east of Vladivostok. Standard tours last 12 days and run through October. Prices are a maximum of US$70 per person.

World Wide Fund for Nature (☎ 310 185) tours support the region's nature reserves. Prices vary but are approximately US$150 per person for a weekend trip for five.

Khankaiski Nature Reserve (☎ 252-231 38) offer ornithological weekends exploring the wetlands of Lake Khanka 250 miles north of Vladivostok near the Chinese border. Tours to the **Ussuriski Nature Reserve** (☎ 241-98 318), 110 km north of Vladivostok, are also possible.

WHERE TO STAY

Hotels in Vladivostok are generally quite expensive. The hotel closest to the station is the basic *Hotel Primore* (☎ 213 182), ul Posetskaya 20, charging US$30/40 for a single/double with attached bathroom.

The most popular centrally located hotel is the rough old *Hotel Vladivostok* (☎ 222 208), ul Naberezhnaya 10. A single costs US$46, doubles are US$75. There are much better rooms on the fourth floor in a concern called *Visit Co Hotel* (☎ 212 053). Rooms here have TV, and attached bathroom; they cost US$90/140.

More basic than the Vladivostok but still centrally located, *Hotel Ekvator* (☎ 212 260) at ul Naberezhnaya 20, charges US$24 for a single room. *Hotel Amurski Zaliv* (☎ 225 520) at ul Naberezhnaya 9, has singles for US$50.

Hotel Gavan (☎ 219 965, fax 226 848, e-mail port@stv.iasnet.com) is at ul Krygina 3, is an upmarket hotel charging US$150/170.

Located about 20 km to the north of Vladivostok around the station Sanatornaya (*sanatorium*) are two good hotels. The *Vlad Motor Inn* (☎ 215 828, satellite ☎ 509-851 5111, fax 509-851 5116) ul Vosmaya 1, is a Canadian/Russian joint-venture, well-run and recommended. A double here costs US$150. The standard *Hotel Pensionat* (☎ 215 639) nearby at ul Devyataya 14, charges US$70 for a double.

Back in the centre of Vladivostok the top hotel is the Japanese owned *Hotel Versailles* (☎ 264 201, fax 265 124) Svetlanskaya 10. Rooms are luxurious and cost US$200/220.

WHERE TO EAT

The best restaurant within easy reach of the railway station is *Café Nostalgia*. They serve genuinely good coffee (most unusual in Russia) and the tiny restaurant next door is clean and has zakuski for about US$3 and main courses for US$5. Right next door, through the ornate Oriental doorway, is the Korean *Restaurant Morambom* which is probably better known for being difficult to get into than for its good food. It's expensive and you will need to book (☎ 227 725).

The cheapest meal in town seems to be at the *Magic Burger*, a McDonald's wanna-be at ul Svetlanskaya 42. Service is reasonably fast although you'll have to queue to get in; burgers cost US$1. The *shashlik stall* in the basement of the Hotel Vladivostok is another good place for a quick meal. There's excellent vegetarian food at *Hare Krishna Restaurant*. It is at pro Okeanski 10/12, open 10:00-19:00 weekdays.

It might be wise to avoid getting into arguments with shady characters in the *Elbrus Café*, ul Ladygina 9. In August 1996 a mafia grenade

The Vladivostok area code is ☎ 4232. From outside Russia dial +7-4232.

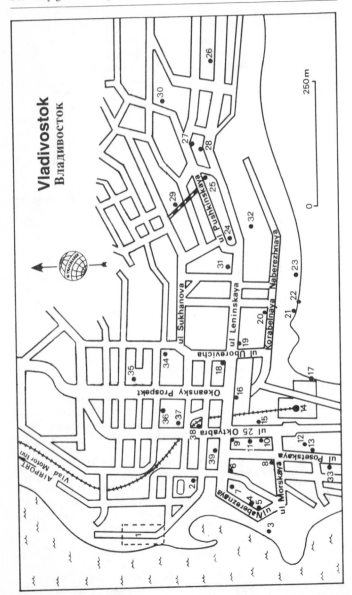

HOTELS AND RESTAURANTS

2 Café Elite Кафе Елите
3 Hotel Amurski Zaliv & Casino
   Гостиница Амурский Залив и Казино
4 Hotel Ekvator Гостиница Екватор
5 Hotel Vladivostok & Indian Consulate
   Гостиница Владивосток и Консульство Индии
6 Hotel Versailles & Casino Amherst
   Гостиница Версалes и Казино
7 Restaurant Okean Ресторан Океан
8 Restaurants Dary Morya/Morambom
   Ресторан Дары Моря/Морамбом
11 Café Ldinka Кафе Льдинк
13 Hotel Primore Гостиница Приморье
19 Magic Burger Кафе Мажик Бургер
26 Restaurant Nagasaki Ресторан Нагасакий
28 Café Nostalgia and Art Saloon Кафе Ностальгия
31 Restaurant Zhemchuzhina Ресторан Жемчужина
38 Restaurant Hare Krishna Ресторан Кришна

OTHER

1 Oceanarium Океанариум
9 Museum of Local Studies Краеведческий Музей
10 House of the Brynner Family Быв. Дом Бриннера
14 Central Post Office Почтамт
14 Railway Station Железнодорожный Вокзал
15 Picture Gallery Картинная Галерея
16 Victory of Soviet Power Monument
   Памятник «Борцам за Власть Советов»

OTHER (cont)

17 Sea Ferry Terminal & Hotel
   Морской Вокзал и Гостиница
18 GUM Department Store ГУМ
20 Submarine Museum & Navy Memorials
   Мемориальный Комплекс «Боевая Слава
   Краснознаменного Тихоокеанского Флота»
21 125th Anniversary of Vladivostok Monument
   Обелиск в Честь 125-летия Основания
   Города Владивостока
22 Krasni Vympel Ship Museum
   Пароход «Красный Вымпел»
23 Local Ferry Terminal
   Морской Вокзал Прибрежных Сообщений
24 American Business Centre
   Американский Коммерческий Центр
25 Pacific Fleet Military Museum
   Музей Тихоокеанского Флота
27 USA Consulate Консульство США
29 Funicular Railway Фуникулёр
30 Catholic Church Католический Костёл
32 Admiral Nevelski Monument
   Памятник Адмиралу Невельскому
33 Aeroflot Office Касса Аэрофлота
34 Australian Consulate Кулсульство Австраилии
35 Market Рынок
36 Japanese Consulate Кулсульство Японии
37 Border Guard Museum Музей «Пограничников»
39 Green Lantern Cabaret House Кабаре

exploded here; no one was injured, however. *Café Elite*, opposite Dynamo Stadium on ul Pogranichnaya, between ul Svetlanskaya and ul Semeonovskaya, is a better place for a coffee.

Upmarket restaurants include the Russian-Japanese *Restaurant Nagasaki* (☎ 269 748), at ul Svetlanskaya 115 and recognisable by the bright mosaic on the doorway; the Japanese *Sakura Restaurant* (☎ 260 305) in Hotel Vladivostok; and the seafood *Okean Restaurant* (☎ 268 186) at Naberezhnaya 3 which is cheaper than these other two.

The city's other top restaurants are further away, in the Sanatornaya district. The *Vlad Motor Inn* serves de luxe hamburgers that actually taste like de luxe hamburgers, for US$6, and some of the biggest steaks you'll ever see for US$30. Advance booking and reasonably smart dress would be a good idea in the evening. Begin the night with an unforgettable cocktail (US$6) from the bar here. Up the block in the Hotel Pensionat is the excellent and cheaper *Captain Cook Restaurant* (☎ 215 341), an Australian/Russian joint venture.

Restaurant Volna (☎ 219 340) on top of the Maritime Terminal, offers splendid views but it usually caters only for pre-booked groups.

WHAT TO SEE

The Pacific Fleet
Don't miss this unique opportunity to see some of the world's finest naval technology, although owing to a lack of funds it's beginning to look a little weatherbeaten now. Locals will tell you that it's all right to take photographs but telephoto lenses and hundreds of pictures of radar fittings may arouse suspicion; a touch of caution is advised. A good place to watch the ships is from the Eagle's Nest Hill (*Orlinoye Gnezdu*). To get to the top, take the **funicular** railway from the Pacific Fleet Museum.

Arsenev history museum
This is the biggest and best of Vladivostok's museums, recounting the history of both the city and the region and named after a local writer. The wildlife display is interesting: local sea life, an Ussuri leopard, a large Amur tiger and a couple of moose locking antlers in the corner. There's a display of the belongings of the early settlers, the robes of a Tungus shaman and the safe from the first bank here, stuffed with old rouble notes. Upstairs there's a small Yul Brynner exhibition (his family lived here before the Revolution), naval memorabilia and local art (the wood carvings are particularly attractive). The museum is at ul Svetlanskaya 20, and is open 10:00-16:30, closed Monday.

Pacific Fleet Military Museum
In an old church surrounded by pieces of heavy artillery, torpedoes, anchors and bombs, this museum isn't difficult to find. The display inside

is small but interesting with miscellaneous items from various conflicts: muskets, model ships, propaganda posters, a flamethrower, an ejector seat and the twisted propeller and gun from a ditched fighter plane. Open 09:30-17:45 daily except Monday and Tuesday.

Submarine Museum

On the waterfront and next to the eternal flame is an old C56 submarine, housing a display covering the history of submarines in Vladivostok. There are early uniforms, ships' instruments, pictures of the earliest submarine (1865) and the first flotillas (1906). The display is largely made up of old photographs, although you can also see some of the gifts made to submarine commanders from foreign hosts including, strangely enough, the key to the Freedom of the City of San Diego and (Tom Cruise fans, take note) a USN Fighter Weapons School Top Gun shield. Open 09:00-18:00, closed Sunday to Tuesday.

Krasnie Vimpel

Although marginally less interesting than the Submarine Museum, the first ship in the Soviet Pacific Fleet is moored just opposite and can also be visited. The *Krasnie Vimpel* was launched on 24 January 1923. Displays include lots of photographs of early crew members, medals, uniforms and various other pieces of salty memorabilia. Some of the machinery is preserved down below. If you're interested in buying bits and pieces of naval uniforms (belt buckles, cap badges etc) the sailors who run the museum may be able to help out. The museum, at nab Korabelnaya, is open 09:30-17:45, closed Sunday, Monday and Tuesday.

Other things to see

The **Primorskaya Art Museum** (open 10:00-18:00 daily, not Monday) at ul Aleutskaya 12 is worth a visit. There's a lot to see in here, most of the art having been donated by the Tretyakov Gallery in Moscow. Almost directly opposite, at No 15, is the **Brynner House**. You can't get inside the former residence of Yul Brynner's family but it's a real pilgrimage for some. In the well-tended **Naval Cemetery** are the graves of the Russians and people from other countries who died fighting the Communists in 1919-20. Unfortunately it's a fair way away, on the hill overlooking the Zolotoi Rog Bay, so you would be wise to take a car.

The **Oceanarium** is interesting, with displays of stuffed birds and marine life and many species of live fish in tanks. Animal lovers might want to avoid the whale pool (400m past the oceanarium) where the whales perform tricks for their food.

Medals, coins and **stamps** can be bargained for at the informal collectors market at Pokrovski Park. The 'swap-meets' occur every Saturday and Sunday from 11:00 to 14:00. You'll see the groups of collectors milling around near the Kronstadt Chapel.

WHAT TO BUY

The best souvenirs in town are sold in the **Nostalgia Café and Art Saloon**, ul 1st Morskaya 6/25. Many of the things here are expensive but they do seem to be of a high standard. The gift shops in the **Art Museum** at ul Aleutskaya 12, open 10:00-18:00, closed Sunday and Monday, or the **Arsenev History Museum** are worth a look. GUM, on ul Svetlanskaya 33, also has quite a good range.

It is best not to buy **vodka** here as there are a number of fake brands on sale that contain more than the legal amount of fusel oil, a by-product of the fermenting process, that will give you very much more than a nasty hangover. These include Avrora, Baren Chezzy, Russkaya, Piezo, Krom and Korona.

ENTERTAINMENT

As well as several theatres. less salubrious places of entertainment include the **Green Lantern Cabaret House**, ul Svetlanskaya 13; **Casino Amurski Zaliv** at the Hotel Amurski Zaliv, ul Naberezhnaya 9 and **Casino Amherst** at the Hotel Versailles.

Films in English are organised by ACTR and IREX educational organisations (☎ 223 798) on Thursday at 6pm at ul Svetlanskaya 150.

Roller blades and skates can be hired on the deck at the Okean Cinema for US$4 an hour between 10:00 and 20:00. Rowing boats (US$2 an hour) can be hired near the barge which doubles as a disco in summer.

❑ **Vladivostok-Japan ferry**
A ferry plies between Vladivostok and Japan, usually from late June to late September. It departs weekly from Vladivostok and travels to the cities of Niigata and Fushiki on alternate weeks. The trip takes about 72 hours. Ferries leaving Japan at 16:00 on Friday arrive in Vladivostok at 09:00 on Sunday, and leaving Vladivostok at 15:00 on Tuesday reach Japan at 09:00 on Thursday.

The prices are ¥33,700 (US$337) in a third class four-berth cabin, ¥35,800 (US$358) for a second class four-berth cabin and ¥77,800 (US$778) for a first class two-berth cabin. These fares include port tax at Vladivostok of US$10 and all meals. There is a 10% discount for round trips and a luggage limit of 100kg per person.

For information contact the United Orient Shipping and Agency Co, (☎ (813) 3740 2061, fax (813) 3740 2085), Level 7 Rikkokai-sogo Building, 2-32-3 Kita-Shinagawa, Shinagawa-ku, Tokyo 140, Japan.

Ulan Bator
Ulaanbaatar

The world's coldest capital is a fascinating place to visit even if it does, at first sight, look like just another Soviet-style city. Among the industrial suburbs and concrete tower blocks there are vibrant splurges of colour in the temples and old palaces. The Mongolian people are charming and cheerful (Luigi Barzini, driving across the country in 1907, was amazed at their high spirits; the nomads he encountered galloped alongside his car roaring with laughter). There are some short stopover tours which are good value and currently the best way to visit the city if you're travelling through on the train.

Ulan Bator sits in a basin surrounded by four mountains: Bogd Uul, Songino Khairkhan, Chingeltei and Bayanzurkh, all part of the beautiful Khentii range, the southernmost boundary of the great Siberian taiga. The city experiences great climatic extremes; the temperature ranges from -49°C (-46°F) in winter to 38°C (93°F) in summer. The average annual precipitation is only 236mm and there are on average 283 sunny days in the year. Ulan Bator is 1350 metres above sea level.

The best time to visit Ulan Bator is during the **Naadam Festival**, usually held between 11 and 13 July. The festival involves the three traditional Mongolian sports of horse riding, wrestling and archery.

HISTORY

Home of the Living Buddha
For much of its 350 year existence the town was little more than a semi-nomadic settlement. From 1639 to 1778, it moved some 30 times, like a migrating *ger* (yurt) city. The Da Khure Lamasery was built here in 1639 and this was the abode of the 'Living Buddha' or Dalai Lama, one of the three incarnations of the Buddha, the other two being in Tibet and Peking. The Dalai Lama at Da Khure was usually a child, who died, or rather was murdered, shortly before reaching maturity, since it was believed that the soul of a deity could dwell only in the body of a child.

From 1639 to 1706 the town was known as Örgöö, from the Mongolian word for palace. From 1706 to 1911 it was Ikh Khuree or Da Khure to the Mongolians and Urga to foreigners.

Independence
When Mongolia declared itself independent of China in 1911, the city was renamed Niislel Khurehe, and by this time it had become a large trading centre on the route between China and Russia. There were, in fact,

three separate cities here: the Chinese, the Russian and the Mongolian. The Chinese and Russian cities were engaged in the tea and silk trades but the Mongolian city's concern was the salvation (or rather the liberation) of souls. There was a population of 30,000 Buddhist monks in the lamaseries here.

Ulan Bator today

After the Communist Party came to power in 1921, the capital was renamed Ulan Bator, meaning 'Red Hero'. With considerable help from the USSR, the city was redesigned and the architectural origins of the austere tower blocks and municipal buildings are recognisably Soviet. In the mid 1990s, the city experienced a private sector boom with new buildings springing up everywhere and shops and restaurants opening. As in Russia, most of this money came from Communist era power brokers who quickly took control of privatised state assets.

VISITING MONGOLIA

Since 1995 Mongolian tour companies have all had to apply for either a category A or B licence. Category A operators have the right to direct foreign contact and issue visa invitations, while B operators can operate only as domestic agents. The largest travel company is **Zhuulchin Foreign Tourism Corporation** (☎ 312 095, fax 320 246, e-mail jlncorp@magicnet.mn, http://www.magicnet.mn/travel/juulchin), Chinggis Khaan Avenue 5B. The former state-owned organisation still has enormous clout but still charges as if it were a monopoly. It's probably best for individual arrangements with car, driver and interpreter. **Nomadic Journeys Ltd** (☎/fax 323 043, e-mail nomadic@magicnet.mn), PO Box 479, Ulan

---

❑ **Visa Registration**

It is essential that all travellers to Mongolia, except transit visa holders, register with the police at the **Citizens' Information and Registration Centre** as soon as possible after arriving and at the very latest within 10 days of arrival. Visitors who fail to register will be stopped at departure, denied exit, and fined. The fine is normally between US$25 and US$60 but will depend on the length of stay. In the summer of 1996, the rare independent traveller who did not know this rule had to pay US$15 for every day in excess of their 10 initial days.

Ulan Bator's Citizens' Information and Registration Centre is hard to find as it doesn't have a street address or look like a police station. It is located about 800 metres up the road which starts opposite the northern end of Eldev-Ochir St. It's on the third floor, on the right, at the end of a hall. It's best to take a Mongolian speaker with you. To register you need your passport and visa and 250 togrog to pay for photocopies. No photo is necessary. The procedure varies but it normally involves filling in a form, taking it to a nearby bank where you pay the money, and then returning to the Centre with the receipt where your visa is stamped. If you are travelling with a group, your hotel will register for you.

Bator 13 is highly recommended. As well as providing a number of local tours, they run Eco Tour Productions' trekking, riding and fishing trips (see p30). **Blue Sky Travel** (☎ 248 65), run by Mrs Cho-Cho Dugrichin, at the Ulan Bator Hotel has been recommended by several readers.

Individual travel vs package tours

While individual travel around Mongolia is possible, the difficulties with language, travel restrictions, accommodation, food and organising travel make joining a group or making one up an option that many travellers go for. If you are visiting only Ulan Bator, you can get by on your own but it's not so easy outside the capital. It is possible to organise personal tours once you arrive in Ulan Bator but they are invariably much more expensive than if you'd booked them before you left your home country.

LOCAL TRANSPORT

There are buses and trolley-buses in Ulan Bator but it is just as easy to walk as most of the sights are in the city's centre. To get a taxi, simply put out your hand by the side of the road and one will stop. Point to the odometer to signify to the driver that you expect to pay the prevailing Mongolian rate of 300 togrogs or US$0.50 per kilometre. Official taxis are also available but they're not in great supply.

ORIENTATION AND SERVICES

From Ulan Bator railway station to Sühbaatar Square is about 1.5km. The majority of people arriving here have pre-booked accommodation and will be met at the station.

Although Ulan Bator is relatively safe compared to some cities in the West, crime is on the increase. You're advised not to wander round the streets after dark and to take particular care at the railway station, where pickpockets and bag-slitters operate on the crowded platforms. The post office has also been reported as a prime location for petty theft.

Post and telecommunications

The **Central Post Office** is on Sühbaatar Square but it's better to buy stamps from the hotels which have a greater range. **International telephone calls** are expensive but can be made from the Post Office, the Business Centre on the fourth floor of the Hotel Ulaanbaatar and from the 24-hour, AT&T direct call telephone in the lobby of the Flower Hotel. International collect calls are not possible. Since 1992, Ulan Bator's telephone system has been slowly upgraded, with most of the old 5-digit telephone numbers becoming 6-digit. Numbers that began with a two usual-

The Ulan Bator area code is ☎ 1. From outside Mongolia dial +9761.

ly are converted by placing a 3 in front of the first digit. However some numbers still retain the 5-digit order. Hotels will send **faxes**: the Flower Hotel charges US$8 per page to the US, the Post Office demands an exorbitant US$25 per page. **E-mail** can be sent for US$2 from Business Centre at the Hotel Ulaanbaatar; they charge US$1.50 to receive a short message

Currency and banks

The togrogs (tugrik) is the Mongolian unit of currency; there are currently 600 togrogs to US$1. Many hotels and banks will change travellers' cheques, exchange hard currency for togrogs, and sell and buy togrogs. The best place to do this is at the new Trade and Development Bank, though the Chinggis Khaan Hotel and Flower Hotel also offer this service. The commission on exchanging travellers cheques into US$ cash is 2% and into togrogs 0%. While there is still a black market for hard currency, you would be foolish to risk your money as there is very little difference between the official and black market exchange rates.

You can get a **cash advance** on Visa and MasterCard in the State Bank of Mongolia, and at several of the biggest hotels for a 4% commission. American Express cash advances attract no commission.

❏ New street names

Finding your way around Ulan Bator is considerably complicated by the fact that not only are Russian names being changed for Mongolian ones but the script used is now Mongolian rather than Cyrillic. The way words are transliterated into English is also different; you're now likely to see Ulan Bator written as Ulaanbaatar. Below is a table of equivalent street names. In Mongolian a street is a *gudamj*, and an avenue is a *orgon choloo* (meaning 'wide space').

Russian	Mongolian	English
Prospekt Lenina	Chinggis Khaan Ave	Ghengis Khan Ave
Ikh Toirog	Ih Toiruu Rd	Big Ring Rd
Ulitsa Stalina	Natsagdori St	Stalin St
Prospekt Mira	Enkhtaivany Ave	Peace Ave
Ulitsa 40-letiya Oktyabrya	Zamchid St	40th Year October
Ulitsa Brezhneva	Khatanbaatar Magsa Iav St	Brezhnev St
Ulitsa Gagarina	Amarsanaa St	Gagarin St
Ulitsa Gorkovo	Ard-Ayush Ave	Gorky St
Ulitsa Konstitutsi	Zanabazar St	Constitution St
Ulitsa Khasbatora	Khuvsgal St	Khuvsgal St
Ulitsa Oktyabrskaya	Khudaldaany St	October St
Baga Toirou	Baga Toyruu Rd	Small Ring Rd
Ulitsa Obedinennykh Natsi	Negdsen Undestnii St	United Nations St
Ulitsa Universitetskaya	Ih Surguul St	University St
Sukhe Bator	Sühbaatar Sq	Sukhe Bator Sq
Prospekt Karla Marxa	Karl Marxyn Ave	Karl Marx Ave
Ulitsa Irkutskaya	Eldiv-Ochir St	Irkutsk St
Ulitsa Kolarova	Baga Toyruu Rd	Baga Toyruu Rd

Diplomatic representation

Embassies here include: **China** (☎ 320 940), Sambuu St, open 9:30-11:30 Monday, Wednesday and Friday; **Germany** (☎ 323 325), 7 Negdsen Undestnii St; **India** (☎ 358 772), 26 Enkhtaivany Ave; **Japan** (☎ 328 112, 328 019), 12 Zaluuchuudyn St; **Russia** (☎ 325 207), 6A Enkhtaivany Avenue; **South Korea** (☎ 321 548, 310 153), 10 Karl Marxyn St; **UK** (☎ 358 153, 327 506) Enkhtaivany Ave, open 9:00-13:00, 14:00-18:00 weekdays; **USA** (☎ 329 095, fax 320 776) Ih Toiruu Rd, open 9:00-13:00, 14:00-18:00 weekdays. The Polish embassy closed in October 1995.

Medical

The first non-government hospital in Ulan Bator, the Yonsei Friendship Hospital, opened in 1994. It is sponsored by the Yonsei University of Korea and various Christian missionary groups.

For those seeking a traditional cure, the Institute for Mongolian Traditional Medicine is at the Manba Datsan. To get to it take bus Nos 5, 9, 10, 20 or 21 or trolley 8.

WHERE TO STAY

Budget accommodation

Dormitory beds at the *Mongolian Technical University* (☎ 527 98) are good value. The rooms are on the fourth floor of the blue building in front of the Chinese shop in Sansar district. (Don't confuse it with the blue and white university building next door). The entrance is at the side through a wooden door with a sign in Mongolian above it. Rooms are US$6 and are clean. They are usually fully booked for July and August, but you might be lucky. No English is spoken at reception. If you get a room facing southwest, you'll be rewarded with a beautiful view of Manba Datsan and Ulan Bator behind it, as well as a spectacular sunset.

When you arrive at the railway station, you may be greeted by someone handing out flyers for *Gana's Guest Yurt* (☎ 367 343, Central PO Box 1017, Ulan Bator-13). For US$5 a night, you can stay in your own ger a stone's throw away from Gandan Monastery. The gers have a wood-burning stove, hot water delivered each morning, a message board for arranging countryside travel, and an external, foot-pumped hot water shower.

The centrally located *Mandukhai Hotel* (☎ 322 204), 19/2 Enkhtaivany Ave, charges US$10 for a double room with shared bathroom. For around the same price there's also the *Zaluuchuud Hotel* (☎ 324 594), 27 Baga Toyruu Rd, basic but quite pleasant but no English is spoken here; the *Ambarbayasgalant Hotel* (☎ 312 391), and the *Hanghay Hotel* (☎ 326 578), 12 Natsagdori St.

Much less pleasant, though better located and ridiculously cheap is the *Hotel of Labour Union* (Partizan St). There's no sign outside and no hot water inside. The *Negdelchin Hotel* (☎ 367209) is located at 25A/1 Enkhtaivany Ave and offers basic rooms for around US$6.

Mid-range and upmarket hotels

The city's most expensive accommodation is the newly completed *Chinggis Khaan Hotel*, (☎ 358 067, fax 313380), 8 Khukh Tengger Ave. A single room is US$120 and a double US$140 but it's not great value as there are insufficient staff to provide much service. Better is the Soviet-styled *Ulaanbaatar Hotel* (☎ 325368, fax 324 485) on Sühbaatar Square, where a single is US$60 and a double room US$140. Rates include breakfast and tax. This is the most popular haunt for foreigners.

Also good value is the recently refurbished, 418-bed *Bayangol Hotel* (☎ 3122 55, fax 326 880) 7 Chinggis Khaan Ave, at US$86 for a single and US$122 a double room with breakfast. The hotel also charges 10% sales tax but the total cost includes breakfast. There are nice rooms with TVs (including CNN), and there's even hot running water in the bathrooms. The hotel has a bureau de change, and accepts credit cards.

The *Tuvshin Hotel*, conveniently located just off Sühbaatar Square, should now be open and worth checking out. The *Geege Hotel* (☎ 51438), formerly the Zuul Hotel, used to be the best deal in town. Recently renovated, the prices of its rooms are expected to rise but it's also worth investigation. Its double rooms have an attached kitchen, bathroom and sitting room.

The *New Capital Hotel* at Enkhtaivany Ave charges US$66 for a double. It is situated between the Indian and British embassies.

The 336-bed *Flower Hotel* (☎ 501 10, fax 358 467), formerly the Altai, at 19/2 Khukh Tengger Ave, is further from the centre but good value at US$40 for a single room with common shower. It has a bank branch and an AT&T direct call telephone in the foyer.

WHERE TO EAT

The best hotel restaurants are in the *Ulaanbaatar*, *Mandukhai* and *Bayangol* hotels. All the hotels have two restaurants; one usually cheaper than the other.

There is a very good Japanese restaurant called *Hanamasa* across from the Geser Temple on Ih Toiruu Rd. There's a buffet: all you can eat for US$8. Similar in style is the *Seoul Korean Restaurant*, in Nairamdal Park. A meal costs about US$12 and if you are there by about 18:00 there's a performance by the Tumen Eh folklore ensemble.

Restaurant Eden serves Bulgarian food. It is located in a brick building behind the Moto Rock disco on Enhktaivany Ave. You get to it through a garden.

Right next door to the Zaluuchuud Hotel is the *Ider Restaurant*, a Russian place serving mutton stews, cold zakuski, potatoes and pasta.

Ulan Bator
Ulaanbaatar

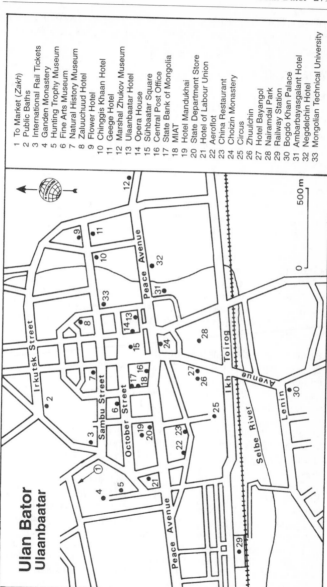

1 To Market (*Zakh*)
2 Public Baths
3 International Rail Tickets
4 Ganden Monastery
5 Hunting Trophy Museum
6 Fine Arts Museum
7 Natural History Museum
8 Zaluuchuud Hotel
9 Flower Hotel
10 Chinggis Khaan Hotel
11 Geege Hotel
12 Marshal Zhukov Museum
13 Ulaanbaatar Hotel
14 Opera House
15 Sühbaatar Square
16 Central Post Office
17 State Bank of Mongolia
18 MIAT
19 Hotel Mandukhai
20 State Department Store
21 Hotel of Labour Union
22 Aeroflot
23 China Restaurant
24 Choizin Monastery
25 Circus
26 Zhuulchin
27 Hotel Bayangol
28 Nairamdal Park
29 Railway Station
30 Bogdo Khan Palace
31 Ambarbayasgalant Hotel
32 Negdelchin Hotel
33 Mongolian Technical University

500 m

0

The food is reasonable and very good value. The *China Restaurant* is on the first floor of the building with the ornate Chinese doorway and serves authentic dishes.

WHAT TO SEE

Sühbaatar Square

A mounted statue of Sühbaatar in heroic pose stands in the centre of this large square, opposite his mausoleum (modelled on Lenin's Mausoleum in Red Square). His preserved body does not receive visitors but newly-weds queue up to have their photos taken at the foot of his statue. In 1990 the square was the scene of the pro-democracy demonstrations that led to the first free elections.

Gandan Monastery

Mongolia once had 700 monasteries but virtually all were destroyed in the communist crackdown at the end of the 1930s. More than 14,000 monks were killed and tens of thousands forced to give up their vows. Following the pro-democracy movement in 1990, restrictions have been eased allowing some monasteries to reopen and Gandan to operate less as a show-piece for tourists.

The first group of new buildings here was put up in 1938 and as well as the main temple there are stupas, a library and accommodation for the monks. Powdered juniper, thrown into the big burner outside the temple as an offering, is dispensed in a side building. It's best to go in the morning (10:00-12:00).

Bogd Khan Palace and Museum

This is a wonderful old place, full of ghosts and rather like Beijing's Forbidden City on a smaller scale. Exploring the palace one gets the impression that the owners walked out a few years ago, leaving it in the hands of rather relaxed caretakers who have forgotten to mow the lawn. Entered through a gateway guarded by four fierce-looking incarnations, the palace comprises two courtyards with small pavilions on each side. There are exhibits of *thangkas* (Buddhist paintings), musical instruments and Buddha figures, as well as the day-to-day furnishings of the buildings.

The museum is beside the palace complex and exhibits include Bogd Khan's throne, fur-lined robes and crown, and his luxurious ger (the exterior covered with the skins of 150 snow leopards and containing stove and portable altar). His collection of stuffed animals is also displayed somewhat haphazardly: a moth-eaten lion sharing the same quarters as a grubby polar bear. Outside is an interesting display of palanquins and carriages. Open Mon, Fri, Sat and Sun from 10:00-18:00; Tues, Wed from 10:00-16:00, closed Thurs and the last Wed of each month. Entry is

US$1. To get here take any bus heading south from the Bayangol Hotel and get off when you see the tank memorial (5 minutes).

Natural History Museum

Mongolia is well known for its dinosaur graveyards and some of the discoveries made in the country are on display here, including several fossilised nests of dinosaurs' eggs. These come in a fascinating range of shapes: cannon balls, ostrich-eggs, even Cornish pasties. Also worth seeing are the displays of stuffed animals arranged in quite imaginative panoramas of the Gobi and the mountains in the west. Here are many of the animals in the *Red Book* for endangered species including the snow leopard, wild Bactrian camel, Gobi bear, khulan (wild ass), red wolf, northern otter, snow griffon and Przewalski's horse. On the top floor are displays of national dress (smelling strongly of moth-balls).

A notice on the door warns: 'Closed last Monday of the month for cleaning'. Hardly surprising that the displays are rather dusty. Open Mon 10:00-16:00 (but not last Mon of the month); closed Tue; other days open 10:00-18:00. Entry is US$0.60 plus about US$10 for using cameras and US$20 for video cameras. Each section of the museum has different camera charges.

Choijin Lama Temple/ Religious Museum

Preserved for many years as a museum of religion, this temple complex has been handed back to the monks in the new spirit of religious freedom. It was the former home of Luvsan Haidav Choijin Lama, the brother of the 8th Bogdo Gegen (Bogd Khan). Both of them were born Tibetans. The temple is brightly decorated and houses a large collection of ornate masks for Buddhist mystery plays. Take a close look at the golden seated Buddha figure, not a statue but the mummified body of a lama, encased in gold. The northern pavilion houses a number of statues graphically depicting Tantric rituals (ie sexual union).

Open daily (except Tues) 10:00-17:00, entry is US$1. Immediately to the south of the museum is a statue of the Mongolian writer Natsagorj.

Fine Arts Museum

The museum includes a comprehensive display of thangkas, one more than 15m long. There are copies of prehistoric cave paintings, robes and masks from Buddhist Tsan dances and a gallery of modern paper-cutting art. Open 10:00-17:00. Entry is US$0.70.

Other museums and sights

Many of the city's smaller, less significant museums have been closed down recently, a fact which seems to have disappointed few visitors. However a few will reopen after renovation or their displays will be moved into other museums. It is no longer possible to visit the Museum in Sühbaatar's Bungalow or the Lenin Museum which has recently suffered the humiliation of being turned into a shopping centre. The former Revolutionary Museum is now the **Museum of Mongolian National History**, open 10:00-17:00, closed Wednesday. The **Marshal Zhukov Museum** is still open, although since it commemorates a Soviet military commander it's unlikely to be packing in the tourists for much longer. This small museum is filled with military and Soviet memorabilia and is easily recognised by the tank outside the front door.

The **Hunting Trophy Museum** near Gandan Monastery focuses on a highly controversial issue: the lucrative industry the Mongolians have set up selling hunting packages to foreign tourists. It's open 09:00-17:00 daily except Monday, but closes at 14:00 at weekends.

Nairamdal Park is where locals go to relax and it has a boating lake, ferris wheel, camel rides and model dinosaurs.

NIGHTLIFE

There has been a radical change to evening activities in Mongolia over the last few years and the city seems to be developing something of a taste for decadence. The Gengko Group operates two discos, Moto-Rock and Hollywood. **Moto-Rock Disco** is in the Saint Petersburg Club (formerly the Russian Club) and its cover charge is usually US$5. Another place to be seen is the **Matisse Art Café** near the the circus. At the Youth and Children's Theatre, it's open nightly 20:00 to 04:00.

More traditional activities include a visit to a ballet or opera in the **State Opera and Ballet Theatre** on Sühbaatar Square; inquire at reception in your hotel for tickets and times, or buy tickets from the box office on the night. The **Song and Dance Show** which is on several times a week at the Drama Theatre, is worth seeing for some excellent traditional dancing. There's also a circus, not usually open in the summer. The bar at the Ulaanbaatar Hotel is popular with foreigners and prostitutes.

PUBLIC BATHS

No hot water in your hotel? Can't face the prospect of another day without soap, shampoo and disinfectant? Then the public bath is the place for you. Entry is US$0.20 and for this you get the use of a sauna and a good hot shower. See map for location.

WHAT TO BUY

Things to buy include leather goods, cashmere shawls and sweaters, sheepskin, carpets, jewellery, dinosaur cards and models. The country is also noted for its wonderfully bizarre, oversize **postage stamps** with naive representations of cars and trains. So many are needed for air-mail postage that there is little room left on the postcard for a message. While the standard postage stamps can be bought from the Post Office for togrog, the oversize stamps can only be bought for hard currency as they are designed for the export market.

The city **market** (*zakh*) some 10km from the railway station is fascinating. You can buy anything from a cowbell to a camel and, of course, heaps of imported Russian and Chinese goods fresh off the train. You can benefit from tough economic times by picking up traditional coats, clothes, hats, silks, thangkas, statuettes, daggers and silver buttons. It's open Wednesday, Thursday, Saturday and Sunday. Watch out for bag-slitters and pickpockets. The market is two roundabouts west of Gandan Monastery on Peace Ave.

Less exciting but more convenient is the **State Department Store**. Here you can buy simple Mongolian toys and souvenirs or a even pair of black riding boots if you are lucky. As these boots are normally custom made, don't be surprised if they sell you a pair and tell you to come back in a few weeks to pick them up. The boots are worn by men as part of their *del*, the national costume. You will also find fur-lined winter and cotton summer Mongolian hats here. There's a bakery selling bread and cakes. A slow system of payment prevails: choose, then pay taking your receipt to exchange for the goods. There's a bookshop opposite the department store.

The 'duty-free' shops in hotels sell Western products and liquor. The best shop is at the back of Hotel Bayangol, a good place to stock up on food for the train journey.

MOVING ON

Rail tickets for travel within Mongolia may be booked at the station. International trains must be booked at the Railway Ticket Booking Office on Sambuu St. It's not easy to find and even harder to buy tickets as few of the staff can be bothered to help and even fewer speak English. The office is open 09:00-14:00 weekdays and until 13:00 on Saturday. Prices quoted from here for hard class coupé berths are: Moscow US$200 (soft: US$ 320) and Beijing US$150 (US$200). Zhuulchin can organise tickets for you but add a service charge of about 5%.

Aeroflot has a weekly Moscow-Ulan Bator **flight** arriving in Ulan Bator on Monday and departing on Tuesday. Air China has twice weekly Beijing-Ulan Bator services arriving and leaving Ulan Bator on Tuesday and Friday. Korean Airlines has a weekly Seoul-Ulan Bator flight on Tuesday. Mongolian Airlines MIAT has services to Seoul, Beijing, Almaty, Irkutsk, Osaka, Hohhot, Berlin and Moscow. MIAT is the most unreliable of the airlines. The best place to get plane tickets is Hotel Bayangol, where Air China and MIAT both have branch offices and

English-speaking staff. Prices are: Moscow (US$390), Beijing (US$200) and Irkutsk (US$99). Aeroflot prices are very similar. Ulan Bator's **Buyant Ukhaa International Airport** has been upgraded considerably in the last few years. Departure tax is about US$8. Passengers arriving in Ulan Bator by plane from Beijing routinely encounter prolonged delays in the delivery of their checked luggage because of the construction work. Take warm clothing and other essentials in carry-on baggage.

Excursions from Ulan Bator

ULAN BATOR AREA

If you really want to see Mongolia you must get out into the countryside. There's no better antidote to the polluted city than a night or two camping in a ger and a few days trekking or riding. For the practical details of exploring beyond Ulan Bator, get a copy of the 2nd edition (released May 1997) of Lonely Planet's *Mongolia – a travel survival kit*. Their excellent Mongolian Phrase Book is also a must for rural travellers.

Terelj
Most groups of travellers are shipped off to Terelj, some 85km from Ulan Bator, where they sleep out under the stars, drink mare's milk for breakfast and sit around campfires lulled by the sound of gently sizzling mutton kebabs. There are two types of accommodation here: gers and hotels. Zhuulchin and a number of other companies offer trips to Terelj. There's no public transport so you'll have to come with a tour group or by car.

Gorhit Mountains Ger Camp
About 65km from Ulan Bator is a small, 30 person ger camp which is considerably more appealing than Terelj. There are no car parks, no concrete buildings within sight, and no fences ringing the camp. As the camp is very popular, it is best to book in advance with Eco Tour Productions . You could also try your luck with Nomadic Journeys in Ulan Bator.

Stars Observatory
A few kilometres west of Ulan Bator is a delightful place called the Stars Observatory. It can be reached on a day trip or with an overnight stay. At the observatory there are two attractive old buildings, one a hotel and the other the observatory. The hotel is clean and charges about US$1 a night. The observatory is open weekdays and at night the staff will let you look through the telescope. The view of the city is also worth the trip.To get there, catch bus 14 going west from the central bus station. Ask to get off

at the first left turn on the main highway after the bus gets out of town. Cross the road and walk south-west toward the big railway bridge over the river. Continue south-west across the field for half an hour until you get to a dirt road which goes all the way to the observatory.

Bogd Uul Nature Reserve

This unique mountain region, directly south of Ulan Bator, was proclaimed a protected area in 1778 making it one of the world's oldest protected parks. Conservation of Bogd Uul, which means Holy Mountain, began well before that when in the twelfth century, Khan Turil declared the mountains sacred and prohibited logging and hunting on them. The mountains of Bogd Uul are the southernmost edge of the great Siberian taiga. Most of the trees are larch. Rolling, hilly, steppe grasslands stretch to the south. Clouds hang over the mountains in summer, and there are frequent thunderstorms. Snow is abundant in winter.

A total of 65,000 hectares of Bogd Uul is being declared a formal biosphere reserve. The area contains 116 species of birds, including 20 endangered bird species. Other species in the area include the musk-deer, ibex, roe-deer, hare and native sable.

The highest peak on Bogd Uul is Tsetsee Gun which is 2268 metres above sea level. It is possible to hike over the ridge to the ruins of the ancient **Manzshir Monastery** and the museum on the southern slope of Bogd Uul. Not far from the monastery is Undur Dov Resort, with about 40 gers.

FURTHER AFIELD

There are numerous places of enormous interest around Mongolia and the best known are the Hustain Nuuru Reserve, Harhorin (Kharakhorum) and the Gobi Desert.

Hustain Nuuru Reserve

About 110 km west of Ulan Bator is the Hustain Nuruu Reserve, dedicated to the reintroduction and preservation of the last truly wild horse, known in the West as Przewalski's horse, and in Mongolia as the *takhi*. Desertification, hunting, cross breeding and competition with domestic livestock resulted in the extinction in the wild in Przewalski's horse by 1969. At that time, the world population was down to 161 animals scattered throughout various zoos. An extensive and carefully monitored breeding programme involving as much genetic interchange as possible has resulted in the population increasing to several hundred. It is possible to organise a visit to the reserve but you will have to do it well in advance. Contact Jan Vegter, Project Manager, Foundation for the Preservation and Protection of the Przewalski's Horse, PO Box 1160, Central Post Office, Ulan Bator 11. Accommodation consists of just two basic guest gers.

Harhorin

This ruined city, formerly known as Kharakhorum, was the capital of the Mongolian Empire in the 13th century. Today, its centrepiece is the **Erdene Zuu Monastery** which was built in 1586 and was the first Buddhist centre in Mongolia. At its height, the monastery housed 1000 monks in 100 temples. During the Stalinist purges of the 1930s, the monastery was badly damaged but it is once again functioning and open to visitors. Entry to the monastery costs US$3.

About 125km away is the beautiful **Orhon Waterfall** which was formed by volcanic activity and earthquakes some 20-30,000 years ago.

Zhuulchin organises a four-day trip to the region by plane which includes visiting Orhon Waterfall, the ruins of the Uighur Kingdom's ancient capital of **Har Balgas**, and several other sites.

If you want to organise a trip yourself, you can hire a driver and the jeep for two or three days from US$80 a day depending on the number of travellers. Another way of getting there is to catch a bus from the long distance bus station. You will need to book the bus in advance and the ticket costs about US$5 one way. Buses leave for Harhorin on Tuesday, Thursday and Saturday and return on Monday, Wednesday and Friday. The trip takes nine hours and the half way stop is at the little village of Sansar. Remember to take your own food and water.

In Harhorin, you can stay in the Hangayin Hotel, next to the movie theatre. A room costs US$10 and the hotel has a restaurant. There are also four tourist ger camps in and around Harhorin.

The Gobi

The Gobi stretches for almost 4000km along the border of Mongolia and China. Only about three percent of the Gobi is true desert; it's said to contain some 33 different ecosystems as well as gazelles, the rare Argali sheep, Asiatic wild ass, wild Bactrian camel, snow leopard and ibex. The site of an ancient inland sea, the Gobi is also a treasure chest of fossilised dinosaur bones and eggs.

Nestled between the beautiful peaks of the Gurvansaikhan (Three Beauties) Mountains towering 3km above the surrounding steppe, is Yol Am Valley. The canyon shelters glaciers which remain frozen in its shadow even on the hottest summer days. Camping is not allowed in the **Gurvansaikhan National Park** but there are plenty of tourist ger camps nearby. National park entry fees are US$3 per day.

Most travel companies organise three-day flying trips to the Gobi from Ulan Bator.

Beijing

Both the Trans-Manchurian and Trans-Mongolian routes, by far the most popular with travellers crossing Siberia, start or finish in Beijing, so you'll probably be spending some time here. The city is well worth exploring, budget accommodation is very cheap and most travellers stay for at least three or four days. You'll find, however, that no matter how much time you allow yourself, you'll still leave having missed some of the sights.

HISTORY

Early history
Remains of China's oldest known inhabitant, Peking Man, were unearthed some 50km to the south of present-day Beijing in 1921, proving that life in this region dates back at least to 500,000 BC. Chinese records go back only as far as the Zhou dynasty (12th century BC to 771BC) but indicate that by this period this region was acknowledged as the country's capital.

The city and its environs were to remain at the heart of Chinese culture and politics, although the role of capital was often lost to other cities, including Xi'an (where the Terracotta Army now draws the tourists) and Luoyang. Beijing's strength, however, lay in its proximity to China's northern frontiers: by ruling from here emperors could keep a close eye on military developments to the north, where 'barbarians' were constantly threatening invasion.

Despite the construction of the Great Wall (a continuous process dating from the second century BC) Genghis Khan marched in in 1215, sacked the city and then proceeded to rebuild it as his capital; the Mongols called this Khanbalik (City of the Khan). It was at this stage that the first Westerners visited, including Marco Polo, who liked the place so much that he stayed for 17 years.

The Mongol collapse; further developments
The Mongol empire fell in 1368 and the Chinese shifted their capital to Nanjing. Following a coup led by the son of the first Ming emperor, the government was moved back here and the city renamed Beijing (Northern Capital).

The Manchurian invasion in 1644 established the final Chinese dynasty, the Qing, which was to rule from here until the abdication of Pu Yi, the 'Last Emperor', in 1912. Although the early years of Qing dynasty rule were successful, corruption, opium and foreign intervention soon undermined Chinese authority and there were major rebellions in the city in the late 19th century.

The Civil War and beyond
The Kuomintang, under Chiang Kai Shek, relocated China's capital to Nanjing in 1928, although following the Communist victory it was moved back here in 1949. In October of that year, Chairman Mao declared the foundation of the People's Republic of China in Beijing. The city has hardly been quiet in the meantime: every major movement in the country since then, notably the mass conventions of the Cultural Revolution and the Democracy rallies (culminating in the Tiananmen Square Incident of 1989, when over 2000 civilians were killed), has had its roots here.

LOCAL TRANSPORT

The metro system is good but stations are not always where you need them. Buses and trolley-buses are cheap but very crowded; watch out for bag-slitters and pick-pockets. Most travellers join the rest of the city's population on two wheels; there are many places to rent bikes from. Taxis are easiest to get outside hotels. They're metered and reasonable value when shared.

ORIENTATION AND SERVICES

Although Beijing is a large city, finding your way around is not too difficult owing to the fact that most streets head either north-south or east-west. The streets are, however, very crowded.

Diplomatic representation
See p38 for information on the Mongolian and Russian embassies in Beijing.

- Australia (☎ 6532 2331) 21 Dongzhimenwai Dajie, San Li Tun
- Canada (☎ 6532 3536) 19 Dongzhimenwai Dajie, San Li Tun
- Czech Republic (☎ 6532 1531) 2 Xiushui Beijie, Jianguomenwai
- Germany (☎ 6532 2161) 5 Dongzhimenwai Dajie
- Hungary (☎ 6532 1431) 10 Dongzhimenwai Dajie, Sanlitun
- Mongolia (☎ 6532 1203) 2 Xiushui Beijie Jianguomenwai
- Netherlands (☎ 6532 1131) 1-15-2, Ta Yuan Office Building
- New Zealand (☎ 6532 2732) 1 Dong Er Jie, Ritan Lu
- Poland (☎ 6532 1235) 1 Ritan Lu, Jianguomenwai
- Russian Federation (☎ 6532 2051) 4 Dongzhimen Beizhong Jie
- Slovakia (☎ 6532 1531) Ritan Lu, Jianguomenwai
- Sweden (☎ 6532 3331) 3 Dongzhimenwai Dajie

- Ukraine (☎ 6532 63 59) Chaoyang Apartment House (near the Great Wall Sheraton Hotel), flat 3, 2nd floor
- UK (☎ 6532 1961) 11 Guanghua Lu
- USA (☎ 6532 3831) 3 Xiushui Beijie, Jianguomenwai

Services

CITS, China International Travel Service, has representatives in many of the larger hotels in Beijing. CITS China head office (☎ 6601 1122) is at 103 Fuxingmennei Dajie; the **Beijing head office** is at 28 Jianguomen Wai, the other end of Chang'an Ave. The Beijing head office can book rail tickets. CAAC (☎ 6601 7755) is on the western side of Chang'an Ave at 15 Fuxingmen Dajie, and there's an efficient bus service to the airport from the stop just across the street.

The main **post office** is on Chaoyangmennan Dajie, the street that runs north off Jianguomen Dajie on the east side of the Beijing International Hotel. There's also a post office opposite the Beijing International Hotel.

Beijing Zhuulchin Office (☎ 6407 9911 ext 209, fax 6507 7397), represents Mongolia's Zhuulchin Foreign Tourism Corporation.

Banks and currency

The unit of currency is the yuan (Y) which is divided into 10 jiao or 100 fen. In May 1997 there were about Y8 to US$1, Y12.5 to £1. For many years there were two types of yuan circulating in China, Renminbi (RMB) used by the majority of the population, and Foreign Exchange Certificates (FEC) used by tourists, diplomats and the few Chinese who could get hold of them. FEC have been phased out and the humble RMB is legal tender everywhere.

If you need hard currency the CITIC Industrial Bank will change travellers' cheques into US$ and allow credit card withdrawals in US$. There's a branch next to the Friendship Store.

Tours

There are tours on offer from most of the larger hotels to all the major sights but you can easily visit the Forbidden City, the Temple of Heaven and Beijing's other tourist attractions independently. It is, however, probably worth taking a tour to see the Great Wall and the Ming Tombs (see below). **Monkey Business** (see p37) are worth contacting.

WHERE TO STAY

Budget accommodation

The standard travellers' haunt is the *Jing Hua Hotel* (☎ 6722 2211) on Nansanhuan Xi Lu (about 1.5 km southwest of the Jingtai Hotel). The dormitories are the best value: beds cost Y28 to Y35 in dorms with thirty, six or four beds. There are also doubles with attached bathroom from

Beijing

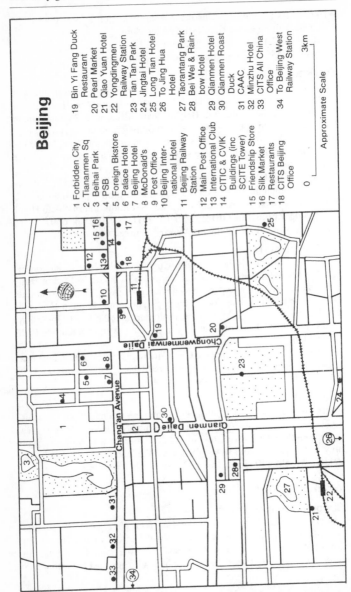

1 Forbidden City
2 Tiananmen Sq
3 Beihai Park
4 PSB
5 Foreign Bkstore
6 Palace Hotel
7 Beijing Hotel
8 McDonald's
9 Post Office
10 Beijing International Hotel
11 Beijing Railway Station
12 Main Post Office
13 International Club
14 CITIC & CVIK Buildings (inc SCITE Tower)
15 Friendship Store
16 Silk Market
17 Restaurants
18 CITS Beijing Office
19 Bin Yi Fang Duck Restaurant
20 Pearl Market
21 Qiao Yuan Hotel
22 Yongdingmen Railway Station
23 Tian Tan Park
24 Jingtai Hotel
25 Long Tian Hotel
26 To Jing Hua Hotel
27 Taorantang Park
28 Bei Wei & Rainbow Hotel
29 Qianmen Hotel
30 Qianmen Roast Duck
31 CAAC
32 Minzhu Hotel
33 CITS All China Office
34 To Beijing West Railway Station

0   3km
Approximate Scale

Y150. There's a travel agency on the second floor; and you can rent bikes from the restaurant next door.

The other budget option is the clean and friendly *Jingtai Hotel* (☎ 6722 4675), Anlelin Lu, south of Tian Tin Park. Doubles are Y90 (Y120 with bath attached). Bus No 40 will drop you off at the end of Anlelin Lu and it's only a five-minute walk from there.

Mid-range hotels

Well-located west of Tian Tan Park, the *Bei Wei Hotel* (☎ 6301 2266) at 13, Xinling Lu, has doubles for Y242. In the same area is *Qiamen Hotel* (☎ 6301 6688) on Hufang Lu, with singles/doubles for Y580/630.

There are two hotels which were once popular with budget travellers but they've now spruced themselves up and raised their prices. The *Long Tian Hotel* (☎ 6771 2244 ext 5888) on Panjiayuan Nan Li, charges Y298 for a standard room and Y370 for a superior room but is not very conveniently located. The *Qiao Yuan Hotel* (☎ 6303 8861), near Yongdingmen railway station, has doubles for Y290.

Upmarket hotels

If you want a really comfortable stay, try one of the following: The *Palace Hotel* (☎ 6512 8899), the *Great Wall Sheraton* (☎ 6500 5566), the *Taiwan Hotel* (☎ 6513 6688) or the famous *Beijing Hotel* (☎ 6513 7766) which is very well located close to Tiananmen Square. All are fairly central and offer first class accommodation. A double in a hotel of this standard will cost you at least US$100.

The *Minzhu Hotel* (☎ 6601 4466), on Fuxingmen Dajie charges US$85 for a single.

WHERE TO EAT

Peking Duck is, of course, the local speciality and there are numerous restaurants to try it at: good places include the *Bian Yi Fang Restaurant* on Chongwenmenwei Dajie near the railway station, and the *Qianmen Roast Duck Restaurant* at 32 Qianmen Dajie.

Cheap food is generally easy to find in Beijing: try any backstreet for noodles or dumplings. There's a cheap *night market* on Donghuamen Dajie, just to the east of the Forbidden City. Spicy-food fans usually head for the *Sichuan Restaurant* in Xirongxian Alley, just to the other side of the City. The *vegetarian restaurant* at 158 Qianmen Dajie has been recommended.

Finally, if you're homesick, visit *McDonald's* on Chang'an Ave and in more than ten other locations, *Kentucky Fried Chicken* on Tiananmen Square, or *Pizza Hut* (two branches, one on Dongzhimenwai, the other south of Tiananmen Square on Zhushikou). For cakes, pastries and croissant go to *Vie de France* (beside the Friendship Store).

WHAT TO SEE

Tiananmen Square and the Forbidden City

Just as Red Square is the best place to start a tour of Moscow, so is Tiananmen Square for a trip around Beijing. In the centre is **Chairman Mao's Mausoleum** (open 08.30-11.30 daily) in which, after joining a long queue which moves surprisingly fast, you can see the great man himself. To the east is the **National Museum of Chinese History**, which also houses the **Museum of the Chinese Revolution**. Both are well worth a morning exploring if you have the time, and are open 08.30-15.30, closed Mon. Opposite the museums on the other side of the square is the Great Hall of the People, used for meetings of the National People's Congress and containing an impressive 10,000 seat auditorium.

To the north of the square is the **Imperial Palace** , better known as the Forbidden City, entered through **Tiananmen Gate**. This enclosure comprising over 178 acres and 1000 buildings takes at least a day to explore to get even a bare impression; there's so much to see here that really you need much longer.

The palace was erected by the Ming emperor Yong Le in the early 15th century and since then has been the home of the last 24 emperors, up until the abdication of Pu Yi in 1911. The best way to get around is to hire a cassette tour at the main gate and have everything explained to you by Roger Moore. It's a good idea to wander round again afterwards, soaking up the atmosphere. The palace is open 08.30-16.30 daily but ticket offices close at 15.30. Entrance is Y55 and the cassette tour costs Y30.

The Great Wall

China's most famous attraction makes an ideal day trip from Beijing. Most tourists visit the Wall at Badaling but it's less crowded at Mutianyu.

The Wall itself was not built in one massive construction project as many believe; in fact the original scheme under Emperor Shih Huang (first century BC) was simply to join extant stretches of individual defensive walls together. It was hoped that the resulting fortification would protect China from marauding foreigners but this was not the case. It's currently responsible for drawing more foreigners to China than ever, as those who visit at **Badaling** or **Mutianyu** will see. It's possible to get to Badaling independently by train (the Trans-Siberian route passes by – see p367) from Xizhimen station but otherwise you'll have to go with a tour group. The travel agency at the Jing Hua Hotel runs popular trips to another section of the Wall: **Simatai**. To get to the least touristy section, Jinshanling, you'll need to hire a minivan.

Tian Tan – the Temple of Heaven

This is the site from which China's emperors conducted the country's most important religious rituals, upon which depended the well-being of

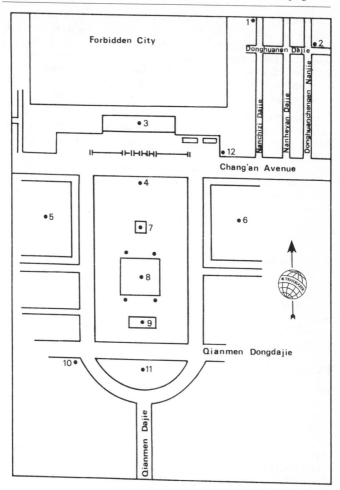

TIANANMEN SQUARE

1 PSB
2 Bank of China
3 Tianan Gate
4 Flagstaff
5 Great Hall of the People

6 Museums of Chinese History and the Revolution
7 Monument to the People's Heroes
8 Mao's Mausoleum

9 Qianmen Gate
10 Kentucky Fried Chicken
11 Arrow Castle
12 Bicycle Park and lavatories

the population. The temple in Tian Tan Park is open from 08.00-17.00 and entry to the park is Y1.50, Y30 for a tourist ticket . Sights worth noting here include the Hall of Abstinence, the marble circular altar, the Imperial Vault of Heaven (where a whisper towards the surface on one side is perfectly audible around the opposite side). The most famous building of the complex is the Hall of Prayer for Good Harvests, to the north, built entirely without the use of glue or nails.

The Summer Palace
The palace (summer retreat of the Imperial family since 1750) covers an area about four times the size of the Forbidden City. Virtually everything in the grounds apart from the lake dates back only to the start of this century, as there has been repeated destruction by foreigners: the entire area was razed in 1860 as retribution for the Opium Wars and then again in 1900 after the Boxer Rebellion. It's a great place to explore slowly and if the weather is good it's well worth spending a whole day here wandering around the Royal Residence, the Dragon King Temple, the Long Corridor, the Tower of Buddhist Virtue and the lake.

WHAT TO BUY

Most people tend to buy souvenirs in the large Friendship Store on Jianguomen Dajie (Chang'an Ave), which has an enormous range. For a more challenging time, visit the shops in the Wangfujing district directly east of the Forbidden City. Another good place is the Qianmen district, where you're likely to have to fight your way through the crowds; bartering is in order here.

MOVING ON

By air Many major airlines maintain offices in Beijing, so it's usually not difficult finding a seat; the problem is that it can be expensive. Most airline offices are in the SCITE Tower opposite the Friendship Store. Sample prices include London (Y5500), Singapore (Y3780), Tokyo (Y4390), and Hong Kong (Y2310). If you want to fly the first leg of your Trans-Siberian journey, MIAT (☎ 6501 8888, ext 807; Room 807, Jing Guang World Hotel, Hujialou, Chaoyanou) charges US$150 for Beijing-Ulan Bator and US$99 for Ulan Bator to Irkutsk.

By rail **Domestic tickets** can be bought from the station at the foreigners' ticket office on the ground floor. Alternatively CITS will book for you for a small fee, saving you the queuing. **International tickets** must be booked either at CITS, or from a registered ticket agency (see p37). If you've just arrived on the Trans-Siberian and feel like clocking up a few more km by rail follow the Silk Route back to Europe (see p124).

PART 5: ROUTE GUIDE AND MAPS

Using this guide

This route guide has been set out to draw your attention to points of interest and to enable you to locate your position along the Trans-Siberian line. On the maps, stations are indicated in Russian and English and their distance from Moscow is given in the text. Note that on the maps there is an orientation symbol (**M**), indicating the direction towards Moscow.

Stations and points of interest are identified in the text by a kilometre number. Note that in some cases these are approximate so start looking out for the point of interest a few kilometres before its stated position. Where something of interest is on only one side of the track, it is identified by the letters **N** (north or left-hand side of the train, going from Moscow east) or **S** (south or right-hand side) after the kilometre number. The altitude of major towns and cities is given in metres and feet beside the station name. Time zones are indicated through the text (MT = Moscow Time). See inside back cover for **key map**.

Kilometre posts
These are located on the southern side of the track. They are sometimes placed so close to the train that they're difficult to see. The technique is either to hang out of the window (dangerous) or press your face close to the glass and look along the train until a kilometre post flashes by. The distance to Moscow is on the west side of the post and the distance to Vladivostok on the other. Note that the distances sometimes given on train timetables are not always accurate and may be out by up to 10km. If you notice any inaccuracies in the distances as shown in this book please write to the author – address on p2.

Station name boards
These are almost as difficult to catch sight of as the kilometre posts since they are usually placed only on the station building and not along the platforms as in most other countries. Rail traffic on the line is heavy and even if your carriage does pull up opposite the station building you may have your view of it obscured by another train.

Stops
Where the train stops at a station the length of the stop is indicated by:
● (1-5 mins), ●● (6-10 mins) or ●●● (11-15 mins). Carriage attendants

will tell you the precise amount of time as this may be reduced if the train is running late. Don't stray too far from the train, as it moves off without a signal or whistle (except in China) and passengers are occasionally left behind. Three of us, our carriage attendant included, were once almost left in sub-zero temperatures on the platform of some tiny Siberian station, when the train left five minutes ahead of schedule.

❏ **Speed calculations**
Using the kilometre posts and a watch, it's possible to calculate how quickly, or more usually how slowly, the train is going. Note the time that elapses between one post and the next and consult the table below. Since the average speed of the train over the seven-day journey between Moscow and Vladivostok is only 69 kph (43 mph), you are unlikely to use the higher speed figures on this table.

Seconds	kph	mph	Seconds	kph	mph
24	150	93	52	69	43
26	138	86	54	66	41
28	129	80	56	64	40
30	120	75	60	60	37
32	113	70	64	56	35
34	106	66	68	53	33
36	100	62	72	50	31
38	95	59	78	46	28
40	90	56	84	43	27
42	86	53	92	39	24
44	82	51	100	36	22
46	78	49	120	30	18
48	75	47	150	24	15
50	72	45	180	20	12

TRANS-SIBERIAN ROUTE

Km0: Moscow Москва
Yaroslavski Station Ярославский вокзал Most Trans-Siberian trains departs from Moscow's Yaroslavski station, pl Komsomolskaya 5. However there are a few trains that go part of the way along the Trans-Siberian and terminate in Central Siberian cities, such as Krasnoyarsk (train Nos 56 & 90), Omsk (No 48), Tomsk (No 38 & 118) and Tyumen (No 60), and **these depart from Kazanski Station nearby**.

If you're arriving from Siberia and leaving Moscow by train the same day, you may need to take the metro or a taxi to one of Moscow's nine other stations. If your journey starts from Moscow, make sure you get to the station early as trains invariably leave on time. If you want to use the station's large waiting halls you have to pay US$0.50. Yaro-slavski station and Kazanski station are on Komsomol Square (metro:

Komsomolskaya Ploshchad). Yaroslavski station is very distinctive; it was built in 1902 as a stylised reproduction of an old Russian *terem* (fort), its walls decorated with coloured tiles. Trains have destination plates fixed to their sides but any railway official will point you in the right direction if you show them your ticket.

Km13: Los Лось Just after this station, the train crosses over the Moscow Ring Road. This road marks the city's metropolitan border and in order to stop the lavatories being used in urban areas loo doors remain bolted until this point.

Km15: Taininskaya Таининская A monument to Russia's last tsar, Nicholas II, was recently unveiled here, bearing the plaque, 'To Tsar Nikolai II from the Russian People with repentance'.

Km18: Mytishchi Мытищи (pop: 154,000) is famous for three factories. The railway carriage factory, **Metrovagonmash**, has manufactured all the Soviet Union's metro cars and is building the new N5 metro carriages that can be seen currently in Moscow's metro. While there is a museum at the factory, the best metro museum is in Moscow (see p148).

The **Mytishchinsky Monument Factory**, the source of many of those ponderous Lenin statues that still litter parts of the country, has at last been forced to develop a new line. It now churns out the kind of 'art' banned in the Soviet era: religious statues, memorials to Stalin's purges and busts of mafia heads. Some of its former achievements which can still be seen in Moscow include the giant Lenin in front of Oktyabrskaya metro station, Moscow's founder Yuri Dolgoruky on horseback on pl Tverskaya and the Karl Marx across from the Bolshoi Theatre.

Production has also slowed at the **armoured vehicle factory**, one of Russia's three major tank factories, with the other two being in the Siberian cities of Kurgan and Omsk.

MAP 1

❑ **Star City**
Just east of Mytishchi a branch line to the right runs 5km to Zvezdny Gorodok (Star City). This city of about 20,000 people is a smaller version of the US Johnson Space Center in Houston and is responsible for controlling all manned spacecraft and space station activities. It is also the main training ground for cosmonauts and contains Soyuz, Prognoz, and Salyut rocket simulators. Other interesting places to visit include the Star City Museum, the Space Station Simulators Hall where mock-ups of all MIR space station modules are kept, the Neutral Buoyancy Simulator, and the main centrifuge with 18 metre arm to imitate g-forces during take off. The area is also home to several military space research institutes so be discreet when taking photos. The town around Zvezdny Gorodok is called Kaliningrad (Калининград). The stations that service Kaliningrad are Podlipki (Подлипки) and Bolshevo (Болшево). Zvezdny Gorodok has a sister city relationship with Nassau Bay, Texas. To organise a visit to the Gagarin Training Center, contact Anton Nemchimov at the Youth Space Academy at Baumann Technical Institute in Moscow (tel (095) 263 6994, fax (095) 262 6511) and mark it Box 4462 for Youth Space Center, email: ipjakk@redline.ru, www http://www.seds.org/ysc/).

The smoking factories and suburban blocks of flats are now left behind and you'll be rolling through forests of pine, birch and oak. Amongst the trees there are picturesque wooden *dacha* (holiday homes where many of Moscow's residents spend their weekends). You pass through little stations with long, white-washed picket fences.

Km30: Pushkino Пушкино This town (pop: 75,600) was founded in 1499 as a resting place for clergy on the road between Moscow and the monastery town of Sergiev-Posad. With the arrival of the railway in 1862, the place became a popular summer holiday destination for Moscow's élite. From 1890 to 1910, Pushkino became known as Russia's summer arts capital with a renowned theatre. While the theatre has gone, the five-cupola St Nicholas Church built in the 1690s remains.

Km36: Pravda Правда To the left of Pravda station, which translates as *truth*, is the village of Zavety Ilicha (Заветы Ильича). This name, which figuratively means the Commandments of Ilich Vladimir Lenin, was a popular name for not only dozens of Soviet towns, but also for collective farms, metro stations and ships.

Km57: Abramtsevo Абрамцево About 3km from the station is the Abramtsevo Estate, one of the most important centres of Russian culture in the second half of the 19th century. Today, the Abramtsevo estate is a museum and well worth a day trip from Moscow (see p168).

Km59: Khotkovo Хотьково This town (pop: 23,400) has a well preserved, historic section on the high bank of the Pazha River

❏ **The Golden Ring**
You are now passing through Russia's most famous historical region; it was from this area that the mighty Russian state was born. The major Golden Ring cities along the Trans-Siberian are Sergiev Posad, Rostov-Yaroslavski and Yaroslavl.

Following the collapse of Kievan Rus, which was the first feudal state in Eastern Europe, its capital was shifted from Kiev to the Golden Ring town of Vladimir in 1169. At that time, Vladimir and the other Golden Ring towns were little more than villages but over the next 200 years they all rapidly grew into political, religious and commercial centres.

The typical Golden Ring town of the 11th to 18th century consisted of a *kremlin*, a *posad* and a *sloboda*. The kremlin, meaning fortress, usually occupied an elevated position and was originally ringed by earth embankments topped with wooden walls. Watch towers were positioned strategically along the walls. Over time, the earth and wooden walls were replaced by stone and brick. Inside the kremlin were the prince's residence, religious buildings and administrative complexes. Outside the kremlin was the undefended posad which was the merchants' and artisans' quarters. Often next to the posad was a sloboda ,a tax-exempt settlement. Sloboda were often established to attract a new workforce.

After the decimation of Russia following the Tatar-Mongol invasion in 1236, Moscow's power had grown even faster since it was the Tatar-Mongols' centre for tax collectors and in 1318, its prince was granted the title of Grand Prince by the invaders. This symbolised the transfer of regional power from Vladimir to Moscow. Gradually Moscow annexed the Golden Ring principalities and used their economic and military power to expand its domination. By the end of the 1500s, Moscow had become a large powerful principality and was fighting to become the capital of Russia. While several of the Golden Ring cities continued to have commercial importance due to their locations on major trading routes, the golden era of these cities was over.

which flows through the centre of the town. The most impressive building here is the large **Intercession of Khotkovo Monastery** which was founded in 1308. Most of the original buildings in the monastery were replaced during the 18th century. The classical **Intercession Cathedral**, built from 1811-1816, is decorated with four Corinthian columns and crowned with a massive round rotunda and four cupolas.

The train crosses over the Pazha River just before it reaches Khotkovo station and you can see these buildings on the left.

Km73 (N): Sergiev Posad Сергиев Посад [See p172]
Have your cameras ready for the stunning sight of the blue and gold domes of the cathedrals of Sergiev Posad (pop: 110,000), known as **Zagorsk** between 1930 and 1993. Look north back to the city just after you leave the station. For many years this was the seat of the Russian Orthodox Church (until it was moved back to Moscow in 1988) and one of the most important seminaries in the country is here. The beautiful buildings of the seminary are much visited by tourists.

Km112: Aleksandrov (●) Александров This little-known town was, for nearly two decades in the 14th century, the real capital of Russia. From 1564 to 1581, Ivan the Terrible lived here and directly ruled the half of the country which he called *Oprichnina* while abandoning the other half to the authority of *boyars* (nobles) and monasteries. The oprichnina was policed by *oprichniki*, mostly low class thugs, mercenaries and foreign adventurers who murdered, pillaged and destroyed at their pleasure.

Ivan ruled from Aleksandrov's **Trinity Fortress Monastery** which was a complex of dungeons, churches, barracks and warehouses. Ivan the Terrible certainly deserved his soubriquet. In his dungeons here he devised and supervised some of the cruellest tortures imaginable. There were racks which broke bones, iron cages for burning victims, pits for burying people alive and frames for whipping prisoners with a *knout* (leather truncheon) which could kill in three strokes. Ivan was a vicious practical joker and would even release his ravenous bears on his own unsuspecting courtiers.

The city's most notable building is the monumental brick **Trinity Cathedral**, built in 1513 in the style of early Moscow architecture. It has two brass doors pillaged from two other churches by Ivan the Terrible during his sacking of Novgorod and Tver.

Despite its vibrant history, Aleksandrov is most famous today for the Rekord brand of TV produced here in enormous numbers. Rekord and Gorizont are Russia's two biggest TV manufacturers.

In the yard just east of the station (N) are six old **steam locomotives**.

The train now enters **Yaroslavskaya Oblast** (administrative district), an area of 36,000 square kilometres in the upper Volga basin, famous for its cheeses and dairy farming. Oats, flax and vegetables are also grown in this region.

Km145: Berendeevo Берендеево There is a 21km branch line to the west from here to the Golden Ring town of Pereslavl-Zalesski.

Km200: Petrovsk Петровск About 15km east of Petrovsk, you will see **Lake Nero** on the right. Rostov-Yaroslavski sits on the western shore.

Km224: Rostov-Yaroslavski Ростов-Ярославский   [See p177]
(pop: 37,000) This is one of the most pleasant Golden Ring cities to visit. It's an interesting place, relatively compact and attractively located beside Lake Nero. About five minutes west of the station you cross over the Ishna River. Five hundred metres downstream (S), where the river flows into Lake Nero, is the St **Jacob Monastery** which guarded the city's southern approach centuries ago. The northern approach was protected by the **St Avraamy Monastery** which you can see about three minutes after leaving the station, on the right by the shores of Lake Nero.

Km240 (N): Amidst the fields and quite close to the track is a sadly neglected but **picturesque church** with five dilapidated domes and a tower.

Km284: Yaroslavl Ярославль (●) [See p181]

(pop: 637,000) Yaroslavl was founded in 1010 by the Christian King Yaroslavl the Wise. It grew quickly into an important trading centre on the Volga shipping route. Many of the ancient cathedrals still stand in spite of the heavy fighting that went on here during the Civil War.

About five minutes after entering Yaroslavl's outskirts, you pass the suburban station of **Kotorosl (Которосль)** and on the left you can see the **Church of St Peter and St Paul** with a 58m bell-tower beside it. The church was built in 1736 by a wealthy textile factory owner, in honour of Peter the Great who was a valuable customer. The church is constructed in the popular St Petersburg Baroque style and in a final sycophantic gesture, it was designed to look like the Cathedral of St Peter and St Paul in St Petersburg. During the communist era it was used as a club.

A minute or so later you cross over the Kotorosl River giving you a good view of several landmarks. On the right of the train, on the southern river bank just before the road bridge is the 15 domed **Church of St John the Baptist**. On the left of the train also on the southern bank is the **Church of St Nicholas** by the Water Mills.

From the square in front of the station, you can see the **Church of the Vladimir Mother of God** built in 1678.

Km289: Volga River

About five minutes after leaving the station, the train changes direction from the north to the east and crosses over the mighty Volga River. The river is about 1km wide at this point. In times gone by Russians regarded this river with such high respect that they would stand and take off their hats to Mother Volga, as the train rattled onto the first spans of the long bridge. Rising in the Valdai hills, **Europe's longest river** meanders 3,700km down to the Caspian Sea. It is to Russia what the Nile is to Egypt: a source of life and a thoroughfare. On the right side of the river you will see the main road bridge across the river and quays on both side of the river. You get a good view of the city of Yaroslavl and its cathedrals looking back south as you go over the bridge

Km357: Danilov Данилов (●●●)

(pop: 19,000) This town is at a railway junction with trains going north to Arkhangelsk and to the east along the Trans-Siberian line. In the town is the Kazan Mother of God Cathedral which was consecrated by the Patriarch Tikhon in 1918. In the early years of the communist state, Lenin was forced for expediency to tolerate such practices but once power was consolidated, churches were rapidly closed.

Km370-378: Some quite good views on both sides of the train in the breaks between the trees. The train soon enters Kostromskaya Oblast, a 60,000 sq km plain in the middle Volga basin. Most of the northern part of the oblast is covered with taiga (swampy forest). There is some cultivation (flax and oats) in the south. Main industries are linen-making and timber-processing.

Km394: Lyubim Любим   Since 1979, Lyubim's population has decreased by 6% to 6900. This makes the town typical of the Russia-wide migration trend from rural villages to large cities. The main reasons for this are the lack of jobs and limited education choices in the country. Following the easing of movement restrictions, many families moved away from country farms.

─────────────── **Km 420-1266 TIME ZONE MT + 1** ───────────────

Km450: Bui Буй (●) (pop: 32,800) There is nothing of interest in this industrial town, specialising in cheese, flax and mineral fertilisers. The two-minute stop here will give you more than enough time to view the silver-painted statue of Lenin on the platform, although by the time you read this he may well have been removed.

Leaving the town, the train follows the southern banks of the Veksi and Holya rivers connected to the Galich Sea which you will see as you approach the town of Galich. The very beautiful lake is ringed with resorts for Moscow's rich and famous. Rotting silt (sapropel) is extracted from the lake and dried to be used as fuel or made into fertiliser.

Local time is now Moscow time + 1 hour.

Km501: Galich Галич If you drive a Lada and need a new door handle, get off the train here. Because of the centralised planning of the communist system, products were often made in huge numbers in only a few locations. Galich's speciality was car door handles.

The town is very ancient and was populated by the Merya tribe of Finno-Ugric peoples before the ethnic Russians arrived. The first mention of the town was in 1238 when the **Galich fortress** was destroyed by the Tatar-Mongol leader, Khan Baty. The fortress was rebuilt and in 1427 amazingly withstood a four-week siege by the Tatar-Mongols. The walls of the fortress can still be seen ringing the central part of the town. The town's centre is a 15-minute walk north from the station. After departing from the station, on the right (S) you pass **Paisiev Monastery**.

Km653: Manturovo Мантурово (pop: 22,400)   After leaving this industrial and forestry town, the train crosses the Unzha River where you may notice the remains of large pits on the banks. These are from the shale oil and phosphate mining operations of a few decades ago.

Km700: Sharya Шарья (●●) (pop: 26,900)
There is usually an 8-10 minute stop at this station where some steam locos are stored (L and Er classes). This town is the biggest timber centre in the region. It has a few interesting old buildings and a Museum of Local Studies.

Km818: Svetcha Светча Roughly mid-way between Sharya and Svetcha, you enter Kirovskaya Oblast. Most of the 120,000 square kilometres of this region are within the basin of the Vyatka River. Since the greater part of the oblast is made up of taiga, the main industry here is logging.

Km870: Kotelnich Котельнич (pop: 38,000)
This station sits at the junction of the Trans-Siberian and the Kirov-Nizhni Novgorod-Moscow lines. If you are changing from one line to the other, don't get off here. Instead go 87km to the east to the major city of Kirov where tickets are much easier to get.

Kotelnich is an ancient trading city on the right bank of the Vyatka River, a major trading route between Arkhangelsk and the Volga region.

Finding your way around the town is not easy as it lies in three ravines with only the town centre being laid out in an orderly fashion. Here the major thoroughfare is ul Moskovskaya and along part of it are a number of buildings built in Vyatka Provincial Style from 1850 to 1880. Sights include the John the Baptist (Predtichi) Monastery and the Presentation of the Virgin (Vvedenski) Nunnery. The town has a museum.

After leaving the station, the train crosses over the Vyatka River which is the 10th longest river in European Russia. It meanders for 1367km and the Trans-Siberian crosses over it several times. When the train first reaches the Vyatka River Basin a few kilometres to the west of Kotelnich, there is a noticeable change in the landscape as the forests give way to fields and more villages.

MAP 2

Монаково MONAKOVO
Антролово ANTROLOVO
Николо-Угол NIKOLO-UGOL
Николо-Полома NIKOLO-POLOMA
Номжа NOMZHA
Еленский YELENSKIY
Нея NEYA
Нельша NELSHA
Брантовка BRANTOVKA
Петрушино PETRUSHINO
Костриха KOSTRIHA
Мантурово MANTUROVO
Вочерово VOCHEROVO
Шекшема SHEKSHEMA
Варакинский VARAKINSKIY
Шарья Vetluga R. SHARYA
Зебляки ZEBLYAKI
Якшанга YAKSHANGA
Бурундучиха BURUNDUCHIKHA
Супротивный SUPROTIVNIY
Метил METIL
Гостовская GOSTOVSKAYA
Шабалино SHABALINO
Свеча SVECHA
Юма YUMA
Капиданцы KAPIDANTSI
Ацвеж ATSVEZH
Даровица DAROVITSA
Котельнич KOTELNICH
Быстряги BISTRYAGI
Оричи ORICHI
Стрижи STRIZHI
Лянгасово LYANGASOVO
Чухломинский CHUKHLOMINSKIY
КИРОВ (kirov)
Поздино POZDINO
Полой POLOY
Бумкомбинат BUMKOMBINAT
Просница PROSNITSA

Km890: Maradykovski Марадыковский Probably sensible not to break your journey here. At the nearby airforce base are stored 7000 out of Russia's 40,000 tons of chemical weapons agents (mustard gas, lewisite, hydrocyanic acid and phosgene). The government has approved a plan for destroying its stocks of chemical weapons but this won't be completed until 2005. It's ironic that the name of the settlement around the station is Mirny (Мирный) which means peaceful.

Km957: Kirov/Vyatka Киров/Вятка (●●●) [See p187]
(Pop: 492,000) Kirov was founded in 1181 on the banks of the Vyatka River, and was originally named Klynov. It's name is now being changed to Vyatka.

Km970: Pozdino Поздино The town around the station is called Novovyatsk (Нововятск) and boasts one of Russia's largest ski factories. During Soviet times, the factory produced 20% of the nation's skis.

Km995: Bum-Kombinat Бум-комбинат This unfortunately-named town gets its name from its principal employer, the paper complex.

Km1062: Zuevka Зуевка (pop: 15,700) Founded in 1895 with the construction of the railway; during WWII hundreds of Leningraders settled here. Their descendants manufacture swings and see-saws.

Km1127: Yar Яр About 20km before this station, you leave Kirovskaya Oblast and cross the administrative frontier into the heavily industrialised Udmurtia Republic. Yar is the first town here and has a number of Udmurt speakers. It sits on a steep river bank (*yar*). There has been a small metallurgical plant here for over 230 years but nothing else of note.

Km1136: Balyshur Балышур Just before arriving at the station, you pass a steam train storage depot.

Km1162: Glazov Глазов (●) (pop: 110,000) Originally an Udmurt indigenous village, Glazov soon became infamous as a desolate and

---

❏ **The Udmurt Homeland**
The Udmurtia Republic is one of 16 republics of indigenous peoples within the Russian Federation. The population of Udmurtia is about 1.6 million, only one third of these being Udmurts. They are descendants of the Finno-Ugric peoples who in turn were descended from the people living in the area in the Neolithic and Bronze Age. The Udmurts started cultivation and stock raising in the 9th century AD, and from 1236 to 1552 were dominated by the Golden Hordes and the Kazan khans. In 1558, Russia incorporated the entire Udmurt area and it was only in 1932 that the indigenous inhabitants were acknowledged when the Udmurt Autonomous Oblast was declared. Today the Udmurt people are the largest Finno-Ugric language group in Russia.

impoverished place of exile. All this was to change with the arrival of the railway and by 1900, there were 102 enterprises and within a few more years the town grew into the region's largest flax, oats and oakum trading centre. Oakum is a fibre used for caulking the seams of ships.

There are still a few wooden Udmurt log huts remaining. Known as *korkas*, they are positioned along an open paved courtyard. The courtyard had a massive gate, which, like the hut, was often decorated with carved geometrical and plant designs. Glazov has a history museum.

Km1190: Balyezino Балезино (●●) Between Yar and Balyezino there are many market-gardens set in this rolling, open countryside. You pass vast fields of grey-green cabbages, and long rows of greenhouses covered in plastic sheeting line the track in some places. There are tiny villages of log cabins with brightly painted front doors.

Km1216: Cheptsa Чепца A few kilometres west of this station, the line crosses the Cheptsa River which the route has been following for the last 250kms. The train begins to wind its way up towards the Urals.

Between Cheptsa and the next station of Vereshchagino is the frontier between the Udmurt Republic and Permskaya Oblast. Permskaya's 160,000 sq km are, like those of Kirovskaya Oblast, lost to the swampy forests of the taiga. However, Permskaya has greater prizes than its millions of pine and birch trees, for the region includes the mineral-rich Ural Mountains. Main industries include mining, logging and paper-making. Agriculture is confined to market-gardening.

──────────── Km 1266-2510 TIME ZONE MT + 2 ────────────

Km1315 (S): Vereshchagino Верещагино (pop: 24,900) Vereshchagino was founded at end of 19th century as a railway depot and today its main industry is still railways. There is a preserved FD21 steam locomotive on a plinth about 1km to the west (Moscow side) of the station near the main rail depot. The town is named after Russia's greatest battlefield painter, VV Vereshchagin, who stopped here on his way to the Russo-Japanese war front in 1905. It was his final and fatal commission.

There are some quite good views south, a few kilometres after Vereshagino.

Km1344: Mendeleevo Менделеево The town is named after the chemist, Dmitri Mendeleev (1834-1907) who developed the periodic table. He often visited this town during his inspections of the region's metallurgical plants. There is a Mendeleev museum in nearby Tobolsk.

Km1309: Chaikovskaya Чайковская
This station is named after the composer Peter Tchaikovsky (1840-1893) who was born about 180km southeast of here at a factory settlement around the Kamsko-Votkinsk industrial plant. Until recently it was

MAP 3

believed that Tchaikovsky died of cholera but researchers have revealed that he was blackmailed into taking poison to prevent his liaison with the nephew of a St Petersburg noble being made public.

The nearby town (a construction settlement for the hydro-electric dam) is called Maiski.

From here to Perm, there are excellent opportunities to get photos along the train as it snakes along the winding railway.

Km1413: Overyata Оверята An 11km branch line leads to the dirty industrial town of Krasnokamsk (Краснокамск) to the south. It was founded in the 1930s and has a large cellulose mill and Russia's only wire netting factory. Surprisingly near the town is the popular Ust-Kachka health resort with medicinal mud baths.

Km1429: Perm freight yard Пермь-Сортировочная This is one of Russia's largest, handling up to 135 trains simultaneously.

Km1431: Kama River Речка Кама Just before the train reaches Perm, you cross over the Kama River. From the bridge, which was built in 1899, you can see Perm stretching into the distance on the left. The mighty Kama River flows over 2000kms from the Urals into the Volga and is one of the great waterways of the CIS. Near the bridge, the river banks are lined with cranes and warehouses. A short distance west of Perm station (to the north of the line) there's a turntable and beside it an ancient green **'O' Class locomotive** (OB 14). Engines of this type were hauling the Trans-Siberian at the turn of the century.

Km1433: Perm 2 Пермь 2 (●●●) [see p189] This city of more than one million inhabitants was founded in 1723 when the copper smelting works were established here. Because of its important position on the Kama River, the Great Siberian Post Road and later the Trans-Siberian Railway, Perm quickly grew into a major trading and industrial centre.

Before the railway reached Perm most travellers would arrive by steamer from Nizhny Novgorod (now Gorky) and Kazan. R L Jefferson (see Part 3) cycled here from London in 1896 on his Siberian ride and was entertained by Gospodin Kuznetsoff, the 60 year old president of the Perm Cycling Club, and fifty enthusiasts. On 20 July 1907, the cyclists came out to escort an equally sensational visitor, the Italian Prince Borghese, who had just driven across Siberia from Peking in his Itala and was on his way to Paris, where he would win the Peking to Paris Motor Rally. One of the wheels of the car was damaged and, when the Prince's chauffeur had replaced some of the wooden spokes, he declared that the wheel needed to be soaked to make the wood expand before the repair could be completed. A local official advised them to send it to one of the bathing establishments along the Kama River. A bathing-machine (of the type used by Victorian swimmers at English sea-side resorts) was hired and the wheel spent the night taking the waters.

Unfortunately, the centre of Old Perm is out of sight, 5km away from Perm 2 station at which the Trans-Siberian train stops. This is a pity as the approaches and area around Perm 2 are dominated by industrial enterprises. Shortly after leaving the station, the train crosses a small bridge over a busy street. This street was once the Siberian *Trakt* which passed through Perm from 1863.

After leaving Perm, the landscape changes abruptly and forests give way to meadows and fields.

Km1458 (S) The attractive, green domed church here might make a good photograph.

Kms1460-1777 The train winds its way up to the highest point in the Urals. One would expect the range of mountains that divides Europe from Asia to be rather more impressive than these hills but they rise up not much more than 500m/1640ft above sea level in this area. R L Jefferson wrote in 1896: 'The Urals certainly are not so high or majestic as the Alps or the Balkans but their wild picturesqueness is something to be seen to be appreciated.' Their wild picturesqueness is somewhat marred and scarred today by open-cast mines at Km1507 (N) and Km1509 (N). There is a large timber-mill at Km1523 (N).

Km1534: Kungur Кунгур Just outside the town is a fascinating and virtually unknown tourist attraction – the Kungur Ice Caves (see p190). The stockade town of Kungur was founded in 1648, 17km from its present site. By the 18th century, the town had become one of the largest centres in the Urals as it was a transit point on the Siberian *Trakt*. It had three big markets a year, numerous factories and the first technical college in the Urals, which opened in 1877. Today the town is much less important but it is still well known in Russia for its guitar factory.

Soon after leaving Kungur, you see the steep banks of the Sylva River which marks the start of the Kungur Forest Steppe. This area is characterised by rolling hills which reach 180-230m, a landscape pitted with troughs and sinkholes, and copses of birch, linden, oak and pine interspersed with farm lands.

Km1537 (N) A picturesque church stands alone on the hill across the Sylva River. The line follows this river up the valley to Km1556 where it cuts across a wide plain. The trees close in again from about Km1584 but there are occasional clearings with villages and timber-mills at about Km1650 (N).

Km1672 Shalya Шаля (pop: 26,900) The forestry town of no special interest. Fifty kilometres west of here, you enter **Sverdlovskaya Oblast**. It covers 195,000 square kilometres, taking in parts of the Urals and extending east onto the Siberian plain. Like most of the other oblasts you have passed though, this one is composed almost entirely of taiga forests. From the rich deposits in the Urals are mined iron ore, copper, platinum, gold, tungsten, cobalt, asbestos and bauxite as well as many varieties of gemstones. The soil is poor so there is very little agriculture in the region.

Km1729: Kuzino Кузино East of the large marshalling yard here the line rises once more, passing a little town built around a freshly white-washed church with a green dome. After about 10km, the train reaches one of the most attractive rivers in the Urals, the Chusavya River. The line follows the course of the river for some 30km.

Km1748: Krylosovo Крылосово A large factory, with rows of apartment blocks for its workers, looks a little out of place amongst the forests up here in the Urals. From Km1764 east the area becomes quite built up.

Km1774: Pervouralsk Первоуральск (pop: 148,000) The city's name translates as 'The First Ural' as it was here in 1727 that the first factory in the Urals was opened. Following the success of its cast iron works, dozens of other factories sprang up, and today the city is home to numerous heavy engineering complexes including one of Russia's largest pipeline factories.

You can see Pervouralsk's main tourist attraction, the **Europe-Asia border obelisk** from the train so there's no reason to get off. If you do, about the only place to stay in the city is *Hotel Pervouralsk* at pro Ilicha 28 (bus No 10 from the station). The hotel has a good restaurant and the other recommended choice is *Restaurant Talaktuka* at ul Trubnikov 52. The city boasts a Museum of Folklore, ul Lenina 65.

Km1777 (S): Europe-Asia Border Obelisk People begin collecting in the corridor long before you reach the white stone obelisk which marks the continental division at this point in the Urals. Just before you get to it, when travelling east, there is a large brick tower beside the track at Km1775-6 (S). The obelisk (see p192) is about 15m to the east of the small Vershina (Вершина) railway platform.

When R L Jefferson reached the point near here where the road crosses the Urals (also marked with an obelisk) he wrote enthusiastically of the view: 'Hills piled upon hills, shaggy mountains and gaunt fir trees, and beyond them dwindling away into the mist of the horizon the great steppe lands of Siberia.' George Kennan wrote in 1887: 'The scenery of the Urals where the railroad crosses the range resembles in general outline that of West Virginia where the Baltimore and Ohio railroad crosses the Alleghenies; but it differs somewhat from the latter in colouring, owing to the greater preponderance in the Urals of evergreen trees'. Unfortunately you won't get much of a view from the train today.

Km1813: Ekaterinburg Екатеринбург (●●●) [see p191]

(pop: 1,370,000)   As soon as you reach the suburbs of Ekaterinburg you see a large lake on the right (Kms1807-9) which feeds the Iset River running through the city. There's a **locomotive depot** west of the station. The train halts in the largest city in the Urals, for a change of engine. Ekaterinburg was formerly known as Sverdlovsk.

After the train leaves the station, on the right along the Iset River a mass of chimney stacks pollute the horizon. This is Ekaterinburg's main industrial region. Here are located the industrial giants of Uralmash (heavy machinery), Uralelectrotiazhmash (heavy electrical equipment) and Uralkhimash (chemical machinery).

For about 70km east of Ekaterinburg, the train winds down and out of the Urals to the West Siberian plain. You are now in Asia (not quite in Siberia yet) but the scenery and houses look no different from those on the European flank of the mountains.

Km1915: Bogdanovich Богданович

There is nothing of interest in this town unless you are want to pick up some fireproof bricks which are the town's biggest products. Clay quarries and other factories make this town and region very ugly.

About 16km from Bogdanovich are the **Kurinsk mineral springs**. The *1900 Guide to the Great Siberian Railway* states 'They are efficacious for rheumatism, paralysis, scrofula and anaemia. Furnished houses and an hotel with good rooms are situated near the baths. There is a garden and a promenade with band; theatricals and concerts take place in the casino'. Such frivolous jollities are hard to imagine in this rather gloomy region today. There's still a hotel, however.

Km1961: Kamyshlov Камышлов

The town was founded in 1668 as a fortress and is one of oldest settlements in the Urals. The original buildings have all gone and today the architecture of the town is predominantly late 19th and early 20th century. There is a museum here dedicated to the locally born poet S P Shchepachev and the writer P P Bazhov, who lived here on and off from 1914-1923.

About 6km to the west of the town, on the banks of the Pyshma River, is the Obukhov sulphur and chalybeate mineral water sanatorium which has been famous since 1871.

❏ The U2 Affair: USSR, 1: USA 0

The U2 affair represented an unprecedented Cold War embarrassment for the West. On 1 May 1960, an American U2 spyplane was shot down from a height of 68,000 feet, some 45km south of Sverdlovsk (as Ekaterinburg was then known). Its pilot, Gary Powers, baled out without activating the plane's self-destruct mechanism for fear that he would blow himself up (criticisms were later raised in Congress that he had not killed himself, either by destroying the aircraft or by pricking himself with the poisoned needle so thoughtfully provided by the CIA). He was picked up shortly after reaching the ground.

Four days later the USA announced that a U2 'meteorological aircraft' had 'gone missing' just north of Turkey after its pilot had reported problems with his oxygen mask. In a detailed press announcement it was speculated that he had fallen unconscious while the plane, automatic pilot engaged, might possibly have flown itself over Soviet territory. Shortly after this announcement, Khrushchev told the Supreme Soviet that a U2 'spyplane' had been shot down over Sverdlovsk. US presidential spokesman Lincoln White commented that 'this might be the same plane', and did his best to cool the situation by explaining the oxygen supply theory again. He concluded: 'there was absolutely no deliberate attempt to violate Soviet airspace and never has been', and he grounded all other U2s to 'check their oxygen systems'.

On 7 May Khrushchev addressed the Supreme Soviet again: 'I must tell you a secret. When I made my first report I deliberately did not say that the pilot was alive and well ... and now just look how many silly things they (the Americans) have said'. Khrushchev exploited his position, revelling in the details of the American cover-up: he was in possession of the pilot ('alive and kicking'), the 'plane, the camera, and had even had the photographs developed. He also had Powers' survival pack, including 7500 roubles, other currencies and gold rings and gifts for women. 'Why was all this necessary?' he asked, 'Maybe the pilot was to have flown still higher to Mars and was going to lead the Martian ladies astray?' He laughed at the US report that the U2 had a maximum height of 55,000 feet: 'It was hit by the rocket at 20,000m (65,000 feet). And if they fly any higher we will also hit them'.

The U2 Affair brought the 1960 Paris Summit to a grinding halt. Following the arrival of the first U2s in England in August 1962, Moscow remarked that they ought to be 'kept far away from us'. In the USSR, Powers was sentenced to ten years but released in exchange for Rudolph Abel, a KGB spy, in 1962. Soviet press maintained that Powers had been sent home as an 'act of clemency'. No mention was made of the exchange. The wreckage of the plane is now on display in Ekaterinburg.   **Dominic Streatfeild-James** (UK)

Km2033: Talitsa Талица (pop: 20,100) The town is famous for its Mayan (Маян) brand of bottled mineral water, believed to be good for stomach disorders. The town, which is 3km south of the station, also produces another drink which is less beneficial: watered down industrial alcohol which is sold as rough vodka.

Km2064: Yushala Юшала The sailors from the battleship *Potemkin* were shot here and buried at nearby Kamyshlov station.

Km2078: Siberia (Сибирь) begins here (ends here, for those going west). The border between Sverdlovskaya and Tyumenskaya Oblasts is the frontier between Siberia and the Urals. Tyumenskaya Oblast comprises 430,000 square kilometres of flat land, tundra in the north, taiga in the south. Until oil was discovered in the region twenty years ago, the inhabitants were engaged in reindeer-herding in the north and farming in the south. Many people have been brought into the oblast recently to work in the petroleum and construction industries.

South of the railway line, the point where the Great Post Road crossed Siberia's frontier was marked by 'a square pillar ten or twelve feet in height, of stuccoed or plastered brick', wrote George Kennan (on his way to research *Siberia and the Exile System* in 1887). He added: 'No other spot between St Petersburg and the Pacific is more full of painful suggestions, and none has for the traveller a more melancholy interest than the little opening in the forest where stands this grief-consecrated pillar. Here hundreds of thousands of exiled human beings – men, women and children; princes, nobles and peasants – have bidden good-by (sic) forever to friends, country, and home ... The Russian peasant even when a criminal is deeply attached to his native land; and heart-rending scenes have been witnessed around the boundary pillar ... Some gave way to unrestrained grief; some comforted the weeping; some knelt and pressed their faces to the loved

MAP 4

soil of their native country and collected a little earth to take with them into exile ... Until recently the Siberian boundary post was covered with brief inscriptions, good-byes and the names of exiles ... In one place, in a man's hand, had been written the words "Prashchai Marya" (Goodbye Mary!) Who the writer was, who Mary was, there is nothing now left to show ...' (see p87).

Km2140: Tyumen Тюмень (●●) (pop: 496,000) [see p200]

Tyumen is the oldest town in Siberia, founded in 1586. It was built on the banks of the Tura River, the site of the former Tatar town of Chingi Tura, said to date back to the fourteenth century. The Russian town was named by Tsar Feodor Ivanovich after Tyumen Khan, who formerly ruled this region. It grew quickly as a trading centre with goods arriving and being shipped on from the large port on the Tura River.

At least one million of the people who passed through this town before 1900 were convicts and exiles. Many were lodged, under the most appalling conditions, in the Tyumen Forwarding Prison. When George Kennan visited the prison in 1887, he was horrified by the overcrowded cells, the dirt and the terrible smell. He wrote: 'The air in the corridors and cells.....was laden with fever germs from the unventilated hospital wards, fetid odors from diseased human bodies and the stench arising from unemptied excrement buckets.....' After a miserable two-week stay

---

❏ **German spy in Ishim**

George Kennan recounts an amusing incident that occurred in Ishim in 1829, when Baron von Humboldt was conducting a geological survey for the Tsar. The famous explorer (who gave his name to the Humboldt Current off the west coast of South America) had by then become more than a little annoyed by the petty Siberian officials who kept him from his studies. He must have been rather short with the police prefect in this little town for the man took great offence and despatched an urgent letter to his governor-general in which he wrote 'A few days ago there arrived here a German of shortish stature, insignificant appearance, fussy and bearing a letter of introduction from your Excellency to me. I accordingly received him politely; but I must say I find him suspicious and even dangerous. I disliked him from the first. He talks too much .... despises my hospitality .... and associates with Poles and other political criminals .... On one occasion he proceeded with them to a hill overlooking the town. They took a box with them and got out of it a long tube which we all took for a gun. After fastening it to three feet they pointed it down on the town .... This was evidently a great danger for the town which is built entirely of wood; so I sent a detachment of troops with loaded rifles to watch the German on the hill. If the treacherous machinations of this man justify my suspicions, we shall be ready to give our lives for the Tsar and Holy Russia.' Kennan adds: 'The civilised world is to be thanked that the brilliant career of the great von Humboldt was not cut short by a Cossack bullet .... while he was taking sights with a theodolite in that little Siberian town of Ishim.'

MAP 5

Вагай
VAGAY

Омутинская
OMUTINSKAYA

Ламенская
LAMYENSKAYA

Голышманово
GOLISHMANOVO

Карасульская
KARASULSKAYA

TYUMENSKAYA OBLAST

Ишим
ISHIM

Ветлуга R.

Маслянская
MASLYANSKAYA

Ново-Андреевский
NOVO-ANDREYEVSKY

Мангут
MANGUT

Называевская
NAZEVAYEVSKAYA

Драгунская
DRAGUNSKAYA

OMSKAYA OBLAST

Любинская
LYUBINSKAYA

Irtysh R.

ОМСК
OMSK

here, convicts were sent on prison barges to Tomsk. Conditions were not much better for the 500,000 emigrants who flooded through the town between 1883 and 1900, but they at least had their freedom. When the new railway reached Tyumen in 1888 prisoners from Russia were no longer herded over the Urals in marching parties but travelled in relative luxury in box-cars used also for the transport of cattle and horses.

Tyumen is becoming increasingly important because of oil and gas discoveries in the oblast. Other industries include ship-building and timber-processing.

Km2222: Yalutorovsk Ялуторовск (pop: 37,000) The town sits on the bank of the wide, 1591km-long Tobol River. In 1639 it was the most easterly fortress of the Tsar's expanding empire. It later became one of the places of exile for Decembrists, who opened the first Siberian school for girls here. It's now a museum and is next to the Decembrists' museum, the house of the most famous exile, Muravev-Apostol.

After crossing over the Tobol River, you will see dozens of small, mostly salt lakes on both sides of the railway.

Km2431: Ishim Ишим (●●) (pop: 65,800) The town sits on the left bank of the Ishim River which was a major trading route before the arrival of the Trans-Siberian at the turn of the century. The strategic location of the town resulted in it hosting one of the largest trading fairs in Western Siberia. The Nikolsk fair was held every December and it attracted more than 2000 traders from as far away as China. The town was founded in 1670 as Korkina village but its name was changed to Ishim in 1782.

North of Ishim, up the Ishim and Irtysh Rivers, lies the city of **Tobolsk**, one of the oldest settlements in Siberia. Yermak (see p84) reached the area in 1581 and established a fort here. The Tsar hoped to develop the region by encouraging colonisation but to the Russian peasant, Siberia was as far away as the moon and no voluntary mass exodus over the Urals occurred. The policy of forced exile was rather more successful. The first exiles that arrived in Tobolsk were former inhabitants of the town of Uglich, who had been witnesses to the murder of Tsarevich Dimitri. With them was banished the **Uglich church bell** which rang the signal for the insurrection that followed the assassination. The bell was reconsecrated in Tobolsk church but in the 1880s the Uglich Town Council decided it would like its bell back. Tobolsk Council refused and the case eventually went to court. The judge ruled that as the bell had been exiled for life, and it was still calling the people to prayers, it had not yet completed its sentence and must therefore remain in Tobolsk.

Km2520 This is the administrative frontier between Tyumenskaya and Omskaya oblasts. **Omskaya** is on a plain in the Irtysh River basin, occupying 140,000 square kilometres. The thick forests of the taiga cover the northern part of the oblast. In the south there is considerable agricultural development, the main crops being spring wheat, flax and sunflowers. As well as sheep and cattle farms, there are many dairy-farming co-operatives. This has been an important butter-producing region since the nineteenth century, when butter was exported to as far away as Turkey and Germany. It is said that butter-making was introduced to the region by the English wife of a Russian landowner. There are many swamps and lakes in the oblast which provide the habitat for a multitude of water birds, including duck, coot, grey goose, swan and crane.

─────────── **Km 2521-2870 TIME ZONE MT + 3** ───────────

Km2565: Nazyvaevskaya Называевская (●●) (pop: 14,400)
Founded in 1910 with the arrival of the railway Nazyvaevskaya rapidly grew with an influx of new agricultural workers during the Khrushchev's Virgin Fields campaign. The plan was conceived following years of chronic grain shortage after WWII and involved the cultivation of 25 million hectares of land in south western Siberia and north Kazakhstan. To put the size of this massive undertaking into perspective, the total surface area of the United Kingdom is only 13 million hectares. By the 1960s over-intensive farming had reduced five million hectares to desert. The Trans-Siberian runs through the very north of the area and, unlike the more fragile south, is still fertile.

This area is famous as much for its insects as for its agriculture. In 1887, Kennan found that travelling through this marshy region was a singularly unpleasant experience. He wrote: 'We were so tormented by huge gray mosquitoes that we were obliged to put on thick gloves, cover our heads with calico hoods and horse hair netting and defend ourselves constantly with leafy branches.' You, however, should be quite safe in your compartment.

Km2707: **Irtyshch River** Речка Иртыщ The Irtyshch rises in China and flows almost 3000km into the Ob River. It's joined here by the Om.

Km2712: Omsk Омск (●●●) (pop: 1,169,000) [see p203]
Omsk is the second largest city in Siberia and great deal of effort has gone into making it the greenest. The 2500 hectares of parks and gardens cannot, however, disguise the fact that Omsk is essentially an industrial city.

Just before reaching the suburbs of Omsk, you see the airport on the left. The first suburban station you pass is Karbyshevo (Карбышево) and this is where the railway from Chelyabinsk joins the Trans-Siberian railway. The train then crosses the 500m wide Irtysh River which gives a view of Omsk to the left. The old centre of Omsk is on the right bank (eastern side). After the bridge, the train makes a left turn and on the right passes an old brick water tower for steam engines, built during the early 20th century. This has been preserved as an architectural monument.

The stretch of line between Omsk and Novosibirsk has the greatest freight traffic density of any line in the world.

For the next 600km the train runs through the inhospitable **Baraba Steppe**. This vast expanse of greenish plains is dotted with shallow lakes and ponds, and coarse reeds and sedge grass conceal swamps, peat bogs and rare patches of firm ground. From the train it appears as if there is a continuous forest in the distance. However if you walk towards it, you will never get there as what you are seeing are clumps of birches and aspen trees that are spaced several kilometres or more apart. The lack of landmarks in this area has claimed hundreds of lives.

In spring, this place is hell as the air is grey with clouds of gnats and mosquitoes. The Baraba Steppe is also a vast breeding ground for ducks and geese and every year hunters bag about five million birds from here. Below the steppe is an enormous natural reservoir of hot water, a geothermal energy supply that is currently being investigated.

Km2760 (S): There is a locomotive storage depot here (mostly electric) and 3km east of it is the station of Kormilovka (Кормиловка).

❏ **The West Siberian Railway (Kms 2716-3343)**
The original line started in Chelyabinsk, south of Ekaterinburg, and ran through Kurgan and Petropavlovsk (both south of the modern route) to Omsk. Work began in July 1892 under the direction of chief civil engineer, Mikhailovski. His task was beset by problems that were also to be experienced along other sections of the line: a shortage of labour and animals, a complete lack of suitable trees for sleepers and inhospitable working conditions (eg swamps that swarmed with insects). However, the first section from Chelyabinsk to Omsk was completed in 1894 and the Omsk to Novo-Nikolayevsk (now Novosibirsk) section opened in October 1895. The total cost of the line was 46 million roubles, one million roubles fewer than the original estimate.

Km2795: Kalachinskaya Калачинская (pop: 25,500) One of the more attractive towns in the Omsk Oblast, this town was founded in 1792 by Russian peasants who were distinct from other settlers because of their unusual dialect – *kalachon* means 'a sharp bend in a river'; *kalach* in modern Russian means 'a small padlock-shaped white bread loaf'. There's a useful bit of information.

Km2870 This is the administrative frontier between Omskaya and Novosibirskaya oblasts. The 178,000 square kilometres of **Novosibirskaya Oblast** extend across the Baraba Steppe region of swamps and lakes. Some of the land has been drained and is now extremely fertile Crops include spring wheat, flax, rye, barley and sun-flowers with dairy farming in many parts of the Baraba region. You might see cowherds rounding up their stock on horseback.

———————— Km 2871-4475 TIME ZONE MT + 4 ————————

Km2880: Tatarskaya Татарская (●) (pop: 30,800) A rather uninteresting small town of apartment blocks and log cabins. The *1900 Guide to the Great Siberian Railway* was not enthusiastic about the place. 'The country is swampy and infested with fever. The water is bad, supplied by a pond formed by spring and bog water.' There was a church, a centre for emigrants, a school and 'the butter manufactures of Mariupolsky, Padin,

---

❑ **The Kirghiz**

South of Omsk and the Baraba Steppe region lie the **Kirghiz Steppes**, the true home of the Kirghiz people. The area extends from the Urals in the west to the mineral-rich Altai Mountains in the south. The Kirghiz are direct descendants of the Turkic-Mongol hordes that joined Ghengis Khan's armies and invaded Europe in the thirteenth century AD. When SS Hill paid them a visit in 1854, they were nomadic herders who professed a mixture of Shamanism and Islam and survived on a diet of boiled mutton and *koumiss* (fermented mare's milk). They lived in *kibitkas* (felt tents or yurts), the doors of which were arranged to face in the direction of Mecca. Fortunately this alignment also kept out the southern winds that blew across the steppe. Of these people Hill wrote: 'The Kirgeeze have the high cheek bones.....of the Mongol Tatars, with an expression of countenance that seemed at least to us the very reverse of agreeable.' However he warmed to his 'new half-wild friends' when they shared their 'brave mess of *stchee*' (soup) with him.

George Kennan found them equally hospitable in 1887. Inside the tent he was offered a large container filled with about a litre and a half of koumiss. For fear of causing offence he swallowed the lot and to his horror, his host quickly refilled the container. Kennan wrote 'When I suggested that he reserve the second bowlful for my comrade, Mr Frost, he looked so pained and grieved that in order to restore his serenity I had to go to the *tarantas*, get my banjo and sing "There is a Tavern in the Town"'. This did not have quite the desired effect and they left shortly afterwards.

Soshovsky, Popel and Weiss, producing annually about 15,000 *puds* (250,000 kg) of cream butter'.

Km2883 (N) An attractive group of colourful log cabins. About fifty kilometres south of the line between Chany and Binsk lies Lake Chany, the centre of a fishing industry. Catches are smaller now but in the nineteenth century it was famous for its abundant stock of large pike (weighing up to 14kg/30lbs) and carp.

Km3035: Barabinsk Барабинск (●) (pop: 36,400) Founded at the end of the 19th century during the construction of the Trans-Siberian. Twelve km to north is the bigger and older town of Kuibyshev (Kainsk-Barabinski).

Km3204: Chulymskaya Чулымская A large railway junction with nothing of interest.

Km3319: Ob Обь Just before reaching this station, you can see Tolmachevo Airport on the left which is one of the two airports which serves Novosibirsk. The city of Novosibirsk can be seen to the northeast of here.

Km3332: The Great Ob River Bridge After nearly a century of operation, many of the steel bridges of the early Trans-Siberian are still in use today. Known as hog-backed bridges because of the hump in the middle of each span, they are supported by massive stone piers, each with a thick buttress that slants upstream to deflect the huge ice chunks as they float down the river in the spring thaw. The 690m long Ob Bridge is a classic hog-backed bridge made up of seven spans.

The writers of the *1900 Guide to the Great Siberian Railway* were clearly impressed by the Ob Bridge, which at the time had only just been completed. They devote almost a whole page to a detailed description of the bridge, beginning: 'At the 1,328 *verst*, the line crosses the Ob by a bridge 327.50 *sazhens* long, having seven spans, the I and VII openings are 46.325 *sazhens*, the II, IV and VI, 53.65 *sazhens*, and III and V, 53.15 *sazhens*. The upper girders of the bridge are on

MAP 6

ОМСК
OMSK

Irtysh R.

Om. R.

OMSKAYA OBLAST

Кормиловка
KORMILOVKA

Калачинская
KALACHINSKAYA

Ивановка
IVANOVKA

161

Каратканск
KARATKANSK

Татарская
TATARSKAYA

Кабаклы
KABAKLY

155

Чаны
CHANY

О.Карачинкое
OZERO KARACHINSKOYE

Кошкуль
KOSHKUL

Ot Chany

Тебисская
TEBISSKAYA

Om. R.

Барабинск
BARABINSK

NOVOSIBIRSKAYA OBLAST

Кожурла
KOZHURLA

Убинская
UBINSKAYA

286

Каргат
KARGAT

Кокошино
KOKOSHINO

Чулимская
CHULIMSKAYA

Дупленская
DUPLENSKAYA

Лесная Поляна
LESNAYA POLYANA

Чик
CHIK

Обь Ob R.
OB

НОВОСИБИРСК
NOVOSIBIRSK

the Herber's system.' If you are unfamiliar with the Russian Imperial units of measurement, a *verst* is 1.06km or 3500ft and a *sazhen* is 2.1m or 7ft.

Work started in 1893 on the bridge with construction of wooden false-work which supported sections of the permanent steel structure until they could be riveted together. Bridge making proceeded all year round and was an extremely hazardous occupation in winter. Gangs were perched 30 or more metres above the frozen river, bolting and riveting without safety lines or protective hoardings. More than a few dropped to their deaths below.

The Ob River is one of the world's longest rivers, flowing more than 4000km north across Siberia from the Altai Mountains to the Gulf of Ob, below the Arctic Ocean.

As you are crossing over the Ob River, you can see Novosibirsk city centre on the left and the Oktyabrski port on the right. The passenger river station is a further 800m upstream from the port. On reaching the right bank, the train turns to the north passing the city's long distance bus station. About 800m onwards on the right, you pass a **steam locomotive** on a plinth (see photo opposite p208).

Km3335: Novosibirsk Новосибирск (●●●)   [see p205]
Novosibirsk (pop: 1,600,000) is the capital of Western Siberia. Most trains stop long enough for you to get a good look at Siberia's largest station, an impressive green, glass-vaulted building that took from 1929 to 1941 to complete.

Travelling east you pass through flat land of fields and swamps with the dachas of Novosibirskians in little groups amongst the trees. Some are particularly photogenic (km3409 (S)). The line traverses an area of thin taiga to Oyash (km3424).

Km3479: Bolotnaya Болотная
The town was founded in 1805 as a stop on the Siberian *Trakt* at a junction of a 250km road south to Barnaul. The town's name means 'swampy', which should please a certain British environmental activist.

Km3485:
This is the **administrative frontier** between Novosibirskaya and Kemerovskaya Oblasts.

Km3498: Yurga 1 Юрга 1 (pop: 94,300)
The town of Yurga 2 is 7km to the south of Yurga 1. A few kilometres east the train crosses the Tom River, which flows an unimpressive (by Siberian standards) 700km (or twice the length of the Thames) from the Kuznetsk basin into the Ob River.

Km3565: Taiga Тайга (●●) (pop: 25,900)
Once this town stood in the

midst of the dense taiga forest. Nowadays the closest taiga is far to the east.

R L Jefferson was here in 1897 and wrote later: 'This little station was bang in the midst of the most impenetrable forest I had ever set eyes on.....in the centre of a pit it seemed, for the great black trunks of pines went up all around and left only a circular space of blue sky visible.' Annette Meakin wrote a few years later that she, 'thought Taiga one of the prettiest stations in Siberia. It is only a few years old, built something after the style of a Swiss chalet.' Unfortunately it has since been replaced by a building that is rather more substantial but aesthetically less pleasing.

The station sits at the junction of a 79km branch line to the ancient city of **Tomsk**, and in retrospect the site of the junction was badly chosen. The basic problem is that there are no rivers or large reservoirs near Taiga so water had to be carted in to feed the steam engines. Tomsk was once the most important place in Siberia. It was founded in 1604 on the Tom River and developed into a large administrative, trading and gold-smelting centre on the Great Siberian Post Road. When it was originally bypassed by the railway, Tomsk began to lose out to the stations along the main line. It is still, however, a sizeable city of half a million people, the administrative capital of Tomskaya Oblast and a large centre of industrial engineering.

Tomsk was visited by almost every nineteenth century traveller who came to Siberia. The city was an important exile centre and had a large forwarding prison. Having almost succumbed to the stench from the overcrowded cells in 1887, Kennan wrote: 'If you visit the prison my advice to you is to breakfast heartily before starting, and to keep out of the hospital wards.' By the time Annette Meakin visited it fourteen years later, the railway had removed the need for forwarding prisons and she could write: 'It was not unlike a group of alms houses. We found very few prisoners.' Tomsk achieved international notoriety

MAP 7

when at nearby Tomsk-7 on 6 April 1993, a radioactive waste reprocessing plant blew up contaminating an area of 120 square km.

Near the station is a **steam engine**, P-360192, built in 1956.

Km3602: Anzherskaya Анжерская (pop: 106,000) This ugly coal mining town is at the northern extremity of the giant Kuzbass coal field which contains a massive 600 billion tons of high quality low sulphur coal. The town, formerly called Anzhero-Sudzhensk (Анжеро-Судженск), was founded in 1897 during the construction of the Trans-Siberian which is also when coal mining started. From the end of the 19th to the beginning of the 20th century, 98% of all coal from the Kuzbass came from here. Most of the original coal miners were Tsarist prisoners and their short and brutal mining life is documented in the Museum of Local Studies.

The railway branch line to the south from here leads to **Novokuznetsk** which is the heart of the Kuznetsk (or Kuzbass) Basin. In the early 1900s, a plan had been put forward to link these coal-fields with the Ural region where iron-ore was mined and coal was needed for the blast furnaces. This plan was not put into action until the 1930s when the so-called Ural-Kuzbass Kombinat was developed. Trains bring iron-ore to the Kuzbass furnaces and return to the iron foundries of the Urals with coal. You will have met (or will meet if you're going west) a good deal of this traffic on the line between Novosibirsk and the Urals.

Kms3613-3623: Several long views south across the fields. The line climbs slowly through birch forests and small fields to Mariinsk.

Km3715: Mariinsk Мариинск (●●) (pop: 41,500) Founded as Kisskoe in 1698, this place was nothing more than a way station for postal riders who carried messages on the Moscow-Irkutsk postal road. In 1826, however, news of a massive gold find brought tens of thousands of fortune seekers. The gold rush lasted for decades and between 1828 and 1917, more than 50 tons of gold were extracted from the region. The town was renamed Mariinsk in 1857 after the German wife of Tsar Alexander II, Maria Alexandrovna.

Just west of the station there are large **engine repair yards** (S). Two kilometres east of the town you cross the Kiya River, a tributary of the Chulim. East of the river the line rises to cross the watershed at Km3760, where there are good views south. The line descends through the market town of Tiazhin (Km3779) to the river of the same name and then climbs over the next water shed descending to **Itat**, another agricultural town.

Km3820: This is the administrative frontier between Kemerovskaya Oblast and Krasnoyarski *Krai*. A krai is a large oblast, usually found in less developed areas of Siberia. This is also the border between West and

East Siberia. **Krasnoyarski** is large, covering 2.5 million square kilometres (an area the size of Saudi Arabia) between the Arctic Ocean in the north and the Sayan Mountains in the south. Most of the krai is covered with taiga, though there is tundra in the region within the Arctic Circle and some agricultural land in the south. The economy is based on timber processing but there are also important mineral reserves.

Km3849: Bogotol Боготол (●●)

This railway town has a **museum** in its locomotive depot which is 1km to the west of the station. There is also a number of **steam locos** here. The town was founded in 1893 as a station on the Trans-Siberian although there is a much older village of the same name 8km away.

Near Bogotol are lignite (brown coal) deposits and open cut mines can be seen scarring the landscape from the train.

About 30km east the line begins to descend, crossing the **Chulim River** at Km3917. R L Jefferson arrived here in the winter of 1897 and described the river as a 'rather a small stream when compared to the Obi, Tom or Irtish but still broad enough to make two of the Thames River at London Bridge'. At the time, the bridge had not been completed but engineers had the brilliant idea of freezing the rails to the thick ice, thus allowing the train to cross the river.

Km3917: Achinsk 1 Ачинск 1 (●)

(214m/700ft, pop: 122,00) Founded in 1642 when a stockaded outpost was built here, on the banks of the Chulim. It was burnt down by the Kirghiz 40 years later but soon rebuilt. In the 18th and 19th centuries Achinsk was an important trading centre, linked by the Chulim to Tyumen and Tomsk. Tea arrived by caravan from China and was forwarded in barges. To the north, in the valleys around the Chulim basin, lay the gold mines. The most valuable mines today, however, are those producing lignite. There's also a giant aluminium production complex which can be seen from the railway.

MAP 8

Kms3932-33 (S): Half-way point on the line from Moscow to Beijing (via Mongolia). There's a **white obelisk** to mark it on the south side of the line but it is difficult to see. The line continues through a hilly region of taiga, winding round sharp curves (Kms4006-12) and past picturesque groups of log cabins (Km4016). There are occasional good views at Km4058 (N) and after the village of Minino (Km4072) at 4078 (N).

Km3960: Chernorechenskaya Чернореченская The name of the town around the station is Novochernorechenskaya (Новочернореченский) meaning 'New Black River'.

Km4098: Krasnoyarsk Красноярск (●●●) [see p215]
(pop: 929,000) This major industrial city was founded in 1628 beside the Yenisei River. (*Yenisei* is also the name of the Moscow-Krasnoyarsk Express which you may see standing in the station). A fort was built and named Krasny Yar. As an important trading centre on the Great Siberian Post Road and the great Yenisei waterway, the town grew fast in the eighteenth century. The railway reached Krasnoyarsk in 1896, some of the rails for this section of the line having been brought from England by ship via the Kara Sea (within the Arctic Circle) and the Yenisei.

Murray would not recognise the town he described as 'pleasantly situated and sheltered by hills of moderate elevation', in the 1865 edition of his *Handbook for Russia, Poland and Finland*.

❏ **The Mid-Siberian Railway (Kms3343-5191)**
Work began on the Mid-Siberian Railway starting at the Ob River in the summer of 1893. Since Tomsk was to be bypassed, part of the route had to be hacked through the thick forests of the taiga regions around the station, which was aptly named Taiga. It would have been far easier to have followed the route of the Great Siberian Post Road through Tomsk but some of that city's administrators wanted nothing to do with the railway, since it would break their trade monopolies and bring down prices, damaging the economy as far as they were concerned. By the time they realised that the effect was quite the opposite it was too late to change the route of the line. Besides, the engineers had discovered that the bypass would save 90km. The tiny village of Novo-Nikolayevsk, (now Novosibirsk) situated where the railway crosses the Ob, grew quickly and soon eclipsed Tomsk as an industrial and cultural centre.

This was difficult territory to build a railway across. The swampy taiga is frozen until mid-July, so the building season was barely three months long. There was the usual labour shortage and 1500 convicts had to be brought in to help. In 1895 a branch line from Taiga reached Tomsk. Although only about 80km long, it had taken a year to build, owing to the virtually impenetrable taiga and the terrible swamps. In 1896 the line reached Krasnoyarsk and work began on the eastern section to Irkutsk. Numerous bridges were needed in this hilly country but by the beginning of 1898 the mid-Siberian was complete and the first trains rolled into Irkutsk. Total cost was about 110 million roubles.

Km4100-2: Yenisei River Речка Енисей Good views (N) and (S).
Leaving Krasnoyarsk, travelling east, the train crosses the great river that bisects Siberia. The Yenisei (meaning 'wide water' in the language of the local Evenki people) rises in Mongolia and flows into the Arctic Ocean, 5200km north of its source.

This bridge, which is almost a kilometre in length, dates from the 1890s and had to be built on heavy granite piers to withstand the huge icebergs which steamroller their way down the river for a few weeks each year. The cement was shipped from St Petersburg, the steel bearings from Warsaw. It took 94,000 workers three years to build. At the World Fair in Paris in 1900, the bridge was awarded a gold medal. The other engineering feat to win a gold medal that year was the Eiffel Tower.

For several kilometres after you've crossed the river the lumber mills and factories blight the countryside. Open-cast mining has slashed ugly gashes into the hills around Km4128 (N).

Km4126: Bazaika Базаиха There is a branch line to the north from here to the closed city of Krasnoyarsk-26, a nuclear waste reprocessing facility. The line goes through Sotsgorod station and terminates at the Gorknokhimicheski Chemical complex. Neither this line nor the city appear on Soviet maps.

Between Krasnoyarsk and Nizhneudinsk the line crosses hilly, picturesque countryside, and the train climbs out of one valley and descends into the next. There are numerous bridges on this section. There are some good places for photographs along the train as it curves round bends at Km4165-7 and Km4176-4177, then the land becomes flatter.

Km4227: Uyar Уяр At the western end of the station is a large strategic reserve of working **steam locos** and also a dump of about ten engines rusting away amongst the weeds. This town's full name is something of a tongue-twister. Try saying 'Uyarspasopreobrazhenskoye' after a few glasses of vodka. In 1897 the station's name was changed to Olgino in honour of grand duchess Olga Nikolaevna. In 1906 it was renamed Klyukvenaya after the railway engineer who built this section of the line but in 1973 its name was changed back to Uyar.

Km4272: Zaozernaya Заозёная (pop: 15,600) A branch line runs north from here to the secret city of Krasnoyarsk-45 (also known as Zelenogorsk) where there's a space centre. East of the station there are huge open cut coal mines beside the track.

Km4343: Kansk-Yeniseiski Канск-Енисейский (pop: 111,000)
This big town, known just as Kansk, had an inglorious start. In 1628 the original Kansk wooden fortress was built about 43km away from the present site on the Kan River. The original site was badly chosen and in

1640, the fortress was moved. It was almost immediately burnt down by the Buryat indigenous people and although it was rebuilt, in 1677 it was again burnt down. Over the following two centuries the town became a major transit point for peasants settling in Siberia. The Russian author, Chekhov, wasn't very impressed with the town and said that Kansk belonged among the impoverished stagnant little towns famed only for an abundance of taverns. It's unlikely he'd change his view if he visited today.

❑ **Ėvenki National Okrug**

About nine hundred kilometres due north of here lies the town of Tura, the capital of the **Evenki National Okrug**, 745,000 square kilometres of permanently frozen land, specially reserved for the indigenous population. The **Evenkis** belong to the Tungus group of people (the names are often used interchangeably) and they were originally nomadic herders and hunters. After the Buryats and the Yakuts, they form the next largest ethnic group in Siberia but they are scattered into small groups, right across the northern regions. They used to live in wigwams or tents and survived off berries and reindeer-meat (a great delicacy being the raw marrow sucked straight from the bone, preferably while it was still warm). They discovered that Christianity fitted in well with their own Shamanistic religion and worshipped St Nicholas as deputy to the Master Spirit of the Underworld. After the Revolution they were organised into collective farms and although most of the population is now settled, there are still some reindeer-herders in the extreme north of the region.

Km4375: Ilanskaya Иланская (●●) (pop: 18,000) The site of the town was selected in 1734 by the Dutch-born Russian naval explorer V Bering (of Bering Straits fame) during the Second Kamchatski Expedition to explore the coast of America. It may seem strange that Bering was surveying central Siberia but he was ordered to make himself useful as he crossed the country to the Russian Far East. There is a **museum** at the locomotive depot with a display of the history of the town.

Between here and Taishet, there are large deposits of brown coal. Our provodnitsa was well aware of this last bit of information and issued four of us with buckets to collect coal (for the carriage boiler) from the piles lying about the platform.

Km4453: Reshoti Решоты This is the junction for the line south to Abakan, an industrial centre in the foothills of the Sayan Mountains.

Km4473: Uralo-Klyuchi Урало-Ключи This small station's name translates as the 'key to the Urals' and it sits near the administrative frontier between Irkutsk and Krasnoyarsk oblasts.

Local time is now Moscow Time + 5 hours. The railway gradually swings round from the east to the south-east as you head towards Irkutsk. For the next 600km you will pass through one of Russia's biggest logging areas. Many of the rivers are used to float down the logs and you can often see log packs being towed down the river or the piles of loose logs washed up on the river banks. This section of the line is very scenic as the train is constantly climbing and descending as it crosses numerous rivers and deep ravines.

Kms4501-02: The river here conveniently marks the **half-way point** for the Moscow to Beijing (via Manchuria) run.

Km4516: Taishet Тайшет (●) This town is at the junction of the Trans-Siberian and BAM (Baikal to Amur Mainline) railways. The 3400km BAM line (see p123) traverses Siberia from the Pacific Ocean to Lake Baikal, and is the gateway to the rarely visited region known as the BAM Zone. The single track line is about 600 to 1000km north of the Trans-Siberian Railway, running parallel to it through pristine taiga, mountain tundra and wide river valley meadows. B e f o r e the 1970s, the BAM Zone was virtually uninhabited taiga dotted with the villages of indigenous people. Today it has a population of about 300,000 involved in extracting natural resources from the region's enormous reserves. Only about 100 Westerners visit the region each year.

Taishet was founded when the Trans-Siberian arrived in 1897. There is nothing to see in the town even though it is famous in Soviet gulag literature. Taishet was a transit camp for Stalin-era prisoners heading east and west, and was a major camp of Ozerlag, the gulag complex which built the Taishet-Bratsk section of the BAM. The building of this section started in earnest following the end of WWII and at the height of construction, there were over 300 camps dotted along the 350km from Taishet to Bratsk with a total population of 100,000 prisoners. In *The Gulag*

MAP 9

Archipelago, Solzhenitsyn wrote that Taishet had a factory for creosoting railroad ties 'where, they say, creosote penetrates the skin and bones and its vapours fill the lungs – and that is death'. The factory which makes the ties (railway sleepers) still operates.

Km4555 (S): Razgon Разгон A small, poor-looking community of log cabins. About a kilometre east of here, the line rises and there are views across the taiga at Km4563 (S), Km4569 (N) and Km4570.

Km4631: Kamyshet Камышет It was here that George Kennan stopped in 1887 for repairs to his tarantass. While the wheel was being replaced, he watched the amazing spectacle of a Siberian blacksmith shoeing a horse. 'The poor beast had been hoisted by means of two broad belly-bands and suspended from a stout frame so that he could not touch the ground', he wrote. Three of the horse's legs had been secured to the frame and 'the daring blacksmith was fearlessly putting a shoe on the only hoof that the wretched and humiliated animal could move'.

Kms4640-4680: The train snakes its way through the foothills of the Eastern Sayan Mountains. The Sayan Mountain Range forms a natural frontier between Siberia and Mongolia.

At Kms4648-9, you have reached the **half-way point** on the line from Moscow to Vladivostok. There are some good views and a number of chances to take photographs of the whole length of the train as it winds around the valleys. The best spots are around Km4657 (S), Km4660 (S), Kms4662-5 and Km4667.

Km4680: Nizhneudinsk Нижнеудинск (●●) (pop: 44,000) The area's best known for saw-mills, swamps and insects. Of the mosquitoes, Kennan complained 'I found myself blotted from head to foot as if I were suffering from some eruptive disease.' Near Nizhneudinsk is a famous Siberian beauty spot, the **Ukovsky Waterfall**, 18km upstream along the Ude River which flows through Nizhneudinsk. About 75km further upstream are the **Nizhneudinski Caves**, which contain ancient paintings.

❑ **The Tunguska Event**
About 800km due north of here, on 30 June 1908, one of the largest (pre-atomic era) explosions in human history took place, in the Tunguska River region. Two thousand square kilometres of forest were instantly destroyed in what came to be known as the Tunguska Event. The sound of the explosion was heard up to 350kms away, the shock waves were registered on seismic equipment right around the world, and the light from the blast was seen throughout Europe.

Newspapers of the time proposed all kinds of theories to explain its cause, from the testing of new explosives to crash-landing Martian space-ships. Scientists now believe that it was caused by a fragment of Encke's Comet, which disintegrated as it entered the Earth's atmosphere, creating a vast fireball.

Siberia's smallest indigenous group, the Tofalar (Tofy), live in the isolated village of Tofalariya, 200km from Nizhneudinsk. Only 500 remain, all living in and around this little settlement. There are no roads to this village and its only regular link with the rest of the world is the helicopter service from Nizhneudinsk.

Between Nizhneudinsk and Irkutsk the country becomes flatter and the taiga not so thick. The train passes through numerous timber-yards.

Km4789 (S): There is a large **graveyard** with a blue fence around it, standing close to the line. Some of the graves are topped with red stars, some with red crosses. Kennan wrote in 1887: 'The graveyards belonging to the Siberian settlements sometimes seemed to me much more remarkable and noteworthy than the settlements themselves.....Many graves (are) marked by three armed wooden crosses and covered with narrow A-shaped roofs.'

Km4794: Tulun Тулун (pop: 53,800) Tulun sits at the road junction of the M55 Moscow-Irkutsk Highway and the main road to the city of Bratsk, 225km to the north. Near the station is the town's centre which still consists of wooden houses. Tulun has a Decembrists museum.

The line follows the river, crossing it at Km4800 and passing a large saw-mill at Km4804 (S) which might make a good photo with the town behind it. For once there are no wires to get in the way. At Km4809 (S) there is a large open-cast mine. You pass through an area of large cultivated fields.

Km4875: Kuytun Куйтун The town's name means 'cold' in the language of the local Buryat people (see p336). There are cold springs in the area.

Km4940: Zima Зима (●●●) (460m/1500ft, pop: 39,400) Zima means 'winter' and this was a place of exile at the beginning of the 19th centu-

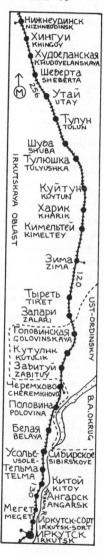

MAP 10

ry for members of the Sectarian sect. When the Tsarevich Nicholas visited Zima on 8 July 1891, the Buryats presented him with a model yurt (tent) cast in silver.

About 3km to the east of the town, the railway crosses the 790km long Oka River. The river runs brown as it cuts through seams of coal and copperas (ferrous sulphate). The mineral rich water and earth have their benefits as the water was used to blacken tanned animal skins, and during epidemics of cholera, the copperas earth was used as disinfectant. However it also causes goitre which many locals suffer from today. Down the Oka River near the village of Burluksk on the river banks are 1000 year old petroglylphs of cattle, horses and their riders.

As the line rises out of one valley, crosses the watershed and drops down to the next river you get several reasonable views: Km4958 (S), Km4972 (N), Km4977 (S) and Km4990 (S).

Km5000-40 You pass through the Ust-Ordinski Autonomous Okrug. There's another graveyard close to the track at Km5010 (S).

Km5027: Kutulik Кутулик This station is the biggest railway town in the **Ust-Orda Buryat Nationality District**. The Ust-Orda Buryats are related to the Buryats to the east of Lake Baikal and to the Mongolians but they have a different language and culture. The best time to be here is during the harvest festival of Surkharban when there are races, archery competitions and the Ust-Orda's peculiar brand of wrestling. Kutulik has a museum which contains information on the Ust-Orda Buryats.

Km5061: Cheremkhovo Черемхово (pop: 73,500) The town revolves around the Cheremkhovo coal deposit, and various mining and industrial complexes are dotted along 10km of the railway. The first mine can be seen from the railway about 20km east of the station.

Thirty-one km to the south is **Belsk (Бельск)** where a blackened watchtower is all that remains of a wooden Cossack fortress built in 1691.

Km5087: Polovina Половина The station's name means 'half' and it once marked the halfway point on the Trans-Siberian between Moscow and Vladivostok. Today Moscow is 5,090km away and Vladivostok is 4,212km. The reason for this discrepancy is that the station was named at a time when the Trans-Siberian ran to Moscow via Chelyabinsk and not Ekaterinburg and to Vladivostok via Manchuria, not along the banks of the Amur.

Km5100: Malta Мальта
It was in a house in Malta, in February 1928, that farmer Platon Brilin was helping a comrade to build a cellar. While he was digging, his spade struck a white object which turned out to be a mammoth tusk carved into

a female form. Excavations revealed dwellings with walls made from mammoth bones and roofs of antlers. He had discovered the remains of an ancient settlement, dating from the thirteenth millennium BC. A grave yielded the body of a child, still wearing a necklace and headband of bones. He may have been a young shaman (see p229) for the gods were thought to select their earthly representatives by branding them with some kind of deformity: the boy has two sets of teeth. Numerous figurines made of ivory have been found at Malta and also at the site in Buret, eight kilometres from here. Many of the excavated artefacts may be seen in the museums in Irkutsk. The oldest settlement in the CIS that has so far been discovered is at Dering Yuryakh (1-2.5 million years old) in northern Siberia near Yakutsk.

Km5124: Usole-Sibirskoe Усолье-Сибирское (pop: 106,900) This

city, sitting on the left bank (western side) of the Angara River, is the salt capital of Siberia. However don't expect to find Siberian salt mines here. Until 1956, all salt was produced by pumping salty water from shallow wells into pans; the water was then left to evaporate. These can still be seen on the left bank of the Angara River and on Varnichnoe Island. Nowadays the salt is produced at the **salt factory**, the biggest in Russia. It manufactures the Russian Extra brand of table salt, common throughout the entire former Soviet Union. The town's other big industrial plant is the 150 year old **match factory**. Nearby is the **Usolye Health Resort** offers salt, sulphur and mud baths to cure afflictions of the limbs.

On the opposite side of the river is the nearly abandoned village of **Alekandrovskoe** which was renowned for the particularly brutal conditions of its Tsarist prison founded in 1873. In 1902 a failed revolt broke out here led by Felix Dzerzhinski. Many of the participants in the failed 1905 Revolution were imprisoned here.

Km5130 (N) There is a large oil refinery here.

Km5133: Telma Тельма Siberia's first textile mill opened here in

1731 and it still operates today, producing work clothing.

Km5160: Angarsk Ангарск (●) (pop: 268,000) Although primarily

an industrial city, Angarsk is well-planned and still very attractive as the industrial and civic parts of it are separated by a wide green belt. From the station, the industrial part is on the left (eastern side) and the civic part on the right. Angarsk's major industry is oil refining and oil is pumped here by pipeline from the West Siberian, Tatarstan and Baskir oil fields. This pipeline can occasionally be spotted running beside the railway.

The city has a river port and from here hydrofoils travel downstream to Bratsk. Ferries also run between Irkutsk and Angarsk, and coming here from Irkutsk makes a pleasant day trip.

❑ **How the post was sent to Siberia**

The building of the Trans-Siberian Railway revolutionised the carrying of mail across the vast Siberian steppes. By 1902 a letter could be carried from St Petersburg to Vladivostok in less than two weeks instead of several months as previously. The first Siberian letter on record was that carried to Moscow in 1582 by some of Yermak's Cossacks, informed Tsar Ivan the Terrible that Siberia was now his. A regular postal system had been established in Siberia by 1600, Russian peasants being encouraged to emigrate to Siberia to work as Post House keepers and post-riders or *yamshchiki* (see p94). The post always had priority for the supply of horses and for right of way on the new post roads. Each Post House keeper had to keep some horses permanently in reserve in case the post should arrive, and on the road a blast of the courier's horn was enough to make other road users pull over and allow the post to pass. Indeed, the yamshchiki were not averse to using their whip on the drivers of carts which were slow to move out of the way.

In April 1829 the German writer, Adolph Erman, travelling down the still-frozen Lena River from Irkutsk to Yakutsk, wrote that he had "the good luck of meeting the postman from Yakutsk and Kamchatka. At my desire he waited until the frozen ink which I carried with me had time to thaw, and a few lines to friends in Berlin were written and committed to his care. The courier, or paid overseer who attended the mail from Yakutsk to Irkutsk carried, as a mark of his rank and office, a sword and a loaded pistol, hanging by a chain from his neck. In winter he obtains from the peasants the requisite supply of sledges and horses; and when the ice-road is broken up he takes boats, sometimes, to ascend the Lena" (*Travels in Siberia*).

By the time Annette Meakin travelled along the Trans-Siberian Railway in 1900, she was able to send letters home speedily by train, but she had evidently heard about dishonest postal officials and she took pains to register all her letters. In *A Ribbon of Iron*, she wrote "If you do not register in Siberia there is every chance that the stamps will be taken and the letter destroyed long before it reaches the border. You cannot register after 2pm, in which case it is advisable to use a black-edged envelope. Superstition will then prevent its being tampered with". Black-edged envelopes were used during a period of mourning.

Much of the mail still travels by train, and passenger trains in Siberia often include a travelling post office coach in which mail is sorted. These have an aperture at platform level, through which letters and cards can be posted.

Philip Robinson (UK)

Philatelists may be interested to know that Philip Robinson is the author of *Russian Postmarks* and *Siberia – Postmarks and Postal History of the Russian Empire Period*. Enquiries to the address on p2 concerning these books will be forwarded to the author.

Km5170: Meget Мегет Just north of Meget, travellers have reported a large strategic reserve (N) of L and Ye 2-10-0s steam engines.

Km5178: Irkutsk Sortirovka Иркутск Сортировка This marshalling yard used to be a small station known as Innokentievskaya, in honour of St Innocent, Archbishop of Irkutsk, who was said to have been the first miracle-worker in Siberia. The **St Innocent Monastery of the Ascension** near here was founded in 1672. The Tsar stopped here on his tour of Siberia in 1891 and the visit was thus described: 'After having listened to the singing, the Tsarevich (sic) knelt at the shrine of the Siberian Saint, kissed the relics and received the image of Innocent, presented to him by Agathangelius, Vicar of Irkutsk. At the same time a deputation from the Shaman Buryats expressed the desire of 250 men to adopt the orthodox religion and to receive the name of Nicholas in commemoration of the Tsarevich's visit to Siberia, which was thus to be preserved in the memory of their descendants. The Imperial traveller graciously acceded to this request.'

Km5185: Irkutsk Иркутск (●●●) [see p220]
(440m/1450ft, pop: 639,000)   Once known as the 'Paris of Siberia' Irkutsk is still a fascinating place and just 65km away is the beautiful Lake Baikal. From the railway you cannot see much of the centre of Irkutsk, located on the other side of the Angara River. In the distance, however, you can see the large Church of the Elevation of the Cross.

Km5214: Goncharovo Гончарово (pop: 49,300)   The town around the station is named Shelekhov (Шелехов) after the Russian merchant who led several trading expeditions to North America in the 1780s. He was made governor of the Russian settlement in America and become one of the richest merchants in Siberia, basing his empire in Irkutsk.

Passing through Goncharovo, you can see the town's main industry, the giant Irkutsk Aluminium Complex, founded in 1956. The train soon starts twisting and turning as it climbs the Primorski Mountains.

Winding through valleys of cedar and pine, and crossing numerous small streams, the train passes **Kultuk**, the junction for the old line from Port Baikal. At Km5228 (N) a giant etching of Lenin waves nonchalantly from the hill above. The line climbs steeply to Km5254 and then snakes downwards giving you your **first glimpses of Lake Baikal** from Kms5274-8. After the tunnel (Km5290) there is a splendid view over the lake at Km5292 (N).

Km5297-8: There is a tunnel as the line curves sharply round the valley and descends to the water's edge. After the junction and goods yard at **Slyudyanka II** (Km5305) the train crawls along a part of the line that is prone to flooding from the lake, and into the main station.

Km5312: Slyudyanka 1 Слюдянка 1 (●●●) (pop: 20,100) As the station is only about 500m from the lake there is just enough time to run down to the water and dip your hand in for good luck (see p236). Check with the carriage attendant that the train is stopping for the usual 15 minutes and hurry down between the log cabins to the lake. You must be

❏ The Circumbaikal Line

The original line from Irkutsk did not follow the route of the present railway but ran to Port Baikal. Until 1904 passengers crossed Lake Baikal on ferries which took them from Port Baikal to Mysovaya. In 1893 it had been decided that this short section of line along the mountainous southern shore of the lake would be impossibly expensive to build, and the plan was shelved in favour of the ferry link. From the English company of Armstrong and Mitchell a specially designed combined ice-breaker and train-ferry was ordered. The 4200 ton ship, christened the *Baikal*, had three pairs of rails laid across her decks for the carriages and could smash through ice up to four feet thick. A sister ship, the *Angara*, was soon brought into service. This ship has now been converted into a museum and is moored in Irkutsk (see p230).

The ferry system was not a great success, however. In mid-winter the ships were unable to break through the ice and in summer the wild storms for which the lake is notorious often delayed them. Since they could not accommodate more than 300 people between them, many passengers were subjected to a long wait beside the lake. The Trans-Siberian Committee realised that, however expensive it might prove, a line had to be built to bridge the 260km gap between the Mid-Siberian and the Transbaikal Railways. Further surveys were ordered in 1898 and in 1901 ten thousand labourers started work on the line.

This was the most difficult section to build on the entire railway. The terrain between Port Baikal and Kultuk (near Slyudyanka) was virtually one long cliff. Thirty-three tunnels and more than two hundred bridges and trestles were constructed, the task being made all the more difficult by the fact that in many places the labourers could reach the route only by boat. Work was carried on simultaneously on the Tankhoi to Mysovaya section.

The labour gangs hacked out embankments and excavated seven kilometres of tunnels but the line was not ready at the time it was most needed. On 8 February 1904, Japan attacked the Russian Navy while it lay at anchor in Port Arthur on the Pacific. Troops were rushed by rail from European Russia but when they arrived at Port Baikal, they found the *Baikal* and *Angara* ice-bound in the severe weather. The only way across the lake was a seventeen-hour march over the ice. It was then that the Minister of Ways of Communication, Prince Khilkov, put into action a plan which had been successful on several of Siberia's rivers: rails were laid across the ice. The first train to set off across the frozen lake did not get far along the forty-five kilometre track before the ice gave way with a crack like a cannon and the locomotive sank into the icy water. From then on the engines had to be stripped and their parts put on flat-cars that were pulled over the ice by gangs of men and horses.

Working as fast as possible, in all weathers, the Circumbaikal line was completed in September 1904 at a cost of about 70 million roubles. The first passengers found this section of the line particularly terrifying, not on account of the frequent derailments but because of the tunnels: there were none in European Russia at that time.

In the 1950s a short cut was opened between Irkutsk and Slyudyanka, which is the route followed by the train today. The line between Irkutsk and Port Baikal is now partly flooded and no longer used. Much of the Port Baikal to Kultuk section, however, is still operational. See p237 for more information.

quick; some people have been left behind. If you're not feeling energetic there are usually interesting things to buy on the platform – sometimes even omul and boiled potatoes, or raspberries and bags of *orecha* (cedars seeds, the classic Siberian snack).

Although there are some photogenic log cabins near the station, Slyudyanka is a rather unattractive mining town; it does, however, have a basic hotel should you miss your train. It's a starting point for hikers and rafters who travel through the Khamar-Daban Mountain Range to the south. Fur-trappers hunt sable and ermine in the forests around this area.

FromSlyudyanka, the 94km **Circumbaikal Railway** branch line runs along the shore of Lake Baikal to Port Baikal.

The train passes through a short tunnel and runs within sight of the water's edge for the next 180km. Some of the best views on the whole trip are along this section of the line.

Km5358: Baikalsk Байкальск (pop: 16,700)
There is a basic hotel here, a base for walks and rafting in the Khamar-Daban Mountains.

About 3km past the town on the left is Lake Baikal's biggest environmental problem: the **Baikalsk Cellulose and Paper Combine**, which makes an extremely strong cellulose used in aircraft tyres and pumps its chlorine contaminated waste water directly into the lake. This has caused the number of crustacean species within a 50km radius of the factory to drop from 57 to 5. Because of the enormous cost of upgrading the plant, and the loss of revenue to the government in closing it down, this destructive operation continues unabated. Not surprisingly, it was the brainchild of that environmental vandal Khrushchev who wanted to 'put Baikal to work'.

Km5390: Vydrino Выдрино
The river just before the station marks the border of the **Buryat Republic**. This region, which is also known as Buryatia comprises an area of about 350,000

MAP 11

square kilometres (about the size of Italy). It was originally set aside for the Buryats (see p332), an indigenous ethnic group once nomadic but now adapted to an agricultural or urban life. Their republic is composed of mountainous taiga, and the economy is based on fur-farming, stock-raising, food and timber-processing and the mining of gold, aluminium, manganese, iron, coal, asbestos and mica. In fact almost all the elements can be found here.

Km5421 (N): The lonely-looking collection of ramshackle buildings by the water's edge might make a good photograph.

Km5426: Tankhoi Танхой (pop: 3000) Tankhoi sits in the middle of the 263,300ha Baikalski Nature Reserve which was created to preserve the Siberian taiga. Occasional ferries travel from here to Listvyanka and Port Baikal.

When Prince Borghese and his team were motoring through this area in 1907, taking part in the Peking to Paris Rally, they found that since the building of the railway, the Great Siberian Post Road had fallen into dis-repair. Most of the post-stations were deserted and many of the bridges were rotten and dangerous. The Italians were given special permission by the governor-general to use the railway bridges. In fact they covered a considerable part of the journey here by driving along the railway line. However, their 40 horsepower Itala was not the only unorthodox vehicle to take to the rails. On his cycle-tour through south Siberia in 1896, RL Jefferson found it rather easier to pedal his Imperial Rover along the tracks than along the muddy roads.

Km5477: Mysovaya Мысовая (pop: 7200) This was the port where the *Baikal* and *Angara* (see p339) delivered their passengers (and their train).

When Annette Meakin and her mother disembarked from the *Baikal* in 1900, they were horrified to discover that the awaiting train was composed entirely of fourth class carriages. The brave ladies commandeered seats in the corner of one compartment but soon they were hemmed in by emigrating peasants. When two dirty moujiks climbed into the luggage rack above them, the ladies decided it would be better to wait at Mysovaya than spend four days in such claustrophobic conditions, and got out. However, the station-master allowed them to travel in an empty luggage-van, which gave them privacy but not comfort.

The village surrounding the town is known as Babushkin (Бабушкин) in honour of Lenin's friend and Irkutsk revolutionary. Ivan Babushkin was executed by Tsarist forces at the railway depot in 1906 and an obelisk marks the spot. While Mysovaya is still a major Baikal port, over 70% of the village's population works for the railways.

Between Mysovaya and Petrovsky Zavod the line skirts around the lower reaches of the Khamar Daban Mountain Range. Around Km5536, the line enters the wide valley of the Selenga River, which it follows as far as Ulan Ude (Km5642).

Km5504: Boyarski Боярский
The hills on the right of the station are all that remain of the volcanoes of the Khamar-Daban foothills. East of the station, the railway moves away from Lake Baikal.

Km5530: Posolskaya Посольская
About 500m west of this station, the train crosses over a narrow, shallow river with the odd name of Bolshaya Rechka (Big Little Stream). Approximately 10km downstream from here the river flows into Lake Baikal at the site of the ancient village of Possolskoe. In previous centuries, Russian ambassadors travelling to Asian countries used to rest here and the rough village got a mention in the papers of Ambassador Fyodor Baikov when he visited it in 1656. In 1681, an abbot and a monk built a large walled monastery here but it has long since disappeared. Today Bolshaya Rechka hosts the Baikalski Priboi (Baikal Surf) Holiday Camp.

The small settlement around Posolskaya station was the site of a brief skirmish between US forces and anti-communist forces in 1920 which claimed two American lives.

❏ **American soldiers die defending communists**
During the Russian Civil War, American, Canadian and Japanese troops occupied parts of eastern Siberia and the Russian Far East helping the White Russian forces battling the communists. The undisciplined White Russians were often little more than bandits and murderers, and the allied forces were often put in the difficult position of supporting the White Army while trying to protect the Russian population from them. What happened at Posolskaya station in January 1920 was just one of many unpleasant incidents that resulted in the allied forces losing complete faith in the White Army.

The White Army General Nicholas Bogomolets arrested the station master at Ulan Ude and announced that he would execute him for Bolshevist activities. The American Colonel Morrow, based in Ulan Ude, threatened to call out 2500 soldiers under his command unless the innocent man was released. Bogomolets retreated with the railway official to Posolskaya in his armoured train, where he opened fire in the middle of the night on the boxcar barracks of a small American garrison comprising one officer and 38 enlisted men. These soldiers swarmed out of their quarters, dropped into a skirmish line and blazed away. Sergeant Carl Robbins disabled the train's locomotive with a hand grenade before being killed. At the cost of two dead and one wounded on their side, the Americans captured the train, the general, six other officers and 48 men.

Bogomolets was released for political reasons and emigrated to Hollywood before being deported to Latvia. Sergeant Robbins and Second Lieutenant Paul Kendall posthumously received the Distinguished Service Cross.

❏ **The Buryats**

The largest ethnic minority group in Siberia, these people are of Mongolian descent. When Russian colonists arrived in the lands around Lake Baikal, the Buryats were nomads who spent their time herding their flocks between the southern shores of the lake and what is now northern Mongolia, in search of pastureland. They lived in felt-covered yurts and practiced a mixture of Buddhism and Shamanism.

The Buryats lived on fish from Lake Baikal, bear-meat and berries. However, their favourite food was said to be *urme*, the thick dried layer of scum skimmed from the top of boiled milk. They hunted the Baikal seal for its fur and in winter, when the lake was frozen, they would track these animals on the ice, wearing white clothing and pushing a white sledge as a hide. Back in their *yurts* the Buryats were not the cleanest of Siberian tribes, lacking even the most basic hygiene as the anthropologists Levin and Potapov point out in *The Peoples of Siberia*. Describing an after-dinner scene, they wrote: 'The vessels were not washed, as the spoons and cups were licked clean. An unwashed vessel was often passed from one member of the family to another as was the smoking pipe. Customs of this kind promoted the spread of various diseases.' Most of the diseases were probably brought by the Russian colonists.

Although at first hostile to the Russian colonists, the Buryats became involved in the fur-trade with the Europeans and a certain amount of inter-marriage occurred. Some gave up their nomadic life and felt-covered *yurts* in favour of log cabins in Verkhneudinsk (now Ulan Ude) or Irkutsk. The Buryats, who number about 350,000, now have their own **Buryat Republic**, around the southern part of Lake Baikal. The capital, Ulan Ude, was opened to tourists in 1990 and is an interesting place to visit.

Km5562: Selenga Селенга   The town was founded as a stockaded outpost in the 17th century on the Selenga River. Unfortunately the wood-pulping factories are rather more in evidence than the 16th century monastery which was the centre for missionaries attempting the conversion of the Buryats. The factories here and in Ulan Ude are notorious for pumping their industrial waste into the Selenga River which flows into Lake Baikal. Pollution from the Selenga and the cellulose and paper mill at Baikalsk has affected over 60% of the lake and even if the pollution stopped tomorrow, it would take 400 years for the waste to be flushed out.

Km5596: Lesovozny Лесовозный   The town around the station is called Ilnika (Ильинка). About 28km east of the station, the train crosses over Selenga River which provides an excellent photo opportunity. At Km5633-4 (N) there's an army camp with some abandoned tanks.

The train approaches Ulan Ude along the right bank (northern side) of the Selenga River and about 1km on the left before the station is a monument to five railway workers executed by the Tsarist forces in 1906 for revolutionary activities.

Km5642: Ulan Ude Улан-Уде (●●●) [see p242]
(544m/1785ft, pop: 366,000)   Ulan Ude is the capital of the Buryat Republic. Stretch your legs on the platform where there is a **steam loco** preserved outside the locomotive workshop (N) at the western end of the station. Turn to p358 for the **Trans-Mongolian route to Beijing**.

Two km east of the station, you cross over Uda River and after another 500m, you can see the Palace of Culture (N) and a WWII memorial.

Km5655: Zaudinski Заудинский   The line to Mongolia branches off from the Trans-Siberian here.

Km5675 (N): Onokhoi Онохой   There is a large number of **steam locos** at the west end of the station. From Onokhoi, the train follows the valley of the river Brian. From Zaigraevo (Km5696), the line begins to climb to Ilka, on the river of the same name. It continues to ascend the Zagon Dar range, reaching the highest point (882m/2892ft) at Kizha.

Km5734: Novoilinski Новоильинский   About 20km past this station, the train crosses the **administrative frontier** between the Republic of Buryatia and Chitinskaya Oblast. The 432,000 square kilometres of the Chitinskaya Oblast comprise a series of mountain ranges interspersed with wide valleys. The dominant range is the Yablonovy (highest peak: Sokhondo, 2510m/8200ft) which is crossed by the Trans-Siberian near Amazar. The mountains are covered in a vast forest of conifers and the climate is dry. The economy is based on mining (gold, tungsten, tin, lead, zinc, molybdenum, lithium, lignite), timber-processing and fur-farming.

─────── **Km 5756-8150 TIME ZONE MT + 6** ───────

Km5784: Petrovski Zavod Петровский Завод (●●●) (pop 28,300)
Local time is now Moscow Time + 6 hours. The name of the station means 'Peter's Factory', after the ironworks founded in 1789 and still going strong. It was built to supply iron for the gold mines in the region. The factory was rebuilt in 1939 next to the railway and from the train you can see the flames from the open-hearth furnaces.

In 1830, the factory was operated by Decembrists brought from nearby Chita and housed in the factory prison. A **monument** and large memorial to them can be seen on the station's platform. There is also a **Decembrist museum** in the former house of Ekaterina Trubetskoi. Princess Trubetskoi (1800-1854) was the first wife of a Decembrist to voluntarily follow her husband into exile. In doing so, she renounced her civil rights and noble privileges. Her name is immortalised in *Russian Women*, a poem by Nekrasov.

Stretching along the railway in the narrow river valley between the mountain ridges, the town makes an interesting day-trip from Chita.

❏ **The Transbaikal Railway (Kms5483-6532)**
In 1895 work was begun to connect Mysovaya (the port on Lake Baikal) with Sretensk, on the Shilka River near Kuenga, where passengers boarded steamers for the voyage to Khabarovsk. Materials were shipped to Vladivostok and thence by boat along the Ussuri, Amur and Shilka Rivers. There was a shortage of labour, for it proved impossible to get the local Buryats to work on the line. Gangs of reluctant convicts were brought in, although they became more interested in the operation after it was decided that they should receive 50 kopecks a day in return for their labour.

The terrain is mountainous and the line meanders up several valleys and over the Yablonovy range. Owing to the dry climate, work could continue throughout the winter, although water was in short supply during these months. Workers were also faced with the problem of permafrost which necessitated the building of bonfires to thaw the ground, or dynamite to break it up. A terrible setback occurred in July 1887, when 350km of track and several bridges were swept away in a freak flood. The line was completed in early 1900 by which time it had cost over 60 million roubles.

East of Petrovsky Zavod, the line turns north-east into the wide, picturesque valley of the Khilok River, which it follows for almost 300kms to Sokhondo, crossing the Yablonovy range between Mogzon and Chita.

Km5883: Look out for the large graveyard of old steam locomotives.

Km5884: Bada Aeroport Бада Аэропорт The little town is clearly a product of the aerodrome and not vice versa: it's built around a large Soviet monument, a Mig fighter plane facing skyward. The runway (N) is interesting for the large numbers of old aircraft that congregate here. These might make an interesting photograph but discretion is advised.

Km5899 (S): A good place for a photo along the train as it travels on higher ground beside the river. Also at Km5908 (S), when the train winds slowly along the water's edge.

Km5932: Khilok Хилок (●) (805m/2640ft, pop: 13,700) East of this small industrial town you continue to climb gently up the valley beside the Khilok. There are pleasant views over the wide plain all along the river. North of the line are the Khogoy and Shentoy mountains, part of the Tsagan Khuntei range. Near the station a granite monument topped with a star commemorates 11 communists slain here during the Civil War.

The train now crosses the Yablonovy Mountains. The eastern escarpment is steeper than the western side and heavy freight trains travelling westwards invariably require extra engines.

Km6053: Mogzon Могзон (●●) (907m/2975ft) There's a steam dump here and, for several km around this town, a number of heavily guarded prisons (Km6055 (N) is one example).

Km6093: Sokhondo Сохондо (944m/3,095ft)
This station is named after the highest peak
(2510m/8230ft) in the Yablonovy range. The line
leaves the river valley and climbs over the
Yablonovy. There is a long view at Km6097 (N).
About 7km east of here you reach the **highest
point on the line** (989m/ 3242ft). In the 1914 edition of his *Russia with Teheran, Port Arthur and
Peking*, Karl Baedeker drew his readers' attention
to the '93 yard tunnel inscribed at its western
entrance "To the Great Ocean" and at its eastern
entrance "To the Atlantic Ocean" in Russian', that
was here. The line has now been re-routed up
onto a huge grassy plain. It then descends steeply
through Yablonovaya and there are several good
views (Kms6107-9).

Km6116 (S): There was a graveyard of **steam
locomotives** here but now most of the engines
have been dismantled. West of the town of
Ingoda, the train enters the narrow winding valley
of the Ingoda River, which it follows for the next
250km east. The line passes through Chernov-
skaya, where lignite is mined.

Km6125: Yablonovaya (Яблоновая)
About 20km south in the settlement of Drov-
yanaya (Дровяная) are 50 nuclear missile silos
which house SS-17 or SS-19 inter-ballistic
nuclear rockets.

Km6131 (S): The line crosses a picturesque
meadow with a stream meandering across it.
Good for a photograph when the flowers are out
in May and June.

Km6197: (N) About 2km west of Chita is the 16
square kilometre Kenon Lake. Only 6m deep, the
lake is warmed by the nearby power station and at
its eastern end there's a popular beach beside the
railway line.

Further on the train crosses the small Chita
River, and about 1km before the main station you
pass through Chita 1 station where a railway factory is located.

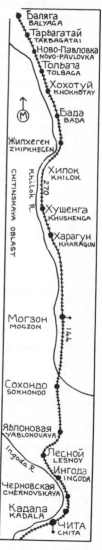

MAP 12

Km6199: Chita Чита (●●●) [see p249]

(655m/2150ft, pop: 376,000) Founded in 1655, the capital of the Chitinskaya Oblast stands beside the Chita and Ingoda rivers, surrounded by low hills. A stockaded fort was built here by the Cossacks at the end of the 17th century and the town became an important centre on the Chinese trade route. In 1827 a large group of exiled Decembrists arrived here and spent the first few months building the prison that was to be their home for the following three years. Many stayed on after they had served their sentence and the development of the town in the 19th century into an industrial and cultural centre was largely due to their efforts.

East of the city of Chita, the train continues to follow the left bank of the Ingoda River downhill, for the next 250kms. The line passes through **Novaya**, where the original community and the whole of the town were wiped out in the great flood of 1897. At Km6225 (S) there's a collection of log cabins (some of them quite photogenic), which look rather vulnerable, being built on the edge of the river flood plain.

Km6265: Darasun Дарасун (●)
Darasun is renowned for its carbonic mineral springs and the water from them has been exported to China and Korea for years. Near the station is a sanatorium where various cardiovascular and intestinal ailments are treated.

About 1km east of the station there's a good view as the train snakes along the river.

Km6270:
Army supply base surrounded by a wooden stockade.

Km6293: Karymskaya Карымская (●●●)
(605m/1985ft) Small industrial town first settled by the Buryats.

Km6312: Tarskaya Тарская
Formerly known as Kaidalovo, this is the junction for the railway to Beijing via Manchuria (see p368). A whitewashed church stands on the hill (S) above the village. Good views along the river at Km6316 (S) and across the wide plains for the next 100km, especially around Km6332 (S) and Km6369 (S). There are large fields around the river and bare hills to the north. The best views are all to the south, across to Mongolia.

Km6417: Onon Онон (515m/1690ft)
A few kilometres east of here the clear waters of the Ingoda River are joined by those of the muddy Onon, on whose banks the great Mongol leader, Genghis Khan, was born in 1162. The Onon and the Ingoda together form the Shilka River, a tributary of the mighty Amur. The railway follows the picturesque valley of the Shilka for the next 120kms.

Km6446: Shilka Шилка (●●●) (505m/1655ft, pop: 18,200)
This village on the Shilka River was founded in 1897 just to serve the railway.

Two years later it became a popular tourist destination with the opening of the Shivanda Health Resort (*shivanda* means royal drink in the local indigenous language). Mineral water was and still is used to treat digestive and respiratory system disorders. A few years later the discovery of gold nearby brought more visitors. In 1954 fluoric spar, a mineral essential in chemistry and metallurgy, was discovered in the area.

There are several interesting-looking wooden buildings near the platform.

Crossing the Kiya River, the train crosses a great wide plain, grazing land for cattle that you may see being rounded up on horseback.

Km6496: Priiskavaya Приисковая The
name means a mine, referring to the gold mining town of **Nerchinsk (Нерчинск)**, 10km down a branch line from here. It was here that the Treaty of Nerchinsk was signed in 1689, depriving the Russians of the valuable Amur region. The treaty gave the Manchurian emperor control over the Russian Far East for the next 170 years.

Nerchinsk was the centre of a rich silver, lead and gold mining district in Tsarist times. The mines were known to the Buryats long before the arrival of the Russians in the seventeenth century. In 1700, a Greek mining engineer founded the Nerchinski Zavod (Works) and the first convict gangs arrived in 1722. George Kennan visited the mine in 1887 and was shown around by one of the convict labourers. Not all the mines were the property of the Tsar and some owners became immensely wealthy. In one mansion he visited in Nerchinsk, Kennan could hardly believe that such opulence and luxury (tapestries, chandeliers, Oriental rugs, silk curtains and a vast ball-room) were to be found in one of the wildest parts of Siberia. From 1826 to 1917, Nerchinsk's mines were a major Tsarist's labour camp.

Today Nerchinsk has 17,000 inhabitants and some interesting sights. These include the early

MAP 13

19th century Resurrection Cathedral and the house of rich merchant, Butin, which was built in the popular Moorish style in the 1860s. Next door is the Hotel Dauriya (closed) where Chekhov stayed in 1890. There is a museum and basic hotel in Nerchinsk.

On the south side of Priiskavaya station is the small village of **Kalinino**. The famous Russian explorer Erofei Pavlovich Khabarov is buried under the walls of the old church. It is believed, however, that the corpse in the grave is actually his brother, Nikifor, the last resting place of Erofei remaining unknown.

Kms6511-2 (S): Standing just across the river is a large deserted church with another building beside it. In the middle of nowhere and with a thick forest of conifers rising behind them, these two lonely-looking buildings make an eminently photogenic scene.

Km6532: Kuenga Куэнга Junction for the line which runs 52km to the east to **Sretensk (Сретенск)**, which was the eastern end of the Transbaikal railway. Sretensk sits on the eastern bank of the Shilka River which flows into the mighty Amur River. The Amur marks the Chinese-Russian border for hundreds of kilometres, before passing through Khabarovsk on its way north to the Pacific. It was this river route that put Sretensk on Russian maps and it was a thriving river-port in the nineteenth and early twentieth centuries (considerably larger than Chita) before the Amur Railway was opened in 1916. Passengers transferred here to the ships of the Amur Steamship and Trade Company. Most of the forty steamers that plied between Sretensk and Khabarovsk were made either in Belgium or the Glasgow yards of Armstrong and Co. Waiting here with her mother in 1900, Annette Meakin caught sight of some Chinese men with their traditional pig-tails. She was not impressed and wrote 'To me their appearance was quite girlish.'

Sretensk (pop: 10,300) is spread over both banks of the river with the centre on the eastern bank and the railway station on the high western bank. The two were joined only in 1986 when a bridge across the river was built. There is a museum and basic hotel in Sretensk. It's not as interesting to visit as Nerchinsk, however. In 1916 the **Amur Railway** was completed and bypassed Sretensk became a backwater.

The line leaves the Shilka River here, turns north, crosses the plain and climbs towards the eastern end of the Yablonovy Mountain Range.

Km6593:Chernyshevsk-Zabaikalski Чернышевск-Забайкальский (●●) Nikolai Chernyshevsky (1828-1889) was a revolutionary who toiled for years at hard labour camps in the region.

After this stop, the train ascends into the foothills of the Yablonovy range towards Zilovo.

❏ **The Amur Railway (Kms6532-8531)**
The building of the Amur Railway was proposed in the early 1890s but surveys showed that it would prove expensive, on account of the difficult terrain. More than one hundred bridges would be needed and many kilometres of embankments. Furthermore much of the region was locked in permafrost. In 1894, when the government signed the treaty with China allowing Russian rails to be laid across Manchuria, from Chita to Vladivostok, the Amur project was abandoned in favour of this considerably shorter route. This change of plan proved to be something of a false economy, for the East Chinese line, despite the considerable saving in distance, was ultimately to cost more than the whole of the rest of the Trans-Siberian Railway.

After Russia's embarrassing defeat by Japan in the 1904-5 War, the government realised the vulnerability of their East Chinese line. Japan was as keen as Russia to gain control of the rich lands of Manchuria and if they did decide to invade, the Russian naval base of Vladivostok would be deprived of a rail link with European Russia. A line within Russian lands was needed. The Amur project was reconsidered and, in 1907, approved.

Construction began in 1908 at Kuenga and for most of the 2000kms the line would follow a route about 100km north of the Amur River, out of range of Manchuria on the southern bank of the river. Winters are particularly harsh in this region and consequently track-laying could only take place over the four warmer months and even in mid-summer considerable amounts of dynamite were needed to blast through the permafrost. There were the usual problems with insects and disease but as the rest of the railway was operating it was comparatively easy to transport workers in from west of the Urals. By 1916 the long bridge over the Amur at Khabarovsk had been completed and the railway was opened. The Japanese were now Russia's allies and in 1918 (as allies to the White Russians) took over the running of the Amur Railway during the Civil War.

Km6629: Bushulei Бушулей This is not the easiest area in which to build a railway as the Trans-Siberian engineers discovered. In winter it was bitterly cold and in the hot summers all surface water dried up. For most of the year, the ground had to be thawed out with gigantic bonfires before the track could be laid.

The complex around the station is a molybdenum ore enrichment plant. The mineral is added to steel to make it suitable for high speed cutting tools. Scattered along the line are other molybdenum and gold mines.

Km6670: Zilovo Зилово (●) The town is called Aksenovo-Zilovskoe (Аксеново-Зиловское). To the south were the gold mines of the Kara region, also visited by Kennan, who found 2500 convicts working under the most appalling conditions. These mines were the property of the Tsar and from them and the other Imperial mines in Eastern Siberia, he could expect an average of 3600 pounds (1630kg) of pure gold each year.

MAP 14

Ульякан
ULYAKAN
Урюм
URYUM

Сбега
SBEGA

CHITINSKAYA OBLAST

Ксеньевская
KSENEVSKAYA

Кислый Ключ
KISLYY KLUG

Артеушка
ARTEUSHKA

Раздольное
RAZDOLNOYE

Могоча
MOGOCHA
Таптугары
TAPTUGARI

Семиозерный
SEMIOZERNYY

Амазар
AMAZAR

Жанна
ZHANNA

Ерофей Павлович
YEROFEY PAVLOVICH

Уруша
URUSHA

AMURSKAYA OBLAST

Тахтамыгда
TAKHTAMIGDA

Бам
BAM   Б.А.М.
Сковородино
SKOVORODINO.

Km6789: Ksenevskaya Ксеньевская The line continues across the forested southern slopes of the Eastern Yablonovy range for the next 200km with occasional good views over the trees.

Km6906: Mogocha Могоча (●) (pop: 17,500) This ugly railway settlement, located in the Bolshoy Amazar River Valley, is probably the harshest place to live on the Trans-Siberian because of the permafrost and the summer sun. In winter the top 10 centimetres of earth that thawed over the summer freezes over again in temperatures as low as -60°C (-87°F), killing all but the hardiest plants while the intense summer sun singes most young shoots. The town was founded in 1910 when this section of the Trans-Siberian was being built and later became the base for geological research expeditions seeking gold in the hills.

The town of **Olekminsk** on the Lena River lies about 700km due north of here (this being no more than a short hike to a Siberian, for as Intourist guides love to tell you, 'In Siberia a thousand kilometres is nothing to travel, a hundred roubles is nothing to spend and a litre of vodka is nothing to drink', although with hyper inflation whittling away the buying power of the rouble they're going to have to rework this favourite saying). As well as holding the world record for greatest temperature range – from minus 60°C (-87°F) to plus 45°C (113°F). Olekminsk was the place of exile in the eighteenth century for a bizarre Christian sect whose followers were known as the Skoptsy. They saw their salvation in abstinence and castrated themselves to be sure of a place in heaven. They lived in mixed communities, which they referred to as 'ships', each having a 'helmsman' and 'crew'. They avoided drink and tobacco and were excellent farmers. Since Olekminsk is experiencing something of a baby-boom at present it must be assumed that the more unconventional practices of the Skoptsy have been abandoned.

Km7010: Amazar Амазар (●) There are the remains of a large strategic reserve of steam engines. About 100km south the Shilka flows into the Amur River ('Heiling Chu' to the Chinese). The Amur rises in Mongolia and flows 2800km along the frontier with China into the Pacific at the Sea of Okhotsk. The river is exceptionally rich in fish and navigable for six months of the year. After initial explorations along the Amur by the Russians in the seventeenth century, following the Treaty of Nerchinsk with the Chinese in 1689, they were kept out of the region for the next 150 years. Colonisation began in the mid-nineteenth century and the Cossacks established garrisons along the river. By 1860 there were 60 villages with a population of 11,000 in the Amur Basin. The Amur is still a vital communications link in the area.

Km7075: The **administrative frontier** between Chitinskaya and Amurskaya Oblasts also marks the border between Siberia and the Far Eastern Territories. **Amurskaya** covers 360,000 square kilometres in the middle part of the Amur basin and extends to the Stanovoy Range in the north. The southern region of the oblast is a fertile plain where wheat, soya-beans, flax and sun-flowers are grown. Most of the area in the north is under thick forest.

Km7119: Yerofei-Pavlovich Ерофей Павлович (●●) Named in honour of the brutal explorer, Yerofei Pavlovich Khabarov (see p85). The river through the town is called the Urka and it was down this that Khabarov travelled with his mercenaries in 1649 to reach the Amur River. The river route opened up a shortcut to the Russian Far East from Yakutsk.

This area is particularly inhospitable with frosts lasting from the middle of October to the beginning of April, with an average January temperature of -33°C. Patches of snow can be found on the shaded sides of mountains as late as July.

At the east end of the station (N) is a **preserved locomotive** (Em726-88) on a plinth.

Km7211: Urusha Уруша (●●) Running mostly downhill, for the next 100kms the line passes through an area of taiga interspersed with uncultivated plains, most of it locked in permafrost.

Km7266: Takhtamigda Тахтамыгда A small settlement with a view (N) across the river valley. The good views to the north continue for the next 150kms. About half a kilometre east of the village, also (N), stands what looks like a prison, surrounded with barbed wire and patrolled by guards in blue uniforms.

Km7273: Bamovskaya Бамовская This is a junction with the Little BAM, the line which runs north to join the Baikal-Amur Mainline (see p123). It is not advisable to get off a train here without knowing when your connecting train up the Little BAM will arrive as only a few head north each day. There is no hotel here.

East of the junction there are good views (S) between Km7295 and Km7300.

Km7306: Skovorodino Сковородино **(●●)** (pop: 14,100) Named after a revolutionary leader killed here in 1920 during the Russian Civil War, Skovorodino is the first stop on the Trans-Siberian line for trains that travel down the Little BAM from Tynda to Khabarovsk. If you are getting off the Trans-Siberian to go up the Little BAM, Skovorodino is better than nearby Bamovskaya as there is a hotel. There's also the railway depot, forestry mills and the permafrost scientific research station.

Km7323: Bolshoy Never Большой Невер On the left (N) side of the railway is the 800km long Amur Yakutsk Highway ('highway' being something of a misnomer) which ends in **Yakutsk** (see p240). Yakutsk is the capital of the Republic of Sakha, formerly known as Yakutia. This must be one of the least pleasant parts of the world to live in, for the region, which is about thirteen times the size of Britain, is entirely covered with permafrost. Even in mid-summer, the soil in Yakutsk is frozen solid to a depth of over 100 metres.

As you leave the station, travelling east, there's a **steam locomotive** (P36-0091) (S).

To the east the scenery becomes more interesting. There are good views at Kms7318-25 (N) and around Km7335 (N). After the tunnel (Kms7343-5) there's a long view (S) down the valley towards China. More views (S) at Km7387 and Kms7426-28.

❑ **The Yakuts**
These people, who number about 300,000, form the largest ethnic group in the Far Eastern Territories. They were originally semi-nomadic herders who roamed around the lands beside the Lena River. What seems to have struck nineteenth-century travellers most about the Yakuts was their rather squalid lifestyle. They never washed or changed their clothes, they shared their huts with their reindeer and preferred their meat and fish once it had begun to rot. They drank a form of *koumiss* (fermented mare's milk) which they froze, sometimes into huge boulders. To give the Yakuts their due, they were considerably more advanced than many other Siberian tribes. Although they were ignorant of the wheel (hardly much use in such a cold climate), they used iron for weapons and tools. Most Yakut clans possessed a blacksmith who was usually also a shaman, since metal-working was considered a gift from the gods. The Yakuts were unique among Siberian tribes in that they made pottery. Russian colonists treated the Yakuts badly and demanded fur tributes for the Tsar. They have now almost completely adopted the Russian culture and although some are still involved in reindeer-herding, most Yakuts work in mining and the timber industry.

Km7501: Magdagachi Магдагачи (●●) The train continues to descend gently, through Magdagachi, out of the taiga and onto a wide plain. There may be a short stop at Tigda about 60kms after Magdagachi.

Km7602: Ushumun Ушумун The border with China is no more than forty kilometres south-west of here. The train turns south-east again and soon crosses an obvious climatic boundary and a not so obvious one marking the southern border of permafrost. From now on the larches grow much taller, reaching 35m, and birches and oaks spring up. These oaks are different from the European oaks as they do not lose their leaves in winter but retain them even though they are stiff and brown.

   The train continues south-east across flat lands with small clumps of trees.

Km7723: Shimanovskaya Шимановская (●) (pop: 26,500) Named after a revolutionary hero, this town played an important part in the development of both the Trans-Siberian and the BAM railways. There's a small museum in Shimanovskaya.

   To the south the land becomes more fertile and parts of the wide plain are under cultivation.

Km7772: Ledinaya Лединая Hidden away in the trees just to the north of this station is the once secret Svobodni-18 Cosmodrome. Until the early 1990s, the base housed sixty SS-11 inter-ballistic rockets (which can each carry a single nuclear warhead 10,000km) but following the START missile reduction agreement, the base has become redundant. All but five of the missile silos has been destroyed. It will not be closed down, however, as the Russian space sector believes that the site has several advantages over the northern Russian Plesetsk Cosmodrome, one of which is that it is at a lower latitude (meaning smaller rockets for the same payload) than Plesetsk.

   If you try to visit the site you will probably not get any further than the station. Good luck.

MAP 15

Km7815: Svobodny Свободный (●) (pop: 81,000) An attractive town sitting on the right bank of the Zeya River, Svobodny has a proud and tragic history associated with the railways. It was founded in 1912 and originally named Alekseyevsk, in honour of the Tsar's haemophiliac son, Alexis. It expanded rapidly into a major railway town with factories building carriages, and with a hospital, schools and an orphanage all sponsored by the railways. By the mid 1930s it was the headquarters of both the Amur section of the Trans-Siberian and the new BAM project. There's a railway museum here.

Beyond the town the line crosses the Zeya River the largest Russian tributary of the Amur River. In the rainy season the water level may rise as fast as 30cm an hour and 10m high floods have been recorded. The area beyond the river, called the Zeysko-Bureinskaya Plain, is the main granary for the Russian Far East. This is the most populated area of the Amur region with villages every 10 to 20km, separated by fields of barley, soya beans or melons. The climate and landscape are very similar to parts of Ukraine and attracted many Ukrainians last century. Today over half the locals are of Ukrainian descent. You can easily spot the Ukrainian houses, which are white-washed *khatas*. The solid log constructions with overlapping log ends are Russian.

Km7873: Belogorsk (●●●) Белогорск (pop: 75,000) Some of the older folk who make up the 70,000 inhabitants of this agricultural centre must find it difficult to remember the current name of their city as it has been changed so many times. It was founded in 1860 with the original name of Aleksandrovka. This stuck until 1935 when the local council decided it should be changed in favour of the rather more impressive Kuybyshevkavostochnaya. Just when everyone had got used to this exotic mouthful, it changed again, to boring Belogorsk.

There's a **branch line** from Belogorsk to Blagoveshchensk (see p349). The only hotel in town is basic *Hotel Zarya* ☎ (24101) 237 50, ul Partizanskaya 23.

Km7992: Zavitaya Завитая (pop: 22,300) This town is famous for soya bean oil and soya flour. There is a 90km branch line to the south which terminates at Poyarkovo on the Chinese-Russian border. Only Chinese and Russian passport holders can cross here.

Km8037: Bureya Бурея (●) On the river of the same name, this town was formerly the centre of a large gold mining region. It now produces tools for the coal mining industry. The area was once inhabited by several different tribes most of whom were Shamanists. The **Manegres** were a nomadic people whose trade-mark was to keep their heads shaven, except for one long pig-tail. The **Birars** lived in hive-shaped huts beside

❑ **The New York of Siberia**

Belogorsk is the junction for the line to **Blagoveshchensk**, the administrative capital of Amurskaya Oblast and a large industrial centre of 190,000 people, sited on the left bank of the Amur River. The name means 'Good News', for it was here in 1858 that Count Muravyev-Amurski announced the success of the treaty with China that granted Russia the Amur region. The city became a centre of colonisation and grew fast in the second half of the nineteenth century. The locals called it the New York of Siberia because its streets were laid out on a grid pattern, American-style. It became the major port on the voyage between Sretensk and Khabarovsk in the days before the completion of the Amur Railway.

In July 1900, Blagoveshchensk was the scene of the cold-blooded massacre of the entire Chinese population of the town (several thousand people) by the Cossack forces. This was in retaliation for the murders of Europeans in China during the Boxer Rebellion. Annette Meakin wrote: 'The Cossacks, who were little better than savages, threw themselves on the helpless Chinese ... and drove them down to the water's edge. Those who could not get across on rafts were either brutally massacred on the banks or pushed into the water and drowned. The scene which followed was horrible beyond description, and the river was black with dead bodies for weeks afterwards. I have this from no less than five eye-witnesses.'

Good relations between the people of Blagoveshchensk and their Chinese neighbours across the river in the city of Hei-Hei have been cemented over the last few years with the development of a major trade route here. Siberian lumber and machinery is ferried across the Amur to be exchanged for Chinese consumer goods.

Hei-Hei is connected by a railway to Harbin and Beijing. There is no bridge over the river but ferries travel six times a day between Hei-Hei and Blagoveshchensk. There are also international flights from Harbin in China and Seoul in South Korea. Blagoveshchensk has enough of interest to occupy a couple of days.

The best accommodation is at *Hotel Zeya* (☎ 416 22-21100), ul Kalinina 8. Travel agents can help organise the river crossing and rail tickets on the other side. They include Intourist (☎ 416 22-45772), ul Lenina 108/2, and Amurturist (☎ 416 22-27798, 90377, 23122, fax 27798, 23122), ul Kuznechnaya 1.

the Bureya and grew vegetables and fruit. North of here lived **Tungus** (Evenki), who were hunters and the **Orochen** who herded reindeer.

To the east were the **Goldi**, described thus in the *1900 Guide to the Great Siberian Railway*: 'They are below average stature, and have a broad and flat face with a snub nose, thick lips, eyes shaped after the Mongolian fashion and prominent cheek-bones ... The women adorn themselves with earrings and pendants. Some of them, as a mark of particular elegance, introduce one or several small rings into the partition of the nose. The people of this tribe are characterised by great honesty, frankness and good will ...Their costume is very various and of all colours; they may at different times be seen wearing a Russian overcoat, a fish-skin suit or the Chinese dress.'

Km8088: Arkhara Архара (●●●) A long stop at the station here is usual, with women selling snacks and fruit on the platform.

Km8118: Uril Урил On the right (S) side of the railway from here to the next station of Kundur is the Khingan Nature Reserve. The sanctuary consists of swampy lowlands dotted with Amur velvet trees and Korean cedar pine woods with a thick undergrowth of hazel trees, wild grapes and wild pepper which is related to ginseng. The sanctuary is rich in Mongol and Siberian animals seldom encountered elsewhere, such as a raccoon-like dog.

Km8170: This is the administrative frontier between Amurskaya Oblast and Khabarovski Krai. **Khabarovski** is, like much of Russia east of the Urals, almost entirely composed of swampy taiga. In the far south, however, there is an area of deciduous trees. The krai is extremely rich in minerals but the economy is currently based on wood-processing, fishing and the petroleum industry.

──────────── **Km 8171-9441 TIME ZONE MT + 7** ────────────

Local time is now Moscow Time + 7 hours. East of this frontier you enter an autonomous oblast within Khabarovski Krai. Between Obluchye and Pryamuskaya, some of the stations have their names written up in Yiddish as well as in Russian, for this is part of the Evreyskaya (Jewish) Autonomous Oblast, otherwise known as **Birobidzhan**, after its capital. This remote region was set aside for Jewish emigration in 1928 (the oblast being formed in 1934) but it never proved very popular. The Jewish population today stands at less than 5% (some say less than 1%) of the total number of inhabitants of this 36,000 square km territory.

A glossy coffee-table book about Birobidzhan (written in Russian, Yiddish and English) used to be sold in the bookshops of Khabarovsk. After pages of smiling cement-factory workers, beaming miners and happy-looking milk-maids, the book ended with the following statement: 'The flourishing of the economy and culture of the Jewish Autonomous Region, the happiness of the people of labour of various nationalities inhabiting the Region, their equality, friendship and co-operation lay bare the hypocrisy (sic) of the propaganda campaign launched by the ringleaders of Israel and international Zionism, about the "disastrous situation" of Jews in the Soviet Union, about the "oppression and persecution" they are supposedly being subjected to. The working people of Jewish nationality wrathfully condemn the predatory policy of the ruling circles of Israel and give a resolute rebuff to the Zionist provocateurs.'

Km8198: Obluche Облучье (pop: 11,700) The town is just inside the border of the Jewish Autonomous Region. The tunnel just after Obluche was the first in the world to be built through permafrost.

Km8234: Izvestkovaya Известковая The name means 'limestone' and there are large quarries in the area. This town sits at the junction of the Trans-Siberian and the 360km branch line to Novy Urgal on the BAM railway. Much of this branch line was built by Japanese POWs until they were repatriated in 1949 and Japanese graves litter the area. Izvestkovaya is a typical small town with a canteen, post office, dairy farm and market but little else. The old part of town, with its rustic wooden buildings and household garden plots, is hidden in the trees to the west.

Km8306: Bira Бира (●●) The obelisk on the platform commemorates the good works of local philanthropist Nikolai Trofemovich and his wife. The railway runs beside the Bira River for about 100km and passes through hills rich with the ingredients of cement.

Km8351: Birobidzhan Биробиджан (●) (pop: 87,600) Originally known as Tikhonkaya, the capital of the 'Jewish' region was founded in 1928 on the Bira River. It is especially famous for its bright red, self-propelled, combine harvesters, made at the Dalselmash factory and exported to Cuba, Mexico, Iraq and now China. Other industries include mining, fish-farming, wood-processing and the manufacture of hosiery, shoes, knitwear and other clothes.

Just east of Birobidzhan, on the left (N) you pass the huge **Iyuan-Koran Memorial** which commemorates a fierce Russian Civil War battle on this site in 1922. Near the memorial are mass graves of the fallen Red Guard.

Km8480: Volochaevka 1 Волочаевка 1 This small station is just a junction of the Trans-Siberian and the 344km railway to Komsomolsk-na-Amure. Volochaevka is famous as the scene of a major battle during the Russian Civil War, which took place in temperatures as low as -35°C. There is a panoramic painting of the battle in Khabarovsk's Museum of Local History. The town of Volochaevka is 9km from the station,

MAP 16

Km8512: Priamurskaya Приамурская This small town is just on the border of the Jewish Autonomous Region.

After crossing 3km of swamp and small streams you reach the 2.6km **bridge across the Amur River**, the longest on the Trans-Siberian and completed in 1916. A new combined rail and road bridge is under construction and until it opens at the end of 1998, cars cross the Amur by ferry. Khabarovsk stretches along the eastern bank of the river and the beaches here are packed with sunbathers at weekends in the summer. The main fishing port is 2.5km upstream.

Km8521: Khabarovsk Хабаровск (●●●) (pop: 614,000) [see p254] Khabarovsk was founded in 1858 as a military outpost against the Chinese. and today it is the most pleasant of the Russian Far East cities.

The train stops here for 20 minutes. Souvenirs and maps are sold in the Intourist Hall at the station. There's an impressive statue of Yerofei Pavlovich Khabarov, the city's founder, outside the station.

From Khabarovsk the line runs south to Vladivostok following the Ussuri River and the border with China. This region is a mixture of hilly country interspersed with wide flat valleys. Two hundred miles east of the line lies the Sikhote Alin mountain range, in which most of the rivers you will cross have their source. In the south, the firs and pines give way to a wide range of deciduous trees. There are good views across the plains to China.

Km8597: The longest bridge on the Ussuri Railway. It crosses the Khor River, one of the widest tributaries of the Ussuri, whose turbulent waters made the construction of the bridge in 1897 extremely difficult.

Km8598: Pereyaslavka Переяславка The town around the station is called Verino (Верино) and was the site of a fierce civil war battle. In front of the station there is a war memorial. There's a museum in Verino.

Km8621: Khor Xop The train crosses the Khor River again. The river marks the southern boundary of the 46,000 hectare **Bolshe-Khekhzirzkiy Sanctuary**. The indigenous Udegeytsy people have a legend to explain why plants from both north and south Siberia are found here. Once two birds flying in opposite directions collided in thick fog and dropped their loads. They'd been sent by the Good Spirit of the South and Good Spirit of the North to throw seeds on the desert plains and mountains respectively. Since then, southern wild grapes wind around northern pine trees and the northern berry *klukva* grows side by side with the southern spiky palm *aralia,* with its metre-long leaves. The vegetation changes considerably with altitude, which you will notice as you

---

(Opposite): Siberia in winter (bottom photo by Tatyana Pozar-Burgar).

travel up and down the mountains. At the foot of the mountains broad leaf species dominate. On the slopes, cedar, Amur velvet ash (cork is produced from the black bark) and Manchurian nut trees take over while on the higher parts of the mountains, angular pine and fir trees dominate.

Km8642: Vyazemskaya Вяземская (pop: 18,200)
This railway town was founded in 1895 and during the Russian Civil War there was fierce fighting around it. There are several memorials and a local history museum. From about 20kms southwards the countryside changes dramatically with forests of maple, alder, willow, and elm.

Km8756: Bikin Бикин
According to the *1900 Guide to the Great Siberian Railway*, the line crossed the river here and followed it south for 30kms. The book states that 'this is one of the most picturesque parts of the line offering an alpine scenery. The cuttings made in basalt rocks seem to be protected by columns of cyclopean construction. Wide expanses lying amidst the cliffs are covered with a most various vegetation, shading numerous Chinese huts. The river is enlivened by the small boats of the Golds and other natives, moving swiftly on the water's surface.' Unfortunately the line does not follow exactly the same route now, traversing rolling hills and marshy land strewn with telegraph poles keeling over at drunken angles.

The railway crosses the Bikin River. Two hundred km upstream is Krasny Yar, the largest village of the indigenous **Udeghe**. Known as the forest people for their lifestyle of fishing, hunting and gathering food from the *taiga*, the Udeghe are facing the end of their way of life because of the voracious logging industry.

Between Bikin and Zvenevoi is the **administrative border** between Khabarovski Krai and **Primorski Krai**. The Krai has a population of over half a million people.

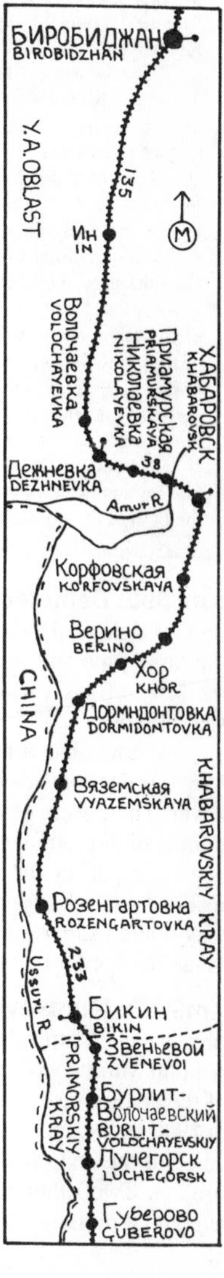

(**Opposite**): Siberia in summer: Listvyanka (top) and Lake Baikal (bottom).

MAP 17

❏ **The Ussuri Railway (Kms8531-9441)**
The first plans for the building of the Ussuri line, as this section between Khabarovsk and Vladivostok was called, were made in 1875 and the foundation stone for the whole of the Trans-Siberian Railway was laid in Vladivostok by the Tsarevich Nicholas in 1891. Priority was given to the Ussuri line as it was seen as vital to ensure that the strategic port of Vladivostok was not cut off by the Chinese. This was difficult territory for railway building. There was a severe shortage of labour. The local Goldi tribe, who at the time were happily existing in the Stone Age, were no help. They were unable to grasp the concept of paid labour and couldn't understand the point of the work, never having seen a train. Prisoners recruited from the jails of Sakhalin Island were not as co-operative as convicts used on other sections of the Trans-Siberian, preferring an evening of robbery and murder in Vladivostok to the railway camps. Like their fellow-workers on other sections of the line, the men here were plagued not only by vicious mosquitoes but also by the man-eating tigers which roamed the thick forests beside the line. Siberian anthrax decimated the already small population of pack animals, and rails and equipment had to be shipped from Europe, taking up to two months to reach Vladivostok.

In spite of these difficulties, the line was opened in 1897, 43 million roubles having been spent on its construction. It was double tracked in the 1930s and the branch line to Nakhodka was built after the Second World War.

Km8890: Dalnerechensk Дальнереченск (pop: 34,600) Founded by Cossacks in 1895 this town quickly became a timber centre thanks to the large pine and red cedar trees there. There is a factory that is one of the few in Russia which still produces wooden barrels for salted fish and seal blubber.

The town has a museum and a memorial to the guards killed in the 1969 border conflict with the Chinese over Damanski Island in the Ussuri River. There were several skirmishes and each country claimed the communist high ground as being the true Marxist revolutionary state. As both began preparing for nuclear war confrontation a political solution was reached when Kosygin, the Soviet premier, stopped off in Beijing on his way home from the funeral of Ho Chi Minh. Although progress has been made the border demarcation has not yet been finalised.

Km8900: Muravevo-Amurskaya Муравьёво-Амурская This station is named after the explorer and governor of Eastern Siberian, Count Nikolai Muravevo-Amurskaya. It was formerly known as Lazo in honour of the communist revolutionary SG Lazo (1894-1920), who was captured in 1920 by the Japanese when they invaded the Russian Far East, and executed at the station allegedly by being thrown alive into a steam engine firebox. Two other revolutionaries, Lutski and Sibirtsev, met a similar fate and a monument to all three stands in front of the station.

Km8991: Shmakovka Шмаковка About 29km from the station is the large, mostly derelict Shmakovski Trinity-St Nicholas Monastery with a very mysterious history. Its valuable land is now being fought over by two groups, both claiming to be its original owners. The Russian Orthodox Church maintains they built the monastery: the Russian military don't deny its religious past, but claim that they constructed the monastery as a front for an espionage academy. It does seem more than a little coincidental that ex-army officer Father-Superior Aleksei, who was commissioned to build the monastery, selected a site next to the remote Tihmenevo telegraph station. This was no ordinary relay station but one that was classified as a 'top secret military object' connected to Khabarovsk by an underground cable. And the monastery was certainly well equipped: there was even a printing press and photo lab. The military sanatorium here still operates today and the monastery is also home to 10 monks and lay brothers who are slowly rebuilding it.

Km9050: Spassk-Dalni Спасск-Дальний (●●) (pop: 52,000) Alexander Solzhenitsyn was imprisoned in this town, where he helped build the large cement works which now supply half of the Russian Far East's cement needs. His experiences formed the basis of his book, *A Day in the Life of Ivan Denisovitch.*

About 40km west is Lake Khanka which has a surface area of 4000 square km but its deepest point is only four metres. The lake is famous for water-nut and the lotus flower *eurea* which has giant buds and leaves two metres wide.

Km9109: Sibirtsevo Сибирцево This area is the centre of an extremely fertile region where wheat, oats, soya beans and rice are grown. Because of labour shortages, these are aerial sown and fertilised. The climate of the southern part of the Russian Far East makes most areas ideal for agriculture as the warm summer rains create a hothouse atmosphere.

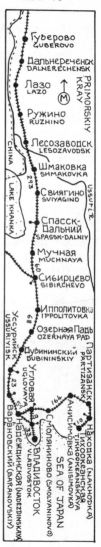

MAP 18

A branch line runs from here through dairy-farming countryside to Lake Khanka. From Sibirchevo south, the line winds down to Ussurisk.

Km9177: Ussurisk Уссурийск (●●) (pop: 161,000) The fertile area around Ussurisk has been inhabited for over a thousand years, first as the legendary kingdom of Bokhai and then by the Manchus. In the mid-nineteenth century, European emigrants began to settle here. At that time the town was called Nikolskoe, in honour of the Tsar. The town stands at the junction of the Ussuri and the Chinese Eastern Railways. When the Tsarevich Nicholas visited it in 1891, there were three wooden churches, a half-built stone cathedral and a population of 8000 people, many of whom were Chinese. Ussurisk is a now an agricultural and engineering centre, home of the 'Okean' brand of refrigerator.

From Ussurisk there are branch lines to Harbin in China via the East Chinese Railway and Pyongyang in North Korea.

The scenery in Ussurisk area is very different from the Siberian taiga. The train winds through the hills in misty forests of deciduous trees (oak, elm, alder, and maple) and across European-looking meadows filled with Friesian cows and willow trees.

Km9221: Amurski Zaliv Амурский Залив A branch line runs from here to the port of **Nakhodka**. Since most passenger ships now leave from Vladivostok there's little reason for visiting. For information on the line to Nakhodka, which is a further 175km, see below.

Km9246: If you're heading east keep a look out on the right (S) for your first glimpse of the Pacific Ocean.

❏ **Decline of the Amur Tiger**

Once the scourge of the railway construction worker, the largest member of the cat family is now just another animal world statistic, dwindling towards extinction. The tigers' habitat used to stretch as far west as Lake Baikal and to Beijing in the south but now only 250-350 cats remain in an area from Vladivostok north into the Sikhote Alin range.

Large scale forest clearance for timber sold to Japan and Korea forces tigers out of their territory. A male tiger can weigh up to 380kg (840lbs), almost twice the size of a lion, and requires about 400 square km of hunting ground. A decline in their food source (deer and wild boar) has also reduced the population and forced remaining tigers to roam even larger areas for prey. In 1987, a train just outside Nakhodka was held up by a tiger that had strayed onto the tracks. An Amur tiger can be worth as much as US$10,000 in China, Korea and Taiwan for the medicinal value that parts of its body are believed to have, and for its skin. Poachers now slip across Russian borders that are no longer tightly patrolled.

The animals are found in and around several nature reserves in this area: Kedrovaya Pad (near Vladivostok), Lazo and Sikhote-Alin, but your chances of seeing a live Amur tiger here are close to zero. There are, in fact, about twice as many of the subspecies in zoos around the world as in the wild.

Km9255: Uglovaya Угловая The town here is known as Trudovoe (Трудовое) and it sits at the northern edge of the Uglovi Bay. The pleasant beaches and the clean water make it a popular swimming spot for Vladivostok's day trippers.

East of the station the railway travels down a peninsula named in honour of the famous Russian explorer, Count Nikolai Muravevo-Amurskaya.

Km9262: Sadgorod Садгород Near Sadgorod (which means 'garden city') was the station called Khilkovo, named in honour of Prince M I Khilkov, Minister of Ways of Communication in the Tsarist government, who was one of the main supporters of the Trans-Siberian. Khilkovo station has long since disappeared.

The accepted date for the start of the building of the Trans-Siberian Railway is 19 May 1891 although the Tsar's son, Nicholas, had already travelled 18km on it from the tip of the peninsula through Vladivostok to Sadgorod. Here he inaugurated it by tipping a barrow of ballast onto the embankment and then returned by train to Vladivostok to unveil a plaque announcing the construction of the railway.

Km9269: Sanatornaya Санаторная The hotels that rate as Vladivostok's best are located here but only local trains will make a stop.

Km9281: Vtoraya Rechka Вторая Речка Vladivostok's main long-distance bus station is here (buses for the airport).

Km9284: Pervaya Rechka Первая Речка According to the original 1880s plan for the Trans-Siberian, this was to have been the line's terminus and a small branch line would extend to Vladivostok. Despite the difficulties of building a multi-track railway along the steep shore, it was decided in the 1890s to extend the Trans-Siberian through to Vladivostok. Near Pervaya Rechka was a small settlement called Convicts' Hamlet, inhabited by exiled settlers who had completed their sentences.

Km9289: Vladivostok Владивосток (pop: 648,000)　　　**[see p263]**
The beginning or the end of your journey.

❏ **The Vladivostok-Nakhodka Railway**
Few travellers visit Nakhodka since the Japanese ferry which connects with Trans-Siberian trains now docks at Vladivostok, which is also the location of the only airport in the region. The 229km-journey from Vladivostok to Tikhookeanskaya (Тихоокеанская), the port 10km east of Nakhodka, runs through Uglovaya (Угловая) at Km47, the mining and industrial city of Artem-Primorski (Артем-Приморский) at Km56, Novonezhino (Новонежно) at Km104, Partizansk (Партизанск) Km183, past the vineyards of the Suchan River Valley to Nakhodka (Находка) Km219, and on to the terminus at Tikhookeanskaya (Тихоокеанская) Km229.

Trans-Mongolian Route

The branch line to Mongolia and China leaves the main Trans-Siberian route at Zaudinsky, 8km east of Ulan Ude. From here it takes five and a half hours to cover the 250km to the Russian-Mongolian border. Between Ulan Ude and the southern border, the train travels through the heart of Buryatia, the Buryat Republic (see p336).

Note that the line now swings due south from its east-west route. However, in order not to confuse readers we shall continue to use (N) and S) to show which side of the train points of interest are located, rather than changing to the more correct compass bearings. Thus (N) means left side of the train if you're coming from Moscow.

Km5642: Ulan Ude Улан-Удэ [see p242]
The suburbs of Ulan Ude extend for several kilometres and there are good views back to the city at Km5659 (S) as the train climbs high above the east bank of the Selenga. The line follows the valley of the Selenga River all the way to the border with Mongolia. The scenery changes remarkably quickly to rolling green hills which are excellent pastures for the many cows in the area. Passing through the little station of **Sayatun** (Km5677) the line crosses to the west bank of the river at Km5689-90 and continues to climb through **Ubukun** (Km5732), stopping briefly at **Zagustay**.

Km5769: Zagustay Загустай
The station sits in the ugly shadow of a factory belching out thick smoke. Six kilometres from this station is the

---

❏ **The Trans-Mongolian Line**
This route to China is an ancient one, followed for centuries by the tea-caravans between Peking and Moscow. Travelling non-stop, foreigners and imperial messengers could manage the journey in forty days of acute discomfort. This was the route of the 1907 Peking to Paris Rally, the great motor race that was won by the Italian Prince Borghese and journalist Luigi Barzini in their 40-horsepower Itala. Until the middle of the present century, a rough track over the steppe-lands of northern Mongolia and the Gobi Desert in the south was the only route across this desolate country. In 1940, a branch-line was built between Ulan Ude and the border with Mongolia. After the Second World War, work started on the line from Naushki south, and in 1949 the track reached the Mongolian capital, Ulan Bator. The line between here and Beijing was begun in 1953 with a mixed work-force of Russians, Mongolians and Chinese. By the beginning of 1956 the work was completed and a regular rail service began between Ulan Ude and Beijing.

large coal mining town of **Gusinozersk** (Гусиноозёрск). The town grew from nothing to today's population of 30,800 following the discovery of a huge coal basin in 1939. The name means 'Goose Lake Town'.

Km5771-99: Goose Lake Between the stations of Zagustaý and Gusinoye Ozero the line passes along the western shore of Goose Lake. Until the Revolution, the most important *datsan* (lamasery) north of Urga (Ulan Bator) was at **Selenginsk**, 20km south east of Gusinoye Ozero and overlooking the lake.

In 1887 George Kennan, who was researching his book on Siberian prisons, arrived in Selenginsk and visited the famous datsan. 'We were tired of prisons and the exile system and had enough misery,' he wrote. Nevertheless he found Selenginsk 'a wretched little Buriat town'. At the datsan, Kennan and his companions were entertained by the Khamba Lama, the chief lama, who claimed through the interpreter that they were the first foreigners ever to visit his lamasery. They were treated to a dinner and a special dance display. The Khamba Lama had never heard of America, Kennan's native land, and was confused when Kennan explained that 'it lies nearly under our feet; and if we could go directly through the earth, this would be the shortest way to reach it'. The lama was completely unaware that the earth was anything other than flat.

Today, the Selenginsk village datsan is operating again.

Km5780: Gusinoe Ozero Гусиное Озеро
The line leaves the lake after this station and continues to climb from one valley to another, passing though **Selenduma** (Km5827) and still following the river.

Km5852 (S): Dzhida Джида There appears to be a small air-base here with hangars dug into hummocks in the ground.

MAP 19

❏ **The old border town of Kyakhta**
The border post for the railway is at the modern town of Naushki. However the old border for the tea-caravans was near the large town of **Kyakhta**, 20kms east of Naushki. In the 18th and 19th centuries this town, together with **Maimachen** (now named Altan Bulak, the Chinese town beside it on the Mongolian side of the border), formed one of the most important trading centres in the world, based almost entirely on the tea trade. Great caravans of camels would transport the precious beverage from Peking across the Gobi Desert to Maimachen and Kyakhta. Kyakhta was a bustling town of wealthy traders and tea-barons but once the Trans-Siberian was built the tea was shipped via Vladivostok to European Russia.

On 24 June 1907 Prince Borghese and his team roared into town in their Itala and were entertained royally by local dignitaries. The morale of the tea-merchants had sunk with the recent decline in trade but was greatly boosted by the arrival of the car and they began making plans for their own motor-caravans. An earlier visitor to these border towns was George Kennan who attended a banquet in Maimachen, where he was served dog-meat dumplings, cocks' heads in vinegar and fried lichen from birch trees, washed down by several bottles of French champagne. He was sick for the next two weeks.

In January 1920 Kyakhta witnessed a particularly appalling atrocity when the sadistic White Army General Semenov despatched 800 people suspected communists using a different method of execution each day.

Today Kyakhta has a population of 18,300, a local museum, the *Hotel Druzhba* (US$12 a room), and little else.

Km5895-0: Naushki Наушки (●●●++) At this Russian border post the train stops for at least two hours, usually for considerably longer. Customs officials collect passports, visas and currency declaration forms, returning them (often to the carriage attendant) after about half an hour. It would be unwise to get off the train before you've got your passport back since guards may not let you back on the train without it. The station tends to be crowded with black marketeers and some may get on the train and start selling roubles to travellers heading west; don't buy too many as the rate is unlikely to be in your favour. There's a **bank** on the platform where you can check the rate. Note that the bank is sign-posted in English but it's a long way down the platform (towards Mongolia). East bound travellers should exchange any unspent roubles here as it's very difficult to exchange them outside Russia.

Note that the loos on the train remain locked until you leave the border. The station lavatories would not win any hygiene awards but are located in the building to the left of the station building.

The **border** is marked by a menacing-looking electrified fence, about five kilometres beyond the Russian border post. The train may stop here while guards search for stowaways. Most trains are timetabled to cross this border at night, which is unfortunate since the landscape is attractive.

To the south is the impressive Selenga River, prone to flooding in the late summer; hills reach up above the track to the north. Have your insect repellent to hand as the air can be thick with mosquitoes in summer.

MONGOLIA

Distances given here follow the Mongolian kilometre markers. For cumulative distances from/to Moscow/Beijing, see timetables: Appendix A).

Km21: Sukhbaatar Сухбаатар (●●●++)
At this Mongolian border town the immigration process used to be a fairly nerve-racking affair. Whole compartments would be rigorously searched, magazines confiscated and film ripped out of cameras. It's all rather tame now for foreigners, although the baggage of local travellers is thoroughly inspected. During immigration and customs procedures a diesel engine is attached. The Mongolian dining-car, however, is not put on until Ulan Bator.

In the past some travellers have managed to get Mongolian visas here but the situation is subject to change; being turned back is not worth the hassle so don't rely on being able to get one here.

The station building is an excellent example of whimsical Mongolian railway architecture. It's an incredible mélange of architectural styles: mock Gothic, Moghul and Modern topped with crenellations and painted what looks like lime green in the artificial light. Strawberry pink is the other popular colour for station buildings in this country.

Situated at the confluence of the Selenga and Orhon Rivers, **Sukhbaatar** was founded in 1940 and named after the Mongolian revolutionary leader Damdiny Sukhe Bator. It grew quickly, superseding the border-town on the caravan route, Maimachen (now named Altan Bulak). Sukhbaatar is now the third largest industrial centre in the country (although in a country as sparsely populated and industrially primitive as Mongolia this is not a particularly impressive fact). Matches, liquor and flour are produced here by some of the 18,000 inhabitants.

Km123: Darhan Дархан (●●●)
It takes about eight hours to cover the 380km between Sukhbaatar and Ulan Bator. The train passes through the town of **Darhan** (capital of Selenga *aimak*) which was founded in 1961 and is now the second most important industrial centre in Mongolia, after Ulan Bator. Darhan is a show town of planned urbanisation and its population increased from 1,500 in 1961 to over 80,000 in 1991. Main sources of employment are open-cast mining, food production, construction and the production of leather and sheepskin coats. The town is an important communications junction with a branch-line running west from here to the big mining complex at **Erdenet**, and the port serves many villages along the Selenga and Orkhon Rivers.

About 120km west of Darhan, in the foothills of Mt Burenkhan is **Amarbayasgalant Monastery**. This vast eighteenth century temple complex, which once housed 10,000 monks and drew pilgrims from many parts of Asia, was desecrated during the anti-religious movement in the 1930s but is now being restored with grants from the Mongolian government and UNESCO.

Km 381: Crossing wide open grasslands, with only the occasional yurt to break the monotony, the line begins to descend into the valley where Ulan Bator is situated. Looking south you catch the first glimpse (Km386) of the ugly factories on the outskirts of the city (Km396).

Km404: Ulan Bator/Ulaanbaatar Улаанбаатар (●●●+) [see p273] (1350m/4430ft) The train spends half an hour at the Mongolian capital, a good chance to stretch your legs. There is a whole **collection of steam and diesel engines** standing outside the locomotive shed on the east side

---

❏ **Mongolia**

Mongolia is one of those countries, like Guyana or Chad, that rarely makes headline news, except when there's a dramatic change of leadership or policy. This was indeed the case with Mongolia in 1989-90 with the pro-democracy movement in the run-up to the first free elections in July 1990.

Mongolia is a sparsely populated place with only 2,250,000 people (50 per cent of whom are under the age of 25) in an area the size of Western Europe. It contains a surprising variety of terrain: the vast undulating plain in the east, the Gobi desert to the south, and in the west snow-capped mountains and extensive forests. Most of the eastern plain is at an altitude of 1500m and in this area the sun shines for around 250 days each year.

For many centuries the deserts and grasslands of Mongolia have been inhabited by nomadic herders living in felt tents (*yurts* or *ghers*). At certain times in the course of world history they have been bound together under a leader, the most famous being Genghis and Kublai Khan in the thirteenth century. Kublai Khan introduced Tibetan Buddhism to the country but it was not until the early seventeenth century that the majority of the population was converted and Buddhism gained a strong grip on the country.

By the end of the seventeenth century, control of Mongolia and its trade routes was in the hands of the Manchus. In 1911 the country became an independent monarchy, in effect a theocratic state since power lay with the 'Living Buddha' (the chief representative of Buddhism in Mongolia) at Urga (now Ulan Bator). In 1921 the communist government that rules today took power and the struggle to modernise a country that was technologically in the Dark Ages began, with considerable help from the Soviet Union. Elections were held for the first time in 1990 and won by the People's Revolutionary Party (Communist Party), who pledged the introduction of a market-style economy. The presidential elections of May 1997 were won by People's Revolutionary Party leader, Natsagiin Bagabandi.

The country is divided into 18 *aimaks* (districts) and the railway-line passes through three of these (Selenga, Tov and Dornogov).

of the line (N). The display includes a 2-6-2 S-116, T31-011 and T32-508 diesels, a 750mm gauge 0-8-0 469, and a 2-10-0 Ye-0266. They are beside the public road but quite accessible even though there is a fence in front of them. In the station building postcards (and weird Mongolian stamps which leave little room for a message on a card) can be purchased at the bar. Black marketeers may approach you on the platform to change money but you should remember that Mongolian currency is of no use on the train. It's US$ only, for food and souvenirs in the dining-car (which is attached here if you're en route to Beijing but is usually detached if you're travelling in the other direction).

Km409: The city extends this far west. At around Km425 the line starts to climb and for the next 50km, to Km470, snakes around, giving good opportunities for photos along the train. Good views over the rolling hills on both sides of the train.

Km507: Bagakangai Багакангай Airfield (S) with camouflaged bunkers.

Km521: Manit Манит (●) The pink station with its tower and weather-vane looks rather like a church.

Km560: Camels are occasionally to be seen roaming across the wide, rolling plain.

Km649: Choyr Чоыр (●●●) Just behind this beautiful pink and white wedding-cake of a station is a statue of Mongolian cosmonaut, VVT Ertvuntz.

Km733-4 (S) The pond here often attracts groups of camels and antelope.

Km751: Airag Аираг The train doesn't usually stop at this small station which is in the middle of nowhere and is surrounded by scrap metal.

❏ **Advice to nineteenth century travellers**
If you'd been doing this part of the journey in the not too distant past before the railway was built, you would now be swaying back and forth in the saddle of a camel, one of many in the caravan you would have joined in Kyakhta.

In the 1865 edition of his *Handbook for Russia, Poland and Finland*, Murray gives the following advice: 'It is customary for caravans to travel sixteen hours a day and they come to a halt for cooking, eating and sleeping ... The Mongols are most trustworthy in their transactions, and the traveller may feel in perfect safety throughout the journey.' He also gives the following useful tips concerning local currency: 'The use of money is as yet almost unknown in this part of the country, brick-tea cut up into slices being the token of value most recognised; but small brass buttons are highly prized.'

❑ **Genghis Khan**
For many decades the name of this famous Mongolian conqueror has been taboo in his home country. The Russians saw Genghis Khan as a brutal invader to be erased from the history books but with their influence rapidly fading there has been a sudden rise in Mongolian nationalism. Genghis Khan, the founder of the thirteenth century Mongolian Empire, is a hero once more, lending his name to the newest (and most luxurious) hotel in town and also to a brand of vodka. The prestigious Mongolian pop group with the wonderful name of 'Honk' recently produced a record in his honour.

Along with his rehabilitation have come a number of interesting characters each claiming to be his legitimate descendant. One of the best publicised was Ganjuurijin Dschero Khan, who claimed to have been smuggled out of the country to escape the Communists when he was four years old. Mongolians were intrigued to meet him, although they didn't quite know what to make of his appearance. He arrived in a military tunic, decked out with medals inscribed 'Bazooka', Carbine', 'Paratroopers' and 'Special Forces', which he claimed to have won in Korea and Vietnam. Support for him waned after it became apparent that he didn't speak Mongolian.

The Gobi Desert

This vast wilderness extends for 1000km north to south and 2400km west to east. Most of the part crossed by the railway is not desert of the sandy Saharan type but rolling grassy steppes. It is impressive for its emptiness: very few towns and just the occasional collection of yurts, herds of stocky Mongolian horses and small groups of camels or gazelles.

While it may not appear so, the Gobi is rich in wildlife although numbers of some species are rapidly dwindling. This is mainly the result of poaching and the destruction of habitat. There are large reserves of coal, copper, molybdenum, gold, uranium and other valuable exports. It's estimated that up to 10 billion tons of coal exist beneath the Gobi, and Japanese and Western companies are negotiating with Mongolia to extract it using strip mining techniques, which could seriously affect the delicate environmental balance. An American conservation group, Wildlife Conservation International, is helping the Mongolian Association for Conservation of Nature and Environment (MACNE) to monitor species at risk in the area. Among these are the 500 remaining wild Bactrian camels, the Gobi bear, the *kulan* (Asian wild ass) and Przewalski's wild horse (the last recorded sighting was in 1962).

Km875 (N): There's a collection of old **steam locos** on display just to the west of Sayn Shand station.

Km876: Sayn Shand Саын Шанд (●●●) (Sajnsand) This is the largest town between the capital and Dzamyn Ude on the southern border. Main industries here include food-processing and coal-mining.

Km1113: Dzamyn Ude Дзамын Уде **(●●●+)** Mongolian border town with a station building that looks like a supermarket at Christmas with all its festive lights. There's a bank and a restaurant, both usually closed in the evening. Customs declaration forms and immigration forms are collected. Customs officers inspect the luggage of Chinese and Mongolian travellers but don't seem too interested in others.

THE PEOPLE'S REPUBLIC OF CHINA

Kilometres below show distance to Beijing.

Km842: Erlyan (Erenhot) (●●●++) The Chinese station master is obviously trying to outdo the show his Mongolian counterpart puts on in the evening over the border, with a full-blown son-et-lumière. There's the Vienna Waltz blaring out of the speakers to welcome the train and the building's decked out in red neon and fairy lights.

Chinese customs officials come on board here. If you're travelling to Beijing you'll be required to fill in a health declaration form and baggage/currency declaration form. Passports are collected.

Bogie-changing: The train spends about 20 minutes at the platform and is then shunted off to the bogie-changing shed. It may be possible to stay on the train until it gets to the shed, get off before they lock the doors (for safety reasons while raising the carriages), and watch some of the bogie-changing operations. The Chinese railway system operates on Standard Gauge (as do Europe and North America) and this is 3.5 inches narrower than Five Foot Gauge used in the CIS and Mongolia. Giant hydraulic lifts raise the carriages and the bogies are rolled out and replaced. Photography is now permitted but take care not to get in the way or the authorities may restore the ban on photography which was in force for many years. You can walk back to the station building but you should be careful at night as the path is not well-lit.

Back in the station you can change money at the bank (passport not necessary but you do need to know your passport number), or visit the Friendship Store (Chinese vodka, Chinese champagne, beer, tea, Ritz crackers, and other snacks) and bar/restaurant (if open). Upstairs is a foreigners' waiting room where fictitious literature (eg *Human Rights in China*) is provided free of charge. The platform is crowded with traders and food and drinks are also sold here.

The Age of the Steam Train has not yet passed in China (a large percentage of its trains are steam-powered) and it is likely that the train will be shunted out of the bogie-changing shed and back to the platform by a puffing Class 2-10-2 locomotive built in Datong (see below). Passports are returned and you depart shortly thereafter, the whole operation taking anything from three to six hours.

❑ **Chinese trains**
Chinese trains ride on the left side of double tracks (unlike the CIS which is right-hand drive). Km markers come in a variety of sizes (usually like little grave-stones down by the track) and there seems to be some disagreement between them and the official kilometre location (on timetables etc) for many places. I've followed the markers where possible but for the last 70km of the journey they are not reliable, altering by 25km at one point.

Passing through towns with Mongolian names like Sonid Youqi and Qahar Youyi Houqi, you reach Jining in about five hours.

Km498: Jining (●) The bulky white station building here is topped by a line of red flags. Beside it is an extensive goods yard full of working steam engines.

Travelling due south from Jining the train leaves the province of Inner Mongolia and enters Shanxi Province. This mountainous area was a great cultural and political centre over a thousand years ago. There are hills running parallel to the west and wide fields either side of the line. The train follows the course of a river which leads it into a valley and more rugged countryside after Fenezhen.

Km415: Fenezhen Between this drab town and Datong you pass through the line of the **Great Wall** for the first time. Occasional glimpses are all you will get until the spectacular crossing at Km82.

Km371: Datong (●●) This large city, founded as a military outpost by Han armies, has a population of more than half a million and stands in the centre of the coal-rich Datong Basin. Its major tourist attraction is the group of Buddhist cave temples known as the **Yungang Grottoes** in the foothills of Wuzhou Mountain (16km west of the city). These caves, dating back to 460AD, are richly decorated and renowned as one of China's three most impressive Buddhist complexes, the others being at Luoyang and Dunhuang.

If you're stopping off here, a visit to the **Datong Locomotive Works** is an interesting and educational experience. Until recently, this was one of the last places in the world where steam trains were made. In the 1980s they were turning them out at the rate of 240 locos per year. The manufacture of the Class QJ 8WT/12WT 2-10-2 engine (133 tonnes; max speed 80kph) ceased in 1986 and the Class JS 2-8-2 (104 tonnes; max speed 85kph) in 1989. Both classes are used for freight haulage and shunting work. The factory now produces parts for steam and diesel locomotives and has customers in many parts of the world. Tours are conducted twice a week and must be arranged through Chinese International Travel Service (CITS).

At Datong the line turns east and follows the Great Wall, running about 20km south of it as far as Zhangjiakou. One hundred kilometres west of Zhangjiakou you leave Shanxi and enter Hebei province. Between Km295 and Km272 (N) the Great Wall can be seen parallel to the line, on the hillside to the east. Best view is at Km284 (N).

Km193: Zhangjiakou (●●) Founded 2000 years ago, this city used to be known by its Mongolian name, Kalgan (meaning gate or frontier). It stands at the point where the old caravan route between Peking and Russia crossed the Great Wall. Luigi Barzini described it as being like one of those 'cities one sees pictured upon Fu-kien tapestries: varied and picturesque, spreading over the bank of a wide snowy river'. He would not recognise it now; it has grown into an industrial city of over one million people. Yet he might recognise the smell he noticed as he drove into town on 14 June 1907, for tanning and leather-work are still major industries here. About 15km south of the city a large factory pollutes the air with orange smoke.

From around Km175 the scenery becomes hilly and more interesting as the line rises over the mountains north of Beijing. There are small valleys of sunflowers, groves of poplars and even some apple orchards. At Km99 you cross San Gan River above which (N) can be seen a small isolated section of the Wall.

Km82: Kanzhuang (●) The train stops for a banking engine to be attached before the steep ascent up through the Great Wall.

Km73: Badaling The first of the stations for the **Great Wall**. To the east is a 2km tunnel beneath the Wall. Look up (N) to the east as you come out for a good view and be ready to get off for the short stop at Qinglongqiao 0.5km further on.

Km70: Qinglongqiao (●●) There are good views of the Great Wall high above this attractive

MAP 20

station. After the stop the train reverses downhill through a spectacular series of tunnels alongside the road. Progress is very slow because of the tortuous bends and the need for heavy braking, which gives some people time to jump off the train and gather the wild marijuana plants which flourish near the tracks in this area. You pass the Tourist Reception Centre at Km68.

Km63: Juyongguan (●) Continuous application of the brake blocks makes them very hot necessitating a stop here.

Km53: Nankou (●●) The name means 'Southern Pass'. After a short stop to detach the rear engine the train speeds off across the fertile plain to Beijing. Something strange has happened to the km markers in this area, with 30km suddenly added around Km35.

Km0: Beijing Turn to p287 for more information.

Trans-Manchurian route

Km6199: Chita Чита (●●●) This is the last major Trans-Siberian station before the Trans-Manchurian trains branches off to China. Detailed information on Chita on p249.

Km6293: Karymskaya Карымская (●) The branch line to Beijing via Manchuria leaves the main Trans-Siberian route at Tarskaya (formerly Kaidalovo), 12kms east of Karymskaya. Leaving Tarskaya, you cross the Ingoda River and head through open steppe-land. Twenty kilometres further south you enter the Buryat Republic (Buryatia).

Km6444: Olovyannaya Оловянная (●●) The 120-flat apartment block by the station was constructed by Chinese labourers using Chinese materials. It was one of many barter deals between the Zabaikalsk (Russia) and Harbin (China) railways. Since 1988, when the first barter contract was signed, most deals have involved Russia swapping fertilisers, old rails and railway wheel sets for Chinese food, clothes and shoes. As confidence has grown, Harbin Railways have provided specialist services such as doctors of traditional Chinese medicine for the nearby Karpovka railway workers, uniforms for Zabaikalsk workers, and the reconstruction specialists for Chita-2 and Petrovski Zavod stations. Leaving this picturesque town you cross the Onon River, which flows north of the main Trans-Siberian line to join the Ingoda and form the

---

(Opposite) Mongolia: Sühbaatar Square (top) and the Bogda Khan Palace (bottom) in Ulan Bator (Ulaanbaatar, p273).

Shilka. Genghis Khan (see p364) was born on the banks of the muddy Onon in 1162. Don't photograph anything from the train in this area as in the town's outskirts are silos housing SS-11 interballistic nuclear rockets and bunkers holding portable SS-20 nuclear rocket launchers. The SS-11 missiles can carry a single nuclear warhead up to 10,000km while the SS-20 can carry three 600 kiloton warheads a mere 5700km.

Between Olovyannaya and Borzya you cross the Adun Chelon Mountain Range, passing through Yasnaya (Km6464) and Birka (Km6477).

Km6486: Mirnaya Мирная At the western end of the station there are two small tanks whose guns appear to be aimed at the train.

Km6509: Khadabulak Хадабулак Small village below a large telecommunications tower on the hill. Long views across the plains to the hills in the north around this area.

Km6543: Borzya Борзя (●●) This town was founded in the 18th century and with the arrival of the railway became the transport hub of south-east Zabaikalsk region. A branch line from here to the west goes all the way to the city of Choibalsan in Mongolia. Black marketeers come aboard (if you're coming from Beijing) to tempt you with army uniforms, military watches and rabbit fur hats. Watch your valuables.

There are several opportunities for photographs along the train as it snakes around the curves between Km6554 and Km6570, and especially Km6564-5 (S).

Km6590: Kharanor Харанор There is a branch line from here to the east which runs to the military towns of Krasnokamensk and Priargunsk.

Km6609: Dauriya Даурия A small village surrounded by a marsh of red weeds.

MAP 21

(Opposite) China: The Great Wall at Badaling (see p367) and Tiananmen Gate, Beijing (see p292).

Km6661: Zabaikalsk Забайкальск (●●●++) This town is within 1km of the border. Customs declarations and passports are checked on the train. If you are leaving Russia, you may still be required to produce your currency declaration form. Any remaining roubles are confiscated so don't admit to having them if you want some as souvenirs.

The train is shunted into the **bogie changing sheds** at the south end of the station. You can either stay at the station, remain in the carriage or get out and watch the bogie changing. Taking photos in the bogie changing shed was once strictly prohibited but now it is possible.

The station has a restaurant, bank and lavatories. ('The 'restaurant' is a joke, no hot food although some good cakes and biscuits are available – and a big hunk of cheese mysteriously appeared while we were there. Anthony Kay, UK). There is another shop, in the building opposite the station and across the line, where vodka, champagne and palekh boxes are sold. There's a small department store next door. You will stay at the station for between one and three hours.

THE PEOPLE'S REPUBLIC OF CHINA

Note that the km markers along this route do not show the distance to Beijing until you reach Harbin. From the border to Harbin they show the distance to Harbin.

Km935 (Bei:2323): Manzhouli (●●●+) (2135ft/651m) At this Chinese border town (formerly known as Manchuria Station) you're required to show officials your baggage and currency declaration form if you're leaving the country, or fill out this form as well as a health declaration form if you're just arriving.

The train spends between one and three hours here so you can visit the **bank** and the **Friendship Store** (tins of high quality peanuts, Chinese vodka and beer). Postcards and stamps are also available. Puffing steam locomotives shunt carriages around the yard, a particularly impressive sight if you arrive in the early hours of a freezing winter morning. Loos stink, less so in winter.

Leaving the station you pass **Lake Dalai Nor** and roll across empty steppe-lands. You may see mounted herders from the train, as did Michael Myres Shoemaker in 1902 when he was passing through this area, on his journey to Peking. Of the first Chinese person he saw, he wrote (in *The Great Siberian Railway from St Petersburg to Pekin*) 'these northern Celestials appear on the whole friendly, and are flying around in all directions swathed in furs, and mounted on shaggy horses.' European newspapers of the time had been filled with reports of the atrocities committed by the anti-foreigner Boxer sect in Manchuria, hence his surprise at the apparent friendliness of the local population.

❏ The East Chinese Railway 1897-1901

The route

The original plans for the Great Siberian Railway had not included the laying of tracks across territories that were outside the Russian Empire. However, when surveyors returned from the Shilka and Amur valleys in 1894 with the news that the Sretensk to Khabarovsk section of the line would prove extremely costly, owing to the difficult terrain, the Siberian Railway Committee were obliged to consider an alternative. Their greedy eyes turned to the rich Chinese territory of Manchuria and they noted that a line straight across this province to Vladivostok would cut 513 *versts* (544km) off the journey to the port. Since the Chinese would obviously not be happy to have Russian railway lines extending into their territory, the Committee had to think up a scheme to win Peking over to the idea.

The Manchurian Deal

It did not take the wily Russian diplomats long to work out a deal the Chinese were forced to accept. After the 1894 Sino-Japanese war the victorious Japanese concocted a peace treaty that included the payment of a heavy indemnity by the Chinese. Knowing that China was unable to pay, the Russians offered them a generous loan in exchange for the right to build and operate a railway across Manchuria. They were granted an 80-year lease on a thin strip of land 1400km long and the project was to be disguised as a Chinese enterprise financed through the Russo-Chinese Bank. The rest of the world suspected Russia of flagrant imperialism and it proved them right in 1897 by annexing Port Arthur.

Work begins

Construction of the Chinese Eastern Railway began in 1897 but it soon became obvious that the project was facing greater problems than any that had arisen during the building of other sections of the railway. There were difficult conditions (the Greater Khingan Mountains had to be crossed); there were not enough labourers; interpreters were needed to translate the orders of the Russian foremen to the Chinese coolies and the area through which the route passed was thick with *hunghutzes* (bandits). It was necessary to bring in a force of 5000 policemen to protect the workers. After the Boxer (anti-foreigner) riots began in the late 1890s it became necessary to protect the rails, too, for when they were not murdering missionaries the Boxers tore up the track and derailed trains.

Set-backs

After the annexation of Port Arthur, another Manchurian line was begun – from Harbin south through Mukden (now Shenyang) to Dalni (now Dalian) and Port Arthur (now Lushun). Work was disrupted in 1899 by the outbreak of bubonic plague although in spite of the Chinese refusing to co-operate with the quarantine procedures, only 1400 people died, out of the total work-force of 200,000. In May 1900, the Boxers destroyed 200km of track and besieged Harbin. The Russians sent in a peace-keeping force of 200,000 men but by the time the rebellion had been put down, one third of the railway had been destroyed.

Despite these set-backs, the line was completed in 1901 although not opened to regular traffic until 1903. It would have been far more economical to have built the Amur line from Sretensk to Khabarovsk, for in the end the East Chinese Railway had cost the government more than the total spent on the entire Trans-Siberian track on Russian soil.

Km749 (Bei:2137): Hailar (●●) (2030ft/619m) From here to Haiman the rolling steppes continue. If you'd been travelling here in 1914, you would have the latest edition of the Baedeker's *Russia with Teheran, Port Arthur and Peking* with you and would therefore be looking out for 'the fortified station buildings (sometimes adorned with apes, dragons and other Chinese ornaments), the Chinese carts with their two high wheels and the camels at pasture'. Modern Hailar is an unexotic city of 180,000 people, the economic centre of the region. Local architecture is a blend of Russian and Mongolian: log cabins, some with 'yurt-style' roofs. The average temperature in this area in January is a cool minus 27°C.

Km674 (Bei:2062): Haiman Also known as Yakoshih, this town stands near the foot of the Great Khingan Mountain Range which extends from the northern border with Russia south into Inner Mongolia. The line begins to rise into the foothills of the range.

Km634 (Bei:2022): Mianduhe (●) The train continues to climb the gently rising gradient.

Km574 (Bei:1962): Yilick Ede (●●) Note that the train does not stop here on the journey **from** Beijing.

Km564 (Bei:1952): Xinganling/Khingan (●) (3140ft/958m) This station stands at the highest point on the line. The long tunnel (3km) that was built here in 1901-2 was a considerable engineering achievement since most of the drilling was done during the winter, with shift workers labouring day and night.

Km539 (Bei:1927): Boketu (●●●) The line winds down through partly-wooded slopes to the town of Balin/Barim (Km7135/1866) and continues over the plains leaving Inner Mongolia and crossing into Heilongjiang Province.

Km270 (Bei:1658): Angangxi (●●●) Forty kilometres south is the ancient city of **Qiqihar** (Tsitsikar). By the time he reached this point Michael Myres Shoemaker had become bored with watching 'Celestials' from the windows of the train and was tired and hungry. He writes 'In Tsitsikar, at a wretched little mud hut, we find some hot soup and a chop, also some coffee, all of which, after our days in lunch baskets, taste very pleasant.' Over their lunch, they may well have discussed the nearby **Field of Death** for which the city was notorious. In this open area on the edge of Tsitsikar public executions were regularly performed. Most of the criminals decapitated before the crowds here were *hunghutzes* (bandits). Since the Chinese believed that entry to Heaven was denied to mortals who were missing parts of their bodies, their heads had to be sewn back in place before a decent burial could take place. However, so as not to lower the moral tone of Paradise, the government ordered that the heads be sewn on the wrong way round, facing backwards.

Twenty kilometres east of Angangxi you pass through a large area of marshland, part of which has been designated a nature reserve. The marsh attracts a wide variety of water-fowl since it is on the migration route from the Arctic and Siberia down to southern Asia. **The Zhalong Nature Reserve**, 20km north of here, is best known for its cranes. Several of those found here (including the Siberian Crane) are now listed as endangered species.

Km159 (Bei:1547): Daqing (●) At the centre of one of the largest oilfields in China, Daqing is a model industrial town producing plastics and gas as well as oil. Higher wages attract model workers from all over the country. Apart from the thousands of oil wells in this swampy district there's very little to see.

Km96 (Bei:1484): Song A small station in an island of cultivation amongst the swamps.

Km0 (Bei:1388): Harbin (●●●) (152m/500ft) Crossing the wide Sungari (Songhua) River (a 1840km long tributary of the mighty Amur to the north) the line reaches Harbin, the industrial centre of Heilongjiang Province. It was a small fishing village until the mid 1890s when the Russians made it the headquarters of their railway building operations in Manchuria. After Michael Myres Shoemaker visited the town in 1902 he wrote: 'The state of society seems even worse at this military post of Harbin than in Irkutsk. There were seven throats cut last night, and now, as a member of the Russo-Chinese Bank expressed it, the town hopes for a quiet season.' The *Imperial Japanese Railways Guide to East Asia* (1913) recommended 'the excellent bread and butter, which are indeed the pride of Harbin' and warned travellers away from the numerous opium dens. After the Revolution, White Russian refugees

MAP 22

poured into the town and the Russian influence on the place continued. There are few onion-domes and spires to be seen today in what is otherwise just another Chinese city. The Russian population is now small. The main tourist attraction is the **Ice Lantern Festival**, which takes place from January to early February. Winters here are particularly cold and during the festival the parks are filled with ice-sculptures: life-size elephants, dragons and horses as well as small buildings and bridges. Electric lights are frozen into these sculptures and when they are illuminated at night, the effect is spectacular.

At the station, good views along the track of the numerous steam locos can be obtained from the bridges between the platforms.

Km1260: The line crosses a wide tributary of the Songhua River. There are numerous small lakes in the area.

Km1146: Changchun (●●) (230m/760ft) Between Harbin and Changchun you cross an immense cultivated plain, leaving Heilongjiang and entering Jilin Province. Changchun is the provincial capital. The station is quite interesting with white concrete sculptures of 'The Graces' and lots to buy from the snack sellers on the platform.

Back in 1913, the *Imperial Japanese Government Railways Guide to East Asia* was reminding its readers (all of whom would have had to change at this large junction) about 'the need of adjusting their watches – the Russian railway-time being 23 minutes earlier than the Japanese'. From 1933 to 1945 Changchun was the centre of the Japanese puppet state of Manchukuo and it has now grown into an industrial metropolis of more than one million people. Local industries include the car factory (where Red Flag limousines are assembled: guided tours possible), the rail-carriage factory and the film studios. If you happen to get off here, the local delicacies include antler broth, hedgehog hydnum stewed with orchid, and the north-eastern speciality, *Qimian*, which is the nose of a moose. However, Changchun is probably more popular with rail enthusiasts than with epicureans. RM Pacifics and QJ 2-10-2s are to be seen here and on the Changchun-Jilin line.

Km1030: Siping Unattractive town but lots of working steam locos in the station. Ten kilometres further south the train crosses the provincial border into Liaoning Province.

Km841: Shenyang (●●●) (50m/160ft) An industrial giant founded two thousand years ago during the Western Han dynasty (206BC- 24AD). At different times during the course of its long history the city has been controlled by the Manchus (who named it Mukden), the Russians, the Japanese and the Kuomintang until it was finally taken over by the Chinese Communists in 1948.

Shenyang is now one of the largest industrial centres in the People's Republic but there are several interesting places to visit between the factories, including a smaller version of the **Imperial Palace** in Beijing. There is also a **railway museum** situated beside Sujiatun shed. The station has a green dome and the square outside it is dominated by a tank on a high pedestal.

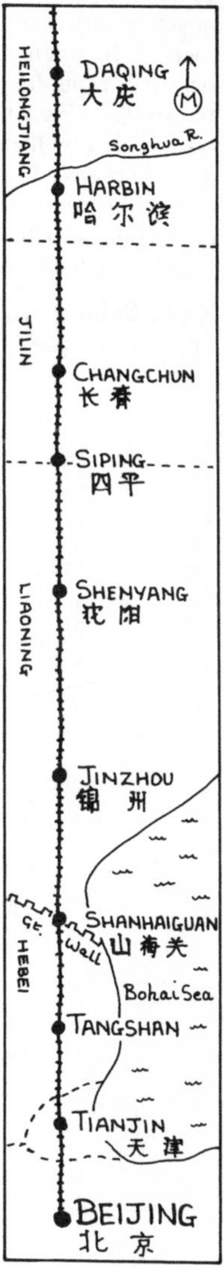

Km599: Jinzhou(●●) From here the line runs down almost to the coast which it follows southwest for the next 300km, crossing into Hebei Province. Beijing is just under eight hours from here.

Km415: Shanhaiguan (●●) As you approach the town from the north, you pass through the **Great Wall** – at its most eastern point. This end of the Wanlichangcheng (Ten Thousand Li Long Wall) has been partially done up for the tourists. Although the views here are not as spectacular as at Badaling (70km north of Beijing and the usual tourist spot on the Wall, see p292), the restoration at Shanhaiguan has been carried out more sympathetically – it is restoration rather than reconstruction. The large double-roofed tower houses an interesting museum.

Km262: Tangshan This was the epicentre of an earthquake which demolished this industrial town on 28 July 1976. The official death toll stands at 150,000 but it is probably as high as 750,000. Many of the factories have been rebuilt and the town is once again producing consumer goods. Locomotives are built here at the Tangshan Works: which until 1991 produced the SY class 2-8-2 steam engine.

Km133: Tianjin/Tientsin (●●) One of the largest ports in China, with a population of seven million. In the mid-nineteenth century the English and the French marched on the capital and 'negotiated' the Treaty of Peking which opened Tianjin to foreign trade. Concessions were granted to foreign powers as they were in Shanghai. England,

MAP 23

France, Austria, Germany, Italy, Belgium, Russia, Japan and the United States each controlled different parts of the city, which accounts for the amazing variety of architectural styles to be found here. Chinese resentment at the foreign presence boiled over in 1870 when (during an incident that came to be known as the **Tientsin Massacre**) ten nuns, two priests and a French official were murdered. To save female babies from being killed by their parents (the Chinese have always considered it far more important to have sons than daughters) the nuns had been giving money for them. This had led the more gullible members of the Chinese population to believe that the nuns were either eating the children or grinding up their bones for patent medicines.

Km0: Beijing The beginning or the end? You are now 9001kms from Moscow. See p287 for information on the city.

PART 6: DESTINATIONS & DEPARTURES

This section contains basic information for those spending a few days in Japan, Hong Kong, Helsinki, Berlin, Budapest, Prague, Poland, Belarus and the Baltic States at the end or beginning of the trip. Details of how to arrange tickets in these cities for the rail journey across Siberia are given in Part 1.

JAPAN: TOKYO

General information
● **Visas** Visas are not necessary for passport holders from the UK, other Western European countries, North America and most British Commonwealth countries. Australia however is an exception and its citizens need Japanese visas.

● **Money/costs** The unit of currency is the yen (¥). Japan has become one of the most expensive countries in the world for foreign visitors. You may need to allow for a minimum of £30/US$50 per day for the most basic accommodation and the cheapest meals.

● **Climate** Japan has four clearly defined seasons: winter being cold and snowy, summer being hot and humid, and both spring and autumn being warm.

● **Language** Since English is taught in the schools and the people are very keen to make contact with foreigners, you will be able to find someone to help you, except in the more out-of-the-way places. If you're stuck dial ☎ 3502 1461 (in Tokyo) for the Tourist Information Center (TIC).

● **Local transport** If you plan to spend some time touring the country, you should purchase a Japan Rail Pass. To get the best price, buy the pass before arriving in Japan. For getting around Japanese cities, the metro system is best although you'll need help with the ticket machines. All stations have signs above the platforms in both Japanese and Latin letters.

Tourist information
Before you leave home, visit the branch of the Japan National Tourist Organisation in your country. A good selection of useful maps and tourist brochures is provided free of charge. JNTO has a Web site at http://www.jnto.go.jp and some of their offices are at:

● **UK**: Heathcourt House (☎ 0171-734 9638), 20 Savile Row, London W1X 1AF

● **USA**: 1 Rockefeller Plaza (☎ 212-757 5640), Suite 1250, New York, NY 10111

● **Canada:** 165 University Ave (☎ 416-366 7140), Toronto, Ontario. M5H 3B8
● **Australia**: Chiefly Tower (☎ 9232 4522), Lvl 33, Sydney, NSW 2000
In Tokyo, the best place for information is the Tokyo Tourist Information Centre (3502 1461) at 1-6-6, Yurakucho, Chiyodo-Ku, open 9:00-17:00 weekdays, 9:00-12:00 Saturday.

Arrival
● **Niigata Port** The Niigata City Tourist Information Center is directly in front of the railway station, at 1-1 Hanazono (☎ 025-241 7914). The Niigata International Friendship Center, at Miyoshi Mansion 3F, Kami-Okwaamae 6 (☎ 025-225 2777) also has tourist information. Note that the boat service between Niigata and Vladivostok does not operate in winter.
● **Niigata Airport** There are flights between Niigata and Khabarovsk, Vladivostok, Irkutsk and Moscow. For information on Aeroflot flights, contact Toyko's Aeroflot Office (☎ 025-244 5935). There is no flight between Niigata and Tokyo, but there is a Bullet train which takes 1.5 hours.
● **Narita Airport (Tokyo)** Transport to the city centre is expensive since the airport is located 60 km outside the capital. The cheapest way to get in is to take the Keisei Limited Express train from the airport to Keisei Ueno Station in Tokyo.

Accommodation in Tokyo
This can be expensive; a bed in a youth hostel will set you back US$20. Youth hostels are cheapest followed by *minshuku* (bed and breakfast) and then business hotels. *Ryokans* (Japanese style hotels) are pricey but often include meals and are an interesting experience for the foreigner. The best way to find somewhere to sleep is to visit the TIC and collect an accommodation list and a map. Then phone the hotel/youth hostel (phone calls are reasonably cheap). Check prices and places and then ask for directions. Some numbers to try for cheap accommodation in Tokyo are:
● Tokyo International Youth Hostel (Iidabashi) (☎ 3235 1107), 18F Central Plaza Building, 1-1 Kagura-kashi, Shinjuku-ku
● Tokyo YMCA (☎ 3293 1919, fax 3293 1926), 7 Kanda-Mitoshirocho, Chiyoda-ku
● Asia Center of Japan (Akasaka) (☎ 3233 0111, fax 3233 0633), 5-5 Saragakucho 2-chome, Chiyoda-ku

Moving on
Flights are expensive in Japan so try to ensure you have made arrangements before arrival. When leaving Japan by air you are required to pay a departure tax ¥2000. For details of ferry services to China and Russia (as well as information about arranging **Trans-Siberian** tickets in Japan), see p36.

HONG KONG

General information

On 1 July 1997, the British will hand over administration of Hong Kong to China. The country will then become a Special Administrative Region of China.

- **Visas** Changes in entry regulations will be introduced gradually. The stay for British citizens drops to six months with no automatic right of employment, and you may need to show proof of onward travel. You'll still need a separate visa to visit China proper but these are easy to get in Hong Kong. Check with the Chinese embassy for the latest information. Before the handover, visas were not necessary for most short-term visitors and most could stay at least a month.
- **Money** The currency of the country is the Hong Kong dollar (HK$). Since the early 1980s, the exchange rate was pegged at US$1=HK$7.70 (£1 =HK$12.60) with small variations tolerated.
- **Climate** Mild with fairly hot and humid summers, and cool winters.
- **Language** Cantonese and English.

Tourist information

The Hong Kong Tourist Association (HKTA) has branches in many countries and can provide you with useful maps and brochures. Branches at the airport and the Star Ferry terminal (Kowloon). There is a telephone information service with multi-lingual operators (☎ 2801 7177).

Arrival

- **Kai Tak Airport** The airport is tucked into Kowloon, beside the bay. Landing here is quite an experience as the tips of the wings seem almost to touch the high-rise blocks. Visit the HKTA office and if you have to visit a bureau de change do not change more than the bus fare. There is an airport bus that runs into Tsimshatsui District (where there is budget accommodation available) in Kowloon and also Hong Kong Island.
- **By rail** There are several options. You can take the 2.5 hour, direct express train which runs between Canton (Guangzhou) and Kowloon (Hung Hom Station). It is cheaper, however, to take local trains, from Canton to Shenzhen; there is also a bus service on this route. You walk across the border into Hong Kong and then take a local train from Lo Wu station to Hung Hom. The new Beijing-Hong Kong and Shanghai-Hong Kong trains became operational in May 1997. Both journeys take 29 hours and they run on alternate days of the week.
- **Ferry/hovercraft from Canton (Guangzhou)** The eight-hour overnight ferry between Canton and Hong Kong arrives and departs from the Tai Kok Tsui Wharf in Kowloon. There is also a three-hour hovercraft service operating between here and Canton. Book tickets from the China Ferry Terminal or through travel agents in Hong Kong.

● **Boat to/from Shanghai** There are about 4 departures a month for this delightful 60 hour trip. The service is popular and heavily booked in the summer, bookings must be made at least two weeks in advance. Contact China Merchants' Steam Navigation Co (☎ ☛815 1006 or 2545 3778), 315 Des Voeux Rd, Central.

Local transport
Most famous is the Star Ferry service which operates between Kowloon and Hong Kong Island. Ask the HKTA information offices for details of ferries to outlying islands. There is also a fast and efficient subway system and the old trams still operate on Hong Kong Island. Taxis are cheap but traffic is slow-moving.

Accommodation
For a cheap place to sleep, **Chungking Mansions** is the best place. In this large block in Kowloon, near the bay and a stone's throw from the famous **Peninsula Hotel**, there are a large number of small hotels with tiny rooms but low prices. Have a look at a few before you settle for the first you see as the rooms vary in size, cleanliness and price. The **Traveller's Hostel** (16f Block A, ☎ 2368 7710) is a popular meeting place for backpackers and has cheap dormitory accommodation, a restaurant and a travel agency that can organise visas for China. There are plenty of other hotels/hostels in A, B and D Blocks. There's also the **YMCA** (next door to the Peninsula Hotel).

Moving on
Visas for China are easy to get in Hong Kong. Either use a travel agent or DIY at the Visa Office (☎ 2827 9569) of the People's Republic of China (counter No 7, 5th floor, Block 26, China Resources Building, 26 Harbour Rd, Wanchai. Remember that you will be without a passport while processing the visa, so if you need to cash travellers cheques do this first. For **Trans-Siberian** tickets, see p37.

FINLAND: HELSINKI

General information

● **Visas** Visas are not necessary for passport holders from most countries including the UK, US, Canada, UK, Australia and New Zealand.

● **Money/costs** The unit of currency is the Finnmark which is divided into 100 penniä. As in most Scandinavian countries, prices are higher here than in many European countries.

● **Climate** Pleasantly warm in summer but winters are long and severe.

● **Language** There are two official languages – Finnish and Swedish (the Swedish name for Helsinki is Helsingfors). Most people also speak English.

Tourist information

There are Finnish Tourist Offices in many capitals of the world including:

● **Canada**: (☎ 964 9159), Box 246 Station Q, Toronto M4T 2MI

● **UK**: (☎ 0171-839 4048), 66-68 Haymarket London SW1Y 4RF

● **USA**: (☎ 949 2333), 665 Third Avenue New York NY 10017

In Helsinki your first stop should be **Helsinki City Tourist Office** at Pohjoisesplanadi 19, (☎ 90-169 3757) on the Esplanadia (the park next to the water-side market square). They are open 08:30-18:00 weekdays, 10:00-15:00 weekends over summer, and provide an accommodation list. You can also get information and a list of youth hostels from the **Hotel Booking Centre-Hotellikeskus** (☎ 90-171 133) at the railway station.

Arrival

● **By sea** If you're arriving from Stockholm on a Viking Line Ship, or from Traveemunde (Germany) on Finnjet, you will dock at Katajanokka on the east side of the bay. If you are arriving from Gdansk, from Tallinn, or from Stockholm on the Silja line, ships dock at Olympialaituri on the west of the bay. Both stops are a 15-20 minute walk from the city centre.

● **By air** Vantaa International Airport is situated 20km north of the city centre. There is a regular bus service (bus No 615 to the railway station). The journey takes about half an hour.

● **By rail** The railway station is six blocks west of the harbour and two blocks north.

Moving on

There are ferries to Germany, Poland and Sweden (which is the usual rail route to the rest of Europe). The Baltic Shipping Company (☎ 3589-665 755) offers cruises from Helsinki to St Petersburg and a one-way, overnight bed in a four-berth room costs about US$70. You can get a bus to St Petersburg from Helsinki. A ticket costs about US$45 and can be bought from Finnord Bus Agency, St Petersburg Express Bus Service and Sovavto. For booking the **Trans-Siberian** in Helsinki see p27.

GERMANY: BERLIN

General information
- **Visas** Not necessary for most nationalities.
- **Money/costs** The Deutschmark (DM) is the unit of currency, divided into 100 pfennigs. Living and travelling costs can be high.
- **Language** It's useful to be able to speak a little German. Most Berliners study English at school and many speak it fluently.

Tourist information
The **Berlin Tourist Office** (☎ 25 00 25) is in the Europa Center, Budapester Strasse 45, (the building with the Mercedes star on the top of it) along Kurfurstendamm and a ten-minute walk from Zoo Bahnhof Railway Station. Maps and accommodation listings are available here. Open daily 08:00-22.00 (21:00 on Sunday). The friendly staff will supply you with brochures and maps including their *Tips für Jugendliche Berlin Besucher* brochure which lists budget accommodation. The **Informationszentrum am Fernsehturm** (☎ 242 4512) is another good information service. It is located beneath the TV tower at Alexanderplatz.

Arrival in Berlin
Zoo Bahnhof (Zoo Railway Station) is the station for international trains. There are left-luggage lockers and a bureau de change. The Berlin Tourist Office is a ten-minute walk away (see above).

Accommodation
The cheapest places are the Youth Hostels which are luxurious by international YH standards but comparatively expensive (from DM30-47).
- Berlin Youth Guest House (☎ 261 1097), Kluck Strasse 3, W-Berlin 30 (Tiergarten)
- Wannsee Youth Guest House (☎ 803 2034), Badeweg 1, corner Kronprinzessinnenweg, W-Berlin 38 (Wannsee)
- Ernst Reuter Youth Hostel (☎ 404 1610), Hermsdorfer Damm 48, W-Berlin north (Hermsdorf)
- Studenthotel Berlin (☎ 784 6720), Meininger Strasse 10, W-Berlin 62, near Rathaus Schoneberg
- Jugendgastehaus am Zoo (☎ 312 9410), Hardenberg Strasse 9a. Under 27s only; accommodation from 35DM. It is located very near the Zoo Railway Station.

Moving on
For cheap flights buy a copy of the weekly magazine *Zitty*, which has several pages of travel deals. A system of car-sharing can be arranged through *mitfahrzentrale* agencies; you pay the agency a fee to find you a ride in a private car to other European cities. To make a booking on the **Trans-Siberian** in Berlin, see pp27-8.

HUNGARY: BUDAPEST

General information

- **Visas** Visas are not necessary for passport holders from USA, UK, Canada and most European countries. Australian and New Zealand passport holders can get a 48-hour transit visa or a 30-day tourist visa on arrival by air or road, but not by rail.
- **Money** The Forint (Ft) is divided into 100 fillérs (f).
- **Language** Magyar is one of the world's more difficult languages to learn. Most people connected with tourism speak a little English though knowledge of German is more widespread.

Tourist information

Information can be obtained from **Tourinforum** (☎ 117 9800), Suto utca 2 (near Deak ter metro station). It is open 08:00-20:00 daily during summer; and any of the national tourism offices, **IBISZ** (see below).

Arrival

- **By rail** Trains from Vienna come into the Keleti Station (East), and there is an IBISZ tourist office here, where you can book accommodation. The Nyugati Station (West) is used for trains to and from Prague. Both have metro stations.
- **By air** The international airport is 22km from the city centre. There is an IBISZ tourist office here and there are shuttle buses every 30 minutes to the city.

Accommodation

Budapest has a wide range of accommodation. At the top end there is the **Hilton** which blends well with the ancient walls of the castle tower it incorporates and stands on the hill above the city. For budget travellers, the city's colleges offer their rooms during the summer holidays. Many local people let rooms in their houses and you can be put in contact with them by visiting one of the tourist offices listed below:

- **IBISZ Hotel Service** (☎ 118 5707, 118 4842), V Petofi ter, open 24hrs. You can also book accommodation at their other offices including those at the Keleti and Nyugati railway stations.
- **Volantourist** (☎ 118 2133), V Belgrad rakpart 6
- **Budapest Tourist** (☎ 117 3555), V Roosevelt ter 5

Moving on

Taking the train back to London requires a change at Vienna (3.5 hours from Budapest) and you reach London the following afternoon. Tickets for the Trans-Siberian are no longer the amazing bargain they were when the communists were in power. For **Trans-Siberian** bookings see p29.

CZECH REPUBLIC: PRAGUE

General information

● **Visas** Visas are not necessary for passport holders from the UK, US and Western European countries. Canadian, Australian, New Zealand, Japanese and Israeli citizens need a visa.

● **Money/costs** The unit of currency is the krown. German DM are accepted in some places. Prices for hotels and restaurants are low. All currency pre-1993 (look for *korun ceskoslovensky* written on the bill) is no longer valid. Beware!

● **Language** Many Czech people involved in tourism now speak English. German and Russian are the other foreign languages spoken.

Tourist information

A good place for tourist information is **Prague Information Service** (☎ 544 444), 20 Na Prikope and 22 Old Town Square. It is open 8:00-20:00 weekdays and 9:00-18:00 weekends. Other places include the **CKM Student Travel Centre** (☎ 268 507), Jidrinsská 28, open 9:00-17:00 weekdays; and the **American Hospitality Centre** (☎ 261 574), Na mustku 7 (bottom of Wenceslas Square).

Arrival

● **By rail** There are four railway stations: **Praha Holesovice** to the north, **Praha Hlavní Nádrazí** (also called Wenceslas Station), **Praha Stred** near the centre, and **Praha Smíchov** to the south (mainly local trains).

● **By air** The international airport is 17km from the city centre. There is a bus departing every hour between 6:00-18:30 between the airport and the airline office (Vltava Terminal, 25 Revollucni).

Accommodation

There's a good range of accommodation but everything gets very crowded in the summer, so start looking for a place to stay early in the day. **Pragotur**, U Obecního Domu 2, has a booking service for private accommodation. It's near the Powder Gate and Metro Náméstí Republiky, open 10:00-17:00. There are also several camp sites around the city, some of which have chalets and dormitories. Full details are available from the tourist information agencies listed above.

Moving on

The cheapest way to get to Britain on public transport is by bus, US$75 on Kingscourt Express, which takes 23 hours and there are daily departures except Sunday. You can get tickets in Prague at ul Antala Staska 6 (☎ 499 456), and in London at 15 Balham High Road (☎ 0181-673 7500). International rail tickets are sold at **Cedok** (☎ 212 7350), 18 Na Príkope, where the queues are often very long. Bring your passport and hard currency. For **Trans-Siberian** bookings, see p27.

POLAND: WARSAW

General information

● **Visas** are not necessary for passport holders from the USA, Germany, Britain or the Netherlands but Canadian, Australian, New Zealand and French citizens need a visa.

● **Money** The zloty is the unit of currency. Avoid exchanging too much money at any one time or you'll end up carrying large denomination notes which are hard to break. Banking hours are 08:00 to 16:00. Travellers' cheques can be difficult to exchange; the most convenient bank for exchanging them is the Bank Pekao SA on the third floor of the Hotel Marriot, opposite the Warszawa Centralna Station. Credit cards are accepted only in Orbis Hotels and expensive restaurants and shops which cater mostly for tourists. For credit card cash advances go to the American Express Office opposite the Hotel Europejski.

● **Language** Polish is the national language. Most people connected with tourism speak English, German or Russian.

Tourist information

The **Warsaw Tourist Information Centre** (☎ 270 000) on Plac Zamkowy 1/13 (Castle Square) can offer assistance, as well as **Orbis Travel Office** (☎ 276 766) on Marszalkowska 142.

Orbis is the national travel service; their offices abroad include:

● **UK**: Polorbis (☎ 0171-637 4971) 82 Mortimer St London WIN 7DE
● **USA**: Orbis (☎ 212-867 5011) 342 Madison Ave, Suite 1512, New York NY 10173

Arrival/departure

● **By rail** Warsaw is a major stopping point between Berlin and Russia. International trains depart from Warszawa Centralna Station.

● **By air** Many airlines fly to Warsaw and the national carrier, Lot Polish Airlines, has services to dozens of places including Bangkok, Beijing, Cairo, Chicago, Damascus, Dubai, Istanbul, Larnaca, Montreal, Newark, New York, Singapore, Tel Aviv and Toronto.

● **By bus** Buses leave regularly for European cities and are cheaper than trains. In Warsaw, ask at the Warsaw Tourist Information Centre or Orbis. From Britain, Eurolines National Express (☎ 0171-730 8235) at 52 Grosvenor Gardens, Victoria London SWIW 0AC, can offer bus information and tickets. Some Polish buses to Ukraine, Belarus, Lithuania and Russia use border crossings still closed to Western tourists: check before you buy your ticket.

● **By ferry** Orbis can assist with information on services to Denmark, Sweden and Finland.

Accommodation

Warsaw has a vast range of accommodation. Central and close to the station is the expensive **Forum Hotel** (☎ 210 270) on ulica Nowogrodzka 24/26. Singles start from US$100. Hotel Metropol (☎ 294 001) on ulica Marszalkowska 99a charges US$50 a room including breakfast. Hotel Saski (☎ 201 115) on Plac Bankowy has rooms from US$16.

For rooms in private homes contact the **Syrena Travel Office** (☎ 628 7540) at ulica Krucza 16/22. Singles start from US$10 and doubles from US$20.

Listings of all youth hostels in Poland are available from **PTSM** (Polskie Towarzystwo Schornisk Młodziezowych), ulica Chocimska 28, 4th floor, suite 426. There are two good centrally located **YHA's** at ulica Smolna 30 (☎ 278 952) and ulica Karolkowa 53a (☎ 328 829). They are often full during the summer, however.

Moving on

International train tickets can be bought from Orbis offices or the train station. ICIS student card holders are eligible for a 25% discount. The Orbis office (☎ 270 105) at ulica Bracka 16 is recommended.

BELARUS
General Information

● **Visas** Visas are necessary for all passport holders except those transiting Belarus who need a Russian visa. To get a Belarusian visa, you need a visa invitation which can be issued only by travel agencies registered by the Belarusian Ministry of Foreign Affairs.

● **Money** The Belarusian rouble is the official currency, replacing the Russian rouble in May 1992. The most widely accepted foreign currencies are US$ and Deutschmarks. Make sure the notes are in excellent condition otherwise changing them may be difficult. In Minsk, you can cash travellers' cheques and receive cash advances on your credit card. Food and entertainment is cheap.

● **Language** In 1990 Belarusian became the country's official language. Belarusian is an Eastern Slavonic language related to Ukrainian and Russian. Russian is still spoken by the majority of people.

Tourist information

There are no tourist information offices in Belarus, only service bureaus and excursion offices within hotels.

● **Belintourist** (Belarus' version of Intourist) (☎ 269 840, fax 231 143) at praspekt Masherava 19, open 08:00-20:00.

● **Hotel Minsk** (☎ 200 132) Praspekt Skaryny 11. This place has the best service bureau and they speak English.

Arrival

● **By rail** Minsk has only one international train station which is located in the south east of Minsk. At the station is the metro station Ploshcha Nezalezhnastsi (formerly Lenin Square).

Accommodation

Hotel Minsk (☎ 200 132) Praspekt Skaryny 11 has small but clean rooms starting from US$38 for a single. **Hotel Svislach** (☎ 209 783) on Vulitsa Kirava 13, has rooms for as little as US$15 for a single. **The Hotel Druzhba** (☎ 662 481) at Vulitsa Tolbukhina 3 has very basic rooms for US$5 a night. One of the nicest hotels is **Hotel Kastrychnitskaja** (☎ 293 910) at Vulitsa Enhelsa 13 where a single room with all amenities costs from US$70. **Hotel Jubileynaja** (☎ 269 171), Praspekt Masherava 19, charges US$50 a single as does **Hotel Planeta** (☎ 267 953), Praspekt Masherava 31.

Moving on

● **By air** The offices of Austrian Airlines, Swissair, SAS and LOT are all at Praspekt Masherava 19. Lufthansa (☎ 973 745) is at Minsk-2 airport. The state-owned Belavia (Belarusian airlines) sells tickets for international flights (☎ 250 231) at vulitsa Chkalova 38, and for flights to the

CIS (☎ 221 882) at Vulitsa Karla Marksa 29. Belavia flights are subject to cancellation because of fuel restrictions.

● **By rail** You can get **international train tickets** on the upper floor of the main railway station. A less stressful place to buy them is the Belintourist (☎ 269 840, fax 231 143), Praspekt Masherava 19; the office is open 08:00-20:00. Another ticket office is at Praspekt Skaryny 18, between Vulitsa Linina and Kamsamolskaya. It is open 08:00-20:00, closed Sunday.

● **By bus** The central long distance bus station is located at Vulitsa Babrujskaja 12. There are two buses a day to Bialystok in Poland, and daily buses to Brest, Kaliningrad, Riga, Kaunas, Klaipeda and Vilnius. The Vostochny Bus station services Homel, Vitsebsk, Pinsk, Polatsk and Warsaw. Bus No 8 travels between these two bus stations.

ESTONIA: TALLINN

General information

● **Visas** are not necessary for passport holders from Australia, Canada, Japan, New Zealand, UK, USA and most European countries. If you do need a visa, you can obtain one on arrival but it's much cheaper if bought in advance. If you need to extend a visa, go to the National Migration Board (☎ 22 664 333) at Lai 40 in Tallinn.

● **Money** The unit of currency is the krooni (EEK). There are exchange offices at the airport and central railway station. If you are carrying hard currency exceeding DM1000, you need to declare it.

● **Language** The official language is Estonian. About 62% of the population are native Estonian speakers, 30% Russian and 3% Ukrainian.

Tourist information

The **Tourist Information Centre** on Raekoja plats (on the Town Hall Square) is open 09:00-17:00 weekdays, and 10:00-15:00 weekends. It offers a wide range of information, maps and guides.

Arrival

● **By air** Tallinn has air links with Riga, Vilnius, Helsinki, Stockholm, Copenhagen, Frankfurt, Amsterdam, St Petersburg and Moscow.

● **By ferry** There are daily ferries between Tallinn and Helsinki and Stockholm.

● **By bus** Buses between St Petersburg and Tallinn are cheap. Routes to Latvia and Lithuania are also serviced. There is one bus a week to Warsaw. Tickets can be purchased at Prnu maantee 24.

● **By rail** Tallinn has direct rail lines to Moscow, St Petersburg, Riga, Vilnius and Warsaw. Trains depart daily from Balti Jaam (Baltic Station). Tickets can be bought from window No 26 (☎ 624 058), located at the back of the main long distance booking hall beside the platform (open 08:00 to 13:00 and 14:00 to 20:00 every day).

❏ **The Baltic States**

Estonia, Latvia and Lithuania lie within easy reach of Moscow and St Petersburg, and any of them makes an interesting staging post for entering or leaving Russia. The Baltics share a 'common visa space' where a visa for any of the three countries allows you to travel back and forth across the shared borders, however stricter border crossing procedures are maintained between Russia and the Baltic States. For in-depth information on the Baltic States the best guides are Lonely Planet's *Baltic States & Kaliningrad – a travel survival kit*; Insight's *Baltic States Guide*; and *A Practical Guide* published by Revalia Publishing, Tallinn.

LATVIA: RIGA

General information
- **Visas** Visas are not necessary for passport holders from the UK and most Eastern European countries. Latvian visas are free to US citizens.
- **Money** The unit of currency is the lati. There are exchange offices at Riga airport and throughout the central city area. Riga's Komerc Banka at Smilsu iela 6 in the Old Riga part of the city exchanges travellers cheques.
- **Language** Latvian is the national language.

Arrival
- **By air** Riga has air links with Helsinki, Stockholm, Copenhagen, Frankfurt, Dusseldorf, Berlin, Hamburg, Prague, Vienna, St Petersburg and Moscow. The airport is 14km west of the city centre at Stulke.
- **By rail** Riga Station is at Stacijas laukums. There are rail connections from Riga to St Petersburg, Moscow, Tallinn, and Vilnius, and to Berlin via Warsaw.

Tourist information
For travel assistance contact the **Association of Latvian Travel Agencies** (☎ 216 201, fax 213 666) at Torna iela 9.

Accommodation
There are hostels all over Riga and information on them can be obtained from the **Latvian University Tourist Club** (☎ 223 114, fax 225 039).

Viesnica Aurora (☎ 224 479) on Marijas iela 5 is conveniently located opposite the station. Good choices are the **Hotel Riga** (☎ 216 000, fax 229 828) on the outskirts of Old Riga at Aspazijas bulvaris 22, and the upmarket **Hotel de Rome** (☎ 216 268) at Kalku iela 28.

LITHUANIA: VILNIUS

General information

- **Visa** Visas are necessary for passport holders from UK, USA, Canada, Australia and New Zealand.
- **Money** The unit of currency is the litas. Money can be exchanged at the airport and railway station. Banks and special currency exchange booths are also located all around town. For Visa credit card cash advances, go to the **Vilnius Bankas** at Gedimino prospekt 12.

Arrival

- **By air** Vilnius has air links with Copenhagen, Warsaw, Frankfurt, Berlin, Hamburg, London, Zurich, Vienna, Budapest, St Petersburg and Moscow. The airport is 4km south from the centre in the suburb of Kirtimai. Bus No 1 runs from the railway station to the airport.
- **By rail** Vilnius is connected by rail to St Petersburg, Moscow, Tallinn and Riga. There is also a service from Berlin to Vilnius via Warsaw and Prague. The station is situated at the south end of the Old Town.
- **By bus** Buses link Vilnius with Estonia, Latvia, Minsk, Berlin, Copenhagen and Warsaw. The long distance bus station is at Sodu gatve 22, next to the railway station. Tickets can be bought in the main ticket hall of the bus station.

Tourist information

For budget accommodation, contact the **Lithuanian Travellers' Union** (☎ 627 118) Didzioji gatve 11. This non-government organisation also offers interesting travel options in Lithuania and can assist with all travel arrangements. Also try **Lithuanian Tours** (☎ 353 931, fax 351 815) at Semyniskiu gatve 18.

Accommodation

Beside the railway station taxi stand is a kiosk, **Viesbutis Ekspresas** (Hotel Express, ☎ 261 717), which arranges rooms in private flats. The centrally located **Hotel Astorija** (☎ 629 914, fax 220 097) at Didzioji gatve 35, has a range of rooms for all budgets. The centrally-located **Viesbutis Vilnius** (☎ 624 157), Gedimino prospektas 20, is also worth checking out.

APPENDIX A: TIMETABLES

Timetables for the most popular trains on the Trans-Siberian, Trans-Mongolian, and Trans-Manchurian routes are given below. Unless otherwise indicated departure times are shown; for arrival times simply subtract the number of minutes shown as the stopping time. Since the timetables are subject to changes from year to year, you should consult the table posted on the wall of the carriage corridor to ensure times are correct. Another useful source of information is the Thomas Cook Overseas Timetable (available from Thomas Cook travel agents or by post from PO Box 227, Peterborough PE3 6SB, UK).

Table 1 Trans-Siberian: Moscow-Vladivostok (Train Nos 1 & 2: *Rossiya*)

Departures are daily.

Station		Km from Moscow	Stop (mins)	Eastbound No 2 MT	LT	Westbound No 1 MT	LT
				Day 1	Day 1		
Moscow's Yaroslavl station	Москва Ярославский вокзал	0		14:15	14:15	6:30	6:30
Aleksandrov	Александров	112	2/-	16:06	16:06	-	-
Yaroslavl	Ярославль	284	5/10	18:33	18:30	2:03	2:03
Danilov	Данилов	357	20/15	20:05	20:05	1:00	1:00
						Day 7	Day 7
Bui	Буй	448	2/8	21:23	21:23	23:10	23:10
				Day 2	Day 2		
Sharya	Шарья	723	-/-	1:16	2:16	19:22	20:22
Kirov	Киров	957	15	5:13	6:13	15:29	16:29
Perm 2	Пермь 2	1437	35/25	13:08	15:08	7:56	9:56
Pervouralsk	Первоуральск	1774	-/-	18:21	20:21	-	-
Ekaterinburg	Екатеринбург	1813	30/15	19:56	21:56	1:47	3:47
				Day 3	Day 3	Day 6	Day 6
Tyumen	Тюмень	2140	-/-	0:20	2:20	20:58	22:58
Ishim	Ишим	2431	-/-	3:58	6:58	17:12	20:12
Nazyvaevskaya	Называевская	2567	11/15	5:59	8:59	15:21	18:21
Omsk	Омск	2712	16	7:50	9:50	13:09	16:09
Barabinsk	Барабинск	3040	15	12:20	15:20	8:45	11:45
Novosibirsk	Новосибирск	3335	15	17:10	20:10	4:12	7:12
Taiga	Тайга	3565	10	21:00	01:00	0:20	4:20
Mariinsk	Мариинск	3719	18/20	23:35	3:35	22:01	2:01
				Day 4	Day 4	Day 5	Day 5
Achinsk 1	Ачинск 1	3917	4/5	2:40	6:40	18:20	22:20
Krasnoyarsk	Красноярск	4098	20	6:19	10:19	15:03	19:03
Ilanskaya	Иланская	4383	20	10:55	14:55	10:02	14:02
Taishet	Тайшет	4516	5/4	13:09	17:09	7:31	11:31
Nizhneudinsk	Нижнеудинск	4683	15	16:15	21:15	4:35	9:35
Zima	Зима	4941	20	20:26	1:26	0:36	5:36
				Day 5	Day 5	Day 4	Day 4
Irkutsk	Иркутск	5185	20/24	1:19	6:19	20:03	1:03

				Day 5	Day 5	Day 4	Day 4
Slyudyanka 1	Слюдянка 1	5312	~/~	3:30	8:30	17:21	22:21
Ulan-Ude	Улан-Уде	5642	~/~	9:00	14:00	12:00	17:00
Petrovski Zavod	Петровский Завод	5784	~/~	11:13	16:13	9:29	15:29
Khilok	Хилок	5932	~/~	13:37	19:37	6:41	12:41
				Day 6	Day 6		
Chita	Чита	6199	20/18	18:27	0:27	2:19	8:19
Karymskaya	Карымская	6293	~/~	20:34	2:34	0:13	6:13
Shilka	Шилка	6451	8	23:34	5:34	21:09	3:09
Chernyshevsk-Zabaikalski	Чернышевск-Забайкальский	6593	15	1:50	7:50	18:24	0:24
						Day 3	Day 3
Amazar	Амазар	7012	~/15	9:53	15:53	10:13	16:13
Erofei-Pavlovich	Ерофей Павлович	7119	~/15	12:51	18:51	8:27	14:27
Skovorodino	Сковородино	7306	10	16:52	22:52	4:17	10:17
				Day 7	Day 7		
Magdagachi	Магдагачи	7501	10	19:50	1:50	0:44	6:44
Belogorsk	Белогорск	7873	27/20	1:58	7:58	19:07	1:07
						Day 2	Day 2
Arkhara	Архара	8088	25/20	5:52	11:52	15:25	21:25
Birobidzhan	Биробиджан	8356	5	10:55	17:55	10:07	17:07
Khabarovsk	Хабаровск	8521	25/23	13:35	20:35	7:48	14:48
Vyazemskaya	Вяземская	8659	17/18	15:46	22:46	5:18	12:18
				Day 8	Day 8		
Ussurisk	Уссурийск	9177	16/18	0:43	7:43	20:27	3:27
Vladivostok	Владивосток	9289		2:45	9:45	17:55	0:55
						Day 1	Day 1

Times shown are departure times – subtract stop for arrival time
MT = Moscow Time; LT = Local Time
hr+ = 1 hour minimum stopping time but invariably much longer
- = not stopping
~ time varies

Table 2 Moscow-Irkutsk (Train Nos 9 & 10 *Baikal*)

Runs daily from late May to mid September and then every second day.

Station		Km from Moscow	Stop (mins)	Eastbound No 10		Westbound No 9	
				MT	LT	MT	LT
				Day 1	Day 1		
Moscow's Yaroslavl station	Москва Ярославский вокзал	0		21:05	21:05	15:37	15:37
Aleksandrov	Александров	112	2/~	23:03	23:03	13:37	13:37
				Day 2	Day 2		
Yaroslavl	Ярославль	282	5/10	1:35	1:35	11:03	11:03
Danilov	Данилов	357	20/15	3:10	3:10	9:38	9:38
Bui	Буй	450	2/8	4:38	4:38	8:00	8:00
Kotelnich	Котельнич	723	~/~	11:21	12:21	1:35	2:35
Kirov	Киров	957	15	12:53	13:53	0:14	1:14
						Day 4	Day 4
Perm 2	Пермь 2	1437	35/25	20:33	21:33	16:29	17:29
				Day 3	Day 3		
Ekaterinburg	Екатеринбург	1818	15	3:26	5:26	9:25	11:25
Tyumen	Тюмень	2144	~/~	8:02	10:02	4:43	6:43
Ishim	Ишим	2433	~/~	11:48	14:48	0:59	3:59
						Day 3	Day 3
Omsk	Омск	2716	15/12	15:24	18:24	20:51	23:51
				Day 4	Day 4		
Novosibirsk	Новосибирск	3343	15	0:53	3:53	11:35	15:35
Taiga	Тайга	3571	10	5:05	9:05	7:21	11:21
				Day 4	Day 4		
Achinsk 1	Ачинск 1	3940	4/5	10:45	14:45	1:20	5:20
Krasnoyarsk	Красноярск	4104	20	14:10	18:10	22:09	2:09
						Day 2	Day 2
Taishet	Тайшет	4522	5/4	21:10	1:10	14:37	18:37
				Day 5	Day 5		
Nizhneudinsk	Нижнеудинск	4683	15	~/~	~/~	~/~	~/~
Zima	Зима	4941	~/~	~/~	~/~	~/~	~/~
Irkutsk	Иркутск	5191	20/24	9:00	14:00	2:53	6:53
						Day 1	Day 1

Times shown are departure times – subtract stop for arrival time
MT = Moscow Time; LT = Local Time
hr+ = 1 hour minimum stopping time but invariably much longer
- = not stopping
~ time varies

Table 3 Irkutsk - Ulan Bator/Ulaanbaatar (Train Nos 263 & 264)

Departures daily.

Station		Km from Moscow	Stop (mins)	Eastbound No 264 MT	LT	Westbound No 263 MT	LT
				Day 1	Day 1		
Irkutsk	Иркутск	0		13:48	18:48	3:46	8:46
Slyudyanka 1	Слюдянка 1	126	2	Day 2	Day 2	Day 3	Day 3
Ulan-Ude	Улан-Уде	457	15	1:20	6:20	16:50	21:50
Gusinoe Ozero	Гусиное Озеро	595	2	5:40	10:40	12:30	17:30
Naushki	Наушки	712	1hr+	12:50	17:50	9:55	14:55
MONGOLIA					**RUSSIA**		
					Day 2		Day 2
Sukhbaatar	Сухбаатар	1hr+	1 hr+		21:10		8:45
Darhan	Дархан	838	10		22:55		3:50
					Day 3		Day 2
Ulan Bator	Улаанбаатар	1119	30		6:20		21:00
							Day 1

Times shown are departure times – subtract stop for arrival time
MT = Moscow Time; LT = Local Time
hr+ = 1 hour minimum stopping time but invariably much longer
- = not stopping
~ time varies

Table 4 Trans-Mongolian: Moscow-Beijing (Train Nos 3 & 4)

One per week in each direction.

Station		Km from Moscow	Stop (mins)	Eastbound No 4		Westbound No 3	
				MT	LT	MT	LT
				Tue	Tue		
Moscow's Yaroslavl station	Москва Ярославский вокзал	0		19:53	19:53	17:10	17:10
				Wed	Wed		
Yaroslavl	Ярославль	282	5/10	0:08	0:08	12:55	12:55
Danilov	Данилов	357	15	1:50	1:50	11:30	11:30
Bui	Буй	450	2/8	3:13	3:13	9:48	9:48
Kirov	Киров	957	15	10:42	11:42	2:39	3:39
						Sun	Sun
Perm 2	Пермь 2	1437	15	18:15	20:15	19:08	21:08
				Thu	Thu		
Ekaterinburg	Екатеринбург	1818	15	0:29	2:29	13:05	15:05
Tyumen	Тюмень	2144	10	4:25	6:25	8:44	10:44
Ishim	Ишим	2433	9	8:03	11:03	5:08	8:08
Omsk	Омск	2716	15	11:47	14:47	1:09	4:09
				Fri	Fri	Sat	Sat
Novosibirsk	Новосибирск	3343	15	21:11	0:11	16:24	19:24
Taiga	Тайга	3571	10	0:52	4:42	12:47	16:47
Achinsk 1	Ачинск 1	3940	4/5	6:15	10:15	6:51	10:51
Krasnoyarsk	Красноярск	4104	22/19	9:57	13:57	3:34	7:34
Ilanskaya	Иланская	4383	20	~	~	~	~
Taishet	Тайшет	4522	2	16:29	20:29	20:22	0:22
Nizhneudinsk	Нижнеудинск	4683	15	~	~	~	~
Zima	Зима	4941	20	~	~	~	~
				Sat	Sat	Fri	Fri
Irkutsk	Иркутск	5185	15/13	4:04	9:04	9:10	14:19
Slyudyanka 1	Слюдянка 1	5312	~/~	6:18	11:18	6:48	11:49
Ulan-Ude	Улан-Уде	5642	20/19	11:49	16:49	1:27	6:23
Gusinoe Ozero	Гусиное Озеро	5800	2	14:46	20:46	22:15	4:15
Naushki	Наушки	5897		18:20	0:20	20:25	2:25
						RUSSIA	
MONGOLIA				Sun		Thur	
Sukhbaatar	Сухбаатар	5925	1 hr+	1:20		22:05	
Darhan	Дархан	6023	10	3:11		19:14	
Ulan Bator	Улаанбаатар	6304	30	9:30		13:50	
Choyr	Чоыр	6551	15	14:06		9:02	
Sayn Shand	Саын Шанд	7778	15	17:52		5:00	
Dzamyn Ude	Дзамын Уде	7013	1 hr+	22:33		0:40	

CHINA					Mon		Thur
Erlan		7023	2 hr+		1:47		20:43
Jining		7356	10		6:29		16:2
Datong		7483	13		8:34		14:25
Zhangjiakou		7661	10		11:00		11:47
Kangzhuang		7771	8		12:34		10:01
Qinglongqiao		7783	10		13:19		9:34
Nankou		7801	14		14:31		8:54
Beijing		7865			15:33		7:40
							Wed

Times shown are departure times – subtract stop for arrival time
MT = Moscow Time; LT = Local Time
hr+ = 1 hour minimum stopping time but invariably much longer
- = not stopping
~ time varies

Table 5 Trans-Manchurian: Moscow-Beijing (Train Nos 19 & 20)

Until recently there were two trains running per week in each direction; currently only one is running in each direction, leaving Moscow on Friday and Beijing on Saturday.

Station		Km from Moscow	Stop (mins)	Eastbound No 20 MT	LT	Westbound No 19 MT	LT
				Fri	**Fri**		
Moscow's Yaroslavl station	Москва Ярославский вокзал	0		20:15	20:15	20:32	20:32
				Sat	**Sat**		
Yaroslavl	Ярославль	284	7	0:33	0:33	16:13	16:13
Danilov	Данилов	357	15	2:25	2:25	14:45	14:45
Bui	Буй	448	15	3:46	3:46	-	-
Kirov	Киров	957	15	11:04	12:04	6:14	7:14
						Fri	**Fri**
Perm 2	Пермь 2	1437	15	18:34	20:34	22:25	0:25
				Sun	**Sun**		
Ekaterinburg	Екатеринбург	1813	15	0:52	2:52	16:23	18:23
Tyumen	Тюмень	2140	8	4:55	6:55	12:11	14:11
Ishim	Ишим	2431	10	8:43	11:43	8:35	11:35
Omsk	Омск	2712	15	12:31	15:31	4:34	7:34
						Thur	**Thur**
Novosibirsk	Новосибирск	3335	15	21:44	00:44	19:43	22:43
				Mon	**Mon**		
Taiga	Тайга	3565	10	1:28	5:28	16:03	20:03
Achinsk 1	Ачинск 1	3917	2	6:53	10:53	10:09	14:09
Krasnoyarsk	Красноярск	4098	18	10:29	14:29	6:43	10:43
Ilanskaya	Иланская	4383					
Taishet	Тайшет	4516	2	17:07	21:07	23:37	2:37
				Tue	**Tue**	**Wed**	**Wed**
Zima	Зима	4941	15				
Irkutsk	Иркутск	5185	20	4:55	9:55	12:14	17:14
Slyudyanka 1	Слюдянка 1	5312	2	7:02	12:02	9:54	14:54
Ulan-Ude	Улан-Уде	5642	15	12:36	17:36	4:19	9:19
Petrovski Zavod	Петровский Завод	5784	12	14:47	20:47	2:06	8:06
Khilok	Хилок	5932	5	17:12	23:12	23:30	5:30
				Wed	**Wed**		
Chita	Чита	6199	15	22:01	4:01	18:36	0:36
						Tue	**Tue**
Karymskaya	Карымская	6293	5	0:01	6:01	17:06	23:06
Zabaikalsk	Забайкальск	6661	1 hr+	14:06	20:06	6:47	12:47

CHINA							
Manzhouli		6678	1 hr+		22:07		7:01
					Thur		
Hailar		6864	10		00:42		2:31
Mianduhe		6979	6		2:23		1:16
Xinganling		7049	10		3:35		0:12
							Mon
Boketu		7074	20		4:22		23:08
Angangxi		7343	12		8:25		18:56
Daqing		7454	10		10:01		17:10
Harbin		7613	15		12:08		14:53
Changchun		7855	12		15:52		11:30
Shenyang		8160	15		19:42		7:20
Jinzhou		8402	12		22:59		4:12
					Fri		
Shanhaiguan		8586	12		1:24		1:53
							Sun
Tianjin		8868	10		5:00		22:19
Beijing		9001			6:32		20:32
							Sat

STOP PRESS: From May 1997 the departure time from Beijing is 22.40: two hours later than shown above.

Times shown are departure times – subtract stop for arrival time
MT = Moscow Time; LT = Local Time
hr+ = 1 hour minimum stopping time but invariably much longer
- = not stopping
~ time varies

APPENDIX B: BUYING A TICKET

Use a pencil to fill in your questions, go to the information window and then go to the booking window

Information	Информация
Please help me. I don't speak Russian. Please read the question I point to and write the answers. MT=Moscow Time *= circle your choice Q=question A=answer	Будьте любезны, помогите пожалуйста, я не говорю по-русски. Пожалуйста, прочтить вопросы на которые я укажу и на пишите ответ. МВ=Московское Время *= Я обвёл мой выбор Воп.=вопрос Отв.=ответ
Q When is the next train with spare SV* coupe* platskatni* tickets to _____? **A** It departs at __:__ (MT) and is Train No. _____.	**Воп.** Когда следущий поезд со свободными местами (СВ* купе* плацкарт*) до _____? **Отв.** Поезд отправляется в __:__ (МВ) и номер у поезда _____.
Q Are there SV* coupe* platskatni* tickets to _____ on Train No. ____? **A** Yes no.	**Воп.** Есть свободные места (СВ* купе* плацкарт*) до _____ у поезда номе _____? **Отв.** Да нет.
Q When does the train depart and arrive? **A** It departs at __:__ and arrives at __:__ (Moscow Time).	**Воп.** Когда поезд отправляется и пребывает' **Отв.** Поезд отправляется в __:__ и пребывает в __:__ (МВ).
Q How much is a SV* coupe* platskatni* ticket? **A** It costs _____ roubles.	**Воп.** Сколько стоит билет в СВ* купе* плацкарт*? **Отв.** Билет стоит _____ рублей
Q Which ticket window should I go to? **A** Ticket window No. _____.	**Воп.** К какой кассе мне подойти? **Отв.** Касса № _____.
Q What platform does the train No. _____ leave from? **A** Platform No. _____.	**Воп.** С Какой платформы отправляется поез № _____? **Отв.** Платформа № _____.
Buying Tickets	
Q May I buy ____ SV* coupe* platskatni* ticket to _____ on train No. _____ departing on _____? **A** Yes, it costs ____ roubles. No.	**Воп.** Можно купить ____ СВ* купе* плацкарт* билет до _____ на поезд № _____ который отправляется до _____? **Отв.** Да, билет стоит ____ рублей Нет
Q Why can't I buy a ticket? **A** There is no train, the train is fully booked, you have to go to ticket window No. _____, or you can only buy a ticket _____ hours before the train arrives.	**Воп.**Почему я не могу купить билет? **Отв.** нет поезда нет мест вы должны купить билет в кассе № _____ вы только можете купить билет за _____ часов по прибытия поезд

APPENDIX C: LIST OF SIBERIAN FAUNA

There are extensive displays of local animals in the natural history museums of Novosibirsk, Irkutsk and Khabarovsk but the labelling is in Russian and Latin. The following translation is given for non-Russian speaking readers whose Latin is rusty or non-existent.

In the list below the letters given beside the animal's English name indicate its natural habitat. NS = Northern Siberia/Arctic Circle; SP = Siberian Plain; AS = Altai-Sayan Plateau/Mongolia; BI = Lake Baikal/Transbaikal region; FE = Far Eastern Territories. Where a Latin name is similar to the English (e.g. Vipera = Viper) these names have been omitted.

Accipiter gentilis	goshawk (AS/SP/NS/BI/FE)
Aegoceras montanus	mountain ram (AS)
Aegoceras sibiricus	Siberian goat (BI)
Aegolius funereus	boreal/Tengmalm's owl (BI/FE)
Aegypius monachus	black vulture (AS)
Aethia cristatella	crested auklet (NS/FE)
Alces alces	elk/moose (SP/BI/FE)
Allactaga jaculus	five-toed jerboa (SP/BI)
Alopex lagopus	arctic fox (NS)
Anas acuta	pintail (BI)
Anas clypeata	shoveler (SP/BI/FE)
Anas crecca	teal (BI/SP/FE)
Anas falcata	falcated teal (SP/BI/FE)
Anas formosa	Baikal teal (BI)
Anas platyrhynchos	mallard (AS/SP/BI/FE)
Anas poecilorhyncha	spotbill duck (AS/BI)
Anser anser	greylag goose (SP/BI)
Anser erythropus	white-fronted goose (AS/SP/BI/FE)
Antelope gutturosa/crispa	antelope (FE)
Arctomis bobac	marmot (AS/SP)
Ardea cinerea	grey heron (AS/SP/BI)
Aquila clanga	greater spotted eagle (SP)
Botaurus stellaris	bittern (SP/BI/FE)
Bubo bubo	eagle owl (BI/FE)
Buteo lagopus	rough legged buzzard (NS/SP/FE)
Butorides striatus	striated/green heron (FE)
Canis alpinus	mountain wolf (AS/FE)
Canis corsac	korsac/steppe fox (BI/FE)
Canis lagopus	arctic fox (NS)
Canis lupus	wolf (SP/BI/FE)
Canis procyonoides	Amur racoon (FE)
Capra sibirica	Siberian mountain goat/ibex (AS/BI)
Capreolus capreolus	roe deer (SP/BI/FE)
Castor fiber	beaver (SP/BI/FE)
Certhia familiaris	common treecreeper (AS/BI/FE)
Cervus alces	elk (AS/BI/FE)
Cervus capreolus	roe-buck (BI/FE)
Cervus elephas	maral deer (AS/BI/FE)
Cervus nippon	sika/Japanese deer (FE)
Cervus tarandus	reindeer (NS/FE)

Circus aeruginosus	marsh harrier (SP/BI)
Citellus undulatus	arctic ground squirrel/Siberian souslik (NS/BI/FE)
Cricetus cricetus	common hamster (AS/SP/BI/FE)
Cygnus cygnus	whooper swan (SP/BI)
Dicrostonyx torquatus	actic lemming (NS)
Dryocopus martius	black woodpecker (SP/BI/FE)
Enhyra lutris	Kamchatka beaver (FE)
Equus hemionus	kulan/Asian wild ass (FE)
Eumentopias Stelleri	sea-lion (NS/FE)
Eutamias sibiricus	Siberian chipmunk (AS/SP/BI/FE)
Ealco columbarius	merlin (NS/SP/BI/FE)
Falco peregrinus	peregrine (NS/SP/BI/FE)
Falco tinnunculus	kestrel (SP)
Falco vesperinus	hawk (SP)
Felis irbis	irbis/panther (FE)
Felis lynx	lynx (SP/BI/FE)
Felis manul	wild cat (AS/BI/FE)
Felis tigris altaica	Amur tiger (FE)
Foetorius altaicus	ermine (SP/BI)
Foetorius altaicus sibiricus	polecat (SP/BI)
Foetorius vulgaris	weasel (SP/BI)
Fulica atra	coot (SP/BI/FE)
Gallinago gallinago	common snipe (SP/BI/FE)
Gavia arctica	black-throated diver/loon (BI)
Gavia stellata	red-throated diver/loon (SP/BI)
Gazella subgutturosa	goitred gazelle (AS)
Grus cinerea	grey crane (SP)
Grus grus	common crane (SP/BI/FE)
Grus leucogeranus	Siberian white crane (NS/SP/FE)
Gulo gulo	wolverine/glutton (SP/BI/FE)
Gypaetus barbatus L.	lammergeyer (AS)
Haematopus ostralegus	oystercatcher (SP/BI/FE)
Lagomis alpinus	rat hare (FE)
Lagopus lagopus	willow grouse/ptarmigan (NS/SP/FE)
Larus argentatus	herring gull (BI/FE)
Larus canus	common gull (BI/FE)
Larus ridibundus	black-headed gull (BI/FE)
Lemmus obensis	Siberian lemming (NS/SP)
Lepus timidus	arctic hare (NS/BI/FE)
Lepus variabilis	polar hare (NS)
Lutra vulgaris	otter (BI/FE)
Marmota camtschatica	Kamchatka marmot (FE)
Marmota sibirica	Siberian marmot (AS/SP/BI)
Martes zibellina	sable (SP/BI/FE)
Melanitta deglandi	American black scoter (BI)
Melanocorypha mongolica	Mongolian lark (BI/FE)
Meles meles	Eurasian badger (AS/BI/FE)
Microtus hyperboreus	sub-arctic vole (NS/SP/FE)
Moschus moschiferus	musk deer (AS/BI/FE)
Mustela erminea	ermine (NS/AS/SP/BI/FE)
Mustela eversmanni	steppe polecat (AS/SP/BI/FE)
Mustela nivalis	common weasel (NS/SP/BI/FE)
Mustela sibirica	kolonok (FE)

Myodes torquatus/obensis	Ob lemming (NS)
Nucifraga caryocatactes	nutcracker (AS/SP/BI/FE)
Nyctea scandiaca	snowy owl (NS)
Ochotona alpina	Altai pika (AS)
Oenanthe isabellina	Isabelline wheatear (AS/SP/BI)
Omul baikalensis	omul (BI)
Otaria ursina	sea bear (NS/FE)
Otis tarda	bustard (SP/BI)
Ovis ammon	argalis (sheep) (AS)
Ovis Argali	arkhar (AS)
Ovis nivicola	Siberian bighorn/snow sheep (FE)
Panthera pardus orientalis	Amur leopard (FE)
Panthera tigris altaica	Siberian/Amur tiger (FE)
Panthera uncia	snow leopard (AS)
Perdix perdix	grey partridge (AS/SP/BI/FE)
Perisoreus infaustus	Siberian jay (BI/FE)
Phalacrocorax carbo	great cormorant (BI/FE)
Phoca barbata groenlandica	seal (NS/FE)
Phoca baicalensis	Baikal seal (BI)
Phocaena orca	dolphin (NS/FE)
Picoides tridactylus	three-toed woodpecker (SP/BI/FE)
Plectophenax nivalis	snow bunting (NS)
Podiceps auritus	Slavonian/horned grebe (AS/BI)
Podiceps cristatus	great crested grebe (AS/SP/BI)
Procapra gutturosa	Mongolian gazelle (FE)
Pteromys volans	Siberian flying squirrel (SP/BI/FE)
Rangifer tarandus	reindeer/caribou (NS/BI/FE)
Ranodon sibiricus	five-toed triton (AS/SP)
Rufibrenta ruficollis	red-breasted goose (NS)
Salpingotus crassicauda	pygmy jerboa (SP/AS)
Sciurus vulgaris	red squirrel (SP/BI/AS/FE)
Spermophilus eversmanni	Siberian marmot (BI)
Spermophilus undulatus	arctic ground squirrel (FE)
Sterna hirundo	common tern (BI/FE)
Strix nebulosa	great grey owl (SP/BI/FE)
Surnia ulula	hawk owl (SP/BI/FE)
Sus scrofa	wild boar (AS/BI/FE)
Tadorna ferruginea	ruddy shelduck (SP/BI/FE)
Tamias striatus	striped squirrel (BI)
Tetrao urogallus	capercaillie (SP/BI/FE)
Tetrao parvirostris	black-billed capercaillie (BI/FE)
Tetraogallus himalayanensis	Himalayan snowcock (AS)
Tetraogallus altaicus	Altai snowcock (AS)
Tetrastes bonasia	hazel grouse (SP/BI/FE)
Turdus sibiricus	Siberian thrush (SP/BI/FE)
Uria aalge	guillemot (NS/FE)
Ursus arctus	bear (SP/FE)
Ursus maritimus	polar bear (NS)
Ursus tibetanus	Tibet bear (FE)
Vulpes vulpes	red fox (AS/SP/BI/FE)

APPENDIX D: BIBLIOGRAPHY

Baedeker, Karl *Russia with Teheran, Port Arthur and Peking* (Leipzig 1914)
Barzini, Luigi *Peking to Paris. A Journey across Two Continents* (London 1907)
Byron, Robert *First Russia Then Tibet* (London 1933)
Collins, Perry McDonough *A Voyage down the Amoor* (New York 1860)
De Windt, Harry *Siberia as it is* (London 1892)
Des Cars J. and Caracalla, J.P. *Le Transsiberien* (1986)
Dmitriev-Mamonov, A.I. and Zdziarski, A.F. *Guide to the Great Siberian Railway 1900* (St Petersburg 1900)
Fleming, H.M. and Price J.H. *Russian Steam Locomotives* (London 1960)
Gowing, L.F. *Five Thousand Miles in a Sledge* (London 1889)
Heywood AJ & Button IDC *Soviet Locomotive Types* (London/Malmo 1994)
Hill, S.S. *Travels in Siberia* (London 1854)
Hollingsworth, J.B. *The Atlas of Train Travel* (London 1980)
An Official Guide to Eastern Asia Vol 1: Manchuria & Chosen (Tokyo 1913)
Jefferson, R.L. *Awheel to Moscow and Back* (London 1895)
Jefferson, R.L. *Roughing it in Siberia* (London 1897)
Jefferson, R.L. *A New Ride to Khiva* (London 1899)
Johnson, Henry *The Life of Kate Marsden* (London 1895)
Kennan, George *Siberia and the Exile System* (London 1891)
Lansdell, Henry *Through Siberia* (London 1883)
Levin, M.G. and Potapov, L.P. *The Peoples of Siberia* (Chicago 1964)
Manley, Deborah *The Trans-Siberian Railway* (London 1988)
Marsden, Kate *On Sledge and Horseback to Outcast Siberian Lepers* (London 1895)
Meakin, Annette *A Ribbon of Iron* (London 1901)
Massie, R.K. *Nicholas and Alexandra* (London 1967)
Murray *Handbook for Russia, Poland and Finland* (London 1865)
Newby, Eric *The Big Red Train Ride* (London 1978)
Pifferi, Enzo *Le Transsiberien*
Poulsen, J. and Kuranow, W. *Die Transsibirische Eisenbahn* (Malmo 1986)
St George, George *Siberia: the New Frontier* (London 1969)
Shoemaker, MM *The Great Siberian Railway –St Petersburg toPekin* (London 1903)
Theroux, Paul *The Great Railway Bazaar* (London 1975)
Tupper, Harmon *To the Great Ocean* (London 1965)

Other guides from Trailblazer Publications

Siberian BAM Rail Guide	1st edn out now
Silk Route by Rail	2nd edn out now
China by Rail	1st edn out now
Trans-Canada Rail Guide	1st edn out now
Japan by Rail	1st edn late 1998
Vietnam by Rail	1st end mid 1998
Asia Overland – A Route & Planning Guide	1st edn late 1997
Cairo to Istanbul Overland	1st edn out now
Trekking in the Everest Region	2nd edn out now
Trekking in the Annapurna Region	2nd edn out now
Trekking in Langtang, Gosainkund & Helambu	1st edn late 1997
Leh & Trekking in Ladakh	1st edn out now

Route guides for the adventurous traveller

APPENDIX E: PHRASE LISTS

English-speaking travellers are unforgivably lazy when it comes to learning other people's languages. As with virtually every country in the world, it's possible to just about get by in Russia, Mongolia and China on a combination of English and sign language. English is spoken by tourist guides and some hotel staff but most of the local people you meet on the train will be eager to communicate with you and unable to speak English. Unless you enjoy charades it's well worth learning a few basic phrases in advance. Not only will this make communication easier but it'll also earn you the respect of local people. You might even consider evening classes before you go, or teaching yourself with books and cassettes from your local library.

The sections here highlight only a few useful words. It's well worth also taking along phrasebooks: Lonely Planet's pocket-size *language survival kits* in Russian and Chinese are recommended.

Russian

CYRILLIC ALPHABET AND PRONUNCIATION GUIDE

It is vital to spend the few hours it takes to master the Cyrillic alphabet before you go, otherwise you'll have trouble deciphering the names of streets, metro stations and, most important, the names of stations along the Trans-Siberian and Trans-Mongolian routes. (Mongolian also uses Cyrillic script.)

The Cyrillic alphabet is derived from the Greek. It was introduced in Russia in the tenth century, through a translation of the Bible made by the two Greek bishops, Cyril (who gave his name to the new alphabet) and Methodius.

Cyrillic letters	Roman letter	Pronunciation*	Cyrillic letters	Roman letter	Pronunciation*
А а	a	(f<u>a</u>r)	П п	p	(<u>P</u>eter)
Б б	b	(<u>b</u>et)	Р р	r	(<u>R</u>ussia)
В в	v	(<u>v</u>odka)	С с	s	(<u>S</u>iberia)
Г г	g	(<u>g</u>et)	Т т	t	(<u>t</u>rain)
Д д	d	(<u>d</u>og)	У у	u/oo	(r<u>u</u>le)
Е е	e	(y<u>e</u>t)	Ф ф	f/ph	(<u>f</u>rost)
Ё ё	yo	(<u>yo</u>ghurt)	Х х	kh	(lo<u>ch</u>)
Ж ж	zh	(trea<u>s</u>ure)	Ц ц	ts	(lo<u>ts</u>)
З з	z	(<u>z</u>ebra)	Ч ч	ch	(<u>ch</u>ill)
И и	ee	(s<u>ee</u>k)	Ш ш	sh	(<u>f</u>ish)
Й й	y	(<u>y</u>ready)	Щ щ	shch	(fre<u>sh ch</u>icken)
К к	k	(<u>K</u>iev)	Ы ы	i	(d<u>i</u>d)
Л л	l	(<u>L</u>enin)	Э э	e/ih	(t<u>e</u>nt)
М м	m	(<u>M</u>oscow)	Ю ю	yu	(<u>u</u>nion)
Н н	n	(<u>n</u>ever)	Я я	ya	(<u>ya</u>k)
О о	o	(<u>o</u>ver)	Ь ь		softens preceding letter

* pronunciation shown by underlined letter/s

KEY PHRASES

The following phrases in Cyrillic script may be useful to point to if you're having problems communicating:

Please write it down for me   Запиши́те это для меня́, пожа́луйста

Help me, please   Помоги́те мне, пожа́луйста

I need an interpreter   Мне ну́жен перево́дчик с англи́йского

CONVERSATIONAL RUSSIAN

Run the hyphenated syllables together as you speak and roll your 'R's:

General

Hello	*Zdrah-stvoo-iteh*
Good morning	*Dob-royeh-ootro*
Good afternoon/evening	*Dobree den/vecher*
Please	*Po-zhalsta*
Do you speak English?	*Gavar-iteh lee vy pa anglee-skee?*
No/Yes	*nyet/da*
thank you	*spasee-ba*
excuse me (sorry)	*izveen-iteh*
good/bad	*haroshaw/plahoy*
cheap/expensive	*deshoveey/daragoy*
Wait a minute!	*Adnoo meenoo-too!*
Please call a doctor	*Vi'zaveete, po-zhalsta, vracha*
Goodbye	*Das-vedahneya*

Directions

map	*karta/schema*
Where is ...?	*G'dyeh ...?*
hotel	*gastee-neetsoo*
airport	*aeroport/aerodrom*
bus-station	*stantsia afto-boosa*
metro/taxi	*metro/taksee*
tram/trolley-bus	*tramvai/trolleybus*
restaurant/cafe	*restarahn/kafay*
museum/shop	*moo-zyey/maga-zyeen*
bakery/grocer's	*boolach-naya/gastra-nohm*
box office (theatre)	*teatrahl-naya kassa*
lavatory (ladies/gents)	*too-alet (zhen-ski/moozh-skoy)*
open/closed	*at-krita/za-krita*
left/right	*na-prahva/na-leva*

Numerals/time

1 *adeen*; 2 *dvah*; 3 *tree*; 4 *chetir*; 5 *p'aht*; 6 *shest*; 7 *s'em*; 8 *vosem*; 9 *d'evat*; 10 *d'e'sat*; 11 *adeen-natsat*; 12 *dve-natsat*; 13 *tree-natsat*; 14 *chetir-natsat*; 15 *pyat-natsat*; 16 *shes-natsat*; 17 *sem-natsat*; 18 *va'sem-natsat*; 19 *d'evat-natsat*; 20 *dvatsat*; 30 *tree-tsat*; 40 *so'rok*; 50 *p'ad-desaht*; 60 *shez-desaht*; 70 *sem-desaht*; 80 *vosem-desaht*; 90 *d'even-osta*; 100 *sto*; 200 *dve-stee*; 300 *tree-sta*; 400 *chetir-esta*; 500 *p'at-sot*; 600 *shes-sot*; 700 *sem-sot*; 800 *vosem-sot*; 900 *devet-sot*; 1000 *tees-acha*.

How much/many?	*Skolka?*
rouble/roubles	*rooble/rooblah/roobley**
Please write down the price	*Nap'eesheet'eh, pazhalsta, tse-noo*
ticket	*beel-yet*
1st/2nd/3rd Class	*perviy/ftoroy/treteey class*
express	*express*
What time is it?	*Kato'riy chahs?*
hours/minutes	*chasof/meenoot*
today	*sevodna*
yesterday/tomorrow	*fcherah/zahftra*
Monday/Tuesday	*pani-dell-nik/ftor-nik*
Wednesday/Thursday	*sri-da/chit-virk*
Friday	*pyat-nit-sah*
Saturday	*sue-boat-ah*
Sunday	*vraski-sen-yah*

*1st word is for 1 unit, 2nd word for 2-4 units, 3rd word for 5 or more.

Food and drink

menu	*menoo*
mineral water	*meenerahl-noi vady*
fruit juice	*sokee*
vodka/whisky	*vodka/veeskee*
beer	*peeva*
wine/cognac	*veenah/kanya-koo*
champagne	*sham-pahn-skoya*
Cheers!	*Zah vasheh zdaro-vyeh!*
caviare	*eek-ry*
salmon/sturgeon	*lasa-seeny/aset-reeny*
chicken/duck	*tsy-plonka/oot-koo*
steak/roast beef	*beef-shteks/rost-beef*
pork	*svee-nooyoo*
veal	*atbeef-nooyoo telyah-choo*
ham/sausage	*vechina/kalba-soo*
bread/potatoes	*khlee-ep/kar-toshka*
butter/cheese	*mah-sla/sir*
eggs/omelette	*yait-sa/amlet*
salt/pepper	*sol/perets*
tea/coffee	*chai/koh-fee*
milk/sugar	*mala-ko/sahk-har*
bill	*shchot*

Questions and answers

What's your name?	*Kak vahs zavoot?*
My name is ...	*Menyah zavoot*
I'm from Britain/USA	*Yah preeyeh-khal eez Anglee-ee/S-Sh-Ah*
Canada/Australia	*Kanadah/Avstralee*
New Zealand/Japan	*Novee Zeelandee/Yaponee*
Sweden/Finland	*Shvetsee/Finlandee*
Norway/Denmark	*Norveggee/Danee*
Germany/Austria	*Germanee/Avstree*
France/Netherlands	*Frantsee/Gollandee*

Where are you going?	Kudah vhee idyotyeh?
I'm going to ...	Yah idoo ...
Are you married?	Vee zhyehnaht/zamoozhyem?*
Have you any children?	Yest ly oo vas dety?
boy/girl	mahl-cheek/de-vooshka
How old are you?	Skolka vahm l'et?
What do you do?	Shto vhee delayetyeh?
student/teacher	stoo-dent/oochee-tel (-neetsa)*
doctor/nurse	vrach/myeh-sestra
actor/artist	aktor/khoo-dozh-neek
engineer/lawyer	een-zheneer/advokaht
office worker	sloo-zhash-chey
Where do you live?	G'dyeh vhee zhivyotyeh?

*(feminine form)

Mongolian

Westerners tend to have difficulty mastering the tricky pronunciation of the national language of Mongolia. Until very recently, Mongolian was written in the same script as Russian (see p405), with two additional characters Θ (pronounced 'o') and Y ('u'). When Mongolian is transliterated into Roman script note that stress is indicated by doubling vowels. You will see Ulan Bator written as 'Ulaanbaatar' to show that the first 'a' in each word is stressed.

Hello	*Sayn bayna uu*
Thank you	*Bayar-lalaar*
Yes/No	*Teem/Ugu-i*
Sorry	*Ooch-laarai*
I don't understand	*Bi oilgokh-gu-i bayna*
What's your name?	*Tani ner khen beh?*
Where do you live?	*Ta khaana ami-dardag beh?*
Goodbye	*Bayar-tai*
Where is ...?	*.....khaana bayna veh?*
hotel/airport	*zochid buudal/nisyeh ongotsni buudal*
railway station/bus station	*galt teregniy buudal/avtobusni zogsool*
temple/museum	*sum/moosei*
lavatory	*zhorlon*
left/right	*zuun/baruun*
soup/egg/mutton	*shoi/ondog/honini makh*
rice/noodles/bread	*budaar/goimon/talh*
cheese/potato/tomato	*byaslag/toms/ulaan lool*
tea/coffee	*tsai/kofee*
beer/fermented mare's milk	*peevo/airag*
How much?	*Khed?*
cheap/expensive	*khyamd/kheterhiy unetiy yum*

1 *neg*; 2 *khoyor*; 3 *gurav*; 4 *dorov*; 5 *tav*; 6 *zurgaar*; 7 *doloo*; 8 *naym*; 9 *ee-us*; 10 *arav*; 11 *arvan neg*; 12 *arvan khoyor*; 13 *arvan gurav*; 14 *arvan dorov*; 15 *arvan tav*; 20 *khori*; 21 *khori neg*; 30 *guchin*; 31 *guchin neg*; 40 *doch*; 50 *tavi*; 60 *zhar*; 70 *dal*; 80 *naya*; 90 *er*; 100 *zuu*; 200 *khoyor zuu*; 1000 *neg myanga*

Chinese

Particularly tricky. The problem with Chinese is one of pronunciation - so much depends on your tone and emphasis that if you do not get the sound exactly right you will not be understood at all. The best way to learn in advance is either to take lessons, or to buy a cassette course (simple ones are under £10/US$15 and come with a useful phrasebook).

The country's main dialect is Mandarin, spoken by about three-quarters of the population. Mandarin has four tones: high tone (–), rising (ʹ) where the voice starts low and rises to the same level as the high tone, falling-rising (ˇ) where the voice starts with a middle tone, falls and then rises to just below a high tone; and falling (ˋ) which starts at the high tone and falls to a low one.

READING PINYIN CHINESE

Pinyin is the system of transliterating Chinese into the Roman alphabet. Pronunciation is indicated by the underlined letters below:

Vowels

a	as in far	e	as in were
i	as in tree	o	as in or
	or as in were	u	as in Pooh
	after c, r, s, z, ch, sh, zh	ü	as in cue

Consonants

c	as in eats	h	as in loch or the kh in an
q	as in cheap		Arabic word, with the sound
r	as in trill		from the back of the throat.
x	as in sheep	z	as in plods
zh	as in jaw		

KEY PHRASES

The following phrases in Chinese characters may be useful to point to if you're having problems communicating:

Please write it down for me 请写下

Help me, please 请帮我

Please call a doctor 请你叫医生

USEFUL WORDS AND PHRASES

General

Hello	Nǐ hǎo
Please	Qǐng
Do you speak English?	Nǐ huì shuō yīng yǔ ma?
Yes/No	Dùi/Bū dùi (literally correct/ incorrect)
Thank you	Xiè xie

Excuse me (sorry)	*Duì bù qǐ*
Excuse me (may I have your attention?)	*Qǐng wèn*
good/bad	*hǎo/bu hǎo*
Wait	*Děng*
Goodbye	*Zài jiàn*
UK/USA	*Yīng guó/Měi guó*
Canada/Australia	*Jīa ná dà/Ào dà lia*
France/The Netherlands/Germany	*Fǎ guó/Hé lán/Dé guó*
I understand/do not understand	*Wǒ dǒng le/Wǒ bù dǒng*
Translator	*Fān yì*

Directions

Where is...?	*Zài nǎr...?*
toilet (ladies/gents)	*cè sǔo (nü/nan)*
airport	*jī chǎng*
bus station	*chē zhàn*
railway station	*hǔo chē zhàn*
taxi	*chū zū qì chē*
museum	*bó wù guǎn*
hotel/restaurant	*lü guǎn/fàn guǎn*
post office	*yóu*
PSB/CAAC office	*Gōng ān jú/Zhōng háng gōngsi*
What time will we arrive at...?	*Liè chē shénme shí jiān dào...?*
What station is this?	*Zhè shì nà yí zhàn?*

Numerals/time

1 *yī*, 2 *èr*, 3 *sān*, 4 *sì*, 5 *wǔ*, 6 *liù*, 7 *qī*, 8 *bā*, 9 *jiǔ*, 10 *shí*, 11 *shí yī*, 12 *shí èr*, 13 *shí sān*, 14 *shí sì*, 15 *shí wǔ*, 16 *shí liù*, 17 *shí qī*, 18 *shí bā*, 19 *shí jiǔ*, 20 *èr shí*, 21 *èr shí yī*, 30 *sān shí*, 40 *sì shí*, 50 *wǔ shí*, 100 *yì bǎi*, 101 *yì bǎi líng yī*, 110 *yì bǎi yī shí*, 150 *yì bǎi wǔ shí*, 200 *èr bǎi*, 500 *wǔ bǎi*, 1000 *yì qiān*, 10,000 *yí wàn*, 100,000 *shí wàn*, 1 million *yì bǎi wàn*,

Monday/Tuesday/Wednesday	*Xīng qī...yī/èr/sān*
Thursday/Friday/Saturday/Sunday	*Xīng qī...sì/wǔ/liù/rì*
How much?	*Duō shao?*
That's too expensive	*Tài guì le*
yesterday/tomorrow/today	*zuó tiān/míng tiān/jīn tiān*

Transport

ticket	*piào*
Hard Seat/Soft Seat	*Yìng Zuò/Luǎn Zuò*
Hard Sleeper/Soft Sleeper	*Yìng Wò/Luǎn Wò*
Please may I upgrade this ticket to....	*Qǐng nǐ huan gao yī ji de piào*

Food and drink

menu	*cài dān*
mineral water/tea/beer	*kuàng quán shuǐ/chá/pí jiǔ*
noodles/noodle soup	*miàn/tāng miàn*
(fried) rice	*(chǎo) fàn*
bread/egg	*miàn bāo/jī diàn*
pork/beef/lamb	*zhū ròu/niú ròu/yáng ròu*
chicken/duck/fish	*jī/yā/yú*
vegetables	*shū cài*
Do you have any vegetarian dishes?	*Nǐ zhèr yǒu sù-cài ma?*

INDEX